D1199011

ADVISORY BOARD

HISTORY IN DISPUTE

Volume 11

The Holocaust, 1933-1945

Edited by Tandy McConnell

A MANLY, INC. BOOK

GALE®

THOMSON ™

GALE

Detroit • New York • San Diego • San Francisco • Cleveland • New Haven, Conn. • Waterville, Maine • London • Munich

History in Dispute
Volume 11: The Holocaust, 1933–1945
Tandy McConnell

Editorial Directors
Matthew J. Bruccoli and Richard Layman

Senior Editor
Karen L. Rood

Series Editor
Anthony J. Scotti Jr.

ISBN 1-55862-455-4

Printed in the United States of America
10 9 8 7 6 5 4 3 2 1

CONTENTS

CONTENTS

CONTENTS

CONTENTS

ABOUT THE SERIES

History in Dispute is an ongoing series designed to present, in an informative and lively pro-con format, different perspectives on major historical events drawn from all time periods and from all parts of the globe. The series was developed in response to requests from librarians and educators for a history-reference source that will help students hone essential critical-thinking skills while serving as a valuable research tool for class assignments.

Individual volumes in the series concentrate on specific themes, eras, or subjects intended to correspond to the way history is studied at the academic level. For example, early volumes cover such topics as the Cold War, American Social and Political Movements, and World War II. Volume subtitles make it easy for users to identify contents at a glance and facilitate searching for specific subjects in library catalogues.

Each volume of *History in Dispute* includes up to fifty entries, centered on the overall theme of that volume and chosen by an advisory board of historians for their relevance to the curriculum. Entries are arranged alphabetically by the name of the event or issue in its most common form. (Thus, in Volume 1, the issue "Was detente a success?" is presented under the chapter heading "Detente.")

Each entry begins with a brief statement of the opposing points of view on the topic, followed by a short essay summarizing the issue and outlining the controversy. At the heart of the entry, designed to engage students' interest while providing essential information, are the two or more lengthy essays, written specifically for this publication by experts in the field, each presenting one side of the dispute.

In addition to this substantial prose explication, entries also include excerpts from primary-source documents, other useful information typeset in easy-to-locate shaded boxes, detailed entry bibliographies, and photographs or illustrations appropriate to the issue.

Other features of *History in Dispute* volumes include: individual volume introductions by academic experts, tables of contents that identify both the issues and the controversies, chronologies of events, names and credentials of advisers, brief biographies of contributors, thorough volume bibliographies for more information on the topic, and a comprehensive subject index.

ACKNOWLEDGMENTS

James F. Tidd Jr., *Editorial associate.*

Philip B. Dematteis, *Production manager.*

Kathy Lawler Merlette, *Office manager.*

Ann M. Cheschi, Carol A. Cheschi, and Linda Dalton Mullinax, *Administrative support.*

Ann-Marie Holland, *Accounting.*

Sally R. Evans, *Copyediting supervisor.* Phyllis A. Avant, Caryl Brown, Melissa D. Hinton, Philip I. Jones, Rebecca Mayo, Nancy E. Smith, and Elizabeth Jo Ann Sumner, *Copyediting staff.*

Zoe R. Cook, *Series team leader layout and graphics.* Janet E. Hill, *Layout and graphics supervisor.* Sydney E. Hammock, *Graphics and prepress.*

Scott Nemzek and Paul Talbot, *Photography editors.*

Amber L. Coker, *Permissions editor and Database manager.*

Joseph M. Bruccoli and Zoe R. Cook, *Digital photographic copy work.*

Marie L. Parker, *Systems manager.*

Kathleen M. Flanagan, *Typesetting supervisor.* Patricia Marie Flanagan, Mark J. McEwan, and Pamela D. Norton, *Typesetting staff.*

Walter W. Ross, *Library researcher.* Tucker Taylor, *Circulation department head, Thomas Cooper Library, University of South Carolina.* John Brunswick, *Interlibrary-loan department head.* Virginia W. Weathers, *Reference department head.* Brette Barclay, Marilee Birchfield, Paul Cammarata, Gary Geer, Michael Macan, Tom Marcil, and Sharon Verba, *Reference librarians.*

PREFACE

There is little to dispute about the facts of the Holocaust. Between 1933 and 1945 approximately fifteen million people, six million of whom were Jews, were murdered by the Nazi government. The vast majority of these killings were carried out after 1941 by the *Schutzstaffel* (Protective Echelon, or SS), an elite, ideologically committed, and racially pure political/military arm of the Nazi regime. Acting under orders from Heinrich Himmler, who was certainly acting with the knowledge and support of Adolf Hitler, the SS combed occupied Europe for Jews, transported them to killing centers, and executed them en masse. Though many killings took place in village squares and remote woods, most victims died in carefully designed *vernichtungslager* (extermination camps), usually by poison gas. A few people evaded capture, finding refuge in Sweden, Britain, China, Japan, South America, or the United States; others hid in Europe with sympathetic non-Jews. Many were sent to Nazi work camps, where conditions were harsh and where the survivors were liberated by invading American, British, and Soviet forces. Survival was the exception. The perpetrators of the Holocaust had a single goal: to murder every Jew and Gypsy in Europe. They failed only because the task was large and Germany lost the war before it could be completed.

Beyond the core fact of fifteen million murders, the Holocaust has been the focus of extended debate. Historians, lawyers, political scientists, theologians, philosophers, and artists have encountered the Holocaust both as inescapable reality and as an impenetrable puzzle. Yet, in seeking to understand what happened and how it came to pass, scholars of the Holocaust have put the evidence together in different ways and examined it from differing perspectives. Not surprisingly, they have reached differing interpretations of these events. This volume presents only a fraction of those arguments.

On 30 January 1933, after more than a decade of political struggle, Adolf Hitler became chancellor of Germany. Fifteen years earlier the German Workers Party had been a fringe political

movement unknown outside of Munich when Hitler, a decorated veteran of World War I (1914–1918), became member number 55. Hitler's gift for persuasion pushed him quickly to the forefront of the right-wing, anti-Semitic party, and in 1921 he became its führer, or leader. He changed the group's name to *National Socialist German Workers Party*, which was quickly abbreviated to *Nazi* in the popular press. Until 1923 Hitler's party remained obscure outside of Bavaria, where it was known mostly for its extreme, if uncertain, views on politics and the economy.

On the night of 8–9 November 1923, the anniversary of the German capitulation in World War I, the National Socialists attempted a putsch, a seizure of power that was supposed to have begun at the Munich Bürgerbräukeller and spread throughout Germany. Events did not develop as hoped, however, and the putsch was put down by police loyal to the Weimar regime. Hitler and his fellow putschists were arrested and tried for treason. The judge was sympathetic, however, and though Hitler was found guilty, he was sentenced to five years in prison, of which he served nine months in comfortable confinement. The trial and imprisonment gave him a certain political cachet as well as an opportunity to dictate his political manifesto, *Mein Kampf* (1925–1927), a rambling monologue on history, politics, Germany's destiny, and his own political journey.

Following the failed coup attempt, the National Socialists under Hitler's leadership emerged from regional obscurity to become a national party. Attacking communists, liberals, Jews, and the "November criminals" who had accepted the terms of the November 1917 Armistice and the subsequent Treaty of Versailles (1919), Hitler played on the anxieties and hopes of ordinary Germans in a nonstop campaign for political power. In 1933 the German electorate gave the Nazi Party a plurality in the Reichstag, and President Paul von Hindenburg reluctantly offered Hitler the post of chancellor. Hitler and the National Socialists seized the opportunity.

The Nazi Party had developed a complex command structure and a host of auxiliary organizations, ranging from the SS, the *Sturmabteilung* (Assault Division, or SA, also known as Storm Troopers or Brownshirts), the Hitler Youth, and the German Maidens Society. The Nazis' stated goal was to remake Germany, to purge the Fatherland of liberalism, communism, and Jewry, to reach back into the distant, heroic past for strong values, and to march into a golden future of prosperity and racial purity. They were less clear on their political agenda but promised to extricate Germany from the bondage of the Versailles Treaty, to end unemployment, and to strengthen the economy. The Nazis did not ride to power on political promises but on personality. Hitler embodied National Socialism in the minds of most Germans and millions of people around the world. Had it not been for member number 55, the German Workers Party would have joined the scores of similar fringe movements that litter the dustbins of history.

Upon seizing control of the government, Hitler instituted a policy of *gleischaltung* (coordination) designed to bring all of German society into harmony with National Socialist ideology. He stopped making payments on Germany's war debts, ignored the limitations on military preparations imposed by the Treaty of Versailles, and launched a program of anti-Semitic legislation designed to leave Germany *judenrein* (free of Jews). He began preparing for a war that would bring Poland and the eastern portions of the Soviet Union under German control. Although Hitler was an astute politician and did not hesitate to modify his strategy, his ideological commitments, revealed in *Mein Kampf,* never wavered.

Based on his ramblings in *Mein Kampf,* one can be reasonably certain of Hitler's worldview. A social Darwinist, he saw humanity as governed by immutable laws of struggle, triumph, and defeat. Societies that attempted to subvert the harsh laws of nature by coddling and encouraging its inferior members, or by admitting lesser races into the community, inevitably weakened themselves. According to Hitler, nature was a harsh and unsympathetic judge, and human societies must be equally unsentimental toward the weak. The alternative was to face inevitable extinction. Hitler was also attracted to the heroic nationalism of Richard Wagner's operas, and he embraced and racialized Friedrich Nietzsche's idea of the superman, the great and unconventional individual who transcends ordinary morality. Hitler transformed this notion into the un-Nietzschean idea of a master race. Little of what Hitler said was completely original, and much seemed completely reasonable to his listeners, which is perhaps why it resonated so broadly among otherwise sane and moral Germans.

Like many of his contemporaries in Europe and North America, Hitler was fundamentally racialist in his understanding of humanity; he understood the Jews not as a religious community but as a special race. Religious anti-Judaism (as distinguished from nineteenth-century racist anti-Semitism) had a long history in Germany—indeed, throughout Europe. The Jews were blamed for rejecting Christ, accused of using the blood of Christian babies in their Passover rituals, and hated for their role as moneylenders and merchants—about the only roles available to them, since most medieval kings forbade their owning land or belonging to craft guilds. Yet, Jew hatred, however virulent, had little to do with race. Jews could and did convert—as in the example of the parents of Benjamin Disraeli, the notable British prime minister—and thereby escaped much of the onus of being Jewish in a Christian world. Enlightenment thinkers, most of whom had little enough patience for Christianity or Judaism, attacked anti-Judaism as unworthy of a civilized people. Revolutionary France was the first state in Europe to emancipate its Jews, and by the end of the nineteenth century, official discrimination against the Jews on religious grounds was outlawed in most of Europe. Religious anti-Semitism did not end in Europe, of course. It continues in the twenty-first century. However, in the late nineteenth century it was transformed into a political movement that drew its acceptance from its association with Charles Darwin's theory of evolution. Using Darwin's explanation of biological diversity and change in human societies, late-nineteenth- and early-twentieth- century anthropologists in Europe and North America conceived of race as a biological rather than a cultural phenomenon. Humanity, they argued, came in three races: Black, Yellow, and White, reflecting three stages of human development. The Black races were less evolved than the Yellow, which were inferior to the White. The White northern European Germanic (or Aryan) races were superior to them all, but this superiority could not be retained without struggle. From the late nineteenth century through the 1950s, eugenicists argued that the offspring of a mixed sexual union would inevitably result in harm to the "superior" race, and they lent "scientific" support to antimiscegenation laws in the United States and elsewhere. To this notion Hitler added an even more sinister interpretation. The White races were invariably creators of culture. Other races, the Japanese and Chinese, for example, existed as the bearers of culture, but some, the Jews above all, were destroyers of culture. The supreme creators of culture were the Aryans, by which Hitler meant the White races of northern and western Europe. Without the Aryans, humanity never would have emerged from barbarism, and should the Aryans be destroyed by mixing with other, lesser races, human culture would be doomed. For Hitler, the

Jews, an Asian, or Yellow, race pretending to be White and European, were the quintessential destroyers of culture. They had no state or national identity of their own, so they insinuated themselves into the cultures created by other, superior people. Like a parasite attacking a healthy host, the Jews were motivated by self-preservation. They could not survive otherwise. Yet, the Aryans must, Hitler believed, recognize the Jews for what they were and isolate their influence. However "German" and civilized they appeared, and however brutal the means necessary, the Jews would have to be treated as an infection of the Aryan body. They would have to be isolated and exterminated to prevent the spread of the infection.

For Hitler, there was simply no choice. The Jews were eternal, racial enemies of the Aryan people. In addition, though they had done nothing to create civilization, they had come to control it from behind the scenes. Thus, there was nothing inconsistent in identifying the Jews with communism as well as predatory capitalism. The Jews dominated the legal professions as they dominated crime. They were dirty and alien. Even when they spoke perfect German and lived hygienic Germanic lives, the Jews were subversive and insidious and would use every means—miscegenation, modern art, democracy, bolshevism, and liberalism—to destroy the Aryan race. According to Hitler, so protean an enemy had to be recognized and annihilated. Ultimately, either the Aryans (and thus civilization) would triumph and the Jews would be destroyed, or the Jews would become masters of the world and the Aryan race would die with civilization.

Similar anti-Semitic views, though perhaps not Hitler's exterminationist version, were widely shared by Americans as well as Europeans. The Dreyfus Affair in the last years of the nineteenth century, in which a Jewish French army officer was imprisoned for treason in spite of compelling evidence of his innocence, demonstrated the strength of anti-Semitism in the most progressive state in Europe. Henry Ford, the American industrialist, was also the publisher of a steady stream of anti-Semitic pamphlets and articles, and he shared Hitler's conviction that the Jews were the hidden string pullers behind the Western economy.

Hitler came to power with a burning desire to do something about the Jews, to resolve the Jewish Question once and for all. However, this issue did not immediately emerge as a major concern of the Nazi State, and it is uncertain whether Hitler had a clear idea of how he would resolve the Jewish Question once he came to power. While campaigning, Hitler—and his future propaganda minister, Joseph Goebbels—had beaten the anti-Semitic drum loudly and often, but Hitler's primary concerns were more traditionally political and economic: to restore the German economy; to repudiate the Treaty of Versailles; to restore Ger-

many's military might; and to coordinate people's civil, political, economic, religious, and social lives in the name of Nazi ideology. The party slogan became *Ein Reich, ein Volk, ein Führer* (One Germany, One German people, One leader).

The problem for Hitler was that Germany's Jews, numbering about 525,000 in 1933, were among the most acculturated in all of Europe. They had enjoyed complete freedom of religion since the 1870s and had prospered as "Germans of the Jewish faith" rather than as an ethnically distinct group. In dress, personal habits, language, and virtually everything else they were Germans above all. Many Jews had served with distinction in World War I, fighting and dying for the Fatherland alongside German Christians. Jews worked as bankers, lawyers, physicians, shopkeepers, laborers, and intellectuals. They were ill prepared for what was about to happen.

Though the Nazi State was violently and stridently anti-Semitic from its inception, few German Jews, or anyone else, anticipated what was to come. Nazi policy from 1933 to 1938 seems to have been aimed at despoiling the Jews and forcing them into exile. This policy was handicapped by the reluctance of most of the rest of the world to accept Germany's Jews as refugees, and by the reluctance of many German Jews to abandon their homes when, surely it seemed, things would have to get better soon. The breaking point came on 9–10 November 1938 when, in a concerted action, Nazi Party thugs across Germany spent the night breaking into Jewish-owned shops and offices, beating Jews in the streets, and rounding up hundreds of men to send to concentration camps where, for a substantial fine, they might be released and allowed to leave the country. German policy was to despoil the Jews and to prevent their leaving Germany with more than a few dollars. Virtually every other country that might have accepted them as refugees, however, exhibited reluctance to admitting penniless refugees. The Jews of Germany were stuck.

German Jews, while suffering increased pressure since 1933, constituted a tiny percentage of European Jewry, which numbered about 9.5 million out of a world population of 15.3 million. Three million Jews lived in Poland; nearly that many lived in the Soviet Union. Only with the invasion of Poland in September 1939 and the subsequent invasion of the Soviet Union in 1940 did Hitler's promised "Final Solution to the Jewish Question" become a reality. Following closely behind the German Army in Operation Barbarossa (the invasion of the Soviet Union) were *Einsatzgruppen,* special units with orders to kill Jews and other enemies of the Third Reich. These murders were impossible to conceal and seemed, even among the most ardent anti-Semites, an inefficient use of wartime resources. Apparently, sometime in 1941 (locating the precise date has consumed hours of scholarly debate) a decision was made at the highest levels of the German government to seek out and exterminate every Jew who could be found within Germany's grasp. Whether this policy was taken because expulsion had failed, because it suddenly seemed possible, or because it had been Hitler's intent from the beginning of his rise to power continues to be debated and will perhaps remain unknowable unless, as is exceedingly unlikely, a document emerges from the archives that indicates Hitler's thinking. *Mein Kampf* notwithstanding, Hitler rarely committed his ideas to paper.

From 1942 until the last days of the Third Reich, Jews from throughout Europe, from states Germany had conquered as well as from its allies, were isolated, imprisoned, loaded onto cattle cars, and transported to concentration camps scattered across Europe. Even here the terminology becomes confusing. The use of concentration camps to isolate (and perhaps to hold hostage) civilian members of a suspect or enemy nationality had been an innovation of the British in the Boer War (1899–1902). The families of Boer fighters were forced into unsanitary concentration camps where many thousands died. The United States used similar camps to relocate Americans of Japanese descent after the attack on Pearl Harbor. Similarly, the Nazis established hundreds of concentration camps throughout Germany within months of taking power. The first facility was the infamous camp at Dachau, located a few miles from Munich. Though Jews were held at such camps, these camps were intended more to intimidate, detain, and punish real or potential enemies of the Third Reich. Communists, Jehovah's Witnesses, homosexuals, Catholic priests, labor-union leaders, and other potential sources of opposition were swept into such camps where, however brutal the regimen, there were no gas chambers and few mass killings.

At the *vernichtungslager,* the extermination camps of Auschwitz-Birkenau, Belzec, Chelmno, Majdanek, Sobibor, and Treblinka, all of which were located in Poland, Jews, as well as Roma and Sinti (Gypsies), were transported to their deaths. Most victims transported here never became inmates per se but were killed within hours of their arrival, usually by poison gas. The most common agent was hydrogen cyanide, packaged and sold by an I. G. Farben subsidiary as an insect and pest fumigant under the brand name Zyklon-B. Those few who were not immediately selected for death were condemned to work, disease, and starvation. Some became subjects of medical experiments. Others were casually killed by guards or capos, the inmate-supervisors, usually common criminals, who led work units and commanded the barracks.

When Allied armies started to close in on the camps, the camp personnel strained to hide the evidence. Many surviving inmates were marched further and further into Germany—and away from rescue—many dying along the way. Even with liberation by British, American, and Soviet forces, many who had survived the horrors of the camps died of typhus or the lingering effects of starvation.

The concentration and extermination camps confronted the victorious Allies with many problems. Survivors often had no home to return to. They joined the wave of Displaced Persons (DPs) that flooded Europe at the end of the war. Some concentration-camp survivors spent years in limbo, awaiting sponsorship to come to the United States, Australia, or Canada to begin life again. Many traveled to Palestine, eventually fighting for and winning independence and recognition as a Jewish state.

The perpetrators, where they could be identified, offered problems of their own. The Allies were not as concerned with crimes against the Jews as they were with war crimes in violation of the Geneva Conventions and other international accords. There was no body of law that had envisioned criminality on such a massive scale. What would come to be called the "Holocaust" was subsumed with other outrages under the rubric "crimes against humanity." Only in later years and decades would the men and women who operated the machinery of murder be prosecuted for crimes specifically against the Jews.

The Holocaust, as a distinct historical event, did not emerge into either popular or scholarly consciousness as separate from World War II (1939–1945) until the 1960s, when the terms *Holocaust* and *Shoah* entered the lexicon of history. Holocaust, a transliteration of a Greek translation of a Hebrew word meaning "a sacrifice to God that is completely consumed by fire," is inaccurate on several points. The destruction of the Jews was far from complete, and just as important, their deaths were not sacrificial. They were murdered. Though there is disagreement on proper usage, for the purposes of this volume "Holocaust" will be used to refer to the German campaign of murder and annihilation targeted at Jews, the Gypsies, Slavs, and other actual and perceived enemies of the Reich who suffered persecution. Victims of Nazi bombing campaigns and retribution killings—however horrific—are not normally thought of as Holocaust victims since their suffering was a result of war.

The Hebrew word *Shoah* means catastrophe. It entered the popular consciousness in the United States in 1985 with the widespread screening of Claude Lanzemann's seven-hour documentary by the same name and with increasingly widespread commemorations of *yom ha-shoah,* the Holocaust

Day of Remembrance held annually in April or May. "Shoah," in this volume as in general usage, refers specifically to Nazi Germany's war of extermination against the Jews and to the Jewish experience of that catastrophe.

The "Final Solution to the Jewish Question," or simply the Final Solution, refers to the Nazi plan to exterminate Europe's Jews. The phrase appears to have first been used in January 1942 at the Wannsee Conference, a meeting of German political, military, and civil officials whose purpose was to coordinate the enormously complex task of finding, isolating, transporting, and murdering every Jew in Europe. It was, of course, a circumlocution, a way of talking about, without actually mentioning, mass murder. It has the same connotations as the more recent phrase "ethnic cleansing."

Genocide, the murder or attempted murder of an ethnically or otherwise identifiable group of people, was coined shortly after World War II and has come to be applied to many such acts: the destruction of Native Americans, the Armenians by the Turks, and more recently, Bosnian Muslims and the Hutu tribespeople in Rwanda. The Holocaust remains the foremost example of genocide, though representatives and survivors of other groups victimized by genocide question the exceptionalism attributed to the Holocaust.

During the 1980s and 1990s, Holocaust studies gained unprecedented funding and attention from scholars, governments, and the media. The United States Holocaust Memorial Museum opened a few blocks from the Washington Monument in 1993, the same year Steven Spielberg's film *Schindler's List* opened in theaters around the country. Both created an air-conditioned and carefully controlled Holocaust experience for millions of customers. Dachau and Auschwitz joined the Anne Frank house in Amsterdam as key points for "Holocaust Tourism," and critics feared that a virtual Holocaust industry was being created.

At the same time, Internet websites, academic sounding journals, and talk-show regulars began to challenge the fundamental historicity of the Holocaust. While much Holocaust denial emanated from openly racist and neo-Nazi organizations, the Institute for Historical Review (IHR), established in 1978, strives to present itself as an academically respectable publisher of revisionist thought. While its literature insists that the IHR is not a Holocaust denial organization, that same literature consistently does precisely that. It argues, for example, that Zyklon-B was never used and would have been ineffective in killing people. It argues that the crematoria were used to dispose of bodies of con-

centration camp inmates who had died of natural causes and that the gas chambers never existed.

Holocaust denial poses a problem for many Holocaust scholars, most of whom would prefer to ignore denial and focus on more mainstream issues. One scholar, Deborah Lipstadt, recently took on the deniers. In *Denying the Holocaust: The Growing Assault on Truth and Memory* (1993) she discussed the career of historian David Irving and referred to him as a Holocaust denier. Irving responded by filing suit against Lipstadt and her publisher, Penguin Books, in a British court where libel laws put the burden of proof on the accused to demonstrate that the allegedly defamatory statement is true. Lipstadt won the case, and the judge called Irving an anti-Semite and Holocaust denier in open court. Yet, though most deniers lack the scholarly sophistication of Irving, Holocaust denial or "revision" continues to intrude into honest debate.

For the purposes of this volume Holocaust denial will not be debated as a subject of scholarly dispute. Its basic tenets, that the Holocaust did not happen, that it was grossly exaggerated, that it is a Jewish or Israeli slander against Germany, are so amply refuted by documentary and eyewitness testimony that there is simply nothing to argue. Holocaust deniers claim that such refusal to engage in debate simply discriminates against an unpopular view. In fact, many of the views argued here are unpopular and exceedingly controversial. However, such controversial views are based on alternative interpretations (one might even call these revisionist interpretations) of historical evidence. Holocaust denial, on the other hand, requires its adherents to ignore or dismiss overwhelming bodies of evidence. Granting legitimacy to a point of view so completely lacking in intellectual merit and historical honesty by treating it as equivalent to a dispute about, for example, the ideological origins of anti-Semitism, would itself be academically dishonest.

Nevertheless, unpopular and controversial views are defended in this text, occasionally by writers and scholars who do not personally hold them but were committed to presenting them fairly, honestly, and persuasively. Many of these debates remain politically explosive. The role of the Holocaust in the foundation of the State of Israel, the liability of German corporations, and the role of the Vatican continue to excite vituperative debate among passionate believers. Yet, in all such cases the debate circles around the best way to interpret data.

–TANDY MCCONNELL
COLUMBIA COLLEGE
COLUMBIA, SOUTH CAROLINA

CHRONOLOGY

Boldface type indicates an entry in this volume.

1933

30 JANUARY: Adolf Hitler becomes chancellor of Germany.

27 FEBRUARY: The Reichstag building is destroyed by fire; Hitler uses this act as a pretext to begin suspending freedom of speech and assembly in Germany.

10 MARCH: Dachau, a concentration camp in Bavaria initially designed to hold political prisoners (primarily Communists and Socialists), is officially opened. (*See* **Nazi Criminality**)

23 MARCH: The Enabling Act is passed, giving Hitler dictatorial power. (*See* **Forms of Power**)

1 APRIL: The Nazis boycott all Jewish businesses. (*See* **Advanced Warning** *and* **Intentional Strategy**)

7 APRIL: The Civil Service Law removes non-Aryans from government and teaching positions. (*See* **Advanced Warning** *and* **Intentional Strategy**)

26 APRIL: The *Geheime Staatspolizei* (Secret State Police, or Gestapo) is formed. (*See* **Forms of Power**)

10 MAY: Books by Jews and other "undesirables" are burned at huge rallies. (*See* **Advanced Warning**)

10 MAY: The Socialist Party in Germany is outlawed.

27 JUNE: The German Nationalist Party is dissolved.

11 JULY: German Protestants unite under the Evangelical Church, but some pastors refuse to submit to a government-appointed bishop for the opposing Confessing Church. (*See* **Confessing Church**)

14 JULY: All political parties, except for the Nazi Party, are banned in Germany.

20 JULY: An agreement between the Catholic Church and Germany provides that Catholic clergy will not participate in politics and that clerical appointments will receive governmental scrutiny. (*See* **Pius XII**)

1934

JANUARY: Individuals considered racially "inferior," especially Gypsies, and the mentally and physically disabled, are forcibly sterilized.

30 JUNE: In an act known as the Night of the Long Knives, or Great Blood Purge, Hitler's supporters murder more than seventy high Nazi Party members and officials suspected of plotting against him. (*See* **Forms of Power** *and* **Nazi Criminality**)

2 AUGUST: Hitler adds the powers of the office of president to his own after the death of Paul von Hindenburg; he also assumes the title *Der Führer* (the Leader). (*See* **Forms of Power**)

1935

13 JANUARY: The German government seeks the return of administrative control of the Saar region from the League of Nations.

1 MARCH: The Saar is returned to Germany.

APRIL: Jehovah's Witnesses are arrested throughout Germany. (*See* **Jehovah's Witnesses**)

21 MAY: Jews are banned from serving in the German military. (*See* **Advanced Warning**)

15 SEPTEMBER: The Nuremberg Laws deprive German Jews of citizenship rights and ban intermarriage with non-Jews. (*See* **Advanced Warning** *and* **Intentional Strategy**)

28 SEPTEMBER: The Protestant churches come under government control. (*See* **Confessing Church**)

1936

4 FEBRUARY: A Jewish assassin kills Swiss National Socialist leader Wilhelm Gustloff; the organization is banned in Switzerland. (*See* **Neutral States**)

MARCH: A special unit of the SS is formed to train guards to staff the concentration camps. (*See* **Nazi Criminality**)

7 MARCH: The Versailles Treaty of 1919 is violated when German troops march into the Rhineland.

17 JUNE: Heinrich Himmler, head of the *Schutzstaffel* (SS, or Protective Echelon), the Nazi paramilitary corps, is made German chief of police with the title of *Reichsführer*. (*See* **Forms of Power** *and* **Nazi Criminality**)

1–16 AUGUST: The Summer Olympic Games are held in Berlin, Germany. The United States participates, and Hitler is embarrassed when African American athletes, including sprinter Jesse Owens, defeat German contenders. Owens wins four gold medals, but German officials, including Hitler, refuse to personally present the prizes. The only Jewish athletes on the U.S. track team, Marty Glickman and Sam Stoller, members of the 4 x 100-meter relay, are not allowed by U.S. officials to run, allegedly because of a Nazi request that Hitler be humiliated no further.

1937

1 JULY: Confessing Church pastor Martin Niemüller is arrested by the Nazis for leading the opposition to Nazi religious policies. (*See* **Confessing Church**)

15 JULY: The Buchenwald prison camp is built in Weimar, Germany, and 149 political prisoners arrive the following day. This concentration camp will grow to be one of the largest on German soil. The first prisoners are charged primarily with political crimes; Jews begin arriving in large numbers in late 1938, followed by Polish prisoners in 1939. Nearly 240,000 prisoners from thirty countries will be housed here during its eight years of existence; nearly 44,000 will be killed. (*See* **Forms of Power** *and* **Nazi Criminality**)

8 AUGUST: More than one hundred protesters against German restrictions on Jews are arrested in Berlin. (*See* **Willing Executioners**)

1938

Jewish poet Mordecai Gebirtig, living in Krakow, writes *Es Brent* (It's Burning) in response to Polish treatment of Jews.

By 1938, more than 150,000 German Jews have fled the country to escape escalating governmental restrictions. (*See* **Advanced Warning** *and* **Intentional Strategy**)

12 MARCH: Germany annexes Austria. Soon after, the Nazis establish the Mauthausen concentration camp near the city of Linz.

16 JUNE: All Jews are required to register their property with the German government. (*See* **Advanced Warning**)

6–15 JULY: Delegates from thirty-two countries meet in Evian, France, to discuss the influx of Jewish refugees into many countries; they fail to achieve any real changes in immigration policies. (*See* **Advanced Warning** *and* **Evian Conference**)

23 JULY: All adult Jews in Germany are required to obtain special identification cards.

11 AUGUST: The synagogue in Nuremberg is destroyed by the Nazis. (*See* **Advanced Warning**)

28 OCTOBER: Approximately seventeen thousand Polish Jews residing in Germany are rounded up and deported to the Polish border. (*See* **Advanced Warning** *and* **Intentional Strategy**)

7 NOVEMBER: A German diplomat is fatally shot in Paris by the son of a Jewish deportee from Germany.

9–10 NOVEMBER: Looting and vandalism of synagogues and Jewish-owned businesses erupts throughout Germany and Austria. The state-sponsored activities become known as *Kristallnacht* (Night of the Broken Glass). (*See* **Advanced Warning** *and* **Intentional Strategy**)

12 NOVEMBER: The German government orders that Jewish businesses be transferred to Aryan ownership. (*See* **Willing Executioners**)

15 NOVEMBER: Jewish students are expelled from non-Jewish schools in Germany. (*See* **Advanced Warning**)

1939

The Ravensbrück prison for women is established near Fürstenberg north of Berlin. More than 130,000 women and children are incarcerated here, many of them executed or experimented upon, during the war. (*See* **Feminist Interpretation, Gender Differences,** *and* **Medical Experiments**)

24 JANUARY: The Germans establish the Central Office Emigration headed by Reinhard Heydrich. (*See* **Advanced Warning**)

15 MARCH: German troops occupy Czechoslovakia.

13 MAY: The *St. Louis,* carrying more than nine hundred Jewish refugees, leaves Hamburg bound for Havana, Cuba. Turned away, the ship sails toward the United States but is refused entry into any port. By June the ship is headed back to Europe. (*See* **Advanced Warning**)

1 SEPTEMBER: Germany invades Poland; World War II officially begins. Polish Jews will be rounded up by the Germans and placed into ghettos; the Warsaw ghetto has nearly 400,000 residents. (*See* **Intentional Strategy** *and* **Jewish Councils**)

1 SEPTEMBER: Switzerland declares itself a neutral state and retains this status throughout the war. (*See* **Neutral States**)

1 SEPTEMBER: Special curfews are imposed on German Jews. (*See* **Advanced Warning** *and* **Intentional Strategy**)

8 SEPTEMBER: Jewish businesses in Germany are required to display the Star of David. (*See* **Advanced Warning**)

OCTOBER: Hitler implements the T–4 program, which sanctions the murder of institutionalized, physically disabled, and mentally handicapped individuals. The religious leadership in Germany reacts negatively to the news, and the government ceases the program in 1941, although by that time more than seventy thousand have been murdered. (*See* **Nazi Criminality**)

12 OCTOBER: Jews are removed from Vienna.

26 OCTOBER: The German government decrees that all Jews can be forced to perform labor for the state. (*See* **Advanced Warning** *and* **Slave Labor**)

23 NOVEMBER: Polish Jews are forced to wear the yellow Star of David on their clothing when out in public. (*See* **Advanced Warning**)

1940

Faced with ever increasing numbers of bodies, which are initially buried in mass graves, the Germans begin to build crematoriums in their concentration camps. (*See* **Nazi Criminality**)

12 FEBRUARY: Germany starts deporting Jews to Polish death camps. (*See* **Intentional Strategy**)

APRIL–MAY: Germany invades Denmark, Norway, the Netherlands, France, Belgium, and Luxembourg.

17 JUNE: Anti-Jewish measures are imposed in France. By October the French Vichy government adopts a set of laws similar to the German Nuremberg laws.

22 OCTOBER: Jews living in the disputed borderlands now controlled by the Germans, such as Alsace-Lorraine and the Saar, are removed to France.

1941

JANUARY: Thousands of Jews in Romania are rounded up and killed; more than ten thousand Romanian Jews will be murdered by government troops by the end of June.

SPRING: Concentration camps are built in Croatia. (*See* **Nazi Criminality**)

14 MAY: Thousands of Parisian Jews are arrested and deported.

JUNE: Hitler invades the Soviet Union, and the *Einsatzgruppen,* mobile killing units of the SS and police, follow the army into captured lands and begin mass executions of Jews. They kill roughly 500,000 Jews, Communists, Gypsies, political leaders, and intelligentsia before the end of the year. (*See* **Führer Order, Irrationality,** *and* **Nazi Criminality**)

JULY: Jewish property in France is confiscated by the Vichy government.

4 JULY–25 NOVEMBER: More than 130,000 Lithuanian Jews are executed by *Einsatzgruppen* units. (*See* **Nazi Criminality**)

31 JULY: Reichsmarschall Hermann Göring commissions Heydrich, security police leader and Himmler's chief deputy, to come up with a comprehensive plan for the Final Solution, the elimination of all Jews in Europe. (*See* **Führer Order, Intentional Strategy, Irrationality,** *and* **Nazi Criminality**)

AUGUST: Anti-Semitic laws against intermarriage are introduced in Hungary. (*See* **Feminist Interpretation**)

SEPTEMBER: The Germans begin experimenting with Zyklon–B (hydrogen cyanide) as a poison to use for mass killing of Jews in the concentration camps. Some victims prior to this point were murdered using carbon dioxide poisoning in mobile gas chambers. (*See* **Irrationality** *and* **Nazi Criminality**)

1 SEPTEMBER: German Jews are required to wear the yellow Star of David on their clothing. (*See* **Advanced Warning**)

29–30 SEPTEMBER: More than 33,000 Jews are executed at Babi Yar, near Kiev, Ukraine, by the *Einsatzgruppen,* who line up the victims along a deep ravine and then machine-gun them. Pro-German Ukrainian militia assist the Germans in several other mass killings in the region. (*See* **Nazi Criminality**)

24 NOVEMBER: A Jewish ghetto is established in Prague. (*See* **Jewish Councils**)

30 NOVEMBER: An estimated fourteen thousand Jews from Riga, Latvia, are murdered and buried in the Rumbuli Forest. (*See* **Nazi Criminality**)

8 DECEMBER: The Germans begin using poison gas to kill Jews in the Chelmno camp in Poland; among the first victims are 5,000 Gypsies (a total of 500,000 to 600,000 Gypsies are killed during the war). Chelmno claims the lives of around 300,000 victims before being shut down in April 1943. (*See* **Führer Order** *and* **Nazi Criminality**)

11 DECEMBER: Germany declares war on the United States following the surprise Japanese attack (7 December) on American forces in Hawaii.

12 DECEMBER: Nearly eight hundred Romanian Jews escape Europe aboard ship and attempt to land in Palestine, but they are turned away by British officials. The ship is later sunk by a Soviet submarine.

1942

Jewish partisans establish a camp in the Naliboki Forest of Poland. More than ten thousand partisans fight the Germans in Poland and Ukraine during the war.

20 JANUARY: Fifteen Nazi senior bureaucrats meet at the Wannsee Conference in Berlin, and they agree on the Final Solution. All Jews throughout Europe are to be sent eastward and formed into labor gangs. Although the word *extermination* is never explicitly mentioned, it is understood that the work and living conditions would be harsh enough to kill large numbers by "natural diminution"; the survivors would be "treated accordingly." Among the leaders present are Heydrich and Adolf Eichmann, chief of Jewish affairs for the Reich Central Security Office. The implementation of the Final Solution is the responsibility of Himmler's SS and Gestapo. (*See* **Eichmann, Führer Order, Irrationality,** *and* **Nazi Criminality**)

MARCH: Sobibor, Belzec, and Auschwitz-Birkenau (all located in Poland) become fully operational death camps for the extermination of Jews. More than 2.5 million people (the Russians estimate that the death toll might have been as high as 4 million) will perish at Auschwitz, which is actually a huge complex of more than forty camps. (*See* **Nazi Criminality**)

17 MARCH: Jews in Lublin, Poland, are rounded up and deported to the concentration camps. By mid April more than thirty thousand Jews from the city have been removed and killed by the Germans. (*See* **Jewish Councils** *and* **Nazi Criminality**)

27 MARCH: French Jews begin to be deported to Auschwitz.

SPRING: Auschwitz begins mass killings of its prisoners using poison gas. (*See* **Nazi Criminality**)

27 MAY: Heydrich is fatally wounded in an assassination plot in Czechoslovakia. In response to his death the Nazis kill more than 1,000 suspected rebels, deport thousands of Jews, and on 10 June wipe out the town of Lidice (killing all 172 men over the age of sixteen and sending the women and children to concentration camps).

MAY–JULY: More than 77,000 Jews (mostly from Poland, but also from Austria, Moravia, Bohemia, and Slovakia) are killed at Sobibor. (*See* **Nazi Criminality**)

JUNE: Gestapo officials order that all traces of murdered Jews be eradicated. This order meant that mass graves have to be dug up and the interred bodies incinerated. (*See* **Nazi Criminality**)

1 JUNE: Jews in all European areas conquered by the Germans are required to wear yellow stars.

30 JUNE: *The New York Times* begins publishing stories of the Holocaust.

7 JULY: German doctors begin experiments on sterilization on Jewish prisoners at Auschwitz. (*See* **Feminist Interpretation** *and* **Medical Experiments**)

14 JULY: Dutch Jews begin to be sent to Auschwitz.

23 JULY: The concentration camp at Treblinka, Poland, becomes operational, and the first Jewish prisoners here are murdered. Initially, between 5,000 and 7,000 Jews arrive daily, but within months that figure rises to more than 10,000 a day. By the end of August nearly 270,000 Jews will be murdered in the gas chambers located here. (*See* **Nazi Criminality**)

AUGUST: Croatian Jews are deported to Auschwitz. (*See* **Nazi Criminality**)

DECEMBER: Belzec stops accepting new prisoners, though the burning of corpses continues until March of the following year; the remaining Jewish prisoners are sent to Sobibor.

10 DECEMBER: The first German Jews arrive at Auschwitz. (*See* **Nazi Criminality**)

1943

Polish Jewish poet and playwright Itzhak Katzenelson composes the poem "Song of the Murdered Jewish People" while in the Vittel camp in France. He later is murdered at Auschwitz.

JANUARY: Himmler visits the Warsaw ghetto and orders that the remaining Jews living there be removed to the concentration camps. The operation is scheduled for April. (*See* **Jewish Councils** *and* **Nazi Criminality**)

FEBRUARY: Greek Jews are forced to move into ghettos.

MARCH: Operations begin to close Treblinka; however, more than 800,000 bodies still need to be incinerated before the Germans can cover up their activities. (*See* **Nazi Criminality**)

Jews from Greece (approximately fifty thousand) and Yugoslavia continue to arrive in Poland to be killed in the camps. (*See* **Nazi Criminality**)

19 APRIL: Jewish rebels in the Warsaw ghetto revolt against the Germans. Although fewer than sixty thousand Jews remain in the ghetto at this time, they fight off superior German military forces until 16 May. (*See* **Jewish Councils**)

MAY: German Dr. Josef Mengele is appointed as a physician to Auschwitz, where he performs medical experiments on inmates. Many of his victims are simply killed to allow for the dissection of organs; he is particularly interested in twins. (*See* **Medical Experiments**)

19 MAY: By this date nearly all known Jews in Berlin have been deported from the city.

JUNE: Himmler orders the liquidation of all the ghettos in Poland and the Soviet Union, with their populations sent to the death camps. (*See* **Jewish Councils** *and* **Nazi Criminality**)

2 AUGUST: Around one thousand Jewish prisoners at Treblinka revolt, but the rebellion is put down; one hundred inmates manage to escape.

OCTOBER: Approximately seven thousand Danish Jews are helped by sympathizers and the underground to escape to Sweden. (*See* **Neutral States**)

14 OCTOBER: Jewish prisoners at Sobibor revolt and kill many of their guards; approximately three thousand escape, although about one hundred are recaptured.

16 OCTOBER: More than one thousand Jews from Rome are sent to Auschwitz. (*See* **Nazi Criminality** *and* **Pius XII**)

17 NOVEMBER: The remaining Jewish prisoners at Treblinka are shot.

2 DECEMBER: Viennese Jews begin to arrive in Auschwitz.

1944

4 APRIL: An Allied warplane photographs Auschwitz for the first time after making a reconnaissance of the fuel and artificial rubber factory at Monowitz, located about 2.5 miles from the camp. Other Allied aerial reconnaissance of the camp occurs periodically until mid January 1945. (*See* **Allied Intervention**)

14 APRIL: More than five thousand Jews from Athens are deported to Auschwitz.

15 MAY: Hungarian Jews begin to be deported to Auschwitz. Within a week more than 100,000 are gassed. In a month and a half nearly one-half of the Jews in Hungary have been deported. (*See* **Nazi Criminality**)

JUNE: The U.S. government has information about the layout of Auschwitz from two former inmates of the camp. (*See* **Allied Intervention**)

6 JUNE: The Allies invade western Europe (D-Day) with a series of landings in Normandy, France.

JULY: Jewish residents in the ghetto in Vilna, Lithuania, revolt; the Germans eventually crush the resistance. (*See* **Jewish Councils**)

Swedish diplomat Raoul Wallenberg arrives in Budapest, Hungary. His efforts result in the saving of more than thirty thousand Jews, but he disappears after the Soviets occupy the country. Despite reports of his incarceration in the Soviet Union, he never returns home. (*See* **Neutral States**)

20 JULY: An assassination attempt on Hitler fails.

24 JULY: Soviet troops liberate Majdanek in Lublin; more than 360,000 prisoners were killed at the camp by the Nazis.

4 AUGUST: Revealed to the authorities, Anne Frank and her family are captured by Gestapo agents in Amsterdam. She dies of typhus in March 1945 at Bergen-Belsen, Germany; her diary is later published by her father.

6 AUGUST: The Lodz ghetto in Poland is destroyed. (*See* **Jewish Councils**)

OCTOBER: German industrialist Oskar Schindler transports his workers from an enamelware and munitions factory in Krakow, Poland, to Moravia. He is credited with saving an estimated 1,200 Jews from the death camps. (*See* **Schindler**)

7 OCTOBER: Jewish rebels at Auschwitz stage a rebellion, but it is quickly put down. Despite the great odds, the rebels destroy one of the incinerators.

26 NOVEMBER: Himmler orders troops to destroy the crematoriums at Auschwitz so as to hide Nazi war crimes.

1945

While retreating from advancing Soviet troops, the Nazis force concentration-camp inmates to march toward Germany, resulting in the deaths of many prisoners.

27 JANUARY: Soviet troops liberate Auschwitz.

6 APRIL: The Germans begin removing prisoners from Buchenwald. Nearly 25,000 people die during the evacuation, which is disrupted by some inmates. (*See* **Nazi Criminality**)

10–11 APRIL: Buchenwald is liberated. American reporter Edward R. Murrow is on hand and reports what he finds. An estimated 50,000 prisoners (including Jews, Gypsies, and Communists) have been murdered in the camp; the liberators find around 21,000 prisoners still alive, approximately 4,000 of whom are Jewish.

15 APRIL: Bergen-Belsen is liberated by the British.

29 APRIL: More than 32,000 prisoners are liberated from the Dachau concentration camp by U.S. soldiers; some of the German guards are executed by the enraged Americans.

Ravensbrück is liberated by Soviet soldiers. (*See* **Feminist Interpretation** *and* **Gender Differences**)

30 APRIL: Hitler commits suicide in Berlin as Russian troops advance on his bunker.

1 MAY: Minister for propaganda Joseph Goebbels and his wife take the lives of their six children and then commit suicide in Hitler's bunker.

5 MAY: Mauthausen is liberated.

7 MAY: Germany surrenders, and the war ends in Europe. Approximately 15 million people (6 million of whom were Jews, representing 63 percent of the Jewish population of Europe) have perished in the Holocaust. (*See* **Nazi Criminality**)

23 MAY: Himmler tries to escape Germany, but he is captured by British soldiers; he then commits suicide by biting a cyanide capsule.

20 NOVEMBER: The International Military Tribunal at Nuremberg begins. Twenty-four Nazi leaders are put on trial for various war crimes, and on 1 October 1946 verdicts are handed down for twenty-two of the defendants: three are acquitted, while the rest receive prison sentences (ranging from ten years to life) or the death penalty. Göring commits suicide before he can be executed. (*See* **Victors' Justice**)

1946

U.S. reports claim that the Nazis had looted an estimated 20 percent of the art treasures in the world, much of it being sold through neutral countries. In addition, Allied authorities estimate that around $579 million of gold (worth more than $5 billion today) was looted by the Nazis, with as much as $400 million being shipped to Switzerland during the war. (*See* **Neutral States**)

More that eleven thousand Jews are housed in the Bergen-Belsen Displaced Persons (DPs) camp (built near the site of the former concentration camp of the same name). An active political cadre pushes for emigration of Jews to British- controlled Palestine. Some Jews begin an exodus to Palestine, but many are stopped by the British and relocated to Cyprus. (*See* **Israel**)

APRIL: The Anglo-American Committee of Inquiry issues a report calling for 100,000 Jewish DPs to be allowed into Palestine. (*See* **Israel**)

JULY: Continued anti-Jewish violence occurs in Poland, convincing many Jews to emigrate.

13 SEPTEMBER: SS officer Amon Goeth, brutal commandant of the Plaszow labor camp in Poland, is hung for causing the murder of more than eight thousand Jews and for the liquidation of the Krakow ghetto. (*See* **Schindler** *and* **Victors' Justice**)

9 DECEMBER: Opening arguments begin in the Doctor's Trial in Nuremberg; twenty-three Nazi scientists and doctors are tried for experiments performed on concentration camp inmates. The trial ends 20 August 1947; sixteen defendants are convicted, seven of whom are given death penalties. (*See* **Medical Experiments** *and* **Victors' Justice**)

1947

The U.N. General Assembly partitions Palestine and creates two states, one for Jews and one for Arabs. (*See* **Israel**)

2 JULY: The Polish parliament creates the Auschwitz-Birkenau State Museum.

13–14 JULY: The First Conference on Holocaust Research is held at the Hebrew University in Jerusalem.

SEPTEMBER: More than four thousand Jewish DPs from Germany, who boarded the ship *Exodus* in an attempt to travel to Palestine, are forcibly removed from the vessel in Hamburg.

22 DECEMBER: Industrialist Friedrich Flick and two other Nazi businessmen are convicted and sentenced to prison terms for using slave laborers. (*See* **Slave Labor** *and* **Victors' Justice**)

1948

Hundreds of former Nazis are recruited by Western intelligence agencies, including the Central Intelligence Agency (CIA), to help provide information about the Eastern bloc.

10 MARCH: Thirteen officials of the Nazi Race and Settlement Office and the Office for the Strengthening of Germandom are convicted of crimes against humanity. (*See* **Victors' Justice**)

9 APRIL: Twenty-four members of the *Einsatzgruppen* (mobile killing units) are convicted of murder and other crimes; fourteen are given death sentences, although ten of the sentences are later commuted. (*See* **Victors' Justice**)

14 MAY: British rule of Palestine ends and Israel is declared an independent state. By the end of the year more than 108,000 Jewish DPs arrive in the new nation. (*See* **Israel**)

30 JULY: Thirteen employees of the I. G. Farben corporation are convicted of war crimes. (*See* **Slave Labor** *and* **Victors' Justice**)

SEPTEMBER: A commemoration is held at Ravensbruck; it will be held yearly thereafter, and in 1993 a museum is established. (*See* **Feminist Interpretation** *and* **Gender Differences**)

1950

By this year, more than 100,000 Jewish DPs have immigrated to the United States and nearly 750,000 have arrived in Israel. (*See* **Israel**)

1951

AUGUST: The last Jewish DPs leave the Bergen-Belsen camp.

1953

18 MAY: The Israeli institution Yad Vashem (The Holocaust Martyrs' and Heroes' Remembrance Authority), devoted to commemorating the Jews who suffered during the Holocaust, is established by the Knesset (Israeli parliament). (*See* **Israel**)

1958

31 January: The United States launches a modified Jupiter–C rocket, carrying the satellite Explorer I, into space. Unknown to most people is the fact that hundreds of scientists and technicians, including Wernher von Braun, were former employees of the Nazi V–2 rocket program, which had employed Jewish slave labor. (*See* **Slave Labor**)

1960

Israeli secret agents kidnap Adolf Eichmann, the architect of the Jewish extermination program, from Argentina and smuggle him to Jerusalem. (*See* **Eichmann** *and* **Israel**)

1961

2 APRIL–14 AUGUST: Eichmann is tried for war crimes. (*See* **Eichmann** *and* **Victors' Justice**)

13 APRIL: Yad Vashem dedicates the Hall of Remembrance in Jerusalem; it is designed by architect Aryeh Elhanani in honor of the six million Jewish victims of the Holocaust.

28 APRIL: Austrian Oskar Schindler, who ran several factories operated by Jewish laborers during the war, is honored by Israel as a Righteous Gentile for saving more than 1,100 Jews from being killed. (*See* **Schindler** *and* **Slave Labor**)

1962

1 May: Trees are planted on the Avenue of the Righteous Among the Nations in honor of non-Jews who saved Jewish lives during the Holocaust.

31 MAY: Eichmann is executed at Ramleh prison. (*See* **Eichmann** *and* **Victors' Justice**)

ADVANCED WARNING

Did German Jews have sufficient warning of the Holocaust to flee Germany prior to 1941 had they chosen to do so?

Viewpoint: Yes. German Jews had many clear indications of what the Nazi regime intended for them.

Viewpoint: No. German Jews did not have enough warning, and, according to William L. Shirer, they were "unduly optimistic" about their circumstances.

Hindsight can be both a blessing and a curse. When one evaluates personal experiences after an event, certain incidents often stand out as important that did not seem so at the time. Equally, while there is a certain pride to be found in reflecting on sound decisions wisely made, mistakes and missed opportunities are often glaringly evident. If one had both complete information and the necessary patience to analyze choices, actions, and responses in sequence, hindsight might also be an effective teacher—assuming that one drew the right conclusions. Strange though it may seem, this challenge is exactly the situation faced by historians.

Historians, for whom hindsight involves the exercise of critical judgment on events often long past, must gather all the available evidence and seek to understand not only what happened but also why it occurred in the way it did. When a situation is examined in the light of subsequent events, it often raises critical questions about what was known, when, and by whom. This inquiry is certainly the case with the complex series of crimes and tragedies commonly called "the Holocaust." Among the many Holocaust issues thus raised by hindsight is the question of why many German Jews remained in the land of their birth even after it came under the rule of an openly anti-Semitic dictator. Did they have enough warning? If they realized their mortal danger, why did they not flee?

Similar questions are raised, of course, after every catastrophe. People have stayed in their homes to face advancing armies, hurricanes, and volcanic eruptions, often with disastrous results. Yet, this seeming bravado is often motivated by quite reasonable fears. If they leave, they might never be able to return home. Given Adolf Hitler's stated goal of making Germany free of Jews, most Jews who did flee the Fatherland assumed that they too would never return. Staying in Germany, even in the face of persecution, seemed to many to be the lesser evil. It should also be emphasized that far more Jews tried to escape Nazi Germany than were able to do so. The Nazi government put up increasingly difficult barriers to emigration. Even more daunting was the prospect of finding a place of refuge outside of Germany, as the Evian Conference made abundantly clear.

Viewpoint:
Yes. German Jews had many clear indications of what the Nazi regime intended for them.

Adolf Hitler was by no means the first virulently anti-Semitic politician to come to power in modern Europe. By the latter half of the nineteenth century, a particularly vicious anti-Semitism was fostered by the government of Russia, while anti-Semitic attitudes were part of the environment for Jewish citizens of Britain, France, Spain, and Italy. Hitler's rise to power in January 1933 was not welcomed by the German Jewish population. But a community that had already survived centuries of extortion, expulsion, forced conversions, and pogroms could not envision the situation becoming any worse than any of those previous persecutions. Germany was, after all, a modern state. Religious and racial discrimination were inconveniences with which Jews would simply have to live until the German nation came back to its senses and democracy was restored. Abandoning Germany to Hitler, especially when his assaults were rhetorical rather than physical, seemed unpatriotic rather than rational. It also meant abandoning professions, businesses, family, friends, and the security of a comfortable place and a familiar language. Even if there were welcoming places of refuge elsewhere in the world—which there were not—any decision to leave would have been filled with uncertainty. Only after *Kristallnacht* (Night of the Broken Glass), the state-sponsored nationwide pogrom on the night of 9–10 November 1938, was any lingering uncertainty erased. By then, however, the catastrophe was already upon them.

In retrospect, the evidence of Hitler's genocidal intent seems apparent, and German Jews should have undertaken every effort to escape. The exterminationist language of *Mein Kampf* (1925–1927) and the triumphant promises by Hitler, Hermann Göring, and others to make the Jews pay for their crimes, to free Europe from their domination, to "hold them under gas" should they start another European war, seem chillingly proleptic. If one reads history as a novel, with a plotline, conflict, and denouement, then German Jews have to be held accountable for not fleeing at the opening scene.

History does not, of course, unfold with the clarity of fiction. In fact, thousands of Jews fled Germany, and thousands more tried unsuccessfully to get out before and after *Kristallnacht*. Failure to perceive that Nazism posed an extreme threat to their existence was only one factor keeping Jews in Nazi Germany. Those

Jews who fled the Reich usually had given up hope in Germany, but not everyone who stayed was optimistic that conditions would improve. Rather, they believed that the conditions could get no worse, or at least that they would not become intolerable. Thousands of Jews and non-Jewish opponents of Nazism were seduced by an unwarranted faith in human progress and civilization. They could not imagine that a civilized, formally Christian state such as Germany could imitate and exceed the barbarity of the Turks during the massacre of the Armenians (1915). The nation of poet Johann Goethe, playwright Johann Schiller, and composers Ludwig von Beethoven and Johann Sebastian Bach might stumble, but it could not fall into complete depravity. Events that in retrospect appear to be the Nazi State tightening the noose around the Jews seemed at the time to be discrete and disparate events, anomalies in the progress of human civilization. Blaming victims of the Holocaust for not interpreting them as one might wish they had—and as they would eventually wish they had—offers no understanding of the thinking of German Jews in the 1930s.

The typical chronology of the Holocaust portrays Nazi policy as, whether by design or because of an unplanned momentum, drawing the Jews inexorably toward Auschwitz. Beginning with the unsuccessful boycott of Jewish businesses in April 1933, and decrees defining Jews as non-Aryans the same month, German Jews were increasingly constrained in their participation in commercial, cultural, and political affairs. In 1938, the Jews having been incrementally isolated from their Aryan neighbors, the Nazis began to implement a policy of identifying Jews and expropriating their assets. This course of action included the practice of arresting Jews, imprisoning them in concentration camps, and then releasing them upon payment of a sufficient fine. In the aftermath of the *Kristallnacht* pogrom Jews were fined one billion German marks, ostensibly to pay for the damage to property their presence in Germany had presumably provoked. In the same year Jewish passports were stamped with a large letter "J," at the request of the Swiss government, and special identification cards were required of all Jews over the age of fifteen. Businesses that remained in Jewish hands were "Aryanized," and the government undertook efforts to keep Aryans from maintaining a fictional ownership of businesses on behalf of Jewish friends. In 1939 German Jews were compelled to give up their silver and gold jewelry and in April were evicted from their apartments and houses. Jews were concentrated in special sections of the cities from which they would later be transported to the east and exterminated. At every point along this path to extermination German Jews moved in two directions

Menorah on an apartment windowsill overlooking town hall, Kiel, Germany, circa 1935

(Bildarchiv Preussischer Kulturbesitz, Berlin)

at the same time. They continued writing friends abroad, applying for permission to emigrate, and undertaking every effort to escape. They also cooperated with their persecutors, on the quite rational (but dangerously mistaken) assumption that traditional laws of civility still applied: "if we cooperate, they will leave us alone." Indeed, it was this faith in civilization, not their misinterpretation of the evidence of Nazi intent, that made them most vulnerable.

Austrian psychoanalyst Sigmund Freud was among the best-known Jewish intellectuals to escape the Holocaust (though he died of throat cancer in exile in 1939). In a series of lectures, published as *Civilization and Its Discontents* (1930), Freud punctured this "myth of civility." Civilization is necessary, he argues, to restrain our most violent passions, but living with these restraints makes us fundamentally unhappy. Had he lived another half decade, Freud would likely have interpreted the Holocaust as a falling away of civilization's pretense. Auschwitz and all that led up to it were not pretense but underlying human reality. That German Jews were unduly hopeful for the future is beyond doubt. They were not failed by their inability to understand where events were leading—no one could have done that—but by their naive trust in humanity and civilization.

Furthermore, even those Jews who had given up on Germany had little opportunity to escape. For the vast majority of German Jews there was no safe refuge. In July 1938 American president Franklin D. Roosevelt convened the Evian Conference under the auspices of the League of Nations. Ostensibly intended to assist beleaguered Jews in their flight from Nazi Germany, the Conference provided the thirty-two nations represented with political cover for their own inaction. In May 1939 the German-owned steamship *St. Louis* sailed from Hamburg carrying 930 Jewish refugees. Almost all had paid extortionate fees, both for a berth on the ship and for permission to reside in Cuba while awaiting resettlement elsewhere. Most hoped to reach the United States. While the ship was at sea, however, the Cuban government rescinded the landing permits that had been issued illegally. Denied permission to dock in Havana, the *St. Louis* steamed back and forth for several days—even getting within sight of Miami Beach—until, short of fuel, it returned to Europe. Britain, Belgium, the Netherlands, and France ultimately agreed to accept the increasingly desperate refugees, some of whom had been released from concentration camps with a promise to leave Germany permanently. Except for the 287 refugees reluctantly accepted by Britain, the passengers

of the SS *St. Louis* found themselves again under Nazi control within the year. The majority of those ultimately perished.

Clearly, those who abandoned the Jews do not share the same culpability as those who perpetrated the Holocaust, and in no sense were the victims to blame for the crimes committed against them. Rather, German Jews accepted without question some of the fundamental premises of all civilized societies: that the government will protect its citizens and that the strong will not be permitted to prey upon the weak. They were not alone in their undue optimism. Nor would it have mattered much had they seen more clearly what lay ahead. Yet, in the face of an implacably exterminationist Nazism and an indifferent world, Jewish faith in civilization proved to be fatal.

–TANDY MCCONNELL,
COLUMBIA COLLEGE

Viewpoint:
No. German Jews did not have enough warning, and, according to William L. Shirer, they were "unduly optimistic" about their circumstances.

German Jews did not have enough warning prior to the beginning of World War II (1939–1945) to have foreseen their destruction by the National Socialist Party. William L. Shirer, American journalist and chronicler of the Third Reich, describes Jews living in Nazi Germany as being "unduly optimistic," and indeed many were, for a variety of reasons. When the doors of emigration closed for Jews in October 1941, a total of 163,696 still resided in Germany. Though many Jews had chosen to emigrate prior to 1941, those who chose to stay later attributed their decisions to a variety of factors: lack of reliable information, denial of the severity of the situation, mixed messages from the Nazi Party and Gentile Germans, a desire to remain optimistic, or an attachment to their Fatherland.

Adolf Hitler's rise to power in January 1933 did not seem particularly alarming to the Jews of Germany. In *The Invisible Wall: Germans and Jews: A Personal Exploration* (1998) Holocaust survivor W. Michael Blumenthal explains that Hitler was dismissed by most Germans as a fanatic; many people thought he was too extreme to pose a real threat to the Jewish population. Furthermore, many Jews did not believe that Hitler would remain in power for long. Even fewer believed that Hitler would actually annihilate the European Jews as he had proposed. Herbert A. Strauss, whose *In the Eye of the Storm: Growing Up Jewish in Germany, 1918–1943: A Memoir* (1999) clearly expresses his surprise at Hitler's actual power and brutality, was one of the disbelieving majority of German Jews. Strauss is hardly an exception; it is documented time and again that Hitler's threats were not taken seriously. Largely because of mixed messages that were conveyed by the Nazi Party, many Jews never believed that Hitler's plan to annihilate the Jews would come to fruition.

The Nuremberg Laws of September 1935 denied Jews their German citizenship. Many Jews lived in fear because of the lack of protection mandated by the new law, for they now had no legal rights of defense against any type of allegation. Nazi policies of "Aryanization," boycotts, and institutionalized anti-Semitism combined to squeeze Jews out of the German culture. While many Jews realized that it was becoming increasingly dangerous to live in Germany and made efforts to emigrate, a vast number remained in the Reich believing that their situation would improve because of their education and influential position in German culture. Not even the November pogrom of 1938 (*Kristallnacht,* or "Night of the Broken Glass") was a warning sufficient to inspire the more well-off German Jews to leave their comfortable homes and homeland for a new life on distant shores.

In his memoir of life in Germany during the Nazi regime, Strauss reiterates the degree to which Jews were deceived by the Nazi Party. He makes special note of the efforts by Nazi propagandists to withhold accurate information from the Jews, thus preventing them from making an informed decision about their future. Once it was no longer possible to emigrate from Germany in 1941, Jews were exposed to a new level of Nazi brutality. Strauss claims that the entire Nazi system was created with the intention of misleading the Jews about what awaited them, either in the early concentration camps or labor camps that were to come. He believes that the deception was based on a multilayered system of Nazi bureaucrats and non-Nazi collaborators who "claimed to be doing nothing more than their jobs." This sort of deception helped Jews remain optimistic and kept them from clearly seeing the reality that would have forewarned them of their impending destruction.

While deception played a key role in the Jews' inability to make an educated decision regarding their future, they were equally hindered by the lack of available information. Shirer documents in *Berlin Diary: The Journal of a Foreign Correspondent, 1934–1941* (1941) that the entire German people were cut off from the world and had little idea of what was going on

politically within their own country. Unless Germans were able to access foreign newspapers such as the *Times* (London), they had no idea of what the Nazi Party was doing apart from its own propaganda claims. In his memoir Strauss goes even further in blaming Nazi propaganda for his lack of knowledge:

> talk about what the Nazi newspapers peddled through well-manipulated headlines every day fell far short of what I would learn later from listening to educated and incisive political commentators over the radio, especially in wartime Switzerland. I lacked the concepts to place events into perspective. Five years of growing up in Nazi Germany had drowned me in political propaganda and turned me into a political ignoramus at the same time. You immunized yourself by adopting a jaundiced cynicism, but you knew of no way of filling the resulting void, you did not know of the void. "They" defined the framework of your opposition and expectations. I should have been afraid of a new war as early as that beautiful summer of 1938.

According to Strauss, German Jews had no idea that they should be afraid.

In fact, on the morning after Hitler's appointment as chancellor in January 1933, a *New York Times* columnist observed that "there is no warrant for immediate alarm. It may be that we shall see the 'tamed HITLER' of who some Germans are hopefully speaking." Perhaps it is only in hindsight that Hitler's threats can be taken seriously, even though his political autobiography *Mein Kampf* (1925–1927) clearly outlined what he would attempt to do in the event that he should gain power. The article in *The New York Times* certainly indicates the general atmosphere outside of Germany when Hitler came to power: he was thought to be neither very frightening nor potentially threatening.

Blumenthal, meanwhile, attributes part of the problem concerning the Jews' need to flee to simple denial. He witnessed the reaction of fellow survivors when they first learned of the enormity of the Holocaust at the conclusion of the war. He reports that few German Jews had seen signs of the oncoming annihilation of their communities. Furthermore, even when the danger signs could no longer be denied, it was expected the hard times would be brief, for few Jews believed that Nazis could maintain control for any length of time. By the time the reality of the situation was apparent, the chances for Jews to flee had greatly diminished, to the point of near impossibility.

Within Germany both non-Jews and Nazi Party members sent mixed messages to their Jewish neighbors that effectively prevented Jews from realizing their precarious position and the threat of impending death. Many of these messages allowed Jews to believe that they could adjust to and eventually prevail over

A Jewish woman, Inge Deutchkron, recalls being forced to wear the Star of David on her clothing during a trip into town:

Alice Licht was my friend. She was a very pretty girl of my own age. She had jet black hair with a centre parting, and was slim and dainty, with the face of a spoilt child. Her big, black eyes could bewitch any man who came near her—and did she know it!

On that morning—September 16—she came to call for me. We had decided to travel to work together. We were going to support each other; for on this particular day, for the first time, we were wearing the Magen David on the left side of our coats, above the heart, sewn on with fine stitches, all according to regulations.

"How do you feel?" I asked Alice.

"Just like you do." She tried to laugh, but her charming child's face was a rigid mask behind which she endeavored to hide her pain and humiliation.

"It's best for us just to make nothing of it," I said. "We'll pretend it's a decoration."

"A decoration!" Alice laughed, but it was a grim laugh.

We went arm-in-arm from the Bayerischen Platz towards the underground station. My heart contracted, because I knew that on the train I'd see a young man who, every morning during the journey to work, used to give me appreciative glances. How would this fair-headed young man behave today? How would he react to the Jewish star?

"Better keep a stiff upper lip," I said, and laughed. But it wasn't a natural laugh.

The train roared into the station and came to a halt; the doors opened with a hiss of compressed air and we got on.

Everyone looked at us; like every morning. Their gaze moved over our faces, our coats. Not an eye fixed itself on the star of David. It was as if we weren't wearing it at all.

There was my young man, too. He stood a couple of paces away from me; and smiled, as always.

I looked around me. I saw dozens of people also wearing the star of David— people one would never have taken for Jews; blond men, red-haired women, a white-haired old gentleman with the boldly etched features of a Viking.

All of them Jews; all wearing the yellow badge of shame which was to stamp them as pariahs.

But we were not pariahs. . . .

One of the passengers made no bones about his sympathy. A middle-aged man, who got up from his seat.

"Please, young lady," he said, pointing to his place.

"I'm not allowed to sit," I said, and remained standing.

"But I insist," he said, in the same polite tone.

I was not allowed to sit; Jews were not allowed to sit. But I could not draw attention to myself, either.

"Please," said the gentleman, who had taken off his hat and now stood before me. "Please sit down. Nothing will happen to you. I'll guarantee that. I offer you my protection."

He said that so confidently that I could do nothing but sit down.

The young man who stood a short distance away smiled again. His smile said: All right. Don't be afraid. It won't be all that bad. But we deceived ourselves, all of us; we Jews and those sympathetic Berliners in the underground that morning. It was going to be very bad for many millions of my co-religionists in Europe, and for millions of Germans, too.

The great massacre was just beginning.

Source: *"The Yellow Star: Mark of Identification and Humiliation," in* Witness to the Holocaust, *edited by Azriel Eisenberg (New York: Pilgrim Press, 1981), pp. 76–77.*

Nazi persecution. Germans who went out of their way to be friendly or helpful toward Jews left the Jews feeling as if their plight were not unbearable. Furthermore, brief interludes in Nazi persecution during the 1930s often gave German Jews false hopes about the future. In an attempt to cope with their persecutors on a day-by-day basis, Jews did not consider the overarching theme of persecution. In the confusing circumstances of the day these mixed messages often made the problems and issues seem manageable, when they were actually entirely out of the control of the intended victims. A common thread seen throughout many Jewish memoirs of this period was hope. In actuality such hope disguised the warning signs.

Optimism prevailed in the minds of many German Jews. Strauss repeatedly notes the optimistic nature to which his fellow Jews clung. He states that he does not believe that he knew anyone who could have imagined the ramifications of the Holocaust. Though people looked less toward the future, Strauss indicates that many Jews still believed they would survive the war. Such optimism is perhaps best summarized by the common refrain for German Jewish leaders during the time: *na also, es geht ja immer besser und besser* (well, things are always getting better and better).

One of the underlying issues that has to be considered when dealing with Jews in Nazi Germany is the status of these residents of the Third Reich; were they, in fact, German? As is apparent from the Nuremberg Laws, Nazified Germans did not believe that Jews were "German." Jews, however, believing in the ideals of *Bildung* (education) and culture, thought of themselves as "Germans" after having become entrenched in German education, history, culture, and ideals throughout the prior centuries. Whereas Nazis defined nationality by blood, Jews defined nationality by a common education in the classics and history. *Bildung,* Jews believed, provided a common ground on which both ethnic Germans and German Jews could meet. In this way Jews residing in Nazi Germany believed that they were as "German" as any "Aryan." Furthermore, they believed that after having made so many contributions to German culture during the Weimar Republic (1919–1933) that they would be fully accepted and welcomed as part of the German nation. The Jews, however, were not as warmly welcomed or received as they had anticipated.

George Mosse, a student of both German and Jewish history, nevertheless argues that their faith in education actually blinded the Jews to Nazi intentions: "*Bildung* and *Sittlichkeit* [respectability], which had stood at the beginning of Jewish emancipation in Germany, accompanied German Jews to the end, blinding them, as many other Germans, to the menace of National Socialism." Inspired by a communal desire to gain equality in predominantly Christian Europe, Jews had long set their sights on attaining *Bildung*. Confronted by the "New Order" of National Socialism, however, German Jews failed to see that *Bildung* was no longer the key to equality. Nor, educated though they were, did they understand what the implications of Nazi control meant for them, their families, and their communities.

Perhaps more than anything else, German Jews felt tied to Germany as their Fatherland and thus were reluctant to leave. The diaries of Victor Klemperer, a German Jewish scholar residing in the Third Reich, repeatedly emphasize the author's inability to leave Germany because of his patriotic ties to the Fatherland. On 18 October 1936, Klemperer recorded:

> [A friend] asked about my work. "Why don't you publish anything in America?" I said: "I am waiting." She: "For what?" Somewhat agitated, my voice and expression perhaps over-theatrical, I said: "For my Fatherland, I have no other!" She, rather surprised and almost pleased: "Oh, so you still think . . . ?" And: "I do not want to emigrate either."

Waiting for the situation to change (and hopeful that it would), Klemperer's frustration is apparent in this passage. Resigned to his fate, Klemperer nonetheless expressed throughout the pages of his diary his hope that Hitler would be defeated. Klemperer, at least in the earlier years of Hitler's control, claimed to be more ashamed of what the German State was doing than fearful of its consequences.

There are many factors that influenced how Jews perceived not only the Nazi regime but also their fate as one of the minorities that Hitler chose to ostracize. The Jews did not have a warning prior to the onset of the war that was sufficient to encourage them to flee. Then, during the two-year gap between September 1939 and the day when the Nazis forbade all Jewish emigration from Germany, there were few destinations open to Jewish migrants. Immigration restrictions to other countries were such that German Jews often could not gain entry visas. In the event that Jews were able to do so, they were often unable to prepare the necessary paperwork within the time limits provided. Essentially, bureaucracy kept them within the bounds of Germany.

Indeed, while relatively few Jews made an effort to leave after 1939, simple fear dissuaded others from making the attempt. Many Jews did not want to leave a country that they understood, despite the grim outlook, for another country where they would not know the language, the culture, the people, or the customs. Klemperer, for example, wrote that he would rather stay in Germany and face danger, with the possibility of having a good life at the conclusion of the war, than go and face the unknown world of the United States. Indicative of their persisitent optimism, some German Jews believed that it took more courage to leave Germany than to stay.

It appears that the "undue optimism" detected by Shirer aptly describes the attitudes of Jews living in Germany during the Nazi years. Contemporary diaries of German Jews and post-war memoirs of Holocaust survivors fairly represent what the majority of Jews were facing during this period. As these documents reveal, no one single factor sustained their optimism more than another. Some combination of factors (a lack of reliable information, mixed messages, denial, optimism, faith in education, attachment to the Fatherland) prompted German Jews to remain hopeful that their situation would improve. In the uncertainty of the times these and many other European Jews stayed put, waiting for the old storm of hatred to blow over them once again. Thus, they became victims of the genocidal hurricane Hitler unleashed on an unsuspecting world.

        –MELISSA JANE TAYLOR,
     UNIVERSITY OF SOUTH CAROLINA

References

W. Michael Blumenthal, *The Invisible Wall: Germans and Jews: A Personal Exploration* (Washington, D.C.: Counterpoint, 1998).

Sigmund Freud, *Civilization and Its Discontents* (New York: Norton, 1961).

Marion Kaplan, *Between Dignity and Despair: Jewish Life in Nazi Germany* (New York: Oxford University Press, 1998).

Victor Klemperer, *I Will Bear Witness: A Diary of the Nazi Years,* 2 volumes, translated by Martin Chalmers (New York: Random House, 1998).

Paul Mendes-Flohr, *German Jews: A Dual Identity* (New Haven: Yale University Press, 1999).

George L. Mosse, "Jewish Emancipation: Between Bildung and Respectability," in *The Jewish Response to German Culture: From the Enlightenment to the Second World War,* edited by Jehuda Reinharz and Walter Schatzberg (Hanover, N.H.: University Press of New England, 1985), pp. 1–16.p

William L. Shirer, *Berlin Diary: The Journal of a Foreign Correspondent, 1934–1941* (New York: Knopf, 1941).

Herbert A. Strauss, *In the Eye of the Storm: Growing Up Jewish in Germany, 1918–1943: A Memoir* (New York: Fordham University Press, 1999).

Ruth Zariz, "Officially Approved Emigration from Germany after 1914: A Case Study," *Yad Vashem Studies,* 18 (1987): 275–291.

ADVANCED WARNING

ALLIED INTERVENTION

Could the Allies have disrupted the Holocaust by bombing extermination camps?

Viewpoint: Allied air raids on extermination camps would have been disruptive, but they also would have prolonged the war by diverting bombers and other military resources needed elsewhere.

Viewpoint: Allied bombing of extermination camps was never a practical option because precise targeting of bombs was not possible.

Jews in Germany came under attack almost as soon as the Nazi Party came to power. They were imprisoned, attacked, and occasionally killed in the streets well before the outbreak of war. However, the mass killing of Jews and other racial enemies of the Third Reich did not begin until the German invasion of the Soviet Union in the spring of 1941. In addition, genocide does not appear to have become a formal part of the Nazi agenda until late in 1941 or early in 1942—by which time American involvement in the European war was a foregone conclusion, and nothing was to be gained (from Adolf Hitler's perspective) in delay. It was no accident that the Holocaust was conducted in a context of total war. The transportation and extermination of Jews and others were easier to hide. Military and diplomatic efforts on the part of the Allies or the neutral states of Europe to hinder or stop the destruction of the Jews became exceedingly difficult. Intervention was further complicated by Soviet indifference. Joseph Stalin was unwilling to cooperate with the western Allies in any mission to alleviate Jewish suffering. And from the perspectives of the western Allies, a substantial diversion of resources to bombing the crematoriums of Auschwitz or the railroads carrying Jews to their deaths would have been politically dangerous, feeding into Hitler's own rhetorical claims that World War II (1939–1945) had been instigated by the Jews and was being fought by the Allies at their behest.

It is also unclear how effective military intervention—aerial bombing was the most likely scenario—might have been. Railroads made exceedingly difficult targets, and any attack on the machinery of death at concentration camps such as Auschwitz would have certainly cost prisoners' lives. Yet, the debate continues precisely because no such attempt was made. Allied war planners argued, both at the time and afterward, that the only effective way to halt the German genocide was to defeat Germany by force of arms, and the only way to do that was to concentrate every effort on destroying Germany's ability to wage war. The concentration camps had little impact on Germany's war-fighting ability, and every bomb dropped on Auschwitz was one less bomb to take out a ball-bearing factory.

Arguments to the contrary have always been handicapped by limited Allied attempts to intervene diplomatically and the complete failure to intervene militarily. There is no way of knowing with any certainty how the concentration-camp bureaucracy would have responded to an air campaign aimed at killing SS guards and bureaucrats and destroying their ability to carry out the war against the Jews. Nor is it knowable how the prisoners, so often disregarded in the discussion, might have responded to such efforts on their behalf. Arguments that even token Allied bombardment might have caused individual camp guards to rethink their commitment to the Final Solution, or emboldened prisoners to make escapes, remain theoretical. More solidly based in documentary evidence, but still controversial, is the argument that Allied failure to take action was based more on political considerations than on military assessments. The issue has received renewed attention in the 1990s, when western failures to intervene effectively to halt ethnic cleansing in the former Yugoslavia and mass murder in Rwanda were also blamed on political cowardice and indifference to human sufferings.

Viewpoint:
Allied air raids on extermination camps would have been disruptive, but they also would have prolonged the war by diverting bombers and other military resources needed elsewhere.

The question of whether the Allies could have intervened to hinder implementation of the Final Solution is straightforward and easily answered, on one level, at least. Certainly, the Allies intervened militarily to disrupt the Holocaust; that military intervention was called World War II (1939–1945). Once the Allies settled upon the "unconditional surrender" of Germany as their wartime policy, they did all in their power, militarily and diplomatically, to make that political aim a reality. To argue that the Allies could have done more to disrupt the many death camps completely misses the point that the entire war effort was designed to bring Germany to its knees as quickly as possible, effectively closing the death camps permanently in the shortest amount of time. Yet, could the Allies have done more than they did? Could innocent lives have been saved had the Allies bombed the crematoriums or cut the rail lines which brought the Holocaust's victims to their deaths? For political, far more than for military, reasons, this alternative remained the road not taken. The Allies could not have stopped the Holocaust without winning the war, but intermediate efforts that were taken saved thousands of lives, and further efforts, however modest, might have saved thousands more.

One must first clarify the term *Allies*. Great Britain, the Soviet Union, and the United States spoke with one voice and acted in concert on some, but by no means all, war-related issues. The Allied leaders stood unanimously behind the policy of defeating Germany first. They were unanimous, too, that no separate peace agreements would be struck with Adolf Hitler. These two policies cannot be separated, and, indeed, the alliance itself could not have survived without such unanimity. Keeping Joseph Stalin's Soviet Union in the war against Germany was indispensable to the entire Allied war effort. Great Britain needed time to recover from the devastating losses imposed on her army on the Continent and on her air forces in the skies over England. The United States needed time to mobilize, train, and deploy its air, ground, and naval forces worldwide. These two policies inextricably linked Allied military efforts, even when such efforts could not always be coordinated globally. Stalin continued to oversee the war in the east while Franklin D. Roosevelt and Winston Churchill focused elsewhere. The Allies agreed, at least in principle, on this division of military labor.

There was no such Allied unanimity regarding the issue of intervening in the Holocaust. Because virtually all of the death camps were in eastern Europe and thus within the Soviet theater of operations—and ultimately within range of Soviet bombers—the Soviet Union was the best situated to intervene. Yet, Stalin was adamant from the beginning: the Jews were absolutely not the only people being persecuted by the Nazis. Millions of Russians were in just as much danger of death, he argued, and to give special treatment to the Jews by intervening solely on their behalf was unacceptable to Stalin. The Soviets would not intervene, nor would Stalin support efforts by the Western Allies. Over time this policy dispute became potentially more, rather than less, contentious among the Allied leaders. Stalin was convinced that his partners, Roosevelt and Churchill, were dragging their feet over starting a second front to relieve the German military pressure on the Soviet Union. American troops could not invade western Europe soon enough to suit Stalin. The suggestion of further diverting inadequate American and British military assets from bombing Germany to bomb, instead, the death camps was too outrageous in Stalin's mind to even consider. Whatever the remaining two Allied leaders determined to do militarily to disrupt the Final Solution would have to be done without Soviet support.

The strategic implications of Stalin's refusal to support such measures crippled any hope of Allied intervention to save the Jews. The majority of the death camps was in the Soviet-controlled eastern theater of operations, not the western areas within comparatively easy reach of American and British air (or airborne) forces. Without ready access to Soviet airfields and logistical support, the ability of Allied forces to effectively project combat power into eastern Europe to disrupt the death camps was problematic at best. Nevertheless, even absent the help of the Soviets, the military mission never became impossible, despite the added difficulties. Nor did these trying circumstances discourage the British and the Americans from considering their military alternatives for disrupting the camps as an adjunct to the broader strategic objective of accomplishing the unconditional surrender of Hitler's Germany.

In pursuing their single-minded objective, the Allies understood that strategic military trade-offs were necessary. President Roosevelt and his joint chiefs understood that every bomber that they dispatched to Europe, for example, was a bomber unavailable to push back the Japanese in the Pacific. Could the war in the Pacific have been ended sooner had the Allies concentrated their combat power in that theater rather than in Europe? Would that have saved lives in the Pacific? The answer to both questions is an unqualified "yes." Nevertheless, the Allies agreed to "Germany First" as their global military policy. Roosevelt and Churchill repeatedly concurred in the difficult strategic choices needed to win the war in Europe while knowingly prolonging the war against Japan. As much as they both wanted to defeat Japan, they understood and accepted that the threat from Germany was greater still. Neither Germany nor Japan could be defeated if the Allies failed to concentrate their forces where it mattered most.

The issue of militarily delaying or hindering the Final Solution involved virtually identical calculations, albeit on a theater, rather than on a global, level. At the behest of concerned parties, first British, then American, strategic planners considered the feasibility and advisability of bombing the death camps. In both cases the military decision making followed a similar evaluation process and came to similar conclusions. Since the British considered bombing the camps before the Americans did, British planning can serve as an example of the overall process.

Several factors initially delayed any military planning. Before the feasibility of air strikes could be determined, planners needed to collect sufficient target intelligence and aerial photographs to begin to consider hitting those sites. Photographic reconnaissance missions were flown on several occasions to collect the needed information. Overcast conditions and film developing problems made these initial photos unusable. While there were target photographs of the camps already in the hands of some Allied strategic planners, those photos, only found in the archives after being collected at the end of the war, were not in the hands of the military planners considering the disruption of the camps

when the information was needed. Strategic targeting during the war years was not nearly so centralized or integrated as it is in modern practice. Having the necessary photographs in the archives decades later and having those same photographs in the right hands in 1943 or 1944 are not the same things. Auschwitz was never a high enough priority target to get the reconnaissance photos into the hands of strategists.

Regardless of what tactical planners did or did not know about the camps, the U.S. government at the highest levels was certainly "in the know." As Secretary of the Treasury Henry Morgenthau, a Roosevelt confidant, said, "We knew in Washington, from August 1942 on, that the Nazis were planning to exterminate all the Jews of Europe." While direct military intervention, in the form of bombing the camps or cutting the rail lines, was being considered and ultimately ruled out, the Allies nevertheless took nonmilitary measures to delay the Final Solution. The most significant was establishment of the Treasury Department's War Refugee Board, founded in January 1944. This organization was designed to help Jews and other refugees resettle in the United States and elsewhere around the world. The board took rescue activities out of the hands of the U.S. Department of State, which, perhaps, had been overly sympathetic toward British concerns about a flood of Jewish refugees bound for Palestine had such rescue taken place.

British reluctance to facilitate a flood of Jewish refugees was well known to President Roosevelt. His own ambivalence to the problem was also fostered by the knowledge that the "Coordinating Foundation," an international corporation to receive Jewish refugees, was opposed by American Jews who believed that these efforts helped Hitler to solve German domestic problems. Thus, Roosevelt was slow to trust in such efforts. Roosevelt was also acutely aware of the view of average Americans on this issue. While complete understanding of the horror of the Holocaust was still known only at the highest levels of the American government, the view on the street recognized the Holocaust for what it was and yet agreed that the best way to stop it was to prosecute the war against Germany as effectively and expeditiously as possible. As Fred Eastman wrote in *Christian Century* in February 1944, in reply to published calls for greater Allied military intervention specifically directed to destroy the Nazi apparatus of the Final Solution:

If this war isn't a big enough fight, just how much bigger would they make it? Our sons are in the service, our incomes are mortgaged for generations to come, and the casualty lists are mounting from week to week. If the spilling of blood and the conversion of our natural resources into instruments of destruction can stop the mass murders and the other depredations of Hitler's cohorts it is being done as rapidly as the generals of the United Nations can manage it.

Further complications, often overlooked today, were the aforementioned policies of unconditional surrender and no separate peace, which virtually precluded open and direct negotiations with the Nazis and other Axis-friendly governments. Instead, the U.S. State Department repeatedly insisted that "rescue through victory" was the best approach, and this attitude became and remained the clear consensus political position that ruled out any other possibilities.

In the interim, military planning continued apace. Since many of the camps were in the vicinity of other industrial targets, photoreconnaissance missions did not have to be diverted widely, but, nevertheless, every photo taken of a concentration camp was a photo not taken of a German combat-aircraft or munitions factory. Once photos were in hand, planners could start to consider the possibilities. At that point military planners ran head-on into many difficult questions with debatable answers. How will bombing the rail lines into the camps save the prisoners already inside? Will not bombing the camps kill the inmates? How many bombers are enough, and how many are too many? How will diversion of bombers to these targets affect the strategic bombing campaign as a whole? How long will the entire war effort be prolonged by such diversion?

Despite running into roadblocks at every step, military strategists diligently considered every option. While bombing might be used to prompt mass escapes, to where would the prisoners escape? Food and medical supplies could be dropped, but it would relieve Germany from any need to feed its own slave labor. Also these supplies would likely have ended up in Nazi hands anyway. Weapons could be dropped to the inmates, but would that not also result in futile deaths? (In March 1944 the Royal Air Force conducted Operation Jericho in occupied France, freeing 150 condemned prisoners. To try the same thing in Poland was far less likely to succeed.) Many lethal and nonlethal options were considered and rejected, sometimes for political and diplomatic reasons. Through it all loomed Stalin's refusal to cooperate with such measures. Even explicit Allied warnings of severe retribution for Nazi atrocities toward the Jews were weakened because the Soviets refused to cooperate, again rejecting special treatment solely for the Jewish victims of the Nazis.

The Allied military planning efforts have been well documented, starting with the initial deliberations in July 1944 of the British Air Ministry, as well as subsequent discussions with U.S. Army Air Force general Carl Spaatz, during which the British handed off the responsibility for such planning to American strategists. The military consensus was crystal clear. British military planners exhaustively considered all options and concluded that the range of such missions, according to Sir Archibald Sinclair, British minister for air, covered the spectrum from "out of our power" to "out of the bounds of possibility." Not surprisingly, American strategists also concluded that accomplishment of these Holocaust-related objectives, to quote John McCloy, U.S. assistant secretary of war, "could only be executed by the diversion of considerable air support essential to the success of our forces now engaged in decisive operations elsewhere and would in any case be of such doubtful efficacy that it would not warrant the use of our resources."

Critics of the Allied military response to the Final Solution often highlight individuals in the Allied governments, what they knew, when they knew it, why they did not act (or act differently), and which realistic alternatives were available to them. The point seems to be that various British and/or American leaders were either anti-Semitic or otherwise uninterested in the fate of the Jews. On that basis, however true, the most common critical argument illogically concludes that this alone resulted in the unnecessary deaths of thousands of Jews.

Notwithstanding personal opinion, however heartfelt, establishing the fact that there was anti-Semitism or indifference in the American and British governments does not resolve the basic issue. Nor does proving that different or additional military options were available to resolve it. The basic issue hinges on whether alternative military measures would have saved additional Jews. There is no proof that more Jews would have been saved had the Allies bombed the camps. It is pure conjecture to contend that bombing the concentration camps or cutting the rail lines would have saved Jews.

However, circumstantial evidence exists that the Allied approach was the most effective and efficient option. The death camps operated at varying levels of production until the final months of the war. It was only the threat of being overrun by Allied troops that caused operations in these camps to cease. That situation points to a grim determination on the part of the Nazis to continue the mass murders until the last possible moment. It certainly does not support the contention that a token number of Allied bombs would cause the Nazis to reconsider and, indeed, jettison their plans for the Final Solution. That token bombing effort is precisely the silver bullet that present-day critics contend was deliberately ignored by Roosevelt, Churchill, and

EVIDENCE OF THE HORROR

On 29 April 1945 American soldiers of I Company, 3rd Battalion, 157th Infantry Regiment, 45th (Thunderbird) Division, liberated the concentration camp at Dachau. Lieutenant Colonel Felix L. Sparks, commander of the 3rd Battalion, left this account:

The initial shock was experienced even before entering the camp. The first evidence of the horror to come was a string of about forty railway cars on a sidetrack near the camp entrance. Each car was loaded with emaciated human corpses, both men and women. A hasty search by the stunned infantrymen revealed no signs of life among the hundreds of still bodies. Few words were spoken as the grim-faced soldiers deployed in battle formation towards the camp itself.

As the main gate to the camp was closed and locked, we scaled the brick wall surrounding the camp. . . . The scene near the entrance to the confinement area numbed my senses. Dante's Inferno seemed pale compared to the real hell of Dachau. A row of small cement structures near the prison entrance contained a coal-fired crematorium, a gas chamber disguised as a shower, and a room piled high with naked and emaciated human corpses. As I turned to look over the prison yard with unbelieving eyes, I saw a large number of dead inmates lying where they had fallen in the last few hours or days before our arrival. Since all the many bodies were in various stages of decomposition, the stench of death was overpowering.

During the early period of our entry into the camp, a number of Company I men, all battle hardened veterans, became extremely distraught. Some cried, while others raged. Some thirty minutes passed before I could restore order and discipline. During that time, the over thirty thousand camp prisoners still alive began to grasp the significance of the events taking place. They streamed from their crowded barracks by the hundreds and were soon pressing at the confining barbed wire fence. They began to shout in a unison which soon became a chilling roar. At the same time, several bodies were being tossed about and torn apart by hundreds of hands. I was told later that those being killed at that time were "informers."

Within about an hour of our entry, events were under control. Guard posts were set up and communications were established with the inmates. We informed them that we could not release them immediately, but that food and medical assistance would arrive soon. The dead, numbering about nine thousand, were later buried with the forced assistance of the good citizens of the city of Dachau.

Source: *Colonel Howard A. Buechner,* Dachau: The Hour of the Avenger *(Metairie, La.: Thunderbird, 1986), pp. 63–64.*

---

their subordinates: to have a limited number of bombers drop a limited number of bombs, thereby forestalling the entire Final Solution.

Allied leaders admittedly responded coldly and calculatedly and put their military resources together in as overwhelming a way as possible in order to bring those assets to bear on the German industrial base. One must never forget, though critics routinely do so, precisely what Allied bombers were doing while they were not bombing the death camps. Weather permitting, American strategic bombers conducted massive bombing runs over German industries during daylight hours. British bombers followed up with nighttime bombing. Intense pressure was maintained on German industry virtually twenty-four hours each day. Despite the broadest strategic bombing campaign in the history of war (before or since World War II), German factories were still producing planes and tanks until the end of the war. Despite the massive Allied bombing, German industry was able concurrently to design and build the world's first operational jet-powered military aircraft. If Allied strategic bombing of this incredible magnitude could not more effectively delay or hinder production of such high-tech weapons, it is inconceivable that Allied bombing of any magnitude could have shut down the relatively low-tech death camps. It was not even remotely possible to destroy every crematorium or cut every rail line into a death camp. Even if it were possible and had been accomplished, the Nazis would have found another way to murder their victims. Hastily dug mass graves across Europe, followed by a spray of machine-gun fire, would have been no less final a solution and equally compliant with the Führer's wish that the Jews be annihilated. No amount of Allied strategic bombing could have changed that outcome.

Yet, the Nazis had abandoned the use of mass graves and machine guns early in the implementation of the Final Solution precisely because such means were less efficient than concentration camps and industrialized factories of death. The work of the *Einsatzgruppen* (mobile killing units) could not be conducted with the secrecy the Final Solution required. It was hard on the morale of troops who witnessed the murders. It left too many witnesses. The killing might have continued, but at a necessarily slower, far less efficient pace. Only in the context of World War II does the potential saving of a few thousand or a few hundred thousand lives count for so little. However, constrained as they were by political and diplomatic considerations, especially by the unwillingness of the Soviet Union to support any such efforts, the Allies did not attempt to intervene militarily to hinder the Holocaust.

–MICHAEL S. CASEY,
GRACELAND UNIVERSITY

Viewpoint:
Allied bombing of extermination camps was never a practical option because precise targeting of bombs was not possible.

In 1940 and 1941, when mass deportations and executions of Jews in the east were just beginning, Germany was well on its way to achieving mastery of Europe. Though the war began in September 1939 with the German invasion of Poland, the mass murder of Europe's Jews did not begin until Operation Barbarossa—the invasion of the Soviet Union—in June 1941. Soviet forces were quickly pushed back to the gates of Moscow and, by the onset of winter, appeared likely to lose the war. By that time British forces had been driven from the European continent at Dunkirk and were desperately preparing for a German invasion of the home islands. France had fallen to Germany in June 1940 and was divided between the collaborationist Vichy regime of Marshal Philippe Pétain and outright military occupation in the north of the country. The United States was distant and neutral until the December 1941 attack on Pearl Harbor. Adolf Hitler's inexplicable declaration of war on the United States brought the Americans into the conflict, but this event would not make much difference for many months. Thus, as the *Einsatzgruppen* (mobile killing units) slaughtered thousands of Russian Jews, as the ghettos and extermination camps developed the machin-

ery of mass murder, as the Holocaust became a reality, there were no Allied forces even remotely capable of intervening. German troops and those of its Axis allies and satellites were triumphant throughout Europe from the Pyrenees to the gates of Moscow. Within Nazi-occupied Europe, millions of Jews were prisoners of Hitler.

Yet, might the Allies not have intervened sooner? The steps by which Nazi Germany reached this hegemonic state of affairs have been endlessly debated, especially the policy of appeasement pursued by Britain and France during the 1930s. Most, but not all, historians today regard appeasement as a relatively rational policy, probably the only one that could have been realistically followed at the time. Two important factors must be kept in mind: until the outbreak of the war Hitler's policy was to expel the Jews, not to kill them, and no Jews were deliberately killed as a matter of systematic Nazi policy until the invasion of the Soviet Union. While the Nazi regime ruled over only Germany, Austria, and the Sudetenland (a German-speaking region of Czechoslovakia), there were only 500,000 Jews living in Germany itself, 265,000 in Austria, and 15,000 in the Sudetenland. Most of these Jews managed to emigrate before the war began. For example, about two-thirds of Austria's Jews emigrated between the *Anschluss* of March 1938 and the early phase of the war, after which emigration was forbidden by the Nazis. The Jews of other parts of Europe, especially the millions of Jews in Poland and the Soviet Union who were to become the chief victims of the Holocaust, were not under Nazi rule or occupation and were not refugees. The overwhelming majority of the Jews who perished in the Holocaust was not under Nazi rule until after World War II (1939–1945) began. Only a preemptive Allied policy that would have prevented Hitler from seizing Poland, Russia, and the rest of Europe would have had any chance of preventing most of these deaths.

Yet, during the 1930s it proved impossible to forge a viable military alliance among Britain, France, and the Soviet Union that might have deterred Hitler from aggression and hence from genocide. Instead, Britain and France pursued policies of appeasement. Though appeasement would ultimately fail, such policies were not without merit. Hitler's aim until 1939 appeared to be the creation of a purely Aryan German Reich in central Europe. The *Anschluss* with Austria and the absorption of the Sudetenland seemed to fulfill that goal. It appeared totally contrary to its aims at the time for Germany to seize other, non-German areas by force, areas with millions of supposedly subhuman Jews and Slavs. Since Hitler's policy toward the Jews in Germany and Austria had been to expel them, it

did not seem likely that he would want to add millions more. The Allies believed that, once Hitler had created a unified pan-German state and thus corrected the injustice of the Treaty of Versailles (1919), he would live at peace with his neighbors. Hitler made just such promises at the 1938 Munich Conference. He had, of course, written about the necessity of acquiring lebensraum (living space) for Germany in the east in *Mein Kampf* (1925–1927), but such language was easily dismissed as the rhetoric of a politician seeking power, not of a successful head of state. Hitler's assertions at Munich that he had no interest in further German expansion were lies, but the Allies had no reason not to believe him.

Unified military action on the part of Britain, France, and the Soviet Union before 1939 might also have preempted both war and genocide, but this too foundered on several factors. Joseph Stalin, a paranoid megalomaniac and mass murderer in his own right, was, in 1937 and 1938, engaged in the Great Purges that resulted in the killing of, among many others, his best military officers. The Soviet Union had no common border with either Germany or Czechoslovakia, and to reach the Czechs during the Sudetenland Crisis of 1938 would have required sending troops through either Poland or Romania. The violently anticommunist governments in both of these countries adamantly refused to

allow Soviet troops to pass through their territories, fearing—with good cause—that Stalin would use the occasion to add their territories to the Soviet Union. The conservative governments of Britain and France feared and mistrusted Stalin, who, in turn, regarded them as "imperialist reactionaries." Presumably, if Britain and France had declared war on Germany at the time of Munich, Anglo-French forces would have invaded the Rhineland area of western Germany, but this offered insurmountable difficulties. France's large army was organized for defense, not invasion, and French policy had been to deter a German attack by building the Maginot Line, a network of fortresses to stop a traditional invasion force from Germany. (It would, in the end, prove worthless against the airborne troops who rendered the line inoperative in a matter of days in 1940.) Britain, relying as always on her navy, had virtually no army. And both countries feared above all a repetition of the bloodbath in the trenches they had experienced in World War I (1914–1918). The United States remained virtually uninvolved until the war, and the Holocaust, were well under way.

Preventing German aggression by preempting the invasion of Poland and the Soviet Union would have been the only realistic means of preventing the Holocaust. Once the war had begun, it is difficult to imagine what the Allies could

Inmates at Dachau hoist an American flag after liberation, 29 April 1945

(Bildarchiv Preussischer Kulturbesitz, Berlin)

have done to halt the Final Solution. The most popular suggestion—and seemingly the most viable since it was discussed at the time—revolves around the bombing of Auschwitz and other extermination camps. The United States Holocaust Memorial Museum pays substantial attention to the debate and to the reasons no such attempt was made. Such proposals were rejected on the grounds that any diversion of bombers from military and industrial targets would lengthen the war and that the only effective way to end the killing of Jews in the camps was to defeat Germany as quickly as possible. Bombing during World War II was far from precise, and only extensive area bombing—of the entire camp—could have had any hope of rendering the railroads, gas chambers, and crematoria inoperative. And given the determination of the SS to finish the task of extermination—even in the face of military collapse—the argument was valid.

The most important point, however, is that no one, anywhere, proposed bombing Auschwitz until April or May 1944. By that time the killing had been going on for years. Furthermore, it is unlikely that, even if practical plans had been available to bomb or otherwise interrupt the work of Auschwitz, no Allied planner would have permitted the diversion of resources from the Normandy invasion. Essentially, the proposal to intervene militarily in the Holocaust became part of the discussion a generation later. It was not, and could not have been, seriously considered at the time.

–WILLIAM D. RUBINSTEIN,
UNIVERSITY OF WALES-ABERYSTWYTH

References

Robert H. Abzug, *America Views the Holocaust 1933–1945: A Brief Documentary History* (Boston: Bedford/St. Martin's Press, 1999).

Yehuda Bauer, *A History of the Holocaust* (New York: Watts, 1982).

Bauer, *Rethinking the Holocaust* (New Haven: Yale University Press, 2001).

Richard Breitman, *Official Secrets: What the Nazis Planned, What the British and Americans Knew* (New York: Hill & Wang, 1998).

Jon Bridgman, *The End of the Holocaust: The Liberation of the Camps* (Portland, Ore.: Areopagitica, 1990).

Jean-Claude Favez, *The Red Cross and the Holocaust,* edited and translated by Beryl Fletcher and John Fletcher (New York: Cambridge University Press, 1999).

Henry L. Feingold, *The Politics of Rescue: The Roosevelt Administration and the Holocaust, 1938–1945* (New Brunswick, N.J.: Rutgers University Press, 1970).

Jack R. Fischel, *Historical Dictionary of the Holocaust* (Lanham, Md.: Scarecrow Press, 1999).

Martin Gilbert, *Auschwitz and the Allies* (New York: Holt, Rinehart & Winston, 1981).

Gilbert, *The Macmillan Atlas of the Holocaust* (New York: Macmillan, 1982).

Walter Laqueur and Breitman, *Breaking the Silence* (New York: Simon & Schuster, 1986).

Nora Levin, *The Holocaust: The Destruction of European Jewry 1933–1945* (New York: Schocken, 1975).

Richard S. Levy, comp., *Antisemitism in the Modern World: An Anthology of Texts* (Lexington, Mass.: Heath, 1991).

Arthur D. Morse, *While Six Million Died: A Chronicle of American Apathy* (New York: Ace, 1967).

Peter Novick, *The Holocaust in American Life* (Boston: Houghton Mifflin, 2000).

William D. Rubinstein, *The Myth of Rescue: Why the Democracies Could Not Have Saved More Jews from the Nazis* (London: Routledge, 1997).

David S. Wyman, *The Abandonment of the Jews: America and the Holocaust 1941–1945* (New York: New Press, 1998).

ANTI-SEMITISM

Did the Holocaust have its origins in the Social Darwinism of the nineteenth century?

Viewpoint: Yes. Racial, as opposed to religious, anti-Semitism originated in the nineteenth century, and it was the underlying cause of the Holocaust.

Viewpoint: No. The Holocaust was a culmination of Christian anti-Judaism dating from the Middle Ages.

Adolf Hitler did not invent anti-Semitism. From the New Testament onward, Christian writings have reflected hostility toward the Jews: it was the Jews who crucified Christ; it was the Jews who opposed the early Church. Unlike Muslims, Hindus, and other non-Christians, Jewish existence (and the Jews' refusal to accept the Christian faith) was a standing reproach to Christianity. Without Judaism, there could have been no Christianity. The writers of the Gospels, especially the author of the Gospel of John, execrated "the Jews" for their hard-heartedness and stiff-necked refusal to believe that Jesus was the long-expected Messiah. The theologians of the early Church—collectively called the Church Fathers—strove to separate their faith from that of the Jews in order to maximize the universal appeal of the Christian Gospel as opposed to the Jewish sense of being chosen.

This Christian, religious anti-Semitism was punctuated, from the Middle Ages through the early twentieth century, with religiously inspired pogroms—outbursts of violence against the purported deicides—murderers of God. However, neither the Nazis in general nor Hitler in particular identified with this religious anti-Semitism. Their hatred of the Jews was based, instead, on racist ideas that emerged in Europe in the nineteenth century. Charles Darwin's phrase "survival of the fittest" was taken out of context and applied to whole groups of people. White, northern Europeans were deemed the most fit to survive and dominate the earth, as the colonial ascendancy of Europe seemed to indicate. The "yellow" and "black" races, in contrast, were inherently unequal to the "white" races. Birth defects, especially Down's Syndrome (or Mongoloidism), was interpreted as proof that white people had advanced through and beyond the black and yellow races. "Mongoloid" children were understood to be "throwbacks" to a more primitive (for example, Mongolian) state of development. That African and Asian children could also suffer from Down's Syndrome did not interfere with the conclusion. It was this "scientific" racism that attracted Hitler and was the basis of his plans for the Master Race. The Jews (members of an Asiatic people, but living and looking like Europeans) were, to racist anti-Semites such as Hitler, not just genetically inferior but biologically subversive to the Aryan race. For this reason the first anti-Semitic laws passed in Nazi Germany were designed to prevent sexual contact between Jews and Aryans. It was also why the Nazis looked at German-speaking Christians of Jewish ancestry as, first and foremost, Jews.

However unpalatable both "theories" might seem, they raise a question of causality: Hitler had no regard for Christianity, but he targeted the Jews for extermination. If extermination ran counter to Christian tradition, hatred for the Jews clearly did not. Was the Holocaust, therefore, a product of nineteenth-century racism, or are its roots to be traced through the Middle Ages to the origins of Christianity?

Viewpoint:
Yes. Racial, as opposed to religious, anti-Semitism originated in the nineteenth century, and it was the underlying cause of the Holocaust.

Anti-Semitism, a term coined only in 1879 and referring to the purported racial inferiority of the Jews, was never a religious notion. Applying Charles Darwin's description of "natural selection" by a natural process of "survival of the fittest" to human history, the nineteenth century witnessed an explosion of such seemingly "scientific" theories of racial superiority and inferiority. The Aryans, the theoretical ancestors of most Europeans, were shown by their accomplishments to be a superior people. Asians, Africans, and virtually everyone else were not only "lesser breeds without the law" but desperately in need of the uplifting hand of European colonialism. One of the first to popularize the superiority of the Aryan race was Count Joseph Arthur de Gobineau, a Frenchman, who used the word *Aryan* to denote a superior and original white race. In *Essai sur l'inégalité des races humaines* (1854–1855), de Gobineau proposed a hierarchy of races and promoted the Germanic peoples to the head of the Aryan race. The Jews, however, posed problems for de Gobineau's schema. They seemed, at least in Europe, to be imminently Aryan. Though their "racial" origins were Asian, they lived and prospered in an increasingly tolerant Europe, where religious discrimination was increasingly frowned upon. Thus, the anti-Semites argued, the Jews were racial parasites who had created no culture of their own. Adolf Hitler seized upon this "scientific" and political anti-Semitism and made it central to his worldview. And it was from this groundwork, not from a Christianity for which an essentially pagan Hitler had only contempt, that the Holocaust arose. Such an assessment need not ignore the influence of almost two millennia of Christian anti-Semitism on the European imagination. The long legacy of Christian anti-Judaism created an intellectual climate of hatred and contempt for the Jews, and racial anti-Semitism did not erupt in a cultural or intellectual vacuum. This new brand of Jewish hatred emerged out of a culture that had fostered and encouraged anti-Jewish sentiment for generations. The Nazis drew from

this deep well of hatred to fuel their policies of genocide, but the "Final Solution to the Jewish Question" did not target Judaism as a religion but the Jews as a race. Conversion to Christianity, which provided medieval Jews an out from the ghetto and rescue from the pogroms, was meaningless as far as the Holocaust was concerned.

This theologically based legacy of contempt began within the earliest centuries of Christianity and can be found in some of the most influential theologians of the Church. Though scholars remain divided over how best to interpret this material given the complex social, intrareligious, and interreligious context of their writing, three crucial anti-Jewish strains are apparent: not only were individual Jews responsible for the death of Christ, but all Jews collectively bear responsibility; as a result, God punished—and continues to punish—them for their crime; and Jews deserve the hatred they are compelled to bear.

In her poignant memoir of World War II (1939–1945), Holocaust survivor Fanya Heller recalls a time when she went to the home of a Christian neighbor and begged for a place to hide for a few hours. The man was on his way to church and stubbornly refused her plea because "The Jews killed Christ," a persistent refrain throughout much of Christian theology. In the New Testament the writer of Matthew's Gospel records that the crowd who demanded the death of Jesus insisted that "His blood be upon us and on our children" (Matthew 27:24). The second-century Latin theologian Tertullian interpreted this passage to say that "all the synagogue of Israel *did* slay Him, saying to Pilate, when he was desirous to dismiss Him, 'His blood be upon us, and upon our children.'" Thus, all Jews, collectively and eternally, were responsible for the crucifixion of Jesus of Nazareth on a Roman cross.

While modern scholars, such as Ellis Rivkin and Paula Fredriksen, caution us that the historical, political, and religious realities that led to the crucifixion are much more complicated than a casual reading of the New Testament indicates, the charge that the Jews killed Christ became regarded as gospel truth as early as the first century. The bishop of Antioch, Ignatius, referred to Jews as "Christ-killing Jews." In the second century, Melito, the bishop of Sardis (in present-day Turkey), wrote a passionate sermon for Easter in which he compared Christ's death to that of the Passover (or paschal) lamb. Historian Marc Saperstein

IS THAT A JEW?

In Mein Kampf *(My Battle, 1925–1927) Adolf Hitler recalls seeing an Orthodox Jew in Vienna and his increasing hatred of Jews:*

Once, when I was walking through the inner city, I suddenly came across a being in a long caftan with black side-locks. My first thought was: Is that a Jew? In Linz they did not look like that. I watched the man stealthily and cautiously, but the longer I stared at that strange countenance and studied it feature by feature, the more the question in a different form turned in my head: Is that a German?

As always on such occasions, I proceeded to try to remove all doubts by means of books. For the first time in my life I bought some anti-Semitic pamphlets for a few heller. Unfortunately, these assumed that the reader had at least some knowledge or understanding of the Jewish question. Finally the tone of most of them was such that I again fell into doubt, because the assertions in them were supported by such flimsy and unscientific arguments. . . .

I could not well continue to doubt that here it was a matter, not of Germans of another religion, but of a separate nation; for, as soon as I began to study the question and to take notice of the Jews, Vienna appeared to me in another light. Now, wherever I went, I saw Jews, and the more I saw, the more strikingly and obviously were they different from other people. The inner city and the parts north of the Danube Canal especially swarmed with a population which bore no similarity to the Germans.

But, though I might still have doubts, my hesitations were dispelled by the attitude of a section of the Jews themselves. A great movement arose among them, asserting the national character of Judaism; this was Zionism. It certainly looked as if only a section of the Jews would approve of this attitude, and that a large majority would condemn, in fact, frankly reject, the principle. On nearer observation, however, this appearance resolved itself into an evil mist of theories, produced purely for reasons of expediency—lies, in fact.

Source: *Adolf Hitler,* My Battle *(Mein Kampf), translated by E. T. S. Dugdale (Boston: Houghton Mifflin, 1937), pp. 19–20.*

notes that Melito made what is often regarded as the first charge of deicide, the killing of God, in Christian literature. Melito claims that "The Master has been outraged. God has been slaughtered. The King of Israel has been slain by Israel's right hand."

Though other ancient Christian writers continued to reiterate the charge that the Jews killed Christ, some theologians moderated the deicide charge. The first great Christian biblical scholar, Origen, reasoned that though the Jews killed Christ, they did not kill God, since "God is not killed." Two centuries later Augustine of Hippo explicitly argued that the Jews did not kill God since they had not realized that Christ was the Son of God. Augustine did, however, hold them responsible for the murder of the man Jesus. While Origen and Augustine exonerated Jews of deicide, they perpetuated the libel that the Jews were responsible for the death of Christ, a distinction lost on a great many Christians. And in the High Middle Ages the great theologian Thomas Aquinas rekindled the ancient deicide charge by asserting that "the Jews therefore, sinned, as crucifiers not only of the Man-Christ, but also as of God." Such sentiments even found expression in official church liturgy, as in this example from the Byzantine Liturgy for Good Friday: "A destructive band of God-forsaken, wicked murderers of God, the synagogue attacked You, O Christ, and dragged You away as an evil doer—the Creator of all, whom we magnify."

Such accusations remain a persistent theme within Christian theology and liturgy well into the post-Holocaust period. Not until the 1960s did the Roman Catholic Church officially begin reversing its position on the issue. In the *Nostra Aetata* (Declaration on the Relationship of the Church to Non-Christian Religions) the Second Vatican Council stated that "what happened in His passion cannot be blamed upon all Jews then living, without distinction, nor upon the Jews of today."

Another recurring theme in Christian writing is the conclusion that the Jews were condemned to a stateless, wandering existence precisely because they had killed the Son of God. Writing shortly after the Roman emperor Hadrian forbade Jews from entering Jerusa-

ANTI-SEMITISM

HISTORY IN DISPUTE, VOLUME 11: THE HOLOCAUST   **19**

lem, the second-century Christian apologist Justin Martyr argued that the Jews deserved such a punishment. According to Tertullian, because of their failure to understand Christ, "their land has been made desert, and their cities utterly burnt with fire, while strangers devour their religion in their sight." He linked the destruction of the Jerusalem Temple with the suffering and death of Christ. Origen similarly writes, "And they also took away the nation, casting them out of the place, and scarcely permitting them to be where they wish even in Diaspora." According to these seminal Christian writers, the *Diaspora* (scattering) of the Jews was caused by their culpability in the death of Christ.

The final leitmotiv in Christian theological portrayals of Jews is the image of them as a sick, God-forsaken, and even devilish people. Justin Martyr called them "a useless, disobedient, and faithless nation." Tertullian argued that since the Jews had forsaken God by rejecting Christ, God removed the divine favor from them. Origen even contended that the Jews were no longer the true Israel and painted the Jews as a "sick" and "feverish" and dying race. He also alluded to Jews as sons of the devil, an image that would grow in popularity in the Middle Ages. From the late fourth century, John Chrysostom, one of the greatest Christian preachers of all time, delivered a set of sermons entitled *Discourses against Judaizing Christians*. These sermons contain some of the most haunting, sinister images of Jews in all of Christian literature. In his first sermon Chrysostom blasted the Jewish synagogues: "Now you give it a name more worthy than it deserves if you call it a brothel, a stronghold of sin, a lodging-place for demons, a fortress for the devil, the destruction of the soul, the precipice and pit of all perdition, or whatever other name you give it."

Though Chrysostom might have intended his invective for Christians in Antioch who continued to participate in Jewish holidays and Sabbaths, his words took on a life of their own in medieval Europe and Russia. The Second Vatican Council sought to correct these traditional images of the Jews when it wrote in *Nostra Aetate*, "Although the Church is the new people of God, the Jews should not be presented as repudiated or cursed by God, as if such views followed from Holy Scriptures." But between Chrysostom and Vatican II lay a continuous history of Christian theologizing and sermonizing that portrayed the Jews as a rejected and accursed people.

Though Jew-hatred was deeply rooted in Christian thinking, ancient and medieval theologians did not speak with a single voice on the subject and made attempts, however futile, to curb violence against the Jews. While Augustine of Hippo perpetuated the libel of the Jews as "Christ-killers," he nevertheless insisted that Jews must not be physically harmed or killed. Arguing that Jews stood under divine protection as preservers of the Old Testament, he cautioned that "not by bodily death shall the ungodly race of carnal Jews perish. For whoever destroys them in this way shall suffer sevenfold vengeance, that is, shall bring upon himself the sevenfold penalty under which the Jews lie for the crucifixion of Christ." Historian Kenneth Stow in 1988 noted that this Augustinian argument had some influence in later centuries and was invoked by Bernard of Clairvaux in an attempt to stem the massacre of Jews during the Second Crusade (1147–1149). However, the behavior of Crusaders, Inquisitors, and frenzied mobs seems to have been little affected by the Augustinian insistence on no violence toward the Jews. And the most famous Augustinian monk of the sixteenth century, Martin Luther, noted his disappointment with the reticence of the Jews to convert to Protestant Christianity with a by-now-familiar invective of 1543:

> First, their synagogues or churches should be set on fire, and whatever does not burn up should be covered or spread over with dirt so that no one may ever be able to see a cinder or stone of it. . . . Secondly, their homes should likewise be broken down and destroyed. For they perpetuate [there] the same things that they do in their synagogues. For this reason they ought to be put under one roof or in a stable, like gypsies, in order [that] they may realize that they are not masters in our land, as they boast, but miserable captives, as they complain of us incessantly before God with bitter wailing.

In 1936, under Nazi auspices, these comments would be published in a collection of Luther's works in German.

Traditional Christian anti-Jewish rhetoric, though it rarely offered the Jews much protection and condemned them to dwell on the fringes of Christian society, never called for their extermination. And the rationale behind Christian anti-Judaism was markedly different from the racial anti-Semitism that inspired Hitler. From the Apostle Paul to Martin Luther, the basis of anti-Judaism was the refusal of the Jews to accept Jesus as their Messiah. As a religious community, but never as a race (as the term would come to be understood in the nineteenth century), the Jews were condemned and despised. Without them, Christianity would have been impossible, but it was their continued rejection of Christ that so tried the Christian mind. In the traditionally anti-Jewish Christian mind conversion would have, with few exceptions, made the "Jewish Question" disappear. One might reasonably argue that, had the European imagination not been inoculated with anti-Judaism for nineteen hundred years, and had the Jews not been marginalized and demonized by church and state alike, the Holocaust would not have happened. But the Holocaust was a product of a modern and distinctly secular, racist ideology that defined Jewishness as a biological rather than as a religious concept. For the Nazis, conversion was never a meaningful solution to the Jewish Question. Only extermination would do.

—LISA UNTERSEHER, COLUMBIA COLLEGE

Viewpoint:
No. The Holocaust was a culmination of Christian anti-Judaism dating from the Middle Ages.

The distinguished scholar Richard Levy defines anti-Semitism—the word itself was invented in the nineteenth century as a polite way to express the bimillennial concept of *Judenhaß* (Jew-hatred)—as the exclusively modern politicization and institutionalization of the willingness to act on a ubiquitous and preexisting anti-Jewish feeling. But a reading of the facts argues that politicization and institutionalization existed continuously and that there is but one tradition of Jew-hatred/anti-Semitism that accounts for the ideology leading to the Holocaust.

Until recently, the principle that the Jewish people were archetypal evildoers, so abhorrent that almost any injustice done to them was justified, has been a permanent element in the fundamental self-identity of Western Christian civilization. Antagonism toward Jews was elaborated by the theological and popular writings and preaching of theologians, popes, and lay believers; enhanced by Christian anti-Jewish myths, beliefs, rituals, liturgy, art, and literature; and institutionalized and politicized by churches and Christian authorities. Supposedly ordained by God, both Church and State created and nurtured in the faithful, even in the only nominally faithful, anti-Jewish moral sensibilities and actions. This religious diabolizing of the Jews supposedly explained the world's evil and conditioned both disorganized movements and organized groups to actualize their Jew-hatred in politicized and institutionalized malediction, degradation, pogroms, and mass murder of Jews.

To show that there was little, if any, change between earlier and more contemporary antagonisms toward Jews, one must examine the continuities of Jew-hatred (anti-Semitism) in European anti-Jewish language, historical parallels, racism, defamations, myths, and fantasies. Christendom considered the Jews monsters, beasts, murderers, betrayers, insects, poisoners, vampires, and devils long before, during, and after the nineteenth century. In the fourth century the great Father of the Church, St. Ambrose, verbally assaulted the Jews in language no less violent than that of the Nazis. He sermonized that the Jews "polluted their pretended bodily purity with the inner feces of their souls." St. Jerome claimed that all Jews were Judases, that is, that they betrayed God for money, as did the young Joseph Goebbels, future head of Nazi propaganda. St. Jerome also called the synagogue, as did the Nazis, worse than "a brothel, a den of vice, the devil's refuge, satan's fortress, a place to deprave the soul, an abyss of every conceivable disaster," or whatever else you will. As did the Nazis, St. John Chrysostom believed that the Jews were congenitally evil people who "danced with the Devil" and "grew fit for slaughter."

The Church Fathers and popes provided a consecrated attack language that political and Church leaders employed against Jews, Judaism, and Jewishness. The Christianized Roman emperors, like the Nazis, referred to Jews as a "plague," "abominable and vile," "enemies of the law," "an alien and hostile perversity," "frightful and hideous." Non-Jews would be "marked by Jewish filth." The medieval popes referred to "blind Jewish perversion," "Jewish treachery," and Jews as "perpetual slaves," "deadly," "malicious," "dangerous," "detestable." Like the Nazis, Crusaders attacked Jews as the "greatest sinners" in Europe and as despised enemies who must be punished and exterminated "down to the last baby at the breast."

The obscene language of street and field pervaded the founder of Protestantism Martin Luther's anti-Jewish rhetoric just as it did the Nazis'. To Luther, the Jews were "learned, shitty." Luther proclaimed that Jews pretend to know God, but in reality read this "out of the sow's ass." Jews were full of "the devil's feces . . . in which they wallow like swine." No longer God's elect, they were "polluted so full of the Devil's shit that it oozes out of them from every pore."

In the *Oxford English Dictionary* fully half the meanings of "Jew" are offensive and repulsive, if not scurrilous. *Jew* is applied to a "grasping or extortionate money-lender or usurer, or a trader who drives hard bargains or deals craftily," whereas "to Jew" means to cheat; a jew-

ANTI-SEMITISM

"Wenn ihr ein Kreuz seht, dann denkt an den grauenhaften Mord der Juden auf Golgatha..."

bird has an "ugly, conspicuous beak"; a jewbush is one "characterized by powerful emetic and drastic properties," that is, it makes a person vomit and die.

It is true that a few political authorities and an occasional pope tried—usually halfheartedly—to protect Jews, but the basic political and ecclesiastical Jew-policy was to allow violence. Although some medieval Christian persecutors allowed Jews to escape death by means of conversion, the Jews' continued existence tested the Christian sense of identity, just as the Jews' presence in Europe between 1933 and 1945 challenged that of the Nazis. Moreover, just as during the Holocaust, medieval synagogues were invaded and

burned, often with Jews in them; Torah scrolls were trampled into the mud, torn, and set afire; and Jewish cemeteries were destroyed, while most church and political authorities sat on their hands. This behavior was also Nazi policy during the Holocaust in regard to attacks on Jews by local anti-Semites.

Both before and after their legal emancipation in the eighteenth and nineteenth centuries, Jews had only a tenuous moral right to live as Jews. Jews were Christendom's public enemies, stateless beings and sinners who must be punished in this world and the next. Antagonism toward Jews was institutionalized and politicized when governments and popes issued edicts, enacted canon laws, and influenced or ordered Christians to discriminate against, expropriate, and exile Jews.

Almost a thousand years before Nazi slave-labor camps, the argument put forward by the church and supported by the political authorities was that the Jews were, or should be, permanent slaves to Christians. That notion is stated clearly by Thomas Aquinas, later acclaimed as the official philosopher of the Roman Catholic Church and favorably quoted during the Holocaust by the French ambassador to the Vatican, Léon Berard.

By the end of the twelfth century the walled ghetto marked most European towns. Not intended as collecting points on the road to mass murder, which was what the Nazis had in mind, the medieval ghettos nevertheless led to increased Jewish stigmatization, and the ghettos' unhealthful locations, overcrowding, and the legal compulsion forcing Jews to live there made them dreadful and dangerous places and in this sense paralleled those the Nazi created in the twentieth century.

The Nazi stipulation that Jews wear an identifying and stigmatic emblem also paralleled requirements of the medieval church. The Fourth Lateran Council (1215) decreed that the Jews had to be distinguished from Christians "by the quality of their clothes." The church pressured secular authorities to impose on the Jews a pariah's badge of shame.

Intellectually, the churches and their theologians had formulated compelling religious, social, and moral *idées forces* that framed Jews as traitors, murderers, plague, pollution, filth, devils, and insects. The National Socialists, and many other modern anti-Semites, also conceived of the Jews in the same way as less than human or inhuman.

Most extraordinary was Luther's program that the Nazis followed almost to the letter. It cannot be an historical accident that both Luther and Hitler advocated the sequential destruction of Jewish religious culture, the abrogation of legal protection, expropriation, forced labor, expulsion, and mass murder. "We are at fault," Luther concluded, "in not slaying them."

The most surprising parallel between pre- and post-nineteenth-century anti-Jewishness is racism. Denying the possibility of change or religious conversion, racism holds that different groups of human beings are permanently different and unequal; that inevitable intellectual, moral, and social consequences derive from these genetically determined differences between groups of people; and that individual members always manifest the same traits as the rest of the group. From the Church Fathers onward, many Christians found an inherent,

permanent, and unchangeable theological and physical repulsiveness in Jews, a clear indication that Jews were forever inferior, Christians eternally superior, and that true conversion was not possible. Writing *Adversus Judaeos* (Against the Jews), St. Augustine observed that no Jew could ever lose the stigma of his forebears' denial and murder of Christ. A St. Jerome homily claimed that all Jews were innately evil creatures. In his *Homilies against Judaizing Christians,* (1979), St. John Chrysostom called Jews "inveterate murderers" who should be slaughtered. St. Isidore of Seville declared that the Jews' evil character never changed. In the twelfth century, perhaps the most outstanding religious figure of the Middle Ages, St. Bernard of Clairvaux, wrote that "it is an insult to Christ that the offspring of a Jew has occupied the chair of Peter." And Thomas Aquinas wrote that the Jews were an inherently cruel people.

Racist ideas led to several massacres of Jews during the Middle Ages, when Crusaders seemed intent on destroying all Jews rather than baptizing them. At Mainz, one of many examples, Count Emicho "showed no mercy to the aged, or youths, or maidens, babes or sucklings—not even the sick . . . killing their young men by the sword and disemboweling their pregnant women."

The most prominent development of the Christian racial idea took place in fifteenth- and sixteenth-century Spain, where it was believed that the Jewish rejection of Christ had corrupted the Jews biologically, even those who supposedly had converted to Christianity. In fact, the government of the most Catholic king, as well as all the major Catholic orders in Spain, adopted racist laws and regulations, even the prestigious Jesuits and Dominicans. No man could become a Jesuit priest, for example, unless non-Jewish heritage could be traced back five generations. Even the National Socialists were less exclusive, defining a Jew as having one parent or two grandparents who were Jewish by religious identity. In 1623 a Portuguese scholar, Vincente da Costa Massos, held that "a little Jewish blood is enough to destroy the world." Later in the century, after calling the Jews carnal, sensualist, and cruel, Friar Francisco de Torrejoncillo, heralding Nazi race laws, warned that Christian children must not be suckled by Jewish wet nurses, "because milk, being of vile and infected persons, can only engender perverse inclinations [in the Christian babies]." Most popes of the period sanctioned this racial discrimination.

Racism developed elsewhere in Christian Europe, as exemplified by the Catholic priest and humanist Erasmus, who wrote in November 1517 that a fully converted Jew could not exist; he was always pernicious. The former priest Luther, arguably the most important religious figure of the sixteenth century, called the Jews "the devil's people" and put them beyond conversion. "From their youth they have imbibed such venomous hatred against the Goyim from their parents and their rabbis," he wrote, "and they still continuously drink it. . . . It has penetrated flesh and blood, marrow and bone, and has become part and parcel of their nature and their life." He also wrote that "It is impossible to convert the devil and his own, nor are we commanded to attempt this." In its Christmas message of 25 December 1941, the Nazi periodical (and Hitler's favorite reading) *Der Stürmer* stated: "To put an end to the proliferation of the curse of God in this Jewish blood, there is only one way: the extermination of this people, whose father is the devil." The last phrase was a quotation from the Gospel of St. John.

From the twelfth to the twentieth centuries, accusations of ritual murder, blood libel, host desecration, and poisoning of wells were made against Jews and resulted in mass murder. The Nazis also used these myths in their propaganda campaign against the Jews.

In the mid fourteenth century, when about one-half of the European population died of the Black Plague, massacres of Jews—accused of conspiring to cause the plague by poisoning the wells—became endemic. During this period tens of thousands of Jews in more than 350 European communities were tortured and murdered as conspirators in the destruction of Christendom. This conspiracy fantasy is paralleled in much modern anti-Semitism, even up to the present day.

Long before the nineteenth century and the Holocaust, the Jews were established as public enemies of Christendom: a tiny minority spread across Christendom; weak, divided, without legal or significant customary rights; and without military or political power of their own. The most terrible things were done to Jews, up to and including mass murder, and these actions were justified by the Church's anti-Jewish doctrines and accepted by most of the populace as well as by most political and religious authorities of the time. The nineteenth century and the Holocaust period added more-efficient organization and weapons of mass destruction to the continuous politicized and institutionalized Jew-hatred called anti-Semitism. As an observer of the Holocaust in Hungary has written, "The anti-Judaism of the Middle Ages is shockingly close to Hitlerian racism."

–ROBERT MICHAEL, UNIVERSITY OF MASSACHUSETTS, DARTMOUTH

References

Walter M. Abbott, ed., *The Documents of Vatican II: In a New and Definitive Translation with Commentaries and Notes by Catholic, Protestant, Orthodox Authorities* (London: Geoffrey Chapman, 1966).

Thomas Aquinas, *Summa Theologiae,* translated by Fathers of the English Dominican Province (Westminster, Md.: Christian Classics, 1948).

Claus-Ekkehard Bärsch, *Der junge Goebbels: Erlösung und Vernichtung* (Munich: Boer, 1995).

Bernard of Clairvaux, *The Letters of St. Bernard of Clairvaux,* translated by Bruno Scott James (Kalamazoo, Mich.: Cistercian Publications, 1998).

Robert Chazan, ed., *Church, State, and Jew in the Middle Ages* (New York: Behrman House, 1979).

John Chrysostom, *Discourses against Judaizing Christians,* translated by Paul W. Harkins (Washington, D.C.: Catholic University of America Press, 1979).

Jeremy Cohen, "The Jews as the Killers of Christ in the Latin Tradition from Augustine to the Friars," *Traditio,* 39 (1983): 1–27.

Norman Cohn, *Warrant for Genocide: The Myth of the Jewish World-conspiracy and the Protocols of the Elders of Zion* (London: Eyre & Spottiswoode, 1967).

Alan Davies, ed., *Antisemitism and the Foundations of Christianity* (New York: Paulist Press, 1979).

Shlomo Eidelberg, ed., *The Jews and the Crusaders: The Hebrew Chronicles of the First and Second Crusades* (Madison: University of Wisconsin Press, 1977).

Gerhard Falk, *The Jew in Christian Theology: Martin Luther's Anti-Jewish Vom Schem Hamphoras, Previously Unpublished in English, and Other Milestones in Church Doctrine Concerning Judaism* (Jefferson City, N.C.: McFarland, 1992).

Edward H. Flannery, *The Anguish of the Jews: Twenty-Three Centuries of Anti-Semitism* (New York: Macmillan, 1965).

Paula Fredriksen, *Jesus of Nazareth, King of the Jews: A Jewish Life and the Emergence of Christianity* (New York: Knopf, 1999).

J. Friedman, "Jewish Conversion, the Spanish Pure Blood Laws, and Reformation," *Sixteenth-Century Journal,* 18 (1987): 3–30.

John G. Gager, *The Origins of Anti-Semitism: Attitudes toward Judaism in Pagan and Christian Antiquity* (New York: Oxford University Press, 1983).

Leonard B. Glick, *Abraham's Heirs: Jews and Christians in Medieval Europe* (Syracuse, N.Y.: Syracuse University Press, 1999).

Solomon Grayzel, ed., *The Church and the Jews in the XIIIth Century,* revised edition (New York: Hermon Press, 1966).

Stephen R. Haynes, *Reluctant Witnesses: Jews and the Christian Imagination* (Louisville, Ky.: Westminster John Knox Press, 1995).

Fredrich Heer, *God's First Love,* translated by Geoffrey Skelton (New York: Weybright & Talley, 1970).

Fanya Gottesfeld Heller, *Strange and Unexpected Love: A Teenage Girl's Holocaust Memories* (Hoboken, N.J.: Ktav Publishing House, 1993).

Raul Hilberg, *The Destruction of the European Jews* (Chicago: Quadrangle, 1961).

St. Jerome, *The Homilies of Saint Jerome,* translated by Marie Liguori Ewald (Washington, D.C.: Catholic University of America Press, 1964).

Werner Keller, *Diaspora: The Post-Biblical History of the Jews,* translated by Richard Winston and Clara Winston (New York: Harcourt, Brace & World, 1969).

David I. Kertzer, *The Popes against the Jews: The Vatican's Role in the Rise of Modern Anti-Semitism* (New York: Knopf, 2001).

Gavin I. Langmuir, *History, Religion, and Anti-Semitism* (Berkeley: University of California Press, 1990).

Richard Levy, *Antisemitism in the Modern World: An Anthology of Texts* (Lexington, Mass. & Toronto: D. C. Heath, 1991).

Franklin H. Littell, *The Crucifixion of the Jews* (New York: Harper & Row, 1975).

Martin Luther, "On the Jews and Their Lies," in *Luther's Works,* translated by Franklin Sherman (Philadelphia: Fortress Press, 1971).

Frank E. Manuel, *The Broken Staff: Judaism through Christian Eyes* (Cambridge, Mass.: Harvard University Press, 1992).

Jacob R. Marcus, *The Jew in the Medieval World: A Source Book, 315-1791* (Cincinnati: Union of American Hebrew Congregations, 1938).

Melito of Sardis, "Paschal Homily," in *The Paschal Mystery: Ancient Liturgies and Patristic Texts,* edited by A. Hamman, translated by Thomas Halton (Staten Island, N.Y.: Alba House, 1969), pp. 26-39.

J. P. Migne, ed., *Patrologiae, Cursus Completus, Series Graeca* (Paris: Imprimerie Catholique du Petit-Montrouge, 1857-1866).

Migne, ed., *Patrologiae, Cursus Completus, Series Latina* (Paris: Imprimerie Catholique du Petit-Montrouge, 1844-1875).

Henry Monneray, *La Persecution des Juifs dans les pays de l'Est* (Paris: Editions du Centre, 1949).

Jacques Nobécourt, *"Le Vicaire" et l'Histoire* (Paris: Seuil, 1964).

Maurice Olender, *The Languages of Politics: Race, Religion, and Philology in the Nineteenth Century,* translated by Arthur Goldhammer (Cambridge, Mass.: Harvard University Press, 1992).

Origen, *Commentary on the Gospel According to John, Books 13-32,* 2 volumes, translated by Ronald E. Heine (Washington, D.C.: Catholic University of America Press, 1993).

Walter Pakter, "De His Qui Foris Sunt: The Teachings of the Medieval Canon and Civil Lawyers Concerning the Jews," dissertation, Johns Hopkins University, 1974.

James Parkes, *The Conflict of the Church and the Synagogue: A Study in the Origins of Anti-Semitism* (London: Soncino, 1934).

Léon Poliakov, *The Aryan Myth: A History of Racist and Nationalist Ideas in Europe,* translated by Edmund Howard (New York: Basic Books, 1974).

Pierre Quillard, *Le Monument Henry Liste des Souscripteurs Classés Méthodiquement et selon l'ordre Alphabétique* (Paris: P. V. Stock, 1899).

Jonathan Riley-Smith, *The Crusades: A Short History* (New Haven: Yale University Press, 1987).

Ellis Rivkin, *What Crucified Jesus?* (Nashville: Abingdon Press, 1984).

Paul Lawrence Rose, *Revolutionary Antisemitism in Germany from Kant to Wagner* (Princeton: Princeton University Press, 1990).

Rosemary Radford Ruether, *Faith and Fratricide: The Theological Roots of Anti-Semitism* (New York: Seabury Press, 1974).

Marc Saperstein, *Moments of Crisis in Jewish-Christian Relations* (London: SCM Press / Philadelphia: Trinity Press International, 1989).

Philip Schaff and Henry Wace, eds., *A Select Library of the Nicene and Post-Nicene Fathers,* 14 volumes (New York: Christian Literature Company, 1890–1900).

A Select Library of the Nicene and Post-Nicene Fathers, series 1, volume 8 (Grand Rapids, Mich.: Eerdmans, 1956).

Marcel Simon, *Verus Israel: A Study of the Relations between Christians and Jews in the Roman Empire, 135–425,* translated by H. McKeating (Oxford & New York: Oxford University Press, 1986).

Shlomo Simonsohn, *The Apostolic See and the Jews: Documents, 492–1404* (Toronto: Pontifical Institute of Mediaeval Studies, 1988).

Kenneth R. Stow, "Hatred of the Jews or Love of the Church: Papal Policy toward the Jews in the Middle Ages," in *Antisemitism through the Ages,* edited by Shmuel Almog, translated by Nathan H. Reisner (New York: Pergamon Press, 1988), pp. 71–89.

Mary Stroll, *The Jewish Pope: Ideology and Politics in the Papal Schism of 1130* (Leiden & New York: Brill, 1987).

Guy G. Stroumsa, "From Anti-Judaism to Anti-Semitism in Early Christianity?" in *Contra Judaeos: Ancient and Medieval Polemics between Christians and Jews,* edited by Ora Limor and Stroumsa (Tübingen: J. C. B. Mohr, 1996), pp. 1–26.

Miriam S. Taylor, *Anti-Judaism and Early Christian Identity: A Critique of the Scholarly Consensus,* edited by David S. Katz (Leiden & New York: Brill, 1995).

Robert L. Wilken, *John Chrysostom and the Jews: Rhetoric and Reality in the Late 4th Century* (Berkeley: University of California Press, 1983).

ANTI-SEMITISM

CONFESSING CHURCH

Did the actions of the Confessing Church (Protestant clergymen opposed to the intrusion of Nazi ideology into the life of the church) constitute resistance to the Holocaust?

Viewpoint: Yes. The Confessing Church, though limited by its own anti-Semitism, provided meaningful resistance to the implementation of the Final Solution.

Viewpoint: No. The Confessing Church was too disorganized, too patriotic, and too anti-Semitic to provide meaningful resistance to the Holocaust.

In a speech broadcast in March of 1933, barely two months after he was appointed chancellor, Adolf Hitler discussed the attitude of the new Reich government toward the Christian churches. Though Hitler's own attitude toward Christianity ranged from cynical indifference to outright hostility, his words were calculated to soothe the anxieties of German Catholics and Protestants. He assured them of the important place of the church in "the work of national and moral renewal of the people recently undertaken by the Nazi state." Hitler promised that his regime would neither infringe on the rights of the churches in Germany nor alter the state's traditional relationship with them. Nevertheless, before the year was out both Catholics and Protestants were being pressured to cooperate with Nazi policies of *Gleichschaltung* (coordination).

The Nazi effort to coordinate the Protestant Church began in May of 1933. The state decreed the creation of a single *Reichskirche* (national church) to replace the existing independent regional synods. The Nazi government then engineered a series of church elections that placed pro-Nazi candidates of the German Christian Movement in control. Although never an official part of the Nazi organization, German Christians were Protestants who agreed with Nazi racial ideology and advocated a nationalist Aryan Christianity. Though they enjoyed a brief period of official favor, the German Christians never had the support of the essentially atheist Nazi leadership or any lasting influence over the German people. From Ludwig Müller, the newly elected Reich Bishop, downward, the *Reichskirche* administration was filled with Nazi sympathizers who were prepared to transform Christianity in Germany into conformity with National Socialist ideology. The *Kirchenkampf* (church struggle) between church and state in Nazi Germany developed as conservative Protestants sought to protect their traditional doctrines and rights of self-government from the intrusions of a totalitarian state.

At the Brown Synod of September 1933 (so named for the many participants in Storm Trooper uniform), the *Reichskirche* assembly appended an article to the church's constitution requiring racial purity of all church officials. Protestant pastors and their wives were to be free of Jewish blood; all baptized Christians of Jewish ancestry were considered non-Aryan Christians and thus excluded from positions of leadership within the church. This

"Aryan Paragraph" was consistent with the Nazi racial laws of the preceding April that removed non-Aryans from the civil service and other secular professions. Yet, while the springtime anti-Semitic legislation drew no protest from the church, the Brown Synod's action was perceived as intolerable state interference in the supposedly independent realm of the church.

Over the next year, Protestant pastors and church leaders banded together to form the *Bekennende Kirche* (Confessing Church) movement to resist the intrusion of Nazi power and ideology into the life of the church. These leaders, united by the Theological Confession of Barmen—which rejected the theological claims of the German Christians–struggled to protect their ecclesiastical integrity. But did their struggle benefit—or was it even intended to benefit—the Jews? Many of the Confessing Church leaders were openly anti-Semitic, and the only part of the "Jewish Question" that the Confessing Church ever formally addressed related to the status of Jewish converts to Christianity. But their opposition, however limited, was not without consequence, and at least some Confessing Christians risked (or lost) their lives on behalf of the Jews. After the war the leadership of the Confessing Church emerged from the ruins of Germany both to rebuild their congregations and to confront their own institutional and personal failings. Yet, without their history of resistance, however compromised, they would almost certainly have lacked the moral authority even for this.

Viewpoint:
Yes. The Confessing Church, though limited by its own anti-Semitism, provided meaningful resistance to the implementation of the Final Solution.

The *Bekennende Kirche* (Confessing Church) offered meaningful resistance to the Nazi program. This conclusion obviously does not mean to suggest that the movement was able to ultimately thwart Adolf Hitler's policies, but credit is due to the pastors and congregants for their courageous opposition. The successes of the Confessing Church appear especially dramatic when one considers the obstacles faced by the movement's leaders.

First, the church had traditionally been close to the German state. During the Second Reich, which failed in the waning days of World War I (1914–1918), the church was openly partnered with the monarchy. In fact, pastors often quoted from the thirteenth chapter of Paul's letter to the Roman church, a passage that admonishes Christians to obey authority. Because the church was so closely tied to the old order, it suffered as a result of Germany's loss in 1918. The disillusionment that followed the war, a feeling that permeated not only German society but also the cultures of many of the victorious nations as well, led to a dramatic secularization of German society. The twin blows of being on the losing side of the war and suffering the cultural fallout from that defeat had left the German church in a considerably diminished condition. Thus, not only was the church as an institution weakened, but the absence of any meaningful tradition of opposition to the state guaranteed that the later

efforts of the Confessing pastors would be that much more difficult.

Second, the Confessing movement was faced with the daunting reality of the Nazi state. Following Hitler's release from prison, where he was serving a sentence for attempting to overthrow the Weimar Republic in 1922, the Nazi Party had quickly gained strength across Germany. When Hitler was named chancellor in 1933, opposition to the Nazi Party rapidly declined. To challenge the regime required considerable political acumen. Complicating matters was the fact that many pastors who were in sympathy with the desire to maintain the church's independence from the Nazi regime were themselves solid nationalists, convinced of the need to revive German power. When taken together, the condition of the church following Germany's defeat in World War I and the sheer power of the Nazi regime make it dramatically clear that real difficulties confronted any resistance movement.

The Confessing Church's opposition to Hitler began to gel following the effort of the Nazis to absorb the church and refashion it into an instrument for the Party. Beginning in 1929, members of the Nazi student movement began openly confronting theologians they deemed to be enemies. A high-profile example was the case of Gunther Dehn, a theology professor who was appointed to the faculty at the University of Heidelberg. Upon arriving to lecture his first class on the opening day of the semester, he was greeted by throngs of angry pro-Nazi students. They proceeded to shout him down. Despite his best efforts to deliver his prepared remarks, he finally succumbed, recognizing that efforts to instruct the class would be futile. He resigned from the university shortly thereafter. When a similar event took place at the University of Halle, even the faculty refused to defend him, and he was forced to surrender his chair there as well. Such episodes were part of a deliberate attempt by the Nazi Party to subvert any possible resistance that might emanate from the nation's religious leaders.

The Nazis recognized that it was not enough to simply intimidate professors, however. The churches themselves would need to be neutralized. With this goal in mind the Party proposed the establishment of a *Reichskirche* (national church). Already, the Protestant churches of Germany were united in an ecumenical body that represented the bulk of non-Catholic Christians. The elections for a new bishop to head the national church were scheduled for 1933. Delegates from across the country were to gather at various polling places to cast their votes. The Nazis, who put their support behind Ludwig Müller, urged the pastors to accept Müller and his "positive theology," a euphemism for a sanitized Protestantism that would offer no theological or philosophical opposition to Hitler. With the help of so-called Brownshirts, members of the pro-Nazi SA movement, Müller was elected. He immediately set about attempting to gain acceptance for what was termed the "Aryan Paragraph," an explicit endorsement of anti-Semitism. It was at this point that many Protestant pastors came to believe that it was impossible to reconcile their Christian confession with the anti-Christian policies of the state.

Adversaries of the Aryan Paragraph, therefore, established the *Pfarrernotbund* (Pastors' Emergency League, PEL) to counter the pro-Nazi drift of the church. Members of the new organization, who were destined to form the backbone of the Confessing Church, rejected what they viewed as the use of Christian terminology to justify decidedly anti-Christian policies. Many of the PEL pastors had been influenced by the writings of Karl Barth, a theologian who had become famous for his rejection of "Liberal Christianity." Liberal theology, which traced its origins back to Friedrich Schleiermacher's early-eighteenth-century efforts to reconcile traditional Christian piety with the tenets of the Enlightenment, was the reigning orthodoxy in Germany at the time of World War I. Barth viewed such an effort as hopelessly doomed in that it drained Christianity of any supernatural claims. He called on Christians to return to a "Christ-centered" Christianity, one that simultaneously recognized the transcendence of God and the responsibility of Christians to be active in the world around them.

Barth himself became an enemy of the Nazi state and with such pastors as Martin Niemöller and Dietrich Bonhoeffer became famous for a willingness to risk everything. He urged pastors to preach that Christ was the only worthy object of devotion. To give Hitler the adulation that he demanded was to abandon the traditional faith and to substitute it for a form of nationalist idolatry. In 1935 Barth and other pastors met with Hitler in an effort to convince him of the need to relax his stringent attempts to manipulate church doctrine. They demanded that Müller be fired and that pastors be free from the censorious policies of the Reich. Hitler proceeded to denounce the pastors and taunt them for their lack of real political power. The Confessing Church and its members were now viewed with heightened suspicion by the Nazi government.

From this point on, Confessing pastors did little to hide their expressed disdain for the regime. While avoiding direct confrontations with Hitler himself, they nevertheless proceeded to offer substantial criticisms of the racial policies being implemented across the country. When Hitler instituted the practice of subjecting the mentally ill and handicapped to euthanasia, much of the country remained silent. The Confessing Church, however, intervened in several cases, attempting to save as many victims as possible. Confessing pastors participated in efforts to shield Jews from the nation's vicious policies. In what was perhaps the most dangerous moment of opposition to the regime, Bonhoeffer, one of the most famous pastors in the Confessing Church, was implicated in the plot to assassinate Hitler in 1944. For this crime he was executed in April 1945, shortly before the conclusion of the war.

In light of the failure of the Confessing Church to actually alter the practices of the Third Reich, how is possible to argue that their opposition was in any way meaningful? The movement itself will forever be remembered for challenging the claims of Nazi ideology. According to the political philosopher Hannah Arendt, in *The Origins of Totalitarianism* (1951), totalitarian governmental systems such as Nazism are based on the idea of the organic polity, which means that the regime claims to speak for a polity that is united in all respects. Opposition is not offered because the people stand in ready approval of all that is done. Further, the policies of the totalitarian regime are said to be grounded on some incontrovertible foundation that no rational person could possibly refute. By opposing Hitler's policies, the Confessing Church demonstrated that these contentions were nothing more than propaganda. In short, Confessing Church opposition served as one of the first voices to declare that the Hitler regime was based on cynical distortions of the truth.

To serve as the initial voice of criticism for the Nazi chapter in world history is no small achievement. When historians look back on a particular time period, they restore to public

THE BARMEN CONFESSION

In May of 1934 Protestant clerics opposed to Nazism and Hitler's attempt to impose Nazi orthodoxy upon the Church issued the following declaration:

1. "I am the way, and the truth, and the life; no one comes to the Father, but by me." (John 14:6).

"Truly, truly, I say to you, he who does not enter the sheepfold by the door but climbs in by another way, that man is a thief and a robber. . . . I am the door; if anyone enters by me, he will be saved." (John 10:1, 9).

Jesus Christ, as he is attested for us in Holy Scripture, is the one Word of God which we have to hear and which we have to trust and obey in life and in death.

We reject the false doctrine, as though the Church could and would have to acknowledge as a source of its proclamation, apart from and besides this one Word of God, still other events and powers, figures and truths, as God's revelation.

2. "Christ Jesus, whom God made our wisdom, our righteousness and sanctification and redemption." (I Cor. 1:30.)

As Jesus Christ is God's assurance of the forgiveness of all our sins, so in the same way and with the same seriousness is he also God's mighty claim upon our whole life. Through him befalls us a joyful deliverance from the godless fetters of this world for a free, grateful service to his creatures.

We reject the false doctrine, as though there were areas of our life in which we would not belong to Jesus Christ, but to other lords—areas in which we would not need justification and sanctification through him.

3. "Rather, speaking the truth in love, we are to grow up in every way into him who is the head, into Christ, from whom the whole body [is] joined and knit together." (Eph. 4:15, 16.)

The Christian Church is the congregation of the brethren in which Jesus Christ acts presently as the Lord in Word and sacrament through the Holy Spirit. As the Church of pardoned sinners, it has to testify in the midst of a sinful world, with its faith as with its obedience, with its message as with its order, that it is solely his property, and that it lives and wants to live solely from his comfort and from his direction in the expectation of his appearance.

We reject the false doctrine, as though the Church were permitted to abandon the form of its message and order to its own pleasure or to changes in prevailing ideological and political convictions.

4. "You know that the rulers of the Gentiles lord it over them, and their great men exercise authority over them. It shall not be so among you; but whoever would be great among you must be your servant." (Matt. 20:25, 26.)

The various offices in the Church do not establish a dominion of some over the others; on the contrary, they are for the exercise of the ministry entrusted to and enjoined upon the whole congregation.

We reject the false doctrine, as though the Church, apart from this ministry, could and were permitted to give to itself, or allow to be given to it, special leaders vested with ruling powers.

5. "Fear God. Honor the emperor." (I Peter 2:17.)

Scripture tells us that, in the as yet unredeemed world in which the Church also exists, the State has by divine appointment the task of providing for justice and peace. [It fulfills this task] by means of the threat and exercise of force, according to the measure of human judgment and human ability. The Church acknowledges the benefit of this divine appointment in gratitude and reverence before him. It calls to mind the Kingdom of God, God's commandment and righteousness, and thereby the responsibility both of rulers and of the ruled. It trusts and obeys the power of the Word by which God upholds all things.

We reject the false doctrine, as though the State, over and beyond its special commission, should and could become the single and totalitarian order of human life, thus fulfilling the Church's vocation as well.

We reject the false doctrine, as though the Church, over and beyond its special commission, should and could appropriate the characteristics, the tasks, and the dignity of the State, thus itself becoming an organ of the State.

6. "Look, I am with you always, to the close of the age." (Matt. 28:20.)

"The word of God is not fettered." (II Tim. 2:9.)

The Church's commission, upon which its freedom is founded, consists in delivering the message of the free grace of God to all people in Christ's stead, and therefore in the ministry of his own Word and work through sermon and sacrament.

We reject the false doctrine, as though the Church in human arrogance could place the Word and work of the Lord in the service of any arbitrarily chosen desires, purposes, and plans.

Source: *"The Theological Declaration of Barmen," EKD: Protestant Church in Germany <http://www.ekd.de/english/3833_barmenengl.html>.*

CONFESSING CHURCH

awareness the various voices that characterized that era. The words and deeds of the Confessing pastors continue to echo from that time period, reminding future generations that the terrible atrocities were not committed without protest. In this sense the Confessing pastors served as reminders of humanity's more noble inclinations in a time of darkness.

When the war ended in 1945, the Confessing Church was one of the few institutions left in Germany with the credibility or contacts to reach out to the rest of the world. Confessing pastors helped to forge the first ties of postwar Germany with the rest of the free world. In 1950 the Confessing Church also began the process of urging the German people to accept their role in the brutality that marked the Nazi period. By helping to move postwar Germany in the direction of reconciliation with the West and by confronting the legacy of the Holocaust, the Confessing Church helped to bury the remaining vestiges of Nazi influence. By resisting the Nazi claims that theirs was a just cause and by assisting Germany in its painful efforts to deal with the memory of the Holocaust, the Confessing Church must be viewed as one of the many spades that were employed in an effort to bury the Third Reich. In this sense the resistance was meaningful.

–JOHN W. WELLS,
CARSON-NEWMAN COLLEGE

Viewpoint:
No. The Confessing Church was too disorganized, too patriotic, and too anti-Semitic to provide meaningful resistance to the Holocaust.

The influential Berlin pastor Martin Niemöller was among the first to protest both the "Aryan Paragraph" and the "German Christian" doctrines that supported it. Niemöller quickly issued a circular letter announcing the creation of a *Pfarrernotbund* (Pastors' Emergency League, PEL), pledging material support to any pastor persecuted by the state and dedicated to preserving pure scriptural teaching guided by the Reformation-era confessions of faith. Based upon these confessions, Niemöller flatly rejected any attempt within the church to discriminate against converts from Judaism or their descendants. He said nothing about the treatment of German Jews who had no connection with the Christian church. The PEL was the response of a devout minister to the false teachings of the "German Christians," not a socially conscious resistance organization, as its founder was well aware:

> This alliance will neither redeem the church nor shake the world; but . . . we owe it to the Lord of the church and to the brethren to do what we can; in these days a prudent retreat to the role of a mere spectator amounts to betrayal, for those under stress have no assurance of our brotherly solidarity. So let us act!

Niemöller's call for action rallied the Protestant community of faith across Germany: 1,300 ministers joined the PEL within weeks of its inception. By the end of 1933 it had a membership of more than 6,000 Protestant pastors (one-third of the total number in the Reich), many of whom enjoyed the whole-hearted support of their congregations. As pastors were suspended, dismissed, or even arrested for resisting the orders of the German Christian Church administration, the PEL stepped in to provide financial and spiritual help as well as whatever political pressure it could muster on their behalf. But the PEL was, at best, an ad hoc organization. Its membership soon realized that the *Reichskirche* (national church), which supposedly represented the theological inheritance of Martin Luther, was betraying its own confessional faith by misguided attempts to "Aryanize" Christianity. The time had come for faithful Christians to reclaim control of the national church.

Representatives from the PEL and other concerned Protestant groups gathered for a "Reformed confessional synod" at Barmen in May of 1934. After heated debate the synod passed the "Barmen Declaration," a theological statement encapsulating the essentials of German Protestantism in six brief points. Based upon the authority of scripture, the declaration firmly rejected both German Christianity and any other state pressure to conform the gospel message to Nazi ideals. While the delegates at Barmen intended to rescue the erring *Reichskirche* rather than break from it, within months their bold statement of faith became the theological foundation for the construction of a separate *Bekennende Kirche* (Confessing Church).

Although the Barmen Declaration implicitly opposed the Aryan Paragraph, it made no reference to the status of Jewish converts to Christianity nor to the plight of other groups tyrannized by the Nazis. According to historian Klaus P. Fischer, in *Nazi Germany: A New History* (1995), the Confessing Church suffered from a "moral myopia" that rendered it unable to see the danger of Nazism beyond its intrusion into religious affairs. The new "true church" was almost too poorly organized to achieve its avowed mission of preserving Protestant doctrine and worship in the Third Reich. It was, therefore, both ill fitted and uninterested in the task of resisting the Nazi persecution of the Jews.

Where organized resistance required participants to act on a shared set of deeply held moral convictions, the leadership of the Confessing Church lacked consensus on everything beyond the basic matters of theology expressed at Barmen. The church was organized as a loose federation of free congregations, assemblies, and regional synods representing three distinct evangelical traditions: the strict Lutheran church, the more liberal Reformed church, and the moderate United church. Matters were not helped by the further division of Confessing Church leaders into "radical" and "moderate" factions, based less on their denominational affiliation than on their status within the church hierarchy or their resentment of coercion. The bishops of Hannover, Bavaria, and Württemburg (the only three regions that escaped German Christian takeover in 1933) were influential moderate voices within the Confessing Church, encouraging a degree of cooperation with state policy. Some outspoken members of the PEL, by contrast, refused to acknowledge any direction of religious matters by either *Reichskirche* or Reich Chancellery. While these moderate bishops held their posts throughout the Third Reich, most PEL "radicals" were detained by the state for varying periods of time. This variety of opinion was not limited to the clergy: individual Confessing congregations included Nazi Party members, pro-Nazi Protestants, and even vocal German Christian propagandists bent on undermining the movement.

Thus divided against itself, the Confessing Church could neither inspire nor coordinate a general protest against Nazi dictatorship. Instead, the church sought to survive as an independent institution by resisting only those government directives that directly infringed on spiritual matters. When the Nazis cut off funding to Confessing congregations, disbanded church youth organizations, censored the religious press, closed seminaries, or subjected Confessing pastors to surveillance and arrest, the actions usually drew angry complaints. But when the Nazis promulgated the virulently anti-Semitic "Nuremberg Laws" (1935), there was no corresponding outcry from Protestant pulpits. Disappointed, the Swiss-German theologian Karl Barth noted that the Confessing Church "still has no heart for millions suffering under injustice. It still speaks . . . only on its own behalf." This narrowly defensive attitude, historian Victoria J. Barnett notes, in *Bystanders: Conscience and Complicity during the Holocaust* (1999), was essentially cooperation with the Nazi plans, for it permitted the state to take an ever tighter

hold on secular society and "undermined the moral credibility" of the church.

The situation was further complicated by the fact that, from the time of Martin Luther onward, the Protestant church historically supported the government. Operating under the "theory of two realms," the church pledged its allegiance to the state (the divinely sanctioned guardian of the temporal realm) and expected in return unquestioned control of the spiritual realm. Consequently, both moderates and radicals understood the Nazi *Gleichschaltung* (coordination) effort as an intrusion by the state into the realm of the church. "Resistance by confession" was a religious matter, not a form of political opposition to the Reich government. When the foreign press characterized the Confessing Church as a "resistance" organization, Confessing pastors reacted "in anger and scorn." Outsiders who "clearly did not understand the situation in Germany" were told to mind their own business. Early reports of Nazi persecution of Christians and Jews were dismissed as "atrocity propaganda," and offers of outside aid were politely refused. From the very first, national pride effectively cut the Confessing Church off from the support of the worldwide Protestant community.

Traditional allegiances, internal dissension, and a defensive mentality all contributed to the failure of the Confessing Church to develop any effective political resistance to Nazism. These "institutional" weaknesses were compounded by the individual sympathies of church members who shared, to greater or lesser degrees, the nationalistic and anti-Semitic attitudes of the Nazis. Both before and after World War I (1914–1918), German Protestant pastors tended to be conservatives who supported the monarchy, distrusted the Social Democratic Party, and feared Communism. Such opinions probably inclined the church to support a Nazi government pledged to destroy the liberal, secular, and socialist "threats" to German culture. Many of the Protestant faithful, one seminary student recalled, "believed during Hitler's first years that his efforts and goals were in the best interest of Germany." Even at the height of the *Kirchenkampf* (church struggle) in the mid 1930s, most Confessing pastors were patriotic citizens who remained loyal to the very regime that attacked them. Radical church leader Niemöller, a submarine commander during World War I, was taken into "protective custody" by the Gestapo in March of 1938 and placed in a concentration camp. Still confined at the outbreak of war the following year, Niemöller wrote a personal letter to Hitler volunteering to resume his commission in the German Navy. Hitler declined the former U-boat commander's request. One wonders if Niemöller's final public sermon, titled "God is my *Führer*," influenced the Nazi leader's decision.

The response of Confessing Christians to their government's wartime call to arms suggests the depth of members' love of the Fatherland, if not necessarily an equal support of the Nazi state. About 2,000 men from the pulpits and (illegal) seminaries of the Confessing Church served in some branch of the *Wehrmacht* (German army). Bonhoeffer, a radical leader whose absolute personal opposition to Nazism eventually cost him his life, nevertheless saw good reasons for his fellow churchmen to volunteer to fight for Germany. According to Bonhoeffer, as recorded in *Letters and Papers from Prison* (1953), active duty provided every young clergyman and student with "an inner liberation from the heavy pressure of political suspicion . . . [and] a long-sought opportunity to prove his inner attitude and readiness for sacrifice as a soldier." And sacrifice they did: half of all Confessing Church seminary students did not return; thousands of pastors' sons (including 2 of Neimöller's boys) also died for "*Führer, Volk* and Fatherland." Of the nearly 8,000 ordained "Protestant" (that is, both Confessing and German Christian) pastors who joined the military, at least 1,855 were killed in action. By contrast, 21 leaders of the Confessing Church were executed during the Nazis' twelve years of rule. It is difficult to justify significant "resistance" by the Protestant church when nearly 2,000 clergymen died fighting for the Nazi regime and only 21 died fighting against it.

Even as Protestant approval of the Nazis' nationalist policies was displayed by its pastors' active participation in the armies of the Reich, so also Protestant ambivalence toward Nazi anti-Semitism was evident when the church failed to act against it. Several things produced this conflicting attitude. Not only was there a long history of Christian anti-Semitism in Europe, but the German religious press joined other groups in making Jews the scapegoats for the nation's contemporary woes. Defeat in 1918, the substitution of a secular democratic republic for the nominally Christian monarchy, and the specter of communist revolution were blamed on elements of "Jewish internationalism." Political observations were buttressed with biblical references, for the New Testament was frequently interpreted to be anti-Semitic in tone. Yet, the church sought to convert the Jews (particularly those who no longer practiced the faith of their ancestors) and thus eliminate the influence of secular political ideologies.

The anti-Semitic point of view taken by church newspapers during the 1920s helped desensitize Protestant audiences to the lethal intent underlying Nazi rhetoric. Although this stance meant that many Christians were favorably disposed to Hitler's message, it did not mean that all Protestants accepted Nazism's pseudoscientific racial ideology. The controversy sparked by early attempts to exclude "non-Aryans" from the *Reichskirche* was one indication of this resistance; some Confessing Christians refused to deny the universal message of the gospel. Nor did tolerance of Nazi speeches equate to support for the murderous "excesses" of anti-Semitic hatred that culminated in the Final Solution. One pastor probably spoke for many German Protestants when he declared in 1933, "Anti-Semitism is justified, but this anti-Semitism must remain within the biblically set limits." In part because of opinions of this sort, the Confessing Church never spoke with unanimity in the defense of the Jews of Europe or of its own Jewish Christian membership.

The controversy sparked by early attempts to exclude "non-Aryans" from the *Reichskirche* exemplifies the complex attitudes of German Protestants toward both Jews and Jewish Christians. In the autumn of 1933 prominent theologians who rejected the doctrines of the German Christian movement nevertheless took opposing positions on the Aryan Paragraph. One group argued that "social and biological differences" between "Aryan" and "non-Aryan" made separate congregations necessary, whereas others reaffirmed the gospel message that all people were equals in the sight of God. One outspoken member of the PEL agreed with the former argument, bluntly declaring that "We want nothing to do with the Jewish race!" Niemöller, meanwhile, grudgingly accepted the latter position:

> Whether it's congenial or not, we have to recognize the converted Jews as fully entitled members through the Holy Spirit. . . . This recognition demands of us a high measure of self-discipline as a people who have had a great deal to bear under the influence of the Jewish people, so that the wish to be free from this demand is understandable.

Both factions were represented at the Barmen synod, which omitted any specific statement on the Aryan Paragraph in its declaration of faith. This initial silence in the face of prejudice set the pattern that still haunts the memory of the Confessing Church.

As Nazi outrages against the Jews escalated toward annihilation, the Confessing Church repeatedly failed to act. When the Nuremberg Laws were enacted in 1935, a moderate Confessing Church bishop warned his fellow believers against bringing "martyrdom" upon themselves by involving the church in the "Jewish Question." Three years later "many pastors and church leaders turned a deaf ear to the cries of anguish from the ghetto" during the anti-Semitic violence of *Kristallnacht*

(Night of the Broken Glass). Instead of vocal
institutional protest, local congregations
responded quietly to the needs of their Jewish
Christian members. Continued Nazi harassment notwithstanding, some clerical and lay
groups discussed, objected to, and (in a few
cases) acted to ease the plight of Jews and Jewish Christians. Yet, for every courageous individual who responded as a private citizen
(rather than as a pastor or church member),
there were many more who stood by in silence,
unable or unwilling to resist the Nazi actions.

Nevertheless, the longer the Third Reich
lasted, the more church leaders were stirred to public protest. Bonhoeffer was among the first to recognize Nazi intentions and to foresee the failure of the
Confessing Church to defend the persecuted. In late
1940, months before the first mass deportations of
Jews, he penned an anguished confession of guilt:

The church confesses to having seen the irrational use of brutal violence, the physical and
spiritual suffering of innumerable innocent
people, oppression, hate, and murder, without
having found a way to hasten to their aid. It

has become responsible for destroying the lives of the weakest and most defenseless brothers of Jesus Christ.

By the time other Confessing Church leaders expressed similar sentiments in public, Bonhoeffer was in prison for his resistance activities. But the young theologian's fate did not deter the members of the regional Prussian synod from speaking out against the Final Solution in late 1943:

> Woe unto us and our nation. . . . when the killing of men is justified on the grounds that they are unfit to live or that they belong to another race; when hate and callousness become widespread. For God says, "Thou shalt not kill." . . . We Christians share the guilt. . . . We have too often kept our silence, we have pled too seldom, too timidly, or not at all, for the absolute validity of God's holy commandments.

Later the same year a leader of the Confessing Church in Württemburg who had long supported the "exclusion" of Jews from German society also began to object to Nazi policies. Bishop Theophil Wurm wrote a highly placed Nazi civic official:

> I must declare, not out of any philosemitic tendencies, . . . that we Christians perceive this policy of extermination conducted against Jewry to be a grievous injustice and an ominous one for the German people.

The belated confession and protest of 1943 had no effect on the murderous Nazi leviathan. The Confessing Church was too disorganized, too preoccupied with itself, too deluded by Nazi propaganda, too patriotic, and—worst of all—too anti-Semitic in outlook to become a significant defender of the Jews. Church resistance to the Final Solution was doomed a decade earlier, the moment Protestants failed to object to the racial ideals behind the Aryan Paragraph as loudly as they objected to state efforts to dictate church policy. Neimöller, who survived the concentration camps to lead the church in postwar West Germany, confirmed this failing in a succinct, if inexact, recollection:

> First the Nazis went after the Jews, but I was not a Jew, so I did not object. Then they went after the Catholics, but I was not a Catholic, so I did not object. Then they went after the trade-unionists, but I was not a trade-unionist, so I did not object. Then they came after me, and there was no one left to object.

–JOHN KUYKENDALL,
UNIVERSITY OF SOUTH CAROLINA

References:

Hannah Arendt, *The Origins of Totalitarianism* (New York: Harcourt, Brace, 1951).

Shelley Baranowski, *The Confessing Church, Conservative Elites, and the Nazi State* (Lewiston, N.Y.: Edwin Mellen Press, 1986).

Victoria J. Barnett, *Bystanders: Conscience and Complicity during the Holocaust* (Westport, Conn.: Greenwood Press, 1999).

Barnett, *For the Soul of the People: Protestant Protest against Hitler* (New York: Oxford University Press, 1992).

Doris L. Bergen, *Twisted Cross: The German Christian Movement in the Third Reich* (Chapel Hill: University of North Carolina Press, 1996).

Eberhard Bethge, *Dietrich Bonhoeffer: Man of Vision, Man of Courage,* translated by Eric Mosbacher (New York: Harper & Row, 1970).

Bethge, *Friendship and Resistance: Essays on Dietrich Bonhoeffer* (Geneva: WCC Publications / Grand Rapids, Mich.: Eerdmans, 1995).

Dietrich Bonhoeffer, *Letters and Papers from Prison,* edited by Bethge, translated by Reginald H. Fuller (London: SCM Press, 1953).

Klaus P. Fischer, *Nazi Germany: A New History* (New York: Continuum, 1995).

Wolfgang Gerlach, *And the Witnesses Were Silent: The Confessing Church and the Persecution of the Jews,* translated by Barnett (Lincoln: University of Nebraska Press, 2000).

Kyle Jantzen, "Propaganda, Perseverance, and Protest: Strategies for Clerical Survival amid the German Church Struggle," *Church History,* 70 (June 2001): 297–305.

Eric A. Johnson, *Nazi Terror: The Gestapo, Jews, and Ordinary Germans* (New York: BasicBooks, 1999).

Klemens von Klemperer, *German Resistance against Hitler: The Search for Allies Abroad, 1938–1945* (Oxford: Clarendon Press / New York: Oxford University Press, 1993).

Peter Matheson, ed., *The Third Reich and the Christian Churches* (Edinburgh: T. & T. Clark, 1981).

Klaus Scholder, *The Churches and the Third Reich* (London: SCM Press / Philadelphia: Fortress Press, 1987).

EICHMANN

Did Adolf Eichmann receive a fair trial?

Viewpoint: Yes. Adolf Eichmann received a fair trial by the standards of international law.

Viewpoint: No. The prosecution's use of the courtroom as a classroom, as well as many procedural irregularities, prevented Adolf Eichmann from receiving a fair trial.

Born in Germany and raised in Austria, Adolf Eichmann had an early life marked by repeated failures and frustrations. The young man was still seeking direction in life when, at age twenty-six, he joined the National Socialist Party of Austria in 1932. Eichmann, a high-school and trade-school dropout, quickly found a purpose and a career within the ranks of the Nazi Party. An early member of the *Schutzstaffel* (SS), the elite guard of the party, he sought assignments that satisfied his personal interest in "studying" the enemies of the Party and (later) the Nazi State. Upon returning to his native Germany in 1933, he began his steady advance from mere SS file clerk to important party official. Working first within the SS branch known as the *Sicherheitsdienst* (Security Service, or SD) and later within its successor organization, the *Reichssicherheitshauptamt* (Reich Central Security Office, or RSHA), Eichmann gained recognition as a Nazi Party specialist on European Jewry and the Jewish Question.

Between 1935 and 1939 SS-*Hauptsturmführer* (captain) Eichmann helped to forcibly "encourage" German Jews to leave the Third Reich, even working closely with Zionist Jews in Germany to facilitate immigration to Palestine. After Austria "came home to the Reich" in 1938, he was transferred to Vienna to participate in the extension of Nazi anti-Semitic policies to the newest part of "Greater Germany." In the former Austrian capital city, Eichmann was instrumental in organizing an efficient bureaucratic process for divesting Jews of their assets and summarily deporting them from the Reich. The outbreak of World War II (1939–1945) brought the SS officer promotions and new, broader responsibilities in dealing with the ever increasing number of Jews under Nazi control. In the autumn of 1941, as an SS-*Obersturmbannführer* (lieutenant colonel), he assumed control of Section IV–B4 of the RSHA. Known as the Office of Jewish Emigration, Section IV–B4 was responsible for organizing the relocation of the Jews of Europe to any site selected by their Nazi oppressors. Thus, between 1939 and 1941, Eichmann administered the "resettlement" of Jews into ghettos and other special zones established in the Reich's newly captured eastern territories. After the mass killings began in the autumn of 1941, he supervised the systematic transportation of European Jews to the death camps in the east.

Surviving records of Section IV–B4 show that Eichmann continued this lethal exercise of his organizational talent up to the close of the war. With the end of Nazi Germany in sight, however, the SS officer prudently began traveling under a false name. In fact, although twice interned by Allied authorities following the capitulation of Germany, Eichmann managed to escape unrecognized. Not until he heard the defendants at the Nuremberg trials mention his name as a key player in the Final Solution did Eichmann decide to flee Germany. With the help of anti-Communist Catholic officials, he was smuggled out of Europe to South America in 1950. Still employing an alias, Eichmann lived a relatively quiet life with his family in Argentina until his discovery and subsequent kidnapping by members of the Israeli security service in May of 1960. Quickly smuggled out of Argentina, Eichmann was taken to Israel to face trial for his role in the terrible crimes of the Nazi regime. Even before it had truly begun, the Eichmann trial became the subject of a controversy that remains unresolved: was it possible for this former Nazi official to receive a fair trial in a court of law presided over by Israeli survivors of the Holocaust?

Viewpoint:
Yes. Adolf Eichmann received a fair trial by the standards of international law.

On 23 May 1960 the prime minister of Israel, David Ben-Gurion, announced to the Israeli Knesset (Parliament), as reported by *The New York Times* (24 May 1960), that

A short time ago one of the greatest of the Nazi criminals, Adolf Eichmann, who was responsible, together with the Nazi leaders, for what they called the final solution to the Jewish problem—that is, the extermination of 6,000,000 of the Jews of Europe—was discovered by the Israeli security services. Eichmann is already under arrest in Israel and will shortly be placed on trial in Israel under the terms of the law for the trial of Nazis and their collaborators.

Ben-Gurion's announcement began a two-year-long process in which Adolf Eichmann, portrayed by the Israelis as the person in charge of carrying out the Nazis' "Final Solution to the Jewish Question," faced justice for crimes he perpetrated against European Jewry during World War II (1939–1945).

Immediately following the Israeli announcement of Eichmann's capture and upcoming trial, observers throughout the world began commenting on the validity of such a proceeding. Commentators voiced opinions concerning the legality of Eichmann's capture from Argentina. They questioned the ability of the Israelis to hold a fair trial. Furthermore, critics maintained that the state of Israel did not exist until 1948, three years after the end of World War II and the commission of these crimes. Finally, many commented upon the enormity of the accusations leveled at Eichmann by Israel.

The first contention, the legality of Eichmann's abduction, caused many to question the validity of the trial. Professor Herbert Wechsler wrote, "Israel's custody of Eichmann was obtained unlawfully in Argentina, where he was kidnapped by Israeli agents. This taints the trial from the beginning." Many observers through-

out the world echoed Wechsler's belief. Yet, several points should be kept in mind regarding the legality of Eichmann's capture. First, Eichmann, upon his detainment, willfully and knowingly signed an affidavit positively identifying himself and agreed to return to Israel. Second, no extradition treaty existed between Argentina and Israel. Finally, Argentina had an abysmal record of extraditing Nazi war criminals to nations that enjoyed an extradition agreement with them, especially West Germany. Argentina protested the Israeli action in front of the United Nations; however, an unspecified reparation was agreed to by all parties involved, and the matter was closed. The Argentineans officially agreed to Eichmann's capture, removing the question of the illegality.

The next contention concerned the belief that Eichmann could not receive a fair trial in Israel and therefore, the Israelis should have handed him over to an international tribunal. Calls for an international tribunal were problematic and were refused by the Israelis. For them, Eichmann's crimes were aimed at Jews for no other reason than that they were Jewish. At the Wannsee Conference (1942) Eichmann and *Reichssicherheitshauptamt* (Reich Central Security Office, or RSHA) chief Reinhard Heydrich identified more than eleven million Jews throughout the world and slated them all for extermination. Therefore, Israel correctly saw it as their right as representatives of the only Jewish state to try Eichmann on their own soil, using Jewish judges and Israeli law as a framework for the trial. Many European countries held "successor trials" after the close of the Nuremberg trials, and the convictions and sentences meted out by such courts were never questioned. The Eichmann trial should be seen as another of these "successor trials."

Connected closely with the question of the impartiality, and perhaps more important of fairness, was the nature of the law that the Israelis accused Eichmann of breaking. The Nazis and Nazi Collaborators (Punishment) Law (1950) passed the Knesset with much debate ten years prior to Eichmann's capture. The law aimed at punishing those individuals suspected of crimes against Jewish people, crimes against

**Adolf Eichmann listening
as an Israeli court
declares him guilty
of war crimes on 15
December 1961**

*(U.S. Holocaust Memorial
Museum, Washington, D.C.)*

humanity, and war crimes. Many, including Eichmann's lawyer, Robert Servatius, argued that the law was invalid because it was retroactive and extraterritorial. According to Servatius, Eichmann's crimes occurred in the late 1930s and 1940s in a sovereign country (Germany) that did not deem his actions illegal. Furthermore, Israel did not exist as a sovereign nation until 1948. Therefore, he concluded, a state that did not exist at the time the crimes were committed could not punish a person under a law enacted fifteen years after the fact. Attorney General Gideon Hausner countered this contention, arguing that the laws used by the Nuremberg Tribunal in 1946 and 1947 were also retroactive. The Israelis established the 1950 law based on precedents set at Nuremberg and, consequently, the court upheld the legality of the Nazi and Nazi Collaborators Law.

The third contention regarding the trial was the broad range of charges arrayed against Eichmann. Israel charged Eichmann with seven counts of crimes against humanity, four counts of crimes against the Jewish people, one count of war crimes, and three counts of membership in criminal organizations. To apply such a broad range of charges to the defendant, Hausner portrayed Eichmann as the sole person

responsible for planning and carrying out the Holocaust. Many objected to the approach taken by the prosecution. Although Eichmann played a key role in the destruction process, most notably in the areas of transportation and the deportation of Hungarian Jewry in 1944, he clearly played a less significant role in the Holocaust than the Israelis attributed to him. When the trial concluded in 1961, the court found Eichmann guilty only of crimes against humanity and crimes against Jews, discarding the membership in criminal organizations and also some specific counts of each indictment.

A reduction of the charges should not, however, have tainted the nature of the trial at all. Faced with the choice of a prosecution based on narrow, specific charges or one based on broad charges, Hausner chose the latter. His reasons were twofold. First, he wished to charge Eichmann with as many crimes as possible. Like most prosecutors, Hausner felt that charging Eichmann with a broad range of crimes helped better ensure a conviction on most, if not all, of the charges. Second, Ben-Gurion and Hausner wished to use the trial for educational and patriotic purposes, "to remind the countries of the world that the Holocaust obligated them to support the only Jewish state on earth." To accomplish this end, Hausner used the trial as a vehicle for recounting the entire story of the Holocaust from 1933 to the end of the war. This strategy included calling 121 witnesses, many of whose testimony had little or nothing to do with the question of Eichmann's guilt. The use of such testimony caused some commentators to voice doubts about the validity of the trial. The prosecution also introduced several hundred documents as evidence that pertained to Eichmann's crimes. In essence, there were two purposes to this public trial of a Nazi fugitive. On the one hand, by using witnesses to tell the whole story of the Holocaust, the prosecution was successful in its educational and patriotic goal. On the other hand, the use of specific documentary evidence satisfied the legal criteria pertaining to the question of Eichmann's guilt.

The documentary evidence offered in Jerusalem clearly established Eichmann's pivotal role in the Nazi machinery of deportation and death. The SS officer's primary responsibility was to organize the transportation of Jews residing in any country or territory selected for Nazi attention. The staff of his Office of Jewish Emigration first calculated the number of Jews to be transported either to a ghetto, a concentration camp, or a death camp. Eichmann then contacted the *Judenrat* (Jewish Council) of the given area from which the Jews were to be transported. The *Judenrat,* in turn, would draw up lists of those to be deported. Meanwhile, Eichmann's office contacted the *Reichsbahn* (German national railway) and hired the trains necessary for the projected transport. Not only did his staff plan for every detail, providing the physical resources necessary for a smooth and efficient transport (trucks, guards, and even meals for the Germans involved). As "immigration agents" they kept meticulous records of the Jews they collected and shipped off to die.

Eichmann carried out his duties with the precision and discipline of a well-trained soldier, enabling this process to continue up to the last days of the war. Even as the German army retreated on all fronts, trainloads of Jews rolled eastward. The mass murders of European Jews, whether by gassings or (following the dismantling of the death camps in late 1944) death marches, lasted almost until the surrender of Germany early in May 1945. Records of the Office of Jewish Emigration introduced at Eichmann's trial left no room for doubt that the defendant had been instrumental in the facilitating the Final Solution.

Although decades have passed since Eichmann's capture, trial, and execution, questions still persist concerning the fairness of the proceedings, and it appears that a consensus will never emerge. Questions surrounding the circumstances of his capture played an important role in clouding the issues involved in the trial and led to many other concerns about how fair the trial could be. However, when one takes into account the thorny issues involved in extraditing Eichmann or returning him to Argentina for trial, a clearer picture develops explaining Israeli actions. Combined with the Argentinian refusal to pursue the matter further within the international community, Israeli actions regarding Eichmann's capture become less important to the matter of his guilt.

Questions also surrounded the issue of the ability of Israel to hold a fair trial for Eichmann. Little or no controversy surrounded the earlier "successor" trials, and guilty verdicts were almost never questioned. Given that fact, why should anyone have questioned the fairness of Eichmann's trial? If the perpetrators' nation was allowed to mete out justice to accused war criminals, why not the nation that represented the victims? Few questioned the impartiality of the Nuremberg judges, who represented the nations victimized by the Nazis.

Finally, many critics wondered at the enormity of the charges arrayed against Eichmann and the broad scope of the trial. The prosecution accused Eichmann of crimes he was not guilty of committing. However, Eichmann's involvement in solving the Jewish Question began in 1935 and lasted until the end of the war, and his participation in the destruction process grew larger with every year. From emigration to transportation, he was deeply involved in the fate of European Jewry in Nazi hands. Although Eichmann himself never killed anyone or commanded a death camp, his actions, especially in the sphere of transportation, played a leading role in the murder of millions of human beings. Eichmann might not have been guilty of all the charges arrayed against him, but he was guilty of the majority of them.

It is also true that Hausner and Ben-Gurion wished to use the trial for purposes other than justice. By utilizing witness testimony and emphasizing the crimes of the Holocaust in their totality, Israel brought the Holocaust into public discourse. Hausner relied heavily on documentary evidence to prove Eichmann's guilt: in effect, holding two trials at once—one broad in its scope and grandly historical in its meaning; the other based on law, legal precedent, and documentary evidence. Although the trial was not perfect, it was fair, and it succeeded in bringing to justice a leading Nazi war criminal, a man fully deserving of his sentence.

—JAMIE WRAIGHT,
UNIVERSITY OF MICHIGAN, DEARBORN

EICHMANN

Viewpoint:
No. The prosecution's use of the courtroom as a classroom, as well as many procedural irregularities, prevented Adolf Eichmann from receiving a fair trial.

The fact of Adolf Eichmann's guilt was never really questioned. The real issues were what institutions and procedures would be utilized to determine that guilt. From the start, there were many procedural irregularities associated with the trial. Eichmann was abducted from Argentina to stand trial in Jerusalem. Israel claimed the legal right to try him, even though the state did not exist at the time of the events in question. In addition, Israel claimed jurisdiction for crimes committed beyond its border, ordinarily a violation of the territoriality principle of international law. The law under which Eichmann was tried, the Nazis and Nazi Collaborators (Punishment) Law (1950), was an ex post facto law; that is, it made a specific act a crime after it had been committed. These irregularities in the trial raise important questions about fairness, but each of these alleged deficiencies are subject to plausible rebuttals. The greatest threat to the fairness of the trial was the attempt by the prosecution to make the trial a vehicle for witness survivor testimony and, thus, push the boundaries of traditional legal forms in favor of collective memory and in support of the Jewish state. The court's struggle with the prosecution, the irregularities of the case, and its attempt to defend its own legitimacy serve to highlight the contending values and interests at stake in the trial, of which fairness was just one. Fairness is not the only consideration in determining the legitimacy of a trial and, in the case of Eichmann, arguably not the most important one.

A key concern in a traditional criminal trial is personal culpability, that is, to place the alleged wrongdoing within the personal control and responsibility of the accused. The prosecutor, Gideon Hausner, directed his efforts not on the personal responsibility of Eichmann but on the documentation of the Holocaust itself. This effort pushed the limits of ordinary criminal proceedings. Instead of producing facts that placed the accused at the scene of the crime or detailed how the accused orchestrated events from behind the scenes, Hausner introduced witness after witness who spoke about individual experiences with deportation, concentration camps, and survival with little regard for witnesses' knowledge of or experience with Eichmann. Documenting the Holocaust as an administrative massacre—describing the Nazi bureaucratic machinery and indicating Eichmann's role in it and connecting this machinery in general to the experiences of scores of survivors—calls for different evidence and a different approach to establishing guilt.

A basic feature of criminal law is "no crime without law." In other words, criminal law should be prospective in nature. Ordinarily, the fact that the charging law is an ex post facto law is enough to call into question the basic fairness and legitimacy of a trial. The concern with the prospective nature of the criminal law is largely that individuals should have prior notice that certain behavior constitutes a crime and serves as protection against an abusive government. This prohibition is not, however, an absolute one. It is plausible to claim, as the prosecution did, that Eichmann's actions were so obviously wrong morally that it can be presumed the law was already in place.

The law under which he was charged, however, led to other irregularities in the trial. Many of the typical devices available to a defendant—calling character witnesses and challenging evidence through friendly witnesses—were not available to Eichmann because the same law that served as the basis for his indictment could also be used for indicting individuals who testified on his behalf. Not only was the law retroactively applied, it was constructed in such a way as to hinder the ability of a defendant to combat the charges against him.

Other features of the law place it outside traditional parameters of criminal procedure. According to the terms of the law, ordinary evidentiary standards do not apply. The standards were relaxed in order to provide the prosecution with greater flexibility concerning the type and reliability of evidence. The law may reflect an attempt to deal with a unique set of circumstances, the Holocaust, in a unique way. Both the legislative history of the Nazis and Nazi Collaborators Law and subsequent judicial interpretation of the law indicate that it was viewed as an extraordinary law responding to a horrific crime. However one might feel about the necessity of such a law as a response to the Holocaust, it seems to run counter to some basic understandings of law, which should be based on general rules and be prospective, not retrospective, in character. This tension highlights the difficulties of evaluating an administrative massacre within a traditional trial format.

Originally the Nazi and Nazi Collaborators Law called for the chief judge of the district court to preside over the trial. The chief judge at the time, Benjamin Halevy, had presided over the emotionally charged and conten-

EICHMANN

A NEW KIND OF MURDER

On 17 April 1961 Israeli attorney general Gideon Hausner, in his opening remarks at the trial of accused Nazi war criminal Adolf Eichmann, stated:

When I stand before you here, Judges of Israel, to lead the Prosecution of Adolf Eichmann, I am not standing alone. With me are six million accusers. But they cannot rise to their feet and point an accusing finger towards him who sits in the dock and cry: "I accuse." For their ashes are piled up on the hills of Auschwitz and the fields of Treblinka, and are strewn in the forests of Poland. Their graves are scattered throughout the length and breadth of Europe. Their blood cries out, but their voice is not heard. Therefore I will be their spokesman and in their name I will unfold the awesome indictment.

Murder has been with the human race since the days when Cain killed Abel; it is no novel phenomenon. But we have had to wait till this twentieth century to witness with our own eyes a new kind of murder: not the result of the momentary ebullition of passion or the darkening of the soul, but of a calculated decision and painstaking planning; not through the evil design of an individual, but through a mighty criminal conspiracy involving thousands; not against one victim whom an assassin may have decided to destroy, but against an entire nation.

In this trial, we shall also encounter a new kind of killer, the kind that exercises his bloody craft behind a desk, and only occasionally does the deed with his own hands. True, we have certain knowledge of only one incident in which Adolf Eichmann actually beat to death a Jewish boy, who had dared to steal fruit from a peach tree in the yard of his Budapest home. But it was his word that put gas chambers into action; he lifted the telephone, and railroad cars left for the extermination centres; his signature it was that sealed the doom of thousands and tens of thousands. He had but to give the order, and at his command the troopers took the field to rout Jews out of their neighbourhoods, to beat and torture them and chase them into ghettoes, to pin the badges of shame on their breasts, to steal their property—till finally, after torture and pillage, after everything had been wrung out of them, when even their hair had been taken, they were transported, en masse to the slaughter. Even the corpses were still of value: the gold teeth were extracted and the wedding rings removed.

We shall find Eichmann describing himself as a fastidious person, a "white-collar" worker. To him, the decree of extermination was just another written order to be executed; yet he was the one who planned, initiated and organized, who instructed others to spill this ocean of blood, and to use all the means of murder, theft, and torture.

He must bear the responsibility therefore, as if it was he who with his own hands knotted the hangman's noose, who lashed the victims into the gas-chambers, who shot in the back and pushed into the open pit every single one of the millions who were slaughtered. Such is his responsibility in the eyes of the law, and such is his responsibility according to every standard of conscience and morality. His accomplices in the crime were neither gangsters nor men of the underworld, but the leaders of the nation—including professors and scholars, robed dignitaries with academic degrees, linguists, men of enlightenment, the "intelligentsia." We shall encounter them—doctors and lawyers, scholars, bankers and economists, in those councils which resolved to exterminate the Jews, and among the officers and directors of the work of murder in all its terrible phases.

This murderous decision, taken deliberately and in cold blood, to annihilate a nation and blot it out from the face of the earth, is so shocking that one is at a loss for words to describe it. Words were created to express what man's reason can conceive and his heart can contain, and here we are dealing with actions that transcend our human grasp. Yet this is what did happen: millions were condemned to death, not for any crime, not for anything they had done, but only because they belonged to the Jewish people, and the development of technology placed at the disposal of the destroyers efficient equipment for the execution of their appalling designs.

The unprecedented crime, carried out by Europeans in the twentieth century, led to the adoption of the concept of a crime unknown to human annals even during the darkest ages—the crime of Genocide.

Source: State of Israel, Ministry of Justice, The Trial of Adolf Eichmann: Record of the Proceedings in the District Court of Jerusalem, *volume 1 (Jerusalem: Ministry of Justice, 1992), pp. 62–63.*

EICHMANN

tious trial of Rudolf Kastner. The Kastner trial focused on collaboration of the Jewish leadership with Nazi leaders, and in particular with Eichmann. Halevy's conduct during the trial raised basic questions about his impartiality and his ability to preside over the trial of Eichmann. In his opinion Halevy wrote that Kastner had sold "his soul to the Devil." The "Devil" was a reference to Eichmann. He was asked to recuse himself from the Eichmann trial but refused. The law was amended to allow a supreme court justice to preside over the district court. Halevy remained as part of the three-judge panel that heard the case. The importance of the appearance of impartiality and objectivity in judicial proceedings often leads to extraordinary efforts to protect against the possibility of partiality and bias. The irregularities present here, Halevy's prior conduct toward the accused, and the unusual circumstances surrounding the amendment of the law, raise serious questions about the possible fairness of the trial.

The setting and atmosphere surrounding the trial raise additional questions about fairness. The trial was not held in the district courtroom, but in a *Beit Ha'am* (community center). Accommodating a large international press corps, spectators, witnesses, and cameras made it necessary to move to a larger and more accessible space. The symbolism behind the need to move to a larger, general-purpose facility tracks the prosecution's attempt to move beyond the normal strictures of criminal law.

Public statements from state officials about the format and purpose of the trial also raise suspicions about the fairness of the trial for the accused. In an interview with *The New York Times* prior to the trial, Israeli prime minister David Ben-Gurion emphasized that the trial was designed to focus on Jewish suffering and to bring Eichmann to face Jewish justice as part of an attempt to place the Holocaust within Jewish history and connect it to the legitimacy of a Jewish State. He saw the trial as an important opportunity "to remind the countries of the world that the Holocaust obligated them to support the only Jewish state on earth."

Hausner, the lead prosecutor, made it clear that he wanted to tell a story about the Jewish community—its victimization, suffering, and resistance—and only secondarily was concerned about the defendant. He argued that determining the guilt of the accused was only one of the purposes of the trial: "I knew we needed more than a conviction; we needed a living record of a gigantic human and national disaster." He made it a conscious goal to mold and shape the consciousness of the Israeli youth—to create sympathy for Holocaust victims and secure a bond for a new nation. The trial in essence would function as a form of political education.

The "living record" generated by the trial was based on survivor testimony; the manner in which it was presented and the degree to which it was emphasized stretched the limits of criminal jurisprudence. The point of the trial for Hausner was telling the story of the Holocaust, not just Eichmann's complicity. Doing the latter would have "simplified the legal argument" but this emphasis would have denied the victims the opportunity to speak and tell their stories. The point was to cover "the whole Jewish disaster." Time and again Hausner encouraged witnesses to speak freely and generally without regard to their knowledge of or experience with the accused. The court struggled to control Hausner and periodically intervened to remind the prosecutor and the witnesses that some connection with the accused had to be made. The basic character of the trial, however, reflected Hausner's insistence that victims tell their stories even if that meant straying from the typical concerns of a criminal trial—for example, linking testimony to the actions of the accused.

The court recognized the pressures that the Nazis and Nazis Collaborators Law, the circumstances surrounding Eichmann's crime, and the prosecution's use of survivor testimony were placing on the judicial process. They were mindful of their role in history as well as the limits of the law in the service of historical understanding. They observed that a court "cannot allow itself to be enticed into provinces which are outside of its sphere. The judicial process has ways of its own, laid down by law, and these do not change, whatever the subject of the trial." Despite the best efforts of the court, however, the subject of the trial had overtaken, to a certain extent, the legal form of the trial.

From the beginning of the trial there were those, such as German philosopher Karl Jaspers, who believed that a trial, especially one held in Jerusalem, was not the appropriate way to confront the meaning and significance of Eichmann's crime. Jaspers argued that "Something other than law is at stake here—and to address it in legal terms is a mistake." Jaspers sounds an important warning about the vulnerability of the law.

American writer Susan Sontag's observations of the trial underscore this concern. Recognizing competing functions within the trial, she suggested that there was a "contradiction between its juridical form and its dramatic function." The trial was "primarily a great act of commitment through memory and the renewal of grief, yet it clothed itself in the forms of legality and scientific objectivity." While capturing a basic tension that runs throughout the trial and that, in particular, is reflected in Hausner's strategy, Sontag's observation misses an important theatrical element of most trials. The rules for a trial provide for and create many dramatic and theatrical opportunities. The key is the purpose served by the rules and in particular why allowances are made for theater and drama in the courtroom: to uncover the facts that support personal culpability for the accused and to shed light on the relevant rules of law. Understood in this light, the juridical function of the Eichmann trial can be said to have been compromised in favor of a larger concern with granting victims the opportunity to tell their stories. Hausner made a conscious decision to organize the trial around survivor testimony and give pride of place to victims. The possible cost of a court's sanction of such an approach is the erosion of the authority and legitimacy of the law. As the Eichmann court observed, if a trial is not bound to the procedures of the judicial process, the law and court procedures will be "impaired . . . and the trial would . . . resemble a rudderless ship tossed about by the waves."

In *Eichmann in Jerusalem: A Report on the Banality of Evil* (1964) Hannah Arendt, while commending the judges for their efforts, argued that the trial, because it focused on the victims and not the accused, failed in its most important function: "the law's main business: to weigh the charges brought against the accused, to render judgment, and to mete out due punishment." According to this standard, the Eichmann trial failed the law and, perhaps, failed justice. However, it is not clear if this standard is appropriate for understanding a trial in general and the Eichmann trial in particular. Might it be possible that the need to "render judgment" in this case required the kind of attention to the voices of the victims that became part of the prosecution's strategy? Did the need to serve justice override an exacting commitment to judicial integrity?

Ultimately, the answer to the question of the fairness of Eichmann's trial may depend upon how one characterizes the Holocaust. If the Holocaust is viewed primarily as a crime against the Jewish people, situated clearly within Jewish history, then a trial held in Jerusalem and conducted by the state of Israel seems not only acceptable, but also necessary. If, however, the Holocaust is viewed, as Arendt would have it, as a crime against humanity, then the explicit partiality of the trial calls into question its legal character and its fairness. Setting aside legal arguments for or against the structure and conduct of the trial, it is clear that all of the parties involved, including those critics of the proceedings, recognized that the trial would play a critical role in what story was told and who would tell that story.

Whatever the failure and deficiencies of the Eichmann trial, it provided a forum for the voice of Jewish victims that was denied to them in the Nuremberg Trials. Because of the decision to place such emphasis on survivor testimony, the trial called attention to the Holocaust in a way that served as a catalyst for future study and debate. As survivors began to speak through the authoritative medium of the law, popular and scholarly debate on the Holocaust began in earnest. The trial and the debate it generated helped, in a way, to make the Holocaust part of our consciousness. Weighed against the complaint of fairness to the accused, the value and legitimacy of the trial as a form of collective memory is undeniable. Whether a trial is a legitimate forum for this exercise remains an important and timely issue as countries such as Rwanda and South Africa struggle with accommodating the need for and value of victim testimony in the context of legal proceedings dedicated to the documentation of administrative massacres and state-sanctioned criminal activity. This testimony is particularly important when such trials are designed to establish the guilt of the accused, and trial procedures serve as important checks on accuracy rather than, in the case of the Eichmann trial, to document what has already been accepted as fact. It would be a mistake to describe the Eichmann trial as fair according to conventional standards of legality and criminal law. Such a mistake runs the risk of obscuring competing and, arguably, more important political, moral, and historical considerations. It also runs the risk of compromising judicial integrity and authority in future cases that look to the Eichmann trial as a precedent.

–BARRY SHARPE, TUSCULUM COLLEGE

References

Hannah Arendt, *Eichmann in Jerusalem: A Report on the Banality of Evil,* revised edition (New York: Penguin, 1964).

David Ben-Gurion, "The Eichmann Case as Seen by Ben-Gurion," *New York Times Magazine* (18 December 1960): 1, 62.

Bruce L. Brager, *The Trial of Adolf Eichmann: The Holocaust on Trial* (San Diego: Lucent Books, 1999).

Randolph L. Braham, *The Eichmann Case: A Source Book* (New York: World Federation of Hungarian Jews, 1969).

Braham, *Eichmann and the Destruction of Hungarian Jewry* (New York: World Federation of Hungarian Jews, 1961).

Shiraz Dossa, "Arendt on Eichmann," *Review of Politics,* 46 (1984): 163–183.

Adolf Eichmann, *Eichmann Interrogated: Transcripts from the Archives of the Israeli Police,* edited by Jochen von Lang, in collaboration with Claus Sibyll, translated by Ralph Manheim (New York: Farrar, Straus & Giroux, 1983).

Eichmann, *The Trial of Adolf Eichmann: Record of Proceedings in the District Court of Jerusalem,* 9 volumes (Jerusalem: Trust for the Publication of the Proceedings of the Eichmann Trial, in co-operation with the Israel State Archives and Yad Vashem, the Holocaust Martyrs' and Heroes' Remembrance Authority, 1992).

Charles Y. Glock, Gertrude J. Selznick, and Joel L. Spaeth, *The Apathetic Majority: A Study Based on Public Responses to the Eichmann Trial* (New York: Harper & Row, 1966).

Gideon Hausner, *Justice in Jerusalem* (New York: Harper & Row, 1966).

Henry R. Huttenbach, "The Eichmann Trial and Beyond: Homage to Hannah Arendt," *Proteus: A Journal of Ideas,* 13 (1996): 19–24.

Peter Z. Malkin and Harry Stein, *Eichmann in My Hands* (New York: Warner, 1990).

Peter Papadatos, *The Eichmann Trial* (London: Stevens / New York: Praeger, 1964).

Jacob Robinson, *And the Crooked Shall Be Made Straight: The Eichmann Trial, the Jewish Catastrophe and Hannah Arendt's Narrative* (New York: Macmillan, 1965).

Yosal Rogat, *The Eichmann Trial and the Rule of Law* (Santa Barbara, Cal.: Center for the Study of Democratic Institutions, 1961).

Tom Segev, *The Seventh Million: The Israelis and the Holocaust,* translated by Haim Watzman (New York: Hill & Wang, 1993).

Barry Sharpe, *Modesty and Arrogance in Judgment: Hannah Arendt's Eichmann in Jerusalem* (Westport, Conn.: Praeger, 1999).

Helen Silving, "In Re Eichmann: A Dilemma of Law and Morality," *American Journal of International Law,* 55 (April 1961): 307–358.

Herbert Wechsler and Benjamin Gassman, "Adolf Eichmann and the Law," *Bar Bulletin,* 19 (January–February 1962).

Stephen J. Whitfield, "Hannah Arendt and the Banality of Evil," *History Teacher,* 14 (1981): 469–478.

Charles Wighton, *Eichmann: His Career and Crimes* (London: Odhams, 1961).

Robert K. Woetzel, *The Nuremberg Trials in International Law with a Postlude on the Eichmann Case* (London: Stevens / New York: Praeger, 1962).

Leni Yahil, "'Memoirs' of Adolf Eichmann," *Yad Vashem Studies,* 18 (1987): 133–161.

Idith Zertal, "From the People's Hall to the Wailing Wall: A Study in Memory, Fear, and War," *Representations,* 69 (2000): 96–126.

EICHMANN

ETHICAL LIMITS

Is the Holocaust a suitable subject for fiction?

Viewpoint: Yes. Serious fiction aspires to a representation of historical truth that supersedes factual accounts.

Viewpoint: No. The facts of the Holocaust and the testimony of survivors carry such profound significance they should not be challenged by fictional truths that blur the historical record.

During the liberation of Europe by the Allies near the end of World War II (1939–1945), *Time* and *Life* magazines and the newsreels began showing images from what would eventually be labeled the *Holocaust*. These now-familiar images of suffering and anguish, however compelling, had to compete with other horrors for popular attention. There was not yet even a word for what these pictures represented, though the Nuremberg War Crimes Tribunal eventually settled on a catchall phrase: crimes against humanity. The French eventually contributed *genocide* to the vocabulary of horror. *Holocaust* and *Shoah* entered the popular vocabulary decades later. However, the horrors of Dachau and Buchenwald (which had been liberated by American and British forces), and eventually the atrocities of Auschwitz (which was inaccessible to the American press and had been liberated by the Soviets), merged quietly into the generalized barbarity of the preceding decade. There were plenty of movies, novels, and short stories set in wartime Europe, but the concentration camps were mentioned peripherally—if at all—and the extermination camps not at all. Survivors were but one part of the mass of Displaced Persons (DP) needing to be fed, sheltered, pitied, and returned to normal life. There was no fiction writing concerning the Holocaust because no one imagined a market for it.

The publication (and unexpected success) of Anne Frank's *Diary of a Young Girl* (1947) in the United States and Britain and its subsequent success as a Broadway play (1955) and Hollywood movie (1959) represented the beginnings of a popular-culture industry: the re-creation of the Holocaust as a setting for film and fiction. The works that followed in the 1970s, 1980s, and 1990s culminated in Steven Spielberg's *Schindler's List* (1993) that, with the opening of the United States Holocaust Memorial Museum in Washington (1993), put the Holocaust firmly into the realm of popular culture. Yet, the fictional representations (even in the Holocaust Museum) were criticized by some Holocaust scholars and survivors for cashing in on a tragedy that they felt ought never be represented except in testimony lest the fictional versions overtake and subvert memories of the actual events. Others pointed out, however, that fictional representations, if undertaken appropriately, served the vital purpose of keeping the Holocaust in public consciousness. In the last decade of the twentieth century—and well into the twenty-first century—the ethical problem of representing the Holocaust in literature and movies remains of central concern to scholars and especially survivors of the Holocaust.

Viewpoint:
Yes. Serious fiction aspires to a representation of historical truth that supersedes factual accounts.

The Holocaust representation debate, which is now going on for its fourth decade, has produced several ethical limitations on the aesthetics of Holocaust representation. These limitations are represented by positions that range from one that is somewhat open to aesthetics to a position that is so stringent that it forbids any aesthetic approach to the Holocaust whatsoever. Insofar as the historical context of this debate has radically changed, many of the ethical limitations that it has produced need to be rethought. In fact, many of the ethical limitations placed on the aesthetics of Holocaust representations are unwarranted today. Experimental post-Holocaust fiction teaches us that the Holocaust debate needs to reassess the ethical limitations it has placed on the aesthetics of Holocaust representation.

The most lenient position in the Holocaust representation debate holds that art can relate to the Holocaust. However, this product is not what one would call traditional art. Rather, it is closer to avant-garde and minimalist art since it exposes its inability to represent the Holocaust. This position establishes a criterion wherein any art that fails to expose its inadequacy is neither legitimate nor able to mourn the Holocaust in a "proper" manner. To represent the Holocaust in a traditional manner is therefore deemed unethical. This stance leads these theorists to argue that the Holocaust cannot be represented by a traditional literary genre such as tragedy or comedy.

The most extreme position is that art cannot represent the Holocaust and must rather be silent. These theorists argue that testimonies and historical accounts take over where art fails—that art acts to make sense of an event, which in this case should remain incomprehensible or sublime. According to this position, art (even art that expresses its inadequacy in the face of the incomprehensible) need not convey this sublimity insofar as it can turn viewers away from a more direct connection to the Holocaust. A more direct relation to the Holocaust can be provided by testimony. The prohibition of art and the affirmation of testimony by these theorists convey their belief that given the failure of human comprehension (through art) one can only bear witness to other witnesses.

In deference to this extreme view that art should remain silent and testimony only should speak, many theorists argue that one of the central tasks of the new form of Holocaust fiction is to convey silence. These theorists contend that

since art is unable to relate to this event through genres such as tragedy or comedy, it ends up saying nothing significant or meaningful in the traditional sense and therefore approaches silence. In order to resolve the dilemma, another position has been created that mediates between the two aforementioned positions and posits that an art form that includes both testimony and this new form of fiction provides an adequate means of relating to and representing the Holocaust.

The most conservative theorists of Holocaust fiction and movies today ascribe to the central premise of all of these positions, but they have changed the focus. Instead of simply arguing that traditional art produces amnesia (anaesthetics), as Jean-François Lyotard contends, they maintain that forgetfulness and its variant, distraction, are primarily products of the entertainment industry and popular culture. What they dislike most is their reduction of reality to fun and cheap thrills. These critics see the dramatization of the Holocaust as trivializing the actual events. This point of view accounts for much of the negative criticism of a movie such as *Schindler's List* (1993). Furthermore, many of the same critics criticize movies such as *La Vita è bella* (Life Is Beautiful, 1997) or Mel Brooks' movie and play *The Producers* (1968) since they employ comedy in relation to the Holocaust and run the risk of trivializing it. The ethical judgment that genres such as comedy and drama are unethical ways of representing the Holocaust is common to Holocaust studies. The judgment is deemed legitimate insofar as these theorists believe that a proper form of mourning cannot be achieved through either drama or comedy whether it is appropriated by the tradition of art or by Hollywood. For these theorists, both the fine-arts culture and Hollywood render natural an event that was completely unnatural. Such re-creating of the Holocaust interferes with the sort of mourning that, for the West, should be the only allowable response.

Experimental post-Holocaust fiction uses a different set of lenses to project and imagine the Holocaust. Instead of focusing on the failure of traditional forms of art and the shortcomings of Hollywood's appropriation of comedy, experimental post-Holocaust fiction concentrates on how the meaning of disaster conveyed by testimony or the failure of art should not be taken for granted. These creators show how neither testimony nor minimalist Holocaust fiction can escape that which the Holocaust theorists condemn by drawing from the very thing that the Holocaust theorists despise most: Hollywood and its appropriation of comedy and drama. Through the use of comic forms such as parody, pastiche, and unreliable narration, experimental

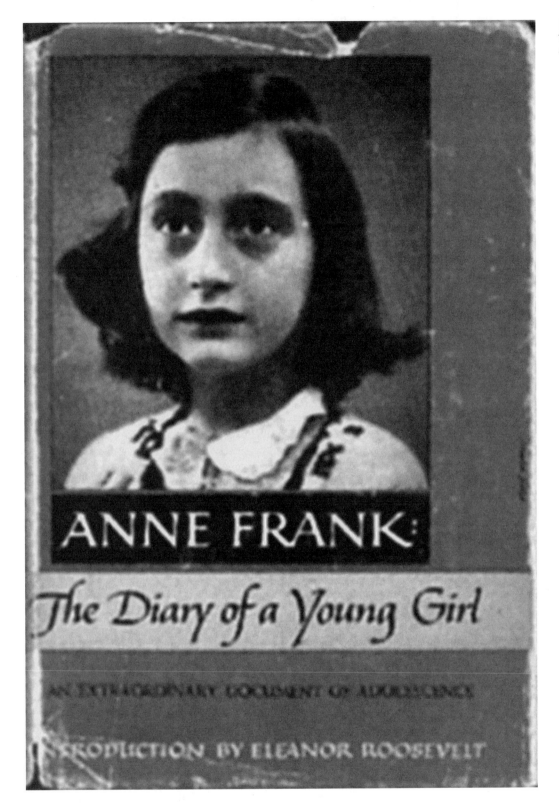

ANNE FRANK:

The Diary of a Young Girl

AN EXTRAORDINARY DOCUMENT OF ADOLESCENCE

INTRODUCTION BY ELEANOR ROOSEVELT

post-Holocaust fiction complicates the notions of authentic witness, realism, and representation (both the failure of representation evinced by the new form of fiction and the claim of realistic/ testimonial representation to be unmediated).

Parody is one of the most powerful tools of post-Holocaust experimental fiction. The employment of parody in literature is nothing new—its roots are in satire, which has served its moral pur-

pose throughout history. Experimental Holocaust writers, however, use parody for a different purpose. Unlike satirical writers who appeal to a proper way of approaching what they parody, creators of experimental post-Holocaust fiction do not make any appeals to a proper approach, in this case, to Holocaust representation. Rather, they use parody in order to deconstruct the notion of a "proper" approach to the Holocaust. Parody, like

satire, deconstructs notions that are given more weight than they can handle. It brings out the relative, rather than the absolute, nature of different concepts that Holocaust criticism emulates. It does this by juxtaposing comic or naive aspects of popular culture with concepts that claim to be absolute, concepts such as authentic witness, realism, and representation.

The parodying of authentic witness, realism, and representation articulates how realistic post-Holocaust fiction, testimony, and history are not free of cultural mediation and exploitation. This practice is troubling to post-Holocaust theorists insofar as they believe that it suggests that the act of witness, and by extension the event itself, is not valid. According to these theorists, to put memory, witness, and representation into question is to prevent the work of mourning. Since experimental fiction parodies realism, authentic witness, and representation, it comes across as parodying memory as well as the act of mourning. In order to combat the threat of parody these critics call for a moral seriousness that they believe is absent from experimental fiction and the elements of popular culture and entertainment that it draws from for its material. Many Holocaust theorists use the same logic with popular movies on the Holocaust. They dislike movies that "appear" realistic, but whose realism is subordinated to and parodied by popular genres, thus reducing the absolute status of realism to a relative status. Movies such as *Schindler's List* and *Life Is Beautiful* and the television miniseries *Holocaust* (1978) are therefore criticized by many Holocaust theorists because they draw on popular genres that employ comedy, suspense, melodrama, and common heroism. They argue that the utilization of popular genres encourages us to be entertained rather than to mourn. Though this may be true to some extent, the mistake of these critics is to underestimate the relevance of popular genres and to place experimental post-Holocaust fiction and these movies into the same category.

Experimental post-Holocaust fiction is not simply out to entertain a wide audience or use the Holocaust as a background for some drama or comedy. Rather, it seeks to use elements of entertainment and popular culture in a way that is much different from movies. Experimental post-Holocaust fiction intentionally appropriates comic elements of the entertainment industry and popular culture in relation to the Holocaust in order to provide readers with a strong sense of what testimony, history, and representation have become in a media age. But, according to many Holocaust theorists, the appropriation of popular culture and the entertainment industry by experimental fiction is no different from these movies since, to their per-

spective, it trivializes the Holocaust, making it into something one can laugh at or be thrilled by. They insist on a realism that adopts a serious moral and academic perspective in relation to the past, a perspective that lacks the ambiguity and playfulness that are characteristic of experimental fiction's appropriation of popular culture and history. What these theorists fail to understand is that post-Holocaust fiction is, quite often, parodying on the one hand the entertainment industry and on the other the moral seriousness of artists, writers, and theorists who convey seriousness in their insistence that the only approach to the Holocaust is one that comments on or communicates the unrepresentable or the sublime.

Many Holocaust theorists see their approach to the entertainment industry and experimental post-1945 fiction as the best defense against trivializing, and thereby forgetting, the Holocaust. What they have not taken into consideration is the possibility that memory has changed and has become something other than serious or realistic. Memory has become a hybrid of entertainment and popular culture. In the media age the act of mourning and the act of memory have changed insofar as memory cannot be separated from popular culture and mass circulation as it might once have been. The implications of this shift are meditated on by experimental post-Holocaust fiction.

The battle against revisionism and the institution of ethical limitations on Holocaust aesthetics has gone on in Holocaust studies for four decades. Now the contest seems to be in its last stages. The fear of forgetting the Holocaust has been curtailed by the entertainment industry. Because of the accumulation of testimonies and historical accounts, and as a result of the popularization of the Holocaust through such movies as *Schindler's List* and *Life Is Beautiful,* Holocaust study now has the opportunity of working through its deeply entrenched fear of revisionism. The Holocaust has entered world history in a way that many other disastrous events involving minority groups—such as slavery and genocide—struggle to do. Holocaust studies can now ask, without fear of sounding revisionist, what it can learn from experimental post-Holocaust fiction. However, Holocaust studies cannot ask such a question as long as Holocaust critics fail to take into consideration the implications of the fact that a large body of work has been developed over the last two decades that establishes the Holocaust as an historical event. The implication of this work is that it has reduced both the possibilities of a revisionist history and forgetfulness. The problem Holocaust theorists have with this development is that it challenges the task they have

ETHICAL LIMITS

allotted to themselves of imposing ethical guidelines about what is or is not a proper way of mourning or representing the Holocaust.

Rather than reestablishing the arguments of the Holocaust debate, Holocaust criticism needs to ask whether the overemphasis on realism that excludes experimental appropriations of the Holocaust or on literature that is obsessed with the Holocaust's unrepresentability has or can become an obstacle. Given the modern world, a better approach to the Holocaust would be one that is more open to, and less judgmental of, the explorations of experimental post-Holocaust fiction. An openness to experimental forms of post-Holocaust literature presents the greatest challenge to the ethical criterion established by these critics since this type of fiction can teach how one can, rather than should, understand the Holocaust. Experimental forms of post-Holocaust literature make the assumption that we are influenced by the complex world: by the entertainment industry, popular culture, capitalism, mass communication, and mass technology.

Experimental post-Holocaust fiction writers' use of literary devices such as parody or satire is not something to look at negatively as many Holocaust critics do, since it allows one to understand how culture mediates disaster. Furthermore, even though experimental post-Holocaust fiction does not take the traditional approach to mourning an event through appeals to realism or its avant-garde variants of the sublime, it teaches one about how the act of remembering or mourning an event has changed radically.

Among the cadre of writers of experimental post-Holocaust fiction, the work of Raymond Federman and David Grossman demonstrate, through their appropriation of parody and popular genres in relation to the Holocaust, how memory has changed. Federman, in *The Twofold Vibration* (1982), uses popular genres such as science fiction, the detective story, travel fiction, melodrama, and slapstick comedy to meditate on the Holocaust. Federman shows how the appropriation of genres usually used by the entertainment industry and popular culture can be used in a way that does not set out simply to entertain and yet is playful in its approach. He shows us how all these genres provide a way of relating to or representing the Holocaust that is not absolute insofar as he parodies each of these genres. In the end none of these genres predominates or makes light of the Holocaust. This emphasis does not bring out the failure of art as it relates to the Holocaust. Neither does it bring out its success. Rather, it employs a pragmatic approach to the Holocaust that is solely interested in making it relevant. It works with the desires people have already invested in popular culture and asks how they can use them in rela-

tion to the Holocaust. Federman does not just write for people who lived through the Holocaust; he also writes for a generation that never went through it and is immersed in popular culture. His fiction addresses a generation that recognizes the Holocaust on the one hand as an historical event but on the other hand as popular phenomena. Federman must therefore forego many of the ethical limitations that are placed on Holocaust representation.

Grossman's novel 'Ayen 'erekh–ahavah (1986), translated as *See Under–Love* (1989), is noteworthy as he employs elements from slapstick comedy, popular magazines, and even cartoons in relation to the Holocaust. The most extreme example of this style of writing is the plot of one of the sections of this book in which a Jewish prisoner is repeatedly subjected to death in a concentration camp but cannot be killed. This plot is used in an imaginative manner insofar as this prisoner is assigned to a Nazi officer who happened to have read his works of popular fiction as a child. Once the Nazi discovers that the prisoner is the writer of these tales he enjoyed as a child, he asks the prisoner to tell a story that is moving. This plot leads to an interesting commentary on the power of art (in this case, popular fiction) to heal or numb the senses. Rather than resist this request, the prisoner decides to tell stories, but the catch is that he never gives any of them a proper ending. Each ending is ambiguous. *See Under–Love* demonstrates how experimental post-Holocaust fiction uses popular culture and entertainment but in a way that neither Hollywood nor a popular magazine would. The goal is not to entertain but to play with the desire to be entertained, which is a trademark of modern times.

In another section of the book Grossman uses mimicry not only to parody a serious approach to the Holocaust but also to bring out a new relationship with the Holocaust that is more pragmatic. The main character is named Momik. The name suggests that his primary trait is mimicry. For the purposes of a post-Holocaust novel, Grossman has him draw on and mime a diversity of popular mediums in his effort to relate to the Holocaust. The act of creating a collage/pastiche of these mediums to relate to the Holocaust demonstrates how art has lost its absolute status and has become relative. Nonetheless, Grossman shows us that art still has a role in relation to the Holocaust, but one that is more concerned with what we can do with the world around us than with how one can or cannot express the Holocaust through traditional genres.

To place ethical limits on either of these experimental post-Holocaust texts would be to forego understanding how one can relate to the

Holocaust or what one can do in order to relate to it, given modern culture. To do so would be to miss an opportunity for making the Holocaust relevant. Therefore, the question is no longer whether or not the aesthetic representation of the Holocaust will lead to forgetfulness or revisionism but how one can relate to it. If the Holocaust debate has taught anything, it is that fears have to be worked through in order for art to resurface in the space of a culture whose image of itself over the last thirty years has changed dramatically.

–MENACHEM FEUER,
STATE UNIVERSITY OF NEW YORK, BINGHAMTON

Viewpoint:
No. The facts of the Holocaust and the testimony of survivors carry such profound significance they should not be challenged by fictional truths that blur the historical record.

One of the central concerns in most of the critical literature is the question as to how to adequately and appropriately represent the Holocaust. In order to decide the appropriateness of various Holocaust representations, one must look at the general debates waged within Holocaust studies about the abilities to represent the Holocaust and the responsibilities such depictions carry. Seen as singular, unique, and exceptional, the Holocaust often is considered nonrepresentable, and any representation thereof is asked to obey a certain moral imperative. The moral imperatives placed upon representations range from the desire to move the Holocaust into an incomprehensible, unintelligible, and thus unrepresentable space that requires writers and artists to approach the events with a reverential silence to the obsessive attempts to recall, represent, and catalogue the events in detail, thus hoping to comprehend and reach a larger truth. In fact, any violation of these supposed rules of author, subject matter, and style immediately draws extensive and vocal criticism. Even though more-recent artists have attempted to broaden the extent of permissible and acceptable Holocaust representations, and critics have begun to consider the problem of relying solely on realist depictions and eyewitness testimonies as artistic expressions, the general stance still seems to favor a traditional, realist, nonexperimental approach, preferably without artistic embellishment and based upon information by an eyewitness. The main points of contention

when dealing with Holocaust representation thus are whether to represent the Holocaust at all, how to represent it, and who should undertake these representations.

This singling out of the Holocaust from any other historical event and from any concerns over textual mediation is fairly characteristic of large parts of Holocaust studies, especially within the historical sciences. The destruction of the European Jews was—and still is—surrounded by an aura of incomprehensibility, a refusal or even inability of representation, and a complete rejection of theoretical tools otherwise easily employed when dealing with narrative history. The Holocaust is thus often raised to an exemplar outside of space and time, an abject event that defies theorization and simply requires that it be witnessed. This mantra of incomprehensibility, disbelief, and inability to represent carries through in much of the writing on the Holocaust and is epitomized in social theorist and philosopher Theodor W. Adorno's claim that poetry is no longer possible after Auschwitz. This often-quoted prohibition is based on the incomprehensibility of the horrors of the camps that, in turn, demands utter silence as its only appropriate response. Possibly the most outspoken representative of such an approach is George Steiner, who describes how art after the Holocaust is confronted with the impossible task of representing an incomprehensible violence and who consequently argues that the only apt response is silence—that is, any artistic object coming out of the Holocaust is already sacrilegious. When he comments that the "world of Auschwitz lies outside speech as it lies outside reason," he moves the Holocaust into a sacred, nonlinguistic realm.

While such a pure and unmitigated response to the Holocaust is theoretically valid, it is not practically viable. Moreover, its principal danger is the repetition and/or completion of the Nazi project of destroying not only the lives but also the knowledge and memory of a people. When acknowledging the need to tell of the Holocaust, however, one immediately faces the next dilemma, namely, how to represent the unrepresentable. At the center of this debate over suitable representations is the question as to whether any fictionalization does not court the danger of negating the facts, that is, whether only the facts pure and simple can adequately tell the "real" story. Most critics therefore agree with a strict separation of fact and fiction, with a clear distinction of memory and testimony against fictional and imaginary (re)creations. As a result, the legitimacy of fictionalizing the Holocaust is repeatedly debated and questioned. Holocaust survivor and scholar Elie Wiesel thus argues that a "novel about Treblinka

"YOU SHOULD NOT BE TOO OBSERVANT"

Pinchus Freudiger, a member of the Hungarian Jewish Council in the 1940s, recalls in testimony, given at the 1961 trial of S.S. officer Adolf Eichmann, his struggle during World War II to believe reports of the annihilation of Jews in the concentration camps and the attempts by the Germans to cover up their activities.

Witness Freudiger: I was always in correspondence with Rabbi Weissmandel—I got a letter nearly every week. . . . Once I received a letter with a report about Auschwitz—I believe the court already heard about this report: the Slovaks who escaped. . . . I received the mail which had been brought by the Slovakian courier. I had quite a number of letters from various people, and from Rabbi Weissmandel. I started to read the report, I kept on reading, studying it; and I asked myself: "Is this really possible, is it credible?" I refused to believe it—it was a letter about the extermination. . . . I see before me the report. It says that up to now 1,000,450 Jews have been exterminated in Poland and other countries, and a further 300,000. . . . And other figures—more numbers. . . . The last sentence says: "Now they are preparing to start with the Jews of Hungary."

Q. Mr. Freudiger, you told us about conversations you had with Krumey, about the fate of the Jews taken out of Hungary. Would you tell the Court something about certain postcards which reached Hungarian Jews at that time from the deportees?

A. Yes. Until this report had been received, we knew they were sent to Auschwitz but we did not know what Auschwitz meant. Krumey always said they were being sent to work. After a fortnight, when the first transports had already been sent—sometimes trains left every day—we received through our liaison officers, who used to go to Schwannenberg almost every day (we had liaison officers to do the routine work), quite a number of postcards written by deported Jews. The postcards were dated, and bore the message: "We are working here. Regards . . ." —or: "We feel well; we are working. Regards

to . . ." Nearly all the postcards were in the same style.

Q. What was the address of the sender—Walze [Waldsee] . . . ?

A. At the top of the postcard there was written 'Walze' and a date—there was no address.

Q. Did you try to establish where this Walze was?

A. I went to Krumey after receiving the postcards and asked him where Walze was. He said in the center of Germany—Thüringen. We searched the map but could not find it, and thought maybe this was such a small place; and the deception continued for three or four weeks, until they realised that it was not worthwhile any longer.

Presiding Judge: Was there a stamp on the postcards?

Witness Freudiger: No, they were not stamped. They said that the Command brought the mail by special bag. Two weeks later I came across a postcard with an erasure. (The postcards were written in pencil.) The word 'Walze' had been rubbed out. As a textile manufacturer I always kept a magnifying glass handy on my desk, and I noticed that the letters "—itz" were visible on the postcard: someone, instead of writing "Walze," had written "Auschwitz," and then erased it—the last letters, "itz," were visible. I took the postcard to Krumey and said: "Our people are in Auschwitz, not in Walze." He said: "How can you say such a thing?" I gave him the postcard and the magnifying glass and said: "Please take a look." He examined it and said: "Freudiger, I know you are a sensible man—you should not be too observant." Then the postcards stopped coming—in fact, there were no people to write those postcards any more.

Source: "Postcards from Waldsee," in Documents of Destruction: Germany and Jewry, 1933–1945, *edited by Raul Hilberg (Chicago: Quadrangle, 1971), pp. 194–195.*

ETHICAL LIMITS

is either not a novel or not about Treblinka," in effect, demanding an authentic realism that precludes any fictional representation of the Holocaust. Furthermore, such a position establishes a clear-cut—though false—dichotomy between facts and fiction and collapses the power of the imagination into falsehood and lies. This approach also implies that only eyewitnesses have the right to narrate the Holocaust.

In fact, Holocaust survivors often are represented as distinguished by their ability to gain unmediated access to their pasts, a fact particularly obvious in depictions of oral testimonies. Emphasizing the particular "knowledge" of survivors suggests that these memories occur extraverbally rather than being remembered and recounted decades after the original experiencing. As many theorists contend that the eyewitness recounts the factual events rather than any narrative accounts, they argue that the experiences of the Holocaust actually short-circuit any traditional modes of mediation. Such an elevation of the eyewitness overlooks much of recent critical theory and denies any consequent generation the opportunity to enter a dialogue with the past, a perspective highly problematic for any number of reasons. Assuming a direct knowledge of the past that can be transmitted to others without manipulation and interpretation, eyewitness testimonies seem to circumvent all limitations imposed by language itself. Holocaust scholars who would like to restrict Holocaust narratives to survivor memories and eyewitness testimonies as the only true and immediate link to the past can do so only by ignoring the media potential of any such memory and account.

The crucial role of the eyewitness is at the center of the recent scandal surrounding Binjamin Wilkomirski's novel *Fragments: Memories of a Wartime Childhood, 1939–1948* (1995). In fact, Wilkomirski's case is exemplary of the moral imperatives and ethical prohibitions that many critics impose upon Holocaust fiction. Wilkomirski's text is a self-described survivor account, only later discovered to be completely fictitious when the author was exposed as a fraud. The text, which supposedly is a product of the author's fragmented and recovered memories of his early childhood in the camps, was initially hailed as one of the great Holocaust testimonies. Critics compared Wilkomirski to Elie Wiesel, Anne Frank, and Primo Levi and awarded the novel a variety of literary prizes. Only three years later, however, research into Wilkomirski's past revealed inconsistencies and raised serious questions about the accuracy of his account and his status as a survivor. Yet, the author maintains that the story is indeed truthful and factual. He explains that his supposed identity as the illegiti-

mate child of a Swiss invalid who was forced to give him up for adoption is in fact one retroactively forced upon him after the war, thereby effectively erasing his own past and Holocaust experience. Accordingly, *Fragments* uses the ambiguity and opaqueness of its production to corroborate the veracity of the text so that the fantastic and fragmentary nature of the work confirms its factuality rather than undermining it. While many supporters initially defended Wilkomirski on the account that Holocaust survivors often could not prove or confirm their stories, further inquiries weakened the author's staunch defense of his account. Critics changed their judgment of his novel from praising it for its simplistically brutal honesty to criticizing its lack of technique. Finally, in 1999, all copies of the novel were removed from bookstores.

The most interesting aspect in the entire debate is the overwhelming literary criticism of the book that had been repressed or ignored when the text was thought to be autobiographical. When *Fragments* was discovered to be a work of fiction, however, critics found the writing, which they previously had described as immediate, poetic, innocent, and magical, to be dilettantish and simplistic with overwrought imagery. In Wilkomirski's case, then, the ethical mandate of Holocaust representation had taken precedence over any aesthetic interests—an oversight now painfully apparent as the text has lost its historical standing and is accused of containing no literary qualities to sustain its existence. In fact, the reception of *Fragments* exemplifies the central problem of Holocaust fiction and its aesthetic and ethical criticism in general. Holocaust survivor and author Ruth Klüger, for example, claims that the literary value of the book deteriorates from shocking to kitsch simply because the extraliterary context is altered. What Klüger suggests—and the altered reception of the novel supports—is that within Holocaust literature the aesthetic is linked with the ethical, that is to say, the aesthetic worth of a literary text is dependent upon its historical truth. Wilkomirski's story reveals the crucial role of the author and identity politics in the reception of Holocaust fiction. The same text is judged completely differently—ethically and aesthetically—depending on whether it is fact or fiction. While it certainly is important from an ethical and factual perspective whether the author tells the truth, it should not diminish the aesthetic value or the emotional impact of the text—yet, according to most of its critics, it does both. Rather than cherishing the text as a powerful testimony of the role of the Holocaust in our contemporary thought and the imaginary power Holocaust imagery holds in our collective unconscious, most critics refuse to engage any longer with the text.

ETHICAL LIMITS

Wilkomirski's case shows that Holocaust literature and its reception do not follow traditional literary criticism but instead establish an aesthetics based on ethical principles. These ethical restrictions on aesthetic practices are particularly apparent when considering postmodern Holocaust fiction. Of course, within a postmodern context, the truth status of the tale and the biographical background of the author should be of little import. After all, postmodernism has long proclaimed the author to be dead and has destroyed the clear lines separating fact from fiction. Furthermore, one of the central tenets of postmodernism, the shifting and uncertain identity of all characters, is particularly appropriate in the context of the Holocaust, where false identities could often save lives. Nevertheless, within the field of Holocaust studies, the author returns with a vengeance and, as in the Wilkomirski scandal, the author's persona, background, and credibility become the ultimate measuring stick for any critical approach. The role of the author thus defines one of the limits of postmodern Holocaust fiction, a limit upheld by many authors who otherwise must be considered postmodernists.

Similarly, some of the better-known postmodern Holocaust texts reveal how their authors resort to a realist aesthetics and maintain the authority of the eyewitness. For example, when confronting the Holocaust directly, postmodern Holocaust novelist D. M. Thomas refrains from the experimental techniques he otherwise employs throughout the text and instead resorts to the documentation of real events, including using testimonies. This practice is most pronounced in *The White Hotel* (1981) where the entire Holocaust chapter is indebted to a survivor testimony, but even in *Pictures at an Exhibition* (1993), he incorporates historically documented events. Similarly, Art Spiegelman, whose graphic novels *Maus: A Survivor's Tale* (1986) and *Maus II: A Survivor's Tale: And Here My Troubles Began* (1991) must be considered one of the most important contributions to Holocaust literature of the past two decades, emphasizes that his texts may be considered literature, but that they should never fall under the rubric of fiction. In the CD-ROM version of *Maus,* Spiegelman also includes several of the taped interviews with his father, thus reiterating the fact that none of the material in his books is made up, that he has done his research and tells us the truth.

Postmodern critic, writer, and poet Raymond Federman provides a particularly interesting case, since he is one of the few survivors who has chosen to recount his experiences in a highly experimental form that questions its own truth status. Repeatedly, he evades questions as to the veracity of his experiences, usually pointing toward his literary texts as answers. Federman's relentless focus on the merging of fact and fiction challenges the ethical imperative of Holocaust fiction that attempts to establish the truth of what happened in the camps in order to counter Holocaust deniers and write a history of the persecuted. Federman's identity as a survivor thus jars with his nonchalant attitude about truth and lies. Yet, for all his merging of truth and fiction, his emphasis on past experiences as only accessible via textual constructs, he is not protected from the reality-demands of the Holocaust. In fact, at one point Federman falls back on a certain ethical imperative of the Holocaust as he maintains the verity and reality of his experiences. When readers accused him of having fabricated the personal events that underlie his texts, Federman resorted to his authority as an eyewitness. As Federman foregoes the ludic ambiguities of fiction and insists on the veracity of his traumatic life experiences, he demonstrates the limits of postmodern Holocaust representation. In so doing, Federman thus reinscribes a boundary between fact and fiction as it relates to his own Holocaust experience, a clear line of separation that most of his literary and theoretical work tends to deny.

While the ever increasing literature within Holocaust studies attests to the fact that few contemporary writers and critics follow the mandate to silence, there nevertheless exists an ethical imperative that guards authorship and modes of representation. In this peculiar case of identity politics, the stakes are high: fictions of the Holocaust quite easily may be mistaken for claims that the Holocaust is a fiction. Similarly, false testimonies, such as Wilkomirski's, question and undermine the legitimacy and trustworthiness of all accounts by eyewitnesses who often have no more than their word to support their memories. As a result, even writers who otherwise subscribe to postmodern theory and practice it in their own writing resort to facts and data and defer to the eyewitness when confronted with the Holocaust. Postmodern theory and practice, with its denial of universalism, its celebration of the imagination, and its emphasis on representation and representability reminds us that even Holocaust testimonies cannot short-circuit the mediacy of language and must be read as critically as any other historical account. Nevertheless, the political, historical, and social weight of Holocaust representations takes precedence over postmodern language games and theoretical detachments. Historical distance may eventually create an environment in which Holocaust fiction welcomes and needs literary experimentation and creative innovations; for now, the Holocaust still demands a certain respect that includes appropriately solemn and serious literary responses.

–KRISTINA BUSSE, ALABAMA SCHOOL
OF MATHEMATICS AND SCIENCE

ETHICAL LIMITS

References

James Berger, *After the End: Representations of Post-Apocalypse* (Minneapolis: University of Minnesota Press, 1999).

Zachary Braiterman, "Against Holocaust-Sublime," *History and Memory,* 3 (Fall/Winter 1999): 7–28.

Paul Eisenstein, "Holocaust Memory and Hegel," *History and Memory,* 2 (Fall/Winter 1999): 5–36.

Sidra DeKoven Ezrahi, *By Words Alone: The Holocaust in Literature* (Chicago: University of Chicago Press, 1980).

Raymond Federman, "Federman on Federman: Lie or Die," in *Critifiction: Postmodern Essays* (Albany: State University of New York Press, 1993), pp. 85–104.

Federman, *The Twofold Vibration* (Bloomington: Indiana University Press / Brighton, U.K.: Harvester Press, 1982).

Saul Friedländer, *Memory, History, and the Extermination of the Jews of Europe* (Bloomington: Indiana University Press, 1993).

Friedländer, *Reflections of Nazism: An Essay on Kitsch and Death,* translated by Thomas Weyr (New York: Harper & Row, 1984).

Friedländer, ed., *Probing the Limits of Representation: Nazism and the "Final Solution"* (Cambridge, Mass.: Harvard University Press, 1992).

Sander Gilman, "Can the Shoah be Funny?" *Critical Inquiry,* 2 (Winter 2000): 279–308.

David Grossman, *See Under—Love,* translated by Betsy Rosenberg (New York: Noonday Press, 1989).

Miriam Bratu Hansen, "*Schindler's List* Is Not *Shoah:* The Second Commandment, Popular Modernism, and Public Memory," *Critical Inquiry,* 22 (Winter 1996): 292–312.

Geoffrey H. Hartman, "Memory.com: Tele:Suffering and Testimony in the Dot Com Era," *Raritran,* 10 (2000): 1–18.

Hartman, "Public Memory and Its Discontents," *Raritran,* 4 (Spring 1994): 24–40.

Hartman, ed., *Bitburg in Moral and Political Perspective* (Bloomington: Indiana University Press, 1986).

Hartman, ed., *Holocaust Remembrance: The Shapes of Memory* (Oxford, U.K. & Cambridge, Mass.: Blackwell, 1994).

Sara Horowitz, *Voicing the Void: Muteness and Memory in Holocaust Fiction* (Albany: State University of New York Press, 1997).

Dominick LaCapra, *History and Memory after Auschwitz* (Ithaca, N.Y.: Cornell University Press, 1998).

Berel Lang, ed., *Writing and the Holocaust* (New York: Holmes & Meier, 1988).

Lawrence L. Langer, *The Holocaust and the Literary Imagination* (New Haven: Yale University Press, 1975).

Langer, *Versions of Survival: The Holocaust and the Human Spirit* (Albany: State University of New York Press, 1982).

Jean-François Lyotard, *The Différend: Phrases in Dispute,* translated by Georges Van Den Abbeele (Minneapolis: University of Minnesota Press, 1988).

Stefan Mächler, *The Wilkomirski Affair: A Study in Biographical Truth,* translated by John E. Woods (New York: Schocken Books, 2001).

Gilead Morahg, "Israel's New Literature of the Holocaust: The Case of David Grossman's *See Under—Love,*" *Modern Fiction Studies,* 2 (Summer 1999): 457–477.

Alvin H. Rosenfeld, *A Double Dying: Reflections on Holocaust Literature* (Bloomington: Indiana University Press, 1980).

Michael Rothberg, *Traumatic Realism: The Demands of Holocaust Representation* (Minneapolis: University of Minnesota Press, 2000).

"Schindler's List: Myth, Movie, and Memory," *Village Voice,* 24 March 1994, pp. 24–31.

George Steiner, *Language and Silence: Essays on Language, Literature, and the Inhuman* (New York: Atheneum, 1967).

Elie Wiesel, "The Holocaust as Literary Inspiration," in *Dimensions of the Holocaust: Lectures at Northwestern University* (Evanston: Northwestern University, 1977), pp. 5–19.

James E. Young, "The Holocaust as Vicarious Past: Art Spiegelman's *Maus* and the Afterimages of History," *Critical Inquiry,* 24 (Spring 1998): 666–699.

Young, *Writing and Rewriting the Holocaust: Narrative and the Consequences of Interpretation* (Bloomington: Indiana University Press, 1988).

Slavoj Zizek, "From Urvater to Holocaust . . . and Back," *Parallax,* 2 (2000): 28–35.

EVIAN CONFERENCE

Did the west do all that it could before the beginning of WWII to assist potential and actual refugees of the Holocaust?

Viewpoint: Yes. Though the Evian Conference failed to provide substantial relief to Jews fleeing Nazi oppression, the failure was systemic rather than intentional.

Viewpoint: No. The Evian Conference was intended only as a politically expedient means of avoiding action to assist the Jews.

Large-scale Jewish emigration from Germany began almost immediately after the Nazi rise to power in 1933. Since this activity was in accordance with Adolf Hitler's dream of a *judenrein* (Jew-free) Germany, Nazi policies tended to encourage emigration, often by imprisoning Jewish heads of household and only releasing them when family members had arranged for an exit visa. Though the Nazis were far from helpful in this process, Jews fleeing Germany were permitted to retain most of their property and were able to transfer sufficient funds out of Germany to ensure a welcome reception in whatever country received them. Between January 1933 and July 1937, more than 137,000 Jews fled Germany, many heading for other European states or the Americas. In most cases their welcome was muted. Anti-Semitism, unemployment, and nativist fear of outsiders were roadblocks to immigration, but given the relatively small number of immigrants, the situation did not seem desperate.

The German *Anschluss* (annexation of Austria) brought thousands more Jews into the Nazi State and coincided with a sharp escalation in persecution. Jews who had been hoping that the situation would normalize now scrambled to find a way out. At the same time, the Nazis instituted a policy of spoliation, effectively preventing Jews from leaving Germany or Austria with any property. German and Austrian Jews were being thrust onto an unwelcoming world without resources. In order to address the crisis, U.S. president Franklin D. Roosevelt, encouraged by his State Department, called for an international conference to meet the present immigration crisis and to create an international organization to address broader problems of immigration. The conference was held 6–15 July 1938 at the French resort of Evian-les-Bains. The thirty-two national governments represented—from Europe and the Americas as well as Australia and New Zealand—were unanimous in their unwillingness to admit more refugees, and the Intergovernmental Committee on Refugees was virtually powerless. The German invasion of Poland in September 1939 brought even that group's minimal efforts to a standstill.

In retrospect, the Evian Conference has been criticized as a purely political endeavor, permitting the Roosevelt administration in particular to seem proactive while, in reality, doing nothing. The following arguments examine this interpretation. Neither, however, finds any evidence that, whatever the intentions of its promoters, the Evian Conference saved anyone from persecution, imprisonment, or death.

Viewpoint:
Yes. Though the Evian Conference failed to provide substantial relief to Jews fleeing Nazi oppression, the failure was systemic rather than intentional.

Modern, sovereign states have limited means to influence each other's behaviors. They can offer incentives, ranging from improved diplomatic relations to outright bribes, to encourage a neighboring state to continue doing something, to stop doing something, or not to begin doing something. They can also threaten or impose sanctions, ranging from a diplomatic snub to a full-scale military assault. When diplomats have neither carrot nor stick, they are left with the far weaker tools of moral suasion, saying, in effect, "you should do this because it is the right thing and will benefit you in the long run even if it seems ill advised right now." Such efforts are rarely effective unless the cost involved—political or otherwise—is small and the perceived moral good is strong.

It was this last, weak diplomatic tool that the administration of President Franklin D. Roosevelt (FDR) had available to it as it tried to find an international solution to the growing refugee crisis sparked by official anti-Semitism in Nazi Germany (which in 1938 included Austria and parts of Czechoslovakia). What came to be called the Evian Conference (6–15 July 1938) failed to provide substantial relief to Jewish refugees, not because it was intended to fail but because the problem—half a million Jews stripped of their financial resources and desperate to flee—could only be resolved by governments not allied with Nazi Germany acting in ways that were, at the time, clearly against their perceived national interest. Only when the full meaning of Nazi tyranny and anti-Semitism became clear near the end of World War II (1939–1945) would some of the barriers to Jewish immigration be rescinded by the same nations that had failed to act at Evian. By then, of course, when the moral necessity could not be evaded, the clock had run out on diplomacy and millions of European Jews were already dead.

The most common criticism of American involvement at Evian holds that the conference was proposed by President Roosevelt as a means of providing political cover for the administration's unwillingness to ruffle isolationist and nativist feathers by increasing the small numbers of refugees admitted to the United States. In 1938, after all, the president

was running for an unprecedented third term in office and could ill afford to antagonize voters who already suspected him of being too willing to get the United States involved in another European conflict. Because the economy had yet to recover from nearly a decade of depression, admitting more than a token number of Jewish refugees, most of whom would need to look for work, would only add to the lingering unemployment crisis. Even Jewish organizations hesitated to support increasing immigration to the United States since the only thing preventing the Nazis from expelling the entirety of Germany's Jewish population was the lack of any place to send them. Certainly what neither Roosevelt nor any other head of state could afford to do was to offer to receive a large number of impoverished refugees. The only possible solution to the refugee crisis that the Nazis were causing, short of a policy change in Germany, was for a substantial number of nations to accept a larger number of Jewish refugees. Any country that tried to solve the problem alone would court political disaster. But a broad-based agreement to share the refugee burden could, Roosevelt had reason to believe, succeed. The challenge became, then, getting governments to the table and persuading them to pay a modest political cost for a substantial moral good. Success was never very likely, but neither was it impossible. The political obstacles simply overwhelmed good intentions.

The political obstacles were substantial. Roosevelt wanted a solution to the refugee crisis but was limited by existing immigration laws. The laws, revised in 1921 and 1924 under Presidents Warren G. Harding and Calvin Coolidge, set specific quotas for foreign countries based on the population origins of Americans residing in the United States in 1890. These laws were directed at eastern Europeans (especially from Russia and Poland), Italians, and Asians. The total number of immigrants allowable per year was set at 153,774 (65,721 from Great Britain and 25,957 from Germany). President Herbert Hoover mandated that no immigrant would be admitted who could become a public charge. This provision, coupled with the Nazis' seizure of Jewish assets and funds, made it difficult for German Jews to enter the country.

FDR had stated that he would not ask Congress to liberalize immigration laws or to increase the size of the quota. He knew that his administration faced political risk in promoting Jewish immigration into the United States. Gallup polls from June 1936 to January 1938, published in *Time* magazine, revealed that approximately 65 percent of Americans were against Roosevelt seeking a third term. A *Fortune Magazine* poll, conducted during June 1938, demonstrated that 67.4 percent of Americans agreed that "with conditions as they are we should try to keep (refugees) out." In addition, 18.2 percent of respondents said, "We should allow them to come but not ruin our immigration quotas," and 4.9 percent favored increasing the quota. The rest were undecided.

Many American Jews were not in favor of admitting refugees. In April 1938 the *Jewish Examiner*, a Brooklyn newspaper, conducted a survey of Jewish opinion. Among the replies only two out of six Jewish congressmen were in favor of easing quotas. Three rabbis feared that any quota increase might arouse a public backlash.

The Great Depression (1929–1941), with its widespread unemployment, fostered anti-immigrant attitudes, prejudice, fear of foreign competition and alien ideologies such as communism, and worries that refugees would become public charges dependent on taxpayer money. An opinion poll for March 1938, at the time of the *Anschluss* (annexation of Austria), revealed that 41 percent of Americans believed that "Jews have too much power in the US"; for example, that they controlled finance, commerce, and entertainment. One-fourth of respondents were in favor of banning Jews from "government and politics," and one-fifth favored expelling Jews from the United States. Nineteen percent were in support of an anti-Semitic campaign in the United States. A Gallup poll conducted the same year revealed that 72 percent of Americans believed "We should not allow a larger number of Jewish exiles from Germany into the US" and 52 percent were opposed to contributing "money to help Jewish and Catholic exiles from Germany settle in other lands."

Nativistic (100 percent Americanism) nationalists within Congress, such as Representative John Rankin (D-Mississippi), Representative Martin Dies Jr. (D-Texas), Senator Robert Reynolds (D-North Carolina), and Senator Rufus Holman (R-Oregon), frequently promoted anti-immigrant and restrictionist legislation. They were concerned that aliens would steal American jobs, consume resources that belonged to American citizens, and endanger American culture. Senator Reynolds, before an immigration subcommittee, asked, "Why should we give up those blessings to those not so fortunate? . . . Let Europe take care of its own people. We cannot take care of our own, to say nothing of importing more to care for." Representative Thomas Jenkins (R-Ohio) complained that Roosevelt had embarked "on a visionary excursion into the warm fields of altruism. He forgets the cold winds of poverty and penury that are sweeping over the one third of our people who are ill-clothed, ill-housed, ill-fed." He said the president was proposing to "violate the immigration policies under which the nation is supposed to have been operating for the past seven or eight years. For years the policy has been to stay within ten percent of quotas."

The natural refuge for many Zionist Jews was Palestine, which in 1938 was administered by the British government as a mandated territory. But because the British government had no wish to alienate the Arab states on whose behalf they were theoretically administering Palestine, they insisted that the subject of Palestine not be raised at Evian. Since no solution to the refugee problem could be achieved without the British present, Myron C. Taylor, the head of the American delegation, agreed not to permit the issue to be raised since, as the American Consul General in Jerusalem, Wallace Murray, wrote, "These questions would stir up bitter passions and might even lead to a disruption of the Committee's labors." Zionist organizations, therefore, lost interest in any proposed solution to dealing with Jewish immigration that would of necessity leave out any discussion of Palestine. While Palestine could not have absorbed more than a small percentage of German Jews, its exclusion from the agenda at Evian set the tone for what was to come.

Furthermore, the countries being asked to accept refugees were, no matter how well intentioned, ill equipped to absorb large numbers of refugees into their economies and cultures. This reality was exacerbated by the racism and anti-Semitism endemic in some of the states, including the United States, most able to absorb refugees. It was this outlook that dominated the conference and continues to give the Evian Conference a reputation for cultivated indifference. Thomas W. White, the Australian delegate, is most often quoted in this context when he defended Australia's policy of not admitting more than a few hundred Jewish immigrants a year. Though Australia was actively seeking immigrants from Britain, Canada, and the United States at the time, the number of Jews admitted could not be increased, "since we have no actual race problem, we are not desirous of introducing one among us by encouraging any sort of plan of foreign migration in considerable proportions." White was clearly not considering Australia's treatment of its Aborigine population as constituting a "race problem," but as distasteful as his words might be, he was diplomatically asserting that the political and social

EVIAN RECOMMENDATIONS

In the proceedings of the Evian Conference (6–15 July 1938) the delegates made the following recommendations:

That the persons coming within the scope of the activity of the Intergovernmental Committee shall be 1) persons who have not already left their country of origin (Germany, including Austria), but who must emigrate on account of their political opinion, religious beliefs or racial origin, and 2) persons as defined in 1) who have already left their country of origin and who have not yet established themselves permanently elsewhere;

That the Governments participating in the Intergovernmental Committee shall continue to furnish the Committee for its strictly confidential information, with 1) details regarding such immigrants as each Government may be prepared to receive under its existing laws and practices and 2) details of these laws and practices;

That in view of the fact that the countries of refuge and settlement are entitled to take into account the economic and social adaptability of immigrants, these should in many cases be required to accept, at least for a time, changed conditions of living in the countries of settlement;

That the Governments of the countries of refuge and settlement should not assume any obligations for the financing of involuntary emigration;

That, with regard to the documents required by the countries of refuge and settlement, the Governments represented on the Intergovernmental Committee should consider the adoption of the following provision:

In those individual immigration cases in which the usually required documents emanating from foreign official sources are found not to be available, there should be accepted such other documents serving the purpose of the requirements of law as may be available to the immigrant, and

that, as regards the document which may be issued to an involuntary emigrant by the country of his foreign residence to serve the purpose of a passport, note be taken of the several international agreements providing for the issue of a travel document serving the purpose of a passport and of the advantage of their wide application;

That there should meet at London an Intergovernmental Committee consisting of such representatives as the Governments participating in the Evian Meeting may desire to designate. This Committee shall continue and develop the work of the Intergovernmental Meeting at Evian and shall be constituted and shall function in the following manner: There shall be a Chairman of this Committee and four Vice-Chairmen; there shall be a director of authority, appointed by the Intergovernmental Committee, who shall be guided by it in his actions. He shall undertake negotiations to improve the present conditions of exodus and to replace them by conditions of orderly emigration. He shall approach the Governments of the countries of refuge and settlement with a view to developing opportunities for permanent settlement. The Intergovernmental Committee, recognizing the value of the work of the existing refugee services of the League of Nations and of the studies of migration made by the International Labor Office, shall cooperate fully with these organizations, and the Intergovernmental Committee at London shall consider the means by which the cooperation of the Committee and the director with these organizations shall be established. The Intergovernmental Committee, at its forthcoming meeting at London, will consider the scale on which its expenses shall be apportioned among the participating Governments.

Source: *"Decisions Taken at the Evian Conference on Jewish Refugees (July 14, 1938)," Jewish Virtual Library <http://www.jsource.org/jsource/Holocaust/evian.html>.*

EVIAN CONFERENCE

cost of opening up his country to Jewish refugees would be greater than the Australian government was then willing to pay. As obsessed as many Australians were with keeping Australia "white" and "British," White's language could be seen more charitably as a statement of fact rather than of indifference. In fact, Australia agreed several months later to receive fifteen thousand immigrants over three years, though only nine thousand were taken in from 1933 to 1943. Most of the thirty-one other governments represented at Evian made similar claims: the economic, social, and political risks involved in becoming a place of refuge for German Jews, no matter how desperate their circumstances, was greater than they could bear. Countries such as Australia and Argentina needed farmers, not businessmen. And no one wanted to admit refugees who would require public assistance.

Nazi policy, however, ensured that most Jews would find it impossible to leave Germany with more than the clothes they wore. German economic policy aimed to impoverish German and Austrian Jews by seizing their assets. In 1933 emigrants from Germany were allowed to retain 75 percent of the value of their assets. This percentage was later decreased to 15 percent, and by 1938 it was reduced to 5 percent. It was this policy of economic spoliation that did the most to prevent the Evian Conference from succeeding.

During the opening of the Evian Conference, the British ambassador in Berlin asked German foreign minister Joachim von Ribbentrop whether the Reich government would allow refugees to retain enough capital to allow resettlement. Von Ribbentrop replied that "This was an internal German problem that was not subject to discussion. The question whether Germany could facilitate the transfer of capital in Jewish hands had to be answered in the negative, since a transfer of the capital accumulated by the Jews—especially after the war—could not be expected of Germany. Cooperation with the powers at present in session at Evian was therefore out of the question for Germany." Germany intended to expel its Jewish population in such a way that the refugees would be seen as an intolerable burden on the rest of the world.

Most of the countries represented at Evian would have increased their refugee quotas—and several ultimately did—but no one was willing to go first and risk solving everyone else's moral problem at the expense of his own political career. This frame of reference was aided, of course, by the assembly's decision not to give the victims a voice in the discussion. In this way, the governments represented at Evian continued to look at Jewish suffering as simply another aspect of the Jewish Question that had become a staple of European diplomacy. Assuming that the Jewish Question had no solution, and not imagining that Adolf Hitler was on the verge of proposing a "final" solution, the Evian Conference met with a "business as usual" attitude, desiring to do something but hoping that someone else would take the first step. When no one did, the conference disbanded. German and Austrian Jews, hemmed in and abandoned, saw their last hope of relief drowned. But the fault was neither with Roosevelt nor with an indifferent international community. The Nazi government, not yet decided on extermination but not wanting the Jews to leave Germany with any resources making resettlement possible, created insurmountable obstacles at Evian. A stronger commitment to justice on the part of the Americans or the British might have made a difference, but such altruism was no more common at Evian than at any other international conference before or since.

–TANDY MCCONNELL,
COLUMBIA COLLEGE

Viewpoint:
No. The Evian Conference was intended only as a politically expedient means of avoiding action to assist the Jews.

The Evian Conference (6–15 July 1938) was planned and implemented to provide political cover to the participating governments and to justify their unwillingness to assist Jewish refugees from Nazi oppression. It was never intended to do anything else.

On 12 March 1938 German troops marched over the Austrian border and received the flowers and cheers of thousands of Austrians. This act, marking the beginning of the *Anschluss* (annexation of Austria) into the Third Reich, drastically altered the situation of the Austrian Jews. Whereas in Germany, beginning in April 1933, anti-Jewish laws and regulations were gradually introduced, within Austria these policies, including the Nuremberg Laws, were enacted rapidly over a two-to-three-month period.

The perilous position of Jews within Austria was widely recognized. *The New York Times* reported on 13 March from Vienna:

Beating of Jews and plundering of Jewish owned stores increased today.

Jews were disappearing from Vienna life. Few, if any, were to be seen on the streets or in the coffee houses. Some were asked to leave streetcars. Others were not molested if they gave the Hitler salute. One man was beaten and left wounded in the street. Another, leaving a café, was beaten while his wife looked on.

Israel Cohen, sent by the World Zionist Organization in London to Vienna, saw "Thousands of Jews . . . besieging the Embassies and Consulates of different Governments in frantic efforts to obtain visas. Their state of despair was evidenced by the fact that they began queuing up at midnight, members of a family relieving one another, so as to make sure of being admitted into the coveted presence the following day."

Austrian Jews, like those whose experience of Nazi rule in Germany had preceded theirs by five years, wanted desperately to flee and looked to British-controlled Palestine, the United States, Great Britain, and elsewhere for refuge. The Jewish population of Germany numbered approximately 500,000 in 1933 and represented less than 1 percent of the total population. By 1938 about 150,000 German Jews had managed to emigrate. After Germany annexed Austria, 185,000 more Jews were brought under Nazi rule. Following the occupation of the Sudetenland, Bohemia, and Moravia in 1938–1939, an additional 115,000 Jews were added to Greater Germany.

The goal of the first phase of Nazi anti-Jewish policy was to make Greater Germany *judenrein* (Jew-free) by means of forced emigration. This goal was to be accomplished by seizing Jewish assets and property, by eliminating Jews from the workforce, and by using terror. The plight of these Jews, and fears of mass migrations, led to calls for an international solution to this refugee crisis.

The U.S. State Department was concerned that these Nazi anti-Jewish policies would force large numbers of Jews to flee the Reich and to seek refuge in the United States. The State Department viewed an international conference as a means of placing President Franklin D. Roosevelt at the forefront of efforts to find places of safety for refugees while avoiding domestic demands for an increase in the immigration quota and a change in American immigration policies. An internal State Department memorandum acknowledged that the purpose of the American proposal was "to get out in front" of liberal opinion, especially commentary from such influential columnists as Dorothy Thompson and

"certain Congressmen with metropolitan constituencies," and attempt to guide the pressure to increase Jewish immigration "primarily with a view to forestalling attempts to have the immigration laws liberalized; to seize initiative before pressure built and to spread responsibility among the 32 nations [which attended the conference] instead of us."

On 25 March 1938 the State Department called for an international conference to discuss the refugee situation. The language proposing the conference was decidedly noncommittal: "Our idea is that whereas such representatives would be designated by the governments concerned, any financing of the emergency emigration referred to would be undertaken by private organizations with the respective countries. Furthermore, it should be understood that no country would be expected or asked to receive a greater number of immigrants than is permitted by its existing legislation."

President Roosevelt indicated that the German and Austrian quotas would be combined, providing approximately twenty-six thousand slots for refugees, but no new slots would be created. In other words, the president was expressly unwilling to take the one action the crisis demanded.

Undersecretary of State Sumner Wells recommended to the president that the American delegation be led by Secretary of State Cordell Hull, accompanied by Francis Perkins, Secretary of Labor, and George Messersmith, head of the Foreign Service Personnel Board. Wells also suggested himself as the other delegate. However, Roosevelt selected a lower profile delegation. Myron C. Taylor—a strong advocate of refugee causes, a Quaker, former head of U.S. Steel, and Roosevelt friend—was named as head of the delegation with the rank of Ambassador Extraordinaire and Plenipotentiary. The other members of the U.S. delegation included James G. McDonald, presidential adviser on refugee affairs; George L. Warren, executive secretary of the Committee on Political Refugees; and several technical assistants. None of these delegates carried much political weight.

There was also concern at the State Department that eastern European countries such as Poland, Rumania, and Hungary were planning to expel their own Jews. Such an action, it was felt, could dissuade other nations from liberalizing their respective immigration policies and lead to more "refugee dumping." The Roosevelt administration therefore planned to limit discussion at the refugee conference strictly to German and Austrian refugees. It also avoided any refer-

**Jewish emigrants waiting
to board a ship,
Hamburg, 1937**

*(Bildarchiv Preussischer
Kulturbesitz, Berlin)*

ence to Jews, choosing instead the more neutral term "political refugees."

The State Department had hoped to hold
the conference in Geneva, Switzerland, but
the Swiss, wary of offending Germany and
conscious of their own restrictive immigration
policies, declined. The French government
offered the Hotel Royal, located in the spa
town of Evian-les-Bains, lying on the French
shore of Lake Geneva, as the conference site.

The U.S. government sent a proposed
agenda to participating governments and to
refugee organizations that wished to be
present as observers:

> To consider what steps can be taken to facil-
> itate the settlement in other countries of
> political refugees from Germany (including
> Austria). The term "political refugees," for
> the purposes of the present meeting, is
> intended to include persons who desire to
> leave Germany as well as those who have
> already done so.

> To consider what immediate steps can be
> taken, within the existing immigration laws
> and regulations of the receiving countries,
> to assist the most urgent cases. It is antici-
> pated that this would involve each partici-

> pating government furnishing, in so far as
> may be practicable, for the strictly confiden-
> tial information of the Committee, a state-
> ment of its immigration laws and practices
> and its present policy regarding the recep-
> tion of immigrants. It would be helpful for
> the committee to have a general statement
> from each participating government of the
> number and type of immigrants it is now
> prepared to receive or that it might consider
> receiving.

> To consider a system of documentation,
> acceptable to the participating states, for
> those refugees who are unable to obtain
> requisite documents from other sources.

> To consider the establishment of a continu-
> ing body of governmental representatives,
> to be set up in some European capital, to
> formulate and to carry out, in cooperation
> with existing agencies, a long range pro-
> gram looking toward the solution or allevia-
> tion of the problem in the larger sense.

Taylor held preliminary discussions in
Europe with other diplomats, which established
further ground rules for the conference:

> Stress should be laid on the fact that Evian
> will be a confidential meeting of representa-

tives of governments and not a public conference where all sorts of ideas will be aired to the press and to the general public. In consequence there should be only one public session at the outset where general statements may be made. Thereafter the meeting should go into executive session and a formal declaration should be given out for publication.

In view of the fact that most of the delegates to the Evian meeting must be in Paris by July 19 when the King of England will make his state visit it will be advisable to adjourn the conference at Evian on July 17 with the understanding that it will resume in Paris if necessary after the King's visit.

The British accepted the invitation with the stipulations that Palestine would not be discussed at the conference and that the United States would guarantee that the United Kingdom would not be pressured to accept more Jewish refugees into Palestine. Taylor, during a preliminary meeting with the British delegation, indicated that American Jewish leaders had approached him to allow Chaim Weizmann, the head of the Jewish Agency for Palestine, to meet him in private session to present the argument that Palestine offered the best haven for Jewish refugees. However, Sir Michael Palairet, deputy head of the British delegation, declared that the British government "would naturally prefer that this meeting should not take place." Taylor agreed and promised not to talk to Weizmann prior to the conference.

The U.S. State Department also agreed to avoid the issue of Palestine. In a cable from the Chief of the Division of Near Eastern Affairs (Wallace Murray) to the Consul General at Jerusalem (Wadsworth), Murray wrote:

It is highly probable that various groups will endeavor to induce the representatives of the governments participating in the meeting to take up the question of immigration into Palestine. It is felt that the Committee should reject any attempts to interject into its considerations such political issues as are involved in the Palestine, the Zionist and anti-Zionist questions. These questions would stir up bitter passions and might even lead to a disruption of the Committee's labors.

The Evian Conference was planned around six public sessions and one private session of all the delegations. Two subcommittees would perform the actual work of the conference. The first subcommittee, chaired by Judge Michel Hansson of Norway, would examine the legal aspects of emigration. It would evaluate the laws of the participating countries regarding the treatment of refugees, the numbers of immigrants each nation would

accept, and details concerning the documentation of aliens. This subcommittee consisted of the United States, Great Britain, France, Canada, Holland, and Switzerland. Unfortunately, many of the delegates, indulging in the recreational activities of the Evian region, did not attend the meetings. Hansson was forced to publicly ask representatives from twenty countries to attend meetings.

The other subcommittee, chaired by Lieutenant Colonel Thomas W. White, the Australian Minister of Commerce, would hear statements from the thirty-nine refugee organizations attending the conference, of which twenty were Jewish. The subcommittee decided to limit its hearings to only "those organizations concerned with the relief of political refugees from Germany (including Austria)." It also determined that each organization would be allowed only one speaker, who could speak for a maximum of ten minutes. Eventually, this time limit was decreased to five minutes. Clearly, hearing, even indirectly, from the refugees on whose behalf the conference had been called was not a priority. The subcommittee refused to allow representatives of Austrian refugee organizations to attend the meetings. An Austrian, Artur Rosenberg, representing the Austrian Refugee Foundation, said this refusal was "scandalous, since the committee was called to discuss our own people."

Nearly twenty-five delegates spoke at the Evian Conference explaining why, although greatly sympathetic, their respective countries were unable to accept refugees. White said that Jewish immigration into Australia numbered annually in the hundreds, but that his country could not take more,

for it is understandable, that in a young country, the human influx that one prefers would be that which comes from the source where the majority of its citizens originated, and it would not be possible to grant unjustifiable privileges to a non-British category of subjects without injustice for the others. It is also no doubt understandable that, since we have no actual race problem, we are not desirous of introducing one among us by encouraging any sort of plan of foreign migration in considerable proportions.

This almost universal reluctance to receive Jewish refugees was not lost on the Nazis. German foreign minister Joachim von Ribbentrop, in a memo to Adolf Hitler, described a conversation he had with French foreign minister George Bonnet:

Bonnet said that in the first place they did not want to receive any more Jews from

Germany and (asked) whether we could not take some sort of measures to keep them from coming to France, and in the second place France had to ship 10,000 Jews somewhere else. They were actually thinking of Madagascar for this. . . . I replied to M. Bonnet that we all wanted to get rid of our Jews but that the difficulties lay in the fact that no country wished to receive them.

Ironically, von Ribbentrop's cynicism was almost matched by some Zionist groups. When Arthur Ruppin, a prominent economist and sociologist, met with Zionist immigration experts to discuss the implications of the Evian Conference, he noted that Palestine had limited potential to absorb immigrants and that the British would not allow increased Jewish immigration there. He recommended that Jews should settle in other areas first in order to expedite their exodus from Germany and Austria. He urged Zionists who would be attending the conference to work toward such a goal.

Yitzhak Gruenbaum, at a session of the Jewish Agency Executive, took a contrary view and stated:

> Palestine might cease totally to be regarded as a country suitable for immigration. . . . There is a danger that in the course of the search for a country of refuge some other, new territory will be found to which, so it will be desired, Jewish migration will be directed. We for our part must defend the principle that it is only in Palestine that Jewish settlement can succeed and there can be no question at all of an alternative to it.

David Ben-Gurion, future prime minister of Israel, agreed with Gruenbaum and felt that acceptance of Ruppin's idea would diminish pressure on the British to open up Palestine for immigration and that it could potentially interfere with Zionism's assertion of an historic right to the land of Palestine. Although Ben-Gurion knew Palestine was not ready to accept large numbers of refugees, he continued to demand a linkage of refugee resettlement to Palestine. Ben-Gurion also believed that the "more we say about the terrible distress of the Jewish masses in Germany, Poland, and Rumania the more damage we shall inflict [on our own position] in the current negotiations [on the future of Palestine]." Thus, German Jews came to be regarded as unwanted pawns in a life-and-death game of meaningless diplomacy. Given Nazi Germany's determination to resolve its "Jewish Question" one way or another, the seeds of the "Final Solution" might reasonably be seen as having been sown at Evian.

The accomplishments of the Evian Conference were virtually null. The final resolution called for the establishment of the Intergovernmental Committee for Political Refugees, based in London and chaired by Lord Winterton, with an American director, George Rublee. The aim of this committee was twofold: to negotiate with the German government to re-establish a system of orderly emigration and to confidentially obtain information regarding the immigration policies of potential countries of resettlement. Neither proved meaningful in actually rescuing Jews from Nazism.

Delegates to the Evian Conference and their respective governments expressed great sympathy for the plight of Jews and non-Jewish "Aryans" who sought to flee Germany. However, this sympathy was not translated into effective action. The democracies lacked sufficient political and moral will to confront the anti-Jewish policies of the German government, which were the ultimate cause of the refugee dilemma. The message sent to the Nazis by the failure of the conference was clear: while the West might criticize the actions of the Reich, these countries did not want the Jews either. It took no great leap for Hitler and Heinrich Himmler to persuade themselves that no one in the West would seriously object to extermination either.

On 12 September 1938 Hitler spoke to a Nazi Party congress in Nuremberg and commented on the hypocrisy of the democracies toward Jewish refugees:

> They complain . . . of the boundless cruelty with which Germany—and now Italy also—seek to rid themselves of their Jewish elements. All these great democratic empires taken together have only a handful of people to the square kilometer. Both in Italy and Germany there are over 140. Yet, formerly Germany, without blinking an eyelid, for whole decades admitted these Jews by the hundred thousand. But now . . . when the nation is no longer willing to be sucked dry by these parasites, on every side one hears nothing but laments. But lamentations have not led these democracies to substitute helpful activity at last for their hypocritical questions; on the contrary these countries with icy coldness assured us that obviously there was no place for Jews in their territory. . . . So no help is given, but morality is saved.

Although the democracies cannot be blamed for the Holocaust, it is clear that their failure to accept Jewish refugees led to catastrophe for German and Austrian Jews. Since the vast majority of Jews murdered by the Nazis was Polish, Lithuanian, and Russian, the Evian Conference could not have affected their fate one way or the other. But

Western indifference to the Jews was not without effect. The 24 November 1938 issue of *Das Schwarze Korps,* the official publication of the SS, described how the progressive impoverishment of Jews would force Jews into a life of crime: "If things were to develop in this way we would be faced with the harsh necessity of having to exterminate the Jewish underground in the same manner as we are used to exterminating criminals in our Order State: with fire and sword. The result would be the actual and definite end of Jewry in Germany—its complete destruction."

The Evian Conference was doomed to fail for a variety of reasons. The American invitation to attend the conference specified that participating nations would not have to change their respective immigration laws and quotas and that any cost would have to be borne by private organizations. Roosevelt selected a nondiplomat with little public standing to head the American delegation. The Roosevelt administration did not attempt to garner public or political support for accepting a larger number of refugees. The Great Depression, unemployment, anti-Semitism, fear of aliens, and isolationism were additional factors fostering anti-immigrant attitudes. The subject of Palestine as a potential haven was not discussed. Jewish groups could not agree on a unified policy toward immigration and failed to send high-level representation to the conference. Finally, the sole accomplishment of the conference, the creation of the Intergovernmental Committee for Political Refugees, failed in its mission to persuade nations to offer realistic opportunities for resettlement or to convince the German government to allow refugees to retain enough financial assets to reestablish themselves in a new life.

Perhaps the essence of the Evian Conference is best expressed by the comments of the Chief Concierge of the Hotel Royal in Evian:

Very important people were here and all the delegates had a nice time. They took pleasure cruises on the lake. They gambled at night at the casino. They took mineral baths and massages at the *Establissement Thermal.* Some of them took the excursion to Chamonix to go summer skiing. Some went riding: we have, you know, one of the finest stables in France. But, of course, it is difficult to sit indoors hearing speeches when all the pleasures that Evian offers are outside.

–DENNIS LAFFER,
TAMPA, FLORIDA

References

Irving Abella and Harold Troper, *None Is Too Many: Canada and the Jews of Europe, 1933–1948* (Toronto: Lester & Orpen Dennys, 1982).

Haim Avni, *Argentina & the Jews: A History of Jewish Immigration,* translated by Gila Brand (Tuscaloosa: University of Alabama Press, 1991).

Yehuda Bauer, *American Jewry and the Holocaust: The American Joint Distribution Committee, 1939–1945* (Jerusalem: Institute of Contemporary Jewry, Hebrew University / Detroit: Wayne State University Press, 1981).

Bauer, *Jews for Sale?: Nazi-Jewish Negotiations, 1933–1945* (New Haven: Yale University Press, 1994).

Norman H. Baynes, ed., *The Speeches of Adolf Hitler,* volume 1, *April 1922–August 1939* (London: Oxford University Press, 1942).

Michael Berenbaum, ed., *Witness to the Holocaust* (New York: HarperCollins, 1997).

Israel Cohen, *Travels in Jewry* (New York: Dutton, 1953).

Complete Presidential Press Conferences of Franklin D. Roosevelt, volumes 11–12 (New York: Da Capo Press, 1972).

Dan Diner, *Beyond the Conceivable: Studies on Germany, Nazism, and the Holocaust* (Berkeley: University of California Press, 2000).

Documents on German Foreign Policy, 1918–1945 (Washington, D.C.: U.S. Government Printing Office, 1949).

Henry L. Feingold, *Politics of Rescue: The Roosevelt Administration and the Holocaust, 1938–1945* (New Brunswick, N.J.: Rutgers University Press, 1970).

Saul Friedländer, *Nazi Germany and the Jews,* volume 1, *The Years of Persecution, 1933–1939* (New York: HarperCollins, 1997).

Robert Edwin Herzstein, *Roosevelt & Hitler: Prelude to War* (New York: Paragon House, 1989).

Holocaust (Jerusalem: Keter Publishing House, 1974).

David Kranzler, *Japanese, Nazis, & Jews: The Jewish Refugee Community of Shanghai, 1938–1945* (New York: Yeshiva University Press, 1976).

Nora Levin, *The Holocaust: The Destruction of European Jewry, 1933–1945* (New York: Crowell, 1968).

Deborah E. Lipstadt, *Beyond Belief: The American Press and the Coming of the Holocaust, 1933–1945* (New York: Free Press, 1986).

Louise London, *Whitehall and the Jews, 1933–1948: British Immigration Policy, Jewish Refugees, and the Holocaust* (New York: Cambridge University Press, 2000).

Michael R. Marrus and Robert O. Paxton, *Vichy France and the Jews* (New York: Basic Books, 1981).

Arthur D. Morse, *While Six Million Died: A Chronicle of American Apathy* (New York: Random House, 1968).

Donna F. Ryan, *The Holocaust & the Jews of Marseille: The Enforcement of Anti-Semitic Policies in Vichy France* (Urbana: University of Illinois Press, 1996).

Ronald Sanders, *Shores of Refuge: A Hundred Years of Jewish Emigration* (New York: Holt, 1988).

Tom Segev, *One Palestine, Complete: Jews and Arabs under the British Mandate,* translated by Haim Watzman (New York: Metropolitan, 2000).

William L. Shirer, *The Rise and Fall of the Third Reich: A History of Nazi Germany* (New York: Simon & Schuster, 1960).

Charles Herbert Stembler and others, *Jews in the Mind of America,* edited by George Salomon (New York: Basic Books, 1966).

United States Department of State, *Foreign Relations of the United States: Diplomatic Papers, 1938,* 5 volumes (Washington, D.C.: U.S. Government Printing Office, 1954–1956).

David Vital, *A People Apart: The Jews in Europe, 1789–1939* (Oxford & New York: Oxford University Press, 1999).

Bernard Wasserstein, *Britain and the Jews of Europe, 1939–45* (London: Institute of Jewish Affairs / New York: Oxford University Press, 1979).

Chaim Weizmann, *The Letters and Papers of Chaim Weizmann,* 23 volumes (New Brunswick, N.J.: Transaction Books / Jerusalem: Israel Universities Press, 1968–1980).

David S. Wyman, *The Abandonment of the Jews: America and the Holocaust, 1941–1945* (New York: Pantheon, 1984).

Wyman, *Paper Walls: America and the Refugee Crisis, 1938–1941* (Amherst: University of Massachusetts Press, 1968).

Leni Yahil, *The Holocaust: The Fate of European Jewry, 1932–1945,* translated by Ina Friedman and Haya Galai (New York: Oxford University Press, 1990).

FEMINIST INTERPRETATION

Did men and women experience the Holocaust differently?

Viewpoint: Yes. Recognition of the significant differences in the perceptions of men and women assist in understanding the complexities of the Holocaust.

Viewpoint: No. To study the Holocaust in terms of gender responses is to diminish its significance as racial genocide.

Human beings come in myriad varieties but two basic forms: male and female. While the first historians of the Holocaust, writing in the 1950s and 1960s, concerned themselves with perpetrators and victims as such rather than as women and men, scholars of the 1980s and 1990s began to wonder about the significance of gender. Particularly to a new generation of feminist scholars, arguing that gender was a salient feature of the Holocaust experience—for perpetrators, victims, or bystanders—was to embrace the obvious. As mothers (or potential mothers) socialized as caregivers and nurturers, and especially vulnerable sexually, women experienced and responded to genocide in ways that men did not.

This extension of the analytical tools and assumptions of feminist and gender studies to the Holocaust was not altogether welcome. Some survivors were particularly put off, arguing, as one survivor did when asked about the lives and deaths of women and men in the camps, "Sex had nothing to do with it." Sex is, of course, about more than sexuality and reproduction. The assumption underlying the feminist analysis was that gender is fundamental to every human experience, no matter how extreme. Critics of gendered analysis pointed out that while women likely experienced the Holocaust differently than did men, so too did children experience the Holocaust differently than adults; intellectuals than laborers; the formerly rich and powerful than those accustomed to hardship and oppression; Jews than Gypsies, Communists, and other ideological opponents.

The debate is not strictly methodological. Modes of analysis, especially gendered ones, are innately political. To many observers, using feminist tools of inquiry to understand the experiences of a segment—or the entirety of the populations—affected by the Holocaust is as reasonable as employing the most modern instrumentation and technologies to address heretofore unanswerable scientific questions. But, the critics counter, using the Holocaust to facilitate and advance women's studies, or feminist modes of inquiry, or gender studies, or men's studies, serves only to re-create a Holocaust that suits the scholar's purposes. Thus, the Holocaust as a gendered event becomes something different than the Holocaust as Shoah, the Holocaust as "yet another example of genocide," or the Holocaust as an exceptional event.

Viewpoint:
Yes. Recognition of the significant differences in the perceptions of men and women assist in understanding the complexities of the Holocaust.

Until the 1970s, scholarly writings about the Holocaust utilized men's experiences of the Holocaust as if they were normative. Gender, as a variable of analysis, was generally ignored. Such neglect suggested that either women's experiences of the Holocaust were the same as men's or that gender was not a significant feature in the shaping of the Holocaust. In the 1970s, however, feminist scholarship began to restore women's experiences to the study of the Holocaust by recognizing that women were indeed historical agents and that gender was as important a difference to examine as a variable as were the varied experiences of Jewish and non-Jewish victims. The point of such study was never to compare and rank sufferings but rather to understand with more specificity the atrocities perpetrated by the Nazis.

The first works to examine the role of gender in the Holocaust were Jill Stephenson's *Women in Nazi Society* (1975) and Leila J. Rupp's *Mobilizing Women for War: German and American Propaganda, 1939–1945* (1978). Both authors suggest that gendered messages for German women were a mixture of tradition and modernity, that while domesticity was glorified by the Nazi regime, women were also advancing in many professions. In the 1980s, feminist scholars such as Renate Wiggershaus, Annette Kuhn, and Valentine Roth argued that the oppression of women under Nazism was yet another manifestation of the long history of women's oppression. Claudia Koonz, however, in her groundbreaking *Mothers in the Fatherland: Women, the Family, and Nazi Politics* (1987), noted ways in which German women benefited from Nazism and collaborated with the Nazis in affirming racial superiority. Historian Gisela Bock argued in *Zwangssterilisation im Nationalsozialismus: Studien zur Rassenpolitik und Frauenpolitik* (1986) that the Nazis did not value motherhood or traditional femininity, as evidenced in policies of compulsory sterilization and eugenic abortion and in German women's involvement as workers in male-dominated professions that directly supported the Holocaust. In examining women's survivor narratives, Joan Ringleheim contended that women's suffering was also gendered and that among Jewish women in particular, Nazi anti-Semitism, racism, and sexism intersected in policies and practices that targeted Jewish women for destruction as both Jews and women.

Women were not simply bystanders in the Holocaust, nor were their experiences subsumed in a generic Holocaust experience as defined by men's narratives. Instead, the historical evidence reveals that gender played an undeniable role in the experiences of German, Jewish, and other European women and that women acted as historical agents in complicity with or resistance to the Nazi regime. As a social construct, gender shaped the ways Nazis thought about women and the ways women thought about themselves. These constructions were evidenced in the various ways Nazis treated both Jewish and non-Jewish women and the ways women responded to Nazi actions. The enactment of Hitler's "separate spheres" ideology ensured that for both Jewish and non-Jewish women, Nazism would create separate and significantly different experiences of the Holocaust.

For elite German Aryan women, Nazi constructions of gender allowed them to be active perpetrators or complicit bystanders who benefited from Nazi anti-Semitism and racism. Thus, while these women held a disadvantaged status as women under Nazism, they also made choices to participate, whether actively or passively, in the advantages gained by Aryan status and therefore bore moral responsibility for their role in the Holocaust. Nazi ideology was especially successful in using religion as a means to enlist women, who were much more actively involved with their churches than men, as complicit participants. Protestant women saw Hitler as a savior, while Catholic women identified with Nazism's emphasis on motherhood. In fact, these Christian women were even able to find in their religion a defense for their anti-Semitism.

As active perpetrators of the Holocaust, women worked for the Nazis, entering into male spheres of power through the institutions of work. In particular, many women became concentration camp guards and joined in the systematic, intentional, and brutal torture and destruction of millions of people, adopting masculine norms of toughness and power. Even more women provided support for Nazi atrocities by creating homes that became sites of collaboration rather than resistance. By enacting traditional feminine roles in providing German men a home to which to retreat and be renewed, Aryan women, in effect, created a refuge for male perpetrators and maintained a sense of normalcy away from the atrocities of the ghettos and concentration camps. Far from being powerless, these women had great opportunity to resist and perhaps stem the brutality and murder. When Nazi propaganda minister Joseph Goebbels rounded up five thousand Jewish men

NOTHING BUT A NUMBER

Some of the experiences of Jewish inmate Helen Kuban (Klein, née Stern), who was from Czechoslovakia, are recalled here, including her transport to and incarceration in Auschwitz:

We were in Patronka for a few days, sleeping on the floor without food, until there were 1,000 of us. They put us on a cattle train, 80 of us in each car. Each transport, as they called the trainload, consisted of 1,000 people.

We still did not know where we were going. We just hoped and prayed that it would be a labor camp. There was no room on the train to lie down. We sat on the ground or stood, body pressed against body, with the door opened about four inches for ventilation.

The train trip seemed endless. There was no water, no food, no lavatories. Girls were fainting and gasping for air because the air was putrid. Finally, the train stopped. When they opened the door, fifteen of the eighty girls had already died. This was my introduction to Auschwitz, a small town in Poland.

It was March 28, 1942. They led us to a common bathroom, stripped us of all our clothing, made us stand naked, and put us into large tubs five at a time. The water became dirtier and dirtier as each group of women entered. They shaved all our hair (everywhere). They gave us uncleaned Russian uniforms which they had stripped from dead Russian bodies. My uniform became my only clothing for the next 10 months. As I looked around, I could not believe what the loss of hair could do to one's looks, even to the prettiest of us. Then they registered us, and from that moment on until after the war I became nothing but number 2282. . . .

Four of us girls befriended each other from the beginning. We tried to stay together because no matter how bad it was, it made the pain more tolerable to suffer with friends. In addition, we were all separated from our families and we all had a need to belong to someone.

We were assigned to barracks which were divided into coops; five of us had to share the space in each coop. Wooden planks were our mattresses and there was one thin blanket to cover the five of us. When we tried to sleep, we would each pull to have part of this blanket. March in Poland was still quite cold.

We worked, slept and ate in the same uniform. We became drenched in it and dried in it. We found that the uniforms which, as I mentioned, were captured from the Russian army, were infected with lice which we learned to call "clothes lice." I never would have believed that they could grow so big. I personally suffered greatly from them especially at night when I felt

them crawling over me, keeping me awake through the night.

Every day we went to work with an armed SS-man or woman and a trained German-Shepherd dog. Each morning before we went to work, and each evening when we returned from work, we underwent a head count, for which we had to stand outside, whether it was raining or snowing. We were lined up five in a row and marched by music out of the camp. We were outfitted with old, poorly-fitting shoes, but were not permitted to wear them to work because they felt we would ruin them too quickly that way. We walked barefoot in the middle of the road as Jews were not allowed to walk on the sidewalk.

We marched about five kilometers to work, and only after we arrived at our destination could we put our shoes back on. I suffered terribly going barefoot as every pebble seemed to hurt. I always prayed it would rain or snow so that I wouldn't feel the stones so much. . . .

Our job was to demolish buildings so that the Germans could re-use the bricks. We formed a chain and tossed the bricks one-to-another. Most of us were very young and inexperienced. It was very cold; the temperature was in the low 20s, and we had no coats or scarves for our freshly-shaved heads. We wore no gloves on our hands, which made catching the bricks particularly difficult. If one of us accidentally dropped a brick when it was tossed to us, the SS-man or woman immediately ordered the dog after us. The dog would jump and bite; the more one cried, the more they would urge the dog on us. I had been raised with dogs and loved them, but I began to hate and fear them.

By evening, we were generally numb, tired and hungry. We would march back to the camp and had to stand outside until the head count was completed (which they called Zaehlappell), after which they gave us our supper. Supper was one slice of bread and a dark liquid which they called "tea." We fought for this food as if we were afraid that they may not have enough for everyone. The menu for the next three years consisted of the same portion: in the morning, plain dark liquid; at noon, squash soup (which they called karpele); and for dinner, a slice of bread and more dark liquid. To this very day, more than 45 years later, I will not have a slice of bread and tea together.

Source: *Helen Kuban (Klein, née Stern), "Born Twice," in* Auschwitz—The Nazi Civilization: Twenty-Three Women Prisoners' Accounts, *edited by Lore Shelley (Lanham, Md.: University Press of America, 1992), pp. 75–77.*

FEMINIST INTERPRETATION

married to Aryan women in an attempt to present Hitler with a "Jew-free" Berlin for his birthday in 1943, the wives organized a protest and demanded the return of their husbands. Each day, more and more women joined the protest until Goebbels was finally forced to back down and release the prisoners.

Not all non-Jewish women were complicit in the Holocaust, however. Many German and other European women became actively involved in resistance to the Nazis. In particular, non-Jewish women demonstrated great courage in hiding Jews. The villagers of the French town of Le Chambon rescued five thousand Jews, following the example of Magda Trocme and her husband, pastor Andre Trocme. Magda explains:

> A poor woman came to my house one night, and she asked to come in. She said immediately that she was a German Jew, that she was running away, that she was hiding, that she wanted shelter. She thought that at the minister's house she would perhaps find someone who could understand her. And I said, "Come in." And so it started. . . . Those of us who received the first Jews did what we thought had to be done—nothing more complicated. . . . There was no decision to make. The issue was: Do you think we are all brothers or not? Do you think it is unjust to turn in the Jews or not? Then let us try to help!

In France, women were particularly involved in the resistance. In fact, the first French person to be killed by the Nazis was a woman who refused to give up her home to them. Usually, French women who harbored Jews and Allied airmen or aided other resisters were immediately executed, while men who committed these same acts were often held as prisoners of war. Nonetheless, women such as Lucie Aubrac were intimately involved in resistance missions. Aubrac organized many rescue missions of resisters held by the Gestapo, one of which even included her husband, Raymond.

Perhaps the most compelling examples of the role of gender in the Holocaust come from the experiences of the victims themselves. From its inception the Holocaust specifically and purposefully targeted Jewish women, based on their status both as Jews and as women. Their extermination was paramount to the Nazi plan for a Jew-free world, for as long as a Jewish woman existed, the possibility remained of new generations of Jews. Therefore, Nazis ultimately deported more Jewish women than Jewish men and killed more women than men, for a variety of reasons, although in the earliest period of the Holocaust more men were deported and murdered than women.

While women and men suffered many of the same humiliations and atrocities under the Nazis, women experienced specific sufferings related to their gender. In particular, women's biology was a site of Nazi abuse. Women, who were taught to be modest, were subjected to nakedness, body shaves, and body searches, quite often by male guards. While men experienced this initiation into the camps as a loss of autonomy and dignity, women often experienced it as sexual assault. The memoirs of concentration camp victims often focus on the sexual intimidation and trauma they experienced at the hands of the Nazis. Jewish women were raped by low-level functionaries (rape by SS officers was rare because Nazi racial laws forbade sexual contact with Jews and because the SS had access to other women in brothels) and forced to exchange sexual favors for food, boots, a better job, or other necessities for survival. Felicia Berland Hyatt was told by her mother, "Do anything anybody asks you to do, just so you save your life." Hyatt added that "the instructions she gave me when we parted were truly a revelation and they became even more meaningful, when months later I was faced with a situation in which I had to make a snap decision about bestowing a sexual favor in exchange for a temporary rescue from the German authorities." Unfortunately, few survivor memoirs document the brutal rapes to which women were subjected. When survivor Judith Isaacson's daughter lamented, "thousands of women were raped during the war, but no one hears about them," Isaacson responded, "the Anne Franks who survived rape don't write their stories." Pregnancy, childbirth, and motherhood were also sites for Nazi abuse and torture. Many women suffered from amenorrhea, and fear of forced sterilization or forced abortion was constant. Pregnancy for Jewish women was a crime against the Reich, and in many ghettos, abortion was compulsory. In Theresienstadt, for example, after the Nazis instituted a compulsory abortion policy, women who refused the procedure were immediately sent to a concentration camp. In forced-labor and concentration camps, pregnant women experienced being beaten with clubs and whips, kicked in the stomach, dragged around by their hair, and murdered. If a pregnant woman survived until she delivered, the Nazis killed both her and the baby. If a woman gave birth away from the awareness of the Nazis, other Jewish women would often smother or drown the newborn to save the mother and other women in her barracks and to prevent the suffering of the baby.

The construction of motherhood played an especially significant role in the deaths of women in the camps. Initial selections upon arrival at the camps were contingent on age, gender, and health. When Lidia Rosenfeld Vago approached the Jewish woman who was head of her block in Auschwitz, she asked, "'Where are our mothers, children, and grandparents?' Hella pointed toward dark clouds of smoke with flames shooting up here and there in the distance. 'There are your mothers and children going up in smoke just now.'" Often, women who had been selected to live as forced laborers refused to abandon their young children and so were sent to the gas chambers with them. Because Nazis disguised the gas chambers as showers, many women were not aware they were choosing death. Nonetheless, when the women of Theresienstadt were sent to Auschwitz-Birkenau, they were given a choice to be selected as workers or to go to the gas chambers with their children, a choice men did not have to make. As one feminist scholar noted, "Being a mother directly affected the chances for survival; being a father did not." Still, all but two of the six hundred women given this choice decided to go to the gas chamber.

Women's socialization might also have played an important role in their survival strategies, although this socialization had also disadvantaged them, particularly before World War II (1939–1945) in their secondary status in family and society. Survivors point to the importance of domestic skills, friendships, and an ethic of caring in surviving the horrors of the concentration camps. While survival was, on the whole, an arbitrary matter, the skills women had learned seemed to provide some small sense of empowerment to them through their connections to and caring for one another.

Women's homemaking skills often allowed them to stretch food supplies, mend clothes, and nurse sick children and friends. Survivor Ruth Bondy recounted the family camp in Birkenau:

> Although men and women lived in separate barracks, they could meet for a few minutes while walking the camp road to the latrines, or they could meet clandestinely for a moment in the barracks. Here, at Birkenau, only a day after their arrival, the differences between the sexes was already striking. The men, in hats with cut-off brims and in trousers and coats thrown to them at random—too short, too long, too wide, too small—looked like sad black storks. The women, also wearing garments that had been distributed to them at random, had somehow succeeded in only twenty-four hours in adjusting them to their bodies and sewing up the holes, using needles made out of wooden splinters and threads pulled out of the one blanket allocated to them.

Women's attention to cleanliness also played a role in their survival as they attempted to lessen the impact of disease-causing germs and bacteria. In one instance, women in a concentration camp pooled their few resources to exchange for a kettle that they then used to boil drinking water. For women, however, the effects of camp life on their appearance were especially traumatic. Socialized to be concerned with their outward manifestations of femininity, women dealt with a great deal of psychological distress about their deteriorating conditions, unlike men, who experienced the filth

and starvation more in terms of loss of strength, health, and power. Nonetheless, most of the women continued to pay attention to hygiene and tried to maintain their appearance as much as possible. For many women, refusing to give in to the filth became a small act of resistance, a way of maintaining dignity despite the Nazis' dehumanizing treatment.

Probably the most striking difference in women's and men's narratives of their Holocaust experience is the role of community. Most memoirs by male survivors tend to focus on the impact of the camps on their individual psyches, although occasional reference will be made to bonding experiences with other inmates. Women's memoirs, however, are filled with stories of connections with other women and solidarity with those around them in the face of the horrors of the camps. While both men and women were well versed in Torahic and Talmudic teachings about Jewish responsibility for one another, the emphasis on bonding in women's memoirs is unparalleled in those by men.

In the camps women often formed surrogate families with unrelated women, "camp sisters," who became instrumental in survival and who often sacrificed themselves for one another. Acting as nurturers and caregivers provided female inmates with understandings and skills that allowed them to build a closeness few men experienced. Women, for example, removed one another's lice and leaned against one another for warmth during the agonizingly long roll calls. They shared food, organized clothes and beds, and helped each other deal with the deprivations of camp life. While many memoirs attest to the fact that some women mistreated others, betrayed their sisters, or even stole bread from other inmates, the overwhelming testimony of survivors is of a sense of comradeship and community that contributed to one's chances of survival. One survivor explained:

> Despite the suffering, the cold, the hunger, the punishments of being forced to stand for long hours with arms raised, despite the roll calls which went on for many hours, and the beatings—life in the Schuh-Kommando [a group of women who sorted prisoners' shoes] was still easier, thanks to the mutual solidarity. One woman would give her slice of bread to her starving friend or another would do her sick friend's work for her. . . . While I had typhus, I was in a state of nervous excitement bordering on madness; I was delirious from fever and unaware of what I was saying. Out of the twilight of high fever, I once asked for an apple. My friends went and exchanged their bread rations for an apple. Thus, solidarity saved my life—and the lives of other women comrades.

Men and women also dealt with their hunger differently. While men focused on their hunger and fantasized about lavish meals they had had, women talked about recipes and shared ways to stretch the meager rations they were given. Sometimes for hours, women talked about foods they had once prepared. Other times, they even wrote recipes down. These conversations played an important psychological role because they both reminded women of their former lives and suggested their commitment to the future. Because conversations about food often were related to Sabbath or holidays, they also affirmed the women's Jewishness and their hope for a future for the Jews.

A final gender distinction was that between gay males and lesbians. Lesbianism was not illegal under the Reich, and so lesbians were not identified by the pink triangle that identified male homosexuals in the concentration camps. Rather, they were designated as asocial or political prisoners. Because Nazi ideology valued women for their reproductive role, lesbians were perceived as women who were not fulfilling their biological destiny. Their persecution, then, stemmed more from Nazi misogyny, while the persecution of gay men resulted from homophobia.

Overwhelmingly, the evidence suggests that, indeed, gender was a salient feature of the Holocaust experience. Men and women had different experiences based on their gender, and social constructions of gender played a significant role in both the ways women and men were perceived and the ways they acted. By no means does scholarly attention to gender seek to minimize the suffering of any group of people in the Holocaust, nor does it seek to rank the sufferings experienced by anyone victimized by the Nazi regime. Instead, a focus on the gendered experiences of the Holocaust reminds one of the complexities of oppression and resistance and offers a fuller glimpse into the wide range of human experiences, both male and female, under the Third Reich.

–SUSAN M. SHAW,
OREGON STATE UNIVERSITY

Viewpoint:
No. To study the Holocaust in terms of gender responses is to diminish its significance as racial genocide.

Adolf Hitler murdered Jews, Gypsies, homosexuals, and the handicapped. He did so because of race. His Final Solution was intended to purify the Aryan nations by removing permanently all inferior races (Jews and Gypsies) while eliminating also the harmful genetic strains (homosexuals and handicapped) that would pollute the genetic pool of his master race. Hitler and his associates did not torture or murder women because they were women but because they were Jews, Gypsies, lesbians, and so forth. To explain the Holocaust as a gendered event is to diminish its significance as racial genocide and at the same time to confuse the issue of gender discrimination.

This statement is not to say that women experienced the Holocaust—whether as victims, perpetrators, or bystanders—in the same fashion as men. Sexuality, socialization, motherhood, and physical strength all affected how women understood and reacted to their conditions. But the same could be argued for all categories of people engaged in or affected by the Holocaust. Women suffered differently than men, but children also suffered differently than adults. Jews had distinct experiences from Gypsies because of their religious socialization, and the able-bodied had more options as victims than the handicapped. There was no singular Holocaust experience by which all can be measured.

While it is important to understand the various perspectives and experiences of individuals, one must not lose sight of the fact that this twentieth-century event was perpetrated by one people against other peoples in the name of race. The horror of the Holocaust was not that it involved genocide—that is not unique to the history of mankind, even in the twentieth century. Pol Pot, communist ruler of Cambodia, murdered one-third of all Cambodians in the mid 1970s. Idi Amin, dictator of Uganda, executed millions of his own people. Serbian president Slobodan Milosevic executed Bosnian Muslims in the 1990s in the name of "ethnic cleansing." Fifteen hundred years earlier Attila the Hun made himself a household word for the ages by his wholesale approach to killing, and it is estimated that the Spanish eliminated nearly 90 percent of the native population of the Americas in the sixteenth century through war, slavery, and disease. From an historical perspective, genocide is a relatively common occurrence, and in all of these other instances, women's experiences have been similar to those encountered by women in the Holocaust. However, the actions of tyrants have often been rationalized by writers and educators as the work of primitive barbarians, thus separating Western sensibilities of civility and morality from the act of mass murder. The horror of the Holocaust lies in the use of Western rational science by a highly civilized, highly educated people to murder nearly fifteen million souls who were, by conventional standards, just as civilized and just as educated as their executioners. In this manner, it was unique. The bureaucracy of the Nazi regime was so efficient and sophisticated that all prisoners were numbered and itemized.

Group of naked Jewish women moments before their execution in the Ukraine, circa late 1942

(Bildarchiv Preussischer Kulturbesitz, Berlin)

FEMINIST INTERPRETATION

To analyze the Holocaust from the perspectives of its many different participants—including those perspectives defined by gender—is a natural expansion of any field of study. As the "facts" and basic interpretations are laid down by the first generation of Holocaust scholars, Raul Hilberg and Lucy Dawidowitz for example, the second generation, scholars who came of age in the 1950s and 1960s, are obligated to ask different questions, to deepen, sharpen, and challenge the dogmas of their own teachers and mentors. It is neither surprising nor distressing that scholars such as Marion Kaplan should focus on differences between the experiences of women and men in building a more nuanced understanding of the Holocaust than was possible for the first generation of scholars. Such scholarship simply applies to the study of the Holocaust contemporary questions and concerns that might not have occurred to earlier scholars. Their answers serve to deepen the level of understanding of all students of the Holocaust.

It is at this micro level that the experience of women provides a lens whereby individual experiences can be understood in the larger whole. If the crimes against women perpetrated by the Nazis differed in degree, in proportion, or in kind from ordinary warfare or ordinary crime, then one could argue that the Holocaust had a gendered nature. Such was not the case; men raped women, women tortured women, and men murdered women and children. The Holocaust was no different than most wars for power or colonization. Nor does one find that the female victims, whether Jewish or Gentile, reacted in an aberrant

sexual fashion. The behavior of the rape victims and the mothers choosing death over abandonment demonstrated historically predictive role behavior. Women reacted according to gendered roles not because the Holocaust was a gendered event but because they were women.

Attempting to analyze the Holocaust as a gendered event also confuses the definition of sex discrimination and places one in the untenable position of arguing that sex discrimination is on the same value level as genocide. In the same instance, it also undermines the validity of the argument that organized gender oppression, such as practiced by the Taliban in Afghanistan, is a crime against humanity. Under the Nazis, women were not raped or tortured because they were women but because they were Jews. Under the Taliban, women were raped and tortured because they were women. While this distinction does nothing to alleviate the pain of the victim nor to reduce the severity of the offense, it does provide definitional clarity to temporal events. The behavior and outcomes may be identical, but the causes are distinct.

A corollary may be seen in the historical position of African Americans in the United States. African American men did not receive the vote until 1870 because they were African American; African American women did not receive the vote until 1920 because they were women. Nevertheless, Sojourner Truth and Harriet Tubman were not held in slavery because they were women but because they were African American. Being female and African American is a double bind stemming from two distinct forms of discrimination. Being female and Jewish (or Gypsy) was also a double bind under the Nazi regime. That the Nazis were misogynist is not debatable, but neither is it explanatory of the Holocaust. The Nazis' choice of particular methods or devices for torture might have been driven by their misogyny, but it was not the reason for the torture.

Arguing that the Holocaust was not a gendered event does not undermine the usefulness of feminist studies of women in the Holocaust. The experiences of women who were victimized by the Holocaust, both those who survived and those who did not, can reveal much about the psychology of women under extreme physical and psychological stress and how the roles that women adopt can aid or impede their survival. Traditionally feminine housekeeping activities such as sewing, cooking, and nurturing created a solidarity among women that traditional male roles of competition denied to men. On this micro level, feminist analysis elucidates the understanding of gender and survival. That is an understanding that comes out of the Holocaust but is not caused by it.

It is also useful to observe and analyze the behavior of female guards. These women were under extreme stress, too, albeit less horrific. Were their behaviors significantly different than those of the male guards? Was it socialization or innate gender attributes that made humans react to external conditions as they did? These are important questions that the events of the Holocaust can help to clarify. Nevertheless, it must be remembered in any analysis that those events involved extreme aberrations of human conditions, and therefore the conclusions drawn from such analysis may be as well.

The Holocaust was a policy of racial extermination planned and executed by civilized people against civilized people, in a war whose goal was eugenics as much as military. Social scientists must be careful not to lose the significance of the Holocaust by subjecting it in a reductionist manner to the microfilters of our modern scholarship on gender.

–ANNE MCCULLOCH,
COLUMBIA COLLEGE

References

Gisela Bock, *Zwangssterilisation im Nationalsozialismus: Studien zur Rassenpolitik und Frauenpolitik* (Opladen: Westdeutscher Verlag, 1986).

Ruth Bondy, "Women in Theresienstadt and the Family Camp in Birkenau," in *Women in the Holocaust,* edited by Dalia Ofer and Lenore J. Weitzman (New Haven: Yale University Press, 1998), pp. 310–326.

Ann Taylor Ellen, "The Holocaust and the Modernization of Gender: A Historiographical Essay," *Central European History,* 30 (1997): 349–364.

Ellen Fine, "Women and the Holocaust: Strategies for Survival," in *Reflections of the Holocaust in Art and Literature,* edited by Randolph L. Braham (Boulder, Colo.: Social Science Monographs / New York: Csengeri Institute for Holocaust Studies of the Graduate School and University Center of the City University of New York, 1990), pp. 79–96.

Myrna Goldberg, "From a World Beyond: Women in the Holocaust," *Feminist Studies,* 22 (1996): 667–687.

Goldberg, "Lessons Learned from Gentle Heroism: Women's Holocaust Narratives," *Annals of the American Academy of Political & Social Science,* 548 (1996): 78–93.

Goldberg, "Memoirs of Auschwitz Survivors: The Burden of Gender," in *Women in the Holocaust,* edited by Ofer and Weitzman (New Haven: Yale University Press, 1998), pp. 327–339.

Felicia Berland Hyatt, *Close Calls: The Autobiography of a Survivor* (New York: Holocaust Library, 1991).

Judith Isaacson, *Seed of Sarah: Memoirs of a Survivor* (Urbana: University of Illinois Press, 1990).

Claudia Koonz, *Mothers in the Fatherland: Women, the Family, and Nazi Politics* (New York: St. Martin's Press, 1987).

S. Lillian Kremer, *Women's Holocaust Writing: Memory and Imagination* (Lincoln: University of Nebraska Press, 1999).

Joan Ringleheim, "Thoughts about Women and the Holocaust," in *Thinking the Unthinkable: Meanings of the Holocaust,* edited by Roger S. Gottlieb (New York: Paulist Press, 1990), pp. 141–149.

Carol Rittner and John K. Roth, eds., *Different Voices: Women and the Holocaust* (New York: Paragon House, 1993).

Leila J. Rupp, *Mobilizing Women for War: German and American Propaganda, 1939–1945* (Princeton: Princeton University Press, 1978).

Jill Stephenson, *Women in Nazi Society* (London: Croom Helm / New York: Barnes & Noble, 1975).

Lidia Rosenfeld Vago, "The Black Hole of Our Planet Earth," in *Women in the Holocaust,* edited by Ofer and Weitzman (New Haven: Yale University Press, 1998), pp. 273–284.

FEMINIST INTERPRETATION

FORMS OF POWER

Was the Holocaust shaped by modern theories of power?

Viewpoint: Yes. Forms of power conceived during the Enlightenment helped produce the Holocaust.

Viewpoint: No. The Holocaust, though dependent on modern technologies and ideologies, was fundamentally medieval and feudal in its structures of power.

Politically, "power" refers to the imposition of one person's will onto the minds and bodies of others, and political philosophers have discussed the nature of such power at least since the writing of Greek philosopher Plato's *Republic* (circa 400 B.C.E.). "Modernity" can refer either to an historical era (beginning either in 1500 [the Early Modern Era] or 1800 [the Modern Era]) or to ideas and lifestyles associated with those periods. In the modern world political power is usually thought of as being transmitted from a centralized and institutionalized source (a king, president, or pope for example) through a self-perpetuating bureaucracy onto the lives of individuals. Pre- and post-modern expressions of power (for example, feudalism or Joseph Stalin's "cult of personality") are structured differently. In feudal political structures, monarchs extended their power through complex relationships based on personal obligation. Stalin extended his power through terror. Adolf Hitler's Germany, though endlessly analyzed, has defied easy categorization.

Though calling a late-twentieth- or early-twenty-first-century politician a "Nazi" may more often be intended as a term of abuse, it also reflects the totalitarian efficiency with which the Nazi Party exercised power in Germany. Whatever else can be said of him, Hitler wielded power effectively, nowhere more so than in the implementation of the Final Solution. He was able, within months of taking office, to seize control of the government and the imaginations of millions of Germans. Hitler projected power through a diverse array of Nazi institutions, influencing the way people worked, how they played, the songs they sang, the sermons they likely heard in church, and, for millions, how and where they died. Though the concentration camps served to terrorize and restrain a determined minority of opponents, the vast majority of Germans more or less willingly acquiesced to Nazi intrusions into their lives. The Nazi policy of *gleischaltung* (coordination) went beyond the German economy to leave virtually no private, unpoliticized space.

In this manner, the Nazi State was, however extreme, far from unique. The Soviet State was, if anything, more ruthless in its demands. Benito Mussolini's Fascist Italy had pioneered the strategies that Hitler would put into practice in Germany, and even the United States and Britain, struggling to get out from under the Great Depression (1929–1941), had imposed far-reaching social and economic controls on their respective populations. And in every case the majority of the affected populations acquiesced to the imposition of state power over their lives. The modern world of the 1930s and 1940s seemed to take centralization for granted. Obedience to authority, whether malignant or benign, was a widely respected virtue.

This centralization, bureaucratization, and radical extension of power into the lives of ordinary people can be understood as "typical" of "modern" states and governments. In the modern world millions of people had been induced to commit terrible acts of savagery—or to suffer from them—because a distant leader wished it so. Modern theories of power, beginning with English philosopher Thomas Hobbes's *Leviathan* (1651), imply that obedience to authority, however malevolent, is necessary to life in civil society and that general disobedience would lead to chaos and a struggle of all against all in which no one was safe. Modern theories of power, therefore, assume some sort of *social contract*—a term invented by eighteenth-century French philosopher Jean-Jacques Rousseau—to account for humanity's willingness to surrender autonomy to institutions and individuals whose legitimacy rests on abstract notions of democratic elections or divine right or the demands of history. Russian novelist Fyodor Dostoevsky forcefully challenges the legitimacy of the social contract in "The Grand Inquisitor" chapter of *The Brothers Karamazov* (1879) as does German philosopher Friedrick Nietzsche in *Also Sprach Zarathustra* (Thus Spoke Zarathustra, 1883–1892). Both writers wondered why people in the modern world seemed so willing to surrender their personal autonomy to distant, often immoral, "sources" of authority. Power, for them, is individual rather than corporate. Modernity, with its concomitant extensions of power from the center into the lives of millions of individuals, was, for thinkers like them, a nightmare. The Holocaust would have surprised neither of them.

The Holocaust, though clearly modern in important ways, was perhaps not "typical" even in comparison with other modern acts of genocide and mass murder—under Stalin, Cambodian leader Pol Pot, or Yugoslavian ruler Slobodan Milosevic. In any discussion of modernity, power, and the Holocaust, one's analysis of the structures of power depends on assumptions about the nature of power and modernity.

Viewpoint:
Yes. Forms of power conceived during the Enlightenment helped produce the Holocaust.

One of the most unsettling moments in the generally sensational 1961 trial against infamous Nazi criminal Adolf Eichmann came when the principal administrator of the Final Solution proclaimed that he was not to be held responsible for the horrendous slaughter he helped execute. Instead, he defended his bureaucratic activities by describing his definition of duty as congruent with the ethical theories of eighteenth-century German philosopher Immanuel Kant. Kant's comprehensive, self-legitimating philosophy created a new version of morals that was not based on concepts of the good but rather emphasized the structural ethics of a generalizable principle. In particular, Kantian ethics revolve around a Categorical Imperative that demands the general applicability of any action: "Act only according to that maxim by which you can at the same time will that it should become a universal law." The sheer perversity of Eichmann aligning his own administrative involvement in the Nazi genocide with the moral and ethical system of one of the founders of modern thinking is shocking; nevertheless, Eichmann's "Act as if the principle of your actions were the same as that of the legislator or the law of the land" does bear an uncanny resemblance to Kant's central doctrine of Enlightenment thought. Moreover, even the persistent universality of Kant can be found in the Nazi administrator

as the latter prides himself in never breaking the law and never claiming an exception. Eichmann, thus, obeyed at the least one of Kant's principal rules of the imperative by showing utter disinterestedness in his respect for the law.

What Eichmann's exclamation in fact suggests is an insight into the complicated and intricate relationship between modernity and Western Enlightenment, on the one hand, and the Holocaust, on the other. In other words, there actually may be a legitimate reading of Kant that invites the response one found so repulsive in Eichmann. Not only does modernity fail to provide a moral system that could have prevented the horrors of the Third Reich, the pure formalism of the Kantian formulas seems to lend itself to be twisted into Eichmann's distorted version thereof. The debate as to how closely the Holocaust is related to modernity has occupied many fields: various commentators on modernity have noticed a link between modern goals, ideas, and principles and the rationale and implementation of the Final Solution. Coming from different disciplines and diverse methodological approaches, all of them recognize the implicit connections between the instrumental rationality of modernity and the ideological underpinnings of Nazism, thereby suggesting that the Holocaust must not be read as an aberrant, exceptional mistake of modernity but that it can be explained in and by the guidelines, rules, and ideas set forth in the Enlightenment. In fact, examining the vital role of modern bureaucracy within the Nazi machinery, the psychological motivations of the Nazi perpetrators that must be understood within a context of modern society, and the relationship between modern science

German civilians
and soldiers giving
the Nazi salute, 1934

*(Bildarchiv Preussischer
Kulturbesitz, Berlin)*

and the Holocaust reveals that the *Shoah* is consistent and compatible with, rather than aberrant, and contrary to the rational Enlightenment.

The same year that Eichmann made his curious confessions linking the basis of his belief system with the philosophical framework of modernity, Raul Hilberg published his groundbreaking in-depth study of the administrative, bureaucratic, and logistic aspects of the Holocaust, *The Destruction of the European Jews* (1961). By focusing on the mechanical, psychological, and bureaucratic means that led to and carried out the Final Solution, Hilberg emphasizes the relation between a scientifically, artistically, and administratively advanced Germany and the structural implementation and logistic execution of a mass murder previously unknown in its range and scope. The study of the modern bureaucratic mode of rationalization is crucial to any understanding of the Holocaust, since the idea of the *Endlösung* (Final Solution) must be understood as an outcry of bureaucratic culture. Looking at the middle echelon of disinterested administrators indicates that Nazi genocide owes more to a Prussian code of obedience and modern alienation than to anti-Semitic prejudices and homicidal urges. In fact, the modern advances of the bureaucratic administration must be held accountable for the emotional distancing and moral evacuation experienced by the perpetrators.

The psychological motivations of the perpetrators can only be fully understood within the context of modernity. In *The Origins of Totalitarianism* (1951) political theorist Hannah Arendt argues that the totalitarian regime could only occur specifically at the intersection of anti-Semitism, imperialism, and modernity. An older anti-Semitism governed by passions and mob rule was replaced with a detached, scientific anti-Semitism in which murder was carried out less through violent riots and pogroms than via a bureaucratically organized campaign of hatred, culminating in the well-planned mass murder of Jews in the Holocaust. As Jewish culture assimilated and became less distinguishable from western Christian culture, the lack of clearly defined markers of difference evoked fears of and consequent wishes to eradicate this uncomfortably familiar otherness. The combination of totalitarian authority and its modern variant of anti-Semitism—with its less passionate, more rational, and organized approach—also explains the willing obedience with which most perpetrators obeyed and carried out their gruesome orders. As the system demanded complete obedience and offered a scientific impetus of racial hygiene for the murders, the perpetrators distanced themselves morally and emotionally from their victims. Stanley Milgram's famous Yale experiments of the early 1960s showed how average Americans were willing to impose extreme pain on others when so ordered. Accordingly, the modern bureaucratic state with its alienated and disenchanted citizens is to blame for Nazi criminals rather than any particular pathological psychology of the individuals. These citizens who simply obeyed the laws and, as a result, committed unspeakable crimes were so immersed in the power structures as often to not realize the actual extent of their murderous actions. Considering that obedience to the law constitutes one of the principle values of the Enlightenment, as it emphasizes the separation of rationality and ethical norms, these experiments clearly suggest that the modern character of the state encouraged this behavior of unquestioning obedience.

Modernity not only created some of the conditions for a new and more severe form of anti-Semitism, this anti-Semitism also employed modern scientific concepts such as studies of race to champion its prejudices. No field may be as guilty in ignoring ethical principles in favor of a value-free rational imperative as the natural sciences. Not only is positivistic scientific discourse the exemplary mode of inquiry and study in modern rational discourse, it also holds a particularly

problematic place within the context of the Holocaust. The extreme valorization of modern science and technology at the same time as any value judgment is suspended, must, of course, be held accountable for some of the most extreme torturous "experiments" within the camps, and it helps explain the previously unknown efficiency and scope of the Final Solution. Many commentators have pointed out the unusual bureaucratic and technical efficiency with which the mass murders took place in the camps and allowed for an emptying out of moral responsibility through a careful division of labor. What is more interesting, however, is the way science and technology played a vital part in the perpetration of the Holocaust by supporting the general ideological environment of the Final Solution. Thus, the racist theories of "social engineering" grew out of a modern scientific mindset that believed that man can change his environment and surroundings to make a better society. If humans can—and ought to—control their environment and the world, how could this attitude not be applied to humans themselves? There exists a continuum between modern scientific ideologies and practices in general and their Nazi instantiation in particular. By severing the bond between innovative and rigorous scientific inquiries and worthy moral causes, Nazi science exemplified the dangers of modern rationality that allowed science to become value free and unconcerned about its impacts on human beings.

While the role of modern bureaucracy, modes of obedience, and understandings of science are crucial to comprehending the execution of the Holocaust, they beg the question as to the interdependency and compatibility of Nazi ideology and the theoretical framework of modernity itself. Sociologist Max Weber's accounts of the instrumental rationality of modernity with its consequent disenchantment of everyday life go far in explaining the bureaucratic efficiency and depersonalization of the Final Solution. In fact, as he describes the dangers of modern disenchantment and the tyranny of Reason, Weber establishes a theoretical framework of modernity that can explain how it could so easily be exploited by Nazi ideology. Even though Weber's theories can offer a framework in which to understand the relationship between modern society and Nazi ideology, sociology in general has failed to fully account for the Holocaust. In his study *Modernity and the Holocaust* (1989), sociologist Zygmunt Bauman blames the fabric of sociological theories for this inability to see the interdependency between modernity and the Holocaust, as classical sociology cannot escape the definite correlation between moral behavior and societal influence. Therefore, sociology by its assumptions cannot theorize a highly antisocial, utterly immoral behavior that nevertheless was completely sanctioned and valorized within the societal laws. In

ORDERS MUST BE SACRED

At the request of one of the presiding judges at his war-crimes trial in Israel in the early 1960s, Nazi official Adolf Eichmann read from a speech by Heinrich Himmler, second in command to Adolf Hitler, on obedience to orders:

In a soldier's life, obedience is required and shown morning, noon and night. The small man in fact always or normally obeys; if he does not, he is locked up. Obedience in the case of higher office-bearers of the state, the Party and the armed forces is a more difficult question; here and there in the SS as well.

Here I would like to say something clearly and unambiguously: It is self-evident that the small man must obey. It is even more self-evident that all the high-placed leaders of the SS, i.e., the entire Gruppenfuehrer corps, are an example of unconditional obedience. If someone believes that an order is based on an erroneous understanding by the superior officer, or on an incorrect foundation, it is self-evident that he, i.e., each one of them, has the duty and responsibility to bring this up, as well as to explain his reasons in a manly and truthful fashion, if he is convinced that they are in conflict with the order.

But once the decision has been taken and the order given by the superior concerned, or by the Reichsfuehrer-SS, which is normally the case for the Gruppenfuehrer corps, or even by the Fuehrer, it must be carried out, not only literally in accordance with its letter, but also according to its spirit. The person who carries out the order must do this as a faithful agent, as a faithful representative of the power issuing the order. If they initially believed that this was right, and that was not right or even wrong, then there are two possibilities: If someone believes that he cannot take responsibility for carrying out an order, he must honestly report that—I cannot take responsibility for that, I request to be released from it. Then in most cases there would be the order, 'But still, you must carry it out, or one may think that the man has lost his nerve, that he is weak.' And then one might say, 'Very well, you will be pensioned off.' But orders must be sacred.

Source: *"The Trial of Adolf Eichmann, Session 106," The Nizkor Project <http://www.nizkor.org/hweb/people/e/eichmann-adolf/transcripts/Sessions/Session-106-07.html>.*

awry with the project of modernity. By turning reason into an instrument of control over nature and other objects, man had opened the door to utilize instrumental rationality over other subjects as well. As a result, Enlightenment's goal to gain further control over one's own destiny by disenchanting one's intimidating environment turned into an abuse of this principle as some men used the concept of instrumental rationality to subordinate and use other human beings. Moreover, as modernity's rational approach was also intended to be turned upon itself, it was constructed to erase its own development and therefore disallow self-critical analysis. Rather than positing its own self-critique, Enlightenment has thus given way to its totalizing, universalizing tendencies, creating a system more totalitarian and all-encompassing than the one it was meant to replace.

For postmodern philosopher Jean-François Lyotard, universalism, order, and unity directly lead to a totalizing and ultimately terrorizing system that can only be prevented by refusing all normative and organizing principles. Unlike other philosophers who attempt to rescue modernity's fragmented remainders to continue its project, Lyotard argues that modernity has destroyed itself, that the terror it produced has foreclosed any possible resurrection or redemption of modernity and its values. Other disciplines similarly recognize the Holocaust as an exemplar that signifies the failure of modernity, consequently initiating postmodernity. Just like Lyotard, who defines the Holocaust as the central break that separates modern and postmodern philosophy, Bauman suggests that the Holocaust provides a test case for traditional sociology insofar as the discipline fails to provide a theoretical framework in which to account for such a crime. Since the Holocaust presents an event that cannot be subsumed under current sociological theories, he argues, it requires new modes of inquiry and, consequently, implies new ways of understanding the sociological discipline as a whole. Within the field of history Hayden White demands a similar disciplinary shift. In his discussion of how to approach the Holocaust within postmodern historical practices, White suggests a new way of writing history when confronted with the Holocaust. Theorizing and studying a so-called metahistory, White emphasizes the textual and narrative quality of historical writing within its specific historical context and consciousness.

other words, "modernity" is incapable of grasping the possibility that a socially sanctioned act may also be a profoundly immoral one.

With the Holocaust so closely tied to the structures of modernity at the same time as it exceeded any theoretical modern framework, it announced the end of modernity and required a new paradigm beyond modern discourses. Within philosophy, Max Horkheimer and Theodor W. Adorno framed their study, *Dialectic of Enlightenment* (1972), as an inquiry into what had gone

Whether rationality itself is to blame or whether modern Reason simply was not powerful enough to hold the irrational at bay, the relationship between modern rationality and the Holocaust has forced scholars in most disciplines to rethink their understanding of modernity, leading many of them to discard it for something different. What is important to realize is that none of

FORMS OF POWER

these thinkers argues that the Holocaust can be traced back to a sinister, antimodern strain that might have found its origins at the same time as the Enlightenment. Rather, they see the dark seed that created the theoretical possibilities to make the Holocaust an historical reality as intricately entwined with the foundation of Enlightenment thought. As such, one must regard modernity with its self-legitimating philosophy, its rigorously structural ethics, its disenchanted social structure, its disinterested rationality, and its scientific positivism as central to the social, philosophical, and psychological context that allowed the Holocaust to happen. While the various modern developments and achievements cannot be blamed for directly causing the Holocaust, they must be recognized as lacking the means to prevent it, thus forcing post-Holocaust thinkers to reinvestigate their respective fields in search not only of models to comprehend this horrendous event but also to contemplate theories that might help preclude similar events in the future.

–KRISTINA BUSSE, ALABAMA SCHOOL OF MATHEMATICS AND SCIENCE

Viewpoint:
No. The Holocaust, though dependent on modern technologies and ideologies, was fundamentally medieval and feudal in its structures of power.

Setting aside their overwhelming immorality, the Nazi Party's anti-Semitic policies were, fundamentally, expressions of power. The Nazi State and its various agents and coconspirators demonstrated, not just in Auschwitz but everywhere it held sway, what a modern, technologically sophisticated state, unconstrained by traditional values of human decency, could accomplish. Without the application of decidedly modern technologies—not just Zyklon–B gas but IBM punch cards, mass communications, and sophisticated transportation infrastructures—the Final Solution would have been inconceivable. Earlier (and later) acts of genocide and mass violence directed against Armenians, the kulaks of Joseph Stalin's Russia, the people of Cambodia, the Hutus, and Kosovar Muslims were hopelessly inefficient and on a necessarily much smaller scale. They depended on starvation and personal acts of violence—a bullet in the back of the head or something similar. The Final Solution, with its finely tuned orchestration of death, represented a macabre triumph of technology.

But the use of modern technology to carry it out does not make the Holocaust a modern application of power. Nor was the bureaucracy that carried it out organized or conceived along modern lines. The Holocaust, like the rest of the Nazi state, was a fundamentally medieval expression of power set within the modern world.

Political power in the modern world is most typically transmitted through bureaucratic channels. These channels tend to become institutionalized, such that one's power (or lack thereof) is determined by one's position in the organization. This pattern is most obvious in military organizations, where rank and responsibility are clearly understood to the point of being displayed on one's uniform, and responsibility for a task is assumed to come with the legal power to carry it out. Modern businesses, governments, schools, and organizations may be less clearly structured, but similar assumptions are at work: an individual may hold power in order to carry out a task, but the power resides in the office, not in the individual. People in a bureaucratic organization, whether military, political, business, educational, or ecclesiastical, carry out directives coming from "above" them in the chain of command. It is not terribly important that they know with whom the command started—the president, the pope, or simply the person in the next office—as long as the one giving the directive has the formal authority to do so. In modern organizations, power resides not with the officer, but the office.

Feudal power structures were (and in some instances remain) extensions of personal, not formal, power. In a feudal power relationship—unlike a modern one—the knight received power from the touch of the lord's hand. A bishop, similarly, received power from the anointing hands of the pope. In neither case was the touch metaphorical but physical. And in either case, the one receiving power—to enjoy the fruits of a feudal manor, or to lead troops in battle, or to perform the sacraments of the Church—became personally obligated to the one from whom the touch was received. They were required, in exchange for the gift of power, to render homage, to become the *homme,* or "man," of the secular or spiritual lord from whom the gift was received. When a king died, his successor normally reconfirmed the sense of personal obligation that came with the office by receiving homage from his father's subjects. Familiar examples abound. In the Anglo-Saxon folk epic *Beowulf* warriors bind themselves to Hrothgar because he has personally bestowed gifts on them. The Merovingian kings of France lost power to the upstart Carolingians because they, as hereditary mayors of the palace, distributed the fruits of conquest to the warriors who became loyal, not to the distant kings but to their immediate leaders. The Investiture Controversy (1075–1077) reflected a conflict between Emperor and Pope over which individual, Henry IV or Gregory VII, would receive homage and obedience from the clergy. The Hundred Years' War (1337–1453) between the kings of France and England reflected similar conflicts over personal relationships and personal obligations. The office, whether king, Holy Roman Emperor, Pope, or bishop, was secondary to the holders of those offices and their personal connections with their subordinates.

Adolf Hitler, though he bore some of the trappings of a modern politician, used his office essentially as would a medieval monarch. He seized control of the *Nationalsozialistische Deutsche Arbeiterpartei* (NSDAP) in 1921 and made himself not a modern leader of a political party but a medieval lord. He encouraged subordinates to call him *der Chef* and ultimately, of course, *der Führer.* Power in the Nazi Party (and after 1933 in the Nazi state) resided not in the office of chancellor or president but in the person of *der Führer.* Perhaps for this reason Hitler found it necessary to destroy anyone whose personal power within the Party (or in German society) might be seen as equally legitimate as that of *der Führer.*

Hitler did not simply appoint men to offices in the Party and the State. He anointed them. He feudalized the workings of the German State, creating conflict and inefficiencies but ensuring, ultimately, that everyone from commanding generals to judges owed final allegiance neither to the ideals of the Party nor to the German state but to *der Führer* personally. German soldiers and sailors took an oath of alliegance to Hitler, as did the Hitler Youth, and virtually everyone else within the Party's sway. Deviance from the resultant *cult of personality* (a term that applies as much to Hitler as to Stalin) was viewed similarly to the medieval *lèse majesté* (a crime committed against the supreme ruler of the State). The orders to initiate the destruction of the Jews—wherever and in whatever context they originated—were always legitimized with the phrase, "*Der Führer wishes. . . .*"

The Holocaust, then, can best be understood as the application of a uniquely modern and criminal goal—the annihilation of the Jews as racial enemies. But the Nazi Party as a whole and the Holocaust in particular were expressions of a distinctly medieval mental world. Power was understood by the Nazis as a personal attribute rather than a formal concomitant of office. The orders to carry it out were understood to have come directly from *der Führer,* whose legitimacy rested not in his official position but in his sense of having been appointed by history. Charlemagne, the eighth-century king of the Franks, might have found Hitler an odious fellow, but he would have understood his theory of power.

–TANDY MCCONNELL,
COLUMBIA COLLEGE

References

Theodor W. Adorno and others, *The Authoritarian Personality* (New York: Harper, 1950).

Hannah Arendt, *Eichmann in Jerusalem: A Report on the Banality of Evil,* revised edition (New York: Penguin, 1964).

Arendt, *The Origins of Totalitarianism* (New York: Harcourt, Brace, 1951).

Zygmunt Bauman, *Modernity and the Holocaust* (Ithaca, N.Y.: Cornell University Press, 1989).

Mario Biagioli, "Science, Modernity, and the Final Solution," in *Probing the Limits of Representation: Nazism and the "Final Solution,"* edited by Saul Friedländer (Cambridge, Mass.: Harvard University Press, 1992), pp. 185–205.

Christopher R. Browning, *Ordinary Men: Reserve Battalion 101 and the Final Solution in Poland* (New York: HarperCollins, 1992).

Daniel Jonah Goldhagen, *Hitler's Willing Executioners: Ordinary Germans and the Holocaust* (New York: Knopf, 1996).

Raul Hilberg, *The Destruction of the European Jews* (Chicago: Quadrangle, 1961).

Max Horkheimer and Adorno, *Dialectic of Enlightenment,* translated by John Cumming (New York: Herder & Herder, 1972).

George Kren and Leon Rappoport, *The Holocaust and the Crisis in Human Behavior* (New York: Holmes & Meier, 1980).

Robert Jay Lifton, *The Nazi Doctors: Medical Killings and the Psychology of Genocide* (New York: Basic Books, 1986).

Jean-François Lyotard, *The Différend: Phrases in Dispute,* translated by Georges Van Den Abbeele (Minneapolis: University of Minnesota Press, 1988).

J. Stanley Milgram, *Obedience to Authority: An Experimental View* (New York: Harper & Row, 1974).

Richard Rubenstein, "Anticipation of the Holocaust in the Political Sociology of Max Weber," in *Western Society after the Holocaust,* edited by Lyman Letgers (Boulder, Colo.: Westview Press, 1983), pp. 166–187.

Hayden White, "Historical Emplotment and the Problem of Truth," in *Probing the Limits of Representation: Nazism and the "Final Solution,"* edited by Saul Friedländer (Cambridge, Mass.: Harvard University Press, 1992), pp. 37–53.

FORMS OF POWER

FÜHRER ORDER

Did Adolf Hitler issue an order to exterminate the Jews?

Viewpoint: Yes. The plan to exterminate the Jews was part of Hitler's original order for the invasion of the Soviet Union.

Viewpoint: No. Although Hitler made his intentions clear to his closest associates, he never explicitly ordered the extermination of European Jews.

Despite the profusion of questions about Nazism and the Third Reich that are still open to debate, few historians doubt that Adolf Hitler was the single most important figure concerned in the development of both the National Socialist Party and the Nazi German state. Hitler laid down the fundamentals of Nazi ideology, from its militant German nationalism to its extreme anti-Semitism. He also established the authoritarian *Führerprinzip* (leadership principle), a doctrine that demanded that one man be granted absolute power to make the difficult decisions required if Germany were to be saved from its many enemies. Such was the position Hitler sought to fill as Führer and Chancellor; and such was the power he exercised over the ranks of the Nazi Party and, later, over the mass of German citizens. Nowhere was this Nazi leadership ideal so clearly expressed as in the common propaganda slogan: *Führer befehl, wir folgen!* (Führer command, we follow!).

Faced with Hitler's own insistence on the centrality of the Nazi *Führerprinzip*, one might well expect to find his signature attached to every important document generated by the bureaucracy of the Third Reich. Yet, even the slightest study of surviving records demonstrates that this level of control was not the case. If few question that Hitler enjoyed the type of absolute power he claimed, some observers are puzzled by how he chose to employ it. The command to implement a "Final Solution to the Jewish Question" is a case in point.

British writer David Irving has offered a large monetary reward to the researcher who can discover a copy of Hitler's personal order for the extermination of the Jews. A *Führer Befehl* (Führer Order) of this sort would offer incontrovertible proof that the Nazi leader not only knew about his subordinates' persecution of the Jews but also actually authorized the murder of millions of human beings. It would, in short, be a powerful blow to the arguments of those who try to deny the reality of the Holocaust or who hope to rehabilitate the reputation of Hitler. Irving, recently declared by a British court of law to be a "Nazi sympathizer" and "Holocaust denier," made his offer because he is confident from his own extensive investigations that no such document exists. Without it, he (and others like him) can attempt to rewrite the history of World War II (1939–1945), ignoring the great crimes Germans committed in the name of their Führer. Yet, as the following essays demonstrate, there is more than one way to explain the absence of a special *Führer Befehl* on the treatment of the Jews without denying that Hitler was uninvolved in or unaware of the Final Solution.

Viewpoint:
Yes. The plan to exterminate the Jews was part of Hitler's original order for the invasion of the Soviet Union.

To the established concepts of "absolute war" and *Vernichtungskrieg* (war of annihilation) in the German military tradition, Adolf Hitler added his own extremist ideology of nationalism based on biological racism. The logical implication of the Nazi leader's conception of warfare was Hitler's "Directive 21," the operations order for an invasion of the Soviet Union. War, to Hitler, was the decisive event in the struggle for racial survival that guided all of history. Hitler further believed that the "Jewish-Bolshevik world conspiracy" was the source of all German misfortunes and that Soviet communism was one important element in this conspiracy. This order suggests that the design of Operation Barbarossa, as the German invasion was known, was also the order that ultimately initiated the Holocaust.

Hitler made it clear, in the next-to-last paragraph of Directive 21, that without proper preparation and implementation, "the most severe political and military penalties will develop." For, as the official diarist of the German Military High Command observed in March 1941, "the coming campaign is more than a mere clash of arms; it is also a conflict between two ideologies." More precisely, Operation Barbarossa was intended to be the final struggle between competing political systems, a National Socialist *Vernichtungskrieg* against the Jewish-Bolshevik world conspiracy. According to Nazi ideology, such a conflict logically demanded the complete and utter destruction of the enemy. Consequently, Hitler's Directive 21 can reasonably be considered the Führer Order authorizing the Final Solution. All that remained in late 1941 and early 1942 was for Hitler's minions to work out the details to implement it.

The *Vernichtungskrieg* was not a new concept when it was embraced by Hitler and his subordinates. From the Wars of Unification (1866–1871) through World War I (1914–1918), German military leaders progressively blurred the lines between combatant and noncombatant by using the terms "absolute war" and *Vernichtungskrieg* for military operations. The German General Staff rationalized that it could best accomplish its goal of saving Germany by expanding warfare to threaten enemy civilians "for strictly military reasons." When employing such ruthless tactics (as in World War I examples of unrestricted submarine warfare, zeppelin raids on cities, and drafting Belgian men as forced labor), the military simply ignored ethical considerations in favor of expediency. This understanding of the nature of warfare predisposed the German military to accept Hitler's extension of the concept of *Vernichtungskrieg* to its darkest extreme: a war for the literal annihilation of an entire people. There would be no such thing as a noncombatant in an absolute peoples' war. Hitler, blending his biological-racist ideology with preexisting military terminology, concluded that an absolute war meant destroying not just an enemy's military power but also the enemy nation itself.

At least initially, the evolution and seriousness of Hitler's racial ideology was not clearly understood by the leaders of the German armed forces. The Nazi leader was not (as now commonly portrayed) simply an irrational psychopath. Rather, certainly before 1941, he appeared to be a sincere German patriot, a decorated hero of World War I, a common soldier who shared much of the outlook of the traditional officer class. Both Hitler and his generals hated the shameful Versailles Treaty (1919) and longed for another war to correct its perceived injustices. As individuals, many generals shared Hitler's contempt for Slavs and Jews, and all utterly despised the Bolsheviks. There were also undeniable tensions between the upstart Führer and the old order: for all his nationalism, Hitler resented the power of the old elite; the generals, meanwhile, were suspicious of the man they derisively called the "little Austrian Corporal." While German military leaders agreed with Hitler that war was a conflict between peoples for superiority, most did not understand that Hitler's racially centered worldview expected such a conflict to include genocide.

The blend of racism and politics at the core of the Nazi leader's personal worldview, the very elements that shaped all his decisions during the destructive years of the Third Reich, emerged as Hitler attempted to understand the defeat of Germany in World War I. When the postwar Social Democratic leadership of the Weimar Republic failed to provide order and stability following the defeat, young Hitler first diagnosed his nation's problem and then devised a cure. Twisted fragments of Nietzschean philosophy and the pseudoscientific ideals of social Darwinism combined in his thought to identify race as the fundamental factor in human history. The former soldier concluded that the existence of a vast Jewish-Bolshevik Conspiracy was the only satisfactory explanation for all the problems of Germany. He firmly believed that Jews were a "declining race" that sought survival by mixing itself with the vital blood of Aryans and by promoting internationalist ideologies such as communism, which would give them access to the seats of power. Hitler was convinced that the Soviet Union was established and controlled by the Jews, an attitude he later kept despite hints that Joseph Stalin had purged Jews from the Communist Party of the U.S.S.R. In Hitler's universe, German Jews and their deluded Social Democratic allies were also the "November criminals" responsible for the German collapse in November 1918. It was a formulaic answer that provided him, he would later claim, with an immediate clarity of vision and a certainty of purpose unavailable through religion or any other ideology.

All human civilization, according to Hitler, was determined by the principle of "survival of the fittest." Furthermore, this theory was not understood in terms of survival of the individual; far more perniciously, it was understood as survival of the fittest race. For Hitler, a person's racial origin dictated how he thought and acted, indeed, determined his very consciousness. Consequently, meaningful existence for an individual German was judged according to the success or failure of the entire "Aryan" race to which he belonged. Thus, all non-Germans (those who thought and acted differently than Aryans) were, by the mere fact of their existence, dangerous to Germans as a race. This worldview not only justified but also actually demanded that all ideas of "morality" be suspended in order to defend the Aryan race against the dangers posed by other races, the Jews in particular. Because Hitler believed there was no higher end than the survival of the German race, all means were legitimate and even necessary (as sixteenth-century Italian political philosopher Niccolò Machiavelli might say) to attain it.

Hitler was determined, from the start of his political career, to gain control of the German state not for mere personal prestige and power but to employ his power to deliver Germany from its racial enemies. Nazi ideology was to direct the state policy of the Third Reich. Many of Hitler's actions during the Nazis' rise to power and in his direction of the German war effort provide evidence of his firm ideological commitment. In the early days, when attaining national office was the goal, Nazi ideology justified all manner of thuggery and voter intimidation as well as deceit and dishonesty in both elections and procedures within the parliament. Later, Hitler's racial worldview determined that his first

wartime objective was not just to win a strategic military victory but also to destroy Poland as a nation. Nazi ideological goals in occupied Poland were pushed forward with a murderous immediacy in the autumn of 1939. By rounding up and executing all teachers, doctors, lawyers, and local officials in Poland, the Nazis sought to decapitate the Polish nation—eliminating forever its intellectual and political leadership. Hitler expected that without ethnic leaders to guide them, the Polish race would be permanently subordinated and would gradually disappear from the earth. Thus, as early as 1939, Hitler understood that true *Vernichtungskrieg* could only be accomplished by the destruction of the enemy's cultural and intellectual leadership.

The regular *Wehrmacht* (German army) of 1939 was not ready to cooperate with this nazified understanding of *Vernichtungskrieg*. Although they had accepted the military expediency of certain forms of terror (such as dive-bomber attacks on refugee columns) during the Polish campaign, the brutality of the SS in conquered Poland horrified *Wehrmacht* officers. Such wanton cruelty was seen as unnecessary bloodlust that undermined military professionalism. Army officers reacted with a peculiar kind of moral indignation, often publicizing their protest by refusing to shake hands with SS leaders at meetings. Hitler had little patience with the army leaders' moral hypocrisy and let them know in no uncertain terms that the actions of the SS were acceptable and necessary in order to permanently destroy the national leadership of the Polish people.

The influence of Hitler's racial worldview on German policies was not limited to the battlefront; it could also be found on the German home front in the months after the defeat of Poland. In the winter of 1939 and spring of 1940, before the great blitzkrieg (lightning war) battles in the west, the Nazis began their experiments in racial engineering within the Reich. By this point, the state was classifying the Aryan racial characteristics of various Germanic peoples and promoting the growth of a stronger, healthier Aryan race through institutions such as the "Fount of Life" homes for unwed mothers. In the same vein, the Nazis took their first notorious step toward mass murder by ordering the euthanasia of German citizens with mental illness or mental and/or physical disabilities in late 1939. There was no practical reason why the sick or disabled, identified by Nazis as "life unworthy of life," needed to be killed: they were neither financially burdensome nor a threat to public safety. Their deaths were,

FÜHRER ORDER

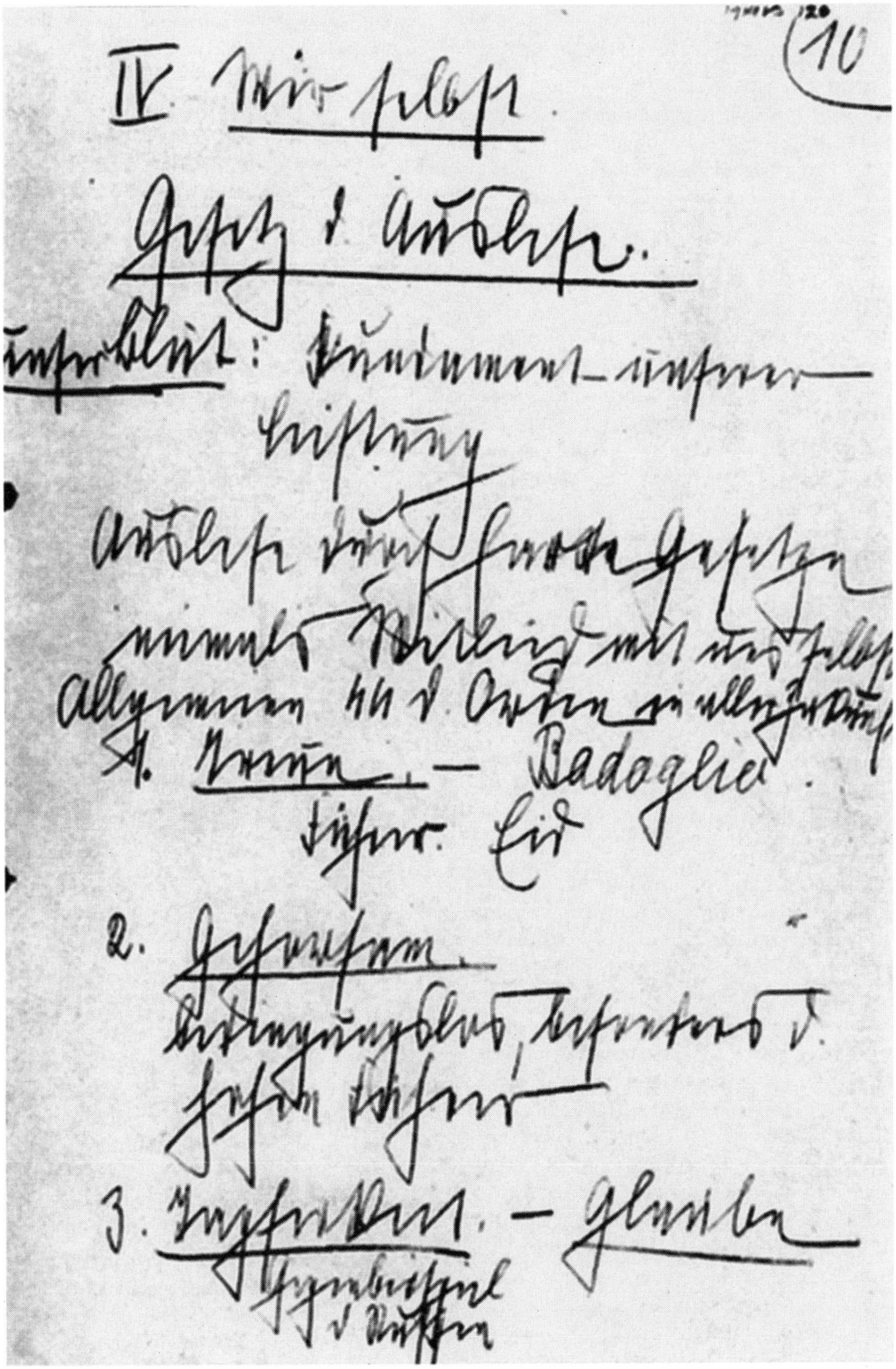

IV. Wir selbst.

Gesetz d. Auslese.

1. Treue. — Badoglio

Führer Eid

2. Gehorsam.

3. Tapferkeit. — Glauben

however, undeniably in keeping with the requirements of Hitler's rigid racial ideology.

These helpless victims of their own government were neither the first nor last Europeans to die because the Führer declared it to be necessary for the future of the German race. When the war resumed in the west in 1940, SS leader Heinrich Himmler acquired the responsibility of governing all those parts of occupied Poland and Czechoslovakia not directly annexed into the Reich. Himmler had many ambitious plans for social and racial engineering that called for the shifting of entire ethnic populations. For example, he intended to collect the *Ostjuden* (Jews of eastern Europe) in isolated areas of the occupied territories and to allow time, disease, inbreeding, and crossbreeding with Slavs to destroy them as a race. The SS leader even expected that many Jews might die during the mass population shifts because he thought they had weak constitutions. Himmler's comments suggest that he initially had no intention of allowing Nazi social engineering to become as barbaric as Stalin's policies of forced collectivization and industrialization: "however cruel and tragic each case may be, this method is still the mildest and best, if one rejects the Bolshevik method of physical extermination of a people out of inner conviction as [being] un-German and impossible."

Himmler's supposedly "humane" efforts to concentrate the Jews soon had to contend with many unforeseen problems created by the population shifts. In particular, lower-ranking Nazi leaders in the occupied territories constantly complained that they had neither the space nor the resources to accept more Jews in their areas. Furthermore, German governors of the eastern provinces complained that they needed to keep local Poles alive as laborers because of the manpower shortage caused by the war. Since it appeared the Jews could not be concentrated into Poland, Himmler sought an alternative. Anticipating a swift victory over the French and British empires, the SS leader even had visions of exiling all Jews to an SS colony on Madagascar, but the British fleet effectively prevented deportation overseas and, consequently, Himmler had to find a place for the unwanted *Ostjuden* as best he could. The inefficiency of the Nazi regime's racial planning is further highlighted by the fact that German Jews were still allowed to emigrate from Germany in 1940 and were not required to wear an identifying badge until September 1941.

In early 1941, however, Hitler's efforts to realize the dreams of Nazi racial ideology and to "purify" Germany of undesirable elements

took an ambitious step forward. Although Britain remained uninvaded and undefeated in the west, the Führer decided to take the war to the heart of the Jewish-Bolshevik Conspiracy. The first decisive step toward the final destruction of European Jewry was his plan to invade Soviet Russia: Operation Barbarossa. By attacking the militarily disorganized and vulnerable Soviet Union, Hitler thought he could smash the communist menace and the Jewish leadership.

One of Hitler's secretaries recalls that, about the time the plan for the invasion was finalized in the spring of 1941, Himmler emerged from a private conference with the Führer, sat down, and muttered that he could not believe what he had been asked to do. Shortly afterward, Himmler began the training for the SS's follow-on forces, known as the *Einsatzgruppen* (mobile killing units). Since the Nazis believed Jews formed the intelligentsia of the Soviet state, the mission of the *Einsatzgruppen* was to eliminate the leadership of the Jewish-Bolshevik Conspiracy—adult male Jews and Communist Party members. In fact, in early June, Hitler's infamous "Commissar Order" instructed all German soldiers to kill Communist Party members immediately upon capture. These plans for operations within the U.S.S.R. are clearly consistent with Hitler's earlier plan to "decapitate" the Polish nation. Where the objective of the French campaign had been primarily revenge for Versailles, the object of war against Soviet Russia required "all efforts," for it was to be the "final struggle between competing political systems."

The invasion of Russia began on 22 June 1941, and by the next day the *Einsatzgruppen* were in action, executing Jews behind the front. Early on, some *Einsatzgruppen* commanders expanded the mass killings of Jewish men to include women and children, whereas other SS commanders simply confined the majority of Soviet Jews in ghettos to be used as laborers. There is a surprising amount of evidence pointing to confusion among these SS officers about whether all Jews were to be killed or some were to be used as forced labor. Leaders of mass killing operations (which sometimes included regular army units) were often rewarded for their "initiative"—and it seems that there was a great deal of initiative displayed. SS officers who thought that noncommunist Jews should be kept alive for employment as slave laborers (in the belief that killing of otherwise innocent women and children was simply murder) received neither rewards nor promotions. Indeed, in his recent study *Nazi Policy, Jewish Workers, German Killers* (2000), historian Christopher R. Browning records at least one case of an officer who refused to round up Jews in ghettos in his area of operations. The officer in question was relieved of duty, sent back to Germany, and shot for disloyalty to National Socialist ideology.

With apparent victory in the east only weeks away, Hitler and the senior Nazi leaders began to consider how best to complete their victory over the Jews. On 31 July 1941 high-ranking SS official Reinhard Heydrich (chief of the Reich Central Security Office) was directed to plan a "Final Solution to the Jewish Question." Then, from August until October, a series of field experiments was conducted to discover how to kill large numbers of Jews most efficiently. Mass shootings were time-consuming and unpopular with the troops (no matter how much they agreed with the Nazi ideology, many soldiers found face-to-face killing to be too much like murder). The Nazis devised less-personal means of murder using gas vans (similar to those first used in the euthanasia program) that killed their passengers with carbon-monoxide fumes. But since vehicles were scarce and fuel a valuable commodity, in September 1941 a purposely built "gas chamber" was tested with a commercial pesticide known as Zyklon-B. The Nazis appear to have been satisfied with the results of the latter test, for construction of the "death camps" began in early November. Finally, with the experiments complete, Heydrich convened the Wannsee Conference in January 1942. Over a light lunch, Heydrich sketched the Führer's wishes, laid out his own plans, and discussed the coordination of resources with several senior state and party officials who would be directly involved in waging a genocidal campaign against European Jews.

Having issued Directive 21, Hitler did not need to compose a separate *Führer Befehl* for the Final Solution. Whether Hitler gave verbal directions that all Jews should be gassed, it cannot be doubted that he had expected the death of the Jews as part of the full implications of his concept of a *Vernichtungskrieg*. The destruction of all Soviet Jewry was clearly implied when, in early 1941, he began planning the invasion of Russia and the elimination of the leadership of the Jewish-Bolshevik Conspiracy. Destroying the Jewish leadership of the Communist state would also destroy the racial threat to Germany. Since Operation Barbarossa was intended to be the complete, final struggle between two competing systems—that is, a *Vernichtungskrieg*—another Führer Order was not necessary: the order had already been given. Hitler had identified the ultimate ideological purpose of the war: the total destruction of the Jewish-Bolshevik Conspiracy. While he personally directed the military side of this operation, the Führer was able to leave details of the genocide to willing and able subordinates, confident that his will would be done.

–CLIFFORD F. PORTER,
DEFENSE LANGUAGE INSTITUTE

Viewpoint:
No. Although Hitler made his intentions clear to his closest associates, he never explicitly ordered the extermination of European Jews.

Adolf Hitler spoke and wrote extensively about his ideas on racial purity and the Jewish Question; during World War II (1939–1945) the Allies spent years decoding and listening to German transmissions; in the closing months of the war they confiscated millions of Nazi documents; hundreds of perpetrators subsequently testified about the orders they received; and historians have spent decades poring through all of this material, but no one has ever found a direct order from Hitler (a *Führer Befehl*) authorizing the extermination of the Jews. Most historians of the Holocaust agree that Hitler never explicitly ordered the extermination of Jews in Germany or in occupied territory. Rather, he and his associates planned and executed the Holocaust without ever directly stating their intentions. Surprisingly enough, given their rabid anti-Semitism, the Nazi leaders used ambiguous language when they discussed their plans for Jews in the areas under their control, probably out of concern that genocide did not enjoy significant popular support. A discussion of Hitler's statements on the Jewish Question makes it clear that, while he intended to rid Germany and eastern Europe of their Jewish populations, he never said so in plain language either in his political writings, in his orders during the war, or in his public speeches.

This lack of written orders does not mean, as David Irving would argue, that the murder of more than six million Jews was carried out without Hitler's knowledge or consent, that Hitler was not ill intentioned toward the Jews, or that the Holocaust did not take place. Nor does it mean that the murder of Jews was the spur-of-the-moment product of necessity as concentration camps became overcrowded. Rather, it indicates that Hitler, like other leaders who have given orders that they knew would be distasteful to many of their supporters, used language that could be interpreted in several ways in his statements and orders dealing with the Jews. There was an established precedent for this circumspect method of command. In 1170, for example, English king Henry II is supposed to have provoked the murder of Thomas à Becket, archbishop of Canterbury, by asking his entourage: "who will free me from this turbulent priest?" More recently, U.S. president Richard Nixon gave the green light to the 1973 assassination of Chilean leader Salvador Allende by telling the "40 Committee" to "do something about him." Similarly, Hitler avoided directly ordering genocide, at least in public. Nevertheless, just as Henry II's courtiers and Nixon's cabinet members understood that they had been ordered to murder the enemies of the men they served, members of the Nazi Party understood that Hitler intended to murder the Jews of Germany and the occupied territories.

Hitler's hatred of Jews developed in his youth. As he would later make clear in *Mein Kampf* (1925–1927), an autobiography and political tract, he already held anti-Semitic ideas when he lived in Vienna, Austria, as a young man (1908–1913). At that time, there were several anti-Semitic groups operating in Vienna, and anti-Semitic tracts circulated widely. Although Hitler would subsequently downplay the importance of this anti-Semitism in his thinking, historian Lucy S. Dawidowicz has argued persuasively that the anti-Semitic newspapers, pamphlets, and magazines available in Vienna played an important role in the development of Hitler's worldview. In Vienna he first learned to articulate his notions about racial purity, particularly about a supposed Jewish conspiracy to bring down the Aryan race. This conspiracy, according to Hitler, took several forms: a political and economic conspiracy of liberals and capitalists on the one hand and an effort to defile Aryan womanhood on the other.

Subsequently, Hitler came to believe that Jews on the political Right and Left alike were conspiring to destroy Germany. In 1918, while in the hospital recovering from wounds suffered in combat, Hitler came to the conclusion that Germany had lost the war because of Jewish sabotage. Although the evidence clearly demonstrates that Germany was forced to surrender because its resources had been exhausted, Hitler preferred to believe that his nation had been betrayed. Already steeped in anti-Semitism, it is hardly surprising that he began to blame Jews for the revolution of November 1918, the uprising that led to the "overthrow of the [German] monarchy, the armistice, and the creation . . . of the Weimar Republic." After leaving the hospital he became

politically active and sought out like-minded people. In the process he began to articulate the argument that an international Jewish community had stabbed Germany in the back.

By 1924 the idea of a Final Solution to the Jewish Question had emerged in Hitler's mind. In the first edition of *Mein Kampf* he made at least two statements that rather explicitly indicated what he would do if given the opportunity. First, he argued that Germany would have won World War I if someone had simply gassed the Jews living within its borders. He wrote, "if at the beginning of the War and during the War twelve or fifteen thousand of these Hebrew corrupters of the people had been held under poison gas, as happened to hundreds of thousands of our very best German workers in the field, the sacrifice of millions at the front would not have been in vain." At the same time, he came to the conclusion that "there is no making pacts with Jews: there can only be the hard either-or." For he believed that "rational anti-Semitism . . . must lead to a systematic legal opposition and elimination of the special privileges which Jews hold, in contrast to the other aliens living among us. . . . Its final objective must unswervingly be the removal (*Entfernung*) of the Jews altogether." These were not simply idle statements; they are indicative, according to Dawidowicz, of Hitler's intention to exterminate the Jews should he ever be given the opportunity to do so.

Although these statements appear to be clear in a post-Holocaust world, they were intentionally obscure to those people who heard them prior to the event. Later, even as thousands of Jews were being marched to the gas chambers, Hitler rarely spoke clearly about what he meant by the Final Solution. Rather, he hinted of "emptying" Germany of its Jewish population. According to Dawidowicz, in his early days Hitler talked of "removing," "eliminating," or "cleaning up" the Jewish problem. Later he referred to "deporting Jews to the east," and, in mid July 1941, of "turning Germany into a Garden of Eden." While the words he chose made it clear that there were to be no Jews in Germany any longer, they did not spell out that those Jews and others were to be exterminated. Rather, he used ambiguous words open to various interpretations, one sense consistent with "driving the Jews out of Germany" and another with murdering all Jews in Germany and the occupied territories.

Did Hitler give the order to kill the Jews? While there appear to be no documents bearing Hitler's signature that give explicit approval of the Final Solution, some assumptions may be made. First, Hitler's plans for the Jews were occasionally outlined in his public speeches. On 30 January 1939, while the world was still at peace,

POSITIVE HARM

An editorial in the German paper Der Stürmer, *published in 1942, calls for the extermination of Jews:*

Another way to solve the Jewish question was for the numerically superior non-Jewish population to absorb the Jewish minority. People believed that close contact between the Jews and the host peoples would, through equality, intermarriage and the mixing of blood, gradually "water down" the Jewish race and lead to its disappearance. The results of this mistake were catastrophic. The Jewish race was not "watered down" and rendered harmless, rather the opposite: the blood of the non-Jewish peoples was poisoned in a grave way.

Experience showed non-Jewish peoples that incorporating the foreign Jewish element into their community not only did no good, but caused positive harm. Gradually people realized that there was only one effective method of dealing with Jewry: consistent separation from their own racial body.

Even during the Middle Ages numerous governments required Jews to distinguish themselves from their non-Jewish host peoples by wearing special clothing such as pointed Jewish hats, yellow symbols, rings, etc. As well-intentioned as these measures were, they had only limited success. Sometimes the Jews wore these symbols with pride. They were pleased that the "stupid Goy" themselves saw to it that only the "chosen people" wore such outward symbols. But other Jews whose business interests were not advanced by making the fact that they were Jews plain continued to go about the country as "non-Jews."

Another way of separating the Jews from the non-Jewish peoples was to force them to live in certain areas. The Jewish quarter became known as the "ghetto."

But this method also failed to achieve its goal. Some Jews welcomed the creation of the ghetto. Once again they had their "community abroad!" In the ghetto, Jewry's secret plans were forged! In the ghetto the Jews had their "staff." Those Jews who carried on their mischief among the non-Jews received their commands from the ghetto. The Jewish danger was greater than ever before.

Realizing that separating the Jews into their own quarter was not sufficient led various peoples to go still further. They expelled the Jews from their countries. This for the first time aroused the Jews. Now they saw a real danger! Now they had to act before it was too late!

Jewry is thousands of years old. Thanks to its devilish cleverness, it has often found a way out of nearly hopeless situations. Here too! The Jews let themselves be expelled without much fuss. They gathered on the other side of the border and waited and waited and waited. They waited for years and decades. They waited for the moment in which the knowledge of the Jewish danger gradually disappeared from people's minds. Then the Jews came back. Then they laid waste to the land more terribly than before.

Today Europe is ready to solve the Jewish question once and for all. It is thus good to learn from past mistakes and remember what history teaches. And what does history teach us? It teaches:

The Jewish question is not only a German matter!

It is also not only a European problem! The Jewish question is a world question! Just as Germany is not safe from the Jews as long as even one Jew remains in Europe, so Europe cannot solve the Jewish question as long as Jews live in the rest of the world.

Jewry is organized world criminality. The Jewish danger will be eliminated only when Jewry thoughout the world has ceased to exist.

Source: Ernst Hiemer, "Wann ist die jüdische Gefahr beseitigt?," Der Stürmer, 19 (1942), in German Propaganda Archive, Calvin College <http://www.calvin.edu/academic/cas/gpa/ds11.htm>.

Hitler uttered a "prophecy" before the assembled Reichstag: "If international Jewish financiers . . . should succeed in once again plunging the nations into a world war, then the result will not be the victory of the Jews, but rather the annihilation of the Jewish race in Europe!" However ridiculous this declaration might have seemed to outside observers, it accurately foretold what Hitler had in store for the Jews. Second, given the method by which power was exercised in the Nazi state, it is unlikely that the extermination process could have taken place without Hitler's prior knowledge. Yet, the Führer often left the duty of interpreting and executing his wishes to like-minded subordinates. Documentary evidence implies that Heinrich Himmler, Reinhard Heydrich, and Joseph Goebbels (among many others) believed they were faithfully adhering to Hitler's

FÜHRER ORDER

desire as they developed the plans necessary to "cleanse" Europe and, eventually, the world of the Jewish population.

It was, nevertheless, a gradual process. It began, in the earliest days of the regime, with Nazi efforts to alienate and isolate the Jewish population of the Third Reich. "*Die Juden sind unser Unglück!*" (The Jews are our misfortune!) had long been a rallying cry in the massive propaganda campaigns by which the Nazis sought to cultivate anti-Semitic fervor. The racially motivated Nuremberg Laws (1935) spelled out legal definitions of "Jewishness" based on blood relations. The pseudoscience of phrenology, based on nineteenth-century Italian physician Cesare Lombroso's theory that criminals had peculiarly shaped heads, was employed to denigrate the physical characteristics of Jewish stereotypes. Goebbels, Reich Minister of Popular Enlightenment and Propaganda, made skillful use of psychology to compose propaganda messages against the Jews. Caricatures of Jews—portraying them with large noses, beady eyes, and claw-like fingers—appeared regularly in Nazi newspapers, on posters, and even in children's stories. The movie *Jud Süss* (1940), likewise, proved to be popular because the audience could relate well to the characters in terms of their own deeply held prejudices and personal experiences with Jews. Nazi anti-Semitic propaganda hit the airwaves as radio commentators warned the German people of the sinister "plans" that the Jews had for the rest of the world: the "bolshevization" of Germany and the economic downfall of Europe. Propaganda of this sort was perfectly matched to the racial decrees that confiscated Jewish wealth and prohibited them from important professions. Nazi action and rhetoric were calculated to fuel the public's animosity toward the Jews. By constant repetition of their message of hate, the Nazis won many converts to their campaign against the Jewish conspiracy that supposedly threatened Germany.

The process sped up with the coming of a new world war, as the Nazis began working to fulfill Hitler's prophecy against the Jews. At first, however, Nazi brutality was directed at the people of Poland in order to remove the possibility of a Polish threat in the newly annexed territories of the Reich. It was in reference to the fate of the Poles that Hitler voiced his approval of genocidal measures and his contempt for world opinion:

> What the weak Western European civilization thinks about me does not matter. Thus for the time being I have sent to the East only my "Death Head Units" with the order to kill without pity or mercy all men, women and children of the Polish race or language. Only in such a way will we win the vital space we need. Who still talks nowadays of the extermination of the Armenians? The German leader fully expected the fate of Polish civilians to resemble that of the Armenians massacred by the Turks during World War One. Some outsiders might object, but time would eventually silence their protests and Germany could enjoy the *Lebensraum* or "living space" provided by its ruthless *Führer*.

Recognizing Hitler's own rabid anti-Semitism, it is not unreasonable to extend his callous remark to the Jews. Even as Slavic Poles were dying, the Nazis rounded up two and a half million Polish Jews and crowded them into ghettos. There can be little doubt that the Nazi leaders knew that Hitler had something worse in store for Jews than the wretched life of the ghettos. As one SS official in occupied Poland remarked in December 1939:

> The creation of the ghetto . . . is, of course, only a transition measure. I shall determine at what time and with what means the ghetto—and thereby also the city of Lodz—will be cleansed of Jews. In the end, at any rate, we must burn out this bubonic plague. Those in charge of carrying out the Nazi policies apparently knew that, sooner or later, they would receive permission to exterminate the Jews.

Hitler was never explicit in his orders for the extermination of the Jews, but he does appear to have deliberated the action. His reasoning may be summarized in the question: if the world had once turned a blind eye to the plight of the stateless Armenians, why should it not also ignore the plight of the equally stateless Jews? The Nazis were convinced that they could employ the cover of the "fog of war" to murder millions and get away with it. But it was a peculiarly open secret, for Hitler reiterated his racial world-view in wartime speeches to large audiences by declaring that he would save the world by annihilating the Jews.

As a prisoner of the Allies in 1945, SS leader Himmler tried to justify the German treatment of the Jews. He maintained that the Nazis "had the moral right vis-à-vis our people to annihilate this people which wanted to annihilate us." Himmler stated that orders to destroy the Jewish threat came directly from Hitler. Convinced of this danger, and of the righteousness of the cause of his Führer, the SS chief acted. The 1941 invasion of the Soviet Union, known as "Operation Barbarossa," was the occasion for the next development in the Holocaust. Himmler dispatched SS units called *Einsatzgruppen* (mobile killing units) into newly conquered Soviet territory with orders to "cleanse" the area of Bolsheviks and to massacre Jews. Like Hitler's intentions toward the Jews, the *Einsatzgruppen* killings were an open secret. Most of these mass executions took place by daylight and in the open, as hundreds of people were machine-gunned into deep ditches or ravines outside of urban areas. Not only were these killings witnessed by many townspeople, but the murderers were sloppy and left survivors. Every now and then a victim, missed by the bullets or sheltered by another body, escaped to tell others about the horror. The stories of *Einsatzgruppen* actions might well have seemed unbelievable in a world where such organized killing was still unusual. Be that as it may, they formed a crucial part in the Nazi plan for the Jews of Europe.

The *Einsatzgruppen* had been murdering Jews in the Soviet Union for six months when a meeting in Berlin between Nazi and non-Nazi German officials laid the foundation for an even more systematic method of killing the Reich's racial enemies. On 20 January 1942, Heydrich (a high ranking SS officer and Chief of Reich Security) arranged the Wannsee Conference to coordinate the efforts of party and state institutions for a "Final Solution to the Jewish Question." Here, he presented the Nazi regime's plans for initiating the program of industrial murder now known as the Holocaust. At Wannsee, Heydrich claimed to be acting on the authority of the Führer, as passed on to him through a memo from the office of *Reichsmarschall* Hermann Göring. Yet, even at this significant gathering, where such proof might well be displayed, no written Führer order was produced to prove Hitler had directed the SS to oversee the extermination of the Jews. Indeed, modern historians do not believe that such an order was ever issued in writing. However, many historians agree that a signal must have come from Hitler to set the Final Solution in motion. In an oral form it could have been either a clear instruction passed on to Göring or to Himmler, or, more probably, a broad hint understood by everybody. Among other things, this contention is supported by the "Wannsee Protocol," a document issued after the conference, which acknowledged that the SS had received "permission" directly from the Führer to deal with the Jewish population of Europe.

At Wannsee, although years of Nazi intentions were converted into specific plans for mass murder, the language employed to authorize the killing was as filled with euphemisms as earlier official references to the Jewish problem. It may be that Hitler first used these ambiguous terms in referring to his long-term plans for European Jews because, early in his career, he was not convinced that it would be possible to exterminate them. While anti-Semitism was common in Europe, support for genocide had to be built. At the same time, what might have been possible in the occupied territories during the war might not have been possible—or at least not so easy—in Germany during peacetime. Thus, during the years prior to war, Hitler and other Nazi leaders worked to solidify popular anti-Semitism. When, in 1941, he realized that it might yet be possible to undertake mass murder of Jews in the occupied territories, the Führer authorized feasibility studies of the gas chambers. That decision does not mean that the idea of exterminating the Jews had just occurred to him, but rather that his old idea finally met the opportunity it required.

When the Nazis began to murder Jews en masse, they did not require a direct order from Hitler to begin. Although Hitler had often obscured his true intentions in public, his inner circle was aware of his diabolical intent and shared it. Within that circle, a radical solution to the Jewish Question had been obliquely discussed since the early 1920s. A world *judenrein* (free of Jews) was the ultimate goal of the Nazis; it was the "dream" Hitler wrote of in *Mein Kampf*. The seed of the Final Solution was sown a full twenty years before the beginning of World War II; fertilized by Nazi propaganda, it sprouted and grew during the 1930s, but it required wartime conditions in which to burst into blood-red blossom. In 1941 motive and opportunity came together; a pitiless feasibility study was conducted; and the killing began. Decisive action, taken only when the circumstances were right, had been the plan from the beginning. For those who shared this understanding, no special *Führer Befehl* was necessary.

–MARY ANN MAHONY, COLUMBIA COLLEGE, AND CYNTHIA KLIMA, STATE UNIVERSITY OF NEW YORK, GENESEO

References:

Yair Auron, *The Banality of Indifference: Zionism and the Armenian Genocide* (New Brunswick, N.J.: Transaction Publishers, 2000).

Christopher R. Browning, *Nazi Policy, Jewish Workers, German Killers* (Cambridge & New York: Cambridge University Press, 2000).

Alan Bullock, *Hitler: A Study in Tyranny,* revised edition (New York: Harper, 1960).

David Cesarani, ed., *The Final Solution: Origins and Implementation* (London & New York: Routledge, 1994).

Lucy S. Dawidowicz, *The War against the Jews, 1933–1945* (New York: Holt, Rinehart & Winston, 1975).

Gerald Fleming, *Hitler and the Final Solution* (Berkeley: University of California Press, 1984).

Joseph Goebbels, *The Goebbels Diaries, 1939–1941,* translated and edited by Fred Taylor (London: Hamilton, 1982).

Geführt von Helmuth Greiner and Percy Ernst Schramm, *Kriegstagebuch des Oberkommandos der Wehrmacht (Wehrmachtführungsstab) 1940–1945,* volume 1, edited by Hans-Adolf Jacobsen (Frankfurt: Bernard & Graefe, 1965).

Raoul Hilberg, *The Destruction of the European Jews* (Chicago: Quandrangle, 1961).

Adolf Hitler, *Mein Kampf,* translated by Ralph Manheim (Boston: Houghton Mifflin, 1943).

International Military Tribunal, *Trial of the Major War Criminals Before the International Military Tribunal, Nuremberg, 14 November 1945 – 1 October 1946,* 42 volumes (Nuremberg: International Military Tribunal, 1947–1949).

Ian Kershaw, *Hitler,* 2 volumes (New York: Norton, 1999, 2001).

George L. Mosse, *Toward a Final Solution: A History of European Racism* (New York: Fertig, 1978).

Alan S. Rosenbaum, ed., *Is the Holocaust Unique?: Perspectives on Comparative Genocide* (Boulder, Colo.: Westview Press, 2001).

Ron Rosenbaum, *Explaining Hitler: The Search for the Origins of His Evil* (New York: Random House, 1998).

Gitta Sereny, *Albert Speer: His Battle with Truth* (New York: Knopf, 1995).

FÜHRER ORDER

GENDER DIFFERENCES

Did Jewish women perceive the dangers of the Nazi threat differently from Jewish men?

Viewpoint: Yes. Women were more likely than men to see the dangers of Nazism and to express a desire to flee Germany.

Viewpoint: No. Though Jewish women and men in Nazi Germany responded differently to the increasingly hostile environment, differences in perceptions of danger and willingness to flee had less to do with gender than with social status and personal experience.

Between 1933, when Adolf Hitler was appointed chancellor of Germany, and 1941, when plans for the extermination of European Jewry were finalized, Jews in Germany and Austria had a narrow window of opportunity to escape (a window that, one must remember, was never opened for Jews in Poland, Russia, or the rest of Nazi-occupied Europe during the war). If they could find a country that would receive them, if they could afford the often extortionate costs of emigration, and if they could negotiate the Nazis' bureaucratic maze and obtain an exit visa, then they could get out. In fact, thousands of German and Austrian Jews did flee their homeland during the Nazi era. For those who left and for those who stayed, the emigration decision was fraught with uncertainty. Many Jews stayed in Germany because they were unable to escape—being too old, or unwell, or poor to be offered refuge elsewhere. Others, however, did not perceive the catastrophe that was about to befall European Jewry until the possibility of escape was no more. It was not easy for Jews to abandon the limited security of the familiar, if increasingly hostile, Germany for the utter unfamiliarity of America, Australia, or Palestine. Abroad, they would be refugees, unable to work or communicate easily. In retrospect, of course, fleeing the Nazis seems wholly logical and reasonable. Staying, for Jews, seems tantamount to suicide. But as the danger of staying became clearer, opportunities for escape diminished. In July 1938, before *Kristallnach* (Night of the Broken Glass), the Evian Conference of thirty-two countries, convened by U.S. president Franklin D. Roosevelt, refused to urge any nation to take on more refugees. Only the Dominican Republic offered to take on twenty thousand Jews. Nowhere is this fact demonstrated more effectively than in the fate of the more than nine hundred Jewish refugees aboard the SS *St. Louis,* which steamed from Germany for Cuba in 1939 with refugees aboard who had obtained an entry visa that the Cuban government rescinded while the ship was in transit. Forbidden entry into Cuba and barred from the United States and every other alternative host, the ship returned to Europe, where many of the refugees eventually fell into the grasp of the Nazis and died.

Marion Kaplan argues that Jewish women were more sensitive than men to the dangers that their families faced as the pressure on Jews mounted and as opportunities decreased. They were less bound by business and social ties to the German community, and their status and sense of self were not usually tied to their work, as was more often the case for men. Having less to lose socially and professionally, women were not blinded by the promises of "good Germans" nor were they likely to believe that "things cannot get any worse," even while the situation deteriorated steadily. As women, they were more eager to get out of Germany than were men. Cynthia Klima argues that, though gendered differences in perceptions of danger did exist, they were less pronounced than Kaplan assumes and were outweighed by factors such as social status and the consequent sense of security that Jews of higher social and economic status seemed to enjoy.

Viewpoint:
Yes. Women were more likely than men to see the dangers of Nazism and to express a desire to flee Germany.

As Nazi political, economic, and social persecution increased in Germany, Jewish emigration became more and more crucial for survival. Women usually saw the danger signals first and urged their husbands to flee Germany. According to one historian, "The role of women in the decision to emigrate was decisive . . . the women were the prescient ones . . . the ones ready to make the decision, the ones who urged their husbands to emigrate."

Why did women want to flee sooner than men? Men and women led relatively distinct lives, men focusing on the public worlds of the economy and politics, and women involving themselves with their families and neighbors. With different vantage points, they often interpreted daily events differently. Raised to be sensitive to interpersonal behavior and social situations, women were more upset when the postman or neighbor no longer greeted them or when former friends avoided them on the street. Women's social antennae were also directed toward more unconventional—what men might have considered more trivial—sources of information. For example, in Hamburg a Jewish woman was alerted to danger by her household help. She wrote, "Any woman knows . . . her best source of information are the servants . . . I received more information from Harold . . . than I could have received at the best . . . intelligence office." Women registered the increasing hostility of their immediate surroundings, unmitigated by a promising business prospect, a loyal employee or patient, or a kind customer. Their constant contacts with their own and other people's children probably alerted them to warning signals that come through interpersonal relations—and they took those signals seriously.

A widespread assumption that women lacked political acumen—stemming from their primary role in the private and domestic sphere rather than the public and political one—gave women's warnings less credibility in their husbands' eyes. One woman's prophecies of doom met with her husband's amusement: "He laughed at me and argued that such an insane dictatorship could not last long." Even after

their seven-year-old son was beaten up at school, he was still optimistic. Many men also pulled rank on their wives, insisting that they were more attuned to political realities. Often the anxious partner heard the old German adage, "Nothing is ever eaten as hot as it's cooked."

Men attempted to see the "broader" picture, to maintain an "objective" stance and to scrutinize and analyze the confusing legal and economic decrees and the often contradictory public utterances of the Nazis. Men mediated their experiences through newspapers and broadcasts. Politics remained more abstract to them, whereas women's "narrower" picture—the minutiae (and significance) of everyday contacts—brought politics home.

Men also felt more at home with German culture. Generally more educated than their wives, they cherished what they regarded as the German Enlightenment heritage. It gave men something to hold on to even as it "blunted their sense of impending danger." In fact, one could argue that men were more "German" than women, more imbued with a sense of patriotism, even in a situation gone awry. When Else Gerstel fought with her husband about emigrating, he, a former judge, insisted that "the German people, the German judges, would not stand for much more of this madness."

Patriotic war veterans refused to take their wives' warnings seriously, especially after President Paul von Hindenburg intervened to exempt them from the "April Laws," which forced the dismissal or early retirement of Jewish doctors, lawyers, judges, and civil servants. The wives of these men typically could not convince their husbands that they, too, were in danger. One woman, who pressed her husband to leave Germany, noted that he "constantly fell back on the argument that he had been at the front in World War I." While the front argument had a deep emotional core to it—many of these men still felt the deep patriotism that the war experience invoked—most men expressed it in terms of having served their country and, hence, having certain rights.

The different attitudes of men and women seem to reflect a gender-specific reaction remarked upon by sociologists and psychologists: in dangerous situations, men tend to "stand their ground," whereas women avoid conflict, preferring flight as a strategy. But men held back for more important reasons: they were the breadwinners of the family. They felt the burden to provide for their wives and children

GENDER DIFFERENCES

Hungarian Jewish
women and children at
Auschwitz, circa 1943

*(U.S. Holocaust Memorial
Museum, Washington, D.C.)*

and knew that in countries of immigration, plagued by the world-wide Great Depression, jobs would be difficult to come by. Moreover, many Jewish men were businesspeople or professionals: they did not have the capital, the qualifications—or even the language—to establish themselves in a foreign country.

As long as men made a living and could support their families, many were unwilling to leave. Men would also have to tear themselves away from their life work, whether a business or professional practice, regardless of the impact on their patients, clients, colleagues, status, or possessions. The daughter of a wealthy businessman commented, "When the Nazis appeared on the scene, he was too reluctant to consolidate everything and leave Germany. He may have been a bit too attached to his status, as well as his possessions." But even businesswomen appeared less reluctant than their spouses to emigrate. One woman, a manufacturer whose husband directed her business, wanted to flee immediately in 1933. He, on the other hand, refused to leave the business. Although the wife could not convince her husband to flee, she insisted that they both learn a trade that would be useful abroad. In light of men's primary identity with their occupation, they often felt trapped into staying. Women, whose identity was more family oriented, strug-

gled to preserve what was central to them by fleeing with it.

Men and women also had gender-specific, distinctive connections to the public world. One man declared in his memoirs that he could not depart from Germany because he thought of himself as a "good democrat" whose emigration would "leave others in the lurch" and would be a "betrayal of the entire Jewish community." Women's memoirs rarely use such lofty language, nor did women see themselves as so indispensable to the public.

Moreover, women were less involved than men in the economy, even though some women had been in the job market their entire adult lives. Since Jewish men worked mostly with other Jews in traditional Jewish occupations (retail trade in specific branches of consumer goods, in the cattle trade, or in independent practices as physicians and attorneys), they might have been more isolated from non-Jewish peers (though not from non-Jewish customers). This isolation spared them direct interactions with hostile peers, but it also prevented the awareness garnered from such associations. As the boycotts of Jewish concerns grew, those Jewish men whose businesses remained intact saw their clientele become predominately Jewish, further isolating them. Moreover, discriminatory hiring meant

GENDER DIFFERENCES

that Jewish blue-and-white collar workers found opportunities only within the Jewish economic sector. In 1937 the Council for German Jewry in London reported that the German-Jewish community lived in a "new type of ghetto . . . cut off from economic as well as social and intellectual contact with the surrounding world." Thus, Jewish men, working increasingly in a "Jewish ghetto," might have been shielded to some extent from "Aryan" hostility, whereas Jewish women (even those who worked in the same "Jewish ghetto") picked up other warning signals from their neighborhoods and children.

Women's subordinate status in the public world and their focus on the household also eased their decision to flee since they were familiar with the kinds of work they would have to perform in places of refuge. One woman described how her mother, formerly a housewife and pianist, cheerfully and successfully took on the role of maid, whereas her father, formerly a chief accountant in a bank, failed as a butler, barely passed as a gardener, and experienced his loss of status more intensely than his wife.

Even when both sexes fulfilled their refugee roles well, women seemed less status conscious than men. Perhaps women did not experience the descent from employing a servant to becoming one to the same degree as men since their public status had always been derivative of their father or husband anyway.

Men's role and status as breadwinner and head of household both contributed to their hesitancy to emigrate and gave them the authority to say "no." Else Gerstel urged her husband of twenty-three years to emigrate. Fearful that he would not find a job abroad, he refused to leave, insisting: "there is as much demand for Roman law over there as the Eskimos have for freezers." She wrote, "I was in constant fury," representing their dispute as a great strain on their relationship. Another wife described her attempt to convince her husband to flee:

A woman sometimes has a sixth feeling . . . I said to my husband, ". . . we will have to leave."

He said, "No, you won't have a six-room apartment and two servants if we do that.". . .

I said, "OK, then I'll have a one-room flat . . . but I want to be safe."

Despite his reluctance, she studied English and learned practical trades. His arrest forced their emigration, and she supported the family in Australia.

Summing up, Peter Wyden recalled the debates within his own and other Jewish families in Berlin:

It was not a bit unusual in these go-or-no-go family dilemmas for the women to display more energy and enterprise than the men. . . . Almost no women had a business, a law office, or a medical practice to lose. They were less status-conscious, less money-oriented than the men. They seemed to be less rigid, less cautious, and more confident of their ability to flourish on new turf.

A combination of events usually led to the final—by then, joint—decision to leave, and, as conditions worsened, women sometimes took the lead. In early 1938 one daughter reported that her mother "applied to the American authorities for a quota number without my father's knowledge; the hopeless number of 33,243 was allocated. It was a last desperate act and Papa did not even choke with anger anymore." (Her parents and young brother were deported and killed.) Still another woman responded to narrowly escaping battering by a Nazi mob in her small hometown by convincing her husband to "pack their things throughout the night and leave this hell just the next day." After *Kristallnacht* (Night of the Broken Glass, 1938), with husbands in hiding, jails, or concentration camps, there were wives who broke all family conventions by taking over the decision making when it was unequivocally clear to them that their husbands' reluctance to leave Germany would result in even worse horrors. Gerstel recalled that although her husband had been arrested on 9 November, he did not have to go to a camp and still "had no intention of leaving Germany, but I sent a telegram to my brother . . . in New York . . . 'please send affidavit'."

Notwithstanding the gender difference in picking up signals and yearning to leave, it is crucial to recognize that these signals occurred in stages. Alice Naunen and her friends "saw it was getting worse. But until 1939 nobody in our circles believed it would lead to an end" for German Jewry. Although women's analyses were often more penetrating, interspersed as they were with personal observations, women, too, could be confused by Nazi policies and events. When Hanna Bernheim's sister, who had immigrated to France, returned for a visit in the mid 1930s, the sister wanted to know why the Bernheims remained in their south German town. Bernheim replied:

First of all it is so awfully hard for our old, sick father to be left by all his four children. Second there are so many dissatisfied people in all classes, professions and trades. Third there was the Roehm Purge and army shake up. And that makes me believe that people are right who told us "Wait for one year longer and the Nazi government will be blown up!"

Moreover, these signals were often profoundly mixed. Random kindness, the most obvious "mixed signals," gave some Jews cause for hope. One woman wrote that every Jewish person "knew a decent German" and recalled that many Jews thought "the radical Nazi laws would never be carried out because they did not match the moderate character of the German people." Confusing signals, often interpreted differently by women and men, as well as attempts by the government to rob Jews of all their assets, impeded many Jews from making timely decisions to leave Germany. Ultimately, however, it was not gendered perceptions that kept Jews in Germany but nations of refuge that shut their doors.

—MARION KAPLAN, NEW YORK UNIVERSITY

Viewpoint:
No. Though Jewish women and men in Nazi Germany responded differently to the increasingly hostile environment, differences in perceptions of danger and willingness to flee had less to do with gender than with social status and personal experience.

Though Jewish women and men experienced the increasing pressures of life in Nazi Germany differently, the decision to flee was determined less by gender than by social role and expectation. And though husbands usually made the final decision about staying or leaving, they did so within the context of family systems in which wives and daughters were enormously influential.

In the decades leading up to the Holocaust, Jewish family life in Germany was in transition. In the latter decades of the nineteenth century, women began to leave the confines of their homes and started to expand their social circles. Indeed, it was during the 1890s that the dominant role of Jewish women as "housewives" began to change into that of their families' "cultural liaison." At the same time, the mass exodus of Jews from the rural areas of Germany into the large cities led to the growth of Jewish communities and hence to the development of social connections that would prove critical during the years of Nazi oppression. These connections facilitated communication among the members of the Jewish community and played an integral role in the decision-making processes during the years 1933–1938, when the danger signals were often unclear but the possibility of immigration still existed.

For women the 1890s brought about a new form of emancipation. They came into social and political roles that could allow for work and career to be combined with the family sphere. Birth control, issues of hygiene, and suffrage (1902) all served to give women a newfound freedom that enabled them to begin to participate in society and in politics, areas that had previously been deemed off-limits to them. These changes were not universally welcomed. In Weimar Germany, "women stood at the nexus of the 'morality question.' They were simultaneously seen as guardians of morality and as the chief agents of a 'culture of decadence.'" While this "sexual revolution" allowed women to be not only creative participants in German culture, such as in theater and cinema, it also created hostility toward them. They were considered great contributors to consumerism, but at the same time, many considered the "new woman" to be responsible for the moral decay in Germany.

This cultural expansion was reflected in the establishment of new organizations for Jewish women. The most important of the Jewish women's groups was the Jewish Women's Union, or *Jüdischer Frauenbund* (JFB), formed in 1902. Many German Jewish housewives joined this "leisured ladies" club, but relatively few Jewish women of eastern European background did so. The JFB was one of the first support and social circles that was exclusively for Jewish women. Universities also opened to women (1908) and allowed them to begin learning and mixing with men not only in academic settings but also in social situations. A majority of the women entering into the university were Jewish. During World War I (1914–1918) women became more emancipated after being thrust into stereotypically male roles while the men were off fighting. As Claudia Koonz argues, in an article for *When Biology Became Destiny: Women in Weimar and Nazi Germany* (1984), "Shebboleths about 'natural' feminine weaknesses dissolved in the face of clear evidence that women could perform men's jobs with only minimal training. War made the anti-feminists' worst nightmares come true: as men marched off to die, women 'stole' their jobs." When men returned from war it was difficult to turn back the hands of time—women had tasted the fruit of what had earlier been the realm of men, and they were not about to turn back. And it is precisely the occasion of their entrance into what was previously the world of men that afforded Jewish women many means by which to gain and share information in ways that would later be critical to their survival. Thus, while the experiences of Jewish women at the beginning of the Nazi era differed from those of men, women were, like men, able to draw upon a variety of networks and interpersonal resources that would help determine their families' fates.

The Nazi Party at first appeared to be somewhat innocuous for the Jews. Anti-Semitic rhetoric was not new in Germany, and Adolf Hitler came to power with the promise of economic support and jobs for all, as well as restoration of the "traditional family." After a long period of worsening economic conditions for Germany in the 1920s, the Nazis pledged to create a stronger Germany and to cure the ills caused by the Treaty of Versailles (1919). But once the Nazis had consolidated power, Jewish women found themselves in an unexpectedly dangerous and ambiguous situation. Since women were the primary caretakers of their families, they were out on the streets shopping more often than men and thus had to weather the brunt of insults and threats. This conduct was alarming for women, who were not used to this sort of treatment and did not know how to react to it. This behavior did not seem to bother men as much, who were more used to the rougher nature of the work world and competition with colleagues. During the early years of persecution, however, women did not think that they would be physically harmed. The Nazis, after all, seemed to ignore Jewish women as if they had no significance. The men were the ones being arrested and confined. But this rough treatment in and of itself had educational benefits for women, for they learned quickly how to weave their way through the Nazi bureaucracy and how to manipulate desperate situations in order to save a family member. They learned the subtle art of bribery, using material possessions and money to gain the release of a husband, son, or father. That they were often successful during the early years of persecution, when Nazi aims seemed to be to encourage rather than to prevent Jewish emigration, gave them more confidence in their abilities to survive.

This situation did not change even when Jews from Poland and Russia living in Germany were deported, starting in 1933. German Jews could look to the unhappy fates of their coreligionists as having little bearing on their own. Often they were unaware that these deportations had begun. Eastern European Jews were poorer and of lower status than German Jews. Their jobs as peddlers and lower-level businessmen did not put them in the same league with German Jews, many of whom were physicians, lawyers, and successful businesspeople; thus, their persecution was not perceived as a threat to the far more acculturated German Jews. Few Jewish women or men gave serious thought to leaving Germany in the mid 1930s.

As hostility toward the Jews intensified, however, the roles played by Jewish women changed immensely. They were forced to enter into the "man's world" and to take care of situations not only on the home front but also outside of the home. When their husbands were arrested, women often found themselves thrust into decision-making roles with which they were unaccustomed. And the most critical decision of all, leaving Germany, often fell upon these women, especially when their husbands were unable or unwilling to make such a move. The doubt and fear were intense. As bad as the situation seemed to be in Germany, many German Jews did not think that they could survive elsewhere. Some swallowed their fear and left to start a new life abroad, but many delayed making a decision or decided upon emigration after it was much too late. Some had to rely on the goodness of family members abroad whom they barely knew to sponsor them. The decision to leave was complex and fraught with difficulties. Though men, in their traditional roles as husbands and fathers, usually made the final decision about immigration, their decisions were reached in the milieu of outside pressures, perceived risks and opportunities, the hope that Hitler would be soon overthrown, and their commitment to their families. Formally or informally, women influenced these decisions and took critical actions to keep the family intact.

The destruction of the Jewish family began between the years 1933–1939 with arrests, deportations, and murders, mainly of men. This displacement of males left women behind to care for children and elderly parents and forced them to "make things work" with few resources and crumbling support networks. Indeed, this period was a time of preparation for women, for with the many restrictions against Jews, women became wondrous inventors and learners. They began to fight for their husbands' freedom and to prepare themselves for menial labor, even apprenticing themselves as laundresses or other domestics in case they had to emigrate. But many women were unwilling to emigrate without male support. The JFB provided some help to such women, who were either too afraid or too poor, to facilitate emigration from Germany. The Nazis began shutting down more women's networks, and the JFB did all it could to educate women and prepare them for emigration. Women began to learn foreign languages in preparation for emigration. However, many Jews, women and men alike, seemed to take the anti-Semitic laws of the Nazis in their stride. They tolerated the situations the Nazis threw before them and hoped that the arrangement would one day end and normality would return. Denial and sublimation set in; for many Jews the situations were simply nightmares that did not exist, and women especially forged ahead with housekeeping duties or other activities that kept their minds off of the current situation. Jewish women were up against their Gentile counterparts, who often had the same goals, wants, and needs. But ethnic lines also separated women; anti-Semitism served to reinforce female differences when common goals might have been a uniting force. According to Susanne Ottenstein, conversations in non-Jewish environments were bland in comparison to the tenser Jewish ones, because of the past history Jews had had with risky situations or because of the temperament of the Jews themselves. Why would a Christian woman need to be as informed as a Jewish woman when the former's life would go on as before and for whom less was at risk? Non-Jewish women had to deal with Nazi misogyny but not with anti-Semitism. The gossip, denunciations, rude behavior, loss of friends, and general social ostracism disturbed Jewish women terribly. And when it came to children, who often came home from a school day rattled from anti-Semitic rhetoric, it was the Jewish mother who had to comfort them. This social upheaval all served to hone the listening and analytical skills of Jewish women. As violence and pressures on their families increased, so did their resolve to leave Germany. But their determination was often conflicted, and husbands most often made the emigration decision for the family.

Jewish women were in denial about their hardships, but they pushed for emigration, often when their husbands would not. Ottenstein's mother suspected that the situation in Vienna had been growing more uncertain since before *Kristallnacht* (Night of the Broken Glass) in November 1938. She had withdrawn the family money from the local bank and had stored it in a secure place in preparation for emigration. Unfortunately, the Nazis arrived and Ottenstein's father was forced to reveal the hidden money to them. It was not until Ottenstein's father was arrested and then released several weeks later from Dachau (at her mother's urging) that the family emigrated in 1939. As Ottenstein said, "Leaving wasn't hard at that time." Her mother organized the family's departure.

In another case sixteen-year-old Ruth Nebel suffered greatly at school from taunts and tried to convince her father to leave rural life for the city, where the family could be more anonymous. "I pleaded with my father to leave for the big city where it was said that life was better, but each time I asked, he would reply, 'What would Hitler want of me? I'm a simple working man, not a scientist or professor. You'll see, things won't be too bad. Maybe soon they'll let you go back to school again'." Many women were forced to take over the role of the husband. Some wealthier women even searched out possible emigration destinations for their families when husbands could not. Women did not arouse as much suspicion as men; they would say they were there for a spa or for shopping or to visit family members. Others urged their families to emigrate when they perceived danger in their community, such as threats on the street or bans from the university. For many Jewish men who were still employed, the thought of emigration did not appeal to them. Starting over in a new land with new customs and a completely

LEAVING GERMANY

Marta Appel described a discussion among Jewish friends in Dortmund about a doctor who had just fled Germany in the spring of 1935. The men in the room, including her husband, a rabbi, condemned him.

A few days after the doctor had left with his family, we were invited to a friend's house. Of course the main subject of the evening was the doctor's flight. The discussion became heated. "He was wrong," most of the men were arguing. "It indicates a lack of courage to leave the country just now when we should stay together, firm against all hatred." "It takes more courage to leave," the ladies protested vigorously. "What good is it to stay and to wait for the slowly coming ruin? Is it not far better to go and to build up a new existence somewhere else in the world, before our strength is crippled by the everlasting strain on our nerves, on our souls? Is not our children's future more important than a fruitless holding out against Nazi cruelties and prejudices?" Unanimously we women felt that way, and took the doctor's side, while the men, with more or less vehemence, were speaking against him.

On our way home, I still argued with my husband. He, like all the other men, could not imagine how it was possible to leave our beloved homeland, to leave all the duties which constitute a man's life. "Could you really leave all this behind you to enter nothingness?" From the heavy sound of his voice I realized how the mere thought was stirring him. "I could," I said frankly, and there was not a moment of hesitation on my part, "I could," I said again, "since I would go into a new life." And I really meant it.

Source: *Monika Richarz, ed.,* Jewish Life in Germany: Memoirs from Three Centuries *(Bloomington: Indiana University Press, 1991), p. 356.*

different career did not seem to be the way to take responsibility for a family. Thus, many men chose not to emigrate. Those who did, such as Clara Isaacman's Uncle Emil, stated, "Everything's going, even my furniture factory. You should come too!" in an effort to convince Clara's father to emigrate. Men who had private enterprises or who had varying job skills found it much easier to emigrate. Those who had worked in offices found it difficult to leave a career. They either did not have the language training that their wives had or the skills that the small, private businessman had (such as Uncle Emil) to convince themselves that they could make it abroad.

If a husband did not see the reason for emigrating, the entire family was in danger. But many wives were also reluctant to emigrate, especially when they had elderly family members to take care of. They did not want to leave because they could not or would not leave their parents behind. The traditions of women as caretakers were not easily broken, and ties to Jewish identity and culture that were strong did not allow for emigration to enter many women's minds. In one Hungarian example from Judith Magyar's testimonial, the Magyar family was about to emigrate, but her mother did not want to miss her sister's wedding. Young women could find jobs easily as domestic servants, teachers, social workers, and in many areas of nurturing or health care, more so than men. But older and married women did not want to leave a home that they had established for their families. They simply could not bear to think of strangers in their houses, using their dishes and sleeping in their beds. Some worried about how suitable their destinations—especially Palestine—would be for raising their daughters.

The year 1938 brought more rules and restrictions on daily Jewish life. The JFB, which had been instrumental in assisting women with education and support, was dissolved. Women continued to write letters in efforts to free their husbands and also to ask for asylum for their families abroad, promising never to be a financial burden. Koonz writes of one conversation with Helen Sachs:

> "Do you know what the number one best-seller among the German Jews was then?" Helen Sachs asked me, her eyes twinkling. I, of course, did not. But I tried. "The Torah? Goethe? Heine? Mann?" All wrong. "It was the Manhattan telephone book. We spent hours, days looking for Jewish-sounding names and writing letters. It was our only chance. And many, many answered back. But not enough."

Kristallnacht forced many Jews to reconsider their stay in Germany. Men who had doubted their wives' "sixth sense" in perceiving danger did so no more. Emigration had clearly become the only way to escape the escalating violence. Unfortunately, for the vast majority, it was simply too late. The only hope left for survival was to go into hiding. Although many German Jews had already immigrated to other European countries, in many cases it was not far enough from the Nazi onslaught.

—CYNTHIA KLIMA, STATE UNIVERSITY OF NEW YORK, GENESEO

References

G. W. Allport, J. S. Bruner, and E. M. Jandorf, "Personality under Social Catastrophe: Ninety Life-Histories of the Nazi Revolution," *Character and Personality: An International Psychological Quarterly,* 10 (September 1941): 1–21.

Avraham Barkai, *From Boycott to Annihilation: The Economic Struggle of German Jews, 1933–1945* (Hanover, N.H.: Brandeis University Press by University Press of New England, 1989).

Ulrich Baumann, "Jüdische Frauen auf dem Land," in *Zerstörte Nachbarschaften* (Hamburg: Dölling & Galitz, 1992), p. 237.

Ruth Eisner, *Nicht Wir Allein: Aus dem Tagebuch einer Berliner Jüdin* (Berlin: Arani, 1971).

John Foster, ed., *Community of Fate: Memoirs of German Jews in Melbourne* (Sydney & Boston: Allen & Unwin, 1986).

Peter Gay, "Epilogue: The First Sex," in *Between Sorrow and Strength: Women Refugees of the Nazi Period,* edited by Sibylle Quack (Washington, D.C.: German Historical Institute / Cambridge & New York: Cambridge University Press, 1995).

Carol Gilligan, *In a Different Voice: Psychological Theory and Women's Development* (Cambridge, Mass.: Harvard University Press, 1982).

Clara Isaacman, *Clara's Story,* as told to Joan Adess Grossman (Philadelphia: Jewish Publication Society of America, 1984).

Judith Magyar Isaacson, *Seed of Sarah: Memoirs of a Survivor* (Urbana: University of Illinois Press, 1990).

Marion Kaplan, "Jewish Women in Nazi Germany: Daily Life, Daily Struggles, 1933–1938," *Feminist Studies,* 16 (Fall 1990): 579–606.

Kaplan, "Keeping Calm and Weathering the Storm: Jewish Women's Responses to Daily Life in Nazi Germany, 1933–39," in *Women in the Holocaust,* edited by Dalia Ofer and Lenore J. Weitzman (New Haven: Yale University Press, 1998), pp. 39–54.

Kaplan, *The Making of the Jewish Middle Class: Women, Family, and Identity in Imperial Germany* (New York: Oxford University Press, 1991).

Kaplan, "Sisterhood Under Siege: Feminism and Anti-Semitism in Germany, 1904–1938," in *When Biology Became Destiny: Women in Weimar and Nazi Germany,* edited by Renate Bridenthal, Atina Grossmann, and Kaplan (New York: Monthly Review Press, 1984), pp. 174–196.

Claudia Koonz, "The Competition for Women's *Lebensraum,* 1928–1934," in *When Biology Became Destiny: Women in Weimar and Nazi Germany,* edited by Bridenthal, Grossmann, and Kaplan (New York: Monthly Review Press, 1984), pp. 199–236.

Koonz, "Courage and Choice among German-Jewish Women and Men," in *Die Juden im Nationalsozialistischen Deutschland,* edited by Arnold Paucker (Tübingen: Mohr, 1986).

Koonz, *Mothers in the Fatherland: Women, the Family, and Nazi Politics* (New York: St. Martin's Press, 1987).

Margarete Limberg and Hubert Rübsaat, *Sie Durften Nicht Mehr Deutsche Sein: Jüdischer Alltag in Selbstzeugnissen, 1933–1938* (Frankfurt & New York: Campus, 1990).

Sybil Milton, "Issues and Resources," in *Proceedings of the Conference on Women Surviving–the Holocaust,* edited by Esther Katz and Joan Miriam Ringelheim (New York: Institute for Research in History, 1983), pp. 10–21.

Ruth Nebel, "The Story of Ruth," in *When Biology Became Destiny: Women in Weimar and Nazi Germany,* edited by Bridenthal, Grossmann, and Kaplan (New York: Monthly Review Press, 1984), pp. 334–348.

Susanne Ottenstein, interview with Cynthia Klima (14 June 2001).

Quack, *Zuflucht Amerika: Zur Sozialgeschichte der Emigration Deutsch-Jüdischer Frauen in die USA 1933–1945* (Bonn: Dietz, 1995).

Sylvia Rothchild, ed., *Voices from the Holocaust* (New York: New American Library, 1981).

Lore Segal, *Other People's Houses* (New York: Harcourt, Brace &World, 1964).

Marga Spiegel, *Retter in der Nacht: Wie eine Jüdische Familie im Münsterland Urberlebte* (Münster: Lit, 1999).

Joseph Walk, ed., *Das Sonderrecht für die Juden im NS-Staat: Eine Sammlung der Gesetzlichen Massnahmen und Richtlinien, Inhalt und Bedeutung* (Heidelberg & Karlsruhe: Müller Juristischer, 1981).

Peter Wyden, *Stella* (New York: Simon & Schuster, 1992).

GENDER DIFFERENCES

INTENTIONAL STRATEGY

Was the progressive isolation of the Jews from German life during the 1930s part of Nazi strategy intended to culminate in extermination?

Viewpoint: Yes. The persecution of the Jews was part of an intentional strategy that resulted in genocide.

Viewpoint: No. Adolf Hitler did not seriously consider the Final Solution until after the invasion of the Soviet Union in June 1941.

So clearly has the history of the *Nationalsozialistische Deutsche Arbeiterpartei* (Nationalist Socialist German Workers' Party, NSDAP) been identified with the Holocaust that people forget that the Final Solution only occupied the last five years of the twenty-five-year history of the NSDAP. And though the Party that Adolf Hitler joined in 1919 (and became leader of in 1921) was already anti-Semitic (as was Hitler), there is little sign in the early agenda indicating interest in the genocide to come. In the "25 points," published in 1920, the NSDAP political platform identified citizenship in the Reich with membership in the German race. Since Jews were explicitly excluded from the German race by the Party, which also believed that only members of the German race should live in Germany, the exclusion of Jews from Germany was implicit—certainly not their mass extermination, nor the elimination of Jews living outside the German Reich from France and Greece to Russia and Norway.

Even when the Nazis seized power in 1933, their anti-Semitic program seemed intent on exiling the Jews and plundering their financial resources rather than destroying them. Is it possible that the Final Solution became Nazi policy only shortly before the conversion of Auschwitz from a labor camp into a death factory? Or was the Holocaust intended, if not from the beginning of Hitler's rise to power, then from early in the Nazi dictatorship? In that case, the apparent scramble in the Party for a solution to the Jewish Question— whether forced emigration, exile to Madagascar, or dumping in "the East"— was part of an intentional strategy that started with rhetorical attacks against Jews and ended in the elimination of Jews in the gas chambers and ovens of Birkenau and Majdanek.

Lucy Schildkret Dawidowicz saw the "War against the Jews" as Hitler's intent from his earliest days in power. If he delayed implementing the Holocaust only until the Final Solution could be carried out under cover of war, then it was not because the Nazis were searching for a solution that only slowly realized itself in annihilation. Rather, anti-Semitic rhetoric, laws, and violence were intended to isolate the Jews and prepare the German people for a process of extermination already taking shape in unrecorded conversations among Hitler, Heinrich Himmler, and other top Party officials.

Yet, an increasing number of historians have interpreted the same evidence to argue against the "intentionalist" thesis and in favor of a "functionalist" interpretation of Nazi planning for the Final Solution. Christopher R. Browning imagines a conversation taking place in mid July 1941, after the *Einsatzgruppen* (mobile killing units) began massacring Jews in the Soviet

Union, in which Hitler turns to Himmler and asks, "My dear Heinie, what about the rest of them? Would it be possible?" However the conversation took place, Browning, Richard Breitman, and other "functionalist" historians argue that planning for the Final Solution did not begin until after the invasion of the Soviet Union (1941).

Viewpoint:
Yes. The persecution of the Jews was part of an intentional strategy that resulted in genocide.

What if Adolf Hitler had died in a plane crash in November 1938? It is possible to argue that the German elite would have rallied around the memory of the Führer and that the Nazi regime might have endured for some time. It is also likely that a war between Germany and other European nations would have occurred, although it could have taken a different form from World War II (1939–1945). However, it is hard to imagine that the Holocaust—the mass slaughter of European civilians, especially Jews, by the Nazis during World War II—would have occurred without Hitler. A Nazi regime without Hitler certainly would have persecuted, expelled, and murdered Jews, but would Hermann Göring, Joseph Goebbels, or even Heinrich Himmler have built Auschwitz? Such an outcome seems dubious. It is simply impossible to account for the Holocaust without according a central role to Hitler. Nazi policy toward the Jews followed an intentional strategy from isolation to genocide, and Hitler was the key strategist.

One important body of historical opinion, dubbed "intentionalist" by historian Christopher R. Browning, argues that the Holocaust was simply the concrete application of Hitler's obsessive hatred of Jews in the form of genocidal policy. The Holocaust happened because Hitler wished it to happen. If his written and spoken threats are to be taken at face value, he intended to carry out such a program of genocide from the beginning of his career. As historian Saul Friedländer put it: "To deny [the central role of Hitler in Nazi] extermination policies requires more explanation than to declare it a major impetus."

Not all Germans shared his obsession; for that matter, not all Nazis shared their leader's point of view. After a careful examination of autobiographical statements written by 581 early Nazis and collected by sociologist Theodor Abel, it was found that only about one in eight respondents even mentioned anti-Semitism as a factor in their decision to join the Nazi Party. Vague political, economic, and social resentments worked to attract a great many members

to the Nazi Party banner. Almost two-thirds of new members in 1930 cited anticommunism as the main factor. Almost all of these new Nazi recruits argued that a revolution was needed since "the system had failed." Biographer Joachim C. Fest commented on the "unmistakable difference between [Hitler's] rigorous obsession with Jews and the lukewarm German anti-Semitism."

Much the same pattern holds true for the Nazi Party leadership. If one looks at the early politics of later Nazi leaders such as Goebbels, Göring, Rudolf Hess, or even Adolf Eichmann, clearly none of these figures joined the Nazis primarily to act upon their anti-Jewish feelings. Historian Sarah Ann Gordon examined the early Nazi elite and concluded that "surprisingly few of the top Nazi leaders were virulent anti-Semites before 1925." In the case of many similarly minded Nazi leaders, they were attracted to anti-Semitism because they were attracted to Hitler. It is difficult to imagine how the Holocaust could have occurred without the unwavering political support of the Nazi Party. In practical terms, the first step toward genocide was Hitler's success in infusing his personal obsessions into the heart of Nazi Party ideology. By the late 1920s, anti-Semitism had become a primary litmus test of loyalty to the Führer.

Hitler was the only figure in the Third Reich with the authority to carry out a policy of genocide. The hypothesis that Hitler used his authority as Führer to implement his lifelong hatred of the Jews in the form of mass murder seemed so obvious to the World War II generation that most scholars spent more time collecting threatening anti-Jewish quotations from Hitler's speeches and conversations than examining the actual record of Nazi decision making leading up to the Holocaust (a term that only came into common usage in the late 1960s). The American prosecutors at the Nuremberg War Crimes Tribunals presented Hitler as the central figure in a criminal conspiracy to carry out crimes against humanity. In brief, the prosecution argued that Hitler set out a coherent plan for the murder of German Jews in *Mein Kampf* (1925–1927) and then proceeded to carry out that plan in a systematic manner. The guilty verdicts of the Nuremberg trials also represented the views of the majority of postwar historians of the Third Reich.

It was only in the late 1970s and early 1980s, as a new generation of scholars replaced those who had lived through the war years, that a competing explanation for Nazi genocide began to emerge. Partially in response to the maverick British historian David Irving, who argued in 1977 that Hitler was largely unaware of mass murders of Jews carried out by Himmler, many scholars decided that the time was right for a fresh look at the origins of the Final Solution, if only to refute the arguments of Irving.

Some younger scholars, mostly social and institutional historians, using the analytic tools of political science, argued that to view the Nazi government as an instrument of Hitler's will was simplistic and, more important, did not seem to reflect the actual nature of the Nazi regime. These scholars, often called "functionalists" or "structuralists," argued that the most notable feature of the Nazi dictatorship was competition for turf, not strict obedience to policy directives from on high, and that Hitler was no more successful than any other dictator in imposing his views on a fragmented, "polycratic" bureaucracy. Functionalists are more impressed by the chaotic decision-making process of the Third Reich and by the tendency of Hitler to retreat into his private world for months at a time while leaving the business of government in the hands of more energetic and ruthless deputies. Structuralist scholars see Hitler as a "Weak Dictator," as Michael R. Marrus expressed it: "a brooding and sometimes distant leader, who intervened only spasmodically, sending orders crashing through the system like bolts of lightning."

Ultimately, the structuralists can only shed light on the lesser question ("how?"), not the larger question ("why?"). Hitler was the driving force behind Nazi anti-Jewish policy from the moment he joined the NSDAP to his final political testament, written hours before he committed suicide. That is not to say that he had a mental blueprint for Auschwitz in mind when he wrote *Mein Kampf.* It is logical to assume that Hitler approached the Jewish Question with the same tactical flexibility that he applied to domestic politics or foreign policy. It is also logical to assume that changes on the diplomatic front—or later, during the war, changes in the military situation facing Germany—would have an impact on Hitler's thinking. Under changing conditions, Hitler's plans for the Jews might seem evolutionary rather than fixed. However, two factors remained constant: Hitler's unrelenting hatred of Jews and his position as primary strategist and policy maker for the German state.

The "twisted road to Auschwitz" that structuralist historians describe corresponds to tactical shifts in Hitler's thinking. For political reasons, or to present a progressive and peaceful image of Germany to the world, Hitler was capable of downplaying his anti-Jewish rhetoric. Under the press of more immediate political and economic crises, Hitler sometimes put his long-range plans for the Jews on the back burner. It is even likely that he envisioned more than one potential Final Solution. In the late 1930s he considered a policy of expulsion: the forced emigration of all German Jews. One possible explanation for the terrible *Kristallnacht* (Night of the Broken Glass) pogrom of November 1938 is that the violence was intended as a clear message to German Jews to get out of the country. As war approached, Hitler began to think beyond the Jewish population of Germany. The final change in his thinking came in the summer of 1941 with the fateful decision to invade the Soviet Union. The German occupation of Poland and the European regions of the Soviet Union brought millions of non-German Jews under Nazi control at the same time that American entry into the conflict closed off all possibility of carrying out a policy of expulsion.

Hitler wanted to win a great war for Germany, and he wanted to eliminate the Jews from Europe. These two goals were intertwined in his mind. Although Hitler's ultimate goals were fixed and nonnegotiable, his tactics and definition of what constituted achievement of these goals were flexible; he was not committed to a rigid schedule of step-by-step persecution leading to the Final Solution. That conclusion is as far as the evidence allows one to go. There were clear limits to Hitler's flexibility. The tactics might be negotiable, but the strategy remained constant. In other words, Hitler might have considered alternate visions of a Total Solution, but he decided upon genocide. He admitted as much in a monologue at his headquarters in October 1941. In a document published in 1980 Hitler mused, "I had to remain inactive for a long time against the Jews too. There's no sense in artificially making extra difficulties for oneself; the more cleverly one operates, the better. It's better to keep silent; unless one doubts the future of the movement! If I believe that the movement will exist in a few centuries then I can wait. I wouldn't have dealt with Marxism either if I hadn't had the power behind me."

Psychologists have repeatedly commented upon Hitler's rigid personality and his stubborn boasting that his vision of the world was set in concrete at an early age. That pattern of rigid consistency certainly is apparent in Hitler's comments about the Jewish Question. From his earliest political speeches, through his autobiographical musings in *Mein Kampf,* to the end of his life, Hitler poured out his venomous hatred of the Jews. It is not necessary to dig deep to find evidence that Hitler was thinking of the mass mur-

FOR THE GOOD OF GERMANY

The demands listed in the program of the Nationalsozialistische Deutsche Arbeiterpartei (Nationalist Socialist German Workers' Party, NSDAP), published 24 February 1920, were:

1. We demand the union of all Germans in a Great Germany on the basis of the principle of self-determination of all peoples.

2. We demand that the German people have rights equal to those of other nations; and that the Peace Treaties of Versailles and St. Germain shall be abrogated.

3. We demand land and territory (colonies) for the maintenance of our people and the settlement of our surplus population.

4. Only those who are our fellow countrymen can become citizens. Only those who have German blood, regardless of creed, can be our countrymen. Hence no Jew can be a countryman.

5. Those who are not citizens must live in Germany as foreigners and must be subject to the law of aliens.

6. The right to choose the government and determine the laws of the State shall belong only to citizens. We therefore demand that no public office, of whatever nature, whether in the central government, the province, or the municipality, shall be held by anyone who is not a citizen.

We wage war against the corrupt parliamentary administration whereby men are appointed to posts by favor of the party without regard to character and fitness.

7. We demand that the State shall above all undertake to ensure that every citizen shall have the possibility of living decently and earning a livelihood. If it should not be possible to feed the whole population, then aliens (non-citizens) must be expelled from the Reich.

8. Any further immigration of non-Germans must be prevented. We demand that all non-Germans who have entered Germany since August 2, 1914, shall be compelled to leave the Reich immediately.

9. All citizens must possess equal rights and duties.

10. The first duty of every citizen must be to work mentally or physically. No individual shall do any work that offends against the interest of the community to the benefit of all.

Therefore we demand: . . .

24. We demand freedom for all religious faiths in the state, insofar as they do not endanger its existence or offend the moral and ethical sense of the Germanic race.

The party as such represents the point of view of a positive Christianity without binding itself to any one particular confession. It fights against the Jewish materialist spirit within and without, and is convinced that a lasting recovery of our folk can only come about from within on the principle:

COMMON GOOD BEFORE INDIVIDUAL GOOD.

25. In order to carry out this program we demand: the creation of a strong central authority in the State, the unconditional authority by the political central parliament of the whole State and all its organizations.

The formation of professional committees and of committees representing the several estates of the realm, to ensure that the laws promulgated by the central authority shall be carried out by the federal states.

The leaders of the party undertake to promote the execution of the foregoing points at all costs, if necessary at the sacrifice of their own lives.

Source: "Program of the National Socialist German Workers' Party," The Avalon Project at Yale Law School <http://www.yale.edu/lawweb/avalon/imt/document/nsdappro.htm>.

der of Jews at an early period in his career. For example, he told a Munich journalist in 1922: "Once I really am in power, my first and foremost task will be the annihilation of the Jews." Nineteen years later, at his dinner table, he mused: "I feel I am like Robert Koch in politics. He discovered the bacillus and thereby ushered medical science onto new paths. I discovered the Jew as the bacillus and the fermenting agent of all social decomposition." Finally, it is only necessary to remind the reader of Hitler's "prophecy" of 30 January 1939—a statement that he repeatedly referred to in later wartime speeches and conversations:

> I have often been a prophet in my life and was generally laughed at. . . . Today I will be a prophet again: if international finance Jewry within Europe and abroad should succeed once more in plunging the peoples into world war, then the consequence will not be the Bolshevization of the world and therewith a victory of Jewry, but on the contrary, the destruction of the Jewish race in Europe.

There is a direct line, in the words of Gerald Fleming, from Hitler's personal hatred "to the liquidation orders that Hitler personally issued during the war." No historian expects to unearth a "smoking gun"—a document ordering the extermination of European Jews personally signed by Hitler. The decision to proceed from escalating persecution to genocide was reached within the senior leadership of the Nazi Party and the German state in such secrecy that historians still debate precisely when, where, and how it was made. It is doubtful that any historical research will ever provide exact answers to that question. The Nazi regime treated the implementation of genocide as a state secret. This lack of direct documentation should not concern the historian nor encourage those who attempt to deny the reality of the Holocaust. There is no contradiction in viewing Nazi policy toward the Jews as both tactically flexible and at the same time committed to a program of annihilation, as long as one remembers that it was Hitler, "the Robert Koch of politics," with his peculiar mix of obsessive hatred and political opportunism, who made the key decisions every step along the way.

One can never know the exact calculations that led Hitler to the decision to implement a policy of extermination any more than one can hope to ascertain precisely why he hated Jews with such intensity. It is even possible, as John Lukacs has argued, that "It [genocide] was Hitler's own secret—a secret to the extent that he pushed that knowledge away from himself. He certainly did not want to know anything about its details." However, it is equally certain that no important decision in the Third Reich could be

made against Hitler's wishes. Did Nazi policy toward the Jews unfold as part of an intentional strategy? Yes. Eighteenth-century English writer Samuel Johnson offered this commonsense maxim: "Intentions must be gathered from acts."

—LARRY L. PING,
SOUTHERN UTAH UNIVERSITY

Viewpoint:
No. Adolf Hitler did not seriously consider the Final Solution until after the invasion of the Soviet Union in June 1941.

The decision to move from persecution to annihilation of the German Jews was not made by the Nazi leadership until after the invasion of the Soviet Union in the spring of 1941. The progressive isolation of Jews within Germany began in 1933, but their increasingly intense persecution, which led to a policy of final destruction, was not the result of a single, well-thought-out policy but of a haphazard evolution of policies. Nazi anti-Jewish thinking before 1941 progressed toward extermination, but there is no evidence that this goal was discussed until after the outbreak of World War II (1939–1945). Adolf Hitler's initial goal was to force Jews to emigrate from Germany. This policy failed for several reasons, not the least of which were the roadblocks set up by the Nazis themselves and the reluctance of other states to accept Jews as refugees. As a result of unsuccessful attempts to force Jewish emigration from Germany and an increase in the number of Jews under German control after the invasion of Poland and the Soviet Union, Nazi officials had to find a more effective way to deal with them. The extermination camps were the next step in an unplanned process that had begun years earlier.

Raul Hilberg was the first historian to argue that the extermination process was not planned. In *The Destruction of the European Jews* (1961) he argues, "The destruction of the Jews did not proceed from a basic plan. . . . The destruction process was a step-by-step operation, and the administrator could seldom see more than one step ahead." Hilberg elaborates on this idea by saying that emigration was the first phase of the destruction process and was carried out in public until 1941. The second phase, Jewish annihilation, began in 1941. This step was done in secret. Karl A. Schleunes, in *The Twisted Road to Auschwitz* (1970), supports Hilberg's thesis. Schleunes contends that the plans for annihilation were not created far in advance, nor did early anti-Jewish

Boycott sign on the window of a Jewish-owned store in Berlin, summer 1933

(Bildarchiv Preussischer Kulturbesitz, Berlin)

activity logically create a direct path to the death camps. Even so, Nazi plans to expel the Jews from Germany did not follow a logical progression. Because of this uneven path, Schleunes deems that the entire process was a "twisted road" rather than a straight course.

A substantial part of Schleunes's argument is based on the assumption that plans leading to the Final Solution were created by several Nazi Party and government agencies, not by Hitler. A variety of policies emerged that were confusing and often

worked at cross-purposes to one another. Hitler did not coordinate the policies; he responded to them. During the postwar years second-ranked *Schutzstäffel* (SS) leaders often referred to a "Führer Order," or a directive that had been given by Hitler for the onset of the extermination process. No one who witnessed that order survived the war, nor is there any record of one being given. Essentially, policies that attempted to deal with the Jewish Question came from Nazi officials, not from Hitler. Since a variety of policies were implemented by various people, who were not always communicating with each other, the Final Solution developed in an unsystematic way. Schleunes argues that this process was actually politically beneficial to Hitler:

> The continued search for a solution to the Jewish problem allowed Hitler to maintain ideological contact with elements of his movement for whom National Socialism had done very little. The situation, which Hitler had created for himself, made the Jewish problem and the promise of its solution a functional necessity. . . . The search had to continue, whatever the obstacles. Out of these circumstances emerged the logic of the boycott [of Jewish businesses], and finally of the extermination camp.

By relying on his officials to create policies, Hitler was free to take a hands-off approach. Hitler, like the German people, eagerly awaited a solution to the Jewish Question. While they waited, Nazi agencies created the circumstances, and later the policies, that would leave no other choice for them than Jewish annihilation.

In 1933, with the Nazi Party increasingly in control of all aspects of German life, Jews found themselves under growing pressure as their political rights were virtually eliminated and their economic opportunities curtailed. First, the Nazi Party promoted emigration. Second was forced evacuation, followed by deportation. Lastly, when these plans had failed, came destruction. Christopher R. Browning, an historian of Nazi Germany, argues that Hitler was trying to create a *judenrein* (Jew free) Germany and that his initial goal was to promote emigration. In an effort to rid Germany of Jews, Nazi policy discouraged Jewish immigration to Germany from other countries, so that the immigration opportunities would benefit Aryans. This policy was maintained until October 1941. Browning further contends that the Final Solution was a "twisted road" rather than an intentional policy because Hitler's early support and encouragement of emigration would have been illogical had he intended ultimately to annihilate the Jews.

The Nazi Party arrived at their extermination solution out of frustration. Schleunes argues that "The search for a solution to the Jewish problem had been set into motion by the anti-Semitic energies which constituted the heart of Nazism; it was driven forward by the frustrations of each successive failure. A more extreme approach appeared to be the only alternative to the less-than-total solutions which had proved unsatisfactory or unworkable." The Nazi Party often had conflicting goals that prevented any of their plans from being truly successful. However, in 1939, Germany began its blitzkrieg (lightning war) in Poland. By acquiring more land for lebensraum (living space), Germany also increased the number of Jews under its control. While acquiring control of Poland fulfilled the ideal of lebensraum, it set back Hitler's goal of creating a *judenrein* Germany. Because emigration was not significantly reducing the number of German Jews, not to mention Polish Jews, a new plan was called for.

The next plan was to create ghettos in which Jews could live. Initially, ghettos were created along rail lines, especially in the area near Lublin, Poland. In June 1940 the number of Jews increased again with the German conquest of Holland, Belgium, and France. Germany hoped to annex the French colony of Madagascar so that a ghetto could be created there for European Jews. However, Great Britain would have to be defeated in order for Germany to gain control of the seas and make this plan a reality. Germany delayed the Madagascar plan when Hitler decided to attack the Soviet Union in June 1941.

Hitler was determined, however, that the conquest of the Soviet Union should not complicate the Jewish Question. He decided that Russian Jews would simply be eliminated. This decision prompted a major change in Nazi policy. Whereas prior to June 1941 the Jewish Question had been handled by the physical removal of Jews, afterward the annihilation of Jews became de facto policy.

Under the direction of Reinhard Heydrich, *Einsatzgruppen* (mobile killing units) followed closely behind frontline troops into Russia, executing Jews, political commissars, and other potential enemies of the Reich. The elimination of Russian Jewry quickly became their primary task. This policy did not, however, extend to Poland or the rest of German-occupied Europe. Heydrich had been commissioned in 1939 to organize first the emigration and later the evacuation of Jews from Germany. However, beginning in 1941, the orders changed, though the chain of command did not. By 1941 Nazi policy on the Jews reached an impasse. Annexation and German military successes brought more Jews into the German sphere, but the possibilities of emigration lessened significantly. Nazi leaders began to think of a far more radical and final solution that might be more practical than emigration.

During the summer of 1941 Hitler decided to turn his recently developed bureaucracy of murder, which had worked efficiently in the Soviet Union, against the rest of the Jews of Europe. On 31 July 1941 Hermann Göring, head of the Gestapo, authorized Heydrich "to make all preparations in organizational, practical and material matters necessary for a total solution (*Gesamtlösung*) of the Jewish question in territories under German influence." The Final Solution was a culmination of the work of the *Einsatzgruppen* and the Wannsee Conference,

INTENTIONAL STRATEGY

which was held in January 1942, to deal with questions regarding how to implement a plan of mass murder.

The murder process was fast and deceptive. First, it was carried out in occupied Russia from June 1941 to October 1942. The destruction extended into Poland from March 1942 to August 1943. Beginning in July of 1942 through August of 1943, genocide was instigated in western Europe. The psychological costs to the killers prompted some changes in how the process was completed. Large-scale shootings, such as those carried out by the *Einsatzgruppen* in Russia, were impractical, and thus, concentration camps were connected into extermination camps.

It can be seen through the progression of changes in Nazi policy concerning the Jewish population that there never was a preformulated plan. As emigration, evacuation, and deportation failed, extermination emerged as the plan that would not need revision. The isolation of German Jews during the Nazi years was not an intentional strategy to annihilate them, nor did they perceive it as such. Most German Jews had become accustomed to life within anti-Semitic German society and could not imagine what was being prepared for them.

So it was that 1941 was the critical year in the evolution of Nazi policy toward genocide. The invasion of Russia created a new Jewish problem for Germany that was solved with mass murder. This decision led to the institutionalization of the Final Solution and its application throughout Europe. Though a *judenrein* Germany was Hitler's aim, how he achieved it was the consequence of the failure of earlier, unfeasible plans, not of a carefully implemented strategy.

–MELISSA JANE TAYLOR,
UNIVERSITY OF SOUTH CAROLINA

References

Uwe Dietrich Adam, "An Overall Plan for Anti-Jewish Legislation in the Third Reich," in *Yad Vashem Studies,* volume 11, edited by Livia Rothkirchen (1976), pp. 35–55.

Yehuda Bauer, "Genocide: Was It the Nazis' Original Plan?" in *The "Final Solution": The Implementation of Mass Murder,* volume 1, edited by Michael R. Marrus (Westport, Conn.: Meckler, 1989), pp. 74–84.

Bauer, *The Holocaust in Historical Perspective* (London: Sheldon Press / Seattle: University of Washington Press, 1978).

Norman H. Baynes, ed., *The Speeches of Adolf Hitler: April 1922–August 1939,* 2 volumes (London: Oxford University Press, 1942).

Richard Breitman, *The Architect of Genocide: Himmler and the Final Solution* (New York: Knopf, 1991).

Christopher R. Browning, "The Decision Concerning the Final Solution," in *The "Final Solution": The Implementation of Mass Murder,* volume 1, edited by Marrus (Westport, Conn.: Meckler, 1989), pp. 188–216.

Browning, *The Final Solution and the German Foreign Office* (New York: Holmes & Meier, 1978).

Browning, *The Path to Genocide: Essays on Launching the Final Solution* (Cambridge & New York: Cambridge University Press, 1992).

Richard J. Evans, *Lying about Hitler: History, Holocaust, and the David Irving Trial* (New York: BasicBooks, 2001).

Joachim C. Fest, *Hitler,* translated by Richard and Clara Winston (New York: Harcourt Brace Jovanovich, 1974).

Gerald Fleming, *Hitler and the Final Solution* (Berkeley: University of California Press, 1984).

Sarah Ann Gordon, *Hitler, Germans, and the "Jewish Question"* (Princeton: Princeton University Press, 1984).

Raul Hilberg, *The Destruction of the European Jews* (Chicago: Quadrangle, 1961).

Adolf Hitler, *Monologe im Führerhaupquartier 1941–1944,* edited by Werner Jochmann (Hamburg: Knaus, 1980).

Ian Kershaw, *The Nazi Dictatorship: Problems and Perspectives of Interpretation* (London & Baltimore: Arnold, 1985).

John Lukacs, *The Hitler of History* (New York: Knopf, 1997).

Marrus, *The Holocaust in History* (Hanover, N.H.: University Press of New England, 1987).

Ron Rosenbaum, *Explaining Hitler: The Search for the Origins of His Evil* (New York: Random House, 1998).

Karl A. Schleunes, *The Twisted Road to Auschwitz: Nazi Policy toward German Jews, 1933–1939* (Urbana: University of Illinois Press, 1970).

J. P. Stern, *Hitler: The Führer and the People* (Berkeley: University of California Press, 1975).

IRRATIONALITY

Was the Final Solution a rationally conceived policy or the result of madness inspired by anti-Semitism?

Viewpoint: The only explanation for the Final Solution was uncontrolled madness inspired by anti-Semitic hatred. The policy offered no discernible political or military advantage.

Viewpoint: The Final Solution was a carefully designed policy to provide Lebensraum (living space) for German settlement in the east and to create a "new order" in Europe.

Adolf Hitler was a political gambler who nearly succeeded. He came to power after a decade-long campaign that no one took seriously. He restored and rearmed Germany in defiance of Britain and France, and got away with it. He seized Austria and destroyed Czechoslovakia with little cost to Germany. In 1941 and 1942, when the destruction of the Jews began in earnest, neither Hitler nor anyone else had much reason to doubt his luck would run out anytime soon. Indeed, it might not have. A better-thought-out strategy toward the Soviet Union, a better understanding of Britain and especially of the United States, and a bit of luck here and there might have made the Nazis masters of Europe from the Atlantic to the Urals.

If that assessment were true, and it certainly seemed so to many millions of people at the time, then Hitler's political, military, and ideological goals, however wickedly conceived, were not madness. Yet, the Final Solution, the annihilation of European Jewry, was of a different order than the military and political calculations that brought world domination within his grasp. It offered no apparent military advantages, nor were the masses of German people (whether they became willing executioners or not) clamoring for the Jews in their midst to be killed. Indeed, the Final Solution, implemented under the covering fog of war, was planned and executed in secrecy. It appears to many historians as a completely irrational spasm of violence. The Jews were killed because Hitler and those who shared his vision of a *judenrein* (Jew-free) Europe were obsessed with an anti-Semitic madness that overrode reason. Once the bureaucracy of murder came into existence, it took on a logic and meaning of its own that continued to kill Jews even when the broader war was clearly lost.

Others argue that however evil their plans, there is no evidence that the Nazis were mad. The Final Solution was, it might be argued, a logical necessity if one intended to create a racially pure Europe. Hitler was, in unleashing the Holocaust, looking ahead to a postwar Europe much as U.S. president Franklin D. Roosevelt and British prime minister Winston Churchill did in the Atlantic Charter (1941). Hitler might well have reasoned that since the goal of the war was to ensure the dominance of the Aryan race, then the seemingly irrational costs of implementing the Final Solution were absolutely necessary. Thus, the redirection of resources and personnel away from the battlefronts, and the wasted labor that might have been put to strategic use, were small sacrifices given the grandeur of the goals. However vile the ideology in which it was rooted, the Final Solution might also be seen as flowing quite logically from the reasonable war aims of the Third Reich. In neither argument, of course, can the rationality—or irrationality—of the Final Solution be seen as a justification for either the attempted conquest of Europe or the destruction of the Jews. A failure of the intellect is not the same as a failure of the heart.

Viewpoint:
The only explanation for the Final Solution was uncontrolled madness inspired by anti-Semitic hatred. The policy offered no discernible political or military advantage.

Adolf Hitler did not ride a popular wave of anti-Jewish hatred to power, nor did he simply unleash the pent-up hatred of the German people to bring about genocide. It is absurd to argue that some sort of genocidal consensus underlay the Nazi dictatorship. German anti-Semitism explains everything and nothing. If those crude generalizations were valid, the story of the Third Reich and the Holocaust would be exclusively a German drama, proceeding toward an inevitable climax, with few moral or political lessons beyond the obvious need to ensure that no repetition of these events occurs. In its simplest formulation, the view that Germany was a society pregnant with hate simply replaces the Nazi formula of the "eternal Jew" with the "eternal German." There are few historical problems as difficult and slippery as that of tracing German public opinion and popular attitudes toward Jews in the Weimar Republic (1918–1933) and the Third Reich (1933–1945).

"In rereading the chronicles of Nazism, from its murky beginnings to its convulsed end," wrote Auschwitz survivor Primo Levi in his memoirs, "I cannot avoid the impression of a general atmosphere of uncontrolled madness that seems to me to be unique in history." The Nazi state undertook to kill every Jewish man, woman, and child in pursuit of a biologically defined utopian vision of a racially purified society. The Nazis employed the most modern and rational means available to the modern state in order to achieve this vision: comprehensive data-bases, in order to list those who were worthy of inclusion in the German racial community; carefully written legislation defining Jewish status, based upon the teachings of "racial science"; and, finally, a rational, industrialized murder machinery to eliminate those deemed unworthy. Ultimately, the Nazi regime was willing to subordinate all political and military goals—even the existence of the German state itself—to the achievement of this racial utopia. It is this shocking juxtaposition of rational means in the service of the most murderous and irrational goal that

takes one to the heart of what Joachim C. Fest called "the solemn insanity" of the Nazi regime.

The necessary starting point for any attempt to account for the intensity of Nazi hatred for the Jews is Hitler. According to one influential view, Hitler was able to inject his personal antipathy into the Nazi movement, thus raising his pathology first to the level of a political program and, ultimately, to state policy. Daniel Jonah Goldhagen in his 1996 best-seller, *Hitler's Willing Executioners: Ordinary Germans and the Holocaust,* wrote, "What Hitler and the Nazis actually did was to unshackle and thereby activate Germans' pre-existing, pent-up anti-Semitism." According to Goldhagen, Hitler's political triumph smashed the legal and political barriers that had dammed up the "virulent" anti-Jewish resentments of ordinary Germans since the nineteenth century. Hitler's political success thus reflected the anti-Semitic consensus of the German people. Does this sweeping generalization hold up under careful scrutiny? The answer is no.

Nazi anti-Semitism was irrational in a political as well as a moral sense. German popular opinion on the Jewish Question ranged from a small minority of fanatic anti-Semites at one extreme; through a silent majority who had no strong feelings on the issue one way or the other; and, finally, to a smaller group of secular and religious people on the other extreme who rejected anti-Semitism. Despite a long tradition of suspicion of and hostility toward Jews and years of Nazi agitation, this basic formation of opinion changed little during the Weimar years and the Third Reich. It is one thing to attempt to manipulate a generalized attitude of public distrust toward a minority group for political gain; it is quite another task to attempt to create a consensus for genocide. Throughout his career Hitler attempted the first—although, arguably, never as part of a consistent, sustained political strategy—but he utterly rejected the second course.

There is a scholarly consensus that anti-Semitism was central to Hitler's personality, but was Hitler's anti-Semitism central to his political appeal? Was there an unspoken consensus in the Third Reich for the persecution of German Jews? Once again, the answer is no. However, both those questions deserve a serious response. Many Germans have argued that public acquiescence to the isolation and persecution of German Jews was more a product of fear than a reflection of consensus. Philosopher Karl Jaspers argued this point forcefully: "Germany under the Nazi regime was a prison. The guilt of getting into it is a political guilt. Once

IRRATIONALITY

British soldier bulldozing corpses in preparation for burial at Bergen-Belsen, 1945

(Bildarchiv Preussischer Kulturbesitz, Berlin)

the gates were shut, however, a prison break from within was no longer possible."

The Third Reich was neither a constitutional state nor a democracy. The decision to proceed from escalating persecution to genocide was a political one, but one that reached within the senior leadership of the Nazi Party and the German state in such secrecy that historians still debate precisely when, where, and how the final decision was made. This commitment to secrecy certainly indicates that Hitler had little confidence that the German public would support his genocidal project. Yet, the regime calculated correctly that a broad section of the German population would accept quasi-legal steps to isolate Jews economically and politically. Once the machinery of dictatorship was firmly in place, however, the political attitudes of ordinary Germans became just one more factor to be manipulated.

If one accepts for a moment the "intentionalist" view that Hitler was committed to a policy of genocide from the beginning of his career, it is apparent that he saw many political dangers in the pursuit of that goal. For proof of that proposition one merely needs to note the gradual escalation from discrimination to murder. Although Hitler's goals were fixed and non-negotiable, his political tactics were flexible, and he was not committed to a rigid schedule of step-by-step per-

secution leading to the Final Solution. He admitted as much at his headquarters in October 1941. In a monologue only published in 1980, Hitler mused, "I had to remain inactive for a long time against the Jews too. There's no sense in artificially making extra difficulties for oneself; the more cleverly one operates, the better."

A major trend in recent literature on the Holocaust focuses upon the problem of finding out what "ordinary Germans" felt about the Jewish Question, both before and after 1933. Fortunately, there is some empirical data available, ranging from electoral statistics to SS and Gestapo reports. The outlawed Social Democratic Party (SOPADE) also attempted to trace public opinion in Germany after 1933. The problem facing the historian is the task of making sense of this ambiguous evidence. It is easier to test the view that the Nazis rode a wave of anti-Jewish hatred to political power. If the electoral statistics are any indication, it is difficult to make the case that anti-Semitism was a viable political issue at all. If anything, the evidence indicates the reverse was the case. As William Sheridan Allen put it, German voters "were drawn to anti-Semitism because they were drawn to Hitler, not the other way around."

One can see this case clearly from an examination of Nazi political tactics. Hitler's earliest speeches centered upon hysterical flights of anti-Jewish hatred. But as the Nazi Party emerged into the political mainstream, Hitler was careful to tone down his anti-Jewish rhetoric in the interest of presenting a more statesman-like image to voters. In the campaign leading up to the vital Reichstag elections of September 1930, Hitler seldom mentioned Jews or the Jewish Question in any of his public speeches. Instead, he stressed the theme of German economic and political collapse under the parliamentary system, which only the National Socialist German Workers' Party (NSDAP) could rectify.

In general, anti-Semitic propaganda did little to enhance the popular appeal of the Nazi Party before 1930. Afterward, Nazi speakers might employ anti-Jewish rhetoric when courting small business or farmers in particular regions, but the Party also regarded anti-Semitism as a political liability when appealing to the German business community for financial support. The Jewish Question might have obsessed Hitler in private, but he clearly recognized that the German electorate did not share his obsession. In the last free election of 1932, some 67 percent of Germans voted against Hitler, although it is certainly possible that some of those who voted against the Nazis also disliked Jews. "It is generally accepted," writes Fritz Stern, "that the more the Nazis tried to widen their appeal, the more they muted their anti-Semitic theme."

After 1933 the regime would have preferred the unquestioned, fanatical support of the German people for their policy of escalating persecution of the Jews, but ultimately, the Nazis settled for indifference. In fact, the Jewish Question only rarely emerged as a political issue on the national stage. For example, amid a loud propaganda campaign, Hitler declared a national boycott against Jewish businesses to begin on 1 April 1933 and to last for four days. Many Berlin shoppers, putting economic self-interest ahead of ideology, simply ignored the Storm Trooper (SA) protestors at the doors of department stores and pushed past to shop as usual. Although the lack of popular support for the boycott was disappointing for Hitler, the public response also held some ominous signs for the future of the Jewish community. Ordinary Germans were apparently not straining (as Goldhagen argues) to unleash their pent-up anger against Jewish businesses. Nevertheless, few individuals protested the harassment of Jewish shopkeepers. The regime concluded that ordinary Germans would be willing to ignore discriminatory policies and even public acts of violence against the Jewish minority so long as those acts were carried out by the state under a facade of legality and did not seem to threaten a general breakdown of law and order.

What did the German public think about Jews? The answer, troubling both to the Nazi regime and to current historians alike, is not much. It is particularly difficult to judge the intensity of public reaction to the Jewish Question. Recent research discredits the view that German society was "intoxicated" with hatred for Jews, but there is no shortage of evidence to indicate that there existed a widespread mistrust of Jews. The problem lies in linking what the historian Michael Müller-Claudius called this "static hatred" of Jews to the Holocaust. To a committed minority of Nazi true believers, the Jewish Question was vital; however, much of the German public remained as indifferent to the anti-Jewish tirades in the Nazi media as they were to the plight of the Jewish minority. As Ian Kershaw put it: "I should like to think that had I been around at the time I would have been a convinced anti-Nazi engaged in the underground resistance fight. However, I know really that I would have been as confused and felt as helpless as most people I am writing about."

The Bavarians studied by Kershaw were remarkably resistant to the Nazi regime's attempt to instill "a dynamic, passionate hatred" of Jews by propaganda. Bavarians simply did not accept the notion that the Jews lay behind current economic or political problems. Kershaw concluded that Nazi anti-Semitism "seemed largely abstract, academic, and unrelated to their own problems." Many historians have been struck by the frequency of complaints in Gestapo reports about ordinary Germans grumbling against the regime and its racial policies or simply doing random acts of kindness, such as giving a Jew one's seat on a streetcar. The Jewish Question only took center stage on rare occasions, such as during the *Kristallnacht* (Night of the Broken Glass) pogrom of 9 November 1938.

From a public relations perspective, *Kristallnacht*—the carefully organized nationwide outburst of anti-Jewish violence—was not a success. Propaganda Minister Joseph Goebbels's claim that *Kristallnacht* was a "spontaneous" expression of public anger at the Jews was widely ridiculed. The Gestapo and the Party noted widespread criticism of the violent, destructive character of the *Kristallnacht* rioting. Yet, once again, few Germans expressed outrage at the assault upon the Jewish minority. One can generalize that Nazi anti-Semitic propaganda failed to mobilize and focus the anger of the public upon Jews. This failure did little to assist Jews or hamper the regime in the push for even more radical means to isolate the Jews from the larger population. Public criticism soon died down. The same calculation of self-interest that might motivate a citizen to continue doing business with a Jewish shopkeeper also worked to deter public protest. The cost of grumbling might well include time in prison or a concentration camp. In other words, the German population did not object to the disenfranchisement and segregation of Jews, but it disliked acts of public violence. Kershaw concluded in a famous sentence: "The road to Auschwitz was built with hate, but paved with indifference."

In the Third Reich, indifference could be a conscious political choice—a decision to put self-interest above empathy and to look the other way. Indifference might also be defined, in the words of Otto Dov Kulka, as "passive complicity." Nazi functionaries might bemoan the public failure to embrace the racial policies of the regime, while police organizations such as the SS and Gestapo might keep a careful watch on those Germans courageous or stubborn enough to undertake public acts of kindness toward Jews, but ultimately, the regime managed to ensure that the German public would choose to look the other way. Nazi Germany was a culture of complicity rather than a culture of anti-Semitism. The widespread existence of anti-Semitism explains neither the political triumph of Hitler nor the Holocaust. To carry out a project of genocide, two groups of people were necessary: a genocidal political elite dominating the German state, and a silent majority willing to turn a blind eye. "In Hitler's Germany," wrote Primo Levi, "a particular code was widespread: those who knew did not talk; those who did not know did not ask questions; those who did ask questions received no answers. In this way, the typical German citizen won and defended his ignorance."

–LARRY L. PING, SOUTHERN UTAH UNIVERSITY

Viewpoint:
The Final Solution was a carefully designed policy to provide Lebensraum (living space) for German settlement in the east and to create a "new order" in Europe.

Attributing rational motives of any kind to the perpetrators of the Holocaust is highly controversial because it may seem to perversely qualify the evil of the Nazi genocide. The attempt to provide a rational explanation for criminality on such a scale may seem misguided, an insult to the memory of millions of innocent victims who died for no other cause than irrational Nazi hatred. If practical reasons and utilitarian judg-

ments contributed to the process that led to the destruction of the Jews, the Nazi leaders who decided on the killings may no longer appear as the monsters that they were. Such a conclusion obviously violates a powerful taboo that has been firmly in place since the end of World War II in 1945.

The obvious horror and irrationality of mass murder seems to require a correspondingly irrational motivation. But to recognize that a degree of rational self-interest and calculation contributed to the process of destruction is not to argue that there was anything rational about the Nazi project of acquiring Lebensraum (living space) and establishing a new order based on a nefarious and spurious doctrine of superior and inferior races. To point to rational motives in Nazi actions is not to credit them with ethical principles or to suggest that what they did was in any way defensible. Indeed, the complex origins of the Holocaust stand as the most graphic warning of the lethal consequences inherent not only in primitive racial bigotry and ethnic hatred, but potentially also in policies of economic rationalization and modernization if ethical judgment is suspended in the ruthless pursuit of efficiency and productivity.

Two postulates underlying the view that the Nazi destruction of the Jews had no rational political function (other than scapegoating a long-persecuted minority to capitalize on popular prejudices) merit closer examination. One is the hypothesis that the anti-Semitism that culminated in the Nazi destruction of the Jews was entirely based on irrational fantasies and imaginary fears. The second questionable postulate is that the Nazis' irrational racial ideology alone is sufficient to explain the causation of the Holocaust. Nazi anti-Semitism, however, cannot be reduced entirely to irrational fantasy or political expediency; rational, utilitarian motives played a significant part in the Holocaust.

Anti-Semitism cannot be reduced to politically expedient scapegoating or irrational fantasy. Nazi leaders were well aware that they could not achieve their goals of national expansion and the domination of Europe without war. The primary lesson they seemed to have derived from World War I (1914–1918) was that national unity was the most important prerequisite for fighting a successful war. It was Jews and the Left (virtually identical in the Nazi mind) that had supposedly deprived Germany of victory in World War I and forced German capitulation. This experience led the Nazis to believe that Germany, with its relatively small population and limited resources, could only win a major war if the effort were fully supported by the national community. The Nazis' major aim, upon Adolf Hitler's accession to power in January 1933, was the creation of

TWENTY-THREE

A German construction engineer, H. F. Graebe, testified at Nuremberg about the systematic murder of Jews at Dubno in the Ukraine in October 1942:

I heard a quick succession of shots from behind one of the mounds of earth. The people who had got off the lorries—men, women, and children of all ages—had to undress upon the order of a SS man, who carried a riding or dog whip. They had to put their clothes on separate piles of shoes, top clothing and underclothing. I saw a heap of shoes that must have contained 800 to 1000 pairs, great piles of clothes and undergarments. Without screaming or weeping these people undressed, stood in family groups, kissed each other, said their farewells, and waited for a sign from another SS man, who stood near the pit, also with a whip in his hand. During the fifteen minutes that I stood near the pit, I did not hear anyone complain or beg for mercy.

I watched a family of about eight, a man and a woman, both about 50, with their children, aged about one, eight and ten, and two grown-up daughters of about 20 to 24. An old woman with snow-white hair was holding the one-year-old child in her arms, singing something to it and tickling it. The child was crowing with delight. The man and wife were looking on with tears in their eyes. The father was holding the hand of a boy of about ten, speaking to him softly. The boy was fighting back his tears. The father pointed to the sky, stroked the boy's head and seemed to explain something to him. At the moment the SS man at the pit shouted something to his comrade, who separated off about 20 persons and ordered them to go behind the mound of earth. Among them was the family that I have mentioned. I still clearly remember a dark-haired, slim girl who pointed to herself as she passed close to me and said "Twenty-three."

I walked to the other side of the mound and found myself standing before an enormous grave. The people lay so closely packed, one on top of the other, that only their heads were visible. Nearly all had blood running over their shoulders from their heads. Some of them were still moving. Some lifted an arm and turned a head to show that they were still alive. The pit was already two-thirds full. I estimated that it contained about 1000 people. I looked round for the man who had shot them. He was an SS man, who was sitting on the edge of the narrow end of the pit, his legs dangling into it. He had a sub-machine gun across his knees and was smoking a cigarette. The people, completely naked, went down some steps which had been cut in the clay wall of the pit and climbed over the heads of those already lying there, to the place indicated by the SS man. They laid down in front of the dead or injured people. Some of them caressed those who were still alive and spoke to them softly. Then I heard a series of shots. I looked into the pit and saw that the bodies were twitching or that the heads lay motionless on top of the bodies which lay before them. Blood was pouring from their necks.

Source: *"From the Ghetto to the Death Pit: Submission or Struggle?"* in Witness to the Holocaust, *edited by Azriel Eisenberg (New York: Pilgrim Press, 1981), p. 269.*

---

the kind of ethnic and ideological unity and top-down authority that would prepare Germany to win the war they would have to wage to achieve their long-term objectives. The chief purpose of Nazi racial legislation and *gleichschaltung* (coordination) was to insure full ideological consensus by purging German society of all ethnic diversity and political dissent. A crucial component of this policy of suppressing democracy, diversity, and dissent—and thereby removing obstacles to the successful prosecution of a war of expansion—was to purge all Jews and opponents of National Socialism from positions of influence and to drive them out of Germany.

Although the Nazi project of territorial expansion and population redistribution was certainly based on a brutal social Darwinist ideology, a fallacious doctrine of racial supremacy, and an unrealistic assessment of German capability and power, the Nazis were not irrational in assuming that their goals could only be achieved by eliminating all liberal and democratic opposition in Germany. Nor were the Nazis irrational in assuming that an essential precondition for the suppression of liberalism and social democracy was the elimination of Jewish influence, and hence the Jewish presence, in German society or in areas under German control. Certainly, the

Nazis built on a long tradition of exploiting popular anti-Semitism for political purposes. As a young man in Vienna, Hitler admired the ability of mayor Karl Lueger to discredit the liberal and social democratic movements by blaming their Jewish leadership for economic problems. But Lueger's anti-Semitism was not just a cynical ploy to attract malcontents. It rested on the fact that most Jews in Vienna tended to support the liberal or social democratic parties. However useful anti-Semitism might have been to the Nazis as a means of scapegoating the Jews and channeling public energies into "purifying" the German "race," at the heart of Nazi anti-Semitism lay the conviction that most Jews would oppose and subvert nationalist efforts to secure German supremacy in Europe (and eventually the world). Irrational though Nazi conspiracy theories might have been in exaggerating Jewish power in Germany or in the world, Right-wing hatred of the Jews rested on the recognition that German (and non-German) Jews overwhelmingly supported the progressive and emancipatory political movements of the Left that promised Jews full civil rights and equality of opportunity. Even though the Nazis' assertion that Jews fostered democracy, liberalism, and socialism to gain political control of their host countries was surely a paranoid fantasy, the point is that the Nazis had to suppress these movements if they hoped to achieve their long-term nationalist and imperialist aims, and neutralizing the influence of the Jews would certainly have the desired effect not only of gaining votes but also of weakening the Left. The Nazis no doubt exaggerated Jewish power and influence, but their assumption that the removal of Jewish influence would fatally weaken the liberalizing or egalitarian political movements that blocked the achievement of Nazi aims was not unfounded.

The Nazi project (which with the benefit of hindsight is now known to have been unattainable) was nothing less than the creation of a new ethnographic order in the vast new territories to be conquered for the expanded Reich in the east. It was in the context of this project that the criminal decision to systematically murder all the Jews of Europe was reached. The research of German historians Götz Aly and Susanne Heim has revealed the strong linkage between German settlement policy in the east and the Holocaust. Their interpretation—epitomized in their provocative phrase, "The economy of the final solution"—is controversial because, in emphasizing bureaucratic plans aimed at economic modernization and rationalization in the causation of the Holocaust, Aly and Heim seem to downplay the significance of irrational racial ideology. In view of the absurdity of Nazi racial ideology, it is not surprising that their contention that intellectuals and social scientists played a leading role in developing plans for mass murder has been greeted with widespread skepticism and even protest. They respond quite persuasively, however, that emphasizing irrationality in the causation of the Holocaust is a way of exculpating the German bureaucratic elite, who after the war claimed that they had no influence on the decision making of the Nazi leadership.

Although Aly and Heim may well have exaggerated the impact of mid-level population experts and planners on Nazi decision making, thus confusing bureaucratic rationalizations with actual motive causes, their conclusion that the Holocaust was conceived as an integral part of a much broader plan of colonization, rationalization, deportation, and murder has been widely accepted by historians—even if the Holocaust was the only part of the plan actually to have been implemented in the course of a war in which growing Allied power increasingly limited German options. The newly acquired Lebensraum was to be progressively Germanized in a grandiose project that involved the expulsion and deportation of millions of ethnic Jews and Slavs and their replacement by German and/or Nordic settlers. From the start German plans to create favorable living conditions for ethnic German settlers in conquered areas were based on the perfidious and cold-blooded premise that many millions of people of non-German ethnicity would have to be "resettled" and that millions would die in the process. The infamous *Generalplan Ost*, drawn up on Heinrich Himmler's instructions in June 1941, called for the resettlement of 45 million Russians, Poles, and Jews to areas east of the Urals in a population transfer in which 30 million people were expected to lose their lives.

Aly and historians of the Hamburg Institut für Sozialforschung have carefully traced the connections between anti-Jewish policy and settlement schemes in the east in the origins of the Holocaust and have demonstrated how the Final Solution evolved after the successive failures of other overly ambitious population resettlement plans. The deportation of Jews from territory controlled by the Reich was the essential condition of all population redistribution plans. From the start of the war until the end of 1940 close to half a million *Volksdeutsche* (ethnic Germans from outside the Reich borders) were brought "home into the Reich" from southeastern Europe, Poland, and the Baltic states. To make way for these new settlers, hundreds of thousands of Jews and Poles were deported from the "incorporated territories" (areas of Poland annexed to the Reich) to the portion of occupied Poland known as the General-Gouvernement. The ghettoization of Jews in 1939–1940 was itself conceived as an interim solution to make Jewish homes and property available for Polish and German resettlement while concen-

IRRATIONALITY

trating Jews in urban areas for future deportation to as yet undetermined destinations. Original Nazi plans calling for the creation of a permanent Jewish reservation in the Lublin area were dropped mainly for economic reasons as German policy shifted in the course of 1940 from treating the General-Gouvernement as a dumping ground for undesirables to making it economically productive for the war effort. Governor General Hans Frank insisted that the General-Gouvernement could never become economically viable, much less the hoped-for granary for the German Reich, if a further influx of Jews were permitted. Even the *Wehrmacht* (German army), which generally gave a much higher priority to the exploitation of Jewish labor than the SS officials in charge of the Jewish ghettos, opposed a further influx of Jews for security reasons, especially after the General-Gouvernement became a staging area for Operation Barbarossa in late 1940. The scheme of resettling Jews on the island of Madagascar (adopted after the fall of France) proved to be even more short-lived when the essential precondition for such an undertaking, peace with Britain on German terms, could not be secured. Once the decision to invade the Soviet Union was made in December 1940, SS planners expected the vast territories east of the Urals to become available for the resettlement of Jews and Slavs. Of course, all German resettlement schemes always included the expectation of massive attrition through forced labor, starvation, and inadequate living conditions, but it was the failure of schemes aimed at economic rationalization and reorganization to permit German colonization that ultimately led to the systematic killing of the Holocaust.

Economic criteria had already played an important role in Nazi anti-Jewish policies before the war. The policy of forced emigration was not solely inspired by racial ideology but was also based on hard-nosed economic calculations (as well as, of course, outright greed). As Aly and Heim point out, national, regional, and local authorities consistently viewed the elimination of Jews as a form of economic relief and as a key to rationalization and "downsizing," especially of the retail sector. The Aryanization program, which became mandatory after the *Kristallnacht* pogrom of November 1938, was certainly a means for Germans to acquire Jewish property, but it was also conceived as a conscious effort to relieve the hard-pressed German *Mittelstand* (middle class) of Jewish competition. The great majority of Jewish businesses in both Germany and Austria was closed entirely in the interests of *gesundschrumpfung* (curtailment of production in order to improve the health of the economy).

Of course, it would be absurd to deny that racial ideology was the crucial determinant in the Nazi persecution of the Jews. But the interconnection of economic and ideological criteria in the selection of victims for destruction is perhaps most clearly apparent in the T-4 euthanasia program that went into effect at the start of the war. The links between the systematic destruction of the mentally and physically disabled and the Holocaust have been clearly demonstrated in the works of many German and American historians. Not only was the technology employed in the Final Solution—the use of poison gas in chambers disguised as shower rooms—pioneered in the T-4 program, the same personnel who carried out the euthanasia program provided the technical expertise in the implementation of the systematic murder of the Jews. It is therefore instructive to examine the genealogy of this program.

If the eugenic purification of the race had been the sole purpose of euthanasia, forced sterilization, already pursued in the 1930s, would have served the purpose equally well. The financial costs to the state and society of caring for the disabled (and other persons unable to earn their own living) provided a major rationale both for eugenic sterilization and for euthanasia. The Nazi government sought to gain public support for eugenic measures mainly by touting its merits as a means of resolving social problems such as crime or alcoholism and of reducing state expenditures for social programs. Already in World War I, mentally and physically handicapped patients had been deliberately allowed to die in order to make food and other resources, including hospital space, available for the war effort. This pattern was repeated in a much more deliberate form and on a much larger scale at the start of World War II (1939–1945). Aly and Heim have documented the close linkage between resettlement plans and euthanasia. At the same time as Jews and Poles from newly conquered Polish territory were deported to permit the resettlement of ethnic Germans from the Baltic states and southeastern Europe, thousands of patients were murdered in mental hospitals—facilities that were then frequently used as temporary housing for ethnic German refugees.

One argument frequently advanced to emphasize the irrationality of Nazi motives is that the Nazis would have served their interests far more effectively by utilizing Jewish labor instead of destroying it. The ideologically motivated destruction of the Jews, so the argument goes, impeded rather than advanced the Nazis' goals of labor mobilization and economic rationalization both in Germany and in conquered areas. It is certainly true that as the Nazis' destructive practices escalated during the war, the criteria of fitness for labor was increasingly ignored in the selection of victims for destruction. However, it must be borne in mind that Nazi experts identified the principal economic problem in central and eastern

IRRATIONALITY

Europe not as a shortage of labor but as agrarian overpopulation leading to low productivity and a shortage of food. Recent research has shown, in the words of Christopher R. Browning, that "food shortages played a crucial role for reaching consensus among the SS, military, and civil administration that the killing of Jews was not only ideologically desirable but economically necessary." Here again, Nazi policies were governed by the specter of the economic blockade of World War I and the internal collapse it precipitated. That the Nazis were more concerned about food shortages than labor shortages may be seen from their treatment of Soviet prisoners of war. Millions of Soviet prisoners of war were deliberately allowed to die of starvation in the first few months of the German invasion in 1941, despite criticism of this policy by some officials of Alfred Rosenberg's Ministry for the Occupied Eastern Territories. It was only after it became apparent that the war would be much longer than originally anticipated that the Nazis turned to a policy of utilizing Soviet labor in 1942. This decision, in turn, reduced the need for Jewish labor. Nazi administrators similarly viewed the Jewish ghettos in the east as an unacceptable economic burden rather than as a source of needed labor.

The strongest argument for the irrationality of the Nazi leadership is that the Holocaust impeded the German war effort and diverted needed resources from the fighting fronts. While the use of railway facilities, manpower, rolling stock, and scarce fuel for transporting victims to the killing sites certainly reduced the number of days that the *Wehrmacht* could hold out against the Allied armies in the closing stages of the war, the argument that the Holocaust was irrational because it compromised the military capability of the Third Reich probably exaggerates the impact of the resources required to implement the killing program. More important, it overlooks the fact that from the start, elimination of the Jews was regarded as an essential means to winning the war. There is no doubt that by the end of the war the killing process had achieved a momentum of its own quite unrelated to the requirements of a *Wehrmacht* plagued by increasing shortages, lack of manpower, and an ever worsening military crisis. But this situation does not change the fact that the killing program evolved in a sequence of events in which economic and utilitarian motives played a prominent role.

It is misleading to think of racial ideology and economic rationalization as mutually exclusive. The relationship between racial prejudice and economic planning was more interactive and dialectical. Of course, racial ideology played a fundamental role in Nazi decisions to target Jews as their primary victims and in removing all moral scruples in the abusive treatment and ultimate murder of Jews. Nazi racial ideology gave social scientists the opportunity to translate their utopian plans of economic rationalization into practice without compromise, thus in turn giving Nazi ideology a rational veneer. At its inception, at least, the Final Solution was not merely the result of completely irrational hatred but was conceived as an essential means of winning the war and achieving fundamental Nazi aims. Once under way, to be sure, the genocide developed a momentum and dynamic of its own. The physical destruction of the Jews became an end in itself, the only war aim the Nazis had any prospect of realizing even in defeat.

Pointing out the rational features of the decision-making process that led to the Final Solution (in the framework of Nazi policies that were indeed irrational, especially given the likelihood of their failure) in no way reduces the moral stigma of this horrendous crime. To understand is not to excuse or forgive or in any other way to suspend moral judgment. But understanding is important to the historian's vocation and is vital to prevention of similar atrocities in the future. To discount utilitarian and practical considerations in the origins of the Holocaust may be reassuring, but it may also blind us to the dangers of practical utilitarian reasoning and the complexity of historical causation. History offers much evidence, not least in the period since the end of World War II, that utilitarian rational thinking in pursuit of efficiency and economic rationalization can be entirely divorced from ethical values and may lead to outcomes that are clearly in conflict with accepted moral norms and universal human rights. To implicate rational utilitarian thinking in the motives of the bureaucratic perpetrators is not to dispute or diminish the immorality of their actions. It may seem a highly disconcerting and unpalatable conclusion, but may be true nonetheless, that most large-scale atrocities, including the genocide of the Holocaust, are committed not by primitive barbarians in the grip of irrational emotions but by rational people pursuing what seemed to them to be rational goals by the most efficient and technologically advanced means available.

–ROD STACKELBERG,
GONZAGA UNIVERSITY

References

William Sheridan Allen, *The Nazi Seizure of Power: The Experience of a Single German Town, 1922–1945* (Chicago: Quadrangle, 1965).

IRRATIONALITY

Götz Aly, *"Final Solution:" Nazi Population Policy and the Murder of the European Jews,* translated by Belinda Cooper and Allison Brown (London & New York: Arnold / New York: Oxford University Press, 1999).

Aly, "The Planning Intelligentsia and the 'Final Solution,'" in *The Holocaust: Origins, Implementation, Aftermath,* edited by Omer Bartov (London: Routledge, 2000), pp. 92–105.

Aly, Peter Chroust, and Christian Pross, *Cleansing the Fatherland: Nazi Medicine and Racial Hygiene,* translated by Cooper (Baltimore: Johns Hopkins University Press, 1994).

Aly and Susanne Heim, *Vordenker der Vernichtung: Auschwitz und die Pläne für eine neue europäische Ordnung* (Hamburg: Hoffmann & Campe, 1991).

Zygmunt Bauman, *Modernity and the Holocaust* (Ithaca, N.Y.: Cornell University Press, 1989).

Christopher R. Browning, *Nazi Policy, Jewish Workers, German Killers* (Cambridge & New York: Cambridge University Press, 2000).

Michael Burleigh, "A 'Political Economy of the Final Solution?': Reflections on Modernity, Historians, and the Holocaust," in *Ethics and Extermination: Reflections on Nazi Genocide* (New York: Cambridge University Press, 1997), pp. 169–182.

Daniel Jonah Goldhagen, *Hitler's Willing Executioners: Ordinary Germans and the Holocaust* (New York: Knopf, 1996).

Adolf Hitler, *Monologe im Führerhauptquartier 1941–1944,* edited by Werner Jochmann (Hamburg: Knaus, 1980).

Karl Jaspers, *The Question of German Guilt,* translated by E. B. Ashton (New York: Capricorn, 1961).

Ian Kershaw, *Popular Opinion and Political Dissent in the Third Reich: Bavaria 1933–1945* (Oxford: Clarendon Press / New York: Oxford University Press, 1983).

Otto Dov Kulka, "Public Opinion in Nazi Germany and the 'Jewish Question,'" *Jerusalem Quarterly,* 25 (1982): 121–144.

Primo Levi, *The Reawakening,* translated by Stuart Woolf (New York: Collier, 1965).

Peter Pulzer, *The Rise of Political Anti-Semitism in Germany and Austria,* revised edition (Cambridge, Mass.: Harvard University Press, 1988).

Fritz Stern, "The Goldhagen Controversy," *Foreign Affairs,* 75 (November–December 1996).

IRRATIONALITY

ISRAEL

Was the Holocaust a decisive factor in the creation of the modern State of Israel?

Viewpoint: Yes. The Holocaust was an important catalyst for the creation of Israel, focusing world attention on the need for a Jewish State.

Viewpoint: No. The political and moral foundation of the modern State of Israel was established long before World War II, and the Jewish nation would have been created eventually whether or not the Holocaust had occurred.

"We are a people—one people. . . . Oppression and persecution cannot exterminate us. No nation on earth has survived such struggles as we have undergone." These words, appropriate to the Jewish experience in the middle years of the twentieth century, were written by Austrian-born Jewish lawyer and journalist Theodor Herzl in *Der Judenstaat* (The Jewish State, 1896). They record with dismay the growth of a modern strain of virulent anti-Semitism in Europe and note its tendency to combine with aggressive nationalism. He was convinced that "oppression and persecution" were certain to continue in coming years, no matter how well the Jews of Europe assimilated with the culture of the nations in which they lived. But, Herzl opined, such anti-Semitism might yet work to the Jews' advantage: "We are one people—our enemies have made us one without our consent. . . . Distress binds us together, and, thus united, we suddenly discover our strength." Indeed, he continued, the Jews were strong enough to form a "model state" of their own, preferably in Palestine ("our ever-memorable historic home"). Convinced though he was that such an independent nation would provide a secure haven for all the Jews in the world, Herzl did not expect to see it created in his lifetime.

Four decades after Herzl's death (1904), both of his predictions were realized. Two events, separated by less than five years, arguably define the history of the Jewish people in the twentieth century. The first was the murder of one-third of the world's 1939 Jewish population in the Holocaust. The second was the emergence in 1948 of the State of Israel as a Jewish national home. Beyond the obvious fact that both events involved Jews, the close chronological sequence suggests a direct link exists between the Holocaust and the formation of Israel. The exact nature of the connection remains open to debate.

Viewpoint:
Yes. The Holocaust was an important catalyst for the creation of Israel, focusing world attention on the need for a Jewish State.

In 1981 Israeli novelist A. B. Yehoshua wrote:

There are some who say . . . that it was the Holocaust that, as it were, begat the State of Israel. This assertion I reject totally, on both factual and moral grounds. The State of Israel could also have been established had there been no Holocaust. In fact, the State of Israel would today be much, much stronger had a third of its people not been wiped out. And on moral grounds, the Holocaust simply cannot be accepted by virtue of the later establishment of the State of Israel. If we were confronted with the choice: no Holocaust and therefore no State of Israel, I doubt that any of us would dare say: Let there be a Holocaust so that the state of Israel can be established.

One year earlier Israeli novelist and Holocaust survivor Aharon Appelfeld contended that:

On that long coast, we, the refugees and survivors, parted to go our various ways. Opposing impulses were intertwined there. Some turned their backs and left everything behind; others held tight to every remaining fragment and Jewish memory. I have not come to judge anyone. But let it be said that the desire of those who made the choice of Eretz Israel [the land of Israel] was for a recovery beyond that of the body.

Yehoshua is correct to insist that the Holocaust should not be considered a direct cause of the establishment of the State of Israel. Indeed, the idea is abhorrent. Certainly, most Jews would have preferred saving the lives of Jews who died in the Holocaust to establishing the Jewish State. Nor did guilt feelings about the murder of two-thirds of European Jewry cause the United Nations to vote for the partition of Palestine in 1947; rather, most of the supporters of partition were motivated by political considerations. Still, Appelfeld is also correct in recognizing a connection between the two most important events in modern Jewish history. However, the connection is broader and more concrete than the spiritual one that Appelfeld describes, and it was recognized by many individuals and groups both during the Holocaust and immediately after it. What is more, it continues to be recognized.

On the one hand, to contemporary Jewry, especially to American and Israeli Jews, the two events seem to mirror each other so that the Holocaust provides an object lesson for the necessity of supporting the state of Israel. As Dr. Chaim Weizmann, who would become the first president of the State of Israel, wrote to President Harry S Truman in 1948, just a few weeks before Truman made his historic decision to recognize the newly independent country:

The choice for our people, Mr. President, is between statehood and extermination. History and providence have placed this issue in your hands, and I am confident that you will yet decide it in the spirit of the moral law.

Thus, the Holocaust stands for the denial of life to anyone and anything Jewish, while the State of Israel stands for the protection of every aspect of Jewish existence. The Holocaust demonstrates Jewish powerlessness and victimization, while the State of Israel demonstrates Jewish power and self-determination. During

the Holocaust, Jewish resistance was tragically restricted by the overwhelming force and organization of the Germans; Israel, a sovereign nation, makes its own decisions, even if it sometimes displeases its allies. Although room is always open for negotiation and compromise, Israel refuses to go along with life-and-death decisions made by others. In addition, during the Holocaust, the reserved and tactful diplomacy engaged in by American Jewry did not exert enough pressure on the U.S. government to provide any meaningful aid to the Jews of Europe. Today, therefore, American Jews have become forceful in pursuing support for their fellow Jews and do not hesitate to use politically sophisticated tactics to defend Israel.

On the other hand, the connection between Jewish suffering under German occupation and Jewish settlement in what was then Palestine was also recognized during World War II (1939–1945), especially as the terrible nature of European Jewry's situation became increasingly clear. Thus, although the Roosevelt administration was unwilling to change American immigration laws to allow large numbers of Jewish refugees fleeing the Nazis to enter the United States, it did try to get Great Britain to modify the White Paper (1939), which had drastically limited Jewish immigration to Palestine. In the mid 1940s several resolutions were passed in the U.S. House of Representatives and U.S. Senate calling for a Jewish State in Palestine. In the presidential election of 1944 both the Republican and Democratic Party platforms called for the establishment of a Jewish state in Palestine. Meanwhile, in separate letters to Senator Robert A. Taft (R–Ohio) and Senator Robert F. Wagner (D–New York) in October 1944, President Franklin D. Roosevelt committed himself personally to a "free and democratic Jewish commonwealth in Palestine."

Harry S Truman, Roosevelt's successor as president, also recognized this connection. As early as 1942, while he was still a senator, Truman called for the admission of Jewish refugees to the United States, and in 1943 he urged that they be allowed to enter Palestine. Upon taking office in April 1945, he made it clear that his sympathies remained with the Jews and that he accepted the Balfour Declaration (1917), in which the British government endorsed the establishment of "a Jewish homeland in Palestine," explaining that it was in keeping with former U.S. president Woodrow Wilson's principle of "self-determination" of nations. Truman also initiated several studies of the Palestine situation that supported his belief that, because of the havoc wrought by the Holocaust, Jews were also in need of a homeland. What is more, he maintained this position in the face of opposi-

DISPLACED JEWS

Earl G. Harrison, who was sent by President Harry S Truman to assess the condition of Jews in the Displaced Persons (DP) camps, wrote in a preliminary report to the president:

While it is impossible to state accurately the number of Jews now in that part of Germany not under Russian occupation, all indications point to the fact that the number is small, with one hundred thousand probably the top figure; some informed persons contend the number is considerably smaller. The principal nationality groups are Poles, Hungarians, Rumanians, Germans and Austrians.

The first and plainest need of these people is a recognition of their actual status and by this I mean their status as Jews. Most of them have spent years in the worst of the concentration camps. In many cases, although the full extent is not yet known, they are the sole survivors of their families and many have been through the agony of witnessing the destruction of their loved ones. Understandably, therefore, their present condition, physical and mental, is far worse than that of other groups.

While SHAEF (now Combined Displaced Persons Executive) policy directives have recognized formerly persecuted persons, including enemy and ex-enemy nationals, as one of the special categories of displaced persons, the general practice thus far has been to follow only nationality lines. While admittedly it is not normally desirable to set aside particular racial or religious groups from their nationality categories, the plain truth is that this was done for so long by the Nazis that a group has been created which has special needs. Jews as Jews (not as members of their nationality groups) have been more severely victimized than the non-Jewish members of the same or other nationalities.

When they are now considered only as members of nationality groups, the result is that special attention cannot be given to their admittedly greater needs because, it is contended, doing so would constitute preferential treatment and lead to trouble with the non-Jewish portion of the particular nationality group.

Thus there is a distinctly unrealistic approach to the problem. Refusal to recognize the Jews as such has the effect, in this situation, of closing one's eyes to their former and more barbaric persecution, which has already made them a separate group with greater needs.

Their second great need can be presented only by discussing what I found to be their wishes as to future destinations:

(1) For reasons that are obvious and need not be labored, most Jews want to leave Germany and Austria as soon as possible. That is their first and great expressed wish and while this report necessarily deals with other needs present in the situation, many of the people themselves fear other suggestions or plans for their benefit because of the possibility that attention might thereby be diverted from the all-important matter of evacuation from Germany. Their desire to leave Germany is an urgent one. . . .

(2) Some wish to return to their countries of nationality but as to this there is considerable nationality variation. Very few Polish or Baltic Jews wish to return to their countries; higher percentages of the Hungarian and Rumanian groups want to return although some hasten to add that it may be only temporarily in order to look for relatives. Some of the German Jews, especially those who have intermarried, prefer to stay in Germany.

(3) With respect to possible places of resettlement for those who may be stateless or who do not wish to return to their homes, Palestine is definitely and pre-eminently the first choice. Many now have relatives there, while others, having experienced intolerance and persecution in their homelands for years, feel that only in Palestine will they be welcomed and find peace and quiet and be given an opportunity to live and work. . . .

(4) Palestine, while clearly the choice of most, is not the only named place of possible emigration. Some, but the number is not large, wish to emigrate to the United States where they have relatives, others to England, the British Dominions, or to South America.

Source: *"Truman's Letter Regarding the Harrison Report on the Treatment of Displaced Jews," Jewish Virtual Library <http://www.us-israel.org/jsource/ Holocaust/truman_on_harrison.html>.*

ISRAEL

tion from his own Departments of War and State. Throughout the Roosevelt and Truman administrations, both of these government agencies routinely advised against American intervention on behalf of the Jews, fearing either a possible Soviet-Arab partnership or potential Arab actions to restrict oil supplies.

President Truman, however, also had personal reasons for supporting the establishment of a Jewish state in Palestine as a haven for European Jews displaced by the Holocaust. His staunch Southern Baptist upbringing led him to believe the Old Testament promise that, after destruction and exile, the Children of Israel would be restored to their ancient homeland. Proud of the fact that by the time he was fourteen years old he had read the Bible "cover-to-cover at least four times," he quoted the opening line of Psalm 137 to express the longing of Jewish exiles for their homeland: "By the rivers of Babylon, there we sat down, yea, we wept, when we remembered Zion." A traumatic incident in the president's family history caused him to identify directly with the plight of displaced Jews. His close relatives had become refugees, their homes and crops destroyed, when Union forces evicted hundreds of farm families in western Missouri during the American Civil War (1861–1865). Truman's own maternal grandmother was forced off her farm and had to move her six children to Kansas City. At the end of the war the exiles returned to discover a degree of devastation so appalling that it remained a taboo subject for years. Out of respect for his grandmother's feelings, the young Truman never wore his National Guard uniform in her home; and after he became president, his mother refused to sleep in the Lincoln Bedroom at the White House. The events of the sixth century B.C.E. and of 1863 made Truman profoundly aware of the suffering of innocents in 1945 and sympathetic to their plight.

This story brings one to the most critical and clearest connection between Jewish suffering during the Holocaust and Jewish existence in a secure homeland in Palestine/Israel: the connection made by Holocaust survivors and refugees themselves—the *She'erith Hapletah* (Surviving Remnant), as they called themselves—especially displaced Jews from eastern Europe. By 1947, two years after the end of World War II, some 250,000 of them were crowded into Displaced Persons (DP) camps in Germany, Austria, and Italy, and 50,000 more were marooned in France, the Netherlands, and Belgium. Some of these people had chosen to remain in western and central Europe after liberation rather than to return to their decimated east European communities. Some had tried to return, only to come up against anti-Semitic violence from their former non-Jewish neighbors and the establishment of totalitarian Soviet-satellite regimes. None of them wanted to remain in Europe, and most of them wanted to immigrate to what was then British-controlled Palestine.

This desire emerged apart from any outside influence almost immediately after liberation in the summer of 1945, while the Allied military organizations were just starting to cope with the enormous task of feeding and sheltering masses of DPs—both Jews and non-Jews—and before Jewish organizations from America and Palestine even entered the camps. Moreover, it emerged because of the overwhelmingly Zionist orientation of the survivors themselves. In the words of historian Yehuda Bauer, "Zionism became what today would be called the civil religion of the [Jews in the] D.P. camps." As a result, Zionists won the elections held to select camp committees representing the Jews in individual DP camps as well as those choosing central committees to represent Jews from all the camps in a particular zone of occupation. The governing bodies so elected immediately began to demand that the DPs be allowed to leave the camps and immigrate to Palestine. Another example of this "grass-roots" Zionism on the part of the "Surviving Remnant" was the *Brichah* (Flight), an organization established by survivors of Zionist youth movements who had spent the war in the Soviet Union. *Brichah* helped nearly 250,000 Jewish survivors move illegally from eastern Europe to DP camps and other places in western and central Europe and to the shores of the Mediterranean with the goal of moving them into Palestine.

This situation played into the development of American policy and practice toward the Jews in the DP camps. From the start, General Dwight D. Eisenhower and his chief of staff, Walter Bedell-Smith, were sympathetic to the Jewish DPs because of what they had seen at the end of the war when they liberated the German concentration camps. This attitude probably influenced the Americans' welcome of David Ben-Gurion, chairman of the Jewish Agency Executive (the organization that represented the Jewish community in Palestine), when he visited Eisenhower's headquarters in Frankfurt in 1945. Ben-Gurion (later the first prime minister of the State of Israel) managed to persuade his hosts not to close the borders of the American zones to the Jews fleeing from eastern Europe with the help of *Brichah*. This policy, in turn, increased the number of Jewish refugees in the U.S. zones and helped Jews to become an even stronger political force.

Then, in late August 1945, Truman sent Earl G. Harrison, a professor of law at the University of Pennsylvania Law School, to investi-

Young Jews traveling to Palestine after being released from Buchenwald

relationship with the Jews, was based on limiting the size of the Jewish population. Thus, the British refusal put the Truman administration in a difficult position. On the one hand, the DP camps were filled with hundreds of thousands of Jews who had nowhere to go. Palestine was closed to them. So, unfortunately, was the United States, as Congress refused to change immigration laws to allow DPs into the country—particularly, Jewish DPs. On the other hand, the Truman administration's inability to find a home for them became the subject of increasingly harsh criticism from the American Jewish community. This reproof was particularly awkward for an administration that needed Jewish votes in the hotly contested 1946 congressional elections, especially in New York, Pennsylvania, Illinois, and California.

This deadlock had a direct impact on the Holocaust survivors still living in Europe. As escape from DP camp existence began to seem increasingly unlikely, despair and discouragement swept the camps. In an effort to deal with this situation the Jewish Agency for Palestine (executive arm of the World Zionist Organization) voted in 1946 to give up its original "hardline" demand that all of Palestine be turned into a Jewish state, in favor of a compromise calling for the partition of Palestine into two states—one for Jews and one for Arabs. They sent Nahum Goldman, an American Zionist leader, to Washington to suggest that the Jewish Agency would support a partition plan if the Americans would propose one to the United Nations. Thus, on 4 October 1946 Truman publicly declared that he favored "a viable Jewish state" that would be a compromise between British plans and those of the Jewish Agency. This stand was not exactly what Goldman had hoped for, but the American media misinterpreted Truman's declaration as favoring partition, and the president became a de facto supporter of Jewish statehood.

Throughout most of 1947, Great Britain kept looking for a compromise that would be acceptable to both Jews and Arabs but that would allow it to maintain its presence in the region. Eventually, however, this issue was forced by the arrival of ships such as the *Exodus 1947;* vessels organized by the *Haganah* (the underground Jewish military organization in Palestine) and filled with Jewish Holocaust survivors willing to risk imprisonment in British detention camps in Cyprus in order to enter Palestine illegally. A series of incidents involving these blockade runners and the Royal Navy marshaled world opinion against the British, increased world support for the Zionist cause, and added force to armed Jewish resistance against the British administration in Palestine. Finally, the British army no longer wanted to remain, and in

gate the situation in the DP camps, with special emphasis on the Jewish DPs. Harrison's report criticized army management of the camps and army policy toward Jews. It called for better food and living conditions, for the establishment of separate camps for Jewish survivors, and for the admission of 100,000 Jewish DPs into Palestine. Truman and Eisenhower acted swiftly on these recommendations, greatly improving the Jews' situation. Truman also asked Great Britain to consider Harrison's recommendation for Jewish immigration to Palestine, which was endorsed in the spring of 1946 by the findings of an Anglo-American Commission of Inquiry, chosen by the two countries to examine the situation of the Jewish DPs and the political situation in Palestine.

Had Great Britain acted on this recommendation, the State of Israel might never have been established, as it might have moderated the DPs' demands and enabled the Truman administration to avoid further direct involvement in Palestine. However, British policy, which called for a continued presence in Palestine coupled with a pro-Arab arrangement that would create an alliance with the Arab states while holding on to a

ISRAEL

February 1947 Great Britain handed the entire "Palestine question" over to the United Nations.

While the Holocaust was not the direct cause of the establishment of the State of Israel, it served as an important catalyst. At its center were the Jewish DPs—Holocaust survivors and refugees—who had formed their own Zionist political and rescue organizations and whose philosophy and activities were directed toward immigration to Palestine. This activity put pressure on the U.S. Army, whose zones of occupation contained most of these DPs, and led the Truman administration to insist that Great Britain accept at least a portion of them into Palestine. The British refusal to do so pushed the "Palestine question" inescapably toward partition and, ultimately, toward the establishment of the State of Israel.

–FRANCES GLAZER STERNBERG, MIDWEST CENTER FOR HOLOCAUST EDUCATION

Viewpoint:
No. The political and moral foundation of the modern State of Israel was established long before World War II, and the Jewish nation would have been created eventually whether or not the Holocaust had occurred.

James Parkes, Anglican theologian and pioneer in the field of Jewish-Christian relations, is reputed to have argued that "bad history does not make good theology." Nor, one may properly argue, does faulty thinking make good history. It would be faulty indeed to assert that the Holocaust was a necessary or critical factor in the creation of the modern State of Israel. Centuries of Jewish religious traditions, theology, and philosophy produced a deep longing among Jewish people to return to the land of their ancestors, to the land in which their faith was born. Zionism means not merely the secular Jewish nationalism that developed in nineteenth-century western Europe but, more fully, the timeless desire of Jews throughout the world for life in a restored homeland at peace and in harmony with their neighbors. This more complete form of Zionism is a product of a long history of victory and defeat, of hopes and fears, and of courage and persecution. Consequently, all of the great events of Jewish history must be remembered and considered in order to provide a proper understanding of the birth of Israel in May 1948.

To understand the events of spring 1948 requires, first of all, a recognition that the Jewish people have dreamed for nearly two thousand years of a return to the land of their ancestors' ancient triumphs. Modern Jews look back with justifiable pride on the kingdom of Israel (circa 1000 B.C.E.). From their palaces in Jerusalem, David and Solomon ruled a territory spreading from modern Lebanon to the Sinai Peninsula and from modern Jordan to the Mediterranean Sea. It was a fertile land, with wealthy cities and profitable trading routes, as well as a rich cultural life centered on the Temple in Jerusalem. For hundreds of years the Jewish people lived, labored, and died within a state of their own; yet, it was too strategically located to remain undisturbed. Beginning with the Assyrian invasions of the eighth century B.C.E., the Jewish people came to know little more than war, exile, and foreign oppression. In the sixth century B.C.E. the Babylonians sacked Jerusalem, destroyed the Temple, and took thousands of Jews into exile. It was the first of many great disasters that would befall the Jewish people and eventually deprive them of their ancestral homeland.

The fall of Babylon to the Persians (539 B.C.E.) allowed the captives to return and rebuild their homes, their Temple, and their civilization. Though the community was often threatened by unscrupulous people, Jews enjoyed a measure of freedom and self-governance as subjects of the Persians. Later, after the collapse of the Persian Empire (331 B.C.E.), the Jewish people struggled to maintain their independence from the arbitrary (and at times sacrilegious) rule of Greek kings and, later, Roman emperors. In their bloody suppression of the Jewish revolt (67–70 C.E.) the Romans destroyed the second Temple, abolished all Jewish self-government in Palestine, and scattered the Jewish people across the known world.

From the point of view of the legionary conquerors of Jerusalem in 70 C.E., the destruction of the Jewish people, their faith, and their civilization must have seemed complete. Yet, for countless generations after this great "Jewish Dispersion," Jews continued to cherish the memory of their ancestral land and the hope of a future return. Year in and year out, in Jewish communities across Europe, North Africa, and into the vastness of Asia, Jews offered the same prayer at the conclusion of their annual Passover celebrations: *"L'shanah ha-ba'ah bIrushalayim"* ("Next year [God willing] in Jerusalem!"). Their liturgy, especially the Book of Psalms, is still filled with references not only to the land itself but also to the obligation to remember. Most often cited are the lines from Psalm 137 concerned with the first great exile of the Jewish people in the sixth century B.C.E.:

By the rivers of Babylon, there we sat down, we, also, wept, when we remembered Zion . . .

How shall we sing the Lord's song in a foreign land?

If I forget you, O Jerusalem, let my right hand forget her cunning:

If I do not remember you, let my tongue cleave to the roof of my mouth; if I do not set Jerusalem above my highest joy.

This common history, instantly recognizable to every Jew of the Dispersion, provided a unique bond of shared dreams and shared promises. The development of Jewish religious literature—the Torah, the Mishnah, the Talmud, and the Midrash—makes clear that it was a universal feature of Jewish civilization. In each of these collections one finds the longing to return to *Eretz Yisrael* (Land of Israel); it was (and, indeed, is) a thread continually woven into the very fabric of Jewish life for generations and in many settings.

In order to understand the creation of the modern State of Israel, it is equally important to recognize the more recent success of Zionism. Historians of the evolving Jewish religious tradition and of the journey of Jewish people agree that Zionism remained an ongoing process. Often thwarted in Europe by the crosscurrents of abiding anti-Jewish prejudice, it was given renewed energy after 1789. Thanks to the spread of the revolutionary ideals of liberty, equality, and brotherhood, French and German Jews emerged from the ghettos to take a more active role in public life and popular culture. Yet, this emancipation of many European Jews neither ended nor diminished the drive of some for a return to the land of their ancestors and the prospect of a reborn Jewish commonwealth. In a largely secular political form, and often represented by the writings of Theodor Herzl, Zionism became the subject of much discussion in western Europe by the end of the nineteenth century. At the same time, however, Jews from eastern Europe began acting on the Zionist ideal. In increasing numbers the oppressed Jews of Poland and Russia migrated back to Palestine to drain the malarial swamps and build cities. They created both the collective agricultural settlements (kibbutzim and moshavim) and the political infrastructure that would be already in place for the moment when a reborn Jewish state would become a reality.

Thanks to the arrival of these early Zionist pioneers, the Jewish population of Palestine (as the land of their ancestors was commonly known) tripled in size between 1882 and 1914, rising from about 24,000 to about 75,000 people. Significant though this migration and settlement was, it was hardly sufficient to establish the Jewish State so long envisioned by Zionists. Those Jews who returned to Palestine during the late nineteenth century found themselves under the indifferent rule of the decrepit empire of the Ottoman Turks. Only the "Great Powers" of Europe could effectively produce a change in Ottoman rule, but it was unlikely that any of these states would upset the delicate balance of power in order to act on behalf of the Jewish people. Thus, in the early years of the twentieth century adherents of Herzl's secular political Zionism met with little success as they lobbied the governments of Europe to gain support for their cause. The crisis of World War I (1914–1918), which drew the Turks into the bloody contest on the side of Germany, provided the opportunity for Zionism to receive the international recognition it required.

In particular, Zionist hopes were buttressed by the Balfour Declaration (1917), which announced that the British government "view[ed] with favor the establishment in Palestine of a national home for the Jewish people." The realization of the timeless dreams of the Jewish people seemed even closer upon the collapse of the Ottoman Empire at the end of the war and the establishment of a provisional British administration in Palestine. British rule, however, also proved to be restrictive, limiting the number of Jewish immigrants to their ancestral homeland. Even as Zionists energetically pressed their case for the creation of an independent state, the rising tide of supposedly "scientific" anti-Semitism in the heartland of Europe and the storm clouds of a new European war were an increasing distraction. As events unfolded in the 1930s, the Zionists' dialogue with those states favorable to Jewish aspirations (Britain, France, and the United States, among others) was drowned out by the demands of war preparation and, later, military conflict. Although the Zionists never ceased promoting their cause, between 1939 and 1945 their claims were a low priority for the Allied powers engaged in a complex global conflict.

With the end of World War II (1939–1945) and the increasing revelations of the horrors of the Nazi genocidal attack upon the Jewish people, Jews redoubled their efforts to find a safe haven for those who survived the catastrophe and were now living throughout Europe in camps for Displaced Persons (DPs). The victorious Allies were, once again, willing to listen (perhaps even somewhat guiltily) to Jewish voices and Jewish claims. Consequently, in November 1947 the United Nations Special Committee on Palestine (UNSCOP) issued a report favoring the creation of both a Jewish state and an Arab state in the region. At long last, almost two thousand years after the destruction of its Temple and the dispersal of its population around the globe, the ages-old Jewish dream was on the verge of realization. The State of Israel emerged, to employ a popular post–World War II metaphor, like a "phoenix arising from the ashes." It sprang as much from the ashes of the Roman burning of Jerusalem as from the more-recent fires of the Nazi crematorium.

To conclude that the Holocaust alone made the formation of the State of Israel possible is, at its most perverse extreme, to regard Adolf Hitler as the true hero of Israel reborn—an argument fictionally placed into his own mouth in George Steiner's brilliant novel *The Portage of A. H. to San Cristóbal* (1981). Furthermore, to assert that without the occurrence of the Holocaust there would be no Israel is to dismiss nearly two thousand years of religious aspirations and political activism. To make such an argument is to regard the murder of almost six million Jews, including one and one-half million of its children eighteen years old or younger, as the premium for Jewish independence. Philosophically, theologically, and—indeed—humanly, one must recognize that if such were the case, then the price paid was far too high: better no Israel and no Holocaust than the Holocaust and the State of Israel.

Nor, it must be remembered, was the Holocaust instrumental in the formation of the State of Israel. This understanding misreads the historical process and totally misinterprets Jewish religious traditions as well as Jewish theological thinking and philosophy. At most, reflection on the unparalleled horrors of World War II made European and American thinkers more sensitive than ever before to the new reality of a diminished Jewish people in Europe. The victorious powers were willing to listen, as perhaps never before, to representatives of those Jewish organizations that had long been campaigning for a Jewish return to Israel. Some, certainly, believed that the apparently endemic problem of anti-Semitism might be solved by supporting the creation of a Jewish homeland in Palestine. But, to ardent inheritors of the Zionist cause, the goal was not one of escape from future persecution or compensation for recent suffering but of fulfillment of the Jewish hopes of two millennia. The Jewish people had been returning to Palestine long before the Holocaust, and had the tragedy never occurred, they would have continued to return in increasing numbers; Israel would have become a state someday. Perhaps the process of return and rebirth would have taken much longer, but it would have happened nevertheless.

–STEVEN LEONARD JACOBS,
UNIVERSITY OF ALABAMA, TUSCALOOSA

References

Aharon Appelfeld, "Witness," *Jerusalem Quarterly*, 16 (Summer 1980).

Yehuda Bauer, *Flight and Rescue: Brichah* (New York: Random House, 1970).

Bauer, "From the Holocaust to the State of Israel," *Rethinking the Holocaust* (New Haven: Yale University Press, 2001).

Bauer, *Out of the Ashes: The Impact of American Jews on Post-Holocaust European Jewry* (Oxford & New York: Pergamon Press, 1989).

Michael T. Benson, *Harry S. Truman and the Founding of Israel* (Westport, Conn.: Praeger, 1997).

Michael J. Cohen, *Truman and Israel* (Berkeley: University of California Press, 1990).

Leonard Dinnerstein, *America and the Survivors of the Holocaust* (New York: Columbia University Press, 1982).

Dinnerstein, *The United States and the D.P.s* (Jerusalem: Yad Vashem, 1990).

Raul Hilberg, *Destruction of the European Jews* (Chicago: Quadrangle, 1961).

Abraham S. Hyman, *The Undefeated* (Jerusalem: Gefen, 1993).

Arieh J. Kochavi, "Britain and the Illegal Immigration to Palestine from France Following World War II," *Holocaust and Genocide Studies*, 6 (1991).

Daniel Landes, "The Holocaust and Israel," Museum of Tolerance and Learning, Simon Wiesenthal Center <http://motlc.wiesenthal.com/>.

James Parkes, *Prelude to Dialogue: Jewish-Christian Relationships* (New York: Schocken Books, 1969).

Monty Noam Penkower, *The Holocaust and Israel Reborn: From Catastrophe to Sovereignty* (Urbana: University of Illinois Press, 1994).

Howard M. Sachar, *A History of Israel: From the Rise of Zionism to Our Time* (New York: Knopf, 1976).

Tom Segev, *The Seventh Million: Israelis and the Holocaust*, translated by Haim Watzman (New York: Hill & Wang, 1993).

George Steiner, *The Portage of A. H. to San Cristóbal* (New York: Simon & Schuster, 1981).

A. B. Yehoshua, "The Holocaust as Junction," in *Between Right and Right*, translated by Arnold Schwartz (Garden City, N.Y.: Doubleday, 1981).

ISRAEL

JEHOVAH'S WITNESSES

Was the Jehovah's Witnesses' commitment to neutrality a defensible response to Nazi tyranny?

Viewpoint: Yes. Political neutrality, as practiced by the Jehovah's Witnesses, was their only viable option.

Viewpoint: No. Neutrality was impossible in the Nazi State.

Jehovah's Witnesses are a minority Christian community that began to organize in the United States in the 1870s. The Jehovah's Witnesses await the establishment of an earthly paradise that they believe will flourish after evil is defeated by God's heavenly Kingdom during the battle of Armageddon. According to the Jehovah's Witnesses, Christians are not to take part in that battle, but they have the commission to herald that Kingdom. Thus, they are widely known for their public preaching, or "witnessing" work, using primarily the complete Bible, as well as their periodicals, *The Watchtower* and *Awake!* (formerly published under the titles *The Golden Age* [1919–1937] and *Consolation* [1937–1946], respectively).

Jehovah's Witnesses have been continuously active in Germany since the mid 1890s. Before 1931 they went by the name *Ernste Bibelforscher* (Bible Students). By 1933 there were about 25,000 practicing Jehovah's Witnesses in Germany. The Nazi regime mounted a violent and sustained assault against the Jehovah's Witnesses. Among the principal reasons for this animosity was the Jehovah's Witnesses' political neutrality—a position involving their nonparticipation in Nazi programs and their refusal to serve in the military. Individual Jehovah's Witnesses would not vote, join the Nazi Party, give the Hitler salute, or hang the swastika flag outside their homes and businesses. The SA (Storm Troopers) and Gestapo responded with ever increasing brutality. Jehovah's Witnesses lost their jobs, saw their businesses boycotted, and were denied pension benefits. Their children were beaten and expelled from school for refusing to share in Nazi activities.

Although the regime banned the religion successively in *Länder* (German states) during the spring of 1933, the Jehovah's Witnesses continued to spread their message and to hold their religious services in secret. The international community of Jehovah's Witnesses, including those in Germany, publicized Nazi atrocities in their literature.

The intermittent arrests, house searches, and harassment of the Jehovah's Witnesses in 1933 and 1934 gave way to a formalized campaign of persecution beginning in 1935. The Gestapo organized mass arrests of Jehovah's Witnesses in 1936 and 1937. Gestapo circular decrees ordered that, immediately upon release from prison, Jehovah's Witnesses should be taken into "protective custody," which usually meant an extended stay in a concentration camp. Consequently, according to Detlef Garbe, director of the Neuengamme Concentration Camp Memorial and author of an exhaustive study on Jehovah's Witnesses, prisoners of this faith made up an average of 5 to 10 percent of the concentration camp population during the prewar period. About 10,000 Jehovah's Witnesses ultimately underwent incarceration. In Nazi camps they wore the purple triangle.

Beginning in 1936, with hundreds of adult male and female Jehovah's Witnesses entering the Nazi camp and prison system, the regime began to send Jehovah's Witnesses' children to Nazi institutions and homes for the express purpose of "reeducation." Jehovah's Witness parents were charged with child endangerment for failing to rear their children according to Nazi norms. Without advance warning the Gestapo, police, or youth-welfare officials picked up the children, some as young as six years old, at school. More than 500 Jehovah's Witness children, primarily from Germany, Austria, France, and Poland, were forcibly removed from their parents' custody.

With the start of the war, Jehovah's Witnesses were hanged, beheaded, or shot for refusing to participate in military activities. The campaign against the Jehovah's Witnesses quickly spread to Nazi-occupied countries. The Nazis executed more than 250 Jehovah's Witnesses as conscientious objectors and more than 100 for other reasons. Altogether, about 2,000 Jehovah's Witnesses perished as a result of maltreatment and incarceration. No other group, religious or political, suffered the execution of such a large number of conscientious objectors.

On several occasions Adolf Hitler vowed that "this brood [Jehovah's Witnesses] will be exterminated in Germany!" Yet, the path leading to the eradication of Jehovah's Witnesses differed from other annihilation programs of the Nazi regime. It is evident from the casualty figures that the concerted assault on the Jehovah's Witnesses community was not aimed directly at complete physical destruction, as was the case with victims of the Nazi racial agenda. Otherwise, many more imprisoned Jehovah's Witnesses would have been killed outright. Nevertheless, the regime sought to destroy the religious community. Persons could be arrested and incarcerated indefinitely, simply for being Jehovah's Witnesses.

As a unique strategy in their ideological campaign against Jehovah's Witnesses, Nazi officials routinely offered these prisoners the opportunity to gain release if they would sign a document of renunciation. By his signature, the prisoner would repudiate his religious beliefs and agree to denounce any Jehovah's Witnesses with whom he came in contact. Nazi captors tried to coerce Jehovah's Witnesses to sign the document by using beatings, torture, public executions, punishment labor, solitary confinement, reduced rations, and other extreme intimidation tactics. Refusal to sign precipitated more abuse. Since the vast majority of Jehovah's Witnesses refused to sign the declaration of renunciation, they were condemned to perpetual detention and, presumably, eventual death in captivity. Thus, although physical extermination might not have been an explicit aim of the regime, Nazi policy regarding Jehovah's Witnesses prisoners effectively condemned them to death.

Whereas millions of victims faced annihilation by the Nazis because of their immutable physical characteristics, Jehovah's Witnesses were harmed and killed because of adhering to their religious convictions. The teachings of Jehovah's Witnesses included elements that diametrically opposed Nazi ideology. Their belief in brotherhood and their repudiation of racism ran directly counter to Nazi racial nationalism; the Jehovah's Witnesses placed the divine law of love ahead of Nazi law; they openly and unequivocally professed loyalty to God rather than to the Führer; they insisted on practicing nonviolence. The regime considered these to be highly deviant and dangerous views, and high-level Nazis ordered a relentless attack on the entire group.

No other Christian group became the object of such intense Nazi persecution. In 1934 the Jehovah's Witnesses sent an official statement to the Hitler government stating: "We have no interest in political affairs, but are wholly devoted to God's Kingdom under Christ His King. We will do no injury or harm to anyone. We would delight to dwell in peace and do good to all men as we have opportunity, but, since your government and its officers continue in your attempt to force us to disobey the highest law of the universe, we are compelled to now give you notice that we will, by His Grace, obey Jehovah God and fully trust Him to deliver us from all oppression and oppressors." When liberation came in 1945, Jehovah's Witnesses were convinced that their God had done just that.

Viewpoint:
Yes. Political neutrality, as practiced by the Jehovah's Witnesses, was their only viable option.

How can one remain neutral in the face of genocide and mass murder? U.S. president John F. Kennedy would likely have replied with a favorite remark: "Dante once said that the hottest places in hell are reserved for those who in a period of moral crisis maintain their neutrality." Kennedy equated neutrality with inaction, a reprehensible refusal to get involved when moral activism seems to be urgently needed.

The Holocaust was just such a moral crisis, raising countless ethical dilemmas for individuals and institutions alike. Sadly, many responses could be characterized by the sort of neutrality Kennedy described. After twelve years of devastating Nazi rule, people offered various explana-

DAS GOLDENE ZEITALTER

Sondernummer über Luzern u.s.w.

DER NEUE GESSLERHUT

monthly — Halbmonatlich
Golden Age — German edition Vol. XIV

Nr. 338

BERN
15. Oktober 1936

JEHOVAH'S WITNESSES

tions for their inaction or collaboration: "I didn't know." "I was in fear for my own life." "What could I have done?" Even notorious perpetrators tried to defend their actions by portraying themselves as helpless cogs in a giant killing machine. Maximillian Grabner, head of the Political Department at Auschwitz concentration camp, stated: "I only took part in this crime because there was nothing I could do to change anything. The blame for this crime lay with National Socialism." Rudolf Höss, commandant of Auschwitz concentration camp, said of his part in the murder of Jews, "I had been given an order, and I had to carry it out."

Such attempts at self-absolution stand in stark contrast to the response of that minority of individuals who dared to oppose the ideology of the Nazi regime. They did so in different ways and with a variety of motivations. As a religious community, Jehovah's Witnesses can be counted among those who rejected Nazi ways and who suffered severe consequences for their firm resolve. Yet, the Jehovah's Witnesses describe their own position as one of "political neutrality." In view of their refusal to conform to Nazi ways, how could the Jehovah's Witnesses claim to have been neutral? On what historical, moral, or theological basis did they adopt this stance? What did they hope to accomplish by remaining neutral? How could they reconcile their neutrality with the fact that they saw innocent people being assaulted and murdered, including many in their own community? Did the Jehovah's Witnesses succeed in adhering to their neutral position as they defined it?

The Jehovah's Witnesses use the term *neutrality* to describe what they believe to be the proper Christian relationship to the state. In analyzing the historical response of Jehovah's Witnesses to the Nazi menace, it is crucial to grasp their special conception of neutrality. Even the most common terms have specific meanings within a given setting. For instance, a child psychologist may use the term *intelligence* in a sense different from the way the word is used by a computer scientist or a military strategist. Jehovah's Witnesses, the Vatican, Switzerland, and for a time the United States all used the word *neutrality* to describe their position toward Nazism. Yet, neutrality had distinct meanings, served different objectives, and produced a wide range of responses to the totalitarian regime.

Before considering what neutrality meant to Jehovah's Witnesses, it is helpful to know what it did not mean. It did not entail moral neutrality. Jehovah's Witnesses consciously took a moral position underpinned by their understanding of certain Christian precepts. Nor did Jehovah's Witnesses' neutrality aim to placate the regime. Of course, during Adolf Hitler's first year in office the Jehovah's Witnesses appealed to the government to recognize that they were not subversives with revolutionary aspirations. At first they believed (incorrectly) that the aggression of Hitler's government against Jehovah's Witnesses stemmed from a misunderstanding of their intentions. As the persecution intensified, Jehovah's Witnesses neutrality did not require them to remain silent about the criminality of the regime. Neutrality did not paralyze their capacity to render help to others. Nor did neutrality obligate the Jehovah's Witnesses to acquiesce to every Nazi demand without protest.

Far from claiming to have originated the concept, the Jehovah's Witnesses trace their doctrine of neutrality back to the founding principles of Christianity. Jesus stated of his disciples: "They are no part of the world, just as I am no part of the world" (John 17:16). That statement may seem enigmatic—the Gospel accounts depict Jesus as being deeply involved with people, teaching great crowds, healing the sick, and feeding the multitudes. Jesus' exhortation to his followers evidently did not call for a monastic retreat from society and a life of pious isolation, if one is to judge by the model he himself set. However, the Jehovah's Witnesses believe that Jesus, despite his keen awareness of the social ills and the plight of the oppressed in his day, remained scrupulously separate from "the world" in one important sense: He never advocated violence, revolution, or political activism as a cure for the world's problems. In fact, Jesus rejected an effort to crown him as a human king. And on the night of his arrest Jesus rebuked Peter, a devoted Jewish disciple, for striking out with a sword to defend his Lord.

Jesus apparently entertained no naive notion that separateness from the world would enable his followers to live a life of peaceful detachment from societal upheavals. Rather, he warned them, "Because you are no part of the world, but I have chosen you out of the world, on this account the world hates you" (John 15:19). Nevertheless, he commissioned his disciples to take to the world a message of hope and reconciliation. The Jehovah's Witness position of neutrality is located in the core of this message: The Kingdom of God.

The Jehovah's Witnesses' fateful decision not to conform to the Nazi New Order can only be understood correctly in light of their firm convictions regarding God's Kingdom. Throughout their history the Jehovah's Witnesses have viewed the heavenly Kingdom of God not as a hypothetical construct but as a tangible government, complete with a sovereign ruler, a body of laws, and loyal subjects. The Jehovah's Witnesses see themselves as emissaries charged with the commission to carry God's invitation to all humanity to become subjects of the Kingdom. The apostle Paul stated that Christians act as "ambassadors substituting for Christ," entreating individuals to "become reconciled to God" (2 Cor. 5:20). Their ambassadorial capacity in the Kingdom of God means that Jehovah's Witnesses will not involve themselves in the political or military affairs of the nations in which they reside. Abstention is not out of apathy or lack of civic responsibility but rather stems from the obligations of an overarching loyalty.

The Jehovah's Witnesses relate to secular governments in a manner similar to the way an ambassador conducts himself while abroad—they respect the laws of the land, but their primary allegiance belongs to God. It is in this special respect that they maintain political neutrality toward temporal governments while taking the side of God's Kingdom. Like most early Christians until the third century, Jehovah's Witnesses do not serve in the armies of any nation, nor do they pledge allegiance to national symbols. In their view a persistent hindrance to world peace has been—not the widespread refusal of religious people to go to war—but the enthusiastic participation of believers. Whether members of the same faith oppose each other on the battlefield or join hands to wage war on "infidels and heretics," mass slaughters in the name of religion bloody the pages of history.

While human governments have been known to increase their realm of influence by means of imperialism and aggression, expansion of the Kingdom realm is predicated on an open-door policy for anyone, of any nationality or ethnicity, who is willing to adopt its ethical code of love. Jehovah's Witnesses in the Nazi realm thus found the *übermensch/untermensch* (superhuman/subhuman) hierarchy absolutely incompatible with their belief that the family of mankind descended from a single set of ancestors. To them, armed disputes over such matters as political borders amount to fratricide. It would be especially unthinkable to them to engage in the slaughter of fellow believers on opposing sides.

The Nazi social order had no room for notions of equality or for proclamations of a Messianic age. The Jehovah's Witnesses' determination to carry on their worship services and preaching work, even in secret, infuriated the Nazi regime and convinced officials of the need to launch a vigorous campaign to stamp out the religion. But the most brutal consequences ensued after Jehovah's Witnesses refused to perform any type of work to support the war effort.

Among the 250 Jehovah's Witnesses executed for their conscientious objection to military service was August Dickmann, a German Jehovah's Witness held in Sachsenhausen con-

centration camp. *The New York Times* of 17 September 1939 reported that Dickmann, age twenty-nine, was the first conscientious objector of World War II (1939–1945) to be executed by the Nazis. Dickmann had refused to sign a declaration renouncing his faith. SS chief Heinrich Himmler approved Dickmann's execution by firing squad in order to intimidate about 400 Jehovah's Witnesses inmates in Sachsenhausen who were ordered to watch Dickmann die. Not one Jehovah's Witness recanted as a result. Eyewitnesses state that just prior to the shooting, camp commandant Hermann Baranowski read the charge: "The prisoner August Dickmann regards himself not as a citizen of the German Reich but a citizen of the Kingdom of God." The Nazi regime could not tolerate such loyalty to another government, even one they viewed as imaginary. The Führer demanded body and soul.

The Jehovah's Witnesses reckoned their debts by a different formula: "Pay back, therefore, Caesar's things to Caesar, but God's things to God" (Matthew 22:21). Jesus here clearly indicated that secular authorities can rightly make demands of a Christian. But if Caesar laid claim to that which belonged to God, the Jehovah's Witnesses were prepared to refuse. The Roman Caesar demanded that Christians burn a pinch of incense on the altar to acknowledge his deity. Early Christians perished in the Roman arena rather than give to Caesar the worship belonging to God.

Jehovah's Witnesses had to weigh every Nazi demand by the same scale. To them, the pinch of incense to the Nazi "Caesar" was the "Heil Hitler" salute, but a subject of God's Kingdom could ascribe salvation only to God's designated king, Jesus. The regime required membership in Nazi organizations, such as the German Labor Front and the Hitler Youth, but Jehovah's Witnesses avoided membership in groups designed to squeeze the populace into the Nazi mold. German homes and businesses had to display the swastika flag, but Jehovah's Witnesses viewed the ceremonious veneration of the quasi-religious symbol as idolatrous. The racist Caesar demanded collaboration and silence as the genocidal program built momentum, but no Jehovah's Witnesses could reconcile murderous bigotry with Jesus' message of brotherhood. Jehovah's Witnesses found the Nazi vision of the Thousand-Year Reich repulsive and blasphemous.

Viewing themselves as emissaries of God's Kingdom, the Jehovah's Witnesses saw an urgent need to counteract such depravity. From a secular standpoint, their preoccupation with "witnessing" about the Kingdom may appear absurd, even foolhardy, especially since such efforts only resulted in more arrests, incarceration, and death. Yet, for earnest Jehovah's Witnesses, the Kingdom held out the only prospect for bringing a permanent end to all injustice. In their view nothing could be of more help to suffering mankind than the knowledge that Almighty God had promised to bring a Messianic Millennium of peace and righteousness.

The fear of death that people said enslaved them to the Nazi machine held little hold on most Jehovah's Witnesses, who believed that God would resurrect them if they remained faithful until death. Secure in the conviction that the Nazis could not deprive them of everlasting life, Jehovah's Witnesses took their conscientious stand despite dire threats and torture. By all accounts Jehovah's Witnesses were ordinary people with ordinary feelings. Yet, the immense and deadly pressure brought to bear by an entire political and social system failed to reconfigure the Jehovah's Witnesses' moral frame of reference. Mature civil societies often seek to imbue their citizens with a similar determination to behave as responsible moral agents.

In one sense it can rightly be said that the Jehovah's Witnesses made no attempt to bring about the downfall of Nazism. From firsthand experience, they had no doubt about the utter evil of the regime. Yet, like Jehovah's Witnesses to this day, they trusted in God to bring about the end of evil. What might seem an unrealistic approach to evil was, to the Jehovah's Witnesses, wholly consistent with their belief system. The question was not "Should evil be stopped?" but "Who is capable of stopping evil?" They reasoned that human warfare inevitably leads to excesses on both sides and sets in motion endless cycles of violence and revenge. Stray bullets and wayward bombs wreak misery and take innocent lives. Those who argue for the efficacy of war hold to the naive presumption that the "good" always triumph and that it is only left for the "good" to become and remain the strongest. Equally dubious is the proposition that the strongest will ever remain the "good."

From the Jehovah's Witness perspective, only God has the wisdom and power to destroy the evil in all its forms while preserving the good. No human is capable of judging who is incorrigibly evil; hence, no Christian has the right to take the life of another, even a mortal enemy. This belief is precisely why the SS trusted only Jehovah's Witness inmates in some camps to shave them with a razor. The SS thus staked their lives on the belief that the Jehovah's Witnesses would never raise a hand against another human.

Although the Jehovah's Witnesses undertook no revolutionary actions, they sought to conquer evil with good, engaging in spiritual resistance, as was consistent with their moral stand. By persistently refusing to participate in Nazi hatred and violence, by submitting to imprisonment and martyrdom rather than taking up weapons against their fellow man, by insisting on preaching a message of love amid a storm of hate, and by treating the denigrated with dignity and respect, the Jehovah's Witnesses took a dangerous and unbending stand, one that the Nazis never succeeded in breaking. After the war some Jehovah's Witnesses demonstrated their determination to rise above feelings of hatred and vengeance by venturing back into the camps to preach to captive Nazis. In their eyes, to see a hateful Nazi transformed into a peaceful Christian would indeed have been a conquest of faith.

The massive crimes of the Nazi regime could not have been perpetrated without the widespread support or acquiescence of millions of people, most of whom professed to adhere to some form of Christianity. Historians generally do not see it as their job to ask "what if" questions. Yet, it is tempting to wonder what course history would have taken if those millions had interpreted their Christian responsibility as the Jehovah's Witnesses did theirs. Whether one agrees with their hopes for Millennial peace, it is clear that the Jehovah's Witnesses' special sense of history and their implicit faith in God enabled them to cling to their ethical moorings and to their distinctive form of neutrality during the quintessential moral crisis of the twentieth century.

–JOLENE CHU, WATCH TOWER SOCIETY, NEW YORK

Viewpoint:
No. Neutrality was impossible in the Nazi State.

The concept of neutrality has a long and complex history of usage, dating back at least to the classic Greeks. Its many applications range from grammar to biology, from expressing the lack of gender of a noun (neither feminine nor masculine) to expressing the asexual status of a category of plants having neither pistils nor stamens. In more recent times, since the High Renaissance and Italian political philosopher Niccolò Machiavelli's *The Prince* (1513), neutrality became a legal term used by statesmen and their diplomats to indicate a country's non-involvement in an international dispute, particularly in times of hostility. In this context, neutrality demanded a strict observance of specific rules of conduct, which if not religiously observed, would lead to the neutral party's being drawn into the very war it sought to avoid. Ideally, assiduous neutrality is also demanded of referees, judges, juries, labor negotiators, and marriage counselors; professionally, they are expected to be nonpartisan. Even more recently, a new usage has been formulated and practiced, namely, grassroots "political neutrality," a concept and policy pioneered by Jehovah's Witnesses.

The idea might seem to be derived from Jesus' admonition to his disciples "to render unto Caesar what is Caesar's and unto God what is God's." On closer examination, however, the Jehovah's Witnesses' brand of political neutrality is almost the antithesis of this New Testament principle of dual loyalty. Whereas the Jehovah's Witnesses profess no direct loyalty to any state, early Christians understood the exhortation to mean a system of complementary or dual loyalties, one owed to the earthly ruler of the City of Man and the other to the divine ruler of the universe, the City of God. Thus, as long as the demands of the ruler do not vitiate the ethical morality ordered by God, there is, in theory, no conflict. However, if predicated on the insistence of the primacy of the divine, or the inverse, those loyalties are bound to clash once one or the other refuses to subordinate itself.

In practice the inherent tensions of Jesus' formula of accommodation inevitably placed Church and State on a collision course, a classic case of a clash of loyalties and values. The result has been a perpetual overt or covert political struggle for primacy, ecclesiastical or secular: for example, would society be ruled by the principle of caesaro-papism or theocracy? Confrontation— a competition for power—was inevitable, if only because what was understood to be the prerogative of Caesar and what was God's due was also subject to rival interpretations by constitutional lawyers of the State and canonic theologians of the Church. Thus, in practice, dual loyalty is unworkable if not self-contradictory.

The closest one can come to a reasonable resolution of this dilemma is in the context of a constitutional, liberal democratic setting that upholds the principle of separation, and not synchronization, of religion and government. Yet, even under such benign circumstances there reigns an ongoing systemic, often bitter, duel over perennial issues—pitting citizens against representatives—such as tax exemption of religions, the legalization or criminalization of abortion, conscientious objection in times of war, the limits of civil disobedience, prayer in public schools, and same-sex marriages. Neither side ever fully bends; compromise is tenuous until the next occasion when the issue is raised anew.

The Jehovah's Witnesses' understanding of neutrality is to remove themselves from the fray of the political arena and to seek sufficient social space in which to carry out their mission, namely, to proselytize unfettered by state and society. Their tactic is to circumvent peacefully any barriers hindering their missionary work while remaining largely apart from sociopolitical disputes that might rage around them. In a flexible (tolerant), democratic, pluralistic culture a head-on collision with the State is unlikely, especially in a richly diverse society such as the United States in which the Jehovah's Witnesses pose no threat, potential or otherwise.

The real test of the Jehovah's Witnesses' principle of political neutrality came in the context of Adolf Hitler's Third Reich. After Hitler's rise to power the principle of political neutrality practiced by the tiny Jehovah's Witnesses minority (about 30,000 worshipers) was sorely tested as it found itself face-to-face with a powerful, implacable, ruthless, totalitarian state determined to impose the racist, atheistic doctrines of National Socialism on all citizens. And what, specifically, did the Nazi State demand of its German citizens? Nothing but total submission to the will of its omnipotent leader, Hitler, and his genocidal racist policies. Herein lay the ultimate challenge to the essence of the Jehovah's Witnesses' concept of political neutrality: Was it rationally and morally possible to attempt a modus vivendi with the Third Reich? Where would the Jehovah's Witnesses find sufficient "space" for their work without offending the ubiquitous Nazi-ridden world of post-1933 Germany?

Jews were being squeezed out of society and increasingly marginalized; socialists and communists were brutally incarcerated if not killed; and the Lutheran Church caved in under pressure, selling its soul by Nazifying Protestantism. One either joined the state or did not. Not to do so was immediately perceived by the Nazis as a political act of defiance and treasonable opposition; in no way was this stance seen as "neutral." Thus, in the absolute authoritarian realm of Nazi Germany there was no room for the slightest deviance from the totalist norms set by the Party. What the Jehovah's Witnesses sought—neutrality—was impossible in the radical context created by the new State.

What did the Jehovah's Witnesses want in Germany? Above all they wanted to proselytize, to spread their faith. Among their teachings was unconditional obedience to God, without qualification, with no limitations placed on them by the Nazi State. The New German Order, however, tolerated no teachings that diluted the citizens' loyalty to the State. To insist on the primacy, if not exclusive loyalty, to religious faith was in the eyes of the Nazis tantamount to political heresy. What the Jehovah's Witnesses

FREEDOM FOR A SIGNATURE

Below is a translation of a statement that Jehovah's Witnesses (International Bible Students) could sign to gain release from imprisonment:

Concentration camp _____

Department II

DECLARATION

I, the _____

born on _____

in _____

herewith make the following declaration:

1. I have come to know that the International Bible Students Association is proclaiming erroneous teachings and under the cloak of religion follows hostile purposes against the State.

2. I therefore left the organization entirely and made myself absolutely free from the teachings of this sect.

3. I herewith give assurance that I will never again take any part in the activity of the International Bible Students Association. Any persons approaching me with the teaching of the Bible Students, or who in any manner reveal their connections with them, I will denounce immediately. All literature from the Bible Students that should be sent to my address I will at once deliver to the nearest police station.

4. I will in the future esteem the laws of the State, especially in the event of war will I, with weapon in hand, defend the fatherland, and join in every way the community of the people.

5. I have been informed that I will at once be taken again into protective custody if I should act against the declaration given today.

_____ , Dated _____

Source: Collection of Henry R. Huttenbach, New York, New York.

---

refused to do was to lend any kind of allegiance to Hitler as the supreme authority. To do so on their part would be to betray their faith. In this respect the Jehovah's Witnesses resembled the German Evangelical Lutherans who, instead of swearing an oath to Hitler, formed a separate congregation of the faithful, the so-called *Bekennende Kirche* (Confessing Church), an act for which they paid a heavy price, including persecution, incarceration, and martyrdom; among them was the young theologian Dietrich Bonnhöffer. However, the members of the *Bekennende Kirche* did not deceive themselves as to their neutrality; they realistically saw their stance was necessarily a provocation, a political act of open opposition. In contrast, the Jehovah's Witnesses interpreted their own refusal to comply with the State's demands as "neutral," never realizing or admit-

ting that there simply was no such "wiggle room." To the Nazis they were anti-Nazi by definition because they remained studiously neutral, or in their eyes, stubbornly uninvolved. The State would not let them be neutral.

What else did the Jehovah's Witnesses in Nazi Germany want specifically? They encouraged the study of the Bible. To that end they disseminated openly and clandestinely the Bible as much as opportunity permitted. However, to circulate any text that made no reference to the legitimacy of the Nazi regime was seen as blatant anti-Nazi propaganda. By this "sin" of omission the Jehovah's Witnesses wantonly ignored the German State, an act perceived as blatant political disobedience. If any text were to be given to the German people, it would have to be Hitler's *Mein Kampf* (1925–1927). Indeed, the Nazis printed millions of copies and distributed them free throughout the country, especially to schools. In contrast, the Jehovah's Witnesses secretly and illegally printed Bibles, covertly as well as overtly distributing them in public places such as railroad stations. To the Nazis this act was purely and simply subversive. Consequently, engaging in this kind of behavior cannot be dubbed "neutral"; on the contrary, to go against the law of the land, no matter the reason, is by definition a political act, by no means neutral. To do what the Jehovah's Witnesses were doing in Hitlerian Germany was none other than engaging in political sabotage. To call it neutral is incorrect by any definition of the term.

The Jehovah's Witnesses' claim of political neutrality within a nondemocratic state is an oxymoron. In fact, to go against such a regime is to undermine its very foundations. Politically, there is no room for both values. The Jehovah's Witnesses, with their religious activism, were challenging the legitimacy of the Nazi State, which naturally responded forcefully, like any other threatened dictatorial state. It struck back violently, seeking to force concessions and promote recantation by means of fear, torture, and death. To no avail, the Jehovah's Witnesses refused to bend, proving they were not neutral; de facto they were at war with Nazism and not caught between two opposing political forces; they were de jure one of the antagonists. For the Nazis, they were the embodiment of the enemy and not a benign neutral bystander. Their proselytizing did not take place between two other protagonists—German society and the Nazi State. No, they were actively part of the political struggle, not by default but by virtue of their beliefs and actions. They were part of the political opposition against the new Aryan Germany. While the Jehovah's Witnesses taught that everyone is a child of God, even the Nazis, the Nazi creed professed an exclusivist faith in race and sought the expulsion of all those who were not of that race or who rejected the essence of the Nazi system and its power elite. There is much politics here, but certainly no neutrality.

Aside from the ideological tyranny imposed by the Nazis, there was no maneuverability for Jehovah's Witnesses, no space except for what they obtained surreptitiously. Neutrality in Nazi Germany was an illusion. It rested on a foundation of zero tolerance. Political neutrality depends entirely on a culture of toleration, which, in turn, demands prudent political activism on the part of those who seek to be tolerated. The more one is noninvolved the less one can count on being tolerated.

The Nazi State was in fact a zero-tolerance society. Everything legitimate was synchronized with the State apparatus. *Gleichschaltung* (coordi-

nation) was the policy of total power of the State. Unions, the press, the military, even the churches were synchronized. Those who refused were, by default, opposing the State and its claim to uncontested supremacy. The Jehovah's Witnesses heroically refused to let themselves be merged into a State system they rejected as morally evil. Thus, in their view their truth was literally at war with the uncompromising State evil embodied in National Socialism. The two faced each other implacably, like David and Goliath; the physically powerless minority versus an all-powerful State; the spiritually energized struggling against the morally impotent might of the Nazis. There was no "in between," no neutral zone, allowing for an apolitical struggle. It was an either-or circumstance, a situation antithetical to neutrality.

In fact, one could cogently argue that to profess this Jehovah's Witness brand of political neutrality in Nazi Germany was itself subtly immoral, according to the Jehovah's Witness value system. As much as political neutrality was deemed illegal by Nazi legal standards, so was neutrality morally wrong in the face of persecution of others by the ethical standards of the Jehovah's Witnesses. Helping Jews, as they did in large numbers, was no act of neutrality but an act in harmony with the central teachings of the Jehovah's Witnesses' faith. Their heroic religious work was in response to a central dictum of decency in the face of an indecent state. Whatever they did or sought to do in Nazi Germany was in the name of the politics of morality against the corrupt abuse of power by the Nazis. To be a Jehovah's Witness in Nazi Germany required not neutrality but moral activism, provocation, defiance, doing right, and being true to humanity and not race. One can conclude that to have done otherwise, to have been truly neutral, would have meant moral surrender, to have neutered oneself. No, the Jehovah's Witnesses in the Third Reich were morally empowered and obliged to say "No!" to the false teachings of National Socialism.

Clearly, this analysis of political neutrality is in extremis. But what happens to the principle of political neutrality in less suppressive political cultures? This inquiry questions the nature of the Jehovah's Witnesses' code of social behavior in an average society where there is some operative room to be (to pretend to be?) neutral, for example, apolitical. Does it mean never to be partisan, to support candidates, to vote, to contribute financially to sympathizers? What does the Jehovah's Witnesses' policy of political disinterest mean? Total disinterest? Does it mean to let others build and maintain the community from which Jehovah's Witnesses profit? Does it mean philosophical pacifism, engaging in no controversy? Or does it mean opportunism, to exploit the conditions of tolerance made possible by the sacrifice of others? Is this stance not unlike the American colonial and postcolonial pseudopacifism of the Quakers, who abhorred violence and war yet had no compulsion to call upon British and then U.S. Federal troops to kill and forcibly remove Indians from their ancestral lands, lands coveted by the Quakers? This surrogate pacifism was, at best, murderous hypocrisy. Is this policy what underlies the Jehovah's Witnesses' principle of noninvolvement in political affairs? It is certainly not the intention of the Jehovah's Witnesses.

If everyone were apolitical, then anarchy would reign. Their reply would be that a god-like society would fill the vacuum: God will provide and supplant Caesar. But that is pure speculative utopianism not too far from the dangerous phantasmagoric idealism of their Nazi enemies. In the end, common sense dictates that without a *civitas mundi* (earthly city) there can be no *civitas dei* (city of God). One must participate in both. To withdraw from the one is to abandon the other.

–HENRY R. HUTTENBACH,
CITY COLLEGE OF NEW YORK

References

Michael Berenbaum, *The World Must Know: The History of the Holocaust as Told in the United States Holocaust Memorial Museum* (Boston: Little, Brown, 1993).

John S. Conway, *The Nazi Persecution of the Churches, 1933–45* (New York: Basic Books, 1968).

Fear Not–Persecution and Resistance of Jehovah's Witnesses under the Nazi Regime (Berlin: Drei Linden Media, 1997).

Detlef Garbe, *Zwischen Widerstand und Martyrium: Die Zeugen Jehovas im "Dritten Reich"* (Munich: Oldenbourg, 1994).

Hans Hesse, ed., *Persecution and Resistance of Jehovah's Witnesses during the Nazi Regime, 1933–1945* (Bremen: Edition Temmen, 2001).

Rudolf Höss, *Commandant of Auschwitz: The Autobiography of Rudolf Hoess,* translated by Constantine FitzGibbon (Cleveland: World, 1959).

Jehovah's Witnesses Stand Firm against Nazi Assault, video, Watchtower Bible and Tract Society of Pennsylvania, 1996.

Jehovah's Witnesses: Victims of the Nazi Era, 1933–1945 (Washington, D.C.: United States Holocaust Memorial Museum, 1995).

Christine Elizabeth King, *The Nazi State and the New Religions: Five Case Studies in Non-Conformity* (New York: Edwin Mellen Press, 1982).

Simone Arnold Liebster, *Facing the Lion: Memoirs of a Young Girl in Nazi Europe* (New Orleans: Grammaton Press, 2000).

New World Bible Translation Committee, *New World Translation of the Holy Scriptures* (Brooklyn, N.Y.: Watchtower Bible and Tract Society of New York, 1961).

Public Papers of the Presidents of the United States, John F. Kennedy: Containing the Public Messages, Speeches, and Statements of the President, January 20, 1961 to November 22, 1963, 3 volumes (Washington, D.C.: U.S. GPO, 1962–1964).

Purple Triangles, motion picture, Starlock Pictures, 1991.

Carol Rittner, Stephen D. Smith, and Irena Steinfeldt, eds., *The Holocaust and the Christian World: Reflections on the Past, Challenges for the Future* (New York: Continuum, 2000).

Gabriele Yonan, "Spiritual Resistance of Christian Conviction in Nazi Germany: The Case of the Jehovah's Witnesses," *Journal of Church and State,* 41 (Spring 1999): 307–322.

JEWISH COUNCILS

Were the *Judenräte* (Jewish Councils) overly cooperative with the Nazi authorities?

Viewpoint: Yes. A variety of motives, ranging from misguided idealism to selfish opportunism, inclined the leaders of the Jewish Councils to be overly cooperative with the Nazi authorities.

Viewpoint: No. The Jewish Councils accommodated Nazi demands in desperate and extraordinary circumstances in order to preserve the lives of fellow Jews.

The new military conflict that occupied the attention of Europe after Germany invaded Poland was more obvious than another kind of war the Nazis began to wage at the same time. In September 1939 the National Socialist leadership in Berlin set into motion a policy process that resulted in the segregation and eventual extermination of millions of Jews across central and eastern Europe. Concurrent with the attack on Poland and subsequent German drive into Russia in June 1941, the Third Reich established a series of nine major ghettos designed to separate the Jews from the remainder of the citizens of the countries it occupied. Established in cities such as Warsaw, Lvov, and Lodz in Poland; Minsk in Belorussia; Riga in Latvia; and Vilna in Lithuania, the ghettos were quickly crowded with Jews expelled from smaller towns and villages. (Within months of its creation, the 1.5-square-mile Lodz Ghetto was home to 165,000 people.) Not only useful as sites in which to "quarantine" the Jewish population of eastern Europe from their German conquerors, the ghettos also served to control, exploit, and ultimately liquidate the vast majority of European Jews during the Holocaust.

After creating each ghetto and walling it off from the general population, the Nazis appointed a *Judenrat,* a council of leading Jews, to assist in governing its inhabitants. The initial (and severe) problems with insufficient housing, poor sanitation, and inadequate supplies of food and medicine proved to be the least of the challenges to these Jewish ghetto administrations. It was not long before the *Judenräte* were under pressure from their German overseers to assist in the implementation of the Nazi's "Final Solution to the Jewish Question." The Jewish Councils were thus faced with an agonizing question: how much, if at all, should they cooperate with Nazi demands? The decisions made by the *Judenrat* leaders are still the subject of controversy and debate.

Viewpoint:
Yes. A variety of motives, ranging from misguided idealism to selfish opportunism, inclined the leaders of the Jewish Councils to be overly cooperative with the Nazi authorities.

The leaders of the *Judenräte* (Jewish Councils) of central and eastern Europe—most notably those presiding over the Warsaw and Lodz Ghettos in Poland—were often overly cooperative with the representatives of the Third Reich during World War II (1939–1945). They worked with Nazi authorities primarily because they had little choice in light of the German superiority in numbers and military assets in the newly conquered territories of the Reich. A variety of motives influenced *Judenrat* leaders to determine how long and how completely they would cooperate with the Nazis. On the one hand, some leaders cooperated in the hopes of guaranteeing the collective security of the Jews in the ghettos under their control. On the other hand, some Jewish leaders helped the Nazis in order to exploit the situation for their personal gain. Ultimately, however, the Germans' shameless but adept manipulation of the *Judenräte* to achieve their own economic, military, and political objectives meant that neither of the councillors' cooperative strategies proved effective. The collective and individual motivations behind Jewish cooperation with Nazi officials are best illustrated by the experiences of the *Judenräte* of the ghettos in Warsaw and Lodz.

Following their conquest of Poland in the autumn of 1939, one of the Germans' first projects was the reorganization of the Jewish communities. The Nazis' standard operating procedure required that Warsaw have a *Judenrat* of twenty-four leading Jewish citizens. Here, as elsewhere, the Nazis selected a well-known Jew as council chairman and demanded that he choose the remainder of the council members from among his peers. Thus, Adam Czerniakow, a sixty-two-year-old teacher and municipal politician, found himself appointed to work with the enemies of his people. Czerniakow, a Warsaw native who studied chemistry and industrial engineering in college and went on to teach at the city's technical high school, had spent most of his life trying to improve the standard of living of Polish Jews. As head of the *Judenrat,* Czerniakow had an opportunity to pursue the same general objective. However, the stakes were considerably higher—physical survival replacing economic prosperity as the task at hand—and the odds against success were all but insurmountable.

Czerniakow's principal responsibilities as chairman of the Warsaw *Judenrat* included the enactment of Nazi decrees, distribution of foodstuffs, record keeping, and resolution of intracommunal disputes. These duties were carried out within the confines of the Warsaw Ghetto, which was established by the Third Reich in October 1940 and housed as many as five hundred thousand Jews before its liquidation in April 1943. The *Judenrat* was often a polarizing force within the ghetto. This situation was especially true on those occasions—which grew ever more frequent between 1940 and 1943—when the Nazis demanded that Czerniakow produce a given number of Jews (ranging from several dozen to hundreds or thousands) for deportation to "labor" camps, where an almost certain death awaited them. For example, Chaim A. Kaplan, who served as diarist of the Warsaw Ghetto, wrote that the members of the *Judenrat* were:

> Strangers in our midst, foreign to our spirit. . . . [Czerniakow] and his advisors are musclemen who were put on our backs by strangers. Most of them are nincompoops whom no one knew in normal times. All their lives until now they were outside the Jewish fold; they did not rejoice in our happiness nor mourn our misfortune.

Notwithstanding the condemnations of his critics, Czerniakow's intentions were reasonably honorable under the circumstances. In short, he believed that by cooperating with the Nazis, whether by supplying Jewish laborers or discouraging open revolt against German authority, the *Judenrat* would serve the collective interests of the community. While Czerniakow recognized that most, if not all, of those individuals he singled out for deportation were unlikely to survive, he was also convinced that if the *Judenrat* did not cooperate fully, even more Jews—men, women, and children alike—would perish. Additionally, Czerniakow felt that the "council might be able to soften Nazi rules if it tried hard enough, and for him, this was a good reason to serve." Unfortunately, Czerniakow's pragmatism did not resonate among the tens of thousands of Jews struggling for daily survival on the streets of the ghetto. As historian Israel Gutman notes, Czerniakow "appealed to people's consciences, expecting them to behave with maturity and a sense of responsibility. He did not understand the difficulty of sustaining such values for desperate people involved in a struggle for existence and survival."

Czerniakow's attempt to administer the ghetto rationally was further complicated by his establishment and subsequent use of a Jewish police force (led by a nonpracticing Jew named Josef Szerynski) to enforce the decrees of the *Judenrat* and maintain general order within the population. Albeit predictably, the members of the two-thousand-man force proved susceptible to bribes from the wealthier residents of the ghetto. Similarly, Czerniakow was reluctant to confiscate the property of the most well-established Jews or to issue deportation orders to the members of their respective families. As Gutman concludes, although Czerniakow's "intentions were honorable, his methods did not suit the reality of the occupation of the ghetto and at times led to disappointing results."

Ultimately, Czerniakow realized the hopelessness of the challenge he had embraced. Faced with a German order to commence mass deportations of all ages to labor camps in July 1942, he acknowledged that cooperation was no longer a useful means to safeguard the Jews' collective interests, and he committed suicide. In a letter written to his wife, Felicia, shortly before his death, Czerniakow wrote, "The SS wants me to kill children with my own hands. There is no other way out and I must die." In the two months following Czerniakow's death, more than three hundred thousand residents of the ghetto were either deported by the Nazis or murdered outright. And, in April 1943, nearly all remaining inhabitants of the Warsaw Ghetto were either killed or captured after staging an uprising that resulted in a massive retaliatory strike by the German army.

Czerniakow's approach to cooperation between the *Judenrat* and the Third Reich was designed to serve the collective interests of the Warsaw Jews. It failed as a result of increasing numbers of Nazi deportation orders and the susceptibility of the council officials and policemen to bribery. By contrast, leaders of other *Judenräte* established in central and eastern Europe during World War II were more prone to develop collaborative relationships with German officials in pursuit of personal gains, whether economic, physical, or political in orientation. This egocentric brand of cooperation was particularly useful to the Nazis, who were adept at manipulating individuals concerned primarily with their own comfort and security rather than the interests of the wider community they had been appointed to govern.

One notable example of such egocentric behavior was the management of Jewish affairs within the Lodz Ghetto between October 1939 and August 1944 by *Judenrat* chairman Mordechai Chaim Rumkowski, who was known to residents as the "Eldest of the Jews." He used the *Judenrat* to administer the ghetto as a de facto one-man autocracy rather than a pseudodemocracy such as Czerniakow's Warsaw. Czerniakow, after meeting Rumkowski for the first time in May 1941, noted in his diary that

the individual does not exist for him. He has special police authority in the ghetto for confiscating and so he has confiscated diamonds and furs. . . . this is an arrogant man, haughty and stupid. He is doing harm, because he tells the authorities that everything is in order in his sector.

Similarly, historian Linda Jacobs Altman concludes that "Rumkowski transformed the ghetto into his own little dictatorship, keeping tight control of everything from work assignments to food rations. They called him 'King Chaim' because of his high-handed style among his fellow Jews."

Only after he presided over the deportation of thousands of people to the concentration camps did Czerniakow eventually recognize that cooperation with the Nazis would not serve the interests of the Jews of Warsaw—either individually or collectively. Rumkowski, however, proved a perpetually willing political figurehead for the Nazis up to the day that the Lodz Ghetto was liquidated. Rather than question Nazi demands—as Czerniakow often did in attempting to reduce the number of deportees required by a given order—Rumkowski chose to cooperate unequivocally in the hope that his own security and that of his family members and close colleagues would be ensured. Consider Rumkowski's response to a Nazi order for the deportation of all Lodz Jews under the age of ten and over the age of sixty-five issued in September 1942, which he recorded in his diary after carrying out the German dictate: "We have to accept the evil order. I have to perform this bloody operation myself; I simply must cut off limbs to save the body! I have to take away the children, because otherwise others will also be taken."

To Rumkowski's credit, the Lodz Ghetto survived longer than any other Jewish ghetto in Poland. One way Rumkowski ensured the relative longevity of his ghetto was by micromanaging its affairs with extraordinary zeal and developing a Jewish police force that—while not composed of the most honorable men—saw to it that his orders were carried out without question or hesitation. Altman observed of this force that the "Jewish police attracted [some] people with few morals, who saw a chance to benefit from the misery of their fellow Jews. Others had a mean streak and simply liked the idea of venting their anger on victims who could not fight back." While these Jewish ghetto police were enforcing Nazi orders, "King Chaim" ensured the short-term survival of his "subjects" by offering them as slave labor for German war industries. More than one hundred ghetto-based factories allowed the Nazis to turn a substantial profit while supplying the German military with the requisite matériel to maintain their control over eastern Europe. One historian has observed that the "organization of labor and the enormous profits the Germans derived from the Jews' toil provide the main explanation for the Germans decision to refrain from liquidating the Lodz ghetto." Ultimately, however, Rumkowski's luck ran out. When the Nazis finally shut down the Lodz Ghetto in August 1944, he was shipped to the concentration camp at Auschwitz, where he subsequently perished.

Neither Rumkowski nor Czerniakow—nor, for that matter, any of their counterparts on *Judenräte* across central and eastern Europe—could have refused to cooperate with the Nazis and also retained their positions (or their lives). The extent of and motives for their cooperation, however, differed appreciably. Fundamentally misunderstanding Nazi intentions, Czerniakow chose to cooperate with the Nazis in order to save the lives of the majority of the residents of the Warsaw ghetto. Once he recognized the futility of that task, he chose to take his own life rather than continue to collaborate. Rumkowski took a considerably more individualistic stance. While he was able to avoid the liquidation of the Lodz Ghetto until late in the war, he did so primarily to preserve his own physical security and political status. It is also significant that neither Czerniakow nor Rumkowski achieved their objectives. Czerniakow's pragmatism, for example, proved unrealistic given the ghetto residents' desperation and resultant willingness to offer and take bribes to improve their living conditions. Rumkowski's egocentrism was even less forgivable and ultimately no more successful in guaranteeing his own survival or saving the lives of his friends and family members. Yet, in rendering judgment on Czerniakow, Rumkowski, and other World War II *Judenrat* leaders, it is important to acknowledge the fact that—irrespective of their motives for cooperation—they and the Jews they governed were all victims of the Third Reich. In the last analysis there were no winners in the context of the Holocaust.

—ROBERT J. PAULY JR.,
MIDLANDS TECHNICAL COLLEGE

Viewpoint:
No. The Jewish Councils accommodated Nazi demands in desperate and extraordinary circumstances in order to preserve the lives of fellow Jews.

Judenräte (councils of leading Jews) in the ghettos during the Holocaust found themselves in precarious situations, for they functioned as the intermediaries between their Nazi oppressors and the Jewish ghetto inhabitants. Much of the power that the *Judenrat* leaders appeared to possess was actually illusory, for they always served under the watchful eye of the Nazi ghetto administrators. The councillors realized that if they incited the wrath of these Nazi oppressors, they, along with their Jewish constituents within the ghetto, would inevitably incur punishment. While the *Judenräte* possessed formal control over their fellow Jews, the horrific and terrible orders that they implemented derived from their Nazi controllers. Some argue that by adhering to and instituting Nazi orders instead of resisting them, this accommodationist policy manifested the evil and treacherous nature of the *Judenrat* leaders, but this view ignores the powerlessness of the Jewish Councils and imposes value judgments made in hindsight. Although *Judenrat* leaders imposed rules that led to the deaths of thousands of Jews, they had no choice and acted in an effort to save lives.

While the Jews who inhabited the ghettos in Europe lived under the control of the *Judenrat*, the *Judenrat* elders, in turn, functioned under the authority of Nazi ghetto administrators and thus possessed little power. They were, to some extent, figureheads of the Nazi regime, employed to provide European Jews with a false sense of security and autonomy. Wanting the Jews to remain isolated within the ghetto so that they could easily observe, control, collect, and ultimately transport them to the concentration camps, Nazi ghetto administrators needed the Jews to feel safe and to maintain the belief that they possessed self-government and that their leaders possessed authority. Thus, they created Jewish Councils that appeared to have authority. Consequently, Jews in the ghetto sometimes blamed the *Judenrat* for adhering to accommodationist policies, unaware that these leaders actually had little or no alternative.

In reality, when Jewish Councils attempted to disobey Nazi orders or acted in a manner contrary to that of Nazi policy, the council members were severely punished and sometimes executed. The punishments incurred by the *Judenrat* leaders demonstrate that challenges to Nazi authority were not permitted and that accommodationist policies were necessary. In the ghetto in Vilna, Lithuania, the Nazis disbanded the *Judenrat* because their actions were considered too democratic. Jacob Gens, head of the Jewish police in the Vilna Ghetto, subsequently took charge. Gens was later executed by the Nazis when he was caught aiding the local partisan organization and even allowing some Jews to escape and join the resistance. A similar fate befell Joseph Parnes, chairman of the *Judenrat* in Lvov, in October 1941 when he refused Nazi orders to round up Jews for transport to a labor camp.

Passive resistance solved nothing. In Elie Wiesel's *The Forgotten* (1992), the elder Malkiel Rosenbaum refuses to become leader of the Jewish Council in the newly constructed Feherfalu Ghetto in Romania. He is beaten up, knocked unconscious, revived, and then tortured for refusing the Nazi officer's request. Shortly thereafter, he must provide the names of ten prominent citizens who will be used by the Nazis as hostages—one of whom will be murdered for every Jew who escapes the ghetto. When Rosenbaum refuses and provides only his name, he is tortured and murdered; the ghetto lasts for a mere month before it, too, is liquidated. Rosenbaum's passive resistance solves nothing, for his people are transported to a concentration camp anyway. Although this work by the author is categorized as historical fiction, it represents the belief that resistance by the Jewish Council (in this case, Rosenbaum), although courageous, was usually futile and only succeeded in angering the Nazis. The historical example of Adam Czerniakow, head of the Warsaw Ghetto *Judenrat*, corroborates this view. Czerniakow committed suicide in 1942 rather than comply with Nazi orders to round up his fellow Jews for deportation.

Although Czerniakow's comportment manifests selflessness and benevolence, his sui-

cide actually expressed his lack of power. His death did not even interrupt the mass deportations in which he was ordered to participate. His refusal to accommodate the Nazi request did not result in the saving of Jewish lives. This result is not in any way to suggest that there were any virtues in open collaboration with the evils of Nazism. Rather, one must recognize that in desperate times some *Judenrat* leaders reluctantly adhered to an accommodationist policy in an effort—sometimes successful—to save Jewish lives. There is a significant distinction to be made between collaborators and accommodationists. Collaborators helped the Nazis out of unscrupulous self-interest and a marked lack of conscience; they wished to profit from providing aid to the Nazis. Accommodationists, however, satisfied Nazi requests not to benefit personally but in order to save Jewish lives. These *Judenrat* leaders hoped that by satisfying some Nazi demands, they could garner sufficient favor with their Nazi superiors to convince them to preserve some Jewish lives, even at the expense of others. Two such accommodationists were Mordechai Chaim Rumkowski, of the Lodz Ghetto, and Gens, of the Vilna Ghetto.

Rumkowski and Gens each faced the terrible decision of whether to permit "selections" in their ghettos. Powerless to save all of the

JEWISH COUNCILS

A BROKEN JEW STANDS BEFORE YOU

After receiving a demand from the Nazis for twenty-four thousand Jews to be delivered for deportation, Mordechai Chaim Rumkowski, chairman of the Lodz Judenrat, *made the following speech to his constituents on 4 September 1942:*

A grievous blow has struck the ghetto. They are asking us to give up the best we possess—the children and the elderly. I was unworthy of having a child of my own, so I gave the best years of my life to children. I've lived and breathed with children, I never imagined I would be forced to deliver this sacrifice to the altar with my own hands. In my old age, I must stretch out my hands and beg: Brothers and sisters! Hand them over to me! Fathers and mothers: Give me your children!

I had a suspicion something was going to befall us. I anticipated "something" and was always like a watchman: on guard to prevent it. But I was unsuccessful because I did not know what was threatening us. The taking of the sick from the hospitals caught me completely by surprise. And I give you the best proof there is of this: I had my own nearest and dearest among them and I could do *nothing* for them! . . .

Yesterday afternoon, they gave me the order to send more than 20,000 Jews out of the ghetto, and if not—"We will do it!" So the question became, "Should we take it upon ourselves, do it ourselves, or leave it to others to do?" Well, we—that is, I and my closest associates—thought first not about "How many will perish?" but "How many is it possible to save?" And we reached the conclusion that, however hard it would be for us, we should take the implementation of this order into our own hands. . . .

I have no thought of consoling you today. Nor do I wish to calm you. I must lay bare your full anguish and pain. I come to you like a bandit, to take from you what you treasure most in your hearts! I have tried, using every possible means, to get the order revoked. I tried—when that proved to be impossible—to soften the order. Just yesterday, I ordered a list of children aged 9—I wanted at least to save this one aged-group: the nine to 10 year olds. But I was not granted this concession. On only one point did I succeed: in saving the 10 year olds and up. Let this be a consolation to our profound grief.

There are, in the ghetto, many patients who can expect to live only a few days more, maybe a few weeks. I don't know if the idea is diabolical or not, but I must say it: "Give me the sick. In their place we can save the healthy."

I know how dear the sick are to any family, and particularly to Jews. However, when cruel demands are made, one has to weigh and measure: who shall, can and may be saved? And common sense dictates that the saved must be those who *can* be saved and those who have a chance of being rescued, not those who cannot be saved in any case . . .

We live in the ghetto, mind you. We live with so much restriction that we do not have enough even for the healthy, let alone for the sick. Each of us feeds the sick at the expense of our own health: we give our bread to the sick. We give them our meager ration of sugar, our little piece of meat. And what's the result? Not enough to cure the sick, and we ourselves become ill. Of course, such sacrifices are the most beautiful and noble. But there are times when one has to choose: sacrifice the sick, who haven't the slightest chance of recovery and who also may make others ill, or rescue the healthy. . . .

I understand you, mothers; I see your tears, alright. I also feel what you feel in your hearts, you fathers who will have to go to work in the morning after your children have been taken from you, when just yesterday you were playing with your dear little ones. All this I know and feel. Since 4 o'clock yesterday, when I first found out about the order, I have been utterly broken. I share your pain. I suffer because of your anguish, and I don't know how I'll survive this—where I'll find the strength to do so.

I must tell you a secret: they requested 24,000 victims, 3,000 a day for eight days. I succeeded in reducing the number to 20,000, but only on the condition that these be children under the age of 10. Children 10 and older are safe! Since the children and the aged together equals only some 13,000 souls, the gap will have to be filled with the sick.

I can barely speak. I am exhausted; I only want to tell you what I am asking of you: Help me carry out this action! I am trembling. I am afraid that others, God forbid, will do it themselves.

A broken Jew stands before you. Do not envy me. This is the most difficult of all orders I have ever had to carry out at any time. . . . So they promised me: If we deliver our victims by ourselves, there will be peace!!!

Source: "Give Me Your Children!" <http://www.data-sync.com/~davidg59/rumkowsk.html>.

JEWISH COUNCILS

Jews in their respective ghettos, these Jewish leaders complied with Nazi orders in the hopes of saving as many lives as possible. Critics of these two men have argued that they were accomplices of the Nazi Final Solution because they willingly sacrificed the lives of many of their constituents, realizing that those picked for selections would be deported to concentration camps. In the case of Rumkowski, it is unclear when he realized that the deportations went to the extermination center at Chelmno and not, as he originally thought, to labor camps. While both men strove to preserve a Jewish "remnant" within a permanent ghetto, their hopes were thwarted by Nazi plans to "liquidate" the enclaves.

The accommodationist policy in Lodz and Vilna was also based on the hope that if the Jews acquiesced to some Nazi demands, the Nazis would allow them to survive until they might be freed by Soviet forces advancing from the east. Although critics of Rumkowski and Gens have pointed out correctly that this policy failed because the Russian advance stopped short of the ghettos, these ghetto leaders could not have predicted this result. (Indeed, if the Soviets had come to the rescue of the Jewish ghettos, Rumkowski and Gens might have been considered heroes.) Isolated in the ghettos, *Judenrat* leaders had access to little information concerning events in the outside world and thus were forced to rely upon rumors, most of which contained little truth. Furthermore, Rumkowski and Gens were immersed in an unprecedented situation with little time for reflection. Critics of these Jewish leaders, meanwhile, possess the advantage of hindsight; it is quite easy to judge others years—and decades—after the events have taken place or when one is not burdened by power and the pressing need to make difficult decisions.

Rumkowski and Gens agreed to the Nazi demand for limited "selections" because the only alternative provided to them by the Nazis was the total liquidation of the ghettos. It seemed better to acquiesce to Nazi orders and choose those who would die from among their own people than to provoke a Nazi invasion of the ghettos and the annihilation of all the inhabitants. In a speech to the residents of the Lodz Ghetto in September 1942, Rumkowski begged his fellow Jews to comply with Nazi demands, because "the part that can be saved is much larger than the part that must be given away!" Thus, the lives of those Jews too ill, too old, or too young to work for the Nazis were traded in order to buy time for those still laboring in the war industries (the Lodz Ghetto, for instance, contained 120 factories). In fact, some *Judenräte* were convinced that once the Nazis

realized that Jews were productive workers and could contribute to the Nazi war effort, the lives of all the Jewish workers eventually would be spared. It is worth noting that Rumkowski appears to have enjoyed some degree of success in his efforts to placate the Nazis, for the Lodz Ghetto remained for some time after all the other Polish ghettos had been liquidated. As those who support Rumkowski's accommodationist policies like to point out, in the words of Shmuel Krakowski, "the five thousand to seven thousand survivors of the Lodz ghetto constituted, in relative terms, the largest among the groups of Holocaust survivors in Poland."

Nevertheless, other historians have reasonable grounds for presenting Rumkowski in an unfavorable light. But they misguidedly conflate his personal character with his accommodationist policies. Inclined to greed and vindictive behavior, the chairman of the Lodz *Judenrat* abused his authority at almost every opportunity. For example, Rumkowski hoarded thousands of extra rations of food while the citizens in the ghetto died of starvation. He ruled as a despot, ensuring that any Jew who opposed him would be punished by inclusion in the next Nazi selection. A megalomaniac, Rumkowski suffered from a messianic complex, considering himself the savior of the Jews; he rode through the ghetto in a horse and carriage and insisted that the postage and currency there should bear his picture. The *Judenrat* leader's personal failings, however grievous, should not have any bearing on the worth of his accommodationist policies. Rumkowski's character and his policies were separate entities.

Gens, like Rumkowski, attempted to save some Jews in his ghetto by allowing others to die, and like the *Judenrat* leader in Lodz, his intentions were good. He reluctantly agreed to Nazi demands for selections, and consequently, he had the power to save some lives. In one case, instead of dispatching the Vilna Ghetto police to collect 1,500 Jews from the nearby Oshmiany Ghetto as he was ordered, he sent the Nazis only 406 Jews who were seriously ill or quite old. Although some would argue that Gens's action constitutes collaboration with the enemy by bringing them 406 people who would be murdered, Gens did not arrange for the mandated 1,500 to die. Furthermore, his action protected the women and children who were most likely to have been selected by the Nazis had he refused to carry out the mission. Thus, his accommodation to the Nazi request actually saved lives. Zelig Kalmanovich, an inhabitant of the Vilna Ghetto and a Yiddish literature and culture archivist, commented on this incident in his diary:

JEWISH COUNCILS

It is horrible, perhaps the worst of all predicaments, still there is no other way. Blessed be the God of Israel, who sent us this man [Gens]. . . . The result: over 400 souls have perished—elderly people, the weak and ill, retarded children. However, 1,500 women and children were saved. If this had been the work of strangers [Nazis], 2,000 people would have perished, God forbid.

Likewise, in the area of armed resistance, Gens saw no alternative to minimal cooperation with the Nazis. He could not fully support the efforts of the United Partisan Organization because he realized that his ghetto police chief, Salek Dessler, was an informant of the Gestapo. After being taken by surprise by the Warsaw Ghetto Uprising in early 1943, the Nazis placed spies in the ghettos to facilitate the rapid detection and destruction of any attempt at armed resistance by the Jews. They were determined not to allow such an uprising to occur again. In Gens's opinion such an uprising was, at best, a futile gesture. Historian Yehuda Bauer agrees, noting that the resisters lacked direct support from Soviet and Allied armed forces as well as sufficient ammunition: "rebellion meant certain death for everyone. A slave labor economy provided at least the possibility of survival."

Angered that some Jews in the ghetto considered him a traitor because of his accommodationist policies, Gens declared in a speech:

I cast my accounts with Jewish blood and not with Jewish respect. If they [Nazi leaders] ask me for a thousand Jews, I give them because if the Germans themselves came, they would take with violence not a thousand but thousands and thousands and the whole ghetto would be finished. With a hundred I save a thousand; with a thousand I save ten thousand. . . . if you'll survive the ghetto, you'll say, "We came out with a clear conscience," but I, Jacob Gens, if I survive, I'll go out covered with filth and blood will run from my hands. Nevertheless, I'd be willing to stand at the bar of judgment before Jews. I'd say I did everything to rescue as many Jews as I could and I tried to lead them to freedom. And in order to save even a small part of the Jewish people, I alone had to lead others to their deaths.

Gens's comments reveal that he considered his accommodationist policies carefully and believed that if he denied Nazi requests to deport some Jews, all of the inhabitants of the Vilna Ghetto would die. Under the desperate circumstances faced by Gens and his colleagues on the other *Judenräte*, the decision to acquiesce to Nazi demands was the only feasible alternative; it was the only option that saved lives.

–ERIC STERLING,
AUBURN UNIVERSITY, MONTGOMERY

References

Linda Jacobs Altman, *The Holocaust Ghettos* (Springfield, Mass.: Enslow, 1998).

Yitzhak Arad, *Ghetto in Flames: The Struggle and Destruction of the Jews in Vilna in the Holocaust* (Jerusalem: Yad Vashem, Martyrs' and Heroes' Remembrance Authority / New York: Ktav, 1981).

Yehuda Bauer, *A History of the Holocaust* (New York: Watts, 1982).

Adam Czerniakow, *The Warsaw Diary of Adam Czerniakow: Prelude to Doom,* edited by Raul Hilberg, Stanislaw Staron, and Josef Kermisz, translated by Staron and the staff of Yad Vashem (New York: Stein & Day, 1979).

Lucjan Dobroszycki, ed., *The Chronicle of the Lodz Ghetto, 1941–1944,* translated by Richard Lourie, Joachim Neugroschel, and others (New Haven: Yale University Press, 1984).

Israel Gutman, *The Jews of Warsaw, 1939–1943: Ghetto, Underground, Revolt,* translated by Ina Friedman (Bloomington: Indiana University Press, 1982).

Gutman, *Resistance: The Warsaw Ghetto Uprising* (Boston: Houghton Mifflin, 1994).

Chaim A. Kaplan, *Scroll of Agony: The Warsaw Diary of Chaim A. Kaplan,* translated and edited by Abraham I. Katsh (New York: Macmillan, 1965).

Emmanuel Ringelblum, *Notes from the Warsaw Ghetto: The Journal of Emmanuel Ringelblum,* edited and translated by Jacob Sloan (New York: McGraw-Hill, 1958).

Isaiah Trunk, *Judenrat: The Jewish Councils in Eastern Europe under Nazi Occupation* (New York: Macmillan, 1972).

Leonard Tushnet, *The Pavement of Hell* (New York: St. Martin's Press, 1972).

Elie Wiesel, *The Forgotten,* translated by Stephen Becker (New York: Summit, 1992).

JEWISH COUNCILS

MEDICAL EXPERIMENTS

Should data derived from Nazi medical experiments be used by contemporary scientists?

Viewpoint: Yes. Scientific evidence has no moral quality, even though it might have been gathered by unethical scientists.

Viewpoint: No. Medical researchers today should dissociate themselves from torturers and murderers who abused their positions of power and privilege in the name of science.

It is well known that medical experimentation unbound by any restraint of ethics or morals was carried out in the concentration camps and that many victims died terrible deaths at the hands of Nazi medical scientists. For example, many victims died of hypothermia as Nazi scientists attempted to determine how long a human might survive in cold oceans; others perished of embolisms in tests of the effects of rapid decompression on humans. These experiments and others like them produced information whose status is questionable. Should it be regarded as scientific data and evaluated on those terms, or should it be judged on ethical terms and thus discarded as irremediably tainted?

Tandy McConnell argues that the data should be available to modern researchers. He acknowledges the criminality of the acts that produced the data but suggests that a distinction be made between the scientists, who merit only condemnation, and the data, which should be evaluated as any other data would be. If, as he notes, the data are flawed, that is a matter for science, not ethics, to determine. The fate of the scientists is a separate matter and is best left to jurisprudence. By pointing out that an anatomical textbook that is still widely used was written by an ardent Austrian Nazi (and may have information based upon autopsies carried out on the bodies of Holocaust victims), McConnell reminds readers that "the bell cannot be un-rung." The data exists and has been, and will continue to be, discussed. To pretend otherwise, he suggests, is not going to make the data go away and will only hinder the practice of future scientists acting ethically in the pursuit of knowledge.

Judith W. Kay, in contrast, argues that the data collected by Nazi "scientists" (the quotes are intended to cast doubt on the status of the experimenters) is permanently tainted by its source in the suffering of tormented victims. Nazi medical research, in her view, is not medical research, because it proceeded outside the bounds of standard, ethical scientific practice of the time. She carefully describes the way that the experimenters violated norms established in early-twentieth-century Germany. In standard German clinical practice of the 1910s and 1920s, no experiment even remotely resembling those carried out in the camps would have been considered to be science. By condemning the experiments based on period conceptions rather than projecting modern standards backward, she makes a strong case for not regarding the results of these experiments as good science. She goes further, based on a well-considered ethical position, to conclude that by banning the use of this evidence, the profession of medical research affirms its moral center—the duty to protect human subjects from torture and murder. The profession ought to refuse to use data obtained through the worst violation of this duty in human history and, by doing so, affirm the dignity of all human life.

Medical and scientific ethics more generally remain crucial issues, particularly in a time when the possibilities for biological research seem to be expanding without limit. With such great opportunities comes the possibility for great abuses. What kind of practices can one condone in the name of progress? What shall be condemned? How does one protect fellow humans from abuse at the hands of science? The Nazi medical experiments raise all these questions.

Viewpoint:
Yes. Scientific evidence has no moral quality, even though it might have been gathered by unethical scientists.

Had the Final Solution been carried out only by mindless thugs and sociopaths, then one might mourn its victims with a clearer mind. Dying at the hands of a psychopathic killer has much the same random, amoral quality as being killed in a tornado or earthquake: sad, and certainly to be prevented if possible, but aberrant and not relevant to the rest of society. But the perpetrators of the Holocaust, as Raul Hilberg has pointed out, were normal people and included police officers, lawyers, judges, and accountants. The Nazi regime was supported by philosophers and theologians. It was not an aberration of an individual killer but of a modern society. Many of the most hideous crimes were carried out by otherwise respectable physicians and scientists laboring under the guise of modern scientific inquiry and the promotion of public health.

Postwar denazification trials sought, with mixed success, to hold these scientific perpetrators accountable for their crimes. During the Doctors' Trial (1946–1949) some of the most gruesome evidence was brought to light: SS physicians performed medical experiments on concentration camp inmates as casually as if they were laboratory rats. Indeed, current regulations on the treatment of laboratory animals would have excluded animals from much of what was perpetrated by Nazi doctors against Jews, Gypsies, and other victims. Clearly, it seemed, Nazi ideology had infected the practice of science and medicine with a bacillus from which it could not hope to recover. Thus, with the perpetrators in prison or, as in the case of Josef Mengele, in hiding, science and medicine in Germany started over again in the 1950s. Books and articles written in the 1930s and 1940s were, if not purged from the shelves, relegated to the realm of curiosity—what could they have been thinking to have done such things? Whatever it was, this atrocity was not science.

One must distinguish between Nazi science and Nazi scientists. Nazi science—specifically the biological sciences—was built on assumptions about the nature of living things that, even in the 1930s and 1940s, were demonstrably flawed. There was no evidence to support Nazi contentions that "race mixing" tended to degrade the gene pool, nor that the Aryan "race" was distinctive in any substantive way from other races. Nazi beliefs about Jews and Gypsies were at the core of many of the most hideous medical "experiments" performed at Auschwitz, and as often happens when a research project is designed to prove a politically potent point, scientists found support for what they were looking for.

Nazi scientists, however, were not without merit. Without Nazi advances made in rocket propulsion and guidance, the American and Soviet space programs would have been delayed for decades. In their efforts to protect the health of the German people, Nazi physicians and public-health officials urged restrictions on tobacco and food additives and labored to protect workers from exposure to workplace toxins, including asbestos, mercury, and radon gas. Nazi doctors identified environmental and genetic causes of cancer. Such public-health concerns were not in spite of Nazi ideology, but because of it, and were not echoed among the Allied states or in postwar Germany for another twenty years. Indeed, Nazi opposition to smoking and interest in whole-food and vegetarian diets has been used to damn a variety of public-health regulations, as if somehow Adolf Hitler's vegetarianism and his abstinence from tobacco and alcohol might somehow threaten to overshadow his wickedness. Hitler was a vegetarian because he believed that such a diet might prevent cancer and other health problems. He was almost certainly right. He was also the perpetrator of genocide and the instigator of a war that nearly destroyed civilization. There is no moral to this story, only complexities.

The Nazi public-health enterprise was rooted in a desire to strengthen the whole German *volk* (people). The well-being of the individual was of importance only as it impinged on the well-being of the race. Thus, Nazi doctors rigorously pursued the chemical causes of cancer and tried to reduce exposure to them. In factories where exposure could not be prevented, slave labor was often imported to do the "dirty work"

MEDICAL EXPERIMENTS

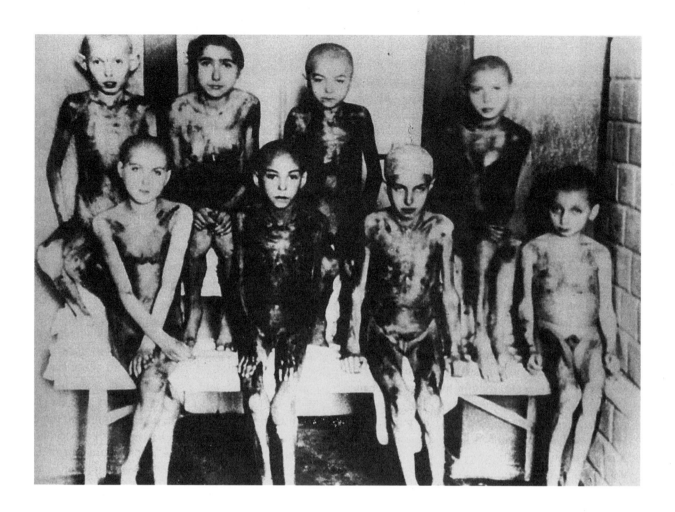

Children who were severely burned in the course of medical experiments at Auschwitz, 1945

(U.S. Holocaust Memorial Museum, Washington, D.C.)

MEDICAL EXPERIMENTS

for which pure Aryans were deemed unfit. The goal was to protect the German workforce and the Aryan gene pool. Smoking, too, was criticized, not as a bad personal habit but as a crime against the good of the whole *volk,* since sick workers could not produce and became, instead, a burden on the nation. It was by this same logic that the incurably handicapped were deemed "unworthy of life," not because they were suffering but because they were a burden on the rest of society. But however inhumane their motives, however wicked their implementation, Nazi health regulations might well have prevented cancers and other environmental diseases and may provide a beginning point for modern epidemiological research.

Nazi scientists prove equally difficult to categorize. Much of the "medical experimentation" associated with Mengele at Auschwitz—sewing together two twins to create artificial Siamese twins or dripping dye in the eyes of brown-eyed people to turn the irises blue—had no conceivable medical or scientific merit. It was more the tinkering of a bored and wicked mind than science. Even the more scientifically—if wickedly—conceived high-altitude and hypothermia experiments at Dachau provided little meaningful scientific knowledge.

The hypobaric experiments are most problematic, and not just because the experimenters casually and callously caused the death and suffering of hundreds of victims. In order to understand the effects of a sudden loss of air pressure—as would happen if a jet pilot were to eject from a pressurized cockpit at high altitude—experimenters reproduced these conditions on concentration camp inmates. Virtually all test victims died. The results—reported at the Doctors' Trial at Nuremberg after World War II (1939–1945)—were that most of the victims died of embolism. Gasses dissolved in the blood under sea-level pressure (32 psi) come out of solution (that is, they form bubbles in the same way a carbonated drink fizzes when the pressure is released). That this process would happen was predictable from the same effect on deep-sea divers who were brought to the surface too quickly. The same thing could have been demonstrated with animal victims. The laws of physics, which had been understood since the eighteenth century, remained unchanged. There simply was not much to be learned.

Concentration camp inmates subjected to cold-water experiments demonstrated the again well-documented, if less well understood, effect of cold water on the human body. Because water conducts heat easily, an unprotected pilot or sailor plunged into icy water would become helpless in minutes and would be dead within an hour. These experiments were less driven by ideology than by practical concerns. Pilots have to be protected with pressure suits at high altitudes; an unprotected sailor or airman in icy water for more than a few minutes is not going to be found alive. Human victims were readily available for Nazi experiments and cost less to use than animals. And unlike animals, for whom the Führer had an affection, Jews, Gypsies, and communists had no advocates to protect them.

The horrible nature of these practices alone does not impugn the data collected in these experiments. Though a court of law might exclude such evidence from consideration, neither history nor science is limited by such rules. Jurisprudence demands that evidence illegally or improperly obtained not be considered in reaching a legal finding of fact. Even though this standard occasionally permits a guilty party to escape punishment, the greater social good—freedom from unrestrained prosecution—generally prevails. Science, unlike law, is fundamentally amoral. Understanding and knowledge are the goals of pure science. Research methods may be constrained by ethical norms, but the quest for knowledge is, at least in theory, unlimited. That means that any data, however obtained, is fair game for scientific inquiry.

The alternative is to lock away the records of the human experiments as a statement that no good, however compelling (and in this case there is no compelling good imaginable), can justify the torture of other human beings. This decision might be ethically satisfying, but it is unlikely that this practice alone would discourage future, unrestrained human experimentation. There may be scientists so lacking in human sympathy and so unrestrained by morality that they could compete with Mengele in brutality. Persuaded that the pursuit of knowledge justifies cruelty or murder, they would follow his path if the opportunity presented itself. Sealing the evidence of sixty-year-old experiments is unlikely to have much effect on them, certainly not compared to the threat of prosecution, loss of status, and denial of access to the tools of research. Mengele was cruel largely because he seems to have enjoyed cruelty. At least, he was unmoved by human suffering, but he was also unimpeded by any threat of legal or professional sanction for his conduct. Had the institutions that restrained him during the first years of his professional life remained in place after he put on an SS uniform, he might never have crossed the line that transformed him from scientist to monster.

Assessing the experimental data reveals little scientific data that is not already known or that could not have been obtained by more-humane methods than murder and torture. But such claims are only valid if the experimental data is, in fact, thoroughly and scientifically analyzed. The value of such data should be determined by physicians, engineers, and anthropologists rather than ethicists. It should, as should all data, be available to anyone with the ability to interpret it for whatever purpose.

Finally, there is no question of releasing gems of knowledge that have been hidden away for decades. In 1995 H. A. Israel, an oral surgeon, became interested in the origins of the *Topographische Anatomie des Menschen: Lehrbuch und Atlas der Regionär-Stratigraphischen Präparation,* or *Pernkopf Anatomy* (1933–1960), an anatomical text widely used by surgeons and anatomists. It had, he discovered, a more than passing association with Nazi science. Begun in 1933 and not completed until 1960, the *Pernkopf Anatomy* was largely the work of Eduard Pernkopf, an anatomist at the University of Vienna and an exuberant Nazi even before the *Anschluss* (annexation of Austria). Though he spent three years in prison after the war, he was never convicted of any crime and continued work on the *Pernkopf Anatomy* until his death in 1955. Many of the anatomical drawings that are the heart of the multivolume work were produced between 1938 and 1945, and one is compelled to wonder about the once-living women, men, and children whose organs are here so artistically and helpfully presented. Probably they were not concentration camp victims, but it is more than likely that Pernkopf followed the time-honored practice of using cadavers of executed criminals. In this case the Wiener Landesgericht prison probably provided the cadavers. During the Nazi era these bodies would have included, according to Simon Wiesenthal, "non Jewish Austrian patriots, communists, and other enemies of the Nazis." The truth may never be known with any precision, but the *Pernkopf Anatomy,* in print and widely distributed, and part of the education of thousands of physicians, is unlikely to be replaced. It is certainly not the only anatomical atlas in print, but it is one of the most widely used. Its existence, and its place in medical literature and education, makes questions of suppression moot. The bell cannot be un-rung. Nazi medical and scientific data, whatever its provenance and however criminally obtained, has not been and will not be ignored. Limiting access to such data, or preventing the publication of contemporary research based on that data, will not make the data go away, it will only hinder and frustrate scientists trying, ethically and responsibly, to create new understandings on a foundation of existing knowledge.

—TANDY MCCONNELL,
COLUMBIA COLLEGE

CRIMINAL EXPERIMENTS

The indictment of Nazi doctors for performing experimentation on concentration camp victims included a list of experiments, in addition to freezing and high-altitude sickness, which are listed below:

(C) Malaria Experiments. From about February 1942 to about April 1945 experiments were conducted at the Dachau concentration camp in order to investigate immunization for and treatment of malaria. Healthy concentration-camp inmates were infected by mosquitoes or by injections of extracts of the mucous glands of mosquitoes. After having contracted malaria the subjects were treated with various drugs to test their relative efficacy. Over 1,000 involuntary subjects were used in these experiments. Many of the victims died and others suffered severe pain and permanent disability. . . .

(D) Lost (Mustard) Gas Experiments. At various times between September 1939 and April 1945 experiments were conducted at Sachsenhausen, Natzweiler, and other concentration camps for the benefit of the German Armed Forces to investigate the most effective treatment of wounds caused by Lost gas. Lost is a poison gas which is commonly known as mustard gas. Wounds deliberately inflicted on the subjects were infected with Lost. Some of the subjects died as a result of these experiments and others suffered intense pain and injury. . . .

(E) Sulfanilamide Experiments. From about July 1942 to about September 1943 experiments to investigate the effectiveness of sulfanilamide were conducted at the Ravensbrueck concentration camp for the benefit of the German Armed Forces. Wounds deliberately inflicted on the experimental subjects were infected with bacteria such as streptococcus, gas gangrene, and tetanus. Circulation of blood was interrupted by tying off blood vessels at both ends of the wound to create a condition similar to that of a battlefield wound. Infection was aggravated by forcing wood shavings and ground glass into the wounds. The infection was treated with sulfanilamide and other drugs to determine their effectiveness. Some subjects died as a result of these experiments and others suffered serious injury and intense agony. . . .

(F) Bone, Muscle, and Nerve Regeneration and Bone Transplantation Experiments. From about September 1942 to about December 1943 experiments were conducted at the Ravensbrueck concentration camp, for the benefit of the German Armed Forces, to study bone, muscle, and nerve regeneration, and bone transplanta-

tion from one person to another. Sections of bones, muscles, and nerves were removed from the subjects. As a result of these operations, many victims suffered intense agony, mutilation, and permanent disability. . . .

(G) Sea-water Experiments. From about July 1944 to about September 1944 experiments were conducted at the Dachau concentration camp, for the benefit of the German Air Force and Navy, to study various methods of making sea water drinkable. The subjects were deprived of all food and given only chemically processed sea water. Such experiments caused great pain and suffering and resulted in serious bodily injury to the victims. . . .

(H) Epidemic Jaundice Experiments. From about June 1943 to about January 1945 experiments were conducted at the Sachsenhausen and Natzweiler concentration camps, for the benefit of the German Armed Forces, to investigate the causes of, and inoculations against, epidemic jaundice. Experimental subjects were deliberately infected with epidemic jaundice, some of whom died as a result, and others were caused great pain and suffering. . . .

(I) Sterilization Experiments. From about March 1941 to about January 1945 sterilization experiments were conducted at the Auschwitz and Ravensbrueck concentration camps, and other places. The purpose of these experiments was to develop a method of sterilization which would be suitable for sterilizing millions of people with a minimum of time and effort. These experiments were conducted by means of X-ray, surgery, and various drugs. Thousands of victims were sterilized and thereby suffered great mental and physical anguish. . . .

(J) Spotted Fever (Fleckfieber) Experiments. From about December 1941 to about February 1945 experiments were conducted at the Buchenwald and Natzweiler concentration camps, for the benefit [page 14] of the German Armed Forces, to investigate the effectiveness of spotted fever and other vaccines. At Buchenwald numerous healthy inmates were deliberately infected with spotted fever virus in order to keep the virus alive; over 90 percent of the victims died as a result. . . .

Source: Trials of War Criminals before the Nuremberg Military Tribunals under Control Council Law No. 10. Nuremberg, October 1946–April 1949 *(Washington, D.C.: U.S. Government Printing Office, 1949–1953), pp. 12–14.*

MEDICAL EXPERIMENTS

**Viewpoint:
No. Medical researchers today
should dissociate themselves from
torturers and murderers who
abused their positions of power and
privilege in the name of science.**

Why should the use of Nazi data by medical researchers be disallowed? First, these data should never have been obtained or used by the Nazis, even by German research ethics of the time. Second, the Nazi data are different from other unethically obtained data, which modern medical research uses. Third, because no good comes from evil, researchers should refuse to legitimize the Nazi doctors' activities as research.

The Nuremberg Code of 1947 is often interpreted as the establishment of standards governing research on humans, given the Nazis' argument that no such rules existed during the Third Reich. Recent work by Susan Lederer, Jochen Vollman, and Rolf Winau demonstrates, however, that researchers recognized ethical constraints in the nineteenth century and that in Germany explicit directives governing use of human subjects were established long before the Nuremberg Code.

In 1900 German lawyers argued that non-therapeutic research on subjects without consent constituted criminal physical injury. Vollman and Winau summarize: "The scientific validity of the experiment did not serve as mitigation. Informed consent was a mandatory precondition for any non-therapeutic research." In 1931 the Weimar Republic issued "guidelines for new therapy and human experimentation." These rules affirmed the principles of beneficence, that physicians ought to do no harm, have autonomy, and practice a legal doctrine of informed consent. Requirements included "proper explanation of the possible negative consequences" of the experiment and "unambiguous consent." These constraints resulted from public outcry and governmental action, not professional initiative. Thus, the practice of medical research consisted of the pursuit of truth through sound science and prohibited experimentation on involuntary subjects. Engaging in medical research meant embodying this practice; researchers were not free to do whatever they wanted and have it recognized as "research."

Was the use of prisoners permissible? The Weimar guidelines indicated, "without exception, non-therapeutic research could be performed only with the subject's informed consent." These guidelines remained binding during the Third Reich. Nevertheless, Sigmund Rascher proposed using "professional criminals"

as subjects to Heinrich Himmler in a 15 May 1941 letter, indicating that he did not expect any volunteers for his high-altitude experiments because of the likelihood of death. Himmler authorized the cooling experiments in May 1942, later explaining, "asocial individuals and criminals . . . deserve only to die." Himmler dismissed Christian (and Jewish) values, disparaging "Christian medical circles" that regarded prisoners' lives as sacred. The highest medical authority in the air force also approved these experiments, although "there were some qualms of conscience."

The official rationale—using "professional criminals condemned to death"—was a ruse. Subjects in Dachau, according to American psychiatrist Leo T. Alexander, were picked generally in the following order: "first Jews, then foreigners, gypsies, stateless persons, foreign Catholic priests, professional criminals and finally political prisoners." Almost all the victims were imprisoned on immoral grounds, and the means of "execution" were disease, starvation, or random brutality—or being selected by Rascher. The Nazis deceived only themselves by using the excuse that the subjects were all going to die anyway. The worst "professional criminals" in the camps were the doctors.

Thus, the practice of medical research included explicit rules about the use of human subjects, contrary to the Nazi doctors' defense. Moreover, several vignettes from before their arrest suggest they knew their activities deviated from acceptable practice. On 5 November 1942 Rascher wrote a memo refusing to use a female prisoner: "My racial conscience is outraged by the prospect of exposing to racially inferior concentration-camp elements a girl who is outwardly pure nordic." Apparently aware that human prisoners should not be mistreated, Rascher did not extend his ethical constraints to "subhuman" prisoners. Perhaps Rascher was following Himmler's distortion of Hippocrates, which was promulgated in a series of short books for SS doctors. Himmler limited to Aryans Hippocrates' injunction to keep "patients from harm and injustice."

When Himmler asked Georg August Weltz to oversee the experiments at Dachau, Weltz anticipated objections from within the Air Force Medical Services, "who he feared might consider such experiments amoral," and delayed the start of the experiments. Weltz later lied about his knowledge of the use of prisoners to a U.S. investigator. Delay and deceit reflect awareness that these activities violated German and/or international practice.

Hubertus Strughold told an American investigator after the war that "he still disapproved of such experiments in non-volunteers on principle: 'I have always forbidden even the thought of such experiments in my Institute, firstly on moral grounds, and secondly on grounds of medical ethics.'" Even if this statement were a lie (since his close associate was involved intimately with the experiments), he lied rather than defend the experiments. Thus, Nazi doctors knowingly departed from the best practices of medical research, selecting only those norms that fitted their depraved agenda and applying them arbitrarily. (Strughold was later chief scientist of the NASA Aerospace Medical Division, having been secretly brought to the United States despite Nuremberg indictments against him.)

Although modern medical research uses data from past exploitation of human subjects, the Nazi abuses exceed any other in scope and lethality. The history of medical research is replete with the abuse of society's most marginalized individuals. Lederer documents experiments perpetrated on unsuspecting people, which produced techniques now standard in clinical practice. For instance, in the early 1930s seventy children died in Germany and nine children in the United States from early trials of polio vaccines (only the German doctors were sued for damages). Robert Proctor also traces the continuities between the racism and classism of the German and American medical communities. The United States was a "leader" in forced sterilization of the mentally ill and prisoners, and "German racial hygienists throughout the Weimar period expressed their envy of American achievements in this area." In 1939 the American Medical Association (AMA) barred black physicians from membership, a year after German physicians prohibited Jews from practicing medicine. The notion of eliminating "lives not worth living" did not begin with the Nazis, having been discussed in eugenics circles since the late 1890s. Medical research is not a marginalized operation, but rather a profession that has often identified its interests with those of the ruling elite. Moreover, individual researchers acquired oppressive attitudes from the surrounding culture and in turn perpetuated them. The Nazis radically extended this oppressive legacy. Rascher alone brutalized and/or killed more than four hundred people between 1942 and 1944. Had the Nazis won the war, such crimes most likely would have been perpetrated on conquered peoples.

The medical profession never made oppression central to its mission—until the Nazis. They ushered exploitation into the heart of the enterprise, by building research around the false distinction between humans and "non-humans." The Dachau hypothermia experiments provide a good example of the thorough perversion of

research practice. Alexander, a neuropsychiatrist and U.S. Army major, compiled the main historical evidence about the cooling experiments. Ernst Holzloehner, Rascher, and Finke conducted the cooling experiments. The only surviving original data are in their final report to Himmler, reproduced in Appendix 7 of Alexander's report. In June 1945, before the full scale of the Holocaust was comprehended, Alexander had already raised doubts about Dachau's "research" enterprise. He noted that the doctors did not provide figures for the total number of experiments or experimental subjects or "comparative figures of their therapeutic trials." The researchers referred to a "great number" of experiments, but the documentation only identified one series of 50 experiments and another series of 57. Thirteen deaths were documented in graphs and tables, although the authors claimed that "none of the experiments were deliberately intended to be fatal." (Later evidence from the Nuremberg trials revealed that in fact 360 to 400 experiments occurred, with at least 80 to 90 deaths.) Age and nutrition level of the men were not noted. The numbers who were immersed while clothed or naked were not differentiated. The end point of the experiments was not stated—were they to be terminated based on length of time in water, body temperature, unconsciousness, or death? Alexander cited several German scientists who reported that Rascher's experiments were conducted with "unreasonable cruelty and waste of life." Only two survivors of the chilling experiments were ever identified.

In language uncharacteristic of Alexander and written on a different typewriter, his two-page summary concluded that the research "satisfies all the criteria of objective and accurate observation and interpretation, despite the fact that precise numbers and percentages are not given." The U.S. Army's eagerness to use these Nazi data led to sweeping statements about "conclusive proof" that "appears to have settled the question of what to do for people in shock from exposure to cold." The American military simultaneously prepared a report to indict the doctors while recommending immediate application of their results. The military might have condemned the doctors' dirty work but was eager to benefit from it—bracketing the ethical question of whether the data should be used at all.

Yet, four years later in 1949, Alexander, writing as a civilian, reversed the position taken in the summary section, and wrote that "The results, like so many of those obtained in the Nazi research program, are not dependable. . . . Obviously, Rascher dressed up his findings to forestall criticism, although any scientific man

MEDICAL EXPERIMENTS

should have known that during actual exposure many other factors . . . would affect the time of survival." Alexander questions the validity of the data—finally condemning both the methodology and the results. Not until 1990 was the validity of the cooling data again severely questioned. Robert Berger highlighted many defects, concluding, "the Dachau hypothermia study has all the ingredients of a scientific fraud, and rejection of the data on purely scientific grounds is inevitable. They cannot advance science or save lives."

Nazi methods were so outrageous that their exploits should not be considered medical research, despite their reliance on medical and scientific traditions. Instead of pursuing truth, they regarded many humans as nonhumans. Some tried to be consistent with their own irrationality, cautioning that the results of research on certain "species" (Jews, Gypsies) were not applicable to humans. Most, however, were selective in their illogic—they tolerated the imprisonment of Jews for committing "race pollution," but assumed data on Jews would apply to humans. They lied to prisoners, promising their release if they volunteered. Many were motivated by greed and hopes for advancement within the Nazi hierarchy, distorting reports to secure Himmler's favor. Although many were technically competent, the profession tolerated members who lacked proper expertise, and no one protested when they reported their findings to colleagues at professional meetings. The result was a practice that authorized cruelty, lacked self-regulation, and used a crude utilitarianism in which harm to members of certain groups counted as zero. They abandoned the inherited practice of medical research and substituted a parody of it, based in racism and tinged with sadism.

Marcia Angell has shown the difference between the validity of a data set and the ethics of its procurement. Proper practice of medical research demands both standards—sound methodology and good ethics. Neither sloppy analysis done ethically nor reliable data gathered unethically constitute "medical research." The label "medical research" should refer to the practice as a whole, not only to the data's reliability. Thus, even when reliable data were produced (such as results obtained by testing the killing power of phosgene gas, although even these data have been called valueless by toxicologists), they ought not to be used. The U.S. Environmental Protection Agency (EPA) has taken this position on the phosgene data, and in 1988 its director prohibited their use, even though they might have protected workers exposed to phosgene.

Nazi data from the camps should never have been produced. Replication of the experiments is impermissible. The experiments were fruits of the same mindset that prompted the attempted annihilation of the Jewish people. Brian Folkner and Arthur Hafner argue that these data have acquired a meaning almost unique in modern science because of their historical associations, which are morally laden. These data should always be linked with crimes against humanity. The attempt to regard the data as morally neutral ignores the fact that the Nazis' choice of "which facts to pursue" and "how to pursue them" were value-laden decisions. These associations and meanings alone make the data unique from all other unethically obtained data—regardless of their validity or invalidity.

Although Nazi knowledge was obtained by cruel exploitation, modern researchers now have it. Many researchers believe that knowledge is better than ignorance, no matter how it is obtained. This belief creates a powerful impetus to proceed, believing that in the long term, usefulness will outweigh all else. Scientists recognize that as the memory of nefarious deeds fades, it becomes harder to connect emotionally with the suffering of the subjects. If superficial moral condemnation after the fact is all that is required, researchers have a powerful incentive to violate human rights. Historian Gerald L. Geison has observed, "dangerous human experimentation . . . has been more easily forgiven if the clinical gains were great and the experimenter turned out to be right." No amount of time will ever make the Nazi experimenters turn out to be right.

By refusing to use Nazi data, researchers can affirm that knowledge is not the highest value. A refusal to use the Nazi data avers that some human goods—such as equal human worth and life itself—should not be sacrificed at the altar of knowledge. Much that could be done ought not to be done because of the potential harm to human subjects, despite the promise of "progress." Often research proposals are revised substantially or never undertaken, to protect human subjects. Researchers are not permitted to know things that can only be discovered by torturing or killing people. They have to wait until their questions can be answered by some other means. The Nazi placement of knowledge above human welfare violated this fundamental code of medical research.

Are future lives more valuable than those in Dachau? One shudders to expose workers to dangerous levels of phosgene gas, and so some researchers are willing to use the information gleaned from murder. However, suppose they were to tell the workers that "colleagues" of theirs murdered many men and this activity was the source of the information used to protect them. The workers might wonder why their lives were worth more than others and tremble at being in the hands of professionals who claim murderers as "colleagues" and who seem to condone the past exploitation of workers.

Some argue that the good produced from Nazi research can outweigh the harmful means used to collect data. Yet, research often produces negligible short-term good, and allusions to "the good of humankind" or "scientific progress" are incalculable. Justice prevents the tally of infinite possible good against time-bound past harm. No degree of benefit should be permitted now from these especially egregious violations of certain fundamental rights perpetrated in the name of medical research.

No good comes from the torture and murder of innocent humans. Contrary to the claim that Nazis "did good in the midst of evil," what they did was evil and "added to the horror of the Holocaust." Any good that happens now is the result of human ability to be good. Fundamentally, researchers must ask themselves what kind of persons they want to be and to what kind of moral community they want to belong. They can be good by refusing to legitimate murder and by creating a moral research community that refuses to use data obtained in violation of everything it professes.

Medical researchers must refuse to place any segment of humanity outside their circle of care and refuse to abuse humans for others' benefit. Refusal to dignify Nazi data as "usable" ultimately rests on the affirmation of the worthiness of all human life. Such affirmation refuses complicity with the despicable and exploitative irrationality at the heart of the Nazi perversion of medical research.

–JUDITH W. KAY,
UNIVERSITY OF PUGET SOUND

References

Leo Alexander, "Medical Science Under Dictatorship," *New England Journal of Medicine,* 241 (1949): 39–47.

Alexander, *The Treatment of Shock From Prolonged Exposure to Cold, Especially in Water, 1945* (Washington, D.C.: Office of the Publication Board, Department of Commerce, Report no. 250, n.d.).

Marcia Angell, "The Nazi Hypothermia Experiments and Unethical Research Today," *New England Journal of Medicine,* 322 (1990): 1462–1464.

Robert L. Berger, "Nazi Science–The Dachau Hypothermia Experiments," *New England Journal of Medicine,* 322 (1990): 1435–1440.

Arthur L. Caplan, ed., *When Medicine Went Mad: Bioethics and the Holocaust* (Totowa, N.J.: Humana Press, 1992).

Brian Folker and Arthur Hafner, "Nazi Data: Dissociation from Evil–Commentary," in *Cases in Bioethics,* third edition, edited by Bette-Jane Crigger (New York: St. Martin's Press, 1998), pp. 171–172.

H. A. Israel and W. E. Seidelman, "Nazi Origins of an Anatomy Test: The Pernkopf Atlas," *JAMA,* 276 (1996): 1663.

Susan E. Lederer, *Subjected to Science: Human Experimentation in America before the Second World War* (Baltimore: Johns Hopkins University Press, 1995).

Robert Jay Lifton, *The Nazi Doctors: Medical Killing and the Psychology of Genocide* (New York: Basic Books, 1986).

Alexander Mitscherlich and Fred Mielke, *Doctors of Infamy: The Story of the Nazi Medical Crimes* (New York: Schuman, 1949).

Robert N. Proctor, "Nazi Doctors, Racial Medicine, and Human Experimentation," in *The Nazi Doctors and the Nuremberg Code: Human Rights in Human Experimentation,* edited by George J. Annas and Michael A. Grodin (New York: Oxford University Press, 1992), pp. 17–31.

Proctor, *The Nazi War on Cancer* (Princeton: Princeton University Press, 1999).

Fred Rosner and others, "The Ethics of Using Scientific Data by Immoral Means," *New York State Journal of Medicine,* 91 (February 1991): 54–59.

Jochen Vollman and Rolf Winau, "Informed Consent in Human Experimentation before the Nuremberg Code," *British Medical Journal,* 313 (1996): 1445–1447.

Nicholas Wade, "Doctors Question Use of Nazi Medical Atlas," *New York Times,* 26 November 1996.

Gerald Weissman and others, "Origins of the Pernkopf Anatomy Atlas," *JAMA* (9 April 1997): 1122.

Jay Zatz and Robert Pozos, "The Dachau Hypothermia Study: An Ethical and Scientific Commentary," in *When Medicine Went Mad: Bioethics and the Holocaust,* edited by Caplan (Totowa, N.J.: Humana Press, 1992), pp. 135–139.

MOVIES

Is the Holocaust an appropriate subject for the movies?

Viewpoint: Yes. Popular representations provide a useful forum for examining the Holocaust.

Viewpoint: No. The study of the Holocaust is best left to professional historians because they are more concerned with truth than entertainment.

Viewpoint: No. Some recent representations such as the movie *Schindler's List* (1993) actually downplay the plight of Holocaust victims.

Movies about World War II (1939–1945) have tended to focus on the course of military campaigns—whether in Europe, North Africa, or the Pacific—and they remain reliably popular, as the success of *Saving Private Ryan* (1998) demonstrates. Holocaust movies, on the other hand, focusing as they do on the central horror of the same period, are fewer and invariably arouse more commentary from the viewing public, professional historians, and survivors. As one of the defining events of the twentieth century, the Holocaust demands representation.

Victor Ehly argues that great historical tragedy is always and inevitably represented in one or another cultural form—whether legend, theater, or myth. This process is not something to be condemned or even avoided but understood. Ehly suggests that historians may be better occupied by thinking about the relation between the kind of history that Hollywood engages in and the works professional historians produce—narratives, he argues, few other than historians come into contact with. Ehly contends that movies can be quite useful to the historian because they can bring the often obscure labor of historians into public discussion, from which it might otherwise be absent. This achievement is no small thing, and rather than condemn Holocaust movies out of hand and dismiss them, Ehly suggests that historians make use of the occasions offered by movies to raise questions, clarify misrepresentations, and correct errors. He argues that without the prompt of popular representations, such opportunities may not arise; debate is preferable to silence or, perhaps worse, obscurity.

J. Michael Butler's essay surveys the history of Holocaust movies and finds them all wanting, though he notes some progress in recent years. From *The Diary of Anne Frank* (1959) to recent television offerings such as *Uprising* (2001), Butler perceives many flaws in Hollywood's treatment of the Holocaust. For Butler, the failures of such movies result from their use of the Holocaust to comment on contemporary issues, their more-or-less universally optimistic endings, and their reliance on stereotypes of both the Jewish inmates and the Nazi guards. Movies trivialize the horrors of the Holocaust in the interest of entertainment, distort history, and prevent a nuanced and respectful understanding of the facts of the Shoah. Butler suggests that rather than memorializing and commemorating the murder of six million European Jews, at worst movies provide ammunition to Holocaust deniers and at best distort understanding of the past—which may lead to the unhappy ending that, as he writes, "Hollywood works hard to avoid."

Lauren Proll's essay focuses on the most successful of recent Holocaust films—Steven Spielberg's *Schindler's List* (1993)—and describes the central problem of the movie as the question of whether a representation of the Holocaust can "ethically center on a non-Jewish hero." The question is not one that is easily answered and leads to a series of related ethical problems, chief among them whether the Holocaust should be represented in fiction at all. Bans being impossible and problematic on their own terms, many artists and thinkers urge, Proll writes, "extreme care." This care usually centers on the basic injunction that any representation of the Holocaust focus on the experience of the victims in such a way as to honor the humanity denied them by the Nazis. The failure to achieve this goal, Proll suggests, is one of the largest problems with Spielberg's film.

In Proll's view, the lionization of Oskar Schindler obscures the individual histories of the Jewish people who surround him. Schindler, as the protagonist, stands apart from the tragedy around him, and the audience's perception is aligned with his. This orientation, Proll argues, makes the Jewish victims of the Holocaust objects, not subjects, "permanently other" and separate from the viewers. Thus, the movie fails to present an "accurate or humane" narrative of the Holocaust and raises what remains an important question: why do viewers respond more favorably to movies about the Holocaust that do not focus more closely on the people whose tragedy the films purport to chronicle?

All three essays deal with a central aesthetic, ethical, and historical question: how should the events at the camps established to carry out Hitler's Final Solution be represented? The representations vary (dramatic movies, documentaries, historical monographs, and so forth) and the question may, in the end, be unanswerable. However, Ehly's query remains compelling: Is it better to have no representations, and thus no discussion, or to have (possibly poor) representations and thus dialogue, whether laudatory or condemning?

Viewpoint:
Yes. Popular representations provide a useful forum for examining the Holocaust.

Every great tragedy in every culture known to human beings is most meaningfully represented in legend, epic, folktale, song, theater, visual art, and most importantly, myth. Of course, events other than great tragedies also provide the content of these cultural forms, but this essay focuses on great tragedy. All these forms of cultural expression and communication are included in the term *Story*, assuming that it is beyond the scope of this essay to differentiate among these many categories. The capital *S* will signal this inclusive use of the term.

The Holocaust of European Jews is one of the greatest tragedies of twentieth-century Western culture. After several decades of denial and shock, it stands to reason that Hollywood, one of the most effective relators of stories in popular culture, would produce a variety of movies with the theme of the Holocaust.

The fundamental task of the historian, on the other hand, is to establish the historical record. This project is carried on within its own dynamic and set of rules. The real work of professional historians is carried out largely outside of the interest of the general public, only occasionally catching the eye of the news media with a

startling, shocking, or otherwise unexpected discovery or especially controversial opinion.

The Holocaust did indeed occur, and it is the task of the historian to search into every available nook and cranny to document it and weave the innumerable strands of documentary evidence into a coherent narrative for the main purpose of identifying what happened. This narrative becomes the historical record. Traditionally, historians are more concerned about the historical record than about public opinion concerning the events in question. Their task is immense, and the problems they encounter are many.

Meanwhile, the business of Storytelling continues in response to one of the most fundamental needs of human beings: the need for meaning. The ancients looked up at the stars and saw not random patterns of light but a bull, a warrior, and gods and goddesses. Whole scenes unfolded before their eyes as they projected their need for meaning onto the night sky. Thus, it is quite predictable that in the case of a crime and a tragedy of such major proportions as the Holocaust, legends arise; tales are told; epics are formed; and creative and artistic expressions arise from every quarter. The contemporary economic structure under which Americans live is a "business culture," and creative people are quick to sense the potential for profit in any powerful Story. Like it or not, Hollywood has become one of the most profitable Storytelling industries the modern commercial world has known.

Much as an oyster needs a grain of sand to begin the creation of a pearl, Hollywood needs a grain of truth—a documented historical incident—with which to create a profitable movie with a story that can be advertised as "historical." The incident can be relatively obscure, such as the takeover of the *Amistad* by its slave cargo, or as well known as the American revolutionary uprising against the British.

Hollywood movies with historical themes are actually quite helpful because they bring the often arcane and highly technical work of the historian into public discussion. Wim Wenders, writing in August 1977 on the German movie *Hitler—eine Karriere* (1977), produced by Joachim C. Fest and Christian Herrendoerfer, observes, "In film (and on television as well) what is actually shown always becomes the main subject [of discussion], while opinions on [the film itself] become secondary. And instead of discussing the methods of Fest's film, how this film was made, they started to argue about the content, about history: what the film was about or supposed to be about." Even as Wenders's point is that such a state of affairs makes it difficult for film critics to focus on the quality and artistry of the production in public discussions, the same phenomenon works in favor of the historian. For it suggests that a movie with an historical subject, which makes a significant impact on the public consciousness, raises the subject itself to public discussion in a way that otherwise would not have been possible. Thus, Hollywood works hand in hand with historians, supporting their purpose while fulfilling its own goals.

Sara R. Horowitz puts it another way, in an article in *The Americanization of the Holocaust* (1999), commenting on Robert Rosenberg's *The Cutting Room: An Avram Cohen Mystery* (1993), about a Jewish Hollywood movie director:

the novel offers a credible critique of the way that popular representations of the Holocaust—and in particular its cinematic portrayal—have functioned as a vehicle for the working out of Jewish American postwar identity. Popular culture constructs and promulgates what might be called a folk discourse of history. It is here, to the chagrin of historians and professors, that most people learn what they "know" about history. The Holocaust too has taken its place in American historical consciousness as much through the vehicles of television, movies, mystery novels, romances, and espionage thrillers as through literature, memoirs, and the work of historians. Cinema in particular has come both to shape and to reflect popular understanding of the Nazi genocide.

Steven Spielberg's *Schindler's List* is often used as an example of Hollywood movies that at best confuse and at worst delude the viewing public about the true nature of the Holocaust. Cinema is both an art form and a language, and by either definition, it is value neutral. Mark Cousins, a British scholar of cinema studies, writing in the June issue of *Prospect Magazine,* sums it up this way:

Take something important in the real world and ask three questions. What if film-makers didn't deal with it? What if film-makers dealt with it, but badly? And what if some film-makers dealt with it successfully, and left other people to make other kinds of movies? Consider the gassings at Auschwitz-Birkenau between 1943 and 1945. Film-makers didn't have to engage with these atrocities and for obvious reasons at the time, they didn't. There isn't a single existing still or moving image of the operation of the gas chambers. This fact leads to further questions: would there be Holocaust deniers if there had been? Would there have been room for doubt? The absence of film helps fuel the case of the doubting Thomases.

On to the second scenario, where the subject was treated, but badly. In the television series *Holocaust,* the process of inserting the Zyklon B gas into the crematoria was so badly portrayed technically—a guy climbs a ladder and pops it in—that revisionists and neo-Nazis had a field day. They watched those scenes and laughed. Granted, this is mainstream television rather than cinema but the dilemma remains the same: audiovisual culture's slip-shod populism led to simplifications which cheated the audience and, no matter how well intentioned, created a new postmodern vagueness around its subject.

What about the third scenario, when cinema tackles the situation and apparently gets it right? *Schindler's List* had the technical brilliance of Steven Spielberg and cinematographer Januscz Koszinski, a source novel like *Schindler's Ark,* a budget to realise [sic] their ambitions, a seriousness of tone, a largely receptive press and a credible back-up programme funded by the Shoah Foundation which is videotaping Holocaust survivor testimony on a massive scale. Still, a few aesthetic mistakes, like the girl in red and the sentimentality of the last act, makes it a flawed work. It is accused of subtly Hollywoodising its subject. The argument to engage falls down if the form is bungled.

It is a sign of weakness when cinema goes all out to deal with the real world but then allows the message to overrun the medium. When content dominates, you can hear B&B [Robert Brasillach and Maurice Bardá in their ground breaking *Histoire du Cinéma*, published in 1935] whispering "what about form?" Form and history are uneasy bedfellows. Form pulls away from content, runs rings around it. Puttnam's *The Killing Fields* had a big political impact; David Lynch's *Blue Velvet* seemed purely personal. Which is best? Or, a rather harder question: which is more valuable to our culture?

MOVIES

ON SCHINDLER

Sol Urback, a Polish Jew and the only survivor of his immediate family of eight persons, was saved because he was one of the workers at Oskar Schindler's factory. Here he recalls his impression of Schindler:

Well, he began to see early on in the war that things are not that great for Germany as he envisioned as a very young man back in Czechoslovakia, that Germany would conquer the world, and he would ride in on that wave and be a big business tycoon. . . . He also recognized that what the Germans were doing was not exactly what he had in mind.

When people were killed in masses, as they were, he began to change his mind as to hanging onto the Germans and helping them. In fact, it turned the other way. But, still, always acting as a loyal German. I mean, he had no way of operating if he did not continue acting as a loyal German.

There was a time during the war that he was jailed, because of suspicions that he was not very loyal. He was kept in jail with another known Nazi concentration camp leader by the name of Goeth, who headed the Kraków/Plaszów concentration camp. But they released him again because of the enormous influence that he had all over the German empire. So they released him, and he came back to the camp and operated again. . . .

From my point of view, he was a fellow who was seeking opportunities, but did not want to join in the ranks of killing people. I have not known him to lift a hand on any inmate or to harm any inmate. So I would have to judge that he was a decent human being, that for a while, was taken by the great anticipation and promise of the German Reich, but certainly did not want to join in and get in on the mass killings and all that.

Source: Joseph J. Preil, ed., Holocaust Testimonies: European Survivors and American Liberators in New Jersey *(New Brunswick, N.J.: Rutgers University Press, 2001), p. 133.*

Cousins's provocative questions can be answered with the admonition to let movies be movies and allow them to deal with historical content when writers and directors so choose for reasons that make sense within the movie industry. In the meantime, historical issues continue to be raised by Hollywood, and talk-show hosts seem ever ready to call on some historian with whom to discuss the content of a particular movie. This forum is where the meeting between history and movies seems to occur, and it is usually a positive opportunity for historians to speak about their craft in a public forum. This arrangement seems to be a healthy state of affairs.

–VICTOR EHLY, NORWICH UNIVERSITY

**Viewpoint:
No. The study of the Holocaust is best left to professional historians because they are more concerned with truth than entertainment.**

The entertainment industry has always capitalized on the American public's fascination with the past. This interest is especially true in motion pictures, where movie creators often use historical events to tell a story. One of the most popular recent themes is the Holocaust, as the movies *Sophie's Choice* (1982), *Schindler's List* (1993), *La Vita è bella* (Life Is Beautiful, 1997), and *Uprising* (2001), to name a few, have demonstrated. Although the productions expose many viewers to an important historical event, no movie can adequately portray the Holocaust. In fact, Hollywood productions often trivialize genocide by oversimplifying the complex issues that the murder of six million Jews presents. For several reasons, therefore, both fictionalized movies and those based on actual events obstruct a more complete understanding of, and distort realities concerning, the Holocaust.

The first movie to use the Holocaust as its theme was *The Diary of Anne Frank* (1959). The movie, which won three Academy Awards, was based on Anne's famous diary and ended on an optimistic note. Although she died in Bergen-Belsen (in 1945), her phrase "In spite of everything I still believe that people are good at heart" summarized the hopeful ending depicted by the movie. In fact, 20th Century-Fox originally ended the picture with a shot of Anne moving numbly through the concentration camp, but it "'was deemed too tough in audience impact' and betrayed the company's wish 'to have the film considered "hopeful" despite all.'" The optimistic conclusion the company used proved both misleading and misplaced because it hid the grim reality of the Holocaust from viewers. The goodness of human nature is not what the Holocaust illuminated, but it is what *The Diary of Anne Frank* stresses.

The next motion picture that addressed an aspect of the Holocaust was *Judgment at Nuremberg* (1961). Filmed while Nazi leader Adolph Eichmann's famous trial progressed in Jerusalem, the movie boasted a spectacular cast featuring Spencer Tracy, Marlene Dietrich, Burt Lancaster, Richard Widmark, Maximilian Schell, Judy Garland, and Montgomery Clift. The movie does not focus on the victims, perpetrators, origins, or consequences of the Final Solution but instead stresses the universal nature of the Holocaust. For example, Jews are mentioned only in passing and do not testify in the movie, while Germans are romanticized or portrayed in a sympathetic light, such as Dietrich's portrayal of the widow of a Nazi officer. Most important, *Judgment at Nuremberg* questions the righteousness of American justice on several occasions. The defense attorney and primary character mentions the U.S. Supreme Court's support of sterilizing mentally handicapped citizens and questions the use of nuclear weapons at Hiroshima and Nagasaki. When the attorney alludes to the hanging of Jewish children, the camera focuses on the disturbed face of a black military-police guard, which subtly reminds viewers of the history of lynching in America. Despite the efforts of defense attorneys to defend their clients, Tracy's character, Judge Dan Haywood, dispenses a just verdict for the accused at the end of the movie.

Judgment at Nuremberg is an unreliable and inaccurate portrayal of the Holocaust because it focuses on and reveals more about the contemporary United States than the event it addresses. The movie, for instance, stresses the triumph of American justice. More important, however, it takes care not to vilify the German population for their roles in the Holocaust. The movie separates Germans such as Dietrich, Garland, and Clift's characters from the Nazis Haywood convicts. Schell's character even demonstrates through his references that America has committed its share of atrocities. *Judgment at Nuremberg* reveals that movie producers often use the Holocaust to reflect contemporary attitudes instead of an accurate view of the past.

A movie that further illuminates how the Holocaust is erroneously used to bring attention to other issues is *The Pawnbroker* (1964). Rod Steiger plays the main character, Sol Nazerman, an unhappy, isolated, and emotionally damaged Jewish concentration-camp survivor who owns a Harlem pawnshop and ruthlessly exploits his destitute customers. Several flashback scenes create a stereotyped image of the average Holocaust survivor: a once happy family man whom Nazis stripped of humanity and dignity in the camp and who now focuses all activity in his miserable life to financial pursuits. Nazerman realizes the error of his ways when his Hispanic assistant, the honest and decent Jesus Ortiz, steps in front of a robber's bullet and saves his employer's life. It is only after Jesus's death that Nazerman demonstrates guilt or remorse. In addition to presenting a disparaging and inaccurate view of Holocaust survivors, *The Pawnbroker* also attempts to elicit sympathy for America's lower classes by using the destruction of European Jewry as its point of reference. Several scenes equate the plight of the urban poor with the experience Nazerman endured. The result is a trivialization of the Holocaust because it becomes an illumination of

contemporary issues and not a focus of attention on its own terms.

Although *The Pawnbroker* was released in 1964, few other movies between 1962 and 1978 utilized Holocaust-related imagery. In 1978, however, the televised NBC miniseries *Holocaust* reintroduced the event into the popular consciousness. The show became a national event as nearly 100 million viewers watched the four-part, nine-and-one-half-hour production. The National Conference of Christians and Jews distributed yellow stars for citizens to wear throughout the monumental day, which observers dubbed "Holocaust Sunday." Although many critics praised the program, *Holocaust* also provoked outrage for using the historical event for entertainment. Auschwitz survivor Elie Wiesel argued the "Holocaust transcends history" and "cannot be explained nor can it be visualized," while the German publication *Der Speigel* denounced the series as "Genocide shrunken to the level of *Bonanza* with music appropriate to *Love Story*." Despite the objections, *Holocaust* inspired the creation of several other televised movies that used the event as its primary theme. As the release of Holocaust-related productions increased, so too did criticism of such programs. Most of the movies downplayed Jewish suffering, focused on survivors, offered positive outcomes, glorified unlikely heroes, or simplified the roles various groups played in the incident. These various themes culminated in the 1993 release of *Schindler's List*, the most popular piece of cultural expression to address the Holocaust.

Steven Spielberg's epic movie traces the efforts of Nazi officer and entrepreneur Oskar Schindler to save 1,100 Jews from death during the Holocaust. Spielberg filmed in black and white on location in Poland to enhance his project's documentary-like effect. *Schindler's List* both reflected and contributed to the fascination with the Holocaust, and audiences responded enthusiastically to the movie. More than 25 million Americans saw it in theaters; the movie won seven Academy Awards in 1994 and grossed $221 million in foreign box-office receipts. In 1997 another 65 million viewed it from home when NBC played it without commercial interruption. While the movie exposed viewers to several graphic and unforgettable moments and opened dialogue concerning the Holocaust, it also reinforced and perpetuated many stereotypes Hollywood previously created surrounding the period.

One of the most blatant oversimplifications in *Schindler's List* is the character Amon Goeth. He personifies evil—he randomly shoots Jews from his balcony before meals, uses a card game to decide the fate of his Jewish maid, and is inhuman in his degree of anti-Semitism. He is a psychotic who kills in a personal manner. Ample moral distance, therefore, exists between Goeth and the viewer. In addition, near the conclusion of the movie he dies by hanging, bringing closure to the terror he inflicts. Although Goeth is a chilling villain, he is an exaggerated, if not unrealistic, portrayal of many Germans involved in the Final Solution. Most perpetrators were more complex in their motivations and actions than Spielberg demonstrates, and the death of one individual does little to resolve the greater issues involved in mass murder.

Schindler's List also glorifies an odd hero at the expense of Holocaust survivors, as do many similar movies. The Nazi and Gentile Schindler becomes the protagonist while Jewish characters remain in the background. Some Jews acquire stereotyped characteristics, such as those who swallow jewels and hide savings to keep Nazis from confiscating them. The movie represents its main Jewish character, Itzhak Stern, as little more than Schindler's greatest admirer and a man who is consumed with finances. Atrocities that confront Jews, moreover, come at a safe distance from viewers. The only Jews with emotional attachments to the audience are a group of women aboard a train mistakenly taken to Auschwitz where water, not gas, comes from the showers. They are ultimately saved by Schindler. The focus of the movie, therefore, is not on murderers and victims but survivors and their savior. Death comes from afar, and exuberance, not depression, comes at the conclusion of the motion picture. Not only does Spielberg create a positive movie concerning the Holocaust, but one that focuses on a most unlikely hero at the expense of many nameless Jews.

Another theme *Schindler's List* repeatedly stresses that distorts understanding of the Holocaust is the triumph of optimism. According to the movie, "right" ultimately succeeds over "wrong" in a variety of ways. At the beginning of the movie, for example, Schindler is portrayed as a person corrupted by power, materialism, and excess. He is clearly a flawed individual. Yet, the death of a young Jewish girl sparks his conscience and transforms Schindler into a man willing to surrender all his material goods in order to save more Jews. In addition, the movie ends on a jubilant note as Schindler's Jews are liberated. A caption reminds viewers that the number of individuals descended from these survivors outnumber all of the Jews living in Poland. This ending highlights the connection between the Holocaust and the creation of Israel. The emphasis of the movie, therefore, is on redemption. Instead of focusing on the six million Jews who died and innumerable horrors that occurred during the Holocaust, *Schindler's List* rejoices

about a minority who lived and searches for value in an event that has no redeeming virtues.

Despite the fact that it presents several comforting and therefore inadequate representations of the Holocaust, *Schindler's List* inspired the creation of many movies that dealt with the topic. Most continued the flawed themes of their predecessors or, worse, created new misconceptions. *Apt Pupil* (1998), for example, uses the Holocaust as a reference point in an effort to focus on the dark side of human nature. The movie strengthens the stereotype of the evil, abnormal Nazi who dons his old SS uniform, gives crisp salutes, and even tortures cats decades after his beloved Reich fell. *Life Is Beautiful* and *Jakob the Liar* (1999) use humor to illuminate similar messages concerning the Holocaust. In the Italian film *Life Is Beautiful,* Roberto Benigni plays a bumbling yet lovable Jewish waiter named Guido who is deported to a concentration camp with his wife and child. To protect him from the harsh realities they face, he convinces his son, Joshua, that the ordeal is a game in which the prize is a new tank. In *Jakob the Liar* the title character, played by Robin Williams, constructs false radio messages of German military defeats to keep the spirits of fellow ghetto residents high. Each movie minimizes the dangers Jews faced during the Holocaust because the protagonist defies Nazi authorities in many ways without detection and successfully protects his loved ones from harm. Both also fail to acknowledge Holocaust actualities by having positive endings. In *Life Is Beautiful* Guido dies offscreen but his family survives, while in *Jakob the Liar* the ghetto is liberated. Televised movies of the early twenty-first century have made more progress than Hollywood movies toward portraying reality, but even they come short.

Nuremberg (2000), a TNT Original movie, commits many of the same errors as the 1961 movie that dealt with the same topic. The latest version of the infamous trial emphasizes the triumph of justice through the diligence of American prosecutor and Supreme Court Justice Robert Jackson, presents the unrepentant Nazi officials on trial as psychologically disturbed, and suggests the verdict brought closure to the Holocaust. Two movies released in 2001 do a better job of accurately depicting Holocaust realities. HBO's *Conspiracy*—depicting the Wannsee Conference (1942), where the German officials discussed the Final Solution—is based on the only transcript of meeting minutes that still exists. The picture successfully portrays Nazi leaders as complicated individuals who made decisions regarding the Final Solution for reasons other than pure anti-Semitism. NBC's four-hour *Uprising* examined the 1943 Warsaw ghetto riots and is one of the first movies to focus on the Holocaust from a Jewish perspective. Although each feature has its shortcomings, they demonstrate that Holocaust-theme movies have begun to diversify their scope.

Nevertheless, the Holocaust has no place in the entertainment industry. The positive characteristics most viewers favor in movies—such as resourcefulness, courage, humor, drama, and suspense—fade in the conditions that surrounded racial genocide. Celebration of the positives ignores historical truths. The Holocaust is best left in the care of professional historians and documenters who strive to understand the event instead of using it to entertain. While motion pictures do open dialogue concerning the Shoah, a misrepresentation of facts is worse than silence in this case. The irony of Holocaust movies is that while many people appreciate the effort to remember and commemorate the topic, it is often a flawed memory that provides ammunition for those who deny the Holocaust occurred. The attempt to recognize the Holocaust through popular mediums, therefore, could lead to the unhappy ending Hollywood so vigorously avoids.

–J. MICHAEL BUTLER,
SOUTH GEORGIA COLLEGE

Viewpoint:
No. Some recent representations such as the movie *Schindler's List* (1993) actually downplay the plight of Holocaust victims.

Practically everyone who has written negatively about *Schindler's List* (1993)—and many have done so—feels the need to apologize. Michael André Bernstein articulates a general critical discomfort in noting that "There is little pleasure in being troubled by what so many have found deeply moving." Indeed, critiquing a movie that world audiences have enthusiastically embraced brings few satisfactions, especially given that *Schindler's List* has, surely, accomplished some good. Certainly the movie has educated millions of people who would not otherwise have confronted the history of the Holocaust, and one can only admire director Steven Spielberg's stated desire to make "a contribution to the memory of this tragedy."

That contribution has been to bring world attention to Oskar Schindler, which is, in itself, a worthwhile project. The historical man saved more than 1,100 Jewish people from transport to concentration camps by employing them in his factories and, as a result, has been honored by Yad Vashem, the Holocaust memorial in Jerusa-

lem, as one of the Righteous Among the Nations. The question of whether the "real" Schindler was a "hero"–whether he was motivated by altruistic or selfish instincts—is a thorny one that continues to be debated by historians. But this question is in many ways the wrong one to ask, because most people know about Schindler not from historians but from the movie Spielberg has produced about the real man, and the depiction of this history in fictional form begs a far more fundamental question: whether the systematic murder of six million innocent people should be fictionalized at all. Even if fictional representation of the Holocaust is judged to be morally palatable, Spielberg's movie raises a second, crucial question: Can such a representation of the Holocaust ethically center on a non-Jewish "hero"?

Some critics argue, for a variety of reasons, that the Holocaust should be off-limits to any fictional representation. The most famous pronouncement has come from the German theorist Theodor W. Adorno, who proclaimed that "nach Auschwitz, ein Gedicht zu schreiben, ist barbarisch" (after Auschwitz, to write a poem is barbaric). In *Thinking about the Holocaust: After Half a Century* (1997), Alvin H. Rosenfeld interprets Adorno's injunction to mean that "it is not only impossible but perhaps even immoral" to write fiction about this human catastrophe. Claude Lanzmann, the director of *Shoah* (1985), the enormously well-respected Holocaust documentary, has spoken out emphatically and passionately against *Schindler's List* on these grounds, arguing for an absolute ban on any fictional representation of the Holocaust.

Other scholars argue that the Holocaust can be represented in fiction, but they urge extreme care. Holocaust survivor and scholar Saul Friedländer, one of the most respected voices in this conversation, allows a place for a fictional representation but cautions that "we are dealing with an event which tests our traditional conceptual and representational categories, an 'event at the limits'." Friedländer stresses an "obligation to bear witness and record this past," but he also observes that

> such a postulate implies, quite naturally, the imprecise but no less self-evident notion that this record should not be distorted or banalized by grossly inadequate representations. Some claim to "truth" appears particularly imperative. . . . in other words, . . . there are limits to representation *which should not be but can easily be transgressed*. (emphasis his)

Definitions of the nature of such limits tend to focus on a basic criterion: that any Holocaust representation honor the humanity of the victims of the Nazi genocide. A hypothetical movie that was in favor of mass murder, for instance,

MOVIES

would clearly be judged immoral and obscene, by any reasonable ethical standards. Less conspicuously, a movie that perpetuated anti-Jewish stereotypes, even as it depicted the mass murder of Jewish people, would also be transgressing the limits upon which Friedländer and others rightly insist.

Yet, these problems are among the most basic with *Schindler's List*. In subtle and even conspicuous ways, the movie tacitly denies humanity to the Jewish victims of the Holocaust at the same time that it valorizes Schindler. In placing Schindler in the position of "hero," *Schindler's List* denies that position to the Jewish people who would otherwise occupy the central position in the narrative; and, in doing so, the movie sets up a dichotomy between Schindler (as "the hero") and the Jews ("the victims") that reduces the Jewish characters to a series of stereotypes that are unflattering at best and actively anti-Semitic at worst.

Most fundamentally, in the shadow of Schindler's heroism the Jews are eclipsed, even erased. While the movie ostensibly seeks to tell the story of the Jewish men and women whose names fill the famous list, the fact is that, with only two exceptions, we barely even know their names. Schindler's name is stressed throughout the film (as witnessed in the first scene, when an exuberant waiter yells, "That's Oskar Schindler!"); at the same time, excepting only Helen Hirsch and the accountant Itzhak Stern, all the Jewish characters remain virtually nameless and almost wholly undifferentiated. The viewer knows everything about the fictionalized Schindler—his background, family life, likes and dislikes—but almost nothing about the Jewish characters who function entirely as supporting cast in the story of Schindler's moral redemption. When dealing with Jews, the movie merely introduces viewers to an array of two-dimensional tokens: a cop, a young married couple, a woman with a bespectacled daughter, and so on. None of these characters approaches the humanity and depth of characterization given to Schindler. Nothing is known about them other than their identifying tags: cop, newlywed, red coat, glasses. Even Stern, as Judith E. Doneson notes in an article in *Spielberg's Holocaust: Critical Perspectives on Schindler's List* (1997), "functions in the film only through his relationship to Oskar Schindler. He exists under no other circumstances. He has no family. No friends. No confidants." Such is the movie's rendition of its central Jewish character, regardless of the fact that, as Doneson notes, the real man "did have a wife who was with him throughout the war." In Lanzmann's *Shoah*, one Holocaust survivor explains that, to the Nazis, "Wir waren eine Masse," meaning that the Nazi guards of the transport trains saw only anonymous bodies, stripped of identities, personalities, and humanity. Spielberg's movie, rather astonishingly, is similarly reductive.

In choosing to focus on the story of the "rescuer hero," Spielberg thus obliterates the point of view of the people to whom this tragedy actually occurred. In the process they become objects, not subjects, of the Holocaust, as the movie solidly positions the viewer outside the Jewish world. Like Schindler watching the liquidation of the ghetto from his position high up on a hill beyond the ghetto wall, the movie audience looks on in horror; but also like Schindler, their view is voyeuristic and removed. Jewish people are rendered permanently "other"; the viewers are shocked at what happens to them only in an abstract way. Actual human identification is reserved for Schindler alone.

More disturbingly, in rendering Jewish people as objects, the movie reduces them to anti-Semitic stereotypes associated with wealth, crime, and a generalized sense of "racial" inferiority. The movie is replete with references to finances, for example, frequently representing both Stern and other Jewish characters as motivated excessively by profit. "Since when does time cost money?" Stern asks; "money's still money," quips a Jewish black marketeer, and these are but the most benign examples. As critics have noted with dismay, Jews are depicted being evicted from expensive apartments, swallowing diamonds to conceal them from the Nazis, and trading all manner of goods—again for profit—on the black market. In these ways the Jewish people in the movie conform to Nazi caricatures of them. As Sara R. Horowitz has commented, the Jews who meet with Schindler in his car to discuss potential profits from the factory "could be straight out of a Nazi propaganda poster on eugenics and racial science. One [actually] appears apelike, with a large jaw covered in stubble." Even Hirsch is reduced to the familiar figure of the Jewish seductress, a stock figure in Western literature associated with an Eastern sensuality and decadence.

The movie also repeatedly paints its Jewish characters as passive victims who contrast greatly with Schindler, the man of action and ability. Jewish people are constantly groveling, apologizing, and begging, as, for instance, does the one-armed machinist who embarrasses Schindler by thanking him with child-like effusiveness for letting him work in the factory. Stern, too, when rescued from a concentration-camp transport train, apologizes to Schindler no fewer than three times for any "inconvenience" Schindler might have incurred in saving him. This kind of characterization only fuels stereotypes of Jewish people as pathologically cowed and weak, play-

ing into anti-Semitic narratives that suggest the Jewish victims of the Nazi genocide somehow brought mass destruction upon themselves through obsequiousness and passivity.

Similarly, it has been argued that the Jewish people in the movie are "feminized" in the most negative sense of the word. That is, they are associated with those qualities that have been misogynistically applied to women: they are helpless and fearful, awaiting a strong male figure who will shelter and save them. Just as the movie depends upon dichotomies between rescuer and victim, it also associates Schindler with extreme masculine traits while tagging his Jewish workers with feminine ones. Stern, the nameless rabbi, and the one-armed mechanic are all represented as old, frail, asexual men, while Schindler embodies the Hollywood vision of the "real hero": handsome, virile, tall, and sexual. In painting Jews as "womanly" victims while representing the Nazi factory owner as powerful and even sexy, the movie once again corroborates Nazi propaganda. Indeed, in his famous study of Nazi

ideology and its representation, *Male Fantasies* (1987), Klaus Thewelheit has noted the ways in which Nazism promoted itself in just these terms: as a hypermasculine realm set over and against the "feminine" and the "Jewish."

Finally, Spielberg's movie also raises problems because Schindler is not just a hero but a particularly Christian hero. Although the movie, admirably, includes snatches of Jewish traditional culture (Hebrew melodies, Sabbath candles, a Jewish wedding in the camp), ultimately it abandons this cultural perspective and retreats to one that would be more comfortable and familiar for most viewers: the Christian narrative of salvation. In the process, Schindler becomes a kind of Christ figure who "saves" the Jews from their otherwise inevitable fate, a theme encapsulated in the final scene, in which the Jews in Schindler's factory gaze up at him in adoration as he tells them of their impending liberation. Standing high above his anonymous Jewish audience, light pouring in from behind, Schindler becomes, as Bernstein notes, a "virtual apotheo-

Scene from the popular 1993 movie *Schindler's List* in which Oskar Schindler (Liam Neeson) and Itzhak Stern (Ben Kingsley) compile a list of Jewish workers to be placed under the factory manager's protection

(Photofest)

MOVIES

sis as a modern Christ figure in his sermon to the awestruck Jews." Earlier in the movie, the Nazi commandant Amon Goeth sardonically asks Schindler, "What are you, Moses?" By the end of the movie, the comparison—with its implicit suggestion not of Moses but of Christ—becomes particularly apt; the Jews are reduced to followers; Schindler is deified.

These are but the most glaring issues that concern scholars with respect to the representation of Jewish people in this movie, but several other serious problems should also be noted. For one thing, the movie is nonrepresentative. The hero, or "rescuer," story is a valuable moral narrative, but it is also one that, in reality, was exceedingly rare: Yad Vashem lists 342 German Righteous Persons; according to Daniel Jonah Goldhagen, the Nazi Party boasted eight million members. Moreover, in its setting in a work camp, as opposed to a concentration camp, the movie completely eliminates any representation of the mass extermination that was at the core of the Nazis' "Final Solution." Those horrors that are represented are vastly watered down, and, as Elinor J. Brecher explains in *Schindler's Legacy: True Stories of the List Survivors* (1994), which focuses on the Jewish people who really worked for Schindler, the movie greatly sanitizes the actuality even of the work camp. None of the Jews looks terribly emaciated, and they often appear ridiculously clean, given their situation and in contrast with the historical reality. They even seem to be well and warmly dressed. These problems pale in significance, though, in comparison with the larger, comforting distortions in the movie. For, as Brecher notes, unlike the reality:

> there were no hangings in *Schindler's List*. No Jews dangled from iron rings in Amon Goeth's office. The dogs wore muzzles; audiences didn't see them gnawing men's genitals and women's breasts like so much hamburger. Spielberg's storm troopers refrained from swinging infants by their feet into brick walls, smashing their skulls like melons. . . .

Above all else, scholars have objected to the shower scene, in which the women of the Schindler factory, erroneously diverted by train to Auschwitz, are forced into huge concrete rooms equipped with metal nozzles. The audience, logically, braces itself for the women's imminent gassing; but, in contrast to what happened to millions of Jewish people, what comes spraying out of the showerheads is, in fact, water. Critics have unanimously condemned this scene for its dangerous potential to fuel the propaganda of neo-Nazi revisionists who want to claim the genocide of European Jewry never occurred at all.

It may not be true that the Holocaust should never be represented in fiction, but *Schindler's List* does not provide a humane or even a terribly accurate narrative. Perhaps in the future a responsible and important fictional representation of the Holocaust will emerge. To date, however, the finest and most profound depictions have come in the form of memoirs and documentaries. Lanzmann's *Shoah*, the extraordinary French documentary *Nuit et Brouillard* (Night and Fog, 1955), and historical memoirs of the concentration camp experience such as Elie Wiesel's *Night* (1960) and Primo Levi's *Survival in Auschwitz: The Nazi Assault on Humanity* (1961) handle the topic with far greater insight, integrity, and factuality. All of these works depict Jewish people as fully realized human beings; none shifts the focus to non-Jewish characters; and each represents the magnitude of the horror that was the Holocaust with far greater sensitivity and accuracy than does Spielberg's movie. Many people argue that Spielberg has accomplished a great deal of good precisely because audiences are much more willing to see a representation that is uplifting and that focuses, more happily, on the "good German" hero and not on tortured Jewish people. Perhaps, above all else, one should ask why this propensity persists more than half a century after the Holocaust, and why contemporary audiences remain uninterested in, and unwilling to identify with, the plight of the people who figured at the center of this terrible history.

—LAUREN PROLL,
WITTENBERG UNIVERSITY

References

Theodor W. Adorno, *Kulturkritik und Gesellschaft*, 2 volumes (Frankfurt: Suhrkamp, 1977).

Jean Améry, *At the Mind's Limits: Contemplations by a Survivor on Auschwitz and Its Realities*, translated by Sidney Rosenfeld and Stella P. Rosenfeld (Bloomington: Indiana University Press, 1980).

Ilan Avisar, *Screening the Holocaust: Cinema's Images of the Unimaginable* (Bloomington: Indiana University Press, 1988).

Michael André Bernstein, "The *Schindler's List* Effect," *American Scholar*, 63 (1994): 429–432.

Tadeusz Borowski, *This Way for the Gas, Ladies and Gentlemen: And Other Stories*, translated by Barbara Vedder (London: Cape / New York: Viking, 1967).

Elinor J. Brecher, *Schindler's Legacy: True Stories of the List Survivors* (New York: Dutton, 1994).

Tim Cole, *Selling the Holocaust: From Auschwitz to Schindler: How History Is Bought, Packaged, and Sold* (New York: Routledge, 1999).

Judith E. Doneson, "The Feminization of the Jew in *Schindler's List,*" in *Spielberg's Holocaust: Critical Perspectives on Schindler's List,* edited by Yosefa Loshitzky (Bloomington: Indiana University Press, 1997).

Doneson, *The Holocaust in American Film* (Philadelphia: Jewish Publication Society, 1987).

Hilene Flanzbaum, ed., *The Americanization of the Holocaust* (Baltimore: Johns Hopkins University Press, 1999).

Saul Friedländer, *When Memory Comes,* translated by Helen R. Lane (New York: Farrar, Straus & Giroux, 1979).

Friedländer, ed., *Probing the Limits of Representation: Nazism and the "Final Solution"* (Cambridge, Mass.: Harvard University Press, 1992).

Daniel Jonah Goldhagen, *Hitler's Willing Executioners: Ordinary Germans and the Holocaust* (New York: Knopf, 1996).

Fanya Gotttesfeld Heller, *Strange and Unexpected Love: A Teenage Girl's Holocaust Memoirs* (Hoboken, N.J.: Ktav, 1993).

Sara R. Horowitz, "But Is It Good for the Jews? Spielberg's Schindler and the Aesthetics of Atrocity," in *Spielberg's Holocaust: Critical Perspectives on Schindler's List,* edited by Loshitzky (Bloomington: Indiana University Press, 1997).

Chaim A. Kaplan, *Scroll of Agony: The Warsaw Diary of Chaim A. Kaplan,* translated and edited by Abraham I. Katsch (New York: Macmillan, 1965).

Lawrence Langer, *The Holocaust and the Literary Imagination* (New Haven: Yale University Press, 1975).

Claude Lanzmann, "Ihr Sollt Nicht Weinen: Einspruch gegen *Schindler's List,*" *Frankfurter Allgemeine Zeitung* (5 March 1994).

Primo Levi, *The Drowned and the Saved,* translated by Raymond Rosenthal (New York: Summit, 1988).

Levi, *The Reawakening,* translated by Stuart Woolf (New York: Collier, 1965).

Levi, *Survival in Auschwitz: The Nazi Assault on Humanity,* translated by Stuart Woolf (New York: Collier, 1961).

Alan Mintz, *Popular Culture in the Shaping of Holocaust Memory in America* (Seattle: University of Washington Press, 2001).

Peter Novick, *The Holocaust in American Life* (Boston: Houghton Mifflin, 1999).

Alvin H. Rosenfeld, "The Americanization of the Holocaust," in *Thinking About the Holocaust: After Half a Century,* edited by Rosenfeld (Bloomington: Indiana University Press, 1997), pp. 119–151.

Rosenfeld, *A Double Dying: Reflections on Holocaust Literature* (Bloomington: Indiana University Press, 1980).

Jeffrey Shandler, *While America Watches: Televising the Holocaust* (New York: Oxford University Press, 1999).

Art Spiegelman, *Maus: A Survivor's Tale* (New York: Pantheon, 1986).

Spiegelman, *Maus II: A Survivor's Tale: And Here My Troubles Began* (New York: Pantheon, 1992).

Steven Spielberg, "Why I Made *Schindler's List,*" *Queen's Quarterly,* 101 (Spring 1994): 27–33.

Klaus Thewelheit, *Male Fantasies,* volume 1, translated by Stephen Conway and others (Minneapolis: University of Minnesota Press, 1987).

Elie Wiesel, *Night,* translated by Stella Rodway (New York: Hill & Wang, 1960).

Yad Vashem website <htttp://www.yadvashem.org>.

James E. Young, *Writing and Rewriting the Holocaust: Narrative and the Consequences of Interpretation* (Bloomington: Indiana University Press, 1988).

MOVIES

NAZI CRIMINALITY

Were the Nazis more evil than other genocidal regimes?

Viewpoint: Yes. Because of the enormous scope of criminal intent exhibited in the totality of their actions, the Nazis were exceptionally evil.

Viewpoint: No. The morals, psychology, and structural context of the genocide sponsored by the Nazi regime did not differ fundamentally from others in history.

The invention of mass murder and genocide did not occur in the twentieth century, but surely its unparalleled proliferation manifested itself during this period. The Armenian massacres in Turkey (1915), the Stalinist purges and massacres in the Soviet Union (1930s), the Holocaust (1933–1945), the Pol Pot regime in Cambodia (1975–1978), the Cultural Revolution in China (1966–1976), the Rwandan massacres (1994), "ethnic cleansing" in the former Yugoslavia (1990s), death squads in Central and South America (1950s to 1980s), and the massacre of Kurds by Iraqi leader Saddam Hussein (1987) punctuate a century already measured by war and the constantly improving technology of violence: aerial bombing, poison gas, germ warfare, and nuclear annihilation. Still, with so much for the popular imagination to choose from, Adolf Hitler has become the archetype for human wickedness and the Nazi State has come to embody the institutionalization of evil as state policy.

The popular conception of the Nazis, comparing all manner of evildoers with an archetypal Hitler and calling any overly zealous police tactic "Gestapo-like," was shared by the first generation of historians of the Third Reich and of the Holocaust. Having lived through and experienced Nazi brutality, they had no doubt that the Nazis were exceptionally evil. The Nazi State, and not simply Hitler, was fundamentally and efficiently wicked. The Holocaust represented the prima facie evidence for this assumption, but not the only evidence. The totalitarian nature of Nazism, its contempt for traditional virtue, its glorification of violence, and the effectiveness of its propaganda in winning the hearts and minds of millions of otherwise inoffensive Germans, put the Nazi regime into an historical and ethical category of its own.

In the 1980s, however, historians, especially in Germany, began to challenge this assumption of exceptionalism. The Nazi regime was, they pointed out, rife with internecine conflicts among different agencies. Lines of authority were unclear. Responsibilities for implementing major policies, including the Final Solution, were divided among competing agencies. That the Nazis came to represent an archetype for criminal despotism has more to do with their geographic location in the middle of Europe and their chosen victims—the Jews. Neither Armenians nor Kurds nor any other victims of genocide have been so capable of drawing attention to their suffering. Only because of the exceptional role of the Jews in the Western historical and religious imagination, and in post–World War II politics, has their destruction come to seem exceptional.

Arguments about the exceptionalism of the Nazi regime differ from those about the Holocaust itself. The latter, while taking into account the actions of the Nazi perpetrators, is more concerned with the experience of the victims. Discussion of the exceptionally criminal nature of the Nazi state focuses almost exclusively on the ideological, social, and political structures of the Nazi state.

Viewpoint:
Yes. Because of the enormous scope of criminal intent exhibited in the totality of their actions, the Nazis were exceptionally evil.

Alas, one does not have to look far, even in the twentieth century, to find evidence of criminality in the highest places. From Third World despots such as François "Papa Doc" Duvalier of Haiti to Russian leader Joseph Stalin, from the dictatorship of Mobutu Sese Seko in Zaire to the regime of apartheid in South Africa, the modern, sovereign state has been an inviting target for those who would violate for their own purposes the fundamental responsibility of political power: to set aside one's own interests, to act lawfully, and to serve the best interests of the governed.

Granted, many political disasters have been caused by leaders who believed themselves to be acting well within this paradigm of responsibility, either because they were incompetent, ill informed, or suffering acutely from bad judgment. Tsar Nicholas II of Russia might be counted among this number, as well as much of the interwar Weimar government of Germany (1919–1933). And petty criminality has been known to afflict otherwise well-intentioned political leaders: U.S. president Richard Nixon acted unlawfully on several occasions, but he has never been accused of intentionally subverting the best interests (as he understood it) of the American people. Some of the most grim ideological despotisms, embodied in Revolutionary France's Republic of Virtue (1793–1794), the Pol Pot regime of Cambodia (1975–1978), or the Cultural Revolution in China (1966–1976), were perpetrated by leaders who, however despicable their actions, believed in the rightness and necessity of their causes.

Of all the modern examples of wickedness in high places one might readily adduce, however, that the Nazi regime was exceptional, not simply in the scale of its crimes—for the Soviet Union might thereby be the winner in the total number of dead, and Pol Pot murdered a greater percentage of his countrymen than did Hitler—but in criminal imagination. The Nazi regime sought to, and nearly succeeded in, destroying the fabric of German and European civilization so that Hitler's imagined "Thousand Year Reich" might be built on its ruins. To this end,

the *Gotterdammerung* of the current age and the creation of a new order in the Aryan image, the Nazis established a totalitarian state in Germany, seized Austria and Czechoslovakia, invaded first Poland and ultimately the bulk of the European continent, and conducted total war without regard to civilian casualties or the laws of civilized warfare. Finally, for this cataclysmic goal of destruction the Nazis planned and implemented the Holocaust. In the specifics, the Nazis were not remarkable; in the totality of their actions, the Nazi regime was unparalleled in criminality.

The Nazi State was remarkable but not exceptional. The Nazi Party came to power in 1933 by promising to solve domestic problems, rebuild the military, and permit Germany once again to enjoy its place in the sun. They fulfilled their promises by centralizing and coordinating the German economy and by attempting to bring every element of people's lives under Party control: religion, recreation, child rearing, education, work, and artistic endeavor. Germany became, under the Nazis, a totalitarian state. The individual was expected to surrender his or her identity for the good of the whole people under the leadership of Hitler. Thus, the slogan *Ein Reich, Ein Volk, Ein Führer* (One Empire, One People, One Leader) was more than effective rhetoric; it was an organizational principle. Benito Mussolini had put similar ideas into place in Italy, and the Soviet Union did the same thing with far greater completeness. But to a degree not seen elsewhere, the Nazi regime managed to subvert the already well established rule of law and cultures of civility with an efficient lawlessness to which neither Stalin nor Mussolini came close. This level of organization is best represented in Leni Riefenstall's *Triumph des Willens* (Triumph of the Will), a propaganda documentary filmed at the 1934 Nuremberg Party rally. The movie captures the tension of Nazism: the uniformed discipline of young boys and men marching in step with banners and torches, singing in cadence and shouting on cue, on the one hand; and the raucous play of the Hitler Youth, the ecstatic joy of young women in der Führer's presence, and the swarming masses of Nurembergers eager to show their devotion to the new Germany and its messianic leader, on the other hand. This tension between chaos and orderly discipline replaced civility and the rule of law in Germany, and this intentional transformation made the Nazi regime exceptionally criminal.

War crimes commission members examining a mobile killing van in which Jews were gassed while being transported to the crematoriums at Chelmno, Poland, 1945

(U.S. Holocaust Memorial Museum, Washington, D.C.)

One of the standard chestnuts about the Nazi State holds that, had Hitler died in 1939, before the invasion of Poland, he would have been remembered as the rebuilder of Germany, a statesman on the order of Otto von Bismarck or even of his American contemporary, Franklin D. Roosevelt. This possibility is eminently unlikely. Roosevelt's tenure as president, to choose a singularly interesting parallel, began and ended within weeks of Hitler's reign. Roosevelt sought, with mixed success, to rebuild the American economy by coordinating the interests of labor and capital, a strategy similar to, if not as complete as, Hitler's policy of *gleichschaltung*. Roosevelt, like Hitler, came to represent the hopes and aspirations of millions of citizens, and both men were willing to sidestep or even ignore established laws and practices when it seemed needful to do so. But had Roosevelt died in 1940, he would have been remembered for having preserved capitalism and the rule of law from catastrophe. Even his Court packing scheme (1937) was legal, if ill advised, and the intent of the New Deal (1933–1941) was never revolutionary. Roosevelt wanted to preserve civilization, not to destroy it.

In the same period, Hitler co-opted capitalism and subverted the rule of law in Germany. He willfully disregarded international obligations and made Germany into a pariah state. The foundations of German economic recovery had been laid before he came to office. His success in moving Germany out from under the restrictions of the Versailles Treaty (1919) had more to do with French and British timidity than with Hitler's statesmanship. Had Hitler died before September 1939, his death would have been greeted with a sigh of relief throughout Germany and Europe. Had he been replaced by a mainstream German politician, the "Hitler Years" would have been remembered as an unusually lawless and embarrassing aberration from long traditions of political and social conservatism in Germany.

Even so, the Nazi regime did not display its fundamental criminality until the outbreak of World War II (1939–1945), and in waging war the Nazi regime was most criminal. The post–World War II International Military Tribunal at Nuremberg accused the Nazi regime of waging aggressive war in violation of international law. Critics of the tribunal—and defense attorneys at the time—argued that there were no clear international laws at the time outlawing aggressive war, and that even if there were, Germany was certainly not the only state to make a preemptive strike against a once and future foe. On a broader time scale, most of the states of Europe had, at one time or another, launched aggressive wars against a neighbor with the intent of seizing land or preempting a future attack. Indeed, the whole of European imperialism might well fall within the language of this indictment. The Nazi invasions of Poland and the Soviet Union, however, were qualitatively different from, for example, Napoleon Bonaparte's conquest of Europe a little more than a century earlier or the seizure of Africa by several European nations in the century thereafter. Both the French Grand Armée and the British, French, and Belgian colonial forces saw themselves, albeit on too little evidence, as heirs of the best of European culture on a mission to expand and extend that culture to other less fortunate peoples. The Nazi invasion of the Slavic nations was meant to be a precursor to cultural and physical genocide. The Slavs, like the Jews, were in the way and had to be pushed aside. The only difference was that the Slavs would be permitted to live as helots, while the Jews would be exterminated. Ancient empires might have attempted similarly bold strokes—the Assyrians come to mind—but they lacked the technology to carry it off. Only the modern world could give play to such criminality.

At the beginning of the war, there was little reason to think the Nazis were qualitatively different from other aggressive regimes. The German armies swept across Europe with frightening efficiency, but the principles by which they waged war were unchanged from those employed on the Somme (1916) a generation earlier, or at Gettysburg (1863) and Chickamauga (1863) a generation before that. The *Wehrmacht* (German army) used technological and other resources to achieve maximum advantage over the enemy. The British, Soviets, and Americans would do the same in their turn. The Allies would kill civilians and noncombatants, especially through area bombing of German and Japanese cities. For the Allies, as it had been for the German armies of Kaiser Wilhelm, civilian deaths were an unavoidable accident of war. For the Nazis, civilian deaths were both a means of waging war and an end in itself.

Again, atrocities are an all too common component of modern war, but one expects such things to take place either among undisciplined troops or among peoples without a tradition of just and limited war. Since the time of St. Augustine of Hippo in the fifth century, warfare in the Western tradition has been governed (albeit loosely) by the idea of just war: war can justly be engaged in only by legitimate authorities (for example, princes) against legitimate targets (such as other combatants), must have a reasonable chance of success, and must avoid excessive force. Specific rules, worked out in the Middle Ages and institutionalized in the Geneva Conventions (1900), tend to be grounded in Augustine's norms. When fighting American or British forces, the Germans generally stayed within the bounds of these agreed-upon rules. Against the Soviets, both ideological and racial enemies, no laws applied. This difference was a conscious decision, again, aimed at destroying not simply the Soviet government and its ability to wage war but the rule of law. That the Nazi regime made such a distinction among enemies suggests as well that they knew that what they did on the Eastern (and Slavic) Front was criminal and tried to avoid the more egregious examples of such behavior in the west, where the enemy was primarily Aryan.

Even more than in their war fighting, the Holocaust distills the essence of Nazi criminality. Avoiding the separate question of the exceptionalism of the Holocaust in a century of genocides, the Nazi implementation of the Final Solution remains an unparalleled example of state criminality. It had no rational motive except hatred; it was intended to be excessively cruel and painful; and it was conducted in secret (away from the eyes even of the Germans, for whose racial future the crimes were being committed). Stalin's destruction of the Kulaks, his purges of real, potential, and imagined enemies, his oppression of national minorities, and his outright murders of opponents clearly put his regime in the same category as the Nazis, but Stalin's crimes had a different quality. For a single example, the murder of the Polish officer corps in the Katyn Forest (1940) was conducted one life, one bullet at a time. It was individual murder repeated over and over with the goal of ridding Poland of its leadership class in order to clear the way for a communist takeover. Stalin used no gas chambers, no crematoriums to hide the evidence. He failed, perhaps for lack of imagination, to create the factories of death that were the hallmark of the Nazi regime.

Such comparisons fail in the end. The destruction of the Armenians by the Turks (1916), of Native Americans by European Americans (late fifteenth century to the nineteenth century), of Hutus by Tutsis (1994), and of the people murdered and persecuted by the Soviets and their satellites, including Pol Pot in Cambodia, were crimes against individuals, for women, men, and children suffered, starved, and died. But criminality is defined not by the wickedness of the act but by the impact of that act on broader society. In the slow development of law

JUST WAIT, IT GETS A LOT WORSE

American soldier Chuck Ferree recalls his introduction to the Nazi horrors at Dachau:

We were at least a mile away maybe more, but we could still smell something very disagreeable. The SHAEF officer climbed into a Command car with another General, and off they went. I hopped into a jeep with a S/Sgt. who wore the shoulder patch of the 45th Infantry Division . . . the Thunderbird Division, which had been in constant combat for almost three years.

We followed the command car. It was cold in the jeep, even though the sun shone brightly, and I wore my fleece-lined flight jacket. It had snowed the night before. The date was April 29th 1945. The Sgt. began telling me what to expect when we reached our destination, which was Dachau, a Nazi concentration camp liberated only that morning. I asked about the bad odor, he said, "just wait, it gets a lot worse."

Dachau had its typical Bavarian attractive homes and neat gardens. This gave me no hint of what lay beyond the landscaped entrance to the death camp.

The first place the Sgt. drove me to was the awful proof of the rumors—boxcars and bodies. The stories we had heard gave no indication of the grotesque forms of the victims and their emaciated condition. These miserable creatures had kept an unusual rendezvous with death. The train loaded with prisoners had been shipped away as the American Liberators approached. The camp at their destination refused to accept them. Without food or water they had been shuttled around from camp to camp and ended up back at Dachau. Most had died on the return trip. The few who had managed to climb from the box cars were shot down by the SS. The bony frames stuck out like skeletons, no meat on those bones. Many of the cars were open gondolas. The dusting of snow gave the cadavers a ghostly aspect.

We passed along a row of imposing homes of camp directors and entered a gate decorated with a large German Imperial eagle. The barracks inside bore lightning-decorated SS insignia. We passed a large kennel, it's occupants lay victims of the wrath of the recently liberated prisoners. Large and once beautiful German Shepherds, throats slashed, heads crushed. We then saw a building appropriately marked "Braus Bad," to lure victims into the gas chamber. Warnings were painted on the building and the door; the international signal for danger . . . a skull with crossed bones.

Leaving the gas chamber we found further proof of the Nazi claim to everlasting infamy—human bodies heaped hodge-podge filling two rooms and sprawling out the doors. It was here that the cold weather worked to the advantage of the witnesses. The stench of the bodies and the accompanying filth would have been unbearable under other conditions. The odor permeated right through my heavy leather jacket.

Between these crowded morgues was the crematorium where four yawning doors stood open and eagerly consumed more victims. Outside there was much evidence of bones and ash where the furnaces had been emptied many times of their gruesome contents. Beyond this scene was a stall which had been used as an execution chamber where many had met death by the firing squad.

This death farm was separated from the main stockades by a high wire fence and a moat. Swarming along the fence were hundreds of the more fortunate prisoners who were now liberated and expressing their gratitude.

Source: Chuck Ferree, "Dachau Liberation," A Cybrary of the Holocaust, Remember.Org <http://www.remember.org/witness/dachlib.html>.

---

in Western society, crimes against persons came to be seen as crimes against the whole people, and the kings took it upon themselves to punish the perpetrators of such crimes in the name of the whole body politic. In the case of the Nazis, and the few other regimes who have come close to their criminality, the victims were and still are all of humanity, for it was the value of humanity the Nazis sought to destroy. Imagining a Nazi victory in World War II and an ascendant Nazism spread across the globe is not to invoke a nightmare; it is to imagine the unimaginable, the collapse of civilization and humanity, and the triumph of apocalyptic wickedness. No other regime, however grimly criminal, ever came so close to making the nightmare a reality.

–TANDY MCCONNELL,
COLUMBIA COLLEGE

NAZI CRIMINALITY

Viewpoint:
No. The morals, psychology, and structural context of the genocide sponsored by the Nazi regime did not differ fundamentally from others in history.

Questions about the nature of Nazi criminality promptly give rise to complex and often heated debates. These debates are held both within and outside the academic world and regularly grow into real polemics. This case regards questions about whether or not Nazi crimes have an exceptional character in comparison with those committed by other regimes. A major cause of this high tension is the inevitable mixture of the different scientific interpretations of these crimes and their respective points of views on the one hand, with various politico-ideological and moral factors playing an important role on the other. This mixture is to a large extent responsible for the enormous susceptibility of the subject, and it makes the task of Holocaust historians more difficult and challenging, since it uncovers the ideological character of historiography.

If one polarizes the different points of view on whether the Nazi crimes have a special character, one quickly comes to the following representation. In the opinion of a first group of historians, the crimes committed by the Nazis are of such a nature or extent and the motivation behind their crimes is so incomprehensibly cruel that they give these Nazi crimes a singular place within history. Without intending to tone down the seriousness of the crimes committed, a second group of historians is of the opinion that this view is not justified and is contradicted by many other genocides in the twentieth century.

The crimes committed by the Nazis during World War II (1939–1945) and the preceding years are diverse in nature. Clearly, not all the crimes committed by the Nazis should be regarded as equally serious. War crimes, such as those committed when battlefield troops got out of hand or by intelligence officers during "hard" interrogations of prisoners of war or resistance fighters, are found in almost any war situation. Any distinction between Nazi and Allied behavior in such cases is at least open to question. There is no claim of exceptionalism on such crimes. Within the group of crimes on which there is a claim, most attention is spent on the various extermination and concentration camps of central and eastern Europe, but the actions by the *Einsatzgruppen* (mobile killing units) against the Jewish civilian population can also be regarded as war crimes. These crimes constitute one of the most notorious episodes in Western history, largely because of the enormous extent of the genocide and its systematic character. The fact that the genocide took place at the heart of Western civilization and that one can represent it visually by means of existing documentation plays an important part in its centrality to modern thinking. Nevertheless, the claim that the Nazis were exceptional in this behavior does not apply to the totality of these crimes. After all, further distinction can be made among the victims. A first group became victims because of its actions, which were regarded as dangerous by the Nazis. Well-known examples are the Russian prisoners of war or the German political opponents of the Nazis, many of whom died in the camps. There are, however, many examples of regimes that have committed similar crimes for the same reasons.

A second group of victims was, however, not confined to the camps because of their actions but because of their existence as a result of their involuntary membership in a group. Well-known examples are the millions of Jewish and Gypsy victims. Furthermore, a policy of active extermination was pursued against this population. Therefore, it is only in this second group that an extra limit was passed by which, according to some historians, a claim of unparalleled wickedness is justified.

This limit is not at the level of the individual victims; classifying individual pain is absurd. The camp experience of a Russian prisoner of war was not necessarily less painful than that of a Jewish fellow-sufferer. If the camps are, however, approached from a philosophical angle and their significance with regard to human civilization is examined, the second category of victims raises many strong questions. The fact that one group decides that another group is no longer entitled to live and tries to achieve this objective at any price defies all imagination. The understanding of the perpetrators' psychology and morals, and the context within which they acted, have, therefore, become objectives for the postwar generations, since these crimes raise fundamental questions regarding the existing views on human nature and human civilization. Although many arguments can be raised against this division of victims, one sticks to it because it is of vital importance for discussion.

Yet, recognition of the implications of the camps for human civilization is still something more than assigning a special status to them. If the Nazi crimes were exceptional, this attribution means that either the perpetrators' psychology and their morals were unparalleled and that they were therefore unequaled in history, or that the context of the Nazi regime and the underlying structures and ideology were special. Without wishing to tone down the horror, one must therefore examine whether such crimes, together with their far-reaching implications, have not been committed in a comparable way anywhere else.

The best-known argument of the advocates of the exceptionalism of Nazi criminality is pithily summarized in Eberhard Jäckel's "The Murder of the European Jews and History" in *The Jews in European History: Seven Lectures* (1993):

> What was novel, and in this respect unique, was solely that until then no state had declined to wipe out as completely as possible a group of people whom it specified. It had included the aged, women, children, and infants, without any examination of individual cases, implementing this decision through the enactments and coercive powers of government.

Although it is highly questionable whether there are still no other genocides falling within this definition, most advocates of this claim remain in one way or another attached to this argument.

A second important argument is not always openly presented, but it is seldom absent from the subtext. Pleas in favor of this contention all too often have the character of dogma. The horror of the Holocaust is indescribable and, consequently, untransferable. When considered in this way, all explanations are liable to serious shortcomings. Belgian historian and philosopher Gie van de Berghe, in *De uitbuiting van de Holocaust* (1990), describes this attitude:

> Even if we were able to know all facts and reconstruct their entire evolution, even then we would not understand. Explanations miss the essence, they weaken and deny reality. Experience is untransferable. Testimonies may only arouse disgust, horror, and humility.

Because the perpetrators' psychology and morals, and the context within which they acted, are said to be totally different from the modern frame of reference, and explanations always require a form of identification, every explanation implies a form of putting things into perspective.

To escape from this difficulty, some historians argue in favor of a shift from "explaining" to "commemorating" or "dealing with" the Holocaust. Thus, they seek to move from an interpretative to an evocative dimension. When commemorating the Holocaust, its exceptionalism is thus introduced as dogma. The representation of Nazi crimes achieves an almost sacral character. The advantage of this explanation is that there is only one frame of reference established by morality. If this attitude found wide acceptance, the division among historians on the interpretation of the Holocaust would be seriously limited. The importance of the limitation of this division should not be underestimated, because negation draws much strength from the existing multilevel interpretation and the productive dialectic of these different points of view.

For the second group of historians, the "explanation" remains central. In their opinion, the risk of putting things to some extent into perspective, which is inherent in every explanation, does not counterbalance the disadvantages of a flight into the moral premise, into an interpretive framework partly inspired by morality. Furthermore, the specter of putting things into perspective can be minimized if historians are aware of this development and also tell their readers about their viewpoint. Admittedly, the pursuit of one clear framework to limited multi-interpretativeness and therefore vagueness is perhaps noble. But this exceptional position for the Holocaust investigation cannot be defended from a scientific-philosophical point of view. There are no objective arguments for approaching this episode differently than any other period of history. Furthermore, in practice, the result of the implementation of this pursuit is often counterproductive with regard to its intended effect. Negation precisely draws a large part of its strength from denouncing this flight into morality; negationists interpret this a priori moral point of view as a lack of daring to enter into an open discussion. The confirmation of the "explanation" with regard to the Holocaust is therefore not only inspired by strictly scientific-philosophical motives, but it is also nourished from this concrete finding.

The fear of too great an openness in interpretation, if the pursuit of one a priori specific framework is given up, is not always justified. Different investigators will come to different insights according to their interpretations, frameworks, and lines of approach. This fact does not mean, however, that every explanation is now possible. Despite the well-known contrast between an intentionalist and a structuralist line of approach, for instance, insights that are no longer questioned and on which a consensus is reached gradually come about.

The first argument of the advocates of the special-status claim can also be considerably nuanced. Although Jäckel's definition applies to the Holocaust, other genocides also fall within this definition. The classic example is the genocide of the Armenians in Turkey. On 24 April 1915 Mehmed Talat Pasa ordered Armenians' deportation on behalf of the Young Turks. On 16 September of the same year the official signal to proceed with their extermination was given. As a result, an officially sanctioned and organized massacre was carried out among the Armenians. In this case as well, the initiative and organization came from the state, and the only criterion was being an Armenian or not. Moreover, one may wonder whether the treatment of slaves by the

Western powers, or the genocide in Rwanda with more than half a million victims in 1994, do not raise equally compelling philosophical questions on human civilization. Every genocide has special characteristics. As far as the Holocaust is concerned, the industrial character of extermination can be pointed out. Yet, these characteristics are not sufficient to assign exceptional status to one of these genocides. Neither the perpetrators' morals and psychology nor the structural context of one of these genocides differed sufficiently from the others to justify doing so.

Those who suffered in the other genocides regard the Holocaust's claim to singleness as a monopolization of the "ultimate unique pain." The other genocides are logically placed at a lower level. This inevitably implies a partial putting of these genocides into perspective, which is precisely what one wishes to avoid at any price with regard to the Holocaust.

One cannot deny that there is an enormous discrepancy between the attention spent on the investigation and commemoration of the Holocaust on the one hand, and the relative silence regarding other genocides and crimes on the other. According to the second group of historians, the reason for this discrepancy is largely to be found in the difference in "power over" and "access to" public opinion by different groups of survivors. With the creation of the state of Israel, the Jews found a powerful defender of their interests. Generally, the Western world listens willingly to the Jewish complaint. This situation is partly because the Holocaust took place in Europe, and therefore it is much more concrete, but partly because of a shared sense of guilt. Therefore, the hierarchy of crimes is often regarded as a Western creation. This hierarchy tells something about the current politico-ideological factors and little about the various genocides themselves.

The stubborn sticking to the monopoly position of the Holocaust, therefore, causes legitimate resentment among the survivors of other, similar genocides. Moreover, one sees once more that negation takes advantage of this controversy and this form of opposed interpretations inspired by politico-ideological motives. The following statement made at the trial of SS leader Klaus Barbie in 1987 is exemplary:

Equally pleased with yourselves as indifferent to the suffering of those who are really oppressed, you do not do anything but cherish your own scratches, and you raise the Jews—that means your own kind—to the dignity of damned people or chosen martyrs in order to make people forget, by means of the

ordeals you suffered, how you have continually ill treated people from the South.

Such arguments, which always contain elements of truth, are all too often fallacies, distorted comparisons, or misrepresentations of narrow-minded points of view. Some of the favorite ingredients of negation are exaggeration, decontextualization, and the repetition effect. The existing vagueness and quarrel within scientific historiography on the interpretation of the crimes, which is inspired to a large extent by policito-ideological factors on both sides, are, however, not conducive to the refutation of negating views.

One can argue that claims of exceptional Nazi criminality run counter to the scientific-philosophical view that is applicable to any other historical phenomena. There are no objective arguments to defend this exceptional position. Furthermore, it appears to be inspired by contemporary politico-ideological reasons. While holders of this point of view contend that they intended to place Jewish suffering respectfully within history, in practice the argument is counterproductive. The hardly defensible pursuit of promoting the exceptional argument all too often turns out to be the weak point at which negationist commentators aim their arrows.

–PIETER FRANÇOIS,
UNIVERSITY OF GHENT

References

Omer Bartov, *Mirrors of Destruction: War, Genocide, and Modern Identity* (Oxford & New York: Oxford University Press, 2000).

Gie van de Berghe, *De uitbuiting van de Holocaust* (Antwerp: Houtekiet, 1990).

Alain Finkielkraut, *La mémoire vaine: Du crime contre l'humanité* (Paris: Gallimard, 1989).

Eberhard Jäckel, "The Murder of the European Jews and History," in *The Jews in European History: Seven Lectures* (Cincinnati: Hebrew Union College Press, 1993).

Samuel Totten, William S. Parsons, and Israel W. Charny, eds., *Century of Genocide: Eyewitness Accounts and Critical Views* (New York: Garland, 1997).

Eric A. Zillmer and others, *The Quest for the Nazi Personality: A Psychological Investigation of Nazi War Criminals* (Hillsdale, N.J.: Erlbaum, 1995).

NEUTRAL STATES

Did the neutral states of Europe act responsibly in the face of the Holocaust?

Viewpoint: Yes. Neutral governments acted within the narrow limits available to them to assist Jewish refugees.

Viewpoint: No. Neutral states, especially Switzerland, benefited from Nazi plunder and expropriation of Jewish assets.

Neutrality in time of war is never easily maintained. This status was particularly true in World War II (1939–1945). The horror of the Holocaust and the perception that a Nazi victory would spell the end of civilization, democracy, and human decency leaves modern observers little patience for those nations that, in the midst of total war, refused to take sides. But did the neutral states of Europe act responsibly and ethically in what was, after all, an impossible situation not of their own making?

Portugal, Spain, Switzerland, and Sweden maintained their neutrality throughout the war. Turkey, a German ally in World War I (1914–1918) and still suspicious of the Soviet Union, made common cause with the Allied Powers only when the defeat of Germany was assured. Other countries, including the United States, maintained their neutrality as long as possible. Franklin D. Roosevelt made no secret of his support for Britain in 1940 and 1941 and waged an undeclared naval war in the Atlantic Ocean to ensure American goods made it safely to Britain. But it was Adolf Hitler, not Roosevelt, who declared war between the United States and Germany on 11 December 1941 a few days after the Japanese attack on Pearl Harbor. Belgium, the Netherlands, and Yugoslavia insisted upon their neutrality in vain before the German blitzkriegs began. In those cases the neutrality of the weak before the strong was worth no more than a scrap of paper. Thus, the nations whose neutrality remained intact until the end of the war were faced with an excruciating set of dilemmas. Refusal to cooperate with the demands of the Third Reich could provoke an invasion. Too friendly an attitude toward the Nazis could result in being treated as a de facto enemy by the Soviets, British, and Americans.

Among the neutrals, Sweden is generally acknowledged as having taken substantial risks to assist Danish and Norwegian Jewish refugees from Nazism. Spain, Portugal, and Turkey also assisted refugees, as did Switzerland, but it was the behavior of the Swiss, surrounded by Axis Powers, which has proved to be most problematic. Switzerland promised that it would defend its historic neutrality if need be and through the Red Cross served prisoners of war, refugees, and the injured on both sides of the conflict. On the other hand, it was at Swiss insistence that German Jews had the letter *J* stamped on their passports. Furthermore, Swiss banks, whose reputations for secrecy were well earned, have been accused of helping finance the Nazi war effort, of laundering gold and other assets stolen from Jews, and of continuing to hide those assets into the twenty-first century.

Viewpoint:
Yes. Neutral governments acted within the narrow limits available to them to assist Jewish refugees.

During the Holocaust the neutral states of Europe were bystanders, unable and in some cases unwilling to prevent the murder of fifteen million men, women, and children. Four major reasons limited the possibility of intervention by these nations: Nazi determination, geography, the vulnerability of the neutrals to German action, and the limited means at their disposal to have an impact on the Holocaust. It is also true that, despite some successes in granting refuge to some individuals attempting to escape Nazi Europe, the neutrals had little incentive or Allied encouragement to interfere with the Final Solution and much to fear from Nazi reprisal if they did act.

Among the neutrals, Sweden, Switzerland, Portugal, Spain, and Turkey had the greatest opportunity to impede the Final Solution. These states were never occupied by either the Axis or the Allies and, with the exception of Turkey, which declared war on Germany in February 1945, did not become belligerents. This neutrality is not to say that their actions were unconstrained. Only Portugal did not share a common border with a Nazi-occupied state. All had to consider the real risk of a Nazi invasion if they too overtly assisted the enemies of the Third Reich, including the Jews. Still, with varying degrees of commitment and effectiveness, all five offered limited avenues of escape for Jews.

No level of commitment on the part of any neutral state could have prevented the vast majority of murders. The most important factor in the implementation of the Final Solution was the Nazis' determination to see it through, no matter what. From 1933 until 1941, the Nazi solution to the Jewish Question had been to force Jews to emigrate. In the summer of 1941, German forces and their collaborators began massacring mostly adult male Jews on the eastern front, using automatic weapons and, eventually, mobile killing vans that poisoned victims with carbon monoxide gas. By late summer the decision had been reached to exterminate the Jews. By late fall of the same year the SS began using poison gas to increase the efficiency of the machinery of killing. Whatever else his goals, Adolf Hitler had no higher priority than these killings.

This determination to destroy European Jewry extended beyond Germany and occupied Europe. At the Wannsee Conference, secretly convened in January 1942 at a lakeside resort outside Berlin in which, as Yehuda Bauer writes, "the entire German bureaucracy became involved in the conscious effort to murder a nation," Jews living in the neutral states were also discussed. Among the data gathered for the meeting were estimates of the number of Jews living in neutral states who would eventually be targeted for destruction: 55,500 in Turkey; 19,000 in Switzerland; 8,000 in Sweden; 6,000 in Spain; and 3,000 in Portugal. The implications of this rough census are clear. Once Germany had conquered Russia and brought the British and Americans to heel, they would then turn their attention to these as-yet-inaccessible Jewish communities.

Whether by accident of geography or genocidal intent, none of the countries in Europe whose neutrality the Nazis respected had substantial Jewish populations, certainly not in comparison with those of the Soviet Union and Poland. The vast majority of European Jews lived to the east and south of Germany, especially in Poland, Hungary, Ukraine, and Lithuania, where they were exposed to the full brunt of Nazi brutality. Of the approximately 11 million Jews whose fate was considered at the Wannsee Conference, more than 9 million lived in these areas. That none of the neutral powers bordered these states with large Jewish populations made any offer of sanctuary virtually meaningless for them. Neutral (albeit fascist) Spain shared a common border with France, whose Jewish population of 350,000 was made up largely of foreign refugees who had fled Germany or Austria. Thousands of Jews managed to cross the Pyrenees into Spain or the Alps into Switzerland. A few fled through the Soviet Union to take refuge in Shanghai and even Japan, but the difficulties and distances were in all cases tremendous. For nearly all of the Jews of Europe, the neutral states were too distant to offer a real hope of refuge.

The most noted exception proves the rule. In late 1943 the Germans were preparing to deport the Jews of Nazi-occupied Denmark to the death camps in "the East." Faced with what the Danes regarded as an attack on their fellow citizens, thousands of Danes organized a massive underground rescue operation that smuggled 8,000 Jews across the fifteen miles of open water into neutral Sweden. The connivance of the Swedes in depriving the Germans of their intended victims angered Hitler, but by then the military position of Germany had become too weak to do anything about it. Also, the proximity of Sweden (about fifteen miles) to Denmark and the relatively benign nature of the German occupation (compared

Jews waiting in front of the Swiss Mission in Budapest, circa 1944

to Poland or Russia, for example) were critical for the success of this rescue, but had the Swedish government not granted the Danish Jews refuge, all would have been for naught. Sweden also granted refuge to almost half of the Jewish community of Norway, but again, the numbers involved were small and the circumstances unique.

Another important factor limiting the ability of neutral countries to rescue Jews was their vulnerability to German reprisal. The neutrals were in a precarious situation. Germany had blithely disregarded the neutrality of Norway, Denmark, Belgium, and the Netherlands in 1940. These examples were not lost on the surviving independent states of wartime Europe. Switzerland endured many German violations of its air space during the Battle of France (1940) and mobilized its army in expectation of imminent attack. Sweden similarly feared a Nazi attack during the German conquest of Norway in April and May of 1940. By mid 1941 all of the neutral states except Portugal shared a common border with Germany or a German-dominated state. Indeed, the Germans developed contingency plans to invade Sweden, Spain, Portugal, Turkey, and Switzerland. Had circumstances led them to attack, it seems doubtful that any of these states could have

offered more than token resistance, especially early in the war. Even as late as 1943, German military planners made serious proposals to send forces against the neutrals, especially pre-emptive strikes to prevent the establishment of bases by the Allies. Spain, in particular, was the subject of several Nazi plans to attack, either to seize the British fortress of Gibraltar, to attack Allied forces in North Africa after November 1942, or to seize the Canary Islands as military bases, with or without Spanish consent. While the Nazis suffered major defeats in 1943 and 1944, from Stalingrad to Normandy, it was by no means clear that the final days of Hitler were approaching until Soviet, American, and British armies surrounded Germany in late 1944. Germany also considered invading Turkey or pressuring the state to enter the war as an Axis power, but the difficulties of the Soviet campaign diminished these possibilities.

The neutral states were, in relation to Nazi Germany, militarily weak and—especially in the cases of Portugal, Spain, and Turkey—economically inferior. Their combined populations were smaller than that of Germany: Spain (twenty-three million), Turkey (eighteen million), Portugal (seven million), Sweden (six million), and Switzerland (four million) were tiny compared with the eighty million Germans living under Hitler. Only in the last years of the war was it safe to flout Nazi wishes. Still, the neutral states frustrated the Final Solution and ignored German protests by allowing thousands of Jews to enter, if only in transit to a more permanent place of refuge. Indeed, more aggressive action in opposition to German wishes would have only invited German invasion and ensured the destruction of yet another Jewish community.

Again, Sweden provides a telling case in point. In addition to its reception of the Danish Jews in 1943, Swedish diplomats were active throughout the war in rescuing Jews. The Second Secretary to the Swedish Legation in Budapest, Hungary, businessman Raoul Wallenberg, was particularly effective. Wallenberg distributed bribes to Hungarian and German officials and Swedish visas and passports to Hungarian Jews with flimsy (or fabricated) connections to Sweden, protecting in 1944 as many as twenty thousand Jews from the SS and the Hungarian pro-Nazi movement, the Arrow Cross. Although twenty thousand lives saved is minimal in comparison to the lives lost, it was near the limits of the Swedes' ability to intervene. Sweden was a small, vulnerable country and could have hardly found room for the millions of Jews who wanted to seek refuge there. Even if the Swedes opened their doors to masses of Jewish refugees, the German army would almost certainly have followed not far behind.

Turkey defied the Germans less directly. During the 1930s Turkey gave refuge and permanent residence to hundreds of dismissed German Jewish professors, scientists, teachers, and other professionals, on the condition that they learn Turkish during their first year or two of residency. During the war more than sixteen thousand Jewish refugees were allowed to pass through Turkey on their way to Palestine or elsewhere. Thousands more passed through illegally, often with the complicity of local Turkish officials. Additionally, more than two thousand Turkish Jews were saved from Vichy France by the intervention of Turkish diplomats, even though most of these Jews had renounced their Turkish citizenship. Pleading poverty, Turkey would only accept refugees with destination visas, not those seeking permanent settlement or without private means of support. Turkey might well have allowed more to pass through their territory had Britain been more willing to allow refugees into Palestine.

The record of Switzerland was more mixed. While maintaining its democratic institutions and territorial independence, Switzerland was hardly a haven for refugees. It was at Swiss insistence that the Nazis began stamping the letter *J* on the passports of Jews. This policy enabled the Swiss to more efficiently turn Jewish refugees away at the border. At least forty thousand Jews were thus prevented from entering Switzerland. The Swiss accepted more than twenty thousand refugees, including many children, but might have accomplished much more, particularly in the final year of the war when there was little to fear from a German invasion. A small country surrounded by Axis Powers, however, Switzerland could not have made a dramatic difference in the Holocaust.

Spain allowed tens of thousands of Jews to pass through its territory, provided they had visas for final destinations somewhere else or the means to support themselves for an extended stay in Spanish territory. Throughout southeastern Europe, Spanish diplomats also extended the protection of Spanish citizenship and passports to thousands of Sephardic Jews whose ancestors had been expelled from Spain in 1492. They still spoke Ladino, a language combining Hebrew and Spanish. By the end of the war the Spanish government had allowed as many as forty thousand Jews to escape through its territory. Spain was willing to tolerate these passages, providing the refugees traveled through Spain "as light passes through a glass, leaving no trace," and thus not attracting any unwanted Nazi attention. Spanish soldiers in the volunteer Blue Division on the Eastern Front also protected some Jews in their military hospitals, but these measures did not survive the evacuation of the Spanish units in early 1944.

Portugal served as a port of embarkation for many Jews who made it out of Hitler's Europe. Portuguese diplomats, often without prior authorization from their governments, also granted visas and passports to Hungarian Jews in the last months of the war, enabling them to escape the Holocaust and allowing Lisbon to become the main point of departure for refugees headed for the Americas.

The neutral states received little encouragement in their efforts to assist Jewish refugees. British, Soviet, and American leaders never pressured the neutrals to accept more refugees, nor did they provide ships or money to encourage further action. Sadly, rescuing Jews was not a priority among the Allies, despite evidence that they had the capabilities to do so. It was the mistaken belief of the Spanish government that the Allies were interested in aiding the Jews that seems to have led to the relatively open door to refugees in Spain.

Could the neutral states have rescued tens of thousands more Jews through diplomatic and humanitarian means? Could their leaders have opened their borders to admit more desperate men, women, and children? Perhaps, and each of these efforts would have been a blessing to the saved. However, the Nazis murdered millions of Jews, most of whom had no capability to reach a neutral border. The Holocaust would still have been the Holocaust no matter what actions the neutral states took. The fate of almost all of the fifteen million killed—with few exceptions—was determined, not in Madrid, Stockholm, or Ankara, but in Berlin.

—WAYNE BOWEN,
OUACHITA BAPTIST UNIVERSITY

Viewpoint:
No. Neutral states, especially Switzerland, benefited from Nazi plunder and expropriation of Jewish assets.

Neutrality was a complicated affair in wartime Europe. For Spain, Turkey, and Portugal, neutrality came as a luxury of geography—all three were on the periphery of Europe and offered too few tactical advantages for either Axis or Allies to risk an invasion. The critical neutrals were the Swiss and the Swedes. In both cases, maintaining neutrality demanded political courage, diplomatic skill, and a fair amount of good luck. Sweden, though circumspect in its relations with the Nazis, and a supplier of some raw materials to the Third Reich, also managed to use its neutral status to shelter thousands of Jews and other refugees from the Nazis. The Swiss, however, though reluctantly offering refuge to a few thousand Jewish refugees, used their strategic location, their traditional neutrality, and their key role in international banking to serve as financial proxies for the Nazis and to benefit handsomely in the process. Contrary to its claims, Switzerland exceeded the role of a wartime neutral by enriching itself through laundering gold stolen from the Jews and expropriated from the treasuries of occupied nations.

Without this gold—with which the Nazis, using the Swiss as intermediaries, purchased goods on the international markets—the ability of Germany to make war would have been seriously hampered. Before the Nazi invasion of the Soviet Union in June 1941, the international credits of the German Reichsbank comprised all the reserves of the countries that Nazi Germany occupied, including Czechoslovakia, France, and the Low Countries. These assets were gone by December 1941. By then Nazi Germany lacked enough hard currency to buy much-needed raw materials on the international

market. To fill the void, the German government made use of the gold it had expropriated from conquered states and stolen from individuals—especially Jews. But such purloined assets could not be readily expended. Like drug money in the twenty-first century, it had to be laundered through the international banking system in order to hide its origins.

The German Reichsbank and several Swiss banks, working through the Bank for International Settlements (BIS) in Basle, Switzerland, provided the laundry service. Reluctant to lose German business, the Swiss National Bank (SNB, the quasi-national bank of Switzerland), together with some private banks, devised a system to accommodate Nazi banking leaders whereby the German Reichsbank, as well as prominent Nazis such as Hitler, Heinrich Himmler, Hermann Göring, and others, maintained Swiss accounts that provided the mechanisms for the international exchange of goods and raw materials required for the war effort. Thus, the victims of Nazism, with Swiss collusion, funded the war effort of the Third Reich.

In addition, Swiss subsidiaries of German firms fronted for many German manufacturing and refinery firms, making it appear that the raw materials and finished goods they sold abroad were Swiss, not German, thus "cloaking" German assets and permitting them to be sold on the world market. Cloaking only worked when the assets involved were not stolen. The Swiss banks facilitated the Nazi war effort by transforming looted assets into usable currency on international markets. This scheme meant that the origins of stolen gold had to be camouflaged from the outside world. As long as gold on the continent of Europe was physically outside Nazi Germany, its ownership could be transferred on paper. Receipts and orders were carried by agents who frequently also represented the Vatican and, thus, retained the diplomatic immunity that allowed them to move back and forth across both Nazi and Allied lines. A few actual shipments of gold bullion from Switzerland to the Iberian Peninsula were made as Third Reich payments for wartime raw materials such as tungsten. Although Swiss banks frequently converted debased bullion, which remained in Switzerland, into Swiss francs for the Nazis to use as international currency, the truck convoy across the Pyrenees from Switzerland illustrates that gold reichsmarks were used to make direct payments during the war. However, certificates of ownership for monetary quality as well as debased gold bars were normally exchanged through the BIS for those countries that were members.

The key differences between bars of monetary and nonmonetary gold derive not only from the exact weight of and stamps on each bar but also from assays of the mercury content in the gold. Monetary gold has only the slightest traces of mercury, while gold used in jewelry manufacture or as dental gold retains a measurable mercury content. Accordingly, at the end of World War II only the actual gold bullion on deposit in the vaults in the United States, Canada, and Great Britain prior to 14 June 1941 (when the United States froze Swiss assets) is unquestionably monetary gold. To be sure, much of the bullion and coins constituting the $263,680,452.94 collected in the Frankfurt Exchange Depository was probably monetary gold, but it is now impossible to determine what proportion of the bars were and were not monetary because the shipments to the Bank of England were not assayed after they arrived.

At the outset, the terms *loot* and *plunder* tend to be used interchangeably as synonyms for what was confiscated by the Third Reich from both individuals as well as from the states they overran. When the word *loot* is limited specifically to those assets in the custody and/or account names of entities including the SS, Joachim von Ribbentrop's Foreign Ministry, and the private holdings of the Nazi leadership, then *plunder* can be reserved to describe what was confiscated by the Third Reich from the national treasuries of the countries that it overran. Indeed, it is not difficult to identify plunder because the Reichsbank records indicate, for the most part, the dispositions of these assets. Loot was stolen from individuals, primarily—but not exclusively—Jews. When it took the form of nonmonetary gold bars, it represented the jewelry, dental fillings, and personal fortunes of victims of the Holocaust. With these assets the SS financed its killing operations. Separating the two is now virtually impossible.

In 1942, when Walter Funk, the head of the Reichsbank, committed the institution to handling what was then called "SS booty," separate records for special deposits made by an SS officer, Bruno Melmer, were kept in an account under the name of Max Heiliger. In theory, the accounting system kept track of the values and amounts of gold, currency, and jewelry deposited. But once the SS loot was resmelted and/or restamped, some nonmonetary bars were intermixed in the seventy-five Melmer shipments of assets that reached Switzerland. However, a shipment of monetary gold was the subject of a postwar controversy concerning 1,526.6 kilograms of fine gold marked for the account of the BIS, which had been located in the Konstanz branch of the Reichsbank awaiting transport over the border into Switzerland. This amount, packed into forty cases, corresponds exactly to the interest accruing on the investments of the BIS for the year 1944. Its value is not included in the $263,680,452.94 collected by "Operation Safehaven" or "Operation Sparkler,"

the two major American missions to locate caches of hidden Nazi loot.

A report about the criminal gold dealings of the Reichsbank was published in *The New York Times* on 29 October 1945. Confirmed by a U.S. Office of Military Government (OMGUS) report to General Lucius Clay from Colonel Bernard Bernstein, dated 30 October 1945, in the three years in which Melmer made a total of seventy-six deliveries of SS loot to the Reichsbank, the SS had to its credit approximately $14,500,000, most of which came from foreign banknotes and gold. However, much of the gold was actually nonmonetary and thus probably stolen from individuals, according to the testimonies of Emil Puhl (vice-president of the Reichsbank and one of the directors of the BIS) and Albert Thoms (in charge of the precious-metals department of the Reichsbank) at Funk's trial at Nuremberg. The problem of separating monetary from nonmonetary gold came about because the Reichsbank deliberately mixed debased bars with authentic bullion and falsified stamps on resmelted gold in export shipments, almost all of which went abroad through Switzerland, where the international currency to pay off the war obligations of the Third Reich and its Nazi entities was purchased.

By early 1941 Germany controlled almost all the wealth of the countries it had overrun. However, American and British freezing orders had shut Germany out from the gold on deposit in the vaults of the United States or the Bank of England. According to the Bergier Report (1998), in November 1939 the BIS sold the Reichsbank $2.3 million worth of gold from the BIS account in Berne at the SNB in order to obtain German currency for payments to German organizations and corporations. In 1946, when the Swiss were preparing to negotiate the Washington Agreement with the Allies, they estimated that in 1939, at the outbreak of the war, Third Reich monetary gold reserves were worth $160 million. By the time the United States declared war in December 1941, this figure had been supplemented by an estimated total of $579 million to $661 million in plundered gold (from Belgium $223 million, from Holland $161 million, from Italy $84 million, from Czechoslovakia $50 million, from Austria $46 million, from Russia $23 million, from Poland $12 million, from Luxembourg $5 million, and from Danzig $4 million). During the war between $398 million and $410 million was shipped from Germany into Switzerland with approximately $138 million of gold ingots reexported to Spain and Portugal. The SNB acknowledged in 1985 that between $185 million and $296 million worth of gold, including all the Belgian gold ($223 million) and $100 million of Dutch gold, had been shipped to Switzerland from Germany. Of the 3,859 gold ingots shipped

GOLD FROM THE DEAD

Benjamin Jacobs, a Jewish inmate and dentist at Auschwitz, recalls in his memoirs being forced to remove gold fillings from victims of the Holocaust:

Another day Dr. König took an impression to replace the bridge of an SS man. Then he asked me if I had enough dental gold to make a new one. That surprised me. How would I have dental gold? I wondered. I said no.

"Don't you take out the gold teeth from the dead inmates?" he asked. "If you are not doing that, plenty of gold is going to waste."

I looked at him in disbelief. "Oh! Herr Haupscharführer," I answered, stunned.

"Why don't you?" he said to me, annoyed.

"I didn't know. No one had ordered me," I said in my defense.

"Be sure that from now on you remove all the gold before they are taken to the Stammlager."

I felt revulsion. I did not think that anyone could stoop that low. Killing people was horrible enough, but tearing out teeth of the dead moved me to disgust. I did not think that I could do it. But it was inevitable. I had no choice. "Jawohl, Herr Hauptscharführer," I said, sickened and scared.

As appalled as I was at having to do it, as repulsive as the thought was, I knew that since I was the only dentist in Fürstengrube, I had to do it. It was by far the hardest thing I had to do in any camp. I often asked myself what would have befallen me if I had not complied with this order. I have never stopped wrestling with that question. When I approached the corpse room for the first time I tried to rationalize that what I was about to do was meaningless to the dead. But it never was to me.

Repugnance preceded each of my trips to the morgue. I never lost that feeling when I went to that small room—two and a half by three meters. When I opened the door, the smell of death greeted me. I shivered. Atrophied bodies lay in a mass on the cement floor. They were grotesquely misshapen, with surprise on their faces, as if they did not know why they had to die. I heard the voices of broken hearts and crushed souls. Some were still clothed. I tried to force myself to believe that they were only bodies and never were human. But as hard as I tried, and as much as I pretended not to care, I could not keep myself from trembling. So many emotions ran through me. I was sickened and unable to begin the task I had come to do. I walked out and went around the building several times. When I returned, I forced myself to approach a middle-aged man's body. His half-open eyes stared up at me, as if to accuse me of the crime I was about to commit. As I tried to pry open his mouth, I felt his ice-cold skin. When I finally forced it open, his jawbones cracked, and that frightened me. Following each turn of the mouth opener was a screeching sound. I imagined this was his way of saying "Don't!" to me. I felt as if the dead would rise up to stop me. Each piece of gold I extracted made me think how shocked they must be. Sometimes I had to pretend, in talking to myself, that what I was doing was normal. The tools I used for this grim task I kept in a red box. Why I painted the box red I didn't know. Most inmates who saw me walking to the morgue with it knew what I was doing and didn't consider it unusual. My father and my brother also knew what I was doing, though I never told them. Now I had enough gold for the SS men's bridges and caps. What I didn't use Dr. König took back with him to the main camp.

Source: Benjamin Jacobs, The Dentist of Auschwitz: A Memoir (Lexington: University of Kentucky Press, 1995), pp.147–148.

---

later from Berne to Lisbon, 1,180 came from Holland (with 318 still in their original Dutch wrappers), and 673 had Belgian stamps.

As to the aid promised by Switzerland in the Washington Agreement (1946) to survivors and claimants to so-called heirless assets—accounts belonging, in many cases, to Jews who had died in concentration camps—Allied negotiators in 1952 turned a blind eye to a Swiss-Polish compensation treaty, which had a secret annex attached. On 22 March 1950 the two countries signed an agreement providing that Polish bank accounts in Switzerland, dormant more than five years, as well as unclaimed life insurance policies, would be turned over to Poland. The funds could then be used to compensate Swiss citizens, banks, and life-insurance companies that had their assets nationalized by the Polish Communist state. The public part of the treaty stipulated that Poland would pay Switzerland Fr 52.1 million to compensate for confiscated

Swiss property. Negotiations for this settlement had been underway before the formation of the Federal Republic of Germany, and on 24 October 1996 *The New York Times* reported that a recently declassified document in the American National Archives referred "to the commercial and financial agreement between Switzerland and Poland of June 25, 1949, which . . . is said to contain a provision whereby the assets in Switzerland of Polish nationals who had died without heirs would be turned over to the Government of Poland." It must be remembered that a large majority of these heirless "Polish nationals" was Jews.

During the Cold War years (1945–1991), when Communism substituted for Nazism as "a mortal threat to Western civilization itself," the former Soviet Union and the menace it posed to European and global stability assumed the ideological basis that redefined policy alternatives. This conflict led the Allies to reduce the number of prosecutions of World War II war criminals, to sidestep the question of whether monetary and nonmonetary assets were fraudulently converted, and to continue the practice of ignoring the cloaking of billions of dollars of capital funding. Assuming the moral superiority of victors over Nazism, the Allies, like the Swiss, tolerated political and financial subterfuge on the international as well as the domestic level of authority at every stage of the Cold War. Governments colluded in the destruction of the reputations and careers of officials who persisted in calling attention to unresolved matters of World War II. Until Edgar Bronfman publicized the World Jewish Congress campaign for financial redress of the billions of dollars of stolen wealth, no nation-state addressed the anti-Semitism and public denial that are at the root of the outrageous claim that the horrific degradation of human beings characterizing the Holocaust has been exaggerated. Isabel Vincent reiterates an anecdote concerning a letter from Yitzak Rabin, former Israeli prime minister who later was assassinated, authorizing Bronfman and the World Jewish Congress "to act on behalf of the Jewish people to seek restitution for Holocaust victims." This directive is Rabin's legacy to the last generation who could cleanse the world community if they resolve the injustices left over from the Holocaust, the defining event of twentieth-century history.

–CAROLSUE HOLLAND,
TROY STATE UNIVERSITY

References

Haim Avni, *Spain, the Jews, and Franco,* translated by Emanuel Shimoni (Philadelphia: Jewish Publication Society, 1982).

Yehuda Bauer, *A History of the Holocaust* (New York: Watts, 1982).

Wayne H. Bowen, *Spaniards and Nazi Germany: Collaboration in the New Order* (Columbia: University of Missouri Press, 2000).

Bowen, "Spanish Protection of Jews on the Eastern Front, 1941–1944," in *Resisting the Holocaust,* edited by Ruby Rohrlich (Oxford & New York: Berg, 1998).

Tom Bower, *Blood Money: The Swiss, the Nazis and the Looted Billions* (London: Macmillan, 1997).

Linus Castelmur, "The Washington Agreement of 1946 and Relations between Switzerland and the Allies after the Second World War," Embassy of Switzerland, London <http://www.swissembassy.org.uk>.

Gordon A. Craig, "How to Think about the Swiss," *New York Review of Books,* 65 (11 June 1998).

Myrna Goodman, "Foundations of Resistance in German-Occupied Denmark," in *Resisting the Holocaust,* edited by Rohrlich (Oxford & New York: Berg, 1998).

Franz Halder, *The Halder War Diary, 1939–1942,* edited by Charles Burdick and Hans-Adolf Jacobsen (Novato, Cal.: Presidio, 1988).

Dale Harrington, *Mystery Man: William Rhodes Davis, Nazi Agent of Influence* (Washington, D.C.: Brassey's, 1999).

Burton Hersh, *The Old Boys: The American Elite and the Origins of the CIA* (New York: Scribners / Toronto & New York: Macmillan, 1992).

Charles Higham, *Trading with the Enemy: An Exposé of the Nazi-American Money Plot, 1933–1949* (New York: Delacorte, 1983).

Raul Hilberg, *Perpetrators, Victims, Bystanders: The Jewish Catastrophe, 1933–1945* (New York: Aaron Asher, 1992).

Adam LeBor, *Hitler's Secret Bankers: The Myth of Swiss Neutrality during the Holocaust* (Secaucus, N.J.: Carol, 1997).

Christian Leitz, *Sympathy for the Devil: Neutral Europe and Nazi Germany in World War II* (New York: New York University Press, 2001).

Itamar Levin, *The Last Deposit: Swiss Banks and Holocaust Victims' Accounts,* translated by Natasha Dornberg (Westport, Conn.: Praeger, 1999).

Alfred Lipson, "Swiss History in Focus," in *The Holocaust: Readings and Interpretations,* edited by Joseph R. Mitchell and Helen Buss Mitchell (New York: McGraw-Hill, 2001).

Michael Marrus and Robert Paxton, "Western Europeans and the Jews," in *The Holocaust: Problems and Perspectives of Interpretation,* edited by Donald L. Niewyk (Lexington, Mass.: D.C. Heath, 1992).

J. Noakes and G. Pridham, eds., *Nazism, 1919–1945: A History in Documents and Eyewitness Accounts* (New York: Schocken, 1990).

Jerrold M. Packard, *Neither Friend nor Foe: The European Neutrals in World War II* (New York: Scribners / Toronto & New York: Macmillan, 1992).

Herman Pedergnana, "Letter to the Editor," *International Herald Tribune,* 21 April 1998.

Christian Pross, *Paying for the Past: The Struggle over Reparations for Surviving Victims of the Nazi Terror,* translated by Belinda Cooper (Baltimore: Johns Hopkins University Press, 1998).

"Report on the Polish-Swiss 1950 Agreement," *New York Times,* 22 October 1996.

Seymour J. Rubin, "Nazi Gold Pact of 1946 Was Badly Implemented," *International Herald Tribune,* 20 May 1997.

Ian Sayer and Douglas Botting, *Nazi Gold: The Story of the World's Greatest Robbery—And Its Aftermath* (London & New York: Granada, 1984).

Hans J. Schaffner, "It's Time to Stop Misrepresenting Swiss Wartime Role," *International Herald Tribune,* 6 April 1998.

Stanford J. Shaw, *Turkey and the Holocaust: Turkey's Role in Rescuing Turkish and European Jewry from Nazi Persecution, 1933–1945* (New York: New York University Press, 1993).

Christopher Simpson, *The Splendid Blond Beast: Money, Law, and Genocide in the Twentieth Century* (New York: Grove, 1993).

Arthur L. Smith Jr., *Hitler's Gold: The Story of the Nazi War Loot* (Oxford & New York: Berg, 1989).

Isabel Vincent, *Hitler's Silent Partners: Swiss Banks, Nazi Gold, and the Pursuit of Justice* (New York: Morrow, 1997).

Sidney Zabludoff, *Movements of Nazi Gold: Uncovering the Trail* (New York: World Jewish Congress, 1997).

Jean Ziegler, *The Swiss, the Gold, and the Dead: How Swiss Bankers Helped Finance the Nazi War Machine,* translated by John Brownjohn (New York: Harcourt Brace, 1998).

NEUTRAL STATES

ORDINARY GERMANS

Were ordinary Germans culpable for the Holocaust?

Viewpoint: Yes. Ordinary Germans were culpable, but not all of them shared the same level of responsibility.

Viewpoint: No. Ordinary Germans did not, as a group, perpetrate the Holocaust.

Soon after the end of World War II (1939–1945), American journalist Milton Sanford Mayer spent a year in a West German village in search of the "average German." The newspaperman expected that interviews with this ideal individual would reveal the subtle deceptions and the measures of intimidation by which the Nazi Party commanded the obedience of millions. He was first disappointed and then surprised by what he found.

Mayer's quest for the "average" German failed because, as he soon realized, there was no such individual. Instead, he cultivated relationships with a diverse collection of Germans "sufficiently different from one another in background, character, intellect and temperament" to represent millions of their fellow countrymen and sufficiently alike to have each supported the Nazis. In the course of his discussions with ten "ordinary Germans" of the middle and lower middle classes, Meyer realized that Nazism "overcame Germany" because "it was what most Germans wanted—or, under pressure of combined reality and illusion, came to want. They wanted it; they got it; and they liked it."

The latter observation—that Germans welcomed and enjoyed their experience of National Socialism—continues to be the subject of controversy and to draw the attention of scholars. If this contention is true, then one must consider its implications for the complicity of the German population at large in the terrible crimes committed by the Nazi regime. The debate between Daniel Jonah Goldhagen (who contends that "ordinary Germans" shared the "eliminationist anti-Semitism" of the Nazis) and Christopher R. Browning (who asserts that Nazi indoctrination, a habit of obedience, and peer pressure influenced "ordinary men" to commit extraordinary acts) is among the most recent examples in this discussion. Explanations for the actions of individuals and groups may differ, but the fundamental issue remains unresolved: were the ordinary people of Nazi Germany guilty of the murders perpetrated by their government?

Viewpoint:
Yes. Ordinary Germans were culpable, but not all of them shared the same level of responsibility.

There were millions of ordinary people living in Nazi Germany between 1933 and 1945. The classification *ordinary Germans* obviously includes those who were not members of the National Socialist German Workers Party (NSDAP), but it could also encompass those people from all social classes who either worked directly for the Nazi government or whose lifestyles or professions brought them into direct contact with the Nazis. In 1933, the year Adolf Hitler was appointed German chancellor, Nazi Party membership averaged 850,000 people; this number rose to more than 6 million by 1942. Thus, in a country with a population of nearly 62 million people before its expansion by wartime conquest, almost 10 percent of the population was directly involved with the Nazi Party at the height of its power. If these Party members knew anything of the NSDAP's quest to exterminate the Jews of Europe, it is probable that their knowledge would be communicated to the German public at large through casual conversation, rumor, and even boasting. In such a situation one is justified in holding different groups of ordinary Germans accountable to varying degrees for complicity in the Nazis' crimes. Those ordinary Germans who worked in the concentration camp system were more culpable than those without official connections sanctioned by the NSDAP and yet who remained silent.

Although there was some resistance to Nazism by German clergy, intellectuals, and university students (among others), the rest of the world took no large-scale action to help the European Jews. Indeed, the responsibility for the Nazis' "Final Solution to the Jewish Question" does not stop at the borders of Germany. Arguably, some level of culpability can also be assigned to countries such as Great Britain and the United States, neither of which took an official stance against the Final Solution. While not all Germans can be blamed for the action of the Nazis, most "ordinary Germans" may be held responsible for tolerating, and not resisting, the crimes committed by the Nazi regime.

Government-sanctioned mass murder on an unfathomable scale, the *Endlösung* (Final Solution) was the Nazi answer to the Jewish Question. As early as 1933, Nazi leaders contemplated ways in which to deal with the Jews in Germany. Between 1933 and 1938 state-sponsored actions against the Jews steadily increased in number and intensity. These measures ranged from the anti-Jewish Nuremberg laws enacted in 1935 to the physical abuse and destruction of property that culminated in 1938 in a pogrom known as *Kristallnacht* (Night of the Broken Glass). With the outbreak of war in 1939, the Nazis were free to take even more violent action.

By March of 1941, when thousands had already been imprisoned or murdered in unsystematic persecutions, top Nazi officials began to consider the complete eradication of all Jews in German-controlled Europe. At the Wannsee Conference in January of 1942, a group of officials from Nazi Party organizations and German government ministries discussed the best ways to rid the world of the problems supposedly tied to the presence of Jews. They agreed to the *Endlösung*–to the total annihilation of the Jewish people. From 1942 until the defeat of Germany in 1945, there would be no other answer to the Jewish Question other than this Final Solution. Nazi officials believed that overt actions against Jews (as well as several other "undesirable" minorities) would meet with almost no resistance on the part of the German people because of the tremendous popularity of the Führer and a general acquiescence to most of the policies of his regime.

Especially after the nation became involved in another war, German public opinion was important to Hitler and his top officials. Any sort of obvious resistance to government or NSDAP policies–in the form of organized, mass, public efforts–might undermine the will of Germany to fight on to victory. Such resistance also would not have allowed the Nazis to proceed with their murderous plans unencumbered. Because the Nazis abhorred domestic unrest, they took whatever measures were necessary to suppress disorder without jeopardizing their popular support (including, in one instance, the release of some Jewish prisoners). While the majority of ordinary Germans did not resist Nazi policies, resistance was not entirely an exercise in futility. Yet, because nearly everyone chose to do nothing in the face of Nazi criminal activity, most ordinary Germans shared some measure of guilt for their leaders' crimes. If the majority of ordinary Germans had resisted the Final Solution, millions of innocent people would not have died.

The Holocaust eclipsed any previous form of genocide in history; yet, ordinary Germans would later claim to have been absolutely unaware of Nazi actions in the concentration and extermination camps. The almost total allegiance of ordinary Germans to Hitler and his policies meant that the official persecution of the Jews was met with little more than passivity, disbelief, and apathy. Hitler's raging hatred of the Jews was tightly bound to his plans for "restoring" a Third German Reich, an empire intended to last

for a thousand years. Along with their appeals to popular nationalist ideas and their glorification of Teutonic heroism, the Nazis inundated ordinary Germans with racist propaganda for more than a decade. By blending their extreme racial ideology into a mixture of common prejudices and opinions, the Nazis prepared ordinary Germans to accept the dehumanization and subsequent extermination of the Jews.

Hitler presented himself to ordinary Germans as their savior from national humiliation, cultural decline, and economic distress. Not only did he blame the Jews for each of these problems, he convinced many people that the Jews worldwide were secretly trying to subjugate and ruin Germany. This aspect of Nazi racial ideology penetrated to all levels of German society because it fit neatly with commonly held anti-Semitic prejudices. No matter how prevalent anti-Semitism already was in Germany, it was not an accepted, government-sanctioned ideology until Hitler came to power. Throughout the Nazi reign of terror, propaganda was widely used to spread the Party's ideology as well as to help gain acceptance among ordinary Germans for Nazi actions and policies. Moreover, skillful use of propaganda to depict the Jew as the enemy of ordinary Germans produced an increase in anti-Semitic opinion and often was accompanied by an escalation in public violence against Jews living in Germany. Nazi propa-

ganda thus made it easier for ordinary Germans to accept the Final Solution.

Hitler's ideology permeated German society through a series of successful racist propaganda campaigns directed by Joseph Goebbels, Reich minister for public enlightenment and propaganda. Goebbels manipulated the German people with brilliant propaganda that delivered a message of German racial superiority, advocated violence against the Jews, and supported the Nazi reign of terror. Party-controlled newspapers, such as Julius Streicher's infamous *Der Stürmer*, regularly espoused contempt, if not open hatred, for Jews. Slogans and campaigns also appeared warning Germans to beware of Jewish "parasites"; several feature movies, such as *Jud Süss* (1940), vilified Jews as liars, thieves, and rapists. Nazi propaganda served to help establish almost total acquiescence on the part of ordinary Germans for the implementation of the Final Solution. Given the prevalence of anti-Semitic rhetoric in official speeches, literature, and many other outlets of Nazi popular culture, it is difficult to see how the German populace could not know what their leader advocated and what his followers (as well as some "ordinary" people) were in the process of implementing.

Among other things, Hitler blamed the Jewish minority for the debilitating economic depression in Germany of the late 1920s and early 1930s. By thus identifying the Jews and

U.S. troops watching a German civilian walk past the bodies of slave laborers executed by the SS at Namering, 1945

(National Archives, Washington, D.C.)

ORDINARY GERMANS

convincing Germans that they were the cause for these financial problems, Hitler moved a step closer to reaching his goal. Hitler claimed that Jews were responsible for the economic, political, and social hardships that Germany endured. Millions accepted Hitler's claim that Germans would enjoy the better life they deserved if Jews were removed from society. As with other issues, Hitler found a willing audience for his anti-Semitic rhetoric by linking it to the promises of a brighter future and economic stability most Germans desired. Hitler promised an end to Jewish "domination" and "manipulation" of German commerce, assuring a return of businesses to German ownership and of profits to German shopkeepers. The various means Hitler used to achieve economic prosperity for Germany, including the expropriation of Jewish property, might have been widely accepted because many ordinary Germans benefited from this practice.

In addition to promising a better life, Hitler's weltanschauung (ideological world outlook) outlined the conditions necessary for converting the dream into reality. First and foremost, he argued, the enemies of civilization must be removed from Germany before true pride and honor could be restored to the German *Volk* (a word meaning both "nation" and "race"). The Führer's ideology asserted that the *Volk* was in need of "purification" from Jewish "contamination." Indeed, he declared that the Jews would eradicate the German race unless every ordinary man and woman stood behind him and fought with him to eliminate the Jewish menace. In addition to Jews, Hitler identified other minority groups as dangerous to the *Volk* for racial reasons (Gypsies, Slavs), "anti-social" tendencies (homosexuals, Jehovah's Witnesses), or debilitating conditions (the handicapped, the mentally ill). Consequently, any members of German society deemed "unfit" by Nazi philosophy were steadily marginalized as Hitler consolidated his political power in the 1930s. It was a marginalization that ultimately facilitated the implementation of the Final Solution.

Ordinary Germans also directly participated in the Final Solution. The longer the Nazi Party was in power, the more average men and women from all areas of Germany (and from every social class) joined its ranks. In 1933 the Party's elite guard, the *Schutzstaffel* (SS), grew from fifty-two thousand members to two hundred thousand in less than a year. By 1942, when the SS had expanded to perform many Party, military, and police functions, its branches boasted a total membership of nearly 1 million Germans. Technically, only men could join this army of dedicated National Socialists, but evidently thousands of ordinary German women also went to work in SS-operated institutions. The legions

of men assigned to SS police and prison guard units were often at the forefront of the killing, transformed by choice or by order into part of the Nazi machinery of death. Hundreds of thousands of others found employment in various government ministries and organizations sponsored by the Nazi Party that played direct parts in enacting the *Endlösung*. After 1939, "ordinary" bureaucrats negotiated the "release" of European Jews in Nazi custody, "ordinary" factory owners accepted Jews for slave labor, and "ordinary" secretaries handled the paperwork that meant dislocation, suffering, and death to millions. By early 1942, the employees of the Reich's railway system were daily accomplices to murder, as they either supervised or witnessed the passage of long trains of boxcars carrying the Jews of Europe eastward to their deaths.

Many of these individuals would later deny any culpability for the Final Solution. The case of Elisabeth Volkenrath, an "ordinary" German woman conscripted for work as an *Oberaufseherin* (Chief Overseer) at several camps, including Auschwitz, offers one example of this attitude. At her postwar trial, Volkenrath admitted to almost nothing about her wartime employment and categorically denied that she performed any role in the extermination of the Jews. Yet, according to the accounts of Auschwitz survivors, Volkenrath actively assisted the SS, abused many prisoners, and took part in the regular "selections" undertaken by guards and doctors to choose prisoners for execution. Not surprisingly, she rejected all the charges leveled against her and denounced all survivors' testimony as lies. Volkenrath said that any blame for the Final Solution lay not with ordinary Germans such as herself but with important men such as Rudolf Höss (commandant of Auschwitz) and *Reichsführer* Heinrich Himmler (head of the SS and Nazi minister of the interior); she was merely doing her job.

The jobs of ordinary Germans were crucial to the Holocaust in another sense as well. The Nazi government had provided the *Volk* with the jobs, economic prosperity, and social stability they long desired. As long as it was believed to be of immediate personal advantage to average people, there was no cause to resist Nazi calls for a Final Solution. Although aware that they lived in a police state, provided one was law-abiding and had no Jewish ancestry, German people did not fear a government that emphasized a return to economic, social, and cultural greatness. The existence of the concentration camps for political prisoners within Germany was no secret at all; they were the subject of positive Nazi news reports from the earliest days of the regime. Thousands of "enemies of the people" were known to be kept in "protective custody" and hundreds were "shot while trying to escape," but

ORDINARY GERMANS

millions of seemingly unconcerned citizens nevertheless lived contentedly within the Third Reich.

In fact, people believed that Hitler knew little or nothing about the specific actions of his followers. The explanation that "the *Führer* does not yet know of these things" was applied to every disagreeable incident in daily life, from the corruption of local Nazi officials to random arrests, unexplained disappearances, and even forced euthanasia. Hitler's personal popularity not only helped the Nazi regime maintain its control over Germany, but it also allowed people to take no action because they were certain that whatever abuses they witnessed were local problems, not part of the Führer's personal policy. Even if they did not approve of the actions of the Nazis, ordinary Germans might have believed that resistance would be unsuccessful. However, one example of successful protest against the Final Solution suggests that that excuse may be baseless.

After ten years of Nazi rule, a few ordinary women resisted the Party's plan to render Germany "free of Jews." The "Rosenstrasse Protest" began in Berlin on 27 February 1943, in response to a *Gestapo* (secret state police) roundup of Jewish men who were married to non-Jewish German women. Within hours of discovering that their husbands were being detained in an office building in the Rosenstrasse, about two hundred women began a noisy protest outside it. They demanded that officials allow them to see their husbands, and when this tactic did not work, the women immediately took matters into their own hands. The women staged a nonstop rally and refused to disperse even under threats. As the women continuously shouted their demands that their husbands be released, others joined in the protest.

These otherwise "ordinary" German women took quick action against the Nazis because they feared what would happen to their Jewish husbands. The women were fully aware that, like other Jews who had been arrested, their husbands would most likely be held for a short period before they were shipped off, never to return. The women held their ground and refused to give up their protests until their husbands were released. Within a week, thanks largely to the Nazi abhorrence of domestic disorder and an unwillingness to further diminish Party popularity in the eyes of ordinary Germans, the men were released at Goebbels's direct order. Indeed, once they recognized that the public and committed way that the women resisted made any further action against these Jewish men extremely unpopular, the Nazis had no choice but to acquiesce to the women's demands. Yet, despite this success, the Rosenstrasse protest was the only large-scale public protest against the Final Solution.

The fact that some small protests against Nazi policies had demonstrable results suggests that ordinary Germans were in a position to either accept or reject most of their governments actions, even during wartime. Since most people did not protest the activities of the National Socialist state at any time, one may justifiably assert that all ordinary Germans were complicit in the Final Solution to some degree. No doubt the twelve-year barrage of Nazi racial ideology played a part in this complicity, but it was effective only so long as people proved willing to listen or were inclined to accept its worldview. Quiet acquiescence was also matched by willful ignorance when, following the collapse of Nazism, ordinary Germans disclaimed any knowledge of what was going on in the concentration camps. Even though, as "victims" of Nazism themselves, some Germans claimed to be innocent of the crimes of the Final Solution, they also bore a measure of guilt as voters and citizens of the Third Reich.

Although levels of responsibility for the Final Solution varied, ordinary Germans were culpable because the majority of people did not resist. It was impossible for average citizens of Germany not to notice when family members, friends, neighbors, clergymen, shopkeepers, teachers, and others disappeared, most never to return. Many could guess the reason, thanks to the widespread propaganda that vilified the Jews, the anti-Semitic speeches by Nazi leaders, and the public actions taken against Jews after 1933. There was plenty of other evidence to inform the curious: the sights and smells of local concentration camps; the wartime roundups of men, women, and children as "enemies of the *Volk*"; the eastward passage of trains filled with captives; and the ceaseless smoking of state crematoriums. An ominous lack of reaction to these clues and provocations affirms the culpability of ordinary Germans. They were guilty, at the least, of ignorance in the face of the terror visited on their fellow citizens.

—WENDY A. MAIER, CHICAGO

Viewpoint:
No. Ordinary Germans did not, as a group, perpetrate the Holocaust.

For nearly two decades following the end of World War II (1939–1945), Germany (East and West) remained a pariah nation. The Germans had killed the Jews. The Germans had, twice in thirty years, made war on civilization itself, and but for the heroism and sacrifice of (depending

BUILDING THE CREMATORIUMS

A German engineer, during testimony given in 1946, testifies about his participation in building crematoriums at Auschwitz:

Q. Who apart from you participated in the construction of the furnaces?

A. From 1941–2, I constructed the furnaces. The technical drawings were done by Mr. Keller. The ventilation systems of the "Kremas" [crematoriums] were constructed by senior engineer Karl Schultze.

Q. How often and with what aim did you visit Auschwitz?

A. Five times. The first time at the beginning of 1943, to receive orders of the SS Command where the Kremas were to be built. The second time in spring 1943 to inspect the building site. The third time was in autumn 1943 to inspect a fault in the construction of a Krema chimney. The fourth time at the beginning of 1944, to inspect the repaired chimney. The fifth time in September–October 1944, when I visited Auschwitz with the intended relocation [from Auschwitz] of the crematoriums, since the front was getting nearer. The crematoriums were not relocated, because there were not enough workers.

Q. Were you the sole Topf engineer in Auschwitz in spring 1943?

A. No, [senior engineer Karl] Schultze was with me in Auschwitz at the time. I saw personally about 60 corpses of women and men of different ages, which were being prepared for incineration. That was at 10 in the morning. I witnessed the incineration of six corpses and and came to the conclusion that the furnaces were working well.

Q. Did you see a gas chamber next to the crematoriums?

A. Yes, I did see one next to the crematorium. Between the gas chamber and the crematorium there was a connecting structure.

Q. Did you know that in the gas chamber and in the crematoriums there took place the liquidation of innocent human beings?

A. I have known since spring 1943 that innocent human beings were being liquidated in Auschwitz gas chambers and that their corpses were subsequently incinerated in the crematoriums.

Q. Who is the designer of the ventilation systems for the gas chambers?

A. Schultze was the designer of the ventilation systems in the gas chambers; and he installed them.

Q. Why was the brick lining of the muffles so quickly damaged?

A. The bricks were damaged after six months because the strain on the furnaces was colossal.

Source: *"Kurt Prufer, senior engineer of Topf and Sohne, testifying in Erfurt, Germany, March 5, 1946 [Quoted from the interrogation transcripts by Gerald Fleming from the University of Surrey, in an NYT article, July 18 1993]," Shamash: The Jewish Network <http://shamash.org/holocaust/denial/testimony.txt>.*

---

on the source of the rhetoric) American, British, or Soviet forces, the swastika would have ruled the world. In movies and literature the Germans were portrayed as a sneering, barbaric race whose genius for music and art was matched only by its passion for violence. Obviously, most of the people who had fought them had no doubt that the German people were, with a few heroic exceptions, complicit in and guilty of the Holocaust. The Germans themselves, especially those who had served as ordinary soldiers or who themselves felt victimized by the Nazi regime, resented the implication.

In the 1970s, as the first post–World War II generation came of age, Volkswagen and Mercedes logos came to replace the swastika as the popular symbol of German genius, at least in the west. The Germans were North Atlantic Treaty Organization (NATO) allies. They were the West's first line of defense against a Soviet invasion. They made interesting music and good beer. The Nazis had been bad, the SS and the Gestapo had been wicked, and Adolf Hitler was the distilled essence of evil. But Germans, ordinary Germans, were people like "us," which, for young Americans in the Vietnam era, meant people unable to affect the criminality of their government. Ordinary Germans were seen, at worst, as passive bystanders to the Holocaust.

There the popular and scholarly consensus lay until the mid 1980s. It was generally held that the Nazis had come to power on the promise of German greatness; they killed the Jews in secret; a few ordinary citizens knew, and more individuals suspected; but there was no reason to blame the whole of the German people for the Holocaust. Subtly, German identity was rehabilitated in the American imagination. The television sitcom *Hogan's Heroes* (1965–1971), with its oafish "ordinary" Germans and officious Nazis, replaced the coldly calculating Nazis of, for example, the wartime propaganda classic *Casablanca* (1942).

In 1985 this easy differentiation between ignorant masses, silent onlookers, and rabid executioners was called into question by Claude Lanzmann's nine-hour motion-picture documentary *Shoah*. Consisting almost exclusively of interviews with perpetrators, survivors, and bystanders, Lanzmann's movie quietly drove home the banality and ordinariness of the functionaries, bureaucrats, and technicians whose participation in the Holocaust was almost accidental. Had they not been assigned to a task that brought them close to the killing, many of these "little men" would have had no connection with it at all. Faced with a job whose implications they could not help but understand—sometimes because they heard the screams of victims—these ordinary Germans and Poles meekly, and sometimes enthusiastically, complied. Resistance, even of a minimal and risk-free nature, could have rendered the Final Solution far less efficient, but because the committed killers could depend on the stolid obedience of ordinary Germans, the killing continued apace.

Lanzmann's documentary was of too long and too leisurely a pace to have shattered the historiographical consensus that differentiated between murderous Nazis and ordinary Germans. The consensus would be shattered, however, in 1996, when a newly minted Ph.D. in Political Science from Harvard University, Daniel Jonah Goldhagen, published *Hitler's Willing Executioners: Ordinary Germans and the Holocaust*. Goldhagen's book was released to great fanfare, was widely and enthusiastically reviewed in the popular press, and became an immediate best-seller, all of which made academic historians suspicious. Goldhagen took direct aim at Christopher R. Browning, a professor at Pacific Lutheran University. Browning's book, *Ordinary Men: Reserve Police Battalion 101 and the Final Solution in Poland* (1992) argued, as its name implied, that the perpetrators whose stories he examined (middle-aged reservists too old for frontline duty) murdered Jews in Poland reluctantly, and only because they had been ordered to do so. Some, in fact, were excused from the terrible task. Only with the passing of time and other executions did most of the men of Battalion 101 become immuned to the horror

of what they were doing. Implicitly, Browning argued that there was nothing extraordinary about these, and presumably many other, perpetrators of the Holocaust. They were not ordinary Germans but ordinary fathers, husbands, policemen, schoolteachers, and laborers. That they were Germans was almost irrelevant: they were soldiers who did as they were told. One wishes that they had behaved otherwise; however, any collection of average men in similar circumstances, whatever their nationality, might have done likewise.

A few years later Goldhagen studied the same evidence and drew a dramatically different conclusion. These same soldier-policemen murdered Jews not because it was their wartime job but because, after centuries of anti-Jewish and anti-Semitic rhetoric, they were eager to do so. German anti-Semitism—unlike the French, English, or American varieties—was distinctly "eliminationist." Ordinary Germans did not kill Jews because Hitler ordered them to but because Hitler gave them permission to do what they had, on some level, long desired to do.

The evidence seemed damning. Ordinary Germans who were not members of the SS or even the Nazi Party helped perpetrate the Holocaust in ways large and small. But though this participation is certainly true, it is equally certain that ordinary Germans also gave shelter to Jews. In numbers beyond counting, subtly and overtly, Germans also ignored the obvious presence of Jews hiding out in a neighboring apartment, or quietly warned the more courageous neighbor that word was getting out and the Jews needed to be moved to another hiding place. Simply put, had there been no ordinary Germans willing to resist the Holocaust on some small level, no German Jews would have survived.

Since the 1964 murder of Catherine "Kitty" Genovese, in full view of scores of New Yorkers who failed to come to her aid despite witnessing three separate attacks, Americans have worried about the culpability of passive bystanders. Undeniably, millions of Germans who would themselves never have been induced to commit murder stood aside for the machinery of extermination. They might have been afraid, or indifferent, or grimly satisfied that now the Jewish Question was being settled once and for all. Before (and perhaps during) the Holocaust, the very idea that a civilized, modern nation-state would organize and direct mass murder on an industrial scale must have seemed like an impossible fantasy to most people, German and non-German alike. At the same time, it was improbable that the Nazis, given their strident anti-Semitism, intended to treat the Jews with any measure of tolerance. Yet, quite likely, millions of ordinary Germans persuaded themselves of the improbable: that European Jews were being shipped to labor camps in the east, where they would be fed, sheltered, and treated humanely. It was easier to credit the Nazis with an improbable plan to "resettle" the Jews than to admit that the death camps were more than the figment of a deranged imagination. It was, in short, far easier to believe the improbable than it was to accept responsibility for one's own inaction. But such culpability does not belong to ordinary Germans alone. The Allies should have done something. The neutral countries should have done something.

Ultimately, the Holocaust happened because a small cadre of committed, eliminationist anti-Semitic racists took advantage of the fog of war, the indifference of the masses, and the blind obedience of soldiers and bureaucrats to execute fifteen million Jews, Gypsies, and other supposed enemies of the Third Reich. Trying to lay a burden of guilt on theoretically "ordinary" Germans adds nothing meaningful to our understanding of history, humanity, the Holocaust, or ourselves.

–TANDY MCCONNELL,
COLUMBIA COLLEGE

References

Hannah Arendt, *Eichmann in Jerusalem: A Report on the Banality of Evil,* revised edition (New York: Penguin, 1964).

Christopher R. Browning, *Ordinary Men: Reserve Battalion 101 and the Final Solution in Poland* (New York: HarperCollins, 1992).

Robert Gellately, *Backing Hitler: Consent and Coercion in Nazi Germany* (Oxford & New York: Oxford University Press, 2001).

Daniel Jonah Goldhagen, *Hitler's Willing Executioners: Ordinary Germans and the Holocaust* (New York: Knopf, 1996).

Sarah Gordon, *Hitler, Germans, and the "Jewish Question"* (Princeton: Princeton University Press, 1984).

Eric A. Johnson, *Nazi Terror: The Gestapo, Jews, and Ordinary Germans* (New York: Basic-Books, 1999).

Robert Jay Lifton, *The Nazi Doctors: Medical Killings and the Psychology of Genocide* (New York: Basic Books, 1986).

Michael Mann, "Were the Perpetrators of Genocide 'Ordinary Men' or 'Real Nazis'?: Results from Fifteen Hundred Biographies," *Holocaust and Genocide Studies,* 14 (Winter 2000): 331–366.

Milton Sanford Mayer, *They Thought They Were Free: The Germans, 1933–45* (Chicago: University of Chicago Press, 1955).

Nathan Stoltzfus, *Resistance of the Heart: Intermarriage and the Rosenstrasse Protest in Nazi Germany* (New York & London: Norton, 1996).

ORDINARY GERMANS

PIUS XII

Was Pope Pius XII culpable in the destruction of the Jews?

Viewpoint: Yes. Though he could have wielded enormous moral influence, Pope Pius XII did little to protect Jewish lives from Nazi genocide.

Viewpoint: No. Pope Pius XII worked effectively to save hundreds of thousands of Jews from the Holocaust.

No modern pope has been more controversial than Pius XII. Born Eugenio Pacelli, the son of a Vatican lawyer, the future Pope spent almost the entirety of his priestly career in the service of his papal predecessors. He served as papal nuncio to the Bavarian kingdom—and by default to the rest of Germany—during World War I (1914–1918) and the Weimar era (1919–1933) and as the Vatican secretary of state. He negotiated a concordat between Nazi Germany and the Vatican that, while guaranteeing the rights of Roman Catholics in Germany, essentially removed the Catholic Center Party as an opposition voice in German politics.

It is Pius's wartime behavior that has been most subject to debate. In a play by Rolf Hochhuth, staged in 1963 in New York as *The Deputy,* the Pope—obviously intended to be Pius—is presented as hostile to the Allies, friendly toward Germany, absorbed in his own affairs, and indifferent to the suffering of the Jews. Even if Hochhuth's condemnation is overstated, Pius, like many politicians of his era, was more concerned with the threat of communism than of Nazism and did not take seriously Adolf Hitler's anti-Semitic rhetoric or reports of genocide. Ever the diplomat, during the opening stages of World War II (1939–1945) Pius tried to preserve the independence of the Vatican—and himself—as a fair arbiter and peacemaker in order to create for himself a significant role in postwar European affairs. Although he spoke harshly against some actions of the Nazis, he did not openly encourage Catholics to disobey Hitler, to save Jewish lives, or to resist the Final Solution.

The Vatican was a small sovereign state—only a few acres—within the capital of an Axis power (Italy). The only forces he had at his disposal were moral and persuasive. He worked quietly on behalf of thousands of Jews, many of whom credit Pius for their survival. Yet, Pius feared that either outspoken condemnation of genocide or overt and open assistance to the Jews would only invite retribution against priests and nuns and would do nothing to protect the Jews. In Holocaust studies it has become customary to categorize nonperpetrators as either bystanders or rescuers. In the case of Pius XII these distinctions are not easily made. Pius's ambiguous legacy received increased attention in the 1990s as Pope John Paul II made known his desire to see Pius XII canonized.

Viewpoint:
Yes. Though he could have wielded enormous moral influence, Pope Pius XII did little to protect Jewish lives from Nazi genocide.

At the end of World War II (1939–1945) Pope Pius XII, to all observers, was an emaciated, frail man. Throughout the war he had placed himself on limited rations and refused to heat the papal apartments. In some way, his self-imposed suffering was penance, perhaps for his near abandonment of European Jewry during World War II. As Pius was living the life of an aesthete, the Jewish population in Europe was being annihilated by the racial policies of Nazi Germany. Even with abundant proof of the Holocaust at hand, the Pope never uttered a clear and specific condemnation of Nazi atrocities. Little was done to support anti-Nazi forces and few words of succor were given to those Catholics who were hiding and protecting Jews.

Pius's pontificate was complex, and his duties were weighty. Determined to defend Catholicism and oppose Communism, he tried to navigate a delicate course of neutrality throughout the war. But his undying belief in papal neutrality, partly based on the misconception that he could negotiate a peaceful conclusion to the war, led to moral ambiguity. Could neutrality be more important than denouncing the great sin of genocide? Would a specific and clear condemnation have helped save Jews? Could Pius have championed policies that would have benefited European Jewry? The Holy See's few vague pronouncements in opposition to the Holocaust were so obtuse that they rarely irritated the Nazis and did nothing to satisfy the demands of Jewish leaders for the Vatican to make a strong statement against the murder and torture of millions of Jews. Instead, the Vatican's reticence helped fulfill the Church's centuries-old acceptance of anti-Semitism, thus making it easy for Nazis and Catholic Germans to justify the persecution of Jews.

Pius XII could have been more vocal in condemning German persecution and could even have used the power of excommunication to pressure Catholics into refraining from anti-Semitic behavior and murder. His most powerful tool, excommunication, was never used as a threat for stopping the violence against European Jewry. However, he wished to be the key figure in preventing a war and, once it was under way, in forging a peace. Therefore, he steadfastly maintained Vatican neutrality, careful not to irritate the Nazis by condemning their actions. His ambition was to elevate the Church by triumphantly negotiating an end to World War II and thus raising the prestige of the Catholic faith in the eyes of the world.

Cardinal Eugenio Pacelli became Pope Pius XII on 2 March 1939. Rarely has a pontificate begun in a time of such great crisis. Pacelli, on the surface, seemed to be the right man for the job. He had extensive diplomatic experience, much of it in Germany, and enjoyed the respect of most in the Vatican. One of his crowning achievements had been negotiating and concluding a concordat with Nazi Germany in 1933. Pius had enjoyed his tenure in Germany and saw his successful negotiation of the concordat as a victory for Vatican diplomacy as well as evidence of his own political skills. Familiar with Germans, he believed that he could do business with Berlin. From his first day in the papacy until September 1939, he devoted himself to preventing the eruption of a European war. Failing in this endeavor, and presiding over Catholics in all the belligerent states, the Pope declared neutrality soon after the German assault on Poland.

London and Paris got a taste of Pius's policy in September 1939, when they failed to convince the pontiff to condemn Germany as an aggressor in its invasion of Poland. Britain and France were outraged that the Pope refused to make any statement damning German actions, a clear-cut case of aggression. But Pius chose to favor neutrality, partly because he was afraid of alienating German Catholics. However, some statement was necessary, especially considering that most German bishops favored the invasion. Pius well understood that the Nazis wished to spread their racial policies throughout Europe; yet, by not condemning Adolf Hitler's actions, he chose to tacitly condone an invasion of staunchly Catholic Poland. In the final analysis Pius was willing to sacrifice Poland to preserve a strong Germany that was, in his opinion, the linchpin for preventing communist expansion.

Early in the war, Pius XII had opportunities to condemn genocides taking place in Poland and Croatia but chose to vacillate rather than denounce the holocausts occurring in these two states. Although never condemning German aggression or directly chastising the Nazis for their treatment of Jews in Poland, Pius noted the suffering of the Polish nation in the encyclical *Summi Pontificatus* issued on 20 October 1939. Little else was voiced until January 1940, when Vatican Radio reported that Polish Jews were being forced into ghettos where living conditions were perilous. This broadcast was the only direct reference to the suffering of the tens of thousands of Jews in Poland voiced publicly by the Vatican. Pius retreated from making any direct and specific appeals for more humane treatment allegedly out of fear of disaffecting German Catholics and concern that Berlin would assault the Vatican if he vocally condemned their activities.

In 1941 Pius XII had a second opportunity to denounce a genocide. Ante Pavelic, a devout Catholic and Croatian nationalist, established, under the auspices of Germany and Italy, the Independent State of Croatia on 10 April 1941. As early as May 1941, Pavelic and his Ustaše (secret police) unleashed a genocide on Orthodox Serbs and Jews that ultimately claimed the lives of 450,000. The Vatican never denounced Pavelic's actions, preferring to look the other way since the new Croatia was destined to be a formally Catholic state. Pius and his advisers were willing to ignore Croatian concentration camps and murders because Pavelic's state was a fledgling concern that needed time to develop into a bulwark of Catholicism in the Balkans. His eyes remained fixed on the establishment of a Catholic state in the Balkans, blind to the heinous massacres perpetrated by the Ustaše. Because Pavelic so eagerly sought Vatican diplomatic recognition and led a movement of zealous Catholics, Pius had the leverage to force Pavelic and the Ustaše to stop murdering Serbs and Jews. The Vatican never attempted to use this leverage to prevent this genocide. Pius XII never condemned the destruction of the Serbian and Jewish population in Croatia, even though he held great sway over Pavelic and his followers. Instead, Pius met twice with Pavelic, a notorious murderer, during the war.

Pius was well informed about the atrocities being conducted by the Nazis against the Jews. Beginning in 1941, an unending string of reports—all raising the same alarm—flowed into Rome from a variety of sources. Jews were being tortured and slaughtered. By December 1942, when information about the genocide against Jews was well known throughout the Western world, British and American representatives to the Holy See requested that the Vatican approve and join the Allies in a declaration condemning the Nazi genocide. Not only did the Holy See reject the Allied declaration, Harold Tittman, American assistant representative to the Vatican, reported that the Church believed that it had condemned atrocities in general, but that "the Holy See was unable to verify Allied reports as to the number of Jews exterminated." The alleged denunciation of atrocities was no more than vague comments in Pius XII's 1942 Christmas message. The language used, however, was so unspecific that even the keenest ears could not discern what Pius intended. In this rather weak condemnation, Pius never mentioned the words *Jew* or *Orthodox,* even though tens of thousands had been both systematically and unsystematically slaughtered.

The Vatican secretary of state, Cardinal Luigi Maglione, was not being forthcoming with Tittman, as it was quite clear through many reports in the media and from Vatican nuncios and others that thousands upon thousands of Jews were being sent to camps for extermination. What is evident is that the Vatican did not want to make any clear statement condemning German actions against the Jews out of fear that it would be construed as destroying Vatican neutrality and potentially unleash attacks against the Vatican itself. As Myron Taylor, the U.S. representative to the Vatican, observed in 1942, the Pope was holding firm to neutrality at the expense of abandoning Christian morality.

There were several avenues that Pius could have taken to aid in mitigating the effects of the Holocaust. One such avenue was through his constant contact with cardinals and bishops throughout Europe. The Pope never issued clear instructions to cardinals and bishops explaining how to handle the Holocaust, although abundant opportunities to do so existed. Historian Michael Phayer has noted that in the Pope's many letters to Bishop Conrad Preysing, Cardinal Adolf Betram, and Cardinal Michael Faulhauber, "Pius never divulged to them the horrible news that the Vatican had learned in 1942 and confirmed in 1943, namely, that Germany had built extermination centers in occupied Poland where millions were being murdered." Rarely did he mention the suffering of Jews in any of his correspondence with them, although Preysing consistently asked for direction from Pius. The Pope intentionally avoided drawing attention to the Holocaust. He did not urge cardinals, bishops, or priests to pursue methods of protecting and saving Jews, preferring to let Catholics make their decisions independently. This policy was out of step with Catholic tradition and did not rally Catholics to the defense of Jews.

Papal restraint was caused by the Vatican's strong desire to stay neutral in the war, a fear of offending the German Catholic population, and a concern that any precise protest would engender worse treatment for Jews and Catholics. These justifications ring hollow when confronted with the reality of the Holocaust. Defenders of Pius often have noted that vocal opposition against the Nazis only engendered a worse form of retaliation. The case of converted Jews being rounded up in Holland after the archbishop of Utrecht condemned Nazi

TAKE CARE, VENERABLE BRETHREN

On 14 March 1937 Pope Pius XI promulgated an encyclical to the German people:

The experiences of these last years have fixed responsibilities and laid bare intrigues, which from the outset only aimed at a war of extermination. In the furrows, where We tried to sow the seed of a sincere peace, other men—the "enemy" of Holy Scripture—oversowed the cockle of distrust, unrest, hatred, defamation, of a determined hostility overt or veiled, fed from many sources and wielding many tools, against Christ and His Church. They, and they alone with their accomplices, silent or vociferous, are today responsible, should the storm of religious war, instead of the rainbow of peace, blacken the German skies. . . .

At a time when your faith, like gold, is being tested in the fire of tribulation and persecution, when your religious freedom is beset on all sides, when the lack of religious teaching and of normal defense is heavily weighing on you, you have every right to words of truth and spiritual comfort from him whose first predecessor heard these words from the Lord: "I have prayed for thee that thy faith fail not: and thou being once converted, confirm thy brethren" (Luke XXII. 32).

Take care, Venerable Brethren, that above all, faith in God, the first and irreplaceable foundation of all religion, be preserved in Germany pure and unstained. The believer in God is not he who utters the name in his speech, but he for whom this sacred word stands for a true and worthy concept of the Divinity. Whoever identifies, by pantheistic confusion, God and the universe, by either lowering God to the dimensions of the world, or raising the world to the dimensions of God, is not a believer in God. Whoever follows that so-called pre-Christian Germanic conception of substituting a dark and impersonal destiny for the personal God, denies thereby the Wisdom and Providence of God who "Reacheth from end to end mightily, and ordereth all things sweetly" (Wisdom VIII. 1). Neither is he a believer in God.

Whoever exalts race, or the people, or the State, or a particular form of State, or the depositories of power, or any other fundamental value of the human community—however necessary and honorable be their function in worldly things—whoever raises these notions above their standard value and divinizes them to an idolatrous level, distorts and perverts an order of the world planned and created by God; he is far from the true faith in God and from the concept of life which that faith upholds.

Beware, Venerable Brethren, of that growing abuse, in speech as in writing, of the name of God as though it were a meaningless label, to be affixed to any creation, more or less arbitrary, of human speculation. Use your influence on the Faithful, that they refuse to yield to this aberration. Our God is the Personal God, supernatural, omnipotent, infinitely perfect, one in the Trinity of Persons, tri-personal in the unity of divine essence, the Creator of all existence. Lord, King and ultimate Consummator of the history of the world, who will not, and cannot, tolerate a rival God by His side.

This God, this Sovereign Master, has issued commandments whose value is independent of time and space, country and race. As God's sun shines on every human face so His law knows neither privilege nor exception. Rulers and subjects, crowned and uncrowned, rich and poor are equally subject to His word. From the fullness of the Creators' right there naturally arises the fullness of His right to be obeyed by individuals and communities, whoever they are. This obedience permeates all branches of activity in which moral values claim harmony with the law of God, and pervades all integration of the ever-changing laws of man into the immutable laws of God.

None but superficial minds could stumble into concepts of a national God, of a national religion; or attempt to lock within the frontiers of a single people, within the narrow limits of a single race, God, the Creator of the universe, King and Legislator of all nations before whose immensity they are "as a drop of a bucket" (Isaiah XI. 15). . . .

Whoever wishes to see banished from church and school the Biblical history and the wise doctrines of the Old Testament, blasphemes the name of God, blasphemes the Almighty's plan of salvation, and makes limited and narrow human thought the judge of God's designs over the history of the world: he denies his faith in the true Christ, such as He appeared in the flesh, the Christ who took His human nature from a people that was to crucify Him; and he understands nothing of that universal tragedy of the Son of God who to His torturer's sacrilege opposed the divine and priestly sacrifice of His redeeming death, and made the new alliance the goal of the old alliance, its realization and its crown.

Source: Pope Pius XI, "Mit Brennender Sorge" (On the Church and the German Reich), 14 March 1937, in Eternal Word Television Network: Global Catholic Network <http://www.ewtn.com/library/ENCYC/P11BRENN.HTM>.

policies is usually cited as proof that Pius made the right decision to remain silent. But even when the war was entering its final stages and millions of Jews had been killed and millions more were being led to their deaths, he failed to assault Nazi atrocities. With German armies reeling in defeat, any statement denouncing Jewish massacres would have saved at least some lives. Even after Rome was liberated and the Pope no longer was concerned with the potential destruction of the city, the pontiff chose to make no direct statements against Nazi abuses. Pius could not bring himself to denounce the murder of Jews because he had become obsessed with the inexorable march of Soviet forces. To Pius, Germany was key to preventing a communist Europe; therefore, he preferred not to say anything that might weaken Germany, even when German resistance was faltering.

Perhaps most telling of all was the pontiff's position during the arrest and deportation of Roman Jews in October 1943. Although approximately forty thousand Jews were hidden in monasteries, churches, and within the Vatican, more than one thousand were shipped off to Auschwitz. Remarkably, Pius never uttered a word denouncing German actions. German officials in Rome treated this silence as somewhat of a victory. German ambassador Ernst von Weizsacker, in a memo to the Wilhelmstrasse, happily reported that Pius "has not allowed himself to be drawn into any demonstrative statement against the deportation of the Jews of Rome." He even recognized that Pius's stance would raise the ire of the Western Allies. In German opinion, Pius was far from hostile to their policies. To the Allies it appeared that Pius was more interested in maintaining neutrality and remaining on good diplomatic terms with the Nazis than denouncing the Holocaust.

Some of Pius's defenders argue that he wielded little power to stop Nazi atrocities. One example contradicts this theory. Beginning in 1942, Bishop Kmetko of Nitra, with the support of the Vatican, strongly voiced protests against the deportation of Jews from Slovakia. These protests began to have an effect. Deportations slowed and then ceased temporarily. Catholic and Protestant opposition to the deportations convinced the majority of Slovaks that anti-Semitic attacks were wrong. This opposition had the effect of forcing the Nazi leadership to retreat from its wholesale attack on Slovak Jewry. Although deportations and executions resurfaced in 1944, it was clear that the Vatican could successfully use its influence to mitigate Jewish persecution in German satellite states.

Excommunication was never used against any Catholic who committed crimes against Jews. Never once did the Pope even threaten its use.

Catholics were free to abuse and kill Jews without any sign that they would be held accountable for their actions. Even though Catholics comprised 43.1 percent of the German population in 1939, Pius refused to threaten excommunication. Although threat of excommunication did not carry the force of the past, it would have induced some Germans to reconsider their actions and perhaps have convinced others to protect Jews.

There were thousands of Catholics who risked their lives to rescue Jews from certain death. These Catholics hid Jews, knowing that if they were discovered they too would face death in a concentration camp. One must believe that if Pius had urged Catholics to intercede on the behalf of Jews, or explicitly condemned Nazi atrocities, then far more Catholics would have ventured to save Jews. Those lone Catholics independently striving to rescue Jews would not have felt so isolated in their moral mission. Other Catholics would have felt compelled to participate in saving Jews, thus most likely creating more-effective rescue networks. The number of Jewish survivors certainly would have been higher than it was. But Pius failed to send such a signal to European Catholics and consequently lost an opportunity to mitigate the consequences of the Holocaust.

Always seeking to defend papal neutrality and wishing to be a major participant in concluding a diplomatic end to the war, Pius never took the step of separating the German people from the Nazis. The Pope had many opportunities to condemn the actions of the Nazis while continuing to support the existence of a strong Germany. He never fully realized that not all Germans wished to support the Nazi cause and that a strong stand against Nazism was not synonymous with attacking the German people. This position was especially true after the war turned against the Nazis. However, Pius chose to ignore reports of Jews being slaughtered rather than even run the risk of alienating any German Catholics who were sympathetic to much of the Nazi agenda.

Pius's concern about the spread of Communism and his belief that Germany could serve as a bulwark against it blinded him to opportunities to save Jews. Likewise, his belief that he could negotiate an end to the war shackled him to neutrality that did nothing to aid Jews. On many occasions the Pope had the opportunity to avoid moral ambiguity and condemn the genocide being perpetrated by Nazi Germany and its satellites. As in Slovakia and Croatia, Pius could wield powerful influence in some of the German satellite states. The pontiff had powerful tools at the ready, but he never used them.

–JOHN DAVIS,
ATHENS, ALABAMA

Viewpoint:
No. Pope Pius XII worked effectively to save hundreds of thousands of Jews from the Holocaust.

In the summer of 1941 the Nazi government introduced a new and sinister policy to deal with resistance to their rule in occupied France. Upon capture, some Frenchmen simply disappeared. No court, no appeal, and no power or person could account for their whereabouts. The policy was called *Nacht und Nebel* (Night and Fog). Because it could happen to anyone, at any time, for no reason, this odious policy cast dread over occupied populations and silenced many with an ominous terror of the unknown. Overt resistance diminished.

The Night and Fog policy was later applied to the greatest goal of Nazism, the destruction of European Jewry. No outside authority would learn of the plan and no appeal would be heard. So classified was this policy that no written document about its origin has ever been found. Such was the atmosphere in Nazi-occupied Europe. How, in this suspicious, deceptive, and capriciously lawless atmosphere did the Vatican, that is, Pope Pius XII and his hierarchy, function? How could the Vatican intervene on behalf of the persecuted Jews in such an atmosphere, a predicament the Vatican had battled since the onset of Nazi power?

Vatican actions to help Jews under Nazi rule from 1933 to l945 were at once diplomatic and formal but also adroitly subtle and covert. In the end, the Vatican was the most successful government entity to act on behalf of Jews during the entire period.

This nuanced policy was rooted in the relationship of the Vatican with prewar Nazi Germany. The Vatican relentlessly emphasized racial equality while actively assisting Jewish emigration from increasing persecution. In addition, the wartime responses of the Vatican to the persecution and murder of Jews in various Axis countries, where dictatorial rule was by no means uniform, was as effective as it could have been under the circumstances. Once the Vatican realized that Jewish lives were at risk, that every method of intervention was a matter of life or death, it spared no effort to rescue them. As the papal nuncio to Turkey, Cardinal Angelo Roncalli, later Pope John XXIII (who saved twenty thousand Jews in the Balkans), stated, "I simply carried out the Pope's orders, first and foremost to save human lives." By analyzing historical realities, one can establish how effective these policies were.

The Vatican represented a Roman Catholic Church that taught the common dignity and equality of man. This belief governed all its policy statements, initiatives, and actions. This fundamental tenet was the core conflict between the Vatican and the Nazi Reich. Repeated Vatican proclamations about the universal family of man flew in the face of Adolf Hitler's "scientific anti-Semitism." Every papal statement against Hitler's racial Darwinism, no matter how refined or oblique, was immediately understood by the adversary, as the Nazi secretary of state Ernst von Weizacker confirmed, "To be sure, the Vatican expresses itself in general terms, but it is perfectly clear who is meant."

One belief, universal and equal, could not coexist with the other, racial and supremacist. The church paid for its limited freedom of action by constant Nazi harassment, arrests, and executions of its priests. An SS document maintained, "A philosophy that assumes human equality . . . is an error or a conscious lie." The Vatican not only continued to present its ideas at every turn but also thereby laid the groundwork for all its subsequent actions on behalf of the Jews.

Upon accession to power, the Nazis simply and clearly defined their program. They would avenge the humiliations of the Versailles Treaty (1919), erase the corrupt Weimar democracy, and end the horrendous joblessness and hunger of depression. Hitler would give Germans their pride back.

The Nazis spoke of reclaiming a wondrous, distant, and mystic Aryan past. In this golden, pre-Christian age the simple *Volksgemeinschaft* (racial community), honest and forthright, characterized what it meant to be born of pure German blood. Brave men protected fair-haired women who cared for home and children. What destroyed this era of virtue, according to the Nazis? Treason. Betrayal. The Nazis contended that the parasitic mongrel race, the decadent and rootless Jew, stabbed the German army in the back in the World War. Such perfidious betrayal heralded the advent of race-defiling postwar cosmopolitanism as embodied in "the Church, Liberalism, Bolshevism, and Jewry." But for National Socialism, with roots in German blood and heritage, the German *Volk* would have succumbed. God himself "sent" Hitler to save Germany. Hitler alone knew how to deal with the Jew. Opposed to this siren song that tempted millions of impoverished, shamed, and despairing Germans, the Vatican knew it had to take care or lose any influence it had.

Hitler firmly believed that British propaganda undermined the German war effort in World War I (1914–1918). He observed the Allies explain their cause in easily understood mottos: "defeat the Hun" and "world liberty." He recalled the Germans had no similar mottos. Together with his propaganda minister Joseph Goebbels, Hitler spread his racial superiority concepts. They employed what by all accounts was incredibly advanced usage of new communications technologies in radio, movies, theater, and literature. With insights from the new science of psychology, the Nazis manipulated the German mentality. For example, Leni Riefenstahl's movie *Triumph of the Will* (1935) recorded Hitler's triumphant arrival at the first Nazi Party congress as if he were a victorious Roman emperor. Hitler, filmed amid resounding music, klieg lights, and cheering soldiers shouting *Sieg Heil* (Hail Victory), embodied victories to come. A banner in every Nazi rally hall proclaimed, *Die Juden sind Unser Ungluck* (The Jews Are Our Misfortune). One leader with one goal demanded total submission. No other belief system could coexist with this exclusionary racism.

Cardinal Eugenio Pacelli, later Pius XII, identified this threat. Pacelli was the papal nuncio (ambassador) to the German kingdom of Bavaria from 1917 through the Weimar years (1919–1933). He saw firsthand the sufferings of the German people. He saw as well that Nazi victory would ruin the country. Philosophically, he was committed to the dignity of each person and understood that "the Church will never come to terms with Nazis as long as they persist in their racial philosophy." Together with Pope Pius XI, he carefully assessed the growing Nazi power.

Pacelli became Papal secretary of state in 1929, and Vatican City was recognized by Italy as an independent state under the Lateran Treaty (1929). The Vatican codified its new international relationships at this time with many national concordats (treaties). These concordats established the ground rules whereby the Vatican functioned in a given country. Vatican diplomacy was conducted through a hierarchy of papal nuncios and apostolic delegates (consuls) who worked through local bishops. Papal guidance was communicated by encyclicals, Latin texts on given themes. These documents were reprinted in the vernacular and read out from pulpits in a given country. Also, Vatican Radio was created in 1931, primarily in response to Italian Fascist efforts to undermine papal rights guaranteed under the Lateran Treaty.

The Vatican reached a concordat with Germany in 1933. Within months the Nazis began to violate its principles. Whereas against the Jews the Nazis were harsh and overt, against the church the Nazis concocted outrageous allegations of sexual deviancy and financial irregularities among Catholic clergy and closed Catholic schools, institutes, and newspapers. The Nazis thus sought to undermine Catholic teaching authority and insidiously diminish Catholic ability to counter Nazi claims on anyone's behalf. In response, Cardinal Pacelli authored and Pius XI proclaimed the only encyclical ever written in the German language, *Mit Brennender Sorge* (With Burning Anguish). It denounced Nazi duplicity, as well as attempts to undermine agreed-upon rules and to usurp Catholic education. The Catholic position of the equality of mankind was restated. As when Pacelli clearly stated in 1935 to 250,000 pilgrims at Lourdes, France, "They are in reality only miserable plagiarists who dress up old errors with new tinsel. It does not make any difference whether they flock to banners of social revolution or . . . whether they are possessed by the superstition of race and blood cult," so again in the encyclical he wrote, "the enemies of the Church, who think their time has come, will see that their joy was premature, and they may close the grave they dug" and "whoever follows that so-called pre-Christian Germanic conception of a dark and impersonal destiny for the personal God . . . denies the Wisdom and Providence of God. . . . Neither is he a believer in God."

Even more powerfully, *Mit Brennender Sorge* proclaimed against the "aggressive paganism" that "Should any man dare in sacrilegious disregard for the essential difference between God and his creature . . . to place a mortal, were he the greatest of all times, by the side of, or over, or against, Christ, he would be called a prophet of nothingness." The Nazis understood immediately who was meant by this text. *Mit Brennender Sorge* undercut racial superiority; indeed, it denounced the German savior, Hitler, and so the Nazi claim to rule. The Nazis moved rapidly to block distribution, confiscating copies and arresting and sending to concentration camps printers who produced the document and priests who read it. In Dresden, copies of the encyclical were passed hand to hand. The conflict lines were drawn for greater battles to come. Pius XI summarized in his 1937 Christmas address, "To call things by their real name: in Germany it is religious persecution . . . it is a persecution lacking neither force nor violence, neither oppression nor threats, neither sly craftiness nor lying."

Every Catholic defense of the defenseless in Germany was met with immediate retaliation. For example, a 1934 Nazi documentary,

Pope Pius XII meeting with American envoy Myron Taylor, 15 March 1940

(U.S. Holocaust Memorial Museum, Washington, D.C.)

Dasein Ohne Leben (Existence Without Life), introduced a euthanasia program. Using apparent scientific rationality, the movie proposed that the state eliminate "beings without life," the mentally handicapped, and devote money thus saved to national revitalization. Catholics resoundingly pilloried this hideous first step in "race purification." When Bishop Clement Count von Galen of Münster denounced the program, his diocesan priests were rounded up and sent to concentration camps, where many died. As with the disabled, so with the Jews, persecution grew. Pacelli implored bishops of the world to encourage their governments to admit the half-million Jews seeking to flee Nazi Germany, but even America declined to provide significant help. The Vatican encouraged the development of national relief foundations for Jews, food shipments, financial assistance, and material help and repeatedly insisted that equal rights be respected. Pius

knew that mere words would not stop the Nazis—action was required.

Upon his succession to the papacy in 1939, among Pius XII's first acts were the raising of an Asian, two Africans, and an Indian to the bishopric. The point was not lost on the Nazis, who closed churches and schools and arrested priests. His first encyclical, *Summi Pontificus,* again condemned racism, reminding that "there is neither Gentile nor Jew." It too was confiscated in Germany. While Hitler could proclaim his views to millions by the ingenious *Volksempfanger* (people's radio) he had mass-produced, the Germans were forbidden on pain of imprisonment, and later death, to listen to Vatican Radio.

Vatican policy in the prewar years was to assist German Jewish "emigration"; to help Jews escape the tightening Nazi noose. The Nazis stripped away Jewish rights with the Nuremberg Laws (1935). Jews were persecuted and expropriated; yet, no country would take them in large numbers as refugees, despite Vatican pleas and admonitions for help. Pius proposed to all ambassadors to the Vatican that their countries admit Jewish refugees. Small numbers were accepted. Pius even appealed to British authorities in Palestine. He proposed a peace conference to avoid war, but no major power agreed to come. He personally worked to have thousands of Jews admitted to Brazil. Then he appealed to all bishops to encourage their governments to help. Vatican emissaries throughout the world worked wherever they had influence to encourage nations to accept refugees. As with all the dozens of protests he formally filed as nuncio, he continued to denounce Nazi Jewish policy. The nuncio in Berlin, Archbishop Cesare Orsenigo, repeatedly intervened in Jewish cases. The Pope continually reemphasized the theme of the equality of man while he actively worked personally and through his nuncios and bishops on behalf of the persecuted. Alone amid governments who would not see or help, he struggled to find escape hatches for the persecuted, vilified scapegoats of Europe.

When World War II (1939–1945) broke out, Nazi themes changed. Now they claimed to be the last bulwark of civilization against Bolshevism. The Nazis saw the Jew behind the Red Menace.

The Vatican declared its neutrality. As neutrals the Vatican could continue to function with formal representatives in warring countries. It could, as in World War I, ensure that prisoners were identified and families notified. It rescued several thousand Jews stranded at sea and transferred them to encampments in southern Italy, where they survived the war. It could assure the movement of emergency food and communication between families, prisoners, and their native countries. It could file diplomatic protests against excesses where identified and privately argue individual cases. Above all, it could try to mediate among enemies and communicate diplomatic and other initiatives for those who could not. Indeed, the Vatican facilitated one German anti-Nazi scheme that foundered when the British refused to communicate, even through Vatican intermediaries. As Vatican peace initiatives failed, the fate of the Jews became ever more tenuous.

Jews were corralled into ghettos, where they died through neglect and malnutrition. Survivors were soon deported to unknown destinations. Where even in wartime, private Vatican entreaties sometimes worked to free concentration camp inmates, in the case of the Jews, however, no formal efforts succeeded. By late 1941 Jews were rumored to have been liqui-

dated behind eastern combat zones. Indeed, the nuncio to Berlin commented with increasing perplexity that in any Jewish case he was now simply ignored by Nazi authorities. Vatican efforts to assist European Jewry under direct Nazi control became increasingly difficult, and no one could pinpoint what had brought about this change. Casimir Papee, Polish ambassador to the Vatican, referring to the liquidation of the Warsaw Ghetto (1943), commented that when even old Jewish men, women, and children were being beaten and brutally deported to the east, grave doubts about their ultimate destination could be inferred.

The Vatican's wartime policy sought to prevent Jewish deportation to "the East." What was the ultimate destination of the Jews? Repeated formal complaints in Berlin merited nothing, neither by the Vatican, the Red Cross, nor any neutral entity. No power could halt these obsessive, ominous deportations, about which no appeal would be heard.

Pius intuited from the hideous treatment of the Jews in the ghettos and the transport stations that lives were at stake. He sent a secret letter, *Opere et Caritate* (By Work and Love), to the Catholic bishops of Europe. It commanded them to help those who "suffered racial discrimination at the hands of the Nazis," in any way that would save them.

The truth behind the mysterious deportations is now known. Reinhard Heydrich, the SS Reich Protector in conquered Czechoslovakia, introduced Hitler's Final Solution at the Wannsee Conference of January 1942. The Nazi leadership agreed to secretly deport and then murder European Jews in remote camps located in occupied eastern Europe. The earlier Night and Fog plan had been effective. So too the Final Solution would work by Night and Fog, and no appeal would be heard. This policy was why the Vatican's appeals for the Jews fell on deaf ears.

In a quixotic Allied attempt to incite resistance, Heydrich, the "Butcher of Prague," was ambushed there in 1942 by Czech parachutists. Hitler commanded a horrific slaughter, massacring or deporting some nine thousand people to avenge Heydrich. Lidice, a Czech village, was plowed, Carthage-like, from the face of the earth. When in 1942 Dutch bishops "in consort with Holy Father" denounced Nazism's "barbarous deportation of the Jews," Hitler responded by rounding up even those Jews who converted to Catholicism. Pius XII was stunned. He observed that had he himself made the proclamation, two hundred thousand would have been taken, rather than forty thousand. The Nazis added, "No intervention will be considered." They communicated a brutal and cynical message. Pius, to succeed in saving lives, had to act with greater discretion. Indeed, in light of the terrible retaliations in the Netherlands and Poland, Jewish organizations and European bishops implored the Vatican to be more circumspect. Pius, though he wanted to "speak words of fire," knew that such "would make the fate of the wretches even worse." In a mid-war letter to Cardinal Conrad Preysing, bishop of Berlin, Pius wrote, "We give to the pastors who are working on the local level the duty of determining if and to what degree the danger of reprisals occasioned by episcopal declarations . . . seem to advise caution, to avoid greater evil, despite alleged reasons urging the contrary."

Pius XII saw how fruitless symbolic or quixotic actions were, not to mention formal or public protests. As in the case of the Dutch bishops, public actions were paid for in vats of blood through Nazi revenge. Thus, to save the Jews, he acted covertly.

Pius gave secret orders to his nuncios to hide Jews in monasteries, to issue false baptismal certificates, to effect escapes, and to influence governments. They were to pay money; give medicine and food where possible; and establish homes, camps, false identities, even false functions for their suffering Jewish brethren. (Three hundred papal guards were disguised Jews!) Pius even spent his personal inheritance to save Jews being blackmailed by the Gestapo, not to mention hiding three thousand Jews in his private residence at Castel Gandolfo.

Across Europe, in every country where German deportation orders were issued, the Vatican fought, by fair means and foul, through the nuncios and bishops and through their proclamations to the faithful. They prevailed far more in Axis client states than where Nazis directly ruled. Cardinal Angelo Roncalli, who saved some twenty thousand Jews marked for death in the Balkans, declared that all he did was "known to the Holy See." Playing for time in Hungary, the Pope interceded with Admiral Miklós Horthy de Nagybánya, whose government swayed to and fro with German demands for compliance, even delivering two thousand Vatican safe-conduct passes to Jews en route to Mauthausen. Archbishop Jules Saliege of Toulouse denounced the deportations in Vichy France and reminded his flock that "the Jews are our brothers. They belong to mankind. No Christian can forget that!" In Spain thousands of Jews were allowed to cross over the border from France, thus saving them. Italian soldiers were influenced to allow Jews to escape deportation orders, so much so that the order was considered useless. Cardinal Luigi Maglione "expressed the Holy See's thinking" on the deportations to the Slovakian government and

"vigorously protested the treatment recently inflicted on hundreds of Jewish women." Regrettably, Vatican appeals to Allied countries to admit Jews often fell on deaf ears.

On and on the Vatican appealed, pleaded, cajoled, implored, and acted—openly, and secretly where necessary. Sometimes successful, often not, it was not for want of trying. Even up to February 1945, in Berlin, Archbishop Orsenigo sought to alleviate Jewish suffering. The nuncio in Bratislava was told to remain in place, in the ruins, so long as "some charity could be done."

Throughout the period of National Socialist rule, the Vatican intervened in any and every way that offered possible success in saving Jewish lives. In prewar Germany the Vatican fought on behalf of Jewish refugees. Formal concordats allowed the hierarchy to function, to influence, and to act to relieve the sufferings of Jews.

With the war, the Vatican remained neutral. This stance allowed it to function in occupied Europe, while nevertheless covertly helping the Jews, saving lives where possible. Absent the treaties, Pius could not continue to communicate with his representatives who understood the local conditions better, which allowed for fine-tuning a policy that had to be correct, since lives were at stake. Nuncios and bishops "on station" were in a better position to help in realistic ways and could remain on duty as representatives of a neutral government. Their actions, directed by Pius XII, were consistent, reminding the faithful that racism "was incompatible with the teachings of the Catholic Church." The hierarchy took any action it could to save Jews, be it hiding, forging documents, funding, assisting, or physically taking the defenseless away to safety. The Catholic principle of the common dignity of man provoked action, while Pius steered it.

Poignantly, Chief Rabbi Isaac Herzog of Palestine wrote in February l945, "The people of Israel will never forget what His Holiness and his illustrious delegates . . . are doing for our unfortunate brothers and sisters." Three months after the end of the war, a petition of some twenty thousand Jewish survivors reached the Vatican. "Allow us to ask the great honor of being able to thank personally His Holiness for the generosity he has shown us when we were persecuted during the terrible period of Nazi Fascism." Indeed, Pinchas Lapide, Israeli consul to the Vatican, summarized, "We Jews are a grateful people. No Pope in history has ever been thanked more heartily by Jews for having saved or helped their brethren in distress."

In the end, it is estimated that some 860,000 Jewish lives were saved by the actions of the Catholic Church. Of course, there is no standard whereby to judge the sufficiency of so many saved while so many died. Who, looking back, could not have hoped for more rescues? Certainly the Pope did, who watched his many efforts wax and wane. Yet, in light of all that was done, perhaps the Jewish proverb that he who saves a single life, saves the world, should suffice.

–ROBERT MCCORMICK,
NEWMAN UNIVERSITY

References

Pierre Blet, *Pius XII and the Second World War: According to the Archives of the Vatican,* translated by Lawrence J. Johnson (New York: Paulist Press, 1999).

John Cornwell, *Hitler's Pope: The Secret History of Pius XII* (London & New York: Viking, 1999).

Thomas J. Craughwell, *The Wisdom of the Popes* (New York: Thomas Dunne Books/St. Martin's Press, 2000).

Carlo Falconi, *Il silenzio di Pio XII* (Milano: Sugar, 1965); translated by Bernard Wall as *The Silence of Pius XII* (London: Faber & Faber, 1970).

Alden Hatch and Seamus Walshe, *Crown and Glory: The Life of Pope Pius XII* (New York: Hawthorn Books, 1957).

Peter Matheson, ed., *The Third Reich and the Christian Churches* (Edinburgh: T & T Clark / Grand Rapids, Mich.: Eerdmans, 1981).

Ralph McInerny, *The Defamation of Pius XII* (South Bend, Ind.: St. Augustine's Press, 2001).

Michael Phayer, *The Catholic Church and the Holocaust, 1930–1965* (Bloomington: Indiana University Press, 2000).

Ronald J. Rychlak, *Hitler, the War, and the Pope* (Huntington, Ind.: Our Sunday Visitor Press, 2000).

José M. Sánchez, *Pius XII and the Holocaust: Understanding the Controversy* (Washington, D.C.: Catholic University of America Press, 2002).

SCHINDLER

Was Oskar Schindler a hero?

Viewpoint: Yes. Schindler was fundamentally altruistic.

Viewpoint: No. Schindler was an opportunist.

With the opening of Steven Spielberg's movie *Schindler's List* (1993), the enigmatic figure of Oskar Schindler (1908–1974) attained mythic proportions. In the movie, and the 1982 novel of the same name by Thomas Keneally, Schindler appeared as a selfish opportunist who transformed himself into an heroic and energetic rescuer of his Jewish employees. More than a thousand of these "Schindler Jews" owed their lives to him. His recognition by Yad Vashem as a "righteous among the Gentiles" seemingly put him into the same category as the Swiss diplomat Raul Wallenberg and others who, for purely altruistic reasons, undertook extreme personal risks in order to keep Jewish women, men, and children from falling into the hands of the SS.

Comparisons between Schindler and Wallenberg raise important questions, however. Wallenberg, like most rescuers, had nothing to gain. Whatever Wallenberg's motivations, he worked to save Hungarian Jews because his government had sent him to Hungary with instructions to do so. By distributing Swedish passports, challenging the SS, and employing every strategy to undermine Nazi genocide, he risked losing his diplomatic immunity or simply being shot. In fact, his actions made him suspect to the conquering Soviet Union, by which he was almost certainly executed as a spy. Schindler rescued Jews, at least initially, because he hoped to turn a profit. The Jews he protected were "his" Jews, not strangers. And while Wallenberg's heroic status was ensured by his disappearance into the Soviet Gulag, Schindler spent the rest of his life as an unsuccessful businessman. If he was a hero, he was never heroic. His righteousness, while real, has to be seen in the context of his whole, rather questionable, life. Additionally, the historical Schindler, unlike the mythic version, points to the often ambiguous relationships among rescuers, survivors, and perpetrators.

Viewpoint:
Yes. Schindler was fundamentally altruistic.

Oskar Schindler was unquestionably a complex and enigmatic historical figure who saved the lives of more than 1,100 Jews. He also was a member of the Nazi Party and allegedly profited financially from the war—at the expense of Jews whose businesses he acquired and who worked for him. Despite these discrepancies in the character of this multifarious man, Schindler was unequivocally a hero who saved Jewish lives and who thus deserves the Righteous Among the Nations honor that he, along with his wife, Emilie, received from Yad Vashem.

Schindler altruistically and courageously saved the lives of approximately 1,100 Jews. In fact, Schindler risked his life often and spent his savings in his crusade to rescue as many Jews as possible. He provided Jews with jobs in his enamel-kitchenware and munitions factories so that they would be considered skilled workers essential to the Nazi war effort, thus saving them from a cruel death at the hands of sinister Nazis such as Plaszow labor-camp commandant Amon Goeth.

Some historians have argued that Schindler actually stole two enamel-kitchenware businesses from Jews and therefore should not be considered a hero. Although Schindler induced Jewish businessmen to hand over their businesses to him, that does not render him a villain or a thief. Because of Nazi restrictions, Jews were no longer permitted to own businesses, so their concession to relinquish their ownership of the factories was inevitable. Other Germans unscrupulously seized Jewish businesses and provided the Jewish owners with nothing in return. Schindler, however, gave the owners something far more valuable than money. Although Schindler could have paid the Jewish business owners money for the factories, the money would have proved useless to them, for they could not have acquired visas or a safe exit from Poland. The money would eventually have been confiscated by Nazi soldiers, and the former owners would have been killed. Instead of compensating the owners with money, Schindler used the businesses and his financial resources to save their lives.

Schindler employed these factories in his clandestine operation of rescuing Jews. The businesses functioned not as a means for Schindler to achieve great wealth but rather as a safe haven for Jews. Those who worked for Schindler survived the Holocaust; the same, unfortunately, cannot be said for those who worked for Goeth: "'When you saw Goeth,' said Poldek Pfefferberg [who worked for Goeth and Schindler], 'you saw death'." In fact, most of the money that Schindler attained from his enamel-kitchenware factory (Emalia) was spent subsequently to bribe Nazis in his efforts to save the lives of the *Schindlerjuden* (Schindler's Jews), rescuing them from the clutches of Goeth and Auschwitz.

Some scholars unwisely object to the classification of Schindler as a hero because he joined the Nazi Party and wore a Nazi pin. This objection manifests a failure to distinguish between membership in, and support of, the Nazi Party; a clear demarcation exists between the two. Some people, such as Schindler, joined the Nazi Party because it was fashionable to do so and because membership afforded them excellent sociopolitical advantages. Others, conversely, joined the Party because they fully supported Nazi ideology and wanted Germany to seize control of Europe and make it *judenrein* (free of Jews), even if this policy meant murdering all of the Jews in Europe, because they considered Jews to be inferior—if not inhuman—beings. Schindler unquestionably belonged to the former group of Nazi Party members. He joined and wore his pin because his membership enhanced his reputation and endowed him with privileges that he would not otherwise have obtained. Schindler sagaciously employed this enhanced reputation and privileges in his quest to save many Jewish lives. Other Good Samaritans who attempted to save Jews were caught and either imprisoned in concentration camps or killed. Schindler, on the other hand, often acted above suspicion and was able to save Jews because of his membership in the Nazi Party; some who might have suspected him gave him the benefit of the doubt because he was a Nazi, which proved to be the ideal cover for someone who wished to undermine the Nazi cause. According to Mordecai Paldiel, Director of the Department of the Righteous Among the Nations, located at Yad Vashem in Jerusalem, Schindler:

> . . . used his good connections with the ABWEHR [Amt Ausland/Abwehr im Oberkommando der Wehrmacht—Foreign Bureau/Defense of the Armed Forces High Command] and with friends in high government positions, as well as his jovial and good humored disposition, to befriend and ingratiate himself with high-ranking SS commanders in Poland. This stood him in good stead when he needed their assistance in extracting valuable and crucial favors from them, such as ameliorating conditions and mitigating punishments of Jews under his care.

Because of his membership in the Party and his concomitant connections with high-ranking Nazi officials, Schindler was able to regain his liberty and continue to help save Jewish lives when he was arrested by Gestapo officers, which happened on several occasions. Thus, Schindler employed his membership not to advance the Nazi cause but instead to subvert and undermine it.

Detractors of Schindler claim that he hired Jews not to save their lives but rather to obtain free labor for his factories. However, Schindler was not a war profiteer; he was a benevolent man who put Jewish lives ahead of acquiring wealth. It is well documented that Schindler hired many Jews who possessed no skills in factory work and some who were even unable to contribute at all to production in the factory because of physical disabilities. Paldiel, for instance, notes that "Schindler used his good connections with high German officials in the Armaments Administration to set up a branch of the Plaszow camp in his factory compound for some nine hundred Jewish workers, including persons unfit and unqualified for the labor production needs. In

THE ANTI-SCHINDLER

Amon Goeth, the Austrian commandant of Plaszow, was well known for his brutal treatment of Jewish inmates. He allowed his guard dogs to kill hapless victims, and he randomly shot prisoners during morning rifle practice. After the war he was executed for his crimes; part of his indictment reads:

The criminal activities of the accused Amon Goeth in the Cracow district were but a fragment of a wide action which aimed at the extermination of the Jewish population in Europe. This action was to be carried out by stages. In the first stage the personal and economic freedom of the Jews was only partly restricted; then they were completely deprived of personal freedom and confined in so-called ghettoes. From there they were gradually transferred to concentration camps and eventually murdered in a wholesale manner by shooting and in gas-chambers. Large numbers of Jews perished in each stage of this action also through inhuman treatment and torture or were individually murdered by German and Ukrainian henchmen.

In the Cracow district, the best known were the ghettoes in Cracow and Tarnow, both of which had been liquidated in an inhumane way by the accused.

The Cracow ghetto was set up on 21st March, 1941, and contained at the outset over 68,000 inmates. Its setting up was preceded by a long series of regulations progressively limiting the rights of the Jewish population. Already on 8th September, 1939, the German authorities ordered all Jewish enterprises to be marked with a star of David. This exposed the owners to robberies and persecutions. On 10th October, 1939, Municipal Registration Offices were ordered to register the Jewish population on special registration forms marked with a yellow band.

On 26th October, 1939, the Governor-General, Dr. Hans Frank, issued a proclamation stating in no uncertain terms that there would be no room for the "Jewish exploiters" in the territories under German administration.

On 26th October, 1939, Dr. Hans Frank introduced compulsory labour for the Jewish population and ordered the setting up of special Jewish labour battalions. The carrying out of this order was entrusted to his deputy for security affairs (der Hohere SS und Polizeiführer). . . .

During the last week of June, 1942, in the course of the liquidation of the Tarnow ghetto about 6,000 Jews were removed to Belzec death camp and nearly the same number murdered on the spot. At the beginning of September, 1943, the ghetto was completely liquidated in this way. It was then, for instance, that the accused Amon Goeth himself shot between thirty and ninety women and children and sent about 10,000 Jews to Auschwitz by rail, organizing the transport in such a way that only 400 Jews arrived there alive, the remainder having perished on the way.

In compliance with the wishes of Dr. Frank who wanted Cracow, the capital of the General Government, to be "purged" of Jews, the German authorities started in July, 1940, their forcible removal from the town. In June, 1942, a large scale action took place in the Cracow ghetto, in the course of which many murders were committed and about 5,000 Jews sent to the death camps on orders issued by Rudolf Pavlu, Stadthauptmann of Cracow. On 28th October, 1942, the barbarous evacuation of the Cracow ghetto and a further reduction of its area took place again. About 7,000 Jews were sent to the death camps and many others murdered on the spot. Of the 68,000 in summer 1940, only 14,000 Jews remained in the ghetto.

On 13th March, 1943, the final liquidation of the Cracow ghetto took place, personally supervised by SS Sturmbannführer Willi Haase and carried out by the accused Amon Goeth with the assistance of Kunde, Heinrich and Neumann, the Security Police experts on Jewish affairs. Wholesale murders were then committed on the spot. The total number of Jews murdered on this occasion reached about 4,000, among which were many women and children. Amon Goeth himself shot many people. The rest, over 10,000 able-bodied people, were accommodated in the Plaszow forced labour camp. . . .

Against this background appeared the person of the accused Amon Goeth, whose life career from the early years was inseparably bound with the Nazi movement, and who was responsible for the atrocities committed as part of a general pattern of the German policy aiming at complete extermination of the Jewish population in Europe.

Source: *"Trial of Hauptsturmführer Amon Leopold Goeth,"* United Nations War Crimes Commission, Law-Reports of Trials of War Criminals, *volume 7 (London: HMSO, 1948), Web Genocide Documentation Centre: Resources on Genocide, War Crimes and Mass Killings <http://www.ess.uwe.ac.uk/WCC/goeth.htm#NATURE>.*

this way he spared them from the horrors of the Plaszow camp."

Because he knew that Plaszow commandant Goeth was a sadistic murderer, Schindler wanted to rescue as many Jews as he could from this camp. Unlike Goeth and other Nazis, Schindler treated Jews humanely and ensured that they stayed alive. Keneally states:

> According to accounts Oskar presented after the war to the Joint Distribution Committee, he spent 1,8000,000 zloty ($360,000) on food for the Emalia camp. Cosmetic entries could be found, written off to similar expenditure, in the books of Farben [I.G. Farben—German chemical manufacturer] and Krupp [armaments factories owned by Gustav Krupp von Bohlen und H albach, where approximately 75,000 Jewish workers died from brutal conditions]—though nowhere near as high a percentage of the profit as in Oskar's account. The truth is, though, that no one collapsed and died of overwork, beatings, or hunger in Emalia. Whereas at I.G. Farben's Buna plant alone, 25,000 prisoners out of a work force of 35,000 would perish at their labor. Long afterward, Emalia people would call the Schindler camp a paradise. Since they were by then widely scattered, it cannot have been a description they decided on after the fact. . . . What it inspired in its people was a sense of almost surreal deliverance.

In Schindler's factories the Jewish workers were fed well—which was unique because the war had created food shortages throughout Europe and because most factory owners did not care if their Jewish workers lived or died—and were treated humanely and provided with medical care.

Furthermore, when Schindler opened his munitions factory in Brinnlitz, Moravia, he ensured that it would not provide any assistance to the Nazi war effort, even though the failure of the factory would cause his business—and consequently his finances—to deteriorate. Schindler made sure that the manufacturing process of shells and rocket casings was faulty; he rejoiced in the failure of his factory to supply the Nazis with weapons. On one occasion Schindler called two of his Jewish workers, Itzhak Stern and Mietek Pemper, into his office to show them a telegram from the armaments assembly plant located in the vicinity of Brno: "It said that Oskar's antitank shells were so badly produced that they failed all quality-control tests. They were imprecisely calibrated, and because they had not been tempered at the right heat they split under testing. Oskar was ecstatic at this telegram." Although Schindler's decision to sabotage his own company was dangerous to him because his failure to manufacture adequate weaponry incurred the wrath of Nazi officials in the Armaments Ministry, notably Armaments Minister Albert Speer, the industrialist took the risk because of his disdain for the Nazi cause.

Schindler's attempt to sabotage the Nazi war effort clearly refutes the notion that he was a proponent of Nazi ideology, and his unwillingness to supply the army with functioning weaponry cost him a fortune, indicating unequivocally that he was in no way a war profiteer.

On many occasions Schindler heroically and selflessly risked his life in order to save Jewish lives. One example occurred when he was contacted by Dr. Sedlacek, an envoy for a Hungarian Zionist rescue organization, who sought definitive information concerning the atrocities in Poland. Schindler's name came to the attention of Sedlacek because the industrialist had already rescued many Jews in Krakow and Zablocie (near Krakow), earning the reputation as a savior of Jews. Schindler willingly went to Budapest to provide eyewitness accounts of the horrors inflicted upon Jews. He warned several Jews, including Dr. Rezso Kastner, about the Nazi mass murders of Jews in Poland. Sedlacek could not find other "Aryans" willing to risk their lives by coming to Budapest and testifying about the atrocities, so he gave to Schindler all of the money that the rescue organization had earmarked for informants (the group considered a reward necessary because conspiring with a Zionist organization was dangerous); Keneally writes that "Oskar behaved impeccably and gave the cash to his contacts in the Jewish community to spend according to their judgment." Schindler later brought Sedlacek and another Jew, known only as Babar, disguised as "Aryan" industrialists to Goeth's labor camp at Plaszow to tour the facilities and to document the atrocities and inhumane activities that occurred in the camp. Babar smuggled a miniature camera into the camp and clandestinely took photographs so that he could present unimpeachable evidence to the Hungarian Zionist rescue organization. Schindler's journey to Budapest and his smuggling of Zionists into a Nazi labor camp to spy on the facilities were activities that, had Schindler been caught, would have resulted in charges of treason and would have led the Gestapo to imprison him in a concentration camp, if not to torture and murder him. But Schindler, a courageous and altruistic man with great convictions, willingly risked his life because he cared deeply about Jews and preserving the lives of innocent people. His valiant and benevolent deeds, committed during an era in which most good people who sympathized with the suffering of the Jewish people chose merely to be bystanders and not to intercede on the behalf of the innocent, manifests unquestionably that Schindler was a heroic man whose actions were not only virtuous and dauntless but also unique.

Some scholars have castigated Schindler for his alleged immorality, stating that his lechery and his frequent employment of bribes signify that he was not a benevolent man, let alone a Holocaust hero. But it is crucial to separate his social behavior from his courageous saving of Jewish lives—to distinguish social law from moral law. Although undeniably Schindler frequently was unfaithful to his wife, this fact in no way detracts from his rescue of Jews, and his personal life, in respect to his munificence during the Holocaust, is irrelevant. In fact, Emilie Schindler, Oskar's wife, accepted her husband's philandering, claiming that it was normal behavior. Schindler also frequently paid bribes to Goeth and other Nazis, but this fact demonstrates the industrialist's benevolence, for Schindler's bribes permitted him to save Jewish lives. When he, for instance, discovered that Goeth was planning to kill a Jewish worker, Rabbi Menasha Levartov, Schindler sent the Nazi some jewelry, and Goeth, instead of murdering the Jew, sent him to work at Emalia. Although Schindler's employment of bribes violated Nazi social codes of behavior, it was nonetheless the morally correct manner in which to act. In fact, Schindler's many bribes actually manifest his heroism and indicate that he saved Jews not because he would benefit financially, but, conversely, out of munificence. In fact, when Schindler discovered that Nazi officials were closing down his factory in Zablocie and the camp in Plaszow and that the Jews located there would be deported (the men to Gross-Rosen and the women to Auschwitz) and, most likely, killed, he worked tirelessly to create a new plant—actually a safe haven—for Jews in Brinnlitz, spending at least 100,000 RM (approximately $40,000) of his own money to bribe Nazi officials to receive permission to do so.

Julius Madritsch, a factory owner and friend of Schindler, also created a safe haven for Jews near Plaszow and was a benevolent man. But he proved unwilling, despite pleas from Schindler, to move his factory—with Schindler's—to Brinnlitz; although he wanted to continue saving Jewish lives, he thought that this move was too dangerous, so he declined. The result was that practically all of his workers were deported. Both Schindler and Madritsch helped Jews a great deal, but Schindler's altruism became an obsession and extended beyond the limits with which Madritsch felt comfortable; Madritsch felt that Schindler's desire to help Jews was so extraordinary that it would become too dangerous. Schindler paid money so that seventy of Madritsch's Jewish workers could be saved, for there was a limit imposed on the number of Jews that could be on his list of those to protect; this distinction between the two righteous men exhibits that Schindler was willing to take risks that other benevolent rescuers of Jews were not prepared to take, that Schindler's actions in saving Jewish lives was not only heroic but also, to some

extent, unprecedented during the Holocaust. For these reasons Schindler, along with his wife Emilie, was honored by being selected for inclusion in the Righteous Among the Nations, located at Yad Vashem, they are file number 20.

—ERIC STERLING, AUBURN
UNIVERSITY, MONTGOMERY

Viewpoint:
No. Schindler was an opportunist.

Few stories of survival during the Holocaust are alike; one exception to this observation may be the case of the group of Polish Jews, more than a thousand strong, known to themselves and to historians as the *Schindlerjuden* (Schindler's Jews). This diverse collection of men and women is quite correct to attribute its survival largely to the efforts of one man, the Sudeten-German industrialist Oskar Schindler. As laborers in one of Schindler's two small factories, these Jews were removed from the harsh conditions of nearby concentration camps, provided better rations than many forced laborers received under Nazi rule, and protected from transport to the extermination centers. A Nazi himself, if never an ideological fanatic, Schindler delivered them from almost certain death at the hands of his fellow Party members. Surely such a man merits his postwar identification as one of the "Righteous Among the Nations." Yet, without questioning his status as a savior of Jews, it is proper to explore what motivated Schindler to behave as he did in the extraordinary surroundings of Nazi-occupied Poland and Moravia.

What led this Nazi businessman to become a rescuer? The complexity of Schindler's character prevents scholars from offering a simple answer to the question; indeed, not even those who directly benefited from his actions know exactly why he protected "his" Jews. It would, however, be a mistake to divorce the characteristics of Schindler the man from Schindler the hero, ignoring the failings of the former while glorifying the virtues of the latter. One must not argue that his perpetual self-indulgence (most obviously in wine, women, and wealth) played no role in the extraordinary selflessness of his later actions to save the Jews in his employ. On the contrary, Schindler worked to protect Jews not in spite of his personal weaknesses but because of them.

As writer Thomas Keneally readily admits, young Oskar was a gambler by nature. It is reasonable to suppose that the thrill-seeking, risk-taking, romantic qualities this lifestyle entailed are directly reflected in every aspect of Schindler's

SCHINDLER

later life: it encouraged his frequent marital infidelity as much as it supported his challenges to Nazi authority by trading on the black market or shielding "his" Jews. As a young man, growing up in rural Czechoslovakia, he had been excited by the prospect of travel, by the speed and daring of amateur motorcycle racing, and by the company of beautiful women. The same rebellious spirit that soured relations with his father and made Schindler resent his obligatory military service, in 1937 prompted him to join the local Nazi organization, the Sudeten German Party. Wearing the swastika lapel badge was an asset to his career as a traveling salesman—facilitating contacts and contracts with German companies before the Nazis brought the Sudetenland "home to the Reich" in the autumn of 1938. After the German "liberation," Party membership was still good for business but no longer something unusual or a risky sign of opposition to the government. The gambler in Schindler was open to any new avenue of excitement that suggested itself.

A willingness to make the most of any opportunity, another feature of Schindler's character that was played out in all spheres of his life, was evident in his response to a chance meeting with a German intelligence officer during a business trip to Poland. When approached, Schindler immediately agreed to serve as a field agent for the *Amt Ausland/ Abwehr*, the Foreign- and Counter-Intelligence branch of the German army. No longer merely a pleasure-loving traveling salesman, he was living an adventure as he gathered military information in southern Poland. Apart from its romantic thrill, Schindler profited from his role as an *Abwehr* operative in a variety of ways: it exempted him from (unwelcome) service in the German army; it gave him a few contacts with influential officials within the Reich; and it required him to visit Krakow—the medieval Polish city in which he would build his short-lived fortune and his long-lived reputation as a rescuer of Jews.

If the rapid German conquest of Poland in the autumn of 1939 was gratifying to Schindler the spy, it was even more satisfying to Schindler the speculator. The Poles' disaster was a golden opportunity for an entrepreneur with a few connections, a good deal of charm, and ambitions to be more than a mere traveling salesman. Short on capital but dressing the part of the wealthy industrialist, Schindler headed for Krakow and began investigating a change of career. His gamble paid off when, within a day of his arrival, the former salesman acquired control of a small factory specializing in enameled kitchenware that the German conquerors had expropriated from its Jewish owners. Unorthodox as he was ambitious, Schindler raised the initial capital for his venture by making contacts with the former owners and

Oskar Schindler in 1949

other local Jews, repaying the investment with a portion of the factory's produce or, occasionally, a job on-site. These early dealings with Polish Jews, which made him an industrialist overnight, were also Schindler's first interaction with a community he would later try to preserve. Yet, there was little altruism in his actions of October 1939; the plight of the Jews was of no concern to a man busily seeking his fortune.

Once he had secured lucrative state contracts to supply German military kitchens with his pots and pans, *Herr Direktor* Schindler of the newly christened *Deutsche Emal Fabrik* (German Enamel Works, DEF, or Emalia) began to enjoy a lifestyle bankrolled by the unlimited profits of an economic boom. In the lean years before it came under Schindler's control, the factory had averaged a quarter of a million reichsmarks a year in Saks (about $100,000 in 1940 U.S. currency); with new equipment, wartime demand, and steady management, Schindler's DEF grossed more than sixteen million reichsmarks ($4 million)

SCHINDLER

between 1939 and 1944. On his substantial income, the former sales manager kept two apartments in Krakow (plus a third in Moravia for his estranged wife). By 1941 he maintained no fewer than five automobiles for his personal use and always spent lavishly on his clothes, food, entertainment, and "gifts" for his friends in the Nazi administration. Even after 1943, when he began spending a substantial amount on bribes to protect his Jewish labor force or on provisions to sustain them, Schindler nevertheless drove away at the end of the war in a fine car with a small fortune in diamonds concealed in the seats. Although life in defeated Germany quickly consumed these remnants of his gains, it should not obscure the fact that Schindler was a war profiteer.

Itzhak Stern, one of the *Schindlerjuden,* recalled that the German once described himself as "a capitalist by temperament" who did not like being "regulated." When one adds this independence of spirit to Schindler's youthful addiction to new thrills, it is hardly surprising that he did not obey Nazi laws prohibiting all black market dealings. Initially, another *Schindlerjude,* Leopold Pfefferberg, provided the link to Krakow's flourishing market in luxury goods. Nazi "party comrade" Schindler might well have been as excited by the act of defiance against the regime that gave him his privileged position as he was at the material comforts he obtained through his dealings. The black market was also an exceptionally good source of the items Nazi officials desired for themselves (jewelry, furniture, carpets, works of art, choice foods, and drinks), a fact not lost on the German entrepreneur. Schindler enjoyed mild celebrity in Nazi-occupied Poland for his uncanny ability to find just the right gift for his many official patrons. From the first days of the DEF, its not-so-law-abiding director cultivated friends in high places—men who, in later years, repeatedly extricated their golden boy from the clutches of the Gestapo.

Just as a compulsive gambler plays for ever higher stakes, so Schindler moved from the thrill of subverting German commercial law to the risk of defying Nazi racial policy. Altruism had little place in Schindler's earliest dealings with the Jews of Krakow. At the same time, his behavior was unusual for a conqueror exploiting the conquered, for his business instincts led him to seek a fair exchange in each case or, better, to leave the other party to the deal somehow in his debt. Thus, Schindler acquired his Emalia plant by promising goods for capital, and he gained the trust of blackmarketeers by consciously overpaying on his earliest dealings. Little wonder, then, that he offered some form of protection to the underpaid Polish and unpaid Jewish laborers who staffed his expanding factory even as he profited from their labors. At best he was protecting them as simple business associates rather than as fellow human beings; at worst he was sheltering them merely to maintain the efficient production guaranteed by an established workforce.

When, in the summer of 1942, the Nazis began their efforts to render Krakow "free of Jews," Schindler was drawn to make the decisions that led him down the path of resistance. At first he continued to operate as the businessman, cajoling the SS into releasing a dozen of "his" Jews from a transport in order to sustain the smooth operation of DEF. Later that summer, however, he witnessed a brutal SS "action" in the Krakow ghetto and resolved to subvert the system that made him wealthy on behalf of the people it was persecuting. Over the coming years Schindler not only retrieved "his" Jews from other labor camps but also employed his entrepreneurial talents and reputation as a "good Nazi" to establish a work camp within his factory walls. Again he took great risks and, yet again, he enjoyed the thrill of flaunting authority and getting away with it. In a way, Schindler indulged his love of gambling, and more than a thousand Jews won. By the end of the war the Jews he was protecting had become real people to the affable German. Ultimately, Schindler ran the greatest risks to save those he knew (or were brought to his attention by those he knew) from the atrocities he had seen inflicted on countless others.

Throughout his life Schindler was neither driven by a rigid moral code nor restricted in the means by which he would achieve any end he desired. In business as in his private life he was impulsive, spontaneous, and flexible in his approach. He often acted at a moment's notice and entirely without scruple. Although not necessarily positive, these traits were vital to Schindler's successful use of charm, bribery, and veiled threats to manipulate the assortment of thugs and bureaucrats who were carrying out the Nazis' Final Solution in southeastern Poland. The *Schindlerjuden* whose lives he saved are right to praise him for his courage and, perhaps, his humanity in an increasingly brutal world. But one must not allow his heroic actions to obscure the less savory parts of his character. In the words of historian Omer Bartov, Schindler was simultaneously a "rather common crook" and the kind of "crook who sets himself against a state of much worse (but officially quite legal) criminals, a man who wishes to profit from evil but also enjoys undermining it." "There are times," *Schindlerjude* Stern is said to have remarked to his German employer, "when the only people left to do business with are crooks."

–JOHN KUYKENDALL,
UNIVERSITY OF SOUTH CAROLINA

SCHINDLER

References

Omer Bartov, "Spielberg's Oskar: Hollywood Tries Evil," in *Spielberg's Holocaust: Critical Perspectives on Schindler's List,* edited by Yosefa Loshitzky (Bloomington: Indiana University Press, 1997).

Elinor J. Brecher, *Schindler's Legacy: True Stories of the List Survivors* (New York: Dutton, 1994).

Mary J. Gallant, "The Social Dimensions of Rescue in the Holocaust," in *Remembering for the Future: The Holocaust in an Age of Genocide,* volume 2, *Ethics and Religion,* edited by Margot Levy (New York: Palgrave, 2001).

Miriam Bratu Hansen, "Schindler's List Is Not Shoah: The Second Commandment, Popular Modernism, and Public Memory," *Critical Inquiry,* 22 (Winter 1996): 292–312.

Thomas Keneally, *Schindler's List* (New York: Simon & Schuster, 1982).

Lionel Kochan, "Krupp von Bohlen und Halbach, Gustav," in *Encyclopedia of the Holocaust,* volume 2, edited by Israel Gutman (New York: Macmillan, 1990), pp. 842–843.

Clifford Marks and Robert Torry, "Herr Direktor: Biography and Autobiography in Schindler's List," *Biography,* 23 (Winter 2000): 49–70.

"Oskar and Emilie Schindler," File 20, Righteous Among the Nations, Yad Vashem, Jerusalem, Israel.

Mordecai Paldiel, "Mordecai Paldiel," in *Voices from the Holocaust,* edited by Harry James Cargas (Lexington: University of Kentucky Press, 1993), pp. 46–55.

Paldiel, "Oskar Schindler," in *Encyclopedia of the Holocaust,* volume 4, edited by Gutman (New York: Macmillan, 1990), pp. 1331–1332.

Paldiel, *The Path of the Righteous: Gentile Rescuers of Jews during the Holocaust* (Hoboken, N.J.: Ktav, 1993).

Paldiel, *Sheltering the Jews: Stories of Holocaust Rescuers* (Minneapolis: Fortress Press, 1996).

Richard L. Rubenstein and John K. Roth, *Approaches to Auschwitz: The Holocaust and Its Legacy* (Atlanta: John Knox Press, 1987).

SCHINDLER

SLAVE LABOR

Do German industries that employed slave laborers have an obligation to pay reparations?

Viewpoint: Yes. Slave laborers were worked to death to enrich private companies supporting the German war effort. Reparations are a moral imperative.

Viewpoint: No. Private industry did not voluntarily employ slave labor, and the workers they did employ would otherwise have gone to the gas chambers.

Full mobilization and a two-front war put tremendous pressure on the German economy. Most pressing was the shortage of labor. Millions of German workers had been drafted into military service. The Nazi-inspired cult of motherhood increased pressure by preventing German women from taking the place of men on the assembly lines and in the fields as they did in Britain and the United States. Germany would have to look elsewhere to keep its factories running. Having gained mastery over most of Europe by 1941, the Nazi government was able to take advantage of the labor—willing or not—of millions of Polish, French, and other conquered peoples to keep its economy on a war footing.

Many of these forced laborers worked for German corporations, building everything from automobiles to the V-1 and V-2 rockets that rained death and destruction on London. They worked long hours in difficult, dangerous conditions with inadequate rations and were considered expendable by their employers, but they were not intentionally worked to death. Jewish and other "racial enemies" of the Third Reich, however, were subjected to slave labor of a different sort. Factory owners could rent the labor of concentration camp inmates—paying the SS, not the workers—and some owners established factories inside or near the concentration camps.

Only in the post–Cold War period have these industries, many of which evolved into global corporations, been pressured to pay reparations to these slave laborers. These industries have argued that their participation in these programs was neither voluntary nor motivated by profit. Indeed, by making use of these concentration camp victims as laborers, they might have saved the lives of women and men who might otherwise have gone to the gas chambers.

**Viewpoint:
Yes. Slave laborers were
worked to death to enrich private
companies supporting the German
war effort. Reparations are a moral
imperative.**

One set piece of Nazi anti-Semitic propaganda before World War II (1939–1945) was to portray Jews as being averse to physical labor. It logically ensued that Jews would be put to work in some punitive, demonstrative fashion. Therefore, among the memorable scenes when Germany annexed Austria in March 1938 was the spectacle of Jews—including many established tradesmen and degree-holding professionals—being forced to scrub the sidewalks of Vienna. No one pretended that this labor had been intended as a normal city sanitation measure. It was, as all understood, an exercise in humiliation. Onlookers are leering and jeering in photographs of the event.

Casual observers might suppose that such degradation, or perhaps extended terms of forced labor, comprised the Nazis' contemplated "solution" to the Jewish Question. Such was not to be the case. Adolf Hitler himself divulged a hint of his plans. In a speech to the Reichstag on 30 January 1939 he warned that if war came, the Jews would disappear from Europe. He did not bother to mention Jewish labor. Whereas no means were specified to bring about this vanishing act, the verb *disappear* is not normally applied to mere work assignments or even to outright enslavement.

As the Führer spoke, however, Germany was already coping with a severe labor shortage. The need for workers worsened when the predicted war duly broke out. Considerable numbers of Jews came under German control with the occupation of the Czech lands (March 1939), followed by the conquest of Poland (September 1939) and then the German triumphs over Belgium, Holland, and France (spring 1940). Before systematic extermination became policy in 1941, the Nazis had set about putting to work both the Gentiles and Jews of these defeated populations, particularly in Poland.

Again came photographic images of these labor tasks, attesting to the separation of Jews from Gentile Poles. Again humiliation, not mere exploitation, was a proudly stated goal of the German masters toward ghetto residents who had been dragged out for corvée details. Hard labor was pointedly scheduled for the Sabbath so as to force religiously observant Jews into profaning their holy day. A principle was thus established in practice well before extermination became policy: Jewish labor held a qualitatively different significance for the Nazis than the labor of those classified as "Aryan" in the ethnic caste scheme of the New Order. It was not merely a matter of economics but of ideology, and it was a special fate reserved for Jews.

Besides racial doctrine and sadistic Nazi activities, the ghettos offered potential for Nazi profit too, as well as material contributions to the German war effort. An edict of the Reich occupation authority in October 1939 imposed forced labor on all Polish Jews. Craft shops and factories were assigned manufacturing tasks, and a Nazi official, Friedrich Wilhelm Krüger, was placed in charge of a bureaucracy to oversee Jewish work for Germany. For some two years, beginning in autumn 1939, Jews incarcerated in the ghettos of Polish towns might hope that their lives, although miserable, could nonetheless be made economically indispensable to the Nazis.

Then came Hitler's invasion of the Soviet Union (1941) and the massacre of Jews on a vast, planned scale. Nazi policy at last caught up with Nazi ideology in mandating the eventual extermination of all Jews throughout German-occupied Europe. It was for the purpose of working out administrative details that the infamous conference was held at Wannsee on 20 January 1942. By that date, six months into the war against Russia, the German wartime labor shortage had not eased. So a question arose. Would Jews, as a proven source of labor, be killed when they could be exploited instead to the greater benefit of the Reich?

Conference chairman Reinhard Heydrich addressed this point:

> Within the framework of the Final Solution, Jews will be conscripted for labor in the eastern territories under appropriate leadership. Large labor gangs of those fit to work will be formed, with the sexes separated. They will be made to build roads as they are led into these territories. A large percentage of them will undoubtedly be eliminated by natural diminution. The remainder who survive—and they will certainly be the ones with the greatest physical endurance—will have to be treated accordingly.

SS labor overseer Krüger had pointedly been invited to Wannsee. Those who put Jews to work were thus informed that their employees had the status of temporaries. The Wannsee note taker was Heydrich's deputy Adolf Eichmann. Two decades later, Eichmann's prosecutor in Israel asked him to clarify what his boss had meant by "treated accordingly." Eichmann responded without hesitation: "Killed, killed. Undoubtedly."

It needed no saying for those present at Wannsee that the sought-after "natural diminution" of "a large percentage" was expected to ensue under conditions of relentless physical effort by malnourished people in the harshest of climates. This postponed-death aspect of the Final Solution

COAL MINING

Benjamin Jacobs recalls labor in the concentration camp designed to aid a large German company:

Then a number of civilians came to the block. They were accompanied by Hauptsturm-führer Rudolf Höss, the Kommandant of Auschwitz. The consensus of our block supervisors indicated that they were from I. G. Farben, a large German pharmaceutical company that already employed prisoners in the nearby Buna camp. At Buna, the I. G. Farben Company was making synthetic rubber. There, we were told, the inmate death rate was very high, and they had a continuous need for replacement workers. We believed that it could only be better than our present situation. We just wanted to get out of there. . . .

About two hundred of us were under Puka's command. After leaving the camp, we passed a cemetery. The gravestones inside were surrounded by withering weeds. Some stones were toppled and sunken. Two and a half kilometers further on, we came to a hut with a slanted roof. At first it did not look like a mine, but when several men in overalls with lights and lunch boxes in hand came out, we knew we were there.

In prewar Poland, this was known as the Harceska Mine, and it had been inoperative for over twenty years. Rubber was crucial to the German I. G. Farben Company. In order to manufacture synthetic rubber, coal was needed. When the Germans occupied this area in 1939, they reopened the mine and renamed it Fürstengrube. Günthergrube, not far away, had a similar history. It had been renamed in honor of Günther Falkenhan, the I. G. Farben director there.

The first thirty men, including Josek, Papa, and me, descended into the mine on a hand-operated elevator. We could smell the coal. I knew that miners worked hard and always faced danger. I respected the danger and did not know what to expect. None of us had ever seen or ever been inside a mine. When the elevator stopped and the doors opened, a thick coal fume greeted us. The air lacked oxygen and was full of coal dust. We could hardly see ahead of us. Before long our eyes adjusted, and we saw a long tunnel with a rail track and carts in the middle. One foreman took my father and me, and another led the rest of the group down the track. We followed our foreman into a cave. There lay coal lumps weighing from a few grams to fourteen kilos. Some were still lodged in the cave walls. "The cave was just blasted yesterday," said the foreman, as he handed us shovels and buckets. Our job was to fill the buckets and load the coal onto the carts.

The cave was barely big enough for both of us to fit into. The only light we had came from our lamps. We began working, on our knees with our heads bent. The smell of coal made us dizzy. At midday a couple of inmates brought down buckets of soup—the usual turnip and water and, if we were lucky, a potato. Then we saw Josek again. He told us that he and two others moved the filled carts to the end of the mine, where a locomotive pulled them further. By then we were all weary and tired, and as black as chimney sweeps. Coal dust had settled in our mouths and noses and had covered our skin. . . .

. . . After a week or two our arms hurt from lifting the heavy shovels. Lugging the coal lumps by hand to the carts was even more difficult, and our hands were now calloused and cracked. The coal dust gradually baked into our skins, and the fat-free soap we used could not wash it off. My eyelids looked as if they were coated with mascara. Papa and Josek didn't look any better. It won't be long before all of us are black Mussulmen, I thought. . . .

. . . At the end of a day's work I could hardly straighten my hands. My knuckles were bruised and oozed blood.

Source: *Benjamin Jacobs,* The Dentist of Auschwitz: A Memoir *(1995), pp. 130, 136–138.*

came to be called *Vernichtung durch Arbeit* (Extermination through Work).

In setting aside some Jews for work, albeit temporarily and at tasks designed to exact a high mortal toll, the SS executive of the Final Solution had made an ideological compromise of sorts. And compromises with reality tend to take on a life of their own. In short order, various tasks besides road-gang work were found for Jews in some places, sparing them—for a while—from being shot or sent to the gas chambers. Many worked for a period of weeks or months only to join their less useful relatives in death by starvation, disease, beatings, or execution.

It is a fact, however, as undeniable as the Nazi murder of six million Jews, that some Jews not only managed to work, even though they suffered greatly, but also to survive and be liberated before they could be "treated accordingly" by the Wannsee precept. Most incidental survivors of such *Vernichtung durch Arbeit* toiled for German industrial corporations until the end of the war.

A cynical argument might then be made along the following lines: millions of innocent European Gentile civilians and Allied prisoners of war were forced to slave for the German Reich. The majority of them survived. All Jews were sentenced to death by the Reich, but one cannot dismiss the fact that a lucky minority also survived through hard work. Owing their lives to this fact of employment, such Jewish survivors are therefore hardly entitled to reparations payments; their survival is compensation enough.

Such reasoning is dispelled by examining the Nazi measures that set Jews apart from other slave laborers. (Some individual Jews managed to endure forced labor while "passing" as Gentiles, but their experience is not the issue here.) Those persons identified by the Nazis as Jews, who were drafted for work, were, as a rule, assigned to all-Jewish detachments. They were marked by a six-pointed star sewn onto their clothing. Rations were calibrated at a lower nutrition level than those provided to Gentiles doing similar work. This policy was aimed at inevitable starvation. Jewish slave laborers therefore constituted a class apart from those millions of other Europeans who had been variously enticed, recruited, conscripted, dragooned, captured, or kidnapped and set to toil for the Third Reich. Many of these Gentile workers enjoyed some limited freedom to come and go from a work site. They could spend a meager wage on some cheap amenities. Not so with Jews, who always worked under strict guard and were barracked in terms of close confinement. Even at a work site Jewish workers labored under sentence of death. The work itself was the means of execution, as sure as gas, a bullet, or the noose, albeit a protracted means designed to extract every last bit of value from the organism before the victim collapsed.

Jewish mortality rates were, as a rule, indisputably far higher than those of Gentiles forced to be laborers. This horrible result is shown from the experiences at such diverse places as Monowitz (an industrial satellite of Auschwitz), Kaufering (a satellite of Dachau), and at the so-called *Südostwall* (Southeast Wall, a fortification attempt using Hungarian Jews to dig entrenchments). The Nazis' systematic killing of Jews through labor continued even after the mass-scale gas chambers ceased operating at Auschwitz in August 1944.

During this closing stage of the Holocaust, death through work characterized the Jewish experience in the Nazis' huge construction agency, the Organisation Todt (OT), which contracted private firms to run its building sites. As at Kaufering, OT operated in close cooperation with the SS, which administered the Jewish work force. The SS had orders to see the Jews enslaved, but they received no orders regarding their freedom. Most German civilian employers cooperated fully with the SS in handing over Jewish workers for execution, on demand. Those industrial employers who resisted, delayed, or prevaricated amounted to a tiny few. Oskar Schindler made the exception that proves the rule.

Where Jewish labor conscripts did not die on the job as intended by *Vernichtung durch Arbeit,* they were sometimes victims of mass executions at the end of the war. There were no death marches of Gentile forced laborers in spring 1945, but Jewish work detachments were herded around without seeming rationale as the Germans retreated, then were shot as Allied troops closed in. Hundreds if not thousands died in this fashion. Here and there some few thousands of emaciated Jewish slaves held on when the Germans gave up.

Compensation for surviving forced-labor victims of the Nazis has been accepted in principle, however belatedly. It follows in keeping with the civilized practice of providing indemnity for victims of false imprisonment, for example, as that suffered en masse by Japanese Americans during World War II or individually by persons exonerated of crimes after wrongful conviction.

In the case of Jewish survivors, though, there is this added factor: the labor they performed was itself calculated as a form of execution. The principle went back to Wannsee. Such Jews had therefore not been granted any reprieve from death by their captors; rather, the death torment was short-circuited by the end of the Nazi State. Justice and reason therefore demand that they be compensated at a commensurably higher rate.

–STEVEN F. SAGE, CONFERENCE ON JEWISH
MATERIAL CLAIMS AGAINST GERMANY

Viewpoint:
No. Private industry did not voluntarily employ slave labor, and the workers they did employ would otherwise have gone to the gas chambers.

The movie *Schindler's List* (1993) called poignant attention to the use of Jewish forced labor during the Nazi regime. In the movie, which was based on real events, Oskar Schindler, a German industrialist, protected and saved the lives of nine hundred Jewish laborers employed as forced laborers in his factory. Though the "list" itself might have been an afterthought, there is no doubt that workers in Schindler's enameling plant were saved by his efforts and by their perceived usefulness to the German war effort. Similar, if less happy, stories abound. Jewish writer Primo Levi attributed his survival to his good fortune at being selected for work in the Buna synthetic rubber plant at Auschwitz. As brutal as the work there was at times, a factory job, however exploitative, was infinitely better than the alternative—punitive and meaningless labor out-of-doors in every kind of weather. Inmates not needed for factory labor were far less likely to survive than those who worked, even as slaves, in German industry. Those individuals found not fit for labor at all were simply exterminated upon arrival at the camps. In the criminal economy of the Nazi camp system, slave labor was a benefit to women and men who, but for their temporary usefulness as workers, would have been murdered immediately.

Thus, if forced labor was not a blessing, it still saved lives. Though the industries that benefited from slave labor were far from virtuous, any obligation on their part to pay reparations must be based on legal, not moral, norms. Because Germany was at war, and because German industry participated in the slave-labor programs as part of the broader war effort, any reparations would be owed to victims by the German government, not the corporations—and certainly not by their current stockholders. Postwar treaties and international agreements confirm this contention. Though the German government and the affected industries signed an agreement to pay such reparations on 17 July 2000, they had no legal—though certainly a moral—obligation to do so.

At the end of World War II (1939–1945) the German economy lay in ruins. Under joint military occupation by France, Britain, the United States, and the Soviet Union, Germany would not be allowed its own government until 1949, when the areas under French, British, and American jurisdiction became the Federal Republic of Germany (West Germany) and the Soviet-controlled sector became the German Democratic Republic (East Germany). Even then the West German economy was dependent on substantial assistance from the United States until the mid 1950s, while the East German economy simply stagnated. The administration of President Harry S Truman was more concerned with rebuilding Europe (including Germany) and preventing the expansion of Soviet influence than with providing compensation for the scattered victims of Nazi slave-labor camps. These priorities are reflected in the postwar agreements that addressed the issue of slave and forced labor and reparations for those affected.

The Potsdam Agreement hammered out in the summer of 1945, shortly after the uncondi-

tional surrender of the Reich in April of that year, was signed by the leaders of the United States, the United Kingdom, and the Soviet Union. It provided that reparation claims were to be paid from specified percentages of seized German industrial capital equipment and shares of German companies. These percentages were set aside to aid the large numbers of stateless peoples released from bondage in concentration camps and German factory camps. The Soviet Union agreed that the claims of Polish nationals would be paid out of the share paid to the Soviet Union and later formalized that agreement in a separate treaty agreement with Poland.

Continuing this approach, the United States and seventeen other nations met in Paris a few months later "to obtain an equitable distribution among themselves of the total assets which . . . are or may be declared available as reparation from Germany." The Paris Agreement recognized that large numbers of now stateless persons had become victims of the German forced-labor program and were in "dire need of aid to promote their rehabilitation." The eighteen signatories to the Paris Agreement, the United States included, agreed that the reparations as determined by the conferees covered all of their claims and those of their citizens against the former German government and its agencies, governmental or private, arising out of the war. Simply put, the United States and other signatory countries waived the rights of their citizens to any reparations from Germany for any reason. The parties to the Paris Agreement did not intend that this arrangement be the final settlement, however. The final settlement for the use of forced labor was to be ascertained through a multilateral peace treaty. All signatories to the Paris Agreement recognized that it might be years or decades before the situation in Europe stabilized to the point that such an agreement might be possible.

In February 1947 the Allies entered into bilateral peace agreements with Romania, Hungary, and Bulgaria, in which these nations waived "all claims against Germany and German nationals outstanding on May 8, 1945, except those arising out of contracts and other obligations entered into, and rights acquired before September 1, 1939," the day Germany invaded Poland.

During 1952 through 1954 a series of agreements were negotiated in Bonn, London, and Paris. The Bonn and Paris conferences established a Transition Agreement, which provided for the following matters pertinent to the subject of reparations of those forced into labor by the Third Reich:

1. Instead of compensation being provided by a fund comprised of assets seized from Ger-

man industry, Germany was now to implement its own plan of compensation.

2. Persons persecuted for reason of nationality who no longer had the benefit and protection of their home country were required to be compensated if permanent injury had been inflicted on their health.

3. The Agreement established in Germany a Supreme Restitution Court to hear the matters related to reparations.

The Transition Agreement recognized that mere money could not compensate the victims of the Nazi regime for the damage done. It also recognized that the new Federal Republic had limited assets and so provided that its ability to pay could be taken into consideration in determining the time and method of compensation. The agreement was not a final settlement of reparation claims and anticipated that a final peace treaty between Germany and its former enemies would resolve the matter. The agreement was delayed by political wrangling until 6 May 1955. In the interim the United States, Great Britain, France, eighteen other Allied nations, and the Federal Republic of Germany concluded the Agreement on German External Debts ("London Debt Agreement") in London on 27 February 1953.

Designed to stabilize the German economy, the London Debt Agreement addressed the subject of German debts arising from World War I (1914–1918), the period between the wars, World War II, and some debts arising after the war. Article 5 set forth "claims excluded from the agreement." Section 2 of Article 2 provided that "consideration of all claims arising out of the Second World War by countries which were at war with or occupied by Germany during that war, and by nationals of such countries, against the Reich, and agencies of the Reich . . . shall be deferred until the final settlement of the problem of reparation."

In the ensuing years the international community has subsumed its claims under the terms of those treaties. The German government has not ignored its responsibilities, paying some $60 billion to claimants for injuries suffered as a result of the actions of the Third Reich.

Negotiated in 1990 and signed in 1991, a final peace treaty ended any obligation that Germany had to pay wartime debts above the amounts already paid. Although the agreement did not speak specifically to the issue of reparations, this arrangement was a settled principle of international and American case law. The most important such case in American jurisprudence, *Ware* v. *Hylton*, found in 1796 that a

treaty of peace abolishes the subject of the war, and that after peace is concluded, neither the matter in dispute, nor the conduct of either party, during the war, can ever be revived, or brought into contest again. All violences, injuries or damages sustained by the government, or people of either, during the war, are buried in oblivion; and all those things are implied by the very treaty of peace; and therefore not necessary to be expressed.

Prisoners working on components for the V-2 rocket at a factory in Nordhausen, Germany, circa 1944

SLAVE LABOR

Much more recently, a German court ruled that in such cases "it is not the affected party himself who is entitled to a claim, but his homeland." Thus, lawsuits claiming damages to an individual can only be brought by the nation in which the individual claims citizenship.

After the final treaty of peace in 1991 there was no liability for any damages from World War II, either to individuals or to nations. There was a strange quirk in the London Debt Agreement that might have opened up the German courts to suits filed by forced and slave laborers. That loophole led to a flurry of slave-labor cases in the German courts and the status of these cases was unsure. All other courts, and all other signatories to the treaties, were now barred as if the crimes had never taken place.

Thus, after 1991 the increasingly elderly survivors of the camps and forced-labor deportment programs faced a difficult battle. A flurry of forced-labor lawsuits beginning in 1998 in the U.S. Federal District Courts drew international attention. Each one was dismissed, most on the grounds that too much time had passed. Legislation was then passed in California, and was pending in Congress, extending the time for Holocaust survivors to bring lawsuits against private companies. A few cases, such as the *Lichtman* case, went much further and were dismissed on the more substantive issue of a political issue, that is, a "question of which courts will refuse to take cognizance, or to decide, on account of their purely political character, or because their determination would involve an encroachment upon the executive or legislative powers." *Lichtman* caught the attention of German law professors, and both Russia and Poland filed friend-of-the-court briefs.

Sizable judgments had been made against Swiss banks for withholding account information, and despite the language of the treaties and the lack of success so far in the courts, German companies began to feel a certain amount of economic nervousness. As more suits began to be filed and more names of German companies who had used slave and forced labor began to be news topics, Chancellor Gerhard Schroeder began to worry about what an international economic boycott of German products would do to the German economy. In a negotiated agreement signed 17 July 2000 between the United States, Germany, and sixty-five German companies, Germany set up a final foundation to compensate forced and slave laborers. This foundation, called *Remembrance, Responsibility and the Future*, had $5 billion to distribute. At the time there were an estimated 240,000 surviving victims of slave labor who were to receive about $7,500

each, and more than 1 million forced laborers who were to receive about $2,500 each. The German government contributed $2.5 billion and German industry contributed the other half.

These contributions were not admissions of liability on the part of the participating companies. German industry claimed, quite rightly, that they had no legal reason to contribute to the fund. Germany, not these private corporations, had fought the war and had enslaved the laborers. According to the peace treaties that ended the war, the German government was responsible for paying all claims of foreigners. The agreement, not quite a treaty and not quite a legal settlement, agreed that a "letter of interest" would be sent to all U.S. district courts, asking that they dismiss all forced-labor suits filed currently and that they bar any future suits. The foundation would not begin payout until this result was accomplished. The foundation began paying survivors in June 2001. Thus, no matter how egregiously some German corporations might have exploited Jewish labor, or labor of any other kind, no reparations were owed to the victims on legal grounds. As for the moral responsibility, the obligation to make amends is more difficult to ignore.

–LESLIE MAGRATH, HOPKINS, S.C.

References

Leopold Banny, *Schild im Osten: Der Südostwall zwischen Donau und Untersteiermark 1944/45* (Lackenbach: L. Banny, 1985).

Christopher R. Browning, *Nazi Policy, Jewish Workers, German Killers* (Cambridge & New York: Cambridge University Press, 2000).

"The Final Reckoning: Businesses Agree to Compensation for Wartime Germany's Forced Labor Policies—But Where's the Money?" *Time International*, 56 (31 July 2000): 16.

Karen Friedman, "Big Business and the Holocaust," *Dimensions: A Journal of Holocaust Studies*, 13.

Edith Raim, "Die Organisation Todt and 'Vernichtung durch Arbeit' in Kaufering und Mühldorf," in *1999 Zeitschrift für Sozialgeschichte des 20, und 21 Jaahrhunderts*, 9 (April 1994), pp. 68–78.

Telford Taylor, *Nuremberg Trials: War Crimes and International Law* (New York: Carnegie Endowment for International Peace, 1949).

SLAVE LABOR

SURVIVAL

Was survival for Jews during the Holocaust purely a matter of chance?

Viewpoint: Yes. Chance alone determined who survived and who perished during the Holocaust.

Viewpoint: No. Even though chance played some role in survival, a wide variety of other factors, such as national origin, race, class, gender, and family, proved much more important.

Convinced that world history was determined by the competition of races, adherents of National Socialist doctrine were obsessed with the concept of survival. Perpetual survival was deemed to be both the right and the duty of the superior Germanic (or Aryan) race. In order to assure this longevity and the racial purity essential to sustain it, any and all actions were justified—including the elimination of those judged "inferior." In the strictest sense, survival of the master race could be guaranteed only if its racial competitors did not themselves survive. Consequently, the Nazis' "Final Solution to the Jewish Question" was the *Judenvernichtung* (annihilation of the Jews); there was to be no surviving remnant of the Jewish people.

The fact that the essays in this section can be written is a testimony to the utter failure of this murderous Final Solution. Despite the often successful efforts of the Nazis and their collaborators to round up and execute millions of Jews, several hundred thousand survived to bear witness to the terrible reality of the Holocaust. Members of this group (as well as later generations of scholars) testify to wonder and surprise at how they managed to outlive a regime that actively sought to destroy them. This problem was of personal interest to writer and poet Primo Levi, whose efforts to answer the question of his survival at Auschwitz inform both sides of the discussion presented below.

"Small causes," Levi wrote in *Moments of Reprieve* (1979), "can have a determining effect on individual histories, just as moving the pointer of a railroad switch by a few inches can shunt a thousand-ton train with two thousand passengers aboard to Madrid instead of Hamburg." The "small cause" that altered his own life was a case of scarlet fever that placed him in the camp infirmary just when the Nazis marched his healthier comrades off to their deaths. Levi believed his infection was the result of a combination of two things: a chance encounter a few days before the Nazis abandoned Auschwitz and the fortunate fact that he had not had scarlet fever as a child. Yet, it can be argued that this "small cause" for his survival (illness at a critical moment) grew out of opportunities he enjoyed because of where he came from, who he was, and what he was trained to do. As an Italian Jew, Levi came to Auschwitz comparatively late in the war; as a young man he was selected for slave labor; and as a professional chemist, he was particularly valuable to his Nazi captors. Was he thus in a better position to survive the Holocaust than his fellow inmates, or was it, as he maintained, mere chance?

Viewpoint:
Yes. Chance alone determined who survived and who perished during the Holocaust.

Virtually everyone who survived the Holocaust asked themselves the same basic question: "Why did I survive when so many others did not?" A few survivors told their stories of escape from the "valley of the shadow of death" with a powerful narrative voice, with poetry, with—one might even say—a terrible beauty. These people, however, were the exceptions. The vast majority of survivors, like most of humanity, had little knack for storytelling. They had their own memories, their own losses, and their own individual obligations demanding they build new lives. If they told their stories at all, it was with reluctance, to family, friends, or the occasional historian with a microphone.

The results, predictably, have been that the most compelling and gifted voices—those of writers such as Elie Wiesel, Primo Levi, and Viktor E. Frankl—have overshadowed the voices of those less talented. This selectivity reflects neither conspiracy nor indifference but the realities of the marketplace of ideas. The powerful message of one articulate voice carries farther than the halting phrases of a million less-articulate survivors. This situation would not be cause for concern if one could be sure that this "survivor intelligentsia" was simply giving voice to the feelings, perceptions, and experiences of the majority of less-articulate but equally important survivors. One cannot. It is the nature of literature and of those who produce it that powerfully written, forcefully spoken words create new meanings. When these words give an account of so terrible and impenetrable an event as the Holocaust, they tend to impose these meanings on perceptions of what has happened. Not only are less-talented voices drowned out, they come to be heard only within the context of what the intelligentsia has already written and said. Indeed, survivors of more-ordinary literary talent often come to speak in terms whose meanings have been determined by the survivor intelligentsia. Yet, intellectual gifts did not predispose anyone to survival; nor did the hunger or fear of a member of the intelligentsia differ from those of a laborer. Indeed, one must be exceedingly careful not to suppose that the voice of the intellectual always reflects the feelings and experiences of all survivors.

Still, it was the intelligentsia who spoke first. They framed the discussion and provided a vocabulary for other survivors and a lexicon for those who hear and read their stories. It was this small, articulate, and supremely gifted survivor intelligentsia who first attempted to answer the question: "Why did we survive when so many others, often better people than we are, lost hope and surrendered to their sufferings?" The answers tended to follow one of two directions: either reflecting Frankl's discovery of a "will to meaning" that made (and continues to make) survival possible in the most extreme situations, or echoing the indifference that Levi summarized in the statement of a nameless camp guard: *Heir ist kein warum* (Here there is no "why").

For both Frankl and Levi, and virtually every other survivor, survival was largely a matter of chance. Being assigned to a dangerous work detail, finding oneself under the command of a brutal Kapo, getting sick right before the SS decided to empty the hospitals and gas the patients, or a million other chances almost always were fatal. Both Frankl and Levi also reported that some inmates seemed to lose interest in their own survival. Such inmates became, in the vocabulary of Auschwitz, *Muselmanner,* or "moslems." Frankl believed that not becoming a "moslem" required a special internal reason to survive, however absurd that reason might be. Based upon this observation, Frankl developed a complex theory of psychotherapy (variously known as "logotherapy" and "existential therapy") that identified this drive to continue living as a "will to meaning." Levi was less sure of the virtue of survivors. For him, the distinction was simple: there were those who perished and those who were saved.

Frankl was a psychiatrist, trained in the psychoanalytic tradition. He built his understanding of the Holocaust experience on the assumptions that the human psyche is a product of submerged strengths and anxieties and that the conscious mind is only the tip of a vast emotional iceberg. Survival, in the concentration camp as in ordinary life, has less to do with rational choice than with an inner purpose (a "will to meaning") that is not necessarily rational. Some inmates, Frankl and almost every other survivor noticed, lost heart almost as soon as they found themselves imprisoned, facing torture, exhaustion, hunger, and filth. They became "moslems" almost immediately. They stopped washing, eating, struggling for life—and they were dead within a week. Other inmates held out with unexpected tenacity against despair. Even in the face of certain death, they never surrendered to it.

Frankl identified this condition of "existential despair," different from resignation to one's fate, as a cause of death equally as lethal as a bullet or Zyklon-B gas. He did not, as is often assumed, assign to it a moral quality:

> On the average, only those prisoners could keep alive who, after years of trekking from

SURVIVAL

camp to camp, had lost all scruples in their fight for existence; they were prepared to use every means, honest and otherwise, even brutal force, theft, and betrayal of their friends, in order to save themselves. We who came back, by the aid of many lucky chances or miracles—whatever one may choose to call them—we know: The best of us did not return.

Thus, for Frankl, random chance and the "will to meaning" were in a constant dance. Most of those who died in the camps were selected for extermination as soon as they got off the train. Among those chosen for immediate execution, the sole benefit of possessing some internal strength was the ability to die with courage. Once one survived the initial "selection," Frankl believed, survival depended on having something to live for—a cause; a loved one who might, by some miracle, still be alive; or a task unfinished (for Frankl, it was a scientific paper that became the beginnings of *Man's Search for Meaning* and logotherapy). Thus, the ideologically committed (whether communists, Zionists, Jehovah's Witnesses, or Catholic activists) had better resources for survival than inmates without an external cause for which to live and fight. Having a cause was more important than the nature of the cause, for by providing order in an otherwise bewildering situation, it was the critical catalyst energizing the will to survive.

Levi, a chemist by training and a poet by vocation, was less inclined to attribute survival to an act of will. For Levi, the camps brought to light a fundamental polarity in human existence, a simple division between the "saved and the drowned." "Other pairs of opposites (the good and the bad, the wise and the foolish, the cowards and the courageous, the unlucky and the fortunate) are considerably less distinct." Levi believed that no one survived in Auschwitz for more than a few months unless he or she exhibited a brutal commitment to live at all costs—whatever inhumanity that commitment demanded—and, simultaneously, was able to benefit from blind chance. There were no rational decisions, no inner "will to meaning," only an animal drive to get enough food, rest, and clothing for another day. One could not choose a survival strategy other than to eat, sleep, and "try to look," as Wiesel reported, "healthy enough to work."

Levi and Frankl, pessimistic poet and optimistic psychiatrist, represent between them the conventional explanation offered by the "survivor intelligentsia." Although they employ the different vocabularies of the artist and the scientist in order to articulate their stories, these two divergent voices describe the same basic reality: a world in which survival seemed to depend on chance. The testimony of lesser-known survivors also tends to support this conviction.

SURVIVAL

A few years ago an elderly couple, survivors of different camps and different Holocaust experiences, addressed a classroom full of high-school teachers gathered to learn how to teach more effectively about the Holocaust. The husband forcefully talked about his months in a work camp. He had told the story often. Answering a question, he said, "we became like animals to survive." His wife, practiced in this disagreement but not keen on speaking in public, shook her head. "No," she objected, "we did not become like animals. We survived because we kept our humanity."

Their disagreement was less profound than customary and probably based on dissimilar but effective responses to the extremity of survival in the camps. It also reflected the semantic differences between Frankl and Levi. They had suffered from different conditions. They had found within themselves differing psychological resources and had employed differing strategies in order to survive. They expressed these differences with a vocabulary they could not share: "We became like animals" and "we retained our humanity in spite of everything" reflect a shared reality. Whether they identified their commitment to survival as a result of human will or of inhuman instinct, they knew their survival depended on what they had done and, equally, on what they had been fortunate enough to avoid. Neither one claimed a "right" to survive.

Scores of other survivor narratives and testimonies reinforce the conclusion: maintaining physical life and holding onto one's psychological strength was dependent on one's health, an adequate diet, enough sleep, and—last, but not least—on a realistic chance of survival. Levi's "drowned" did not actually die of despair, though they might have despaired of life long before the end. They died of gas, bullets, disease, exposure, or exhaustion. To suggest otherwise is to blame the dead for their own moral failure. The dead might have surrendered well before they died, they might have become "moslems"; the survivors might have had something for which to live; but neither answer offers a complete explanation. When one seeks to understand why some survived and some did not, one must not overlook the fundamental point that Frankl, Levi, and most survivors—whether intelligentsia or illiterate—are trying to make: the Holocaust was not a random catastrophe. It was not a psychological attack. It was a targeted act of violence. The dead were like victims of a sniper attack. They got in the way of death. They were, as a group, neither more nor less than survivors; they were simply dead.

–TANDY MCCONNELL,
COLUMBIA COLLEGE

Viewpoint:
No. Even though chance played some role in survival, a wide variety of other factors, such as national origin, race, class, gender, and family, proved much more important.

Survival during the Holocaust was a matter of origin, age, class, gender, and family status. As recent scholarship has looked more carefully at the composition of Jewish camp survivors, many formerly overlooked factors have come into play. For instance, most east European and Russian Jews were sent directly to extermination camps in Poland (Treblinka, Belzec, Sobibor, Chelmno, and others), while most west European Jews arrived at concentration camps (Auschwitz, Bergen-Belsen, Dachau, and others). All people arriving at extermination camps were gassed immediately, meaning that most eastern European and Russian Jews were not even given a chance to survive. Some historians have noted, however, that a larger number of Jews survived in countries where the nominally pro-Nazi government refused to expel Jews (such as Bulgaria or Old Romania) or in cities where the German police could not mobilize sufficient transports for deportation (such as Budapest or Paris).

In the concentration camps, chances of survival were not much higher, as Jews were literally worked to death: the life expectancy of a working Jew in Auschwitz was a few months. Hunger, thirst, cold, heavy labor, disease, and torture were such severe threats to one's life that chances of survival were best for those who spent a minimal amount of time in the camps. In other words, those who arrived at the camps at a relatively late date were most likely to survive until the camp was abandoned or liberated. Once again origin, class, and family status were significant, since persecution hit certain disadvantaged groups earlier and more severely while arriving at other, advantaged groups more slowly or in milder forms.

Although absolutely nothing could protect a Jew from death in the camps, historian Raul Hilberg maintains that "survival was not altogether random," and he enumerates advantages that, particularly in the early stages of the war, could prolong lives and lessen maltreatment. According to Hilberg, these advantages included some special status, such as foreign nationality, marriage to a non-Jew, or military service in World War I (all of which were reasons for transfer to the "model" camp at Theresienstadt); public position, such as a seat on a Jewish Council; occupation (physicians, carpenters, shoemakers, and policemen were needed in the ghettos as well as in the concentration camps); and money, which could enable emigration in the 1930s or improve one's standard of living within the ghettos. While these advantages were in no way a guarantee for survival, they effectively counter the perception that survival was solely a matter of luck.

Nowhere are the characteristics requisite for survival more apparent than in those camps that combined extermination facilities with war industries employing vast amounts of slave labor. For most arriving Jews, the infamous "selection" remained the first and last impression of the camps. Without consideration for friends and families, the guards first separated men from women and then those deemed capable of hard work from those "unfit to work." The old or weak, women with small children, and older children and adolescents—80 to 90 percent of the arriving Jews—were immediately sent to their deaths. Survival chances for women were considerably less than those for men: although the Nazis considered most women capable of work, they chose not to separate mothers from their young children, fearing that such separations would cause too much of a disturbance. Thus, motherhood was directly linked to extermination in a way not equally true of fatherhood. For Jewish children, survival chances in the camps were minimal. Even if they were able to escape the initial selection, they consistently ran the chance of being discovered and killed.

From these bleak statistics, one can conclude that luck or any internal characteristic had little to do with one's chance of survival. But what about the small percentage of prisoners initially selected to work in a camp such as Auschwitz? Were some of those inmates "lucky" to survive? Not quite. In *Survival in Auschwitz: The Nazi Assault on Humanity* (1961), Primo Levi argues that in this ruthless environment, survival was possible only because of special advantages:

> There remained only the doctors, tailors, shoemakers, musicians, cooks, young attractive homosexuals, friends or compatriots of some authority in the camp; or they were particularly pitiless, vigorous and inhuman individuals, installed . . . in the posts of Kapos, *Blockältester,* etc.; or finally, those who, without fulfilling particular functions, had always succeeded through their astuteness.

Levi's identification of certain privileged professions has been confirmed by the extensive research of Hilberg, among others. In fact, Levi himself survived by working as a chemist at I. G. Farben's Buna rubber factory, purposefully constructed next to Auschwitz to exploit Jewish labor. Levi's second hypothesis, that only the most ferocious survived, has been the subject of much discussion. Were survivors "better" or "worse" than other inmates, or not any different from their peers? This question is misleading because it reduces survival to a moral issue. Instead of focusing on moral categories, one needs to discover and emphasize the different and complex factors that influenced survival.

As Hilberg contends, youth, health, and physical strength were necessary conditions for survival:

> In sheer physical terms, the veterans of camps, hideouts, and partisan units had two attributes. They were relatively young, concentrated in the age group from the teens to the thirties, and that is to say that those who were middle-aged were even fewer. They also had to be in good health at the start of the ordeal.

Those physically healthy and strong were simply much better equipped to endure the hardships of camp life. Aside from sheer physical attributes, another crucial factor for survival was a will to survive, a mental attitude that Hilberg defines as a "psychological profile." Hilberg suggests that three psychological traits—realism, rapid decision making, and a determination to live—let inmates adapt to pain, cold, heat, hunger, and thirst. Survivor Viktor E. Frankl seems to agree when remarking that the prisoners' fate was not solely decided by external circumstances but also "the result of an inner decision."

A careful examination of various testimonies indicates those attitudes, skills, and ways of thinking that the survivors believe contributed to their survival. The importance of care of the body, regular human interactions with others, and mental engagement stand out as particularly important in this context. While there is a great deal of truth in the simple explanation of one former inmate, that "surviving was just day by day—there was no long-term 'survival strategy,'" even the "day by day" activities exhibit some common patterns in the lives of the survivors. Although no single strategy, skill, or mind-set could guarantee survival, the testimonies reveal that inmates played an active role in using some or all of these behaviors to aid their survival.

The day-to-day effort of prisoners to care for their bodies is but one such behavior. The use of the word *care* in the context of the camps is misleading since prisoners—if they had the opportunity at all—could only wash in filthy water, without soap. But in spite of the horrendous sanitary conditions, several survivors identify cleansing as a crucial factor in self-determination and survival. Levi claimed to have lost the "instinct for cleanliness" after only one week at Auschwitz, but a friend (a fifty-year-old former sergeant honored with the Iron Cross) washed himself busily and lectured Levi on the importance of washing. The younger man, although not fully convinced by this kind of military discipline, must agree: In that place it was practically point-

FICKLE FINGER OF FATE

A prisoner at Dachau recalls his efforts to save his father and himself:

You stood *Appel* in the morning and then you went up to the kitchen to pick up your so-called lunch which was soup. One day I'm standing on *Appel* and somebody's asking if I am around. This guy says your father is here in Barrack 30, a different section of the camp. Dachau had 31 barracks. On the right hand side were six or seven hospital barracks. You weren't allowed in there. Barrack 13 was the whorehouse. That was for the Germans only. Barrack 27–30 was isolation. People were just left there to starve. 30 was the worst one.

It was like the fickle finger of fate. My father stayed at Auschwitz. It was evacuated and he went on the march to Gross Rosen. From there he was shipped to Dachau. That night I met him through the fence. It was quite an experience. He sneaked up to the fence and kissed me and I kissed him. We talked. How are you? When did you eat last? He looked very bad—very bad—very bad. At this point I got into trading.

I was able to feed my father plus a couple of his buddies. But sometime in the month of March, around March 15th I came down with typhus. I went on sick call and they put me in the hospital barracks. The beds had sheets on them. They gave me an injection once a day, something in the vein. I don't know what it was, but it made my heart beat awful fast. I crapped blood for a couple of

weeks and I finally got better. They shipped me out to the recovery barracks. There was a Dutch fellow there, a hospital orderly, fatter than hell. He had Red Cross packages and he fed me every day. I said to him I want to get out of here. I want to go back to work. But I said not only I'm going to starve, but my father's going to starve. So a couple of days later he signed me out. When I left he told me he expected me to get him some food—not for himself—but for all those people there. And I did whatever I could. One day he asked me for a knife and that's how the knife came in.

I was carrying bread, coal and a knife through the main gate at Dachau. The bread I carried inside my pants, this was civilian bread, not the two pound loaf, the long loaf. The knife I had inside the bread. And I had a bucket full of coal. I was going to get it in camp in the soup kettle. The SOB SS corporal took the coal off me for his own use. Then he said, "What else have you got?" I said, "One loaf of bread." He said, "Let's have it." I said, "Please let me keep some of the bread." He didn't find the one with the knife. I gave him the other loaf. If he had found that one that would have been it. I could have been killed right there. So he beat me up and chased me back and that was the end of that.

Source: Saul S. Friedman, Amcha: An Oral Testament of the Holocaust (Washington, D.C.: University Press of America, 1979), pp. 296–297.

---

less to wash every day in the turbid water of the filthy washbasin for purposes of cleanliness and health, but it was most important as a symptom of maintaining vitality and necessary as an instrument of moral survival.

Likewise, Charlotte Delbo, a political prisoner who arrived at Auschwitz in 1943 in a convoy of 230 French women, described her first opportunity to wash since the shower she received upon her arrival at Auschwitz sixty-seven days earlier. When the Kapo of her column surprisingly allowed the women to wash in a nearby icy stream, Delbo examined her soiled body with detached curiosity and found her toenails sticking to her stockings. Instead of remaining shocked, a desire for cleanliness took over and led her to scrub her body to the point of bleeding. To contemporary readers, this con-

cern for cleanliness may seem irrelevant, if not strange. Washing and caring for one's body helped self-preservation for several reasons. In the camps, sickness most often meant death; at Auschwitz, for example, a prisoner was allowed to remain in the infirmary only up to six days. Anyone not recovered within that time was sent to the gas chambers. Not only obvious sickness but also appearance played a crucial role in survival. Outer characteristics such as gray hair or sunken cheeks made selection as a death candidate more likely. Testimonies describe how women pinched their cheeks to give them more color before "selections" that the guards periodically executed to separate the sick and weak from the healthy.

Prisoners sought to maintain physical appearance not only to escape selection for death but also to maintain inner resistance. Hindered from washing themselves and their clothes, inmates were forced to confirm Adolf Hitler's stereotype of "the filthy Jew," a theme Terrence Des Pres illuminates in his testimony *The Survivor: An Anatomy of Life in the Death Camps* (1976). In the ghettos as well as in the camps Nazi officials made conscious use of this strategy: they first removed any means of hygiene and health and then complained about Jews being dirty and having diseases. The act of cleaning one's body defied this strategy and demonstrated self-determination, a will to survive, and thus a will to resist. Any sign of caring for mind or body necessarily attested to the failure of the purpose of the camps: to kill the prisoner's spirit and body and erode the will to live.

Individuals who consistently sought out human interaction with their family, friends, or fellow prisoners were also resisting the dehumanizing effects of the concentration camps. The separation of men and women—husbands and wives, siblings, parents, and children—was aimed at destroying existing bonds between families and friends as well as eliminating a means of communication. Surely, the Nazis realized that these ties would embody a source of strength to the inmates. Interactions among the segregated family members with old and newfound friends and with other prisoners played a crucial role in survival for men and women alike. To Hungarian Judith Magyar Isaacson, the most important focus in the camps became staying with her mother and aunt Magda. Two of the women even risked death when they switched from a line to which they had been assigned upon spotting the third in another line. Since family members felt they needed to stay united at all costs, familial ties not only motivated but also pressured one to stay alive. Elie Wiesel eloquently describes this pressure as an obligation to another family member:

My father's presence was the only thing that stopped me. . . . He was running at my side, out of breath, at the end of his strength, at his wit's end. I had no right to let myself die. What would he do without me? I was his only support.

For Delbo, national ties among the French formed the most important support system. Communication focused on personal, immediate needs: "To talk meant that we could make plans about going home, because to trust we would return was a way of forcing luck's hand. The women who had stopped believing they would return were as good as dead." Other interactions among the prisoners included singing and the exchange of recipes, rituals that became sources of self-esteem and outlets for creativity, as Isaacson remembers:

The pessimists predicted our stay would end in death, but we told them to keep it to themselves. A group of us huddled together in a corner, some in rags, some in prisoners' garb, trying to amuse ourselves. Mostly we sang or exchanged recipes. I recall a lengthy discussion about *retes,* the incredibly flaky Hungarian strudel.

Obviously, constant hunger in the camps motivated the sharing of recipes. Since one typically thinks of food when enduring hunger, imagining culinary feasts offered a mutual outlet from these conditions. In addition, it provided inmates with an imaginary world that offered an escape from daily life. One's familiar food symbolized one's national and spiritual home in perhaps the most accessible, yet nonthreatening, way. Whereas thinking of one's family and friends, even of one's house and belongings, could evoke fear and despair, thinking of one's food at home was easier and more neutral. Like singing, sharing and exchanging recipes also created a sense of community and sustained former religious, family, or national ties. To remember songs and recipes meant to return to one's roots and traditions, links that the Nazis had tried to eradicate. Such ties helped maintain an identity within the identityless world of the camp.

Whereas singing and exchanging recipes were elements of daily camp life according to women's testimonies, men's testimonies rarely mention these practices. If mentioned at all, such rituals do not have a positive connotation; for instance, to Levi it is simply meaningless to dwell on food that is beyond reach. It seems that men and women made use of different socialized behavior. Cooking in prewar times was reserved primarily for women, which may explain men's prevailing lack of interest in customs that women formed into a survival tool. It is to be expected that female inmates used those behaviors society had taught them to use, behaviors that in the camps surprisingly emerged as an advantage and helped them to survive. But Levi, too, emphasizes social contact as a means of survival, maintaining that his friendship with Lorenzo, "an Italian civilian worker who brought me a piece of bread and the remainder of his ration every day for six months," made survival possible:

I believe that it was really due to Lorenzo that I am alive today; not so much for his material aid, as for his having constantly reminded me by his presence, by his natural and plain manner of being good, that there still existed a just world outside our own for which it was worth surviving.

Lorenzo's generosity, as well as the women's sharing of recipes, serves as a reminder of a healthy world outside the camps and sparks hope that such a world still exists.

Remaining mentally engaged in the world, whether the greater one beyond the physical barriers imposed by the Nazis or the lesser one inside the camps, was another significant aid to survival. Psychoanalyst Bruno Bettelheim, a political prisoner in Dachau, studied mass behavior in extreme situations and reported how his "research" helped him to survive. Bettelheim argued that prisoners had to stay actively involved in order to survive. In a similar vein Frankl reveals that his attempt to understand the psychology of victims and perpetrators became a coping mechanism. For instance, when facing attacks of delirium, Frankl attempted to reconstruct the manuscript for his book that had been lost at Auschwitz. By trying to search for meaning in his precarious position, he was able to transcend his situation. Not only research served as a survival tool; many testimonies mention literature in this context. Like songs, recipes, and former family/friends, literature offered a link to the past, to the language, culture, values, and customs of the former world.

Recalling this literature, especially poems, helped to occupy the mind during the endless hours of the daily *Appell* (roll call). Although camp inmates were most often busy with hard work, they also experienced many hours of senseless waiting. In the early mornings and late afternoons inmates had to stand motionless for several hours at roll call, often in cold, rain, snow, or searing heat. A slight movement or stumble could lead to immediate death. Sometimes the SS guards awoke all prisoners at night and forced them to endure yet another *Appell*. Since prisoners could not communicate during roll call, those who survived were able to protect themselves from destructive thoughts by engaging in some sort of mental activity, such as practicing one's memory and reciting poetry. One survivor recalled:

Since Auschwitz, I always feared losing my memory. To lose one's memory is to lose oneself, to no longer be oneself. I had invented all kinds of exercises to put my memory to work: memorize all the telephone numbers I used to know, all the metro stations along one line, all the boutiques along the rue Caumartin between the Athènèe theater and the Havre-Caumartin metro station. I had succeeded, at the price of infinite efforts, in recalling fifty-seven poems. I was so afraid they might escape my mind that I recited them to myself every day, all of them, one after the other, during roll call.

Ruth Klüger also used poetry to endure the roll call, revealing that forcing herself to remember provided desperately needed "mental exercise" in a camp with no mental stimulation, no schooling, and no friends of similar age. During roll call and at other times, engaging the mind also distracted inmates from bodily deprivations caused by hunger, thirst, cold, or torture. Poems provided a structure, focus, and time line in an otherwise limitless and timeless world. During the endless waiting, marching, or work, poems divided the time into smaller segments and revealed how much time had passed. The use of recalled literature extends far beyond escapism; rather, survivors were strengthened through evoking cultural ideals and thus employed literature as a tool of resistance.

The prisoners' treatment in the concentration camps was aimed at, and in most cases succeeded in, destroying their core personalities, including any former characteristics and behavior. Survival depended on many tangible and intangible factors (physical and mental stamina, the presence of family, friends, or other supporting groups) as well as upon the various coping strategies adopted by individual inmates. If survivors had pondered their survival chances and allowed themselves to be fully aware of their hopeless situation, they might not have found the strength to stay alive. Realistically, their chances of survival were nil, and no one could survive by keeping this fact in mind. Activities such as singing, culinary discussions, or reciting poetry distracted prisoners from oppressive thoughts and were used specifically to aid survival. Each testimony poses a specific set of contingencies that finally leads to survival; there existed no single uniformly successful survival strategy. Yet, Holocaust testimonies by men and women reveal that inmates played active roles in their own survival. Hilberg argues "in the final tally, women were most probably more than half of the dead, but men died more rapidly." Lacking evidence for the concentration camps, Hilberg uses statistics from the Jewish ghettos in Poland, noting that "in the age group twenty to twenty-five the death rate of the Lodz Ghetto men was three and a half times that of the women." Likewise, Myrna Goldenberg claims that the mortality rate of women was substantially lower once they had passed the initial selection. The question of why women survived both ghettos and camps longer and in greater numbers than men has startled researchers and has led to an animated debate. Some researchers have claimed that quintessential "feminine" qualities facilitated survival, a statement that has been criticized by others as valorizing and thus essentializing women. Unfortunately, the discussion of whether women had superior survival skills has drawn much attention and led to many generalizing statements. Rather than positing members of one sex as "better" survivors, the debate only underscores the need for further studies on this topic. Luck played an additional but not an exclusive role.

—CAROLINE SCHAUMANN,
EMORY UNIVERSITY

SURVIVAL

References

Bruno Bettelheim, *Surviving and Other Essays* (New York: Knopf, 1979).

Charlotte Delbo, *Auschwitz and After,* translated by Rosette C. Lamont (New Haven: Yale University Press, 1995).

Terrence Des Pres, *The Survivor: An Anatomy of Life in the Death Camps* (New York: Oxford University Press, 1976).

Debórah Dwork, *Children with a Star: Jewish Youth in Nazi Europe* (New Haven: Yale University Press, 1991).

Viktor E. Frankl, *Man's Search for Meaning: An Introduction to Logotherapy* (Boston: Beacon, 1959); revised edition of *From Death-Camp to Existentialism: A Psychiatrist's Path to a New Therapy,* translated by Ilse Lasch (Boston: Beacon, 1959).

Raul Hilberg, *Perpetrators, Victims, Bystanders: The Jewish Catastrophe 1933-1945* (New York: Aaron Asher, 1992).

Judith Magyar Isaacson, *Seed of Sarah: Memoirs of a Survivor* (Urbana: University of Illinois Press, 1990).

Ruth Klüger, *Still Alive: A Holocaust Girlhood Remembered* (New York: Feminist Press, City University of New York, 2001).

Primo Levi, *Survival in Auschwitz: The Nazi Assault on Humanity,* translated by Stuart Woolf (New York: Collier, 1961).

Elie Wiesel, *Night,* translated by Stella Rodway (New York: Hill & Wang, 1960).

SURVIVOR NARRATIVES

Are survivor narratives of the Holocaust reliable as historical evidence?

Viewpoint: Yes. Survivor narratives are a rich source of evidence that provides both eyewitness testimony and a measure of the emotional effect of the Holocaust.

Viewpoint: Not necessarily. While their importance is undeniable, survivor narratives are filtered by the emotional trauma of the Holocaust, which can distort memories and limit perspectives.

The status of survivor narratives as historical evidence is an often-debated question in work on the Holocaust. In the absence of extensive Nazi documents about the operation of the camps or copies of orders to exterminate the Jews, survivor testimony becomes a centrally important resource for historians and laypeople attempting to understand the events of the Holocaust. Some scholars have emphasized these narratives, taking them to be transparent documents of the horrors they discuss, while others subject them to the same scrutiny any other historical documents receive. These positions tend to be represented as mutually exclusive—in other words, either you accept the narratives as evidence or you do not, and if you do not you are questioning the whole of the Holocaust. This question is one of the more divisive in studies about the Shoah.

Traditionally, historians treat all documentary evidence with a degree of skepticism as they develop an understanding of the past—viewpoints are partial; stories can be either deliberately or unintentionally distorted; and documents can be forged. The Holocaust—one of the most singular events of the twentieth century, if not of all western history—can either be regarded as a unique event, inexplicable except as horror, or as a particularly evil outgrowth of tendencies within western culture. Those who regard the Holocaust as unique tend to view survivor narratives as the best access to what happened, while those who see the Holocaust as an expression of latent tendencies in the culture look at the narratives as documents subject to scrutiny.

Both essays in this section hold that survivor narratives offer insights into the horror of the camps. Neither contributor, in other words, questions the evidentiary use of the narratives. However, the writers take different positions on the status of narratives as evidence. Both suggest that their positions have political resonances, though again of different kinds.

Caroline Schaumann argues that survivor narratives are the best evidence of what happened in the camps and that to question them provides fodder for Holocaust denial. Her argument is two-pronged. First, in the absence of Nazi documents about the Final Solution, the only real evidence is the narratives of guards and inmates. These narratives, she argues, show both the facts of the Holocaust—the images of horror—and "something fundamental about its nature" that other documents cannot. That fundamental something is the way the Holocaust breaks radically with normal experience, taking the events somehow outside history and into the narrative of trauma. To downplay the narratives is thus to downplay the horror, what Schaumann calls the "magnitude of the horror." Second, by questioning the validity of the narratives, one questions the reality of the events narrated. Following Jean François Lyotard, she suggests that raising questions about the "truth" of the narratives effectively silences and marginalizes the victims and thus enables those who would deny the Holocaust to make their cases. For her, the choice to give added weight to survivor narratives is both historical (they are better documents than anything else) and political (their veracity disables those who would deny the Holocaust happened).

Meili Steele begins from the premise that survivor testimony provides invaluable information about the Holocaust and that the question is not whether such testimony is important but if it is adequate. Is the testimony of survivors, in other words, sufficient to the project of understanding the Holocaust, or does it need to be supplemented by other forms of evidence? Steele answers in the affirmative, asserting that historians and citizens need context to supplement the powerful impact of the writing of survivors. Looking at Hannah Arendt's *Eichmann in Jerusalem: A Report on the Banality of Evil* (1963), Daniel Jonah Goldhagen's *Hitler's Willing Executioners: Ordinary Germans and the Holocaust* (1996), and Christopher R. Browning's *Ordinary Men: Reserve Battalion 101 and the Final Solution in Poland* (1992), Steele argues that historical and philosophical works that supplement the testimonies of survivors with other kinds of evidence offers a way for readers to think about the trauma of the genocide. In other words, the survivor narratives by themselves show the trauma of the Holocaust but do not allow one to truly understand what it means in political, historical, and ethical terms. Steele writes: "testimony alone is never enough. It is only the beginning of our reengagement with the past and ourselves." In this view, testimony offers guidelines for that reengagement, but the reengagement needs to go beyond that testimony in order to do full justice to it.

Neither essay questions the importance of the testimony of survivors; they differ on what to do with it. This distinction is an important one and characterizes the work of history in many areas. The historian's or the citizen's relation to evidence is a matter for careful thought and has ramifications beyond the immediate confines of discipline or period.

Viewpoint:
Yes. Survivor narratives are a rich source of evidence that provides both eyewitness testimony and a measure of the emotional effect of the Holocaust.

To prevent and counter attempts of Holocaust denial, one needs to recognize survivors as the most reliable eyewitnesses to the Holocaust. Since few authentic documents exist that are historical proof of the Holocaust, people depend on survivor testimony for its documentation. Survivor testimony teaches not only the historical facts of the Holocaust but also something fundamental about its nature that cannot be conveyed in other historical documentation.

While historians usually rely on archival data, material evidence, and authenticated documentation, those sources are not available to prove the Holocaust. There exists no written order by Adolf Hitler pertaining to the final extermination of Jews. Nazi documents carefully avoid unmistakable terminology, using euphemisms such as "Final Solution of the Jewish Question," "special treatment," "resettlement," or "euthanasia" for murder, killing, and extermination. There is also no extant formal authorization by Hitler delegating to Heinrich Himmler the execution of his plans, perhaps because after public protest and the abandonment of the

"euthanasia" program, Hitler was concerned that evidence of another mass murder could reduce his popularity. Furthermore, during the last weeks of World War II (1939–1945), the Nazis conscientiously destroyed any evidence of their crimes. As Hannah Arendt has pointed out, SS men destroyed "the paper mountains that testified to six years of systematic murder," and Adolf Eichmann's department methodically burned possibly incriminating files. When the threat of advancing Russian troops put an end to further gassing of prisoners, Himmler immediately ordered the crematoria in Auschwitz destroyed. Thus, the material and documentary record of the Holocaust has not been fully established and can never be sufficiently documented. This lack of incriminating evidence for the extermination of the European Jews has made the prosecution of Nazi perpetrators difficult and has led to endless debates by revisionist historians about the exact numbers of people killed. It has also deeply affected scholarly approaches to the Holocaust, as primary sources for understanding the Holocaust are the testimonies by survivors.

Jean-François Lyotard points out a perpetual dilemma for the Holocaust witness. In his philosophical inquiry on the public reception of Holocaust testimonies, Lyotard reveals that the term "testimony" originates in the judicial system where it constitutes a demand for reparation of damages, addressed to a third party, namely a judge. Since the U.S. legal system is based on the presumption of innocence, the prosecution must establish the facts of the crime and prove that it has happened, while the accused does not have to prove anything. Lyotard points out that this legal practice has put Holocaust survivors in an impossible situation; according to its logic, the only eyewitness who could prove the facts of Auschwitz would be ones who died in its gas chambers. Since the Nazis themselves proclaimed that nobody could return alive from a death camp, there could in theory not be any such thing as a survivor, which also renders their testimonies invalid. Ruth Klüger supports this sentiment, pointing out that her contemporaries often doubt the severity of the horrors she experienced: *Ehre den Toten, den Lebenden eher Mißtrauen* (honor to the dead, but mistrust to the living). While the dead are final proof of persecution and mass murder, the living cannot supply such proof. Therefore, Lyotard concludes, the reality of Auschwitz cannot be established. Indeed, the dismantling of the crematoria by the SS, the destruction of incriminating files, and the absence of written orders by Hitler quite literally efface the murderers' instruments and impair the ability to grasp the magnitude of the crimes committed. In *Auschwitz and After* (1995) Charlotte Delbo candidly declares:

> You don't believe what we say
> because
> if what we say were true
> we wouldn't be here to say it.
> We'd have to explain
> the inexplicable

Lyotard suggests that putting the burden of proof on survivors has led to their silencing and marginalization. To leave survivors in this precarious condition and thus effectively silence them, the Nazis would have committed the perfect crime, one that Himmler envisioned in his infamous speech of 3 October 1943 as *ein niemals geschriebenes und niemals zu schreibendes Ruhmesblatt unserer Geschichte* (a never-written and never-to-be-written page of glory in our [SS] history).

Lyotard's analysis and Himmler's words emphasize that one needs to listen to the survivors' stories if they are to defy the Nazi goals. The events of the Holocaust are frightfully close to "the perfect crime" in that most stories could not have been written; history lost forever the possibility of hearing more than six million stories of those murdered. The world cannot afford to lose or forget the stories of the few remaining survivors, even though they cannot replace or make up for the millions of untold stories. As James Young illustrates, Holocaust witnesses have not only the choice but also the obligation to tell what they know. In this way Holocaust testimonies become historiographic contributions, each one extending knowledge of the Holocaust,

and at the same time they underscore that one can never fully come to know the Holocaust.

In the immediate postwar era, survivors faced great difficulties when trying to speak about the Holocaust. As the postwar societies of Germany, Israel, and the United States were concerned with their new roles in world politics, they remained for a long time ignorant of survivors' damages and needs. It was not until 1953 that Germany passed its restitution law, its first official admission of guilt. Although physically sick persons were now entitled to reparations, in order to receive payments survivors had to be examined by German doctors and had to prove a causal link between their symptoms and their maltreatment in the camps. As incomprehensible as it sounds, psychiatrists and psychoanalysts in Germany and the United States did not view the Holocaust as a cause of psychological damage. In the United States, according to Aaron Hass, survivors "encountered a culture which glorifies success, optimism, and happiness, while shunning failure, pessimism, and suffering." Even though Israel created commemoration days such as Yom Hashoah in 1951, the Holocaust was not discussed publicly, taught in schools, or researched at universities. As a whole, neither perpetrators nor bystanders took responsibility for their actions. Raul Hilberg observes:

> The postwar societies of Israel and the United States were forward looking, and these countries were also confronted with new adversaries: Israel with the Arabs, the United States with the Soviet Union. The survivor had no audience and frequently felt the isolation of someone who cannot be understood. Many memoirs were written, but not for large audiences.

Elie Wiesel, who composed *Night* in 1955, had trouble finding a publisher, and Primo Levi's *If This Is a Man* (1959) was first published in an edition of only 2,500 copies. In the 1960s the success of Wiesel and Levi gave way to a wave of interest in the Holocaust, making the current attention to the Holocaust in history, literature, politics, philosophy, religion, and psychology partly the result of their extraordinary testimonies.

While survivors, as Lyotard suggests, have been criticized for not adhering to historical facts, many incorporate a discussion of historical truth in their testimonies. In *Survival in Auschwitz,* Levi never disputes the truth-value and the cohesion of his text, but belatedly, in an interview in 1985, he asserts:

> Please grant me the right to inconsistency: in the camp our state of mind was unstable, it oscillated from hour to hour between hope and despair. The coherence I think one notes in my books is an artifact, a rationalization a posteriori.

In this belated reflection, Levi reveals that the traumatic experience of camp life caused discrepancies in his memory and that the organization and rationalization of his account are artificial. Levi's initial insistence on a "coherent" style may be attributed to the burden of proof Lyotard describes, and to the need to validate the facts of the Holocaust. In contrast to Levi, Delbo from the outset questions a definition of truth based solely on historical facts. Prefacing her memoir, she writes: "Today, I am not sure that what I wrote is true. I am certain it is truthful." Delbo reveals that "truthful" can be different from "true." "Truthful" encompasses her experiences and her interpretations of the facts, but "true" corresponds only to the facts. Delbo also suggests that "truthful" may indicate a state of flux, different from one day to the next. As Young adds, "truthfulness" may also mean something different for each survivor: "But each victim "saw"—i.e. understood *and* witnessed—his predicament differently, depending on his own historical past, religious paradigms, and ideological explanations."

Each testimony represents a different way of understanding the Holocaust. In contrast to historical data, Holocaust testimonies thus narrate not only the events but also their impact on the human body and soul, as well as disclose the interpretative framework through which the author understands the Holocaust. As historian Omer Bartov observes, "the experience and memories of survivors give them insight not only into the event itself, but also into some aspects of human behavior and psychology, into the potential of each of us and into the potential of human society to create hell on this earth." This argument is perhaps the strongest reason for reading Holocaust testimonies in addition to history books. People have come to view the Holocaust as the most influential crime of the twentieth century, as an event that cannot be compared to other man-made disasters and that has led to the limits of understanding, interpretation, and representation. In such an "exceptional situation," Saul Friedländer argues, one cannot, and should not, separate the events from their moral implications:

> Let me clarify the questions raised by such limitations on interpretive strategies by one simple illustration: Could one write the history of the science produced by experiments made on human beings in Nazi camps as genuine history of science, or can one use the results of such experiments as elements in ongoing, normal scientific discourse?

In other words, one should look not only at the events themselves but also ethical and moral considerations. By focusing exclusively on the factual record of the Holocaust, one will fail to see its most crucial impact, namely the reality of the victims' experiences. A survivor undoubtedly knows more about the Holocaust than an historian. Holocaust testimonies can convey more adequately a sense of the magnitude of the horrors than documentary data ever could. When Levi calls survivors' testimonies "stories of a new Bible," he suggests that both texts provide humankind with paradigmatic parables that reveal something fundamentally true that cannot be verified. The Bible and Holocaust testimonies thus convey not only facts but also their existen-

Polish Jews captured by German troops after the Warsaw uprising in 1943

tial interpretations, since without interpretation, the Holocaust can neither be represented by the survivors nor can it be grasped by their audience. In this way Holocaust testimonies not only further knowledge of the Holocaust but also reveal something about the nature of the Holocaust; people depend on the survivors' memories, since they cannot imagine such evil.

If the Holocaust takes one to the limits of understanding and interpretation, then perhaps new approaches to representation must be found. Holocaust survivors had to arrange their isolated, traumatic memories into coherent stories and give them a dimension in space and time, thus transforming and distorting the events. But their testimonies often show an increased awareness of this distortion. Many witnesses, faced with the dilemma of having to narrate the inexplicable, were led to reflection on and analysis of the process of writing itself. Questioning the capacity of language, survivors use styles that demand the readers' involvement. Instead of simply recounting their memories in chronological and linear order, they interrupt their texts to examine both the process of remembering and the problems of representing their memories. For instance, Delbo's narrative is no chronological, cohesive story but consists of poems, autobiographical vignettes, and fiction, and it often blurs the boundaries between these genres. Delbo also frequently interrupts her text to contrast her memories with a critical analysis of her present life: "Presently I am writing this story in a café—it is turning into a story." Sitting in the café and remembering the Holocaust are two different realities that seem impossible for her to think of simultaneously. As a result, Delbo recognizes that she is making her memories into a story, thus necessarily structuring and transforming them. Some testimonies also contain reflections on the capacity of language. Instead of regarding language as a tool for expression, survivors come to see it as an impediment. Even worse, words can distort and displace the reality and authenticity of events. Levi comments on the fallible character of language:

> Just as our hunger is not that feeling of missing a meal, so our way of being cold has need of a new word. We say "hunger," we say "tiredness," "fear," "pain," we say "winter" and they are different things. They are free words, created and used by free men who lived in comfort and suffering in their homes.

Similarly, Delbo asserts: "There are people who say, 'I'm thirsty.' They step into a café and order a beer." While readers think they know what the words "hunger," "thirst," "cold," or "pain" mean, such language is insufficient to express the atrocities in the camps. Since those words are typically used in an ordinary context,

they are inadequate to represent something completely inconceivable to those who have not shared the experience. Just as historical facts acquire meaning only if they are interpreted and put into a context, words by themselves are empty and need the readers' emotional involvement to convey meaning.

Some scholars have reasoned that each testimony is a product of traumatic circumstances and thus represents a highly biased and fragmentary perspective. Bartov claims, "Hence, while we must take into account what survivors tell us about human behavior, we must also remember that this is a partial view, formed under the most extreme conditions," while Michael André Bernstein concludes, "Moreover, since one of the Nazi mechanisms of controlling the prisoners depended on isolating each of them as much and for as long as possible to keep them ignorant of the full scale of their predicament, the testimony of any single survivor, no matter how vivid and thoughtful, will be fragmentary and in need of supplementation from other sources and narratives." This perspective is indeed true; each survivor faced a different camp reality and absorbed these experiences differently, and as a result there are many different, perhaps even contradictory, testimonies instead of one single true story. All information on the Holocaust remains to a certain degree fragmentary, and any attempt to present a uniform picture would be presumptuous at best. If the process of remembering traumatic events interprets and transforms the original experience, tools for expressing that experience distort it even further. The writing of memories is not an impartial activity; it is dependent on context and subject to conscious and unconscious selection and interpretation. Instead of presenting the illusion of complete stories, the authors of Holocaust testimonies are aware that coherence and closure are impossible. Hence, the narrators make little attempt to cover up gaps and omissions in their texts. For instance, Wiesel at times uses an elliptical style to describe Auschwitz: "An open tomb / A hot summer sun." Rather than attempting a long and detailed description, Wiesel uses only fragments. These fragments, left open to readers' interpretations, responses, and emotions, demand active involvement rather than passive reception.

As Kenneth Seeskin and Irving Howe point out in articles in *Writing and the Holocaust,* edited by Berel Lang (1988), the fundamentally unintelligible nature of the Holocaust leaves anyone concerned with Holocaust testimony disarmed and helpless. Even survivors, who should know the most about the horrors they endured, acknowledge the inexplicability of the Holocaust. If the survivors themselves cannot explain what has happened to them or how the Holocaust could have happened, how then can listeners and readers of their testimonies or anyone else ever come to such an understanding? In a similar vein, Bartov wonders how one can teach the Holocaust; neither author nor reader, neither teacher nor student can ever hope to understand. Yet, one cannot leave this dilemma as it stands. Silence or withdrawal from these questions cannot be an option; something so fundamentally horrifying as the Holocaust demands attention and engagement. Roger S. Gottlieb asserts:

> There will always be a painful gap between theoretical *explanation* and human *understanding*. We cannot master the Holocaust with our thinking, we can only deepen ourselves in our relation to it. Even if all our intellectual questions were answered, we would still cry: "But how can this be?" Nevertheless, if we are to find meanings as well as sorrow and despair, to alter our lives as well as mourn the victims, we must try to *think* this unthinkable event.

While scholars might be inclined to intellectually process information, the Holocaust forces scholars to go beyond a purely intellectual analysis and to incorporate emotional responses. Emotions are needed to access the nature of the Holocaust, but if these emotions are not intellectually processed, one will remain overwhelmed by them. Thus, the topic of the Holocaust challenges one to become involved both intellectually and emotionally, a task with which Holocaust testimonies can help best.

–CAROLINE SCHAUMANN,
EMORY UNIVERSITY

Viewpoint:
Not necessarily. While their importance is undeniable, survivor narratives are filtered by the emotional trauma of the Holocaust, which can distort memories and limit perspectives.

The question of survivor testimony in the interpretation of the Holocaust is not whether it is important but whether it is adequate. Survivor testimony undoubtedly contributes indispensable documentary evidence at the same time that it helps one orient oneself toward these events. However, it should not replace research into the social, political, economic, and cultural processes at work during this period and modern times.

While survivor testimony helps in confronting the historical, interpretive, ethical, and political questions posed by the Holocaust, the

significance and interpretation of these testimonies depend upon many other factors. The simplest way into the debates is to note that the survivor testimony breaks with the basic presupposition of normal testimony—that speaker and listener share meaning and a world. Does one require a new language of representation to capture what took place from either the victim's or the perpetrator's perspective?

On the one hand, there are those who make the world of the Holocaust contiguous with the everyday world, such as Tzvetan Todorov, who investigates the moral world of the camps, or Zygmunt Bauman, who seeks to explain how the Holocaust "brings together some ordinary factors of modernity which normally are kept apart. . . . Only the combination of factors is unusual and rare, not the factors that are combined." In this case, survivor testimony becomes part of a larger picture that includes perpetrator testimony and sociopolitical analysis. On the other hand, there are those who think the Holocaust is such a profound rupture in the fabric of history that people have a moral and epistemological obligation not to attempt to re-create it. Claude Lanzmann, who made the documentary movie *Shoah* (1985) says that between the preexisting conditions and the Holocaust there is "a gap, an abyss, and this abyss will never be bridged." Even to try to understand and represent the Holocaust is to become complicit with making it acceptable: "It is enough to formulate the question in simplistic terms—Why have Jews been killed?—for the question to reveal right away its obscenity. There is an absolute obscenity in the very project of understanding." Others such as Elie Wiesel, while less extreme than Lanzmann, nonetheless, want to place the Holocaust beyond historiography, "Auschwitz cannot be explained nor can it be visualized. . . . [T]he Holocaust transcends history." Writers and movie makers such as Wiesel and Lanzmann are not interested in establishing facts and explanatory mechanisms but in exploring a new vocabulary that will touch off a new psychological ethical, psychological, or referential relationship to these events. These challenging forms of testimony do not stand by themselves as self-evident forms of meaning; they depend upon the discourses that they are calling into question. Thus, whether one is using survivor testimony as part of an account of modernity or as a way to reconfigure the languages of representation, the testimony never stands by itself. It is always about how to understand the relationship of these texts to other texts and historical factors.

To give some concreteness to this point, one can look at survivor testimony and the dispute between intentionalists and functionalists in the explanation of the Holocaust. This

SHE DIED WITH OPEN EYES

Roma Tcharnobroda, a Polish Jew, recalls in a 1946 interview a hanging she had witnessed while she was interned at Dachau:

Tcharnobroda: A . . . that happened . . . that was soon . . . two months . . . March . . . April, May, in May, a woman was brought in. She must have . . . all at once we noticed that in the middle of the field something was standing. We really did not know what it meant. And so they had . . . what do you call it?

Boder: The gallows . . .

Tcharnobroda: the gallows erected, and this woman . . . we all had to stand for appell, we stood forming a square, facing the gallows, and then . . . the woman was compelled to fetch the chair herself. She stood upon the chair and then the SS man asked: what would be her last wish.

Boder: Yes.

Tcharnobroda: I stood then very near. She said she had no wish from the Germans. So he asked her whether she regretted her deed. So she said, she was not attempting to escape, because that was absurd. But if she only had a chance, she would have done it. She regrets nothing at all, because life at any rate has no worth, and she dies readily. But to slap him in the face, she probably was too weak. She died calmly without a single outcry. That woman was twenty three years old. Then we had to stand as punishment,—we don't know what for—but as punishment we had to stand and look at the dead woman for three hours. When the appell was over . . .

Boder: Who performed the hanging?

Tcharnobroda: An SS man. He . . .

Boder: Did she suffer much?

Tcharnobroda: No. He only swung the noose around her neck and pushed the chair away with his foot.

Boder: Did he first cover her face?

Tcharnobroda: No. She died with open eyes.

Boder: So you saw the dead woman afterwards and the face of the dead woman?

Tcharnobroda: I stood for two hours afterwards, directly in front of her at a distance of about ten meters.

Boder: How did she look?

Tcharnobroda: Perfectly calm. Her hands were stretched downward and folded.

Boder: And her face?

Tcharnobroda: . . . her face downward, fixed like this looking downward and perfectly calm as if she would have been . . . no, perfectly calm as if she slept.

Boder: No.

Tcharnobroda: Afterwards we had to stand for several hours and look at the dead. When the appell was over we did not go away. There were at that time twenty thousand women at the appell.

Source: Interview with Roma Tcharnobroda, 24 September 1946, Munich, Germany, transcribed by David P. Boder, Spool 155-B, Voices of the Holocaust: A Documentary Project by Illinois Institute of Technology <http://voices.iit.edu/frames.asp?path=Interviews/&page=tchar&ext=_t.html>.

debate hinges on the interpretation of testimony by victims and perpetrators. On one side are those who claim that the anti-Semitic intentions of the German leadership and/or general populace were the principal cause of the Holocaust. On the other side are those who think that the principal causes of the Holocaust cannot be located in individuals or in their cultural beliefs but in the general processes of modernity that deprived perpetrator and victim of a world of moral action. Intentionalists portray perpetrators as "monsters," while functionalists portray them as "ordinary."

The most recent turn in this debate is the controversy surrounding Daniel Jonah Goldhagen's *Hitler's Willing Executioners: Ordinary Germans and the Holocaust* (1996). Goldhagen maintains that the principal cause of the Holocaust was the intentions of the historical actors, intentions that were released in the political turmoil of the Third Reich. "My explanation—which is new to the scholarly literature on the perpetrators—is that the perpetrators, 'ordinary Germans,' were animated by antisemitism, by a particular type of antisemitism that led them to conclude that the Jews ought to die." Goldhagen is not just saying that widespread anti-Semitism was an enabling condition of the Holocaust but that Germans made their "choices as members of an assenting genocidal community, in which the killing of Jews was normative and often celebrated." Goldhagen offers a dramatic phenomenology of perpetrators' minds during killings in order to assign them "responsibility" for their actions.

On the other side are the alternative phenomenologies of the perpetrator, provided by Hannah Arendt and Christopher R. Browning as well as the testimony of victims such as Levi. In their view, both perpetrator and victim "lost a world." This concept does not mean that their situations are similar or that that they should be presented in a similar way. Indeed, distinguishing victim and perpetrator is crucial. However, as Levi reminds his readers, if the perpetrators become inhuman monsters, then one can easily seal oneself off from the ways in which this potential is within modern society and the modern subject.

In *Ordinary Men: Reserve Battalion 101 and the Final Solution in Poland* (1992) Browning attempts to show that it was not preexisting anti-Semitism but the extraordinary circumstances that produced their actions: "If the men of Reserve Police Battalion 101 could become killers in such circumstances what group of men cannot?" Arendt broadens the horizon of historical questions in *Eichmann in Jerusalem: A Report on the Banality of Evil* (1963). She aims to show that Adolf Eichmann was an empty shell, a totalitarian subject whose depravity resulted from "thoughtlessness." Her notorious "banality of evil" does not mean that totalitarianism is not radically evil, only that the perpetrators' actions cannot be understood by referring only to his/her internal processes or even to German culture. Rather, totalitarianism is the culmination of the modern demands for freedom, not its opposite.

Goldhagen directly contests Arendt's claim that the perpetrators had lost a world. "Contrary to Arendt's assertions, the perpetrators were not such atomized, lonely beings. They decidedly belonged to their world and had plenty of opportunities, which they obviously used, to discuss and reflect upon their exploits." However, what accompanies this reading is a different account of modernity. For Goldhagen, the historical forces that shaped these events can be localized in an ideology and worked on; from Arendt's point of view, the forces, institutions, and self-understandings that produced the Holocaust continue to damage people today. These are not just matters for professional historians but for citizens trying to decide what politicians to vote for and what kinds of textbooks should be used.

Both survivor and perpetrator testimony are thus part of what Paul Ricoeur has called the "historiographical operation." There are three moments: the documentary phase, the phase of explanation and understanding, and the historical representation in an historian's text. These moments are not linear, but recursive—for example, the historian comes to the archive with some preconceptions about historical representation. Survivor testimony contributes to all three of these phases, not just the documentary one, for it suggests or blocks certain modes of explanation and representation. Moreover, survivor testimony figures in the second-order philosophical reflection on the conditions of these discourses—that is, on historicity, one's historical condition. Ricoeur shows how the speculative historical questions of the citizen and philosopher can never be driven out by historiographical operations of historians; rather, they must accompany such explanatory concerns.

Nevertheless the danger of occasional mistaken identity exists in using survivor narratives. The most notorious case involves John Ivan Demjanjuk, suspected of being the infamous Nazi guard "Ivan the Terrible." Stripped of his U.S. citizenship, Demjanjuk was extradited to Israel in 1986. He was convicted there of war crimes and sentenced to death, but in 1993 the Israeli Supreme Court overturned that decision because of inconsistencies in corroborating documents and the testimony of eyewitnesses.

The importance of the context of interpretation to survivor testimony comes to the fore with the issue of trauma because it brings out an important dimension of the modern relationship to these testimonies. Trauma, as Cathy Caruth explains, is not an experience at all, but a skip in experience, in which the subject must shut down emotionally in order to survive. Traumatized persons, says Caruth, "become the symptom of history they cannot entirely possess." When survivors give their testimonies, they manifest the trauma, but they do not fully describe it. As Dori Laub articulates in his work with survivors, the task of the listener is to hear what cannot be spoken, to help the survivor reconstruct a self, a witness to the events that he/she had to leave psychically in order to survive. The effects of these traumas are passed on from generation to succeeding generations, as Art Spiegelmann's graphic novel *Maus: A Survivor's Tale* (1986) shows so well. The continuing appeal of survivor testimonies is that they bring one back to the events that have marked everyone in ways that they are still trying to understand. They serve as ethical guides when historians try to relativize the Holocaust by making comparisons with Stalinism or when artists trivialize it by making it the background noise in the depiction of life in the Third Reich. Testimony alone is never enough. It is only the beginning of our reengagement with the past and with ourselves.

—MEILI STEELE,
UNIVERSITY OF SOUTH CAROLINA

References

Hannah Arendt, *Eichmann in Jerusalem: A Report on the Banality of Evil*, revised edition (New York: Penguin, 1963).

Peter Baldwin, ed., *Reworking the Past: Hitler, the Holocaust, and the Historians' Debate* (Boston: Beacon, 1990).

Omer Bartov, *Murder in Our Midst: The Holocaust, Industrial Killing, and Representation* (New York: Oxford University Press, 1996).

Zygmunt Bauman, *Modernity and the Holocaust* (Ithaca, N.Y.: Cornell University Press, 1991).

Michael André Bernstein, *Foregone Conclusions: Against Apocalyptic History* (Berkeley: University of California Press, 1994).

Randolph L. Braham, *The Psychological Perspectives of the Holocaust and of its Aftermath* (Boulder, Colo.: Social Science Monographs / New York: Csengeri Institute for Holocaust Studies of the Graduate School and University Center of the City University of New York, 1988).

Christopher R. Browning, *Ordinary Men: Reserve Battalion 101 and the Final Solution in Poland* (New York: HarperCollins, 1992).

Cathy Caruth, *Trauma: Explorations in Memory* (Baltimore: Johns Hopkins University Press, 1995).

Lucy S. Dawidowicz, ed., *A Holocaust Reader* (New York: Behrman House, 1976).

Charlotte Delbo, *Auschwitz and After*, translated by Rosette C. Lamont (New Haven: Yale University Press, 1995).

Saul Friedländer, *Memory, History, and the Extermination of the Jews of Europe* (Bloomington: Indiana University Press, 1993).

Friedländer, ed., *Probing the Limits of Representation: Nazism and the "Final Solution"* (Cambridge, Mass.: Harvard University Press, 1992).

Daniel Jonah Goldhagen, *Hitler's Willing Executioners: Ordinary Germans and the Holocaust* (New York: Knopf, 1996).

Roger S. Gottlieb, ed., *Thinking the Unthinkable: Meanings of the Holocaust* (New York: Paulist Press, 1990).

Michael Halberstam, *Totalitarianism and the Modern Conception of Politics* (New Haven: Yale University Press, 1999).

Aaron Hass, *The Aftermath: Living with the Holocaust* (Cambridge & New York: Cambridge University Press, 1995).

Raul Hilberg, *Perpetrators, Victims, Bystanders: The Jewish Catastrophe 1933–1945* (New York: Aaron Asher Books, 1992).

Irving Howe, "Writing and the Holocaust," in *Writing and the Holocaust*, edited by Berel Lang (New York: Holmes & Meier, 1988), pp. 175–199.

Ruth Klüger, *Weiter leben: eine Jugend* (Göttingen: Wallstein, 1992).

Lawrence L. Langer, *Holocaust Testimonies: The Ruins of Memory* (New Haven: Yale University Press, 1991).

Primo Levi, *The Drowned and the Saved*, translated by Raymond Rosenthal (New York: Summit Books, 1988).

Levi, *Survival in Auschwitz: The Nazi Assault on Humanity*, translated by Stuart Woolf (New York: Collier-Macmillan, 1961).

Jean-François Lyotard, *The Différend: Phrases in Dispute*, translated by Georges Van Den Abbeele (Minneapolis: University of Minnesota Press, 1988).

J. Noakes and G. Pridham, *Nazism, 1919–1945: A History in Documents and Eyewitness Accounts*, volume 3 (New York: Schocken, 1990).

Paul Ricoeur, *La Mémoire, l'histoire, l'oubli* (Paris: Seuil, 2000).

Kenneth Seeskin, "Coming to Terms with Failure: A Philosophical Dilemma," in *Writing and the Holocaust*, edited by Lang (New York: Holmes & Meier, 1988), pp. 110–121.

Tzvetan Todorov, *Facing the Extreme: Moral Life in the Concentration Camps*, translated by Arthur Denner and Abigail Pollak (New York: Metropolitan, 1996).

Elie Wiesel, *Against Silence: The Voice and Vision of Elie Wiesel*, edited by Irving Abrahmson (New York: Holocaust Library, 1985).

Wiesel, *Night*, translated by Stella Rodway (New York: Hill & Wang, 1960).

James Young, *Writing and Rewriting the Holocaust: Narrative and the Consequences of Interpretation* (Bloomington: Indiana University Press, 1988).

VICTIM PSYCHOLOGY

Did the concentration camp experience rob the victims of what Bruno Bettelheim called their "psychic independence"?

Viewpoint: Yes. The concentration camp experience had the effect of rendering its victims dependent on the guards and unable to assert their full humanity in the face of extremity.

Viewpoint: No. Reliable eyewitness accounts cite many examples of dignified and courageous behavior on the part of concentration camp inmates who, despite all odds, refused to allow their humanity to be debased.

Psychologist Bruno Bettelheim argued that the dehumanizing nature of the concentration camp rendered its victims increasingly dependent on the guards, capos, and institutional order of the camps themselves. This condition, Bettelheim argued, was also true of modern mass society, which endeavored to render its inmates immature and dependent on a sometimes malevolent authority. His thesis proved to be exceedingly controversial. Survivors, in particular, felt that Bettelheim was calling upon his own relatively mild experiences as a detainee to make claims about victims of the slave-labor and death camps whose extremity, and perhaps whose courage, was far greater than his own.

Viktor E. Frankl, an Austrian psychiatrist and inmate of Auschwitz, also used his experiences in the camp to build a theoretical model of human behavior in extremis. He was particularly interested in the difference between those inmates who succumbed to despair (*musselmänner,* in camp slang—muslims) and those who, in the face of the same gnawing hunger, fear, and filth, held onto their humanity. The difference, he argued, between survivors and those who surrendered to despair was a sense of having something to live for—a will to meaning. The greatest threat to life was, oftentimes, not the gas chamber but despair, which was the aim of the concentration camp system.

Critics of both views argue that Bettelheim and Frankl allowed their theoretical frameworks rather than the evidence to determine their conclusions. People died, not because they no longer wanted to live, but because they were shot, gassed, or worked to death. The evidence, however, cuts both ways. Some concentration camp inmates surrendered their identities to the point of adopting the behaviors and values of the SS. Bettelheim pointed out that even when it might have been possible, inmates almost never resisted their captivity and rarely attempted to escape. This reaction might have reflected a survival strategy, or the physical exhaustion of inmates, or a loss of identity. Others died—or more rarely survived—because they resisted the conformity imposed on them by the camp system but, in living or dying, retained their full humanity and maturity. Most, perhaps, did a little of both.

**Viewpoint:
Yes. The concentration camp
experience had the effect of
rendering its victims dependent
on the guards and unable to
assert their full humanity in
the face of extremity.**

It is never safe to generalize about the concentration camp experience. For many—perhaps most—of the women and men who passed through the gates of Auschwitz and Sobibor, their stay was brief. They never became prisoners, just transients on their way to the gas chambers and the crematoriums. For others, especially for political prisoners and ordinary criminals, the camps were brutal—and often deadly—but the surviving individuals emerged fundamentally unchanged. Even in the slave-labor camps there were degrees of privation and abuse. Responses to the concentration camp experience varied as well. It is safe, however, to suggest that those inmates who were not given special privileges or who were not murdered outright on their arrival experienced a system in which they were subjected to a regimen designed to dehumanize and paralyze the human psyche. Though many inmates retained a vital spark of independence and though survivors of the camps were able to reassert their autonomous humanity after liberation, under the extreme conditions of the Nazi concentration camps, inmates came to surrender a degree of psychic integrity as the price of (even temporary) survival.

Survival in the camps required inmates to live by the camp rules made by the SS. Standing up for oneself, insisting on one's autonomy, or refusing to submit to the horrors of life in the camp was to invite torture and death. Many—perhaps most—inmates retained a secret reserve of independent will, but survival meant recognizing one's absolute dependence on guards and administrators. External subservience came to shape the inmates' internal attitudes toward the guards and toward themselves. The terror of the concentration camp, hunger, overwork, the constant threat of death, and the sense that none of this treatment would ever end forced long-term inmates to bury their autonomy as the price of survival. Those who survived the camps and rejoined the land of the living had to struggle to restore their psychic independence before they could feel at home in the post-Holocaust world.

This thesis is widely associated with Bruno Bettelheim, a psychoanalyst and survivor of a year and a half in Nazi concentration camps. Bettelheim's critics have pointed out that though he claimed to have based his arguments on his own experiences in Dachau and Buchenwald and on conversations he had with other inmates, his experience, however terrifying, was far less extreme than those of inmates in Auschwitz and other death and slave-labor camps. It is far from clear what Bettelheim experienced as a prisoner. He received packages and assistance from home and was eventually released thanks to the influence of family and friends. His work assignments in the camp were also far less life-threatening than those imposed on many inmates. Furthermore, some critics have contended that many of the experiences he cites to support his contentions were fabricated. Even more problematic, Bettelheim seems to be using his concentration camp experience to buttress a larger argument about the totalitarian nature of modern mass society. The camp, Bettelheim argued, put inmates into an impossible situation: surrender your identity; become a number, a unit in this seething mass of not-humanity; accept your not-humanness and in so doing live a little longer and a little less painfully. Or die. It did not matter because an inmate had already joined the ranks of the not-human. In surrendering one's individual autonomy as the price of survival, one has lost the struggle already. Thus, he argued, the concentration camp serves as a human laboratory in which trends already implicit in modern mass society are rendered in their most extreme forms. Inmate behavior in the extreme situation of the camps reflects the sort of behavior to be expected in any other totalitarian society.

Bettelheim's interpretation of inmate behavior has been seen as an implicit criticism of the Nazis' victims, most of whom, it seemed to Bettelheim, went passively to their deaths. Had they asserted their autonomy, even in the face of certain death, they could have slowed the workings of the machinery of extermination, saved others, and gone to their own deaths as free, autonomous individuals. This interpretation has been harshly criticized—and for good reason—but Bettelheim's underlying argument that inmates became psychologically dependent on their tormentors remains valid. One does not need to blame the victims of Nazi oppression to measure the psychological impact of that oppression or to argue that people responded differently in the face of extremity.

Discounting Bettelheim's rather suspect evidence, one still finds substantial support for his thesis. Viktor E. Frankl argued that "an abnormal reaction to an abnormal situation is normal," and in the circumstances of Auschwitz, apathy became a "necessary defense mechanism." Indeed, according to Frankl, the constant strain of camp life, "coupled with the constant necessity of concentrating on the task of staying alive, forced the prisoner's inner life down to a primitive level." Frankl identified this as "regression"—a retreat to a more primitive form of mental life.

A man's character became involved to the point that he was caught in a mental turmoil that threatened all the values he held and threw them into doubt. Under the influence of a world that no longer recognized the value of human life and human dignity, which had robbed man of his will and had made him an object to be exterminated (having planned, however, to make full use of him first—to the last ounce of his physical resources)—under this influence the personal ego finally suffered a loss of values. If the man in the concentration camp did not struggle against this in a last effort to save his self-respect, he lost the feeling of being an individual, a being with a mind, with inner freedom and personal value. He thought of himself then as only a part of an enormous mass of people; his existence descended to the level of animal life.

This reaction is clearly demonstrable in far less extreme situations. Military recruits, if they are to succeed as soldiers, must quickly abandon their civilian values and behaviors and adopt those of the drill sergeant. New prisoners in even the most "normal" and humane of penal institutions are pressed to lose their autonomy—in effect, their adulthood—as the cost of getting along in such a society.

Frankl and others have pointed out that those who most readily survived were the ideologically and intellectually motivated, those who had something outside of themselves to live for—a cause, a faith, anything. Yet, prisoners could survive only by becoming invisible, by seeing nothing, by blending into the crowd, and by losing the virtues that made them mature.

The unavoidable problem of Auschwitz is that people indeed walked, under their own power and without overt resistance, into the gas chambers. They obeyed the guards even when they knew, or suspected, what awaited them inside the heavy metal doors. Why? Were there no options? Could they not have resisted? Fought back even if only to retain their honor? Bettelheim implicitly blamed this seeming failure of nerve in the moment of extremity on the Jewishness of most of the victims—resistance is futile, just try to get along, and wait until the pogrom is over so that the nation can survive. This conclusion has been rightfully criticized and rejected. It was not the Jewishness of the victims that rendered them like sheep led to the slaughter, but their civility. Nothing had prepared them for this reality. Communists, Jehovah's Witnesses, and others who had previously come to expect persecution and hardship seem to have held onto their psychic integrity better than many middle-class Jews who had little psychological preparation for the extremity of the camps.

RESISTANCE BY FAITH

In 1944 some female inmates at Auschwitz-Birkenau practiced a form of resistance by performing a rite on a Jewish holiday:

But this particular year, in 1944, when I was there, one day, some of the older women—and by older I mean they could have been 35 or 40 years old (to a 15 year old anyone who is over 30, looks old)—asked these two specific *Kapos* (high-ranking prisoners) for permission to do something for *Kol Nidre* (the Eve of Yom Kippur) . . .

So, we asked for and received, one candle and one *siddur* (prayer book). We were about 800 women jam-packed in one barrack. Everybody came: the believers, the atheists, the Orthodox women, the agnostics, women of all descriptions and of every background. We were all there.

The two *Kapos* gave us only ten minutes and they were guarding the two entrances to the barrack to watch out for any SS guard who might happen to come around—unexpectedly.

Then, someone lit this lone candle—and a hush fell over the barrack. I can still see this scene: the woman, sitting with the lit candle, started to read the *Kol Nidre* passage in the *siddur*. Incredibly, all of this happened in a place where, we felt, it was appropriate that instead of we asking forgiveness from God, God should be asking for forgiveness from us.

And yet, we all wanted to gather around the woman with the lit candle and *siddur*.

She recited the *Kol Nidre* very slowly, so that we could repeat the words if we so desired. But we didn't. Instead, the women burst out in a cry—in unison. Our prayer was the sound of this incredible cry of 800 women.

Source: *Judy (Weissenberg) Cohen, "A Most Memorable Kol Nidre," Women and the Holocaust: A Cyberspace of Their Own <http://www.interlog.com/~mighty/>.*

The women and men who survived the dehumanization of the concentration camp experience could not immediately pick up the threads of their interrupted lives and move on. The psychological, not to mention physical, impact of the camp experience was too great. Having been so radically deprived of their autonomy, the task of restoring it required as much courage and strength of will as surviving the camps in the first place. In many ways, recovering from the Nazi assault on their humanity became the work of a lifetime.

—TANDY MCCONNELL,
COLUMBIA COLLEGE

Viewpoint:
No. Reliable eyewitness accounts cite many examples of dignified and courageous behavior on the part of concentration camp inmates who, despite all odds, refused to allow their humanity to be debased.

A Kansas City neighbor of Holocaust survivor Jack Mandelbaum, director of the Midwest Holocaust Education Center in Overland Park, Kansas, once asked him what kinds of games he played in the concentration camp. The shocked survivor replied, "There was only one game in the concentration camp. The Nazis were trying to kill me and I was trying to stay alive." Perpetrators of the Holocaust knew that for their victims to survive it was necessary for those detainees to hold on to their identity as integral human beings. The Nazis therefore attempted to dehumanize the inmates in every way possible. The inmates did everything they could to preserve a sense of human dignity. When reading memoirs of Holocaust survivors, a dialectic between dehumanization and human dignity is clearly observable: between the techniques of dehumanization of concentration camp detainees and the methods used by the concentration camp survivors to resist the fate intended for them.

Despite the cruel and efficacious methods of dehumanization, many inmates attempted to rehumanize themselves in order to maintain their will to live. Many inmates refused to succumb to the thought that their deaths were inevitable. According to Primo Levi:

> Sooner or later in life everyone discovers that perfect happiness is unrealizable, but there are few who pause to consider the antithesis: that perfect unhappiness is equally unattainable. The obstacles preventing the realization of both these extreme states are of the same nature: they derive from our human condition which is opposed to everything infinite. Our ever-insufficient knowledge of the future opposes it: and this is called, in the one instance, hope, and in the other, uncertainty of the following day. The certainty of death opposes it: for it places a limit on every joy, but also on every grief. The inevitable material cares oppose it: for as they poison every lasting happiness, they equally assiduously distract us from our misfortunes and make our consciousness of them intermittent and hence supportable.

The unpredictability of the future and the realization that the Nazi tyrants were at war with the Allied Powers planted the seeds of resistance in many inmates who tenaciously clung to life even under the most desperate circumstances. It is necessary to examine the ways in which concentration camp inmates tried to maintain their humanity in order to hold on to that quintessential recognition of their dignity, without which survival was impossible. Such means included religion, literature, semiorganized instruction, and acts of defiance.

Ruth Klüger recollects seeing the famous rabbi Leo Baeck preaching from the roofs of Theresienstadt, trying to console the inmates. He gave theological sermons on the fact that God's time is not man's time and that humankind must have patience with God's calendar, implying, in a subtle way, that the Nazis would not last forever. Klüger felt personally inspired by the sermon, and she also remembers Zionist discussions among her Jewish coreligionists. Her conscious thoughts were saturated with Zionism because it was the philosophy that made the most sense to her. She recalls singing Zionist songs with companions her own age.

Semiorganized instruction was also a vehicle for rehumanization. Although organized instruction for the children of Theresienstadt was forbidden, there were clandestine attempts to calm the children's fears by imparting knowledge of art and literature to them. This teaching was forbidden because the Jewish intellect was viewed by the Nazis as being a danger even in a concentration camp situation because of its power to revitalize the victims they wanted to destroy. The ban on learning made the children value learning all the more. Theresienstadt contained people of a variety of intellectual endeavors and ideological leanings who were capable of providing instruction. Teachers, professors, rabbis, and museum curators led discussion groups of eager children, who learned to break up quickly when a German inspection was imminent.

Klüger also writes about the consoling effect that her knowledge of the German classics had on her. Knowing the best of what German classicism had produced helped give her the strength to survive the worst of what German barbarism had produced. She poignantly describes the importance poetry had for the inmates' survival:

> I am not telling anything unusual when I say I would have recited and composed poems anywhere where I would have been. Many concentration camp inmates found consolation in the verses they knew by heart. . . . Most of them mention poems with religious or philosophical themes or such poems that had a special emotional value during their childhood. Incidentally, it appears to me that the theme of a poem was of secondary importance: the most important thing in giving us support was the form of the verse, the rhyme itself.

VICTIM PSYCHOLOGY

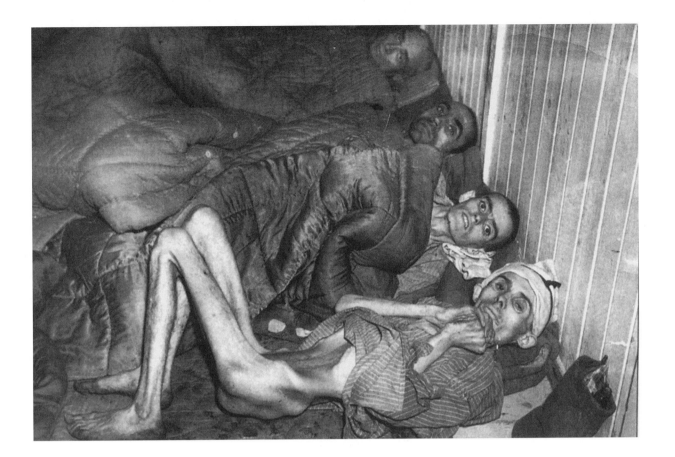

Survivors of the
Buchenwald
concentration
camp, 1945

She writes about using verse and rhyme to convince herself that continued life was a worthwhile goal. Simcha Bunem Unsdorfer similarly recalls how he took solace as a concentration camp prisoner in Auschwitz by rewriting the Jewish sacred texts of the Haggadah on scraps of paper and how it kept him from dwelling on the likelihood of a tragic future: "Happy memories were brought back to my mind of my childhood, and of the *Seder Nights* at home, when I sat at our table listening excitedly and attentively to Father's recital of the *Haggadah* which he always did so beautifully and inspiringly." He specifically credits his rewriting of Jewish lore with helping him to survive: "It was a reminder that our people have gone through many difficult and tragic experiences in our long history, and have been freed each time, by the will of God, from bondage and slavery."

Those people facing the worst scourges of humanity could increase their chances of survival by recalling the best that humanity had accomplished, because it had a consoling and benevolently animating effect. Literary scholar Andrea Reiter writes that withdrawal into art offered the detainees a welcome opportunity to forget temporarily the brutal reality of the concentration camps and thereby conquer their fears. It should be mentioned that literary activity seldom took the form of reading or writing but usually reminiscing about favorite books, reciting memorized

poems, or trying to create original poems and then committing them to memory.

Another factor that had a rehumanizing effect on the victims and increased their chances of survival were clever acts of defiance. Such an act is described by Anja Lundholm. The privileged inmate Wanda, who served as a brothel madam for the SS, was killed by several female inmates in retaliation for her sexual exploitation of them. An organized group of inmates subsequently decided to confiscate her foodstuffs and distribute them to other inmates. A kapo had custody of Wanda's goods, but during an air raid the inmates were able to break into the kapo's apartment and confiscate fruit preserves, bread, butter, salami, and chocolate. The women ate their fill and, after realizing that they could not keep their stolen goods in secrecy, decided to distribute them to women and children in different barracks, where the presence of the stolen goods was less likely to arouse suspicion. This act in turn had a rehumanizing impact on the women and led them to put forth a greater moral resistance to the forces threatening their survival.

The dialectic between dehumanization and preservation of human dignity is portrayed most vividly by Klüger in her account of the Nazi evacuation of the last concentration camp at which she was detained, Christianstadt, a satellite camp of Gross-Rosen. The Nazis, fearing an impending liberation by the Allies, wished to erase all traces of the brutal concentration camp. When the Nazis knew that the liberation of the concentration camps was imminent, it was their policy not to abandon the detainees to the would-be liberators but to forcibly march them to other concentration camps. Many prisoners perished as a result of these inhumane procedures intended to thwart their impending liberation. As Klüger and her mother were subjected to a death march, her mind turned toward escape, while her mother was reticent to risk it. Klüger describes the events that led them to flee from the Nazi tyrants:

> There was an alluring feeling coming from the land. It was early February 1945, and despite the cold weather, the air had a feeling of early spring and the seductive draw of this season to it. There outside was a feeling of comfort that did not make its way toward us, but nonetheless seemed within reach. We could sense it, mere steps away from the unnaturalness of our existence, from the misery of the camp, that we bore on our back, together with our blanket and eating utensils. Very near to us was nature, silent, organic. Away, now, immediately. My mother wanted to wait for the next bread ration. I argued against her bitterly and with conviction. As much to eat as they were giving us, especially recently, could be easily found. Now or never, no one is looking, they are busy and are probably tired themselves.

During the early stages of the death march Klüger found herself healthy enough to feel spring fever, which intensified her desire to be free of her captors. Klüger, who was an avid reader of eighteenth-century dramatist Friedrich Schiller and who credits her knowledge of his work with helping her to survive the camps, was perhaps thinking of Schiller's phrase, "It is better to fall into God's hands than men's." Her mother's life, however, revolved around bread rations, and she was reluctant to surrender this vestigial tracing of security. Klüger's youthfulness prevailed, and the women, along with four fellow inmates, made their dramatic escape from the snares of Adolf Hitler's apocalyptic henchmen.

Levi describes organized acts of resistance at Auschwitz-Birkenau, including the blowing up of a crematorium:

> Last month one of the crematoriums at Birkenau had been blown up. None of us knows (and perhaps no one will ever know) exactly how the exploit was carried out: there was talk of the *Sonderkommando*, the Special Commando attached to the gas chambers and the ovens, which is itself periodically exterminated, and which is kept scrupulously segregated from the rest of the camp. The fact remains that a few hundred men at Birkenau, helpless and exhausted slaves like ourselves, had found in themselves the strength to act, to mature the fruits of their hatred.

Levi counteracts the stereotype of cowering, infantile concentration camp inmates by demonstrating that some inmates greeted the camp administration with an organized show of force. Internees sometimes reacted to the forces of death with dignity and heroism, even under the most unbearable and degrading of circumstances:

> The man who is to die in front of us today in some way took part in the revolt. They said he had contacts with the rebels of Birkenau, that he carried arms into our camp, that he was plotting a simultaneous mutiny among us. He is to die before our very eyes: and perhaps the Germans do not understand that this solitary death, this man's death which has been reserved for him, will bring him glory, not infamy. . . . Everybody heard the cry of the doomed man, it pierced through the old thick barriers of inertia and submissiveness, it struck the living core of man in each of us: *Kamaraden, ich bin der Letz!* (Comrades, I am the last one!).

The condemned man's amazing show of courage and resoluteness at the moment of his death demonstrates the limits of the Nazis' ability to dehumanize and infantilize the inmates. Olga Lengyel, a former medical student who was detained at Auschwitz, also witnessed the blowing up of the crematorium, and she explained it thusly:

> The revolt was organized by a young French Jew named David. Knowing that he was condemned to death anyway, since all members of the *Sonderkommando* were liquidated every three or four months, he decided to employ usefully what little time of life remained to him. It was he who had obtained the explosives and he who had hidden them.

It is clear from the descriptions of both Levi and Lengyel that this David was a man of great moral suasion and inner strength who preserved his humanity under the bleakest of circumstances unto the moment of his public execution. It was the observation of people such as David that led Lengyel to comment:

> I saw many internees cling to their human dignity to the very end. The Nazis succeeded in degrading them physically, but they could not debase them morally. Because of these few, I have not entirely lost my faith in mankind. If, even in the jungle of Birkenau, all were not necessarily inhuman to their fellowmen, then there is hope indeed. It is that hope which keeps me alive.

–PETER R. ERSPAMER,
FORT HAYS STATE UNIVERSITY

References

Bruno Bettelheim, *Freud's Vienna and Other Essays* (New York: Knopf, 1990).

Bettelheim, *The Informed Heart: Autonomy in a Mass Age* (Glencoe, Ill.: Free Press, 1960).

Peter R. Erspamer, "Women before Hell's Gate: Survivors of the Holocaust and their Memoirs," in *Literature and Ethnic Discrimination,* edited by Michael J. Meyer (Amsterdam & Atlanta: Rodopi, 1997), pp. 171–186.

Michel Foucault, *Discipline and Punish: The Birth of the Prison,* translated by Alan Sheridan (London: Allen Lane, 1977).

Viktor E. Frankl, *Man's Search for Meaning: An Introduction to Logotherapy* (Boston: Beacon Press, 1963), revised edition of *From Death-Camp to Existentialism: A Psychiatrist's Path to a New Therapy,* translated by Ilse Lasch (Boston: Beacon, 1959).

Otto Friedrich, *The Kingdom of Auschwitz* (New York: HarperPerennial, 1994).

Ruth Klüger, *Weiter Leben: Eine Jugend* (Göttingen: Wallstein, 1992).

Olga Lengyel, *I Survived Hitler's Ovens: The Story of Auschwitz* (New York: Avon, 1947).

Primo Levi, *Survival in Auschwitz: The Nazi Assault on Humanity,* translated by Stuart Woolf (New York: Collier, 1961).

Anja Lundholm, *Das Höllentor: Bericht einer Überlebenden* (Hamburg: Rowohlt, 1988).

Richard Pollak, *The Creation of Dr. B.: A Biography of Bruno Bettelheim* (New York: Simon & Schuster, 1997).

Theron Raines, *Rising to the Light: A Portrait of Bruno Bettelheim* (New York: Knopf, 2002).

Andrea Reiter, *Auf daß sie entsteigen der Dunkelheit: Die literarische Bewältigung von KZ-Erfahrung* (Vienna: Löcker, 1995); translated by Patrick Camiller as *Narrating the Holocaust* (London & New York: Continuum, 2000).

S. B. Unsdorfer, *The Yellow Star* (New York: Yoseloff, 1961).

THE VICTIMS

Did the Nazi T–4 euthanasia program discriminate among victims in the targeted groups?

Viewpoint: Homosexuals received different treatment from other targeted groups.

Viewpoint: Trial Nazi extermination programs initially targeted the disabled, sick, and aged, but their function was to develop procedures for the indiscriminate extermination of non-Aryans.

Nancy C. Unger and J. Michael Butler take up the question of the targeting of Jews for elimination in the Holocaust. Was this emphasis a special case or part of a broader spectrum of elimination policies designed to rid Germany of all groups designated as undesirable by Nazi ideology—including homosexuals, Gypsies, and the mentally ill?

Unger argues for the specificity of the targeting of the Jewish population for extermination by comparing it to the case of homosexuals. Homosexual men were incarcerated in the death camps, and many were killed in the course of the Holocaust, but, Unger argues, their targeting was quite different and far more selective than that of Jews. As she notes, not all homosexual men were incarcerated, and their treatment in the camps was substantially different from that of Jews. This difference in treatment does not minimize the brutality or depravity of the victimization of male homosexuals but marks it as a specific case, not to be identified simply with the assault on European Jewry that was the central feature of German exterminationist policy. Unger's article suggests that each target of the Holocaust was special and that to imagine otherwise is a simplification that does not do full justice to the victims of the death camps.

Butler argues that though the final structure of the extermination camps was centrally focused on the Jewish population, the techniques and practices that camp directors employed derived from a more conceptually broad eugenic euthanasia program initiated in 1939. Looking back to nineteenth-century German race theory, Butler suggests that an intellectual climate increasingly friendly toward the goal of a spurious racial purity in Germany enabled a euthanasia program to begin that initially targeted disabled children, the chronically ill, and the aged. Jews became a target as the program became more successful, as Germany expanded, and as public outcry about the initial targets of the T–4 program (collective euthanasia programs headquartered in a Berlin villa at Tiergarten Street Number 4) grew. Carefully describing the tools developed by the T–4 program, Butler asserts that the Holocaust was a more successful and larger-scale version of extermination programs that were already under way in Germany.

Is the Holocaust different from other genocidal assaults? Or, are there common features in all genocides? These are among the questions raised in this section—questions that remain vital as contemporary society grapples with the aftermaths of genocides in many different places. Questions about history and debates about answers are crucial in understanding not only the past but also the present as well.

Viewpoint:
Homosexuals received different treatment from other targeted groups.

The Jews were not the only victims of the Holocaust. While homosexuals were indeed targets of Nazi hatred, those persecuted expressly for their homosexuality were victimized in drastically smaller numbers, in different ways, and for different reasons than were Jews. Several factors distinguish the treatment of homosexuals from the persecution of Jews, and also from fellow non-Jewish prisoners, including trade unionists, communists, Gypsies, and Jehovah's Witnesses. Among the non-Jewish prisoners in the camps, homosexuals marked by the pink triangle lacked the racial, religious, or ideological identity and unity of their fellow prisoners. Moreover, they suffered some of the harshest conditions and were frequently treated as the lowest of the low. But more than their harsh treatment, small numbers and lack of group identity set them apart.

During the period of Nazi domination, some men known to the authorities to be homosexuals, including several prominent members of the art world, were (unlike Jews, prominent or otherwise) expressly excluded from persecution. Another major difference between the persecution of Jews and the persecution of homosexuals was that the total number of people sent to concentration camps exclusively for the crime of homosexuality (somewhere between 5,000 and 15,000, with 10,000 being the generally agreed-upon best estimate), virtually all were men. Although lesbians were sometimes designated as such within the camps, sexual relations between women were not illegal under German law. Men convicted of homosexual acts (under the infamous Paragraph 175 of the German criminal code, expanded in 1935 to include all forms of male homosexual contact) and sent to prison were not deemed "unworthy of life," a designation applied to Jews. In the majority of cases men convicted of homosexuality were spared the camp experience. Those who were not spared landed in concentration, rather than extermination, camps, although the end result—death—was frequently the same. The final distinction between the Jewish and homosexual experiences was that the legal persecution of homosexuals continued for decades following World War II (1939–1945), while the story of their victimization at the hands of the Nazis remained, until quite recently, zealously repressed.

Much of the pioneering work on sexuality, including same-sex sexuality, was carried out by German Jews. For decades prior to the Nazi rise to power, leading sex researcher Magnus Hirschfeld promoted homosexual rights, engendering much controversy even among his fellow sexologists. His Scientific-Humanitarian Committee sought to alter Paragraph 175, which, beginning in 1871, defined sexual activities between men (or between men and animals) throughout the German Empire as perverse offenses, punishable by imprisonment for up to four years in conjunction with a loss of citizenship. In 1910 Hirschfeld abandoned his belief that homosexuals constituted a biologically distinct gender. However, an unintentional result of his previous, tireless efforts to identify homosexuals as a "third sex" was wide acceptance of homosexuals as not just medically unique but morally inferior.

The confluence of anti-Semitism, antifeminism, and homophobia in the sexual ideology of Nazism first curtailed, then prevented, and finally destroyed all German sex research and a flourishing sex-reform movement. Although the same-sex sexual activities of early Nazi leader Ernst Röhm and others active in Adolf Hitler's rise to power were hardly secret, Hitler never approved of homosexuality, which he considered a weakness. Some six years before the Night of the Long Knives (1934)—that resulted in the death of Röhm and other high-ranking SA officials, including several known to be homosexual—Hitler's National Socialist Party formally declared, "Those who are considering love between men or between women are our enemies. . . . Therefore, we reject all immorality, especially love between men, because it deprives us of our last chance to free our people from the chains of slavery." In 1933, in one of their earliest official acts of terror, the Nazis plundered the Institute for Sexual Science in Berlin, established by Hirschfeld in 1919, destroying an enormous body of research and photographs.

The 1935 redrafting of Paragraph 175 expanded the range of sexual acts that were punishable offenses to include same-sex kissing and fondling, and even passive observance of such acts. The following year the Federal Security Department for Combating Homosexuality and Abortion was created in the Berlin Gestapo headquarters. Along with a comprehensive antihomosexual propaganda campaign came many acts of terror and brutality as police and the Gestapo targeted meeting places, clubs, and associations reputed to be frequented by homosexuals.

The 1936–1937 show trials were designed to discredit the Catholic Church by presenting it as a hotbed of sexual depravity. However, the Nazis were disappointed in the results. Of a total of 4,000 members of monastic orders, for example, only seven were found guilty of crimes under Paragraph 175. The effort to

Article titled "Wandering Race: Combating the Gypsy Plague," from *NS-Rechtsspiegel,* **Munich, 21 February 1939**

(Bildarchiv Preussischer Kulturbesitz, Berlin)

Fahrendes Volk

Die Bekämpfung der Zigeunerplage auf neuen Wegen

Die Zigeuner sind für das Reich, für Volk und Staat eine akute Gefahr. Wer sie erfolgreich bekämpfen will, muß die Zigeuner zunächst — frei von allen romantischen Vorstellungen und Gefühlsduseleien — nach ihrer Herkunft, ihrer Rasse, ihren Sitten, ihrer Lebensart kennenlernen und sie sehen, wie sie wirklich sind.

Zigeuner, die als mehr oder weniger „heldische" Gestalten durch moderne Operetten und Zigeunerfilme gaukeln, sind Romanfiguren, die unser Mitgefühl und unsere Sympathie erwecken sollen. Sie können uns nicht irre machen im Kampf gegen jene Zigeuner, die, nie seßhaft, immer in Horden auf Fahrt mit Karren und Wohnwagen, neuerdings sogar mit Kraftwagen umherziehen, jede ernste und ehrliche Arbeit ablehnen und unter dem Deckmantel des Hausierens oder als Schirmflicker, Scherenschleifer, Kesselflicker, Korbflechter, Siebmacher als Wahrsager, kleine Schausteller, stets aber in Wirklichkeit durch versteckten Bettel und Eigentumsdelikte ihren Lebensunterhalt suchen.

Nicht jeder allerdings, der als „Fahrender" ein „Zigeunerleben" führt, ist auch ein Zigeuner. Die echten Zigeuner sind eine eigene, der unseren artfremde Rasse. Es sind die stammechten Zigeuner, die sich schon in ihrem Aussehen, ihrer Sprache und in ihren Sitten von anderem „fahrenden Volk" unterscheiden, und zwar stolz unterscheiden. Denn stolz ist der echte Zigeuner auf die Zugehörigkeit zu seinem Volk und zu seiner Rasse.

Heute wissen wir*, daß die Zi-

* Vgl. R. Ritter: „Zigeuner und Landfahrer" in „Der nichtshafte Mensch", C. H. Beckse Verlagsbuchhandlung München 1938.

geuner aus Indien stammen. Nach alten Chroniken tauchen sie um das Jahr 1417 zum erstenmal in Deutschland auf; damals noch in großen Gemeinschaften geführt von Zigeuner„königen" und „grafen". Der Weg, den sie von Indien zu uns nahmen, läßt sich aus der Zigeunersprache, die im wesentlichen indoarischen Ursprungs zu sein scheint, und zwar aus den vielen Ausdrücken feststellen, die der persischen — auch der Name „Zigeuner" wird von dem persischen Wort cengi, d. h. Musikant, hergeleitet —, arabischen, armenischen, türkischen, griechischen und ungarischen Sprache entstammen.

In Deutschland sind sie dann besonders im Süden, und zwar im Böhmer Wald, im Schwarzwald, in Ober- und Niederbayern, in der Pfalz

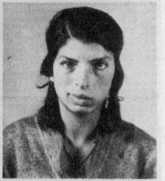

und in Hessen, aber auch im Braunschweigischen, im Harz und in Thüringen hervorgetreten. Hier sind ihre Wanderbezirke, in denen sie früher in großen Sippschaften und Stämmen, oft unter Stammeshäuptlingen, umherzogen und wo sie heute noch „zu Hause" sind. Es entstanden auch

Die Lichtbilder zeigen drei typische Zigeuner. Sie gehören einer Zigeunerbande an, die seit Jahren mit Wohnwagen als Werkzeugschleifer im Reich umherzog und 1937 aufgelöst wurde. Ihre wirklichen Namen und ihre Staatsangehörigkeit waren bisher trotz umfangreicher, auch mit ausländischen Behörden geführter Verhandlungen nicht einwandfrei festzustellen. Alle drei befinden sich seit fast zwei Jahren im Arbeitshaus.

---

spur a massive exodus of the faithful from the church was a colossal failure. The persecution of homosexuals, however, remained a Nazi mainstay. In 1937 head of German police Heinrich Himmler declared, at his elite SS training academy, that homosexuals were not just "cowards" but also warned, "If this vice continues, it will be the end of Germany," because only "nations with many children can gain supremacy and mastery of the world." By this logic, German male homosexuals were a greater threat to national security than were gay men of the countries conquered by the Nazis (where treatment of homosexuals following occupation varied from place to place). The systematic registration and persecution of

homosexuals increased as the Gestapo registered some 90,000 German homosexual men (of an estimated total of 1.2 million) from 1937 to 1939 alone.

Persecution of German homosexuals intensified and targeted virtually all levels of society. Scholar Richard Plant estimates that between 50,000 and 63,000 males, including nearly 4,000 juveniles, were convicted of homosexuality from 1933 to 1944. Even members of the German military were not exempt. Of the roughly 4,800 men sentenced for same-sex activities in 1941, more than 1,100 were in the armed forces. Although ever stricter directives were enacted to punish gay men in the military, with the increasing manpower shortages after 1943, these policies were not enforced. Accusations of homosexuality, however, continued to be frequently included in charges against persons perceived as enemies of the Reich.

Conviction on charges of homosexuality guaranteed punishment but usually not detention in a concentration camp. In one study of Gestapo files from three German regions, about 80 percent of men accused of homosexuality were sent to prison. The length of sentence depended upon the number of proven sexual partners. So-called protective custody and detention in concentration camps was ordered in 7 to 10 percent of the cases, with 325 of 413 men in "protective custody" placed in Lichtenburg concentration camp. In July of 1940 Himmler declared that men who had engaged in sexual practices with more than one male partner were to be taken into "police preventive custody" after their release from prison. Exceptions included men who had been castrated and medically proved not to be at risk for homosexual relapse.

To designate convicted homosexuals within the camps, badges imprinted with "175," or insignia bearing a large letter "A" (generally understood to indicate anal intercourse) were replaced from about 1937 forward with pink triangles sewn onto camp uniforms. The bearer of a pink triangle could be considered "incurably sick" and therefore a candidate for extermination. There was, however, another alternative. While Jews were targeted for extinction because of their alleged inherent and unchangeable inferiority, the Nazi goal was, ostensibly, to eliminate homosexuality by the "reeducation" of homosexuals. Experiments designed to cure homosexuality included those carried out by Danish SS Sturmbannfuhrer and endocrinologist Caril Vaernet. With the German SS Haupsturmfuhrer and surgeon Gerhard Schiedlausky, Vaernet implanted synthetic hormones in fifteen human subjects, resulting in more than one death. Homosexual prisoners in Buchenwald were also subjected to castration (some on a "voluntary" basis, in the hope of being released) and others were made the subjects of experiments to develop immunization against typhus fever, resulting in many agonizing deaths.

The Nazis targeted every Jewish man, woman, and child for extermination. Homosexuals were targeted on a far more selective basis. Affection between German Aryan women was generally accepted as evidence of women's more emotional and affectionate nature. Unlike their male counterparts, women who preferred intimate relations with their own sex were perceived as not precluded from the heterosexual activities vital to the much-desired rising birth rate. Generally, German women were perceived to be carrying out their "natural sphere" as dedicated wives and mothers, providing soldiers for future Nazi conquests and "outbreeding inferior races." Lesbianism alone was rarely the cause of persecution, since it was not a crime. Nonetheless, six lesbians were arrested from 1933 to 1944. And although technically exempt from Paragraph 175, women thought to be sexually involved with other women exclusively (as with men suspected of sexual involvement with other men) were considered generally suspect, closely scrutinized, and subject to arrest on other charges. Lesbians identified as such within the camps, like their male counterparts, suffered unspeakably and were subjected to, among other tortures, repeated rapes.

A case study of male homosexual inmates in Buchenwald reveals that the first prisoner listed as a "175er" was registered in January 1938. The numbers declined to just a few in the early part of 1940 because 27 homosexuals were sent to the notorious Mauthausen, a concentration camp for "serious criminals, inmates with little chance of reeducation." Altogether, some 500 men were brought to Buchenwald as punishment for their homosexuality, representing about 25 percent of the total inmate population. During 1942 there was a peak in the number of homosexuals sent to camps, accounting for about 25 percent of their commitals, but information on the numbers, treatment, and ultimate fate of gay men sent to all camps remains fragmentary.

Incomplete records are not the only barrier to learning about homosexual victims of the Holocaust. With homophobia rampant, and sexual acts between consenting males remaining a criminal offense in Germany for decades, survivors were often reluctant to come forward to tell their stories. Certainly, the Nazis' ability to tap into and intensify preexisting homophobia ensured that gay men sent to camps were not just brutalized by their captors but distrusted and ostracized by their fellow prisoners. Homosexuals were almost never, for example, granted the minor positions of power among the prison population that came with tasks such as the distribution of food or labor assignments. The heterogeneity of homosexuals, who came from all walks of life and were in all other ways equally diverse, made difficult any bonding through group identification among themselves. Although homosexual practices existed throughout the camps among members of virtually all designations of prisoners, men marked with the pink triangle were ostracized, frequently segregated, and consigned to the lowest caste in camp. Attractive young men, homosexual and heterosexual alike, could sometimes curry favor as *Puppenjungen* (toy boys) to more powerful inmates, or even guards and camp officers, but such relationships were frequently unstable and fraught with danger.

The surviving records reveal the mortality rate of homosexuals to be higher than that of political prisoners or Jehovah's Witnesses. Wolfgang Roll's study of Buchenwald reveals that about 50 percent of inmates identified by the pink triangle died, exclusive of the unknown percentage who died among the 238 transferred from Buchenwald to other camps. Homosexual men sent to Buchenwald were targeted for "extermination through work" in the quarry with the result that 75 percent of the homosexual deaths recorded by the SS occurred within a period of six weeks after the prisoners' arrival in camp. Although the Nazis distinguished among "normal" homosexuals, "relapsed" heterosexuals, and "homosexual Jews" (the last being doubly stigmatized throughout the camps), the number of homosexuals not designated as such among the Jewish (and non-Jewish) dead remains unknown.

While all Holocaust survivors suffered immeasurably, those persecuted expressly for their homosexuality faced unique difficulties after liberation. Unlike Jews, many were the only members of the families to have been in a camp; yet, their release was frequently met with ongoing ostracism rather than reunion. Others suffered from the judicial decision of some of the liberation armies that time served in a camp did not constitute prison time, and therefore jail terms for the crime of homosexuality still needed to be completed. None were granted even the minimal restitution made available to Jews, political prisoners, or other former inmates.

Efforts continue to eliminate the ongoing persecution of homosexuals and rectify the denial of their victimization under the Nazis. Scholars have stepped up the investigations that began in earnest in the 1970s concerning the Nazi persecution of homosexuals. In the 1980s the pink triangle was adopted as a symbol of defiance against discrimination against people with AIDS and against homophobia in general. Along with the rainbow flag, the pink triangle serves as an international symbol of gay and lesbian people.

Not until 1994 were the criminal provisions against homosexual acts finally removed from German law. In 2002 the Paris-based Foundation pour la Memoire de la Deportation released a report indicating that 210 French homosexuals had been deported to Germany to serve as laborers during the war, contradicting the claims of the French government that there is no evidence of such a deportation. Jean Le Bitoux's *Les Oublies de la Memoire: Le Persecution des Homosexuels en Europe au temps du Nazisme* (Erased from

Memory: The Persecution of Homosexuals in Europe During the Nazi Era, 2002) gives special consideration to the French experience. Finally, in 2002 the German Society for Research into Sexuality, in its efforts to achieve collective rehabilitation and compensation for homosexual victims, continued to press for recognition that the injustices suffered at the hands of the German government by no means ended with the fall of the Nazis.

Those victimized for their homosexuality by the Nazis should neither be ignored nor simply (and belatedly) identified as targets of the Holocaust substantially similar to Jews in their treatment. Unlike the Jews of Europe, most homosexuals survived the Holocaust. Additional aspects of their experience set them apart from others who were oppressed, especially Jews: persecution was limited almost exclusively to males; not all males convicted on homosexual charges were sent to camps or targeted for death; and prisoners wearing the pink triangle made up only a tiny portion of Holocaust victims. The fact that homosexuals were so ostracized, both during their camp experience and beyond, also sets them apart. Homosexuals were indeed victims of the Holocaust, but in ways that were frequently substantially different from their fellow prisoners.

–NANCY C. UNGER,
SANTA CLARA UNIVERSITY

Viewpoint:
Trial Nazi extermination programs initially targeted the disabled, sick, and aged, but their function was to develop procedures for the indiscriminate extermination of non-Aryans.

The quest for racial purity dominated National Socialist ideology. After Adolf Hitler became German chancellor in 1933, the Nazis implemented many policies to guarantee the survival of a racially pure Aryan state that culminated in the Final Solution. Yet, before six million Jews were murdered in camps throughout eastern Europe, the German government had established programs to eliminate groups they identified as inferior, such as the mentally and physically handicapped, chronic alcoholics, and habitual criminals. Compulsory sterilization and euthanasia laws were two policies that proved indispensable to initiating racial genocide in Nazi Germany. Each policy provided the institutional groundwork, trained medical professionals, and justified the eliminationist mind-set required for the elimination of people Nazis identified as racially undesirable. Sterilization and euthanasia, therefore, established an atmosphere where the annihilation of particular groups was accepted, anticipated, and even desired. The policies Nazis established legally to sterilize and euthanize selected groups were essential in the eventual implementation of the Final Solution.

Racial identity fascinated Germans for decades before the Nazis assumed power. In 1815, for instance, author Ernst Moritz Arndt argued that "mish-mash and bastardization are the main source of degeneration and decline of a people." In 1899 Houston Steward Chamberlain, an Englishman who became a German citizen, argued that Germans belonged to a racially pure and superior group he called the Aryan race. Aryans, Chamberlain maintained, were the originators of Western culture and the mental and physical "lords of the world." Their descendants had thus to save society from inferior groups such as Jews and Gypsies. The national obsession with racial purity continued into the twentieth century, as German scientists used eugenics, "the science of fine breeding," to link racial traits to heredity. The interest in eugenics, or, as Germans called it, "racial hygiene," increased in 1920 when attorney Karl Binding and psychiatrist Alfred Hoche published *Die Freigabe der Vernichtung lebensunwerten Lebens* (Authorization for the Destruction of Life Unworthy of Life). In their influential book, the scholars reiterated their belief in Aryan superiority and proposed the legal euthanasia of those with hereditary mental and physical ailments to secure a racially pure German state. Binding and Hoche justified euthanasia, Greek for "fine death," because it maintained healthy Aryan specimens worthy of reproduction and relieved Germany of the social and economic drain that sustaining the handicapped brought. Hoche became the foremost proponent of selective euthanasia during the Weimar era (1919–1933) as his views grew in popularity. German schoolteachers, for instance, had their children calculate the costs of institutional care for the disabled in math classes, while biology students toured state hospitals and wrote essays on the effects of mental degeneracy. Many German citizens in the early twentieth century, therefore, supported euthanizing the infirm for racial and humanitarian reasons. One such person, Adolf Hitler, detailed a belief in Aryan superiority, a commitment to ensuring German racial purity, and a hatred of inferior races such as Jews in his autobiography *Mein Kampf* (1925–1927). When Hitler assumed power in 1933, the racial cleansing of Germany became the Nazi Party's main priority.

The elimination of racially inferior German citizens began on 26 July 1933 when Hitler enacted the Law for the Prevention of Offspring with Hereditary Diseases. The measure, popularly called the "sterilization law," took effect on 1 January 1934, demanded compulsory sterilization of the disabled, and led to the sterilization of about 360,000 Germans, about 1 percent of the total population. Those selected for sterilization were defined as "feeble minded" because they possessed mental illnesses such as manic depression and schizophrenia, but the law also targeted epileptics, those with physical deformities, severe alcoholics, the blind, and deaf individuals. Nazi officials provided crude intelligence tests for state hospitals, special schools, and nursing homes to determine who qualified for sterilization, which occurred primarily through radiation exposure or chemical injection. On 26 June 1935 the law broadened to provide abortions for women not beyond the sixth month of a "hereditarily diseased" pregnancy. The sterilization law provided a crucial precursor to the extermination of racial inferiors in an idealized Aryan state by identifying those with undesired features and preventing their reproduction. The measure also demonstrates that the State and social welfare took precedence over individual rights in Nazi Germany.

The next step in the effort to control reproduction in Nazi Germany came approximately one month after the establishment of the infamous Nuremberg Laws. On 18 October 1935 the Marriage Health Law prohibited marriage if either partner suffered from diseases the sterilization law named. In addition, couples had to earn a Marriage Fitness Certification before obtaining a marriage license. Nazi officials intended to use the law to begin a national registry that contained hereditary information concerning every German citizen. The Marriage Health Law extended Nazi control over the reproduction of German citizens and justified the intrusion with racial arguments. During the same year the Marriage Health measure passed, Hitler informed Reich physician leader Gerhard Wagner that he intended to kill the German disabled when war began in Europe. Wagner became a prominent supporter of the euthanasia programs as he and his successor, Leonardo Conti, ensured the medical community would become one of the key instruments in the Nazi war against racial impurities.

German euthanasia programs began with the mass murder of children who had mental or physical handicaps. In 1938 Hitler received an appeal from the parents of a child who wanted their disabled infant mercifully euthanized. The 1938 "Knauer baby" incident inspired the Reich to establish thirty Special Children's

AFRAID TO STIR UP MEMORIES

Gay Frenchman Pierre Seel, in his autobiography, describes the murder of his lover while they were incarcerated in a German concentration camp at Schirmeck:

Days, weeks, months wore by. I spent six months, from May to November 1941, in that place where horror and savagery were the law. But I've put off describing the worst ordeal I suffered. It happened during my earliest weeks in the camp and contributed more than anything else to making me a silent, obedient shadow among the others.

One day the loudspeakers ordered us to report immediately to the roll-call. Shouts and yells urged us to get there without delay. Surrounded by SS men, we had to form a square and stand at attention, as we did for the morning roll call. The commandant appeared with his entire general staff. I assumed he was going to bludgeon us once again with his blind faith in the Reich, together with a list of orders, insults and threats—emulating the infamous outpourings of his master, Adolf Hitler. But the actual ordeal was worse: an execution. Two SS men brought a young man to the center of out square. Horrified, I recognized Jo, my loving friend, who was only eighteen years old. I hadn't previously spotted him in the camp. Had he arrived before or after me? We hadn't seen each other during the days before I was summoned by the Gestapo.

Now I froze in terror. I had prayed that he would escape their lists, their roundups, their humiliations. And there he was before my powerless eyes, which filled with tears.

Unlike me, he had not carried dangerous letters, torn down posters, or signed any statements. And yet he had been caught and was about to die. What had happened? What had the monsters accused him of? Because of my anguish I have completely forgotten the wording of the death sentence.

The loudspeakers broadcast some noisy classical music while the SS stripped him naked and shoved a tin pail over his head. Next they sicced their ferocious German Shepherds on him: the guard dogs first bit into his groin and thighs, then devoured him right in front of us. His shrieks of pain were distorted and amplified by the pail in which his head was trapped. My rigid body reeled, my eyes gaped at so much horror, tears poured down my cheeks, I fervently prayed that he would black out quickly.

Since then I sometimes wake up howling in the middle of the night. For fifty years now that scene has kept ceaselessly passing and re-passing though my mind. I will never forget the barbaric murder of my love—before my very eyes, before our eyes, for there were hundreds of witnesses. Why are they still silent today? Have they all died? It's true that we were among the youngest in the camp and that a lot of time has gone by. But I suspect that some people prefer to remain silent forever, afraid to stir up memories, like that one among so many others.

Source: Pierre Seel, I, Pierre Seel, Deported Homosexual: A Memoir of Nazi Terror (New York: BasicBooks, 1995), pp. 42–44.

Departments that began the legal execution of racial undesirables in Nazi Germany. The Chancellery of the Führer (KdF) office governed the endeavor. Hitler appointed his personal physician, Karl Brandt, to supervise the operation, and Brandt appointed Viktor Brack to implement a process of efficient euthanasia. To mask its true intentions, the children's programs existed under the official yet ambiguous title "Reich Committee for the Scientific Registration of Severe Hereditary Ailments."

Before the infant euthanasia enterprise was well underway, Hitler ordered the execution of disabled adults as well. The KdF also supervised the second undertaking and placed it under several agencies that resembled the structure created to

euthanize children. Brack presided over both killing programs, headquartered in a Berlin villa at Tiergarten Street Number 4. The collective euthanasia programs thus operated as the T–4 program. Although KdF directed T–4, the organization cooperated closely with the SS and operated secretly under nonexistent agencies such as the Reich Cooperative for State Hospitals and Nursing Homes, the Community Foundation for Institutional Care, and the Charitable Corporation for the Transport of the Sick. The convoluted bureaucracy that supervised the murders of disabled Germans became a pattern Nazis employed over and again during the execution of many other groups defined as eugenically and socially flawed, such as Jews, homosexuals, communists, and Gypsies.

THE VICTIMS

The processes of euthanizing children and adults worked in similar ways. In 1939 the Reich minister of the interior compiled information on all German institutions that provided care for the disabled. Staff members at each institution, such as administrators, doctors, nurses, and midwives, had to answer questionnaires concerning each of their patients. The forms were returned to the KdF, where approximately forty physicians, most of them psychiatrists who were paid by the number of cases they reviewed, examined the documents and determined who died. They labeled condemned children as "idiots," "Mongols," "valueless," or "malformed," while adults were often declared "incurable." A panel of three physicians endorsed each decision the review board recommended. Those selected for euthanasia early in the program, particularly children, usually died from a barbiturate overdose or starvation. About 6,000 children died as a result of the euthanasia campaign. Physicians commonly experimented on subjects prior to their death, removed their organs for observation afterward, and took valuables from the dead bodies.

Once the euthanasia programs began, they spread rapidly to remote provinces within the nation. Instead of bringing victims to Berlin or distant urban centers, though, operation leaders began using large vans in mass murder. Patients in outlying hospitals who had no relatives or whom physicians declared "incurable" became the first victims of the gas vans; they were loaded in the vehicles and driven around their territories as carbon monoxide poured from a steel bottle in the driver's compartment through a hose and into an airtight section where inmates inhaled the noxious fumes. The van operation proved immensely successful to euthanasia directors because it eliminated degenerate citizens in distant provinces without the cost of transporting them to urban areas. In one operation, for example, 1,558 handicapped residents in East Prussian hospitals died during a two-week period in May 1940. Although mass murder first targeted the German handicapped, the techniques T-4 officials utilized became an indispensable aspect of the Final Solution.

As the conquest of Poland progressed and Germany attained more Lebensraum (living space) for its mythic Aryan peoples, the nation simultaneously encountered more people it considered mentally, physically, and culturally inferior to them. In the fall of 1939, therefore, German euthanasia programs began to evolve into a Final Solution for the nation's perceived racial enemies, particularly Jews. A new method of execution was needed to kill large numbers simultaneously, and T-4 doctors began to experiment with gas executions. An example of how euthanasia and the Final Solution converged

occurred at the Owinski psychiatric hospital in Poland on 15 November 1939 when 1,100 residents were murdered with poisoned gas. It marked one of the first times Nazis used gas for mass murder and set a precedent for future extermination. On 7 December 1939 Germans used mobile gas vans for the first time to kill 7,120 patients at the Tygenhof psychiatric hospital in Germany. The new method of eugenic purging proved so successful to T-4 directors that they launched "Operation Euthanasia" in January 1940 and approved mass gassing as the most efficient method of killing.

The KdF established euthanasia centers for adults at Brandenburg, Grafeneck, Hartheim, Sonnenstein, Bernburg, and Hadamar. One physician managed each facility, all of which contained a receiving area, gas chambers built to resemble shower rooms, a crematorium, and staff lodging. Staff members examined victims upon their arrival at the center, verified their paperwork, took photographs of the condemned, and escorted them to the shower chambers, where pipes pumped carbon monoxide into the enclosures. Doctors observed the deaths through a window, ordered the room ventilated approximately thirty minutes after the procedure began, and pronounced the victims dead. Workers often looted the corpses before their cremation. Approximately 71,000 patients died during "Operation Euthanasia." To hide their activities, T-4 officials often sent condolence letters and death certificates with fraudulent reasons for and dates of death to each victim's family. Program directors often collected premiums from the dead's insurance companies or charged their relatives for burial fees. As the enterprise continued, however, protests from relatives, clergymen, and the judiciary increased. Hitler officially ended the T-4 program in August 1941 because of its public unpopularity, but the work T-4 began increased its scope as World War II (1939-1945) progressed.

In July 1941 Reinhard Heydrich took control of the Final Solution, the official response of Nazi Germany to the Jewish Question, and transferred some euthanasia technology and personnel to the killing of Jews. When Hitler officially ended the T-4 program a month later, Heydrich had the entire operation at his disposal and quickly placed its experts, bureaucracy, machinery, and discoveries to work against Jews. T-4 initially placed Jews and non-Jews together in its facilities but began placing them in separate hospitals in early 1940. Within months, Jews died without the required examination those at euthanasia centers received. The murders continued after the termination of T-4 as program directors visited concentration camps and selected prisoners to be executed at chambers that continued to operate. The gassing of concentration-camp inmates, predominantly Jews, was declared "Special Treatment 14f13." The gas van became an essential instrument in the earliest stage of the Final Solution. As the German army moved into Russia in 1940, *Einsatzgruppen* (mobile killing units) followed closely behind, eradicating Jews and others perceived as racially inferior. The execution method *Einsatzgruppen* units initially used was the firing squad, but the gruesome massacres had a detrimental effect on the perpetrators. SS leaders, therefore, sought a new method capable of mass murder while distancing most soldiers from the disturbing slaughters. They found a solution in the mobile gas vans KdF officials used in their euthanasia program. Heydrich first used T–4 personnel and their death vehicles against Jews at Chelmno, where the vans executed 152,000 inmates. Operation 14f13 continued until the killing capabilities at facilities such as Auschwitz-Birkenau rendered the T–4 methods obsolete, and the operation provided a clear link between Nazi euthanasia laws and the Final Solution.

Those individuals associated with T–4 who did not assist Operation 14f13 nevertheless contributed to the Final Solution in several ways. T–4 chemists, for example, conducted experiments with several different gases and execution techniques, while the masons who constructed the gas chambers and crematoriums at Sonnestein and Hartheim were transferred to the new facilities when T–4 ended. Several T–4 administrators and physicians were reemployed in Jewish extermination camps and occupied positions at Belzec, Sobibor, Chelmno, and Treblinka. The euthanasia of undesirable Germans provided a critical step to the Final Solution, as Heydrich himself recognized and acknowledged with the appointment of crucial T–4 personnel to assist in the Jewish death factories.

The most important function of early Nazi sterilization and euthanasia programs, however, was that they created an atmosphere where the experimentation on and elimination of humans not defined as racially pure Aryans was acceptable. The sterilization and euthanasia policies also trivialized the death of selected groups who lived within the Third Reich by rewarding those who proved most dedicated to cleansing Germany of racial impurities. Administrators were awarded and recognized for their murderous efficiency, physicians received promotions or new facilities, chemists were granted enhanced research funding, and bureaucrats were given monetary bonuses for the number of individuals they processed through gas chambers each day. In other words, the euthanasia of those designated as racially degenerate in Nazi Germany

operated in a manner that made genocide seem normal. The T–4 program killed between 70,000 and 95,000 individuals but indirectly led to the deaths of millions more because of the tremendous influence it had on the implementation of the Final Solution.

–J. MICHAEL BUTLER,
SOUTH GEORGIA COLLEGE

References

Gad Beck and Frank Heibert, *An Underground Life: Memories of a Gay Jew in Berlin,* translated by Allison Brown (Madison: University of Wisconsin Press, 1999).

Christopher R. Browning, *Fateful Months: Essays on the Emergence of the Final Solution* (New York: Holmes & Meier, 1985).

Michael Burleigh, *Death and Deliverance: "Euthanasia" in Germany, c. 1900–1945* (Cambridge & New York: Cambridge University Press, 1994).

Burleigh, *Ethics and Extermination: Reflections on Nazi Genocide* (Cambridge & New York: Cambridge University Press, 1997).

David Cesarani, ed., *The Final Solution: Origins and Implementation* (London & New York: Routledge, 1994).

Rob Epstein and Jeffrey Friedman, *Paragraph 175,* A Telling Pictures production with Home Box Office, 2000 (video).

Henry Friedlander, *The Origins of Nazi Genocide: From Euthanasia to the Final Solution* (Chapel Hill: University of North Carolina Press, 1995).

Günter Grau, ed., with a contribution by Claudia Schoppmann, *The Hidden Holocaust?: Gay and Lesbian Persecution in Germany 1933–45,* translated by Patrick Camiller (London: Cassell / Chicago: Fitzroy Dearborn, 1995).

Erwin J. Haeberle, "Swastika, Pink Triangle, and Yellow Star: The Destruction of Sexology and the Persecution of Homosexuals in Nazi Germany," in *Hidden from History: Reclaiming the Gay and Lesbian Past,* edited by Martin Bauml Duberman, Martha Vinicus, and George Chauncey Jr. (New York: New American Library, 1989), pp. 365–379.

Heinz Heger, *The Men with the Pink Triangle,* translated by David Fernbach (London: Gay Men's Press / Boston: Alyson, 1980).

James W. Jones, "Pink Triangle," in *Gay Histories and Cultures: An Encyclopedia,* edited by

George Haggerty (New York: Garland, 2000), pp. 691–692.

Rudiger Lautmann, "Categorization in Concentration Camps as a Collective Fate: A Comparison of Homosexuals, Jehovah's Witnesses and Political Prisoners," *Journal of Homosexuality,* 19 (1990): 67–88.

Jean Le Bitoux, *Les Oublies de la Memoire: Le Persecution des Homosexuels en Europe au temps du Nazisme* (Paris: Hachette, 2002).

Richard Plant, *The Pink Triangle: The Nazi War against Homosexuals* (New York: Holt, 1986).

Wolfgang Roll, "Homosexual Inmates in the Buchenwald Concentration Camp," *Journal of Homosexuality,* 31 (1996): 1–28.

Karl A. Schleunes, *The Twisted Road to Auschwitz: Nazi Policy toward German Jews, 1933–1939* (Urbana: University of Illinois Press, 1970).

Claudia Schoppmann, *Days of Masquerade: Life Stories of Lesbians during the Third Reich,* translated by Allison Brown (New York: Columbia University Press, 1996).

Pierre Seel, *I, Pierre Seel, Deported Homosexual: A Memoir of Nazi Terror,* translated by Joachim Neugroschel (New York: BasicBooks, 1995).

James Steakley, "Homosexuals and the Third Reich," *The Body Politic,* 11 (January/February 1974): 1, 20–21.

Paul Weindling, *Health, Race, and German Politics between National Unification and Nazism, 1870–1945* (Cambridge & New York: Cambridge University Press, 1989).

THE VICTIMS

VICTORS' JUSTICE

Were Nazis tried for war crimes subjected to victors' justice?

Viewpoint: Yes. The prosecution of German war criminals was judicially unfair because the United States was more concerned with geopolitical issues than the rule of law.

Viewpoint: No. Trials of Nazi war criminals constituted reasonable efforts to achieve justice in the immediate postwar period.

Viewpoint: No. In spite of charges of victors' justice and the questionable inclusion of Soviet judges, the Nuremberg trials were fair.

Even before the collapse of the Nazi State, it was apparent that neither a German defeat nor a new Versailles treaty would fulfill Allied goals. The leaders of Nazi Germany could not be permitted to live. Sending Adolf Hitler into exile and imposing reparations on Germany would not suffice. From the perspective of the Allies, the Nazi regime was unprecedented. Hitler was not simply the leader of a nation against whom the Allies waged war; he and his lieutenants were criminals. With complete disregard for the rule of law, for the customs of war, and for human decency, they were directly responsible for the deaths of an estimated forty million people, many of whom, like the Jews, had been rounded up and executed with no military justification whatsoever. It seemed obvious to many soldiers and politicians, among them Dwight D. Eisenhower, Franklin D. Roosevelt, and Winston Churchill, that the best and most expedient course was to execute Hitler, Heinrich Himmler, and other top Nazi leaders summarily as they were captured and identified.

As appealing as this course might have been, the lawyers argued more persuasively that an Allied victory needed, above all, to restore the rule of law to Europe, and extrajudicial executions, however justified and satisfying, would not advance that effort. Thus were born the International Military Tribunal at Nuremberg and subsequent trials by the U.S. Army and other civil and military authorities in the aftermath of the war. Similar trials continued for half a century after World War II (1939–1945), whenever concentration camp guards, Nazi doctors, collaborationist police officers, and other Holocaust and war-crimes perpetrators were brought into the light. The principle of an international court of criminal justice was made permanent in 2002 with the establishment of the International Criminal Court in The Hague.

These trials were controversial from the beginning. Contemporaries argued that, however culpable the perpetrators of genocide and war crimes might have been as human beings, they had not violated existing law. And even if they had, an extraordinary military tribunal had no jurisdiction over such crimes. Summary executions of the key Nazi leadership and local trials under local law—for example in Poland, Germany, or the Soviet Union— would have better restored the rule of law. Above all, skeptics feared that an International Military Tribunal, for which the judges were drawn from the victorious allies and the accused were a defeated enemy, would be condemned by history as victors' justice. No matter how rigorously fair the trials, the results could be dismissed by future generations as vengeance against a prostrate foe rather than a restoration of law and order. Even though the convening authority of the International Military Tribunal was mindful of this skepticism, and the court avoided any appearance of partiality, debate about the legitimacy of such courts continues into the twenty-first century, when accused perpetrators of other crimes against humanity find themselves facing similar courts and making similar challenges.

Viewpoint:
Yes. The prosecution of German war criminals was judicially unfair because the United States was more concerned with geopolitical issues than the rule of law.

At the conclusion of the European segment of World War II in May 1945, the administration of American president Harry S Truman faced three related challenges in developing and implementing policies to manage the occupation of defeated Germany effectively. First, the administration had to collaborate with its wartime allies in administering punitive measures to the remnants of the Third Reich's leadership for the prosecution of the war, generally, and the ghastly horrors of the Holocaust that unfolded therein, specifically. Second, it had to strike a balance between justice and pragmatism in dismantling the National Socialist German Workers' (Nazi) Party and disciplining its adherents without unduly hampering either the reconstruction of the vanquished state's physical and economic infrastructure or the cultivation of democratic values among Germans populating the Western Zones of Occupation. Third, it had to foster a spirit of reconciliation between the Germans under American, British, and French occupation and their former enemies across western Europe in order to consolidate a united transatlantic front in the nascent Cold War pitting the United States against the Soviet Union. The dispensation of justice to Nazis who served in a variety of civilian and military wartime leadership positions, which transpired in the contexts of the 1945–1946 Nuremberg trials and subsequent U.S. Army and denazification trials between 1946 and 1949, was central to meeting the above challenges effectively. However, in spite of their political importance, the prosecution of German war criminals was judicially unfair because the Truman administration ceded primacy to geopolitical pragmatism over the rule of law in conducting the Nuremberg and U.S. Army trials and orchestrating the denazification process. Nonetheless, the administration's decision to proceed in that manner was both understandable and prudent given its indispensability to facilitating the processes of reconstruction and reconcilia-

tion and resultant consolidation of a Western democratic front to oppose the Soviet Union in the opening stage of the Cold War.

The conduct of World War II entailed devastating costs in terms of physical destruction and lives lost for both the victors and the vanquished. Such costs were most notably evident in the European theater, where more than 41 million soldiers and civilians died as a direct result of the war, including 6 million Jews and other victims of the unspeakable atrocities of the Holocaust. Once hostilities had ended, the populations of the triumphant Allied states—as well as the broader international community—demanded the public apportionment of blame and resultant punishment of those deemed responsible for the outbreak and prosecution of the war. The question facing Allied leaders was not whether to act punitively but how. As historian Joseph E. Persico notes, the "dilemma the victors faced at the time was simply to determine what to do after the Nazis had caused the deliberate deaths of some six million Jews and millions of others in killings divorced from any military necessity. Could the Allies merely walk away from murders so vast and so calculated?"

Understandably—and justly, given the outcome of the war, scale of its costs and nature of the Nazi regime—the Allies concurred on the need to exact justice in a relatively swift manner. However, at least initially, they disagreed on the means to that end. British prime minister Winston Churchill, for instance, suggested summary executions of Nazi leaders in order to avoid the complexities and delays of formal judicial proceedings. The United States and the Soviet Union, on the other hand, favored the use of a multilateral military tribunal to try the Third Reich's most high-profile figures. The Truman administration insisted on this approach primarily because of the centrality of the rule of law to the American domestic political system. The Soviets, for their part, were more interested in the internationalization of the proceedings, the outcome of which—guilty verdicts for the accused—would presumably be all but predetermined. Eventually, representatives of the United States, Britain, the Soviet Union, and France settled on the establishment of the International Military Tribunal (IMT), agreeing in principle in May 1945 in San Francisco and formalizing that decision at the Potsdam Conference three months later.

VICTORS' JUSTICE

Hermann Göring on the
stand before the
International Military
Tribunal, Nuremberg,
13 March 1946

(Bildarchiv Preussischer
Kulturbesitz, Berlin)

The IMT, the administrative and judicial particulars of which were developed primarily by American officials, opened for proceedings at Nuremberg in November 1945. The tribunal was composed of representatives from the four victorious powers, with U.S. Supreme Court justice Robert H. Jackson serving as chief American prosecutor and Sir Geoffrey Lawrence of Britain serving as president of the court. In all, twenty-two Nazi leaders stood before the IMT on four charges associated with the planning and conduct of the war and attempted extermination of Jews and other opponents of the Third Reich: conspiracy to commit war crimes; war crimes; crimes against peace; and crimes against humanity. The accused ranged from diplomats (Foreign Minister Joachim von Ribbentrop and German ambassador to Austria and Turkey Franz von Papen) to military leaders (Chief of Staff Alfred Jodl and Field Marshal Wilhelm Keitel), political figures (Reichstag president Hermann Göring and Minister of Arms and Munitions Albert Speer), and propagandists (Gauleiter of Franconia Julius Streicher and head of German radio Hans Fritzsche), all of whom served in reasonably high-profile positions in Hitler's regime.

Those on trial were prosecuted over a twelve-month period ending in October 1946 under the unrelenting scrutiny of the interna-tional media, which ensured global publicity for—and thus enhanced the perceived legitimacy of—the proceedings. Ultimately, the trial resulted in nineteen guilty verdicts and three acquittals. Twelve defendants were sentenced to death. One, Göring, cheated the hangman by committing suicide on 15 October.

The rest, including Nazi foreign minister Ribbentrop, Chief of the Armed Forces High Command Operational Staff Jodl, Keitel, and Streicher, who published the Nazi Party's anti-Semitic newspaper, *Der Stürmer,* were hanged on 16 October. However, contrary to pretrial assumptions, former commander of the navy Karl Dönitz—Hitler's personally appointed successor as chancellor—received a ten-year sentence, Speer was given twenty years, and Papen, Fritzsche, and economics minister Hjalmar Schacht were acquitted.

The nature and variety of the sentences passed was demonstrative of the purpose of the IMT, as envisioned by American policymakers in particular. Executing the majority of the highest profile Nazis at Nuremberg served as a necessary punitive catharsis for Allied leaders' domestic constituents (most notably those in western Europe). Ultimately, that helped the Truman administration to better facilitate its subsequent shift in emphasis to the reconstruction of defeated Germany and reconciliation between former World War II adversaries. In hindsight, the trial itself was reasonably just, especially in light of the relatively even balance between death sentences, on one hand, and jail terms and acquittals, on the other. As Persico explains, "no saint or statesman lost his life or his freedom at Nuremberg. All the men who went to prison or mounted the gallows were willing, knowing and energetic accomplices in a vast and malignant enterprise. . . . The one indisputable good to come out of the trial is that, to any sentient person, it documented beyond question Nazi Germany's crimes." Nonetheless, the fact that the process was administered by the victorious powers rather than a neutral body rendered its judicial legitimacy open to challenge in the contexts of subsequent debates among policymakers, scholars, and laypeople alike.

Notwithstanding the symbolic and practical relevance of its conduct and outcome, the IMT was by no means the only—and perhaps not even the most historically significant—example of American involvement in the prosecution of German war criminals. The United States also participated in judicial proceedings against Nazis with lower profiles than the Nuremberg defendants in the course of governing its Zone of Occupation in southern and western Germany between 1945 and 1949. These adjudication processes included a series of trials of low- and mid-level Nazi civilian officials and military officers administered by the U.S. Army at Dachau and the related development and implementation of the denazification process by the Office of Military Government for Germany, United States (OMGUS).

Concurrent with and subsequent to the events at Nuremberg, the U.S. Army conducted a series of trials under military legal auspices at Dachau, which was the site of one of the Third Reich's many notorious concentration camps. Carried out in 1945–1949, these trials were designed to punish less-high-profile Nazis than the defendants at Nuremberg—most notably concentration camp guards, policemen, minor officers, and soldiers—charged with specific crimes against Holocaust victims and captured Allied soldiers. In all, the Dachau trials resulted in 1,416 convictions and 256 acquittals. Of those convicted, 426 were sentenced to death. However, 326 of those sentences were thrown out, commuted, or reduced by American general and military governor Lucius D. Clay, who personally reviewed all death-penalty cases before the court. Clay's judicial fastidiousness, in turn, reflected his own concerns over allowing the Allies—rather than neutral third parties, if not Germans untainted by association with the Nazi Party—to try war criminals at all. As he later recalled, the "point is, don't lose the war. . . .

You've always had, since the beginning of time, penalties to be paid by those who were defeated, sometimes in the form of reparations and damages, frequently in the form of punishments for those who took part. . . . This was a punishment for losing."

Clay expressed—and acted upon—similar misgivings with respect to the implementation of the denazification process in the American Zone of Occupation. In short, denazification was conceived by the Truman administration and formalized in the context of Joint Chiefs of Staff directive 1067 as a means to purge German society of any lingering remnants of National Socialism. To achieve that end, the OMGUS was charged with the daunting (and, for practical purposes, logistically unfeasible) task of removing from positions of leadership all individuals associated with a Nazi Party that had more than six million members at the end of the war. Denazification procedures entailed the distribution of elaborate questionnaires to the approximately twelve million individuals over the age of eighteen under OMGUS jurisdiction beginning in February 1946. On the basis of the questionnaires, individuals were classified as (a) major offenders; (b) offenders; (c) lesser offenders; (d) followers; or (e) nonoffenders, with those distinctions eventually to be made by German officials—albeit under American supervision—in the context of the nascent postwar German legal system. From there, class (a) and (b) offenders would be removed from positions of authority.

Ultimately, the denazification process proved unworkable—both judicially and politically—and was discontinued by Secretary of Defense James Forrestal (after recommendations to that end by Clay) in August 1947 and terminated in March 1948, at which point just 600,000 cases had been processed. Judicially, denazification proceedings were often arbitrary. For instance, personal vendettas between Germans excluded many alleged Nazis from playing productive roles in society, while others found themselves in influential positions on the basis of the indispensability of their practical knowledge in the reconstruction of Germany's physical and industrial infrastructure. As historians Dennis L. Bark and David R. Gress assert, "What began as a grandiose plan to purge all Nazis from leading roles in public life and to punish severely persons who had held responsible positions in the Third Reich was, in practice, transformed into a procedure by which the major offenders were slapped on the wrist and minor offenders exonerated." Politically, the Truman administration chose to forego denazification so that it could concentrate almost exclusively on the democratization of occupied Germany as a means to counter the emerging Soviet bloc in

VICTORS' JUSTICE

the East. The balance favoring geopolitical pragmatism over the rule of law thus became progressively more pronounced as the division of Europe grew increasingly unavoidable between 1946 and 1949.

In order to prevent Soviet advances beyond Moscow's control of the Eastern Zone of occupied Germany and the states of central and eastern Europe in the aftermath of World War II, the United States had to cultivate western European economic and political cohesion within an American-led military alliance. The creation of such an entity, in turn, demanded multilateral economic, political, and military cooperation and thus the willingness of western Europeans to overcome bitter interstate animosities, particularly with respect to the Germans. The success of the project hinged on the western Europeans' desperate need of immediate economic assistance for the reconstruction that would necessarily precede the process of reconciliation. As scholar Simon Serfaty explains, "Unity among the nation-states of Europe was a precondition for economic reconstruction not from one but two world wars; reconstruction was also the precondition for political unity not only within each European nation-state but among all of them as well."

American support for western European reconstruction, which was manifested in the provision of more than $12 billion in economic assistance through the Marshall Plan between 1948 and 1952, was part of a multistep bargaining process between the United States and its allies across the Atlantic. First, the Truman administration proposed and the western Europeans accepted the Marshall Plan in exchange for a pledge to administer the aid multilaterally as the first step in a long-term regional integration project. Second, the western Europeans requested that the United States maintain a long-term military presence on the Continent in order to mitigate, if not eliminate, any security threats posed by their Soviet adversaries and recently reformed but still distrusted German partners. Third, Washington complied by establishing the North Atlantic Treaty Organization (NATO) in April 1949, with the guarantee of collective defense serving as a security blanket under the cover of which the Western Europeans could deepen and widen the integration process in the future.

The reconstruction and subsequent inclusion of the American, British, and French Zones of Occupation in Germany within the NATO alliance were central to these agreements. As a result, it was essential that the United States dispense with the punitive phase of the occupation—particularly the prosecution of the Nazi leadership at Nuremburg—expeditiously and

focus on the interconnected reconstruction and reconciliation processes in anticipation of the impending Cold War. This policy stance was manifested in American secretary of state James Byrnes's rhetoric in an address in Stuttgart in September 1946 and the subsequent consolidation of the American and British Zones of Occupation into a unified Bizone in January 1947. Similarly, the abandonment of denazification was conditioned by rising East-West tensions that culminated in the Soviet Union's imposition of a road and rail blockade of Berlin in June 1948 and the resultant Western Allied airlift of supplies to the American, British, and French sectors of the city over the ensuing eleven months. Breaking the blockade, in turn, helped to foster a common sense of purpose among the western Europeans that was reinforced by the establishment of a west German state (the Federal Republic of Germany)—largely at Washington's behest—in May 1949.

This essay's purpose was to consider the judicial fairness—or lack thereof—of the prosecution of German war criminals by the United States in the aftermath of World War II. It pursued that end by examining the connections between two related sets of issues: the conduct of the IMT at Nuremberg and subsequent U.S. Army and denazification trials in the American Zone of Occupation; and the geopolitical transformation of the European continent generally and the defeated German state specifically.

In light of the evidence uncovered and presented in the three main sections of the essay, the following three conclusions are instructive in the development of a clearer understanding of those connections. First, on balance, the Truman administration unquestionably ceded primacy to geopolitical imperatives over the rule of law in dispensing justice to Nazi leaders and their followers from 1945 to 1949. Second, that approach detracted from the judicial fairness of the proceedings, albeit to variant degrees. The broad range of sentences passed and carried out by the IMT, despite the general culpability of the Nazi leadership in provoking and conducting the war and carrying out the crimes of the Holocaust on its margins, indicate that there was no gross miscarriage of justice at Nuremberg. However, the central role of the victors—as opposed to neutral parties—in trying German leaders was certainly prejudicial. These arguments hold true with respect to the U.S. Army trials at Dachau as well. The denazification process, on the other hand, was rendered more defensible in theory by the transfer of legal responsibilities to Germans deemed untainted by National Socialism in trying their peers. Yet, it proved unworkable in practice and was sensibly abandoned after a mercifully short period.

Third, the positions American policymakers took in each of these judicial contexts were geopolitically prudent given their indispensability to the reconstruction and reconciliation processes that enabled the United States to consolidate a democratic Western front against the Soviet Union in the Cold War.

–ROBERT J. PAULY JR.,
MIDLANDS TECHNICAL COLLEGE

Viewpoint:
No. Trials of Nazi war criminals constituted reasonable efforts to achieve justice in the immediate postwar period.

Between 1945 and 1949 the United States tried almost 1,900 Germans in more than 500 trials for violations of international law during World War II (1939–1945). Asking whether these trials were fair is a bit like asking whether trials of U.S. citizens under the American judicial system are fair. Some are and some are not, and reasonable people will disagree over which is which, according to a wide variety of criteria. And to whom were the trials fair? Moreover, courts reflect the values of their societies, and these values are not static. Condemning to death a man proved guilty of theft in eighteenth-century England might have been fair in the context of that time and place, but it is unthinkable in the twenty-first-century United States. Yet, it is reasonable to ask if the American trials of Germans suspected of crimes associated with the Holocaust constituted reasonable efforts to achieve justice in the historical context of the immediate postwar period. They were.

Germans had inflicted on the world horrors of staggering dimensions during World War II. Crimes against humanity, of which the Holocaust is the most notorious example; war crimes, including the deaths of a majority of the 5,700,000 Soviet prisoners of war taken by Germany; and World War II itself, unleashed upon Europe by German aggression, cost the lives of tens of millions of people. To be sure, the Allies had not waged a uniformly clean war. British and American bombers devastated German cities, killing hundreds of thousands of noncombatants, the Soviet secret police murdered thousands of captured Polish army officers, and the Soviet Army slaughtered huge numbers of German civilians in the last months of the war, while casual killings of German prisoners of war by Allied forces, including those of the United States, were common. The fact that Allied crimes usually went unpunished suggested to many Germans that the trials of accused German war criminals were nothing more than victors' justice. There was much hypocrisy in the approach of the United States to dealing with wartime atrocities. Yet, ideologically motivated German crimes, particularly the racist extermination of millions of Jews, Gypsies, and Slavs, had been unmatched on the Allied side, even in the Pacific war, where racial hatred of the Japanese was much in evidence. Once resistance to American forces ceased, the killing of enemy nationals by American forces also ceased. Nonresistance to German forces by Jews, Gypsies, and Slavs, on the other hand, simply made their destruction easier.

During the war some American leaders argued that the magnitude of Nazi crimes was so enormous, and the identity of those responsible for them so obvious, that the appropriate Allied response was to execute high-ranking German political and military figures summarily when they were captured and identified, a policy advocated by Secretary of the Treasury Henry Morgenthau Jr. and supported by General Dwight D. Eisenhower, supreme Allied commander in Europe, who urged the execution of the entire German general staff without trial. Secretary of War Henry Stimson, however, argued that summary execution would be likely to create Nazi martyrs in the eyes of the German people, and that it would be far better to hold trials that would create a record of Nazi criminality that the German people would be forced to confront. This position eventually prevailed and became the official policy of the United States and the other leading Allied powers. In assessing the fairness of American war-crimes policy toward Germany, therefore, it would be well to remember that there was a widely supported alternative to the trials that might have been adopted—the firing squad, with no trials at all.

The centerpiece of Allied war-crimes justice in regard to Nazi Germany, largely the work of U.S. planners, was the "Trial of the Major War Criminals before the International Military Tribunal," opened in Nuremberg, in November 1945 and concluded at the beginning of October 1946. Twenty-two defendants were tried (one, Martin Bormann, in absentia) before a panel of eight judges from Britain, France, the Soviet Union, and the United States. The indictment included four counts: conspiracy; crimes against peace; war crimes; and crimes against humanity. Critics of the trial have argued that it was unfair to charge the defendants with conspiracy, an offense generally not recognized under Continental, including German, law, and that crimes against peace, the waging of aggressive war, and crimes against humanity, such as genocide, had not been forbidden by international law at the time those acts had been committed. The inclusion of conspiracy at the insistence of the United States was an unfortunate and unnecessary complication. Yet, it is hard to argue plausibly that aggressive war was not an offense under international law in 1939, in light of the Kellogg-Briand Pact of 1928, which outlawed war as an instrument of national policy and to which Germany was a signatory. In addition to the claim that exterminating millions of human beings because of their racial or ethnic identities was not a crime because it had not been specified as such in positive law is to be guilty of the worst kind of pettifoggery. Murder does not cease to be murder if committed on a colossal scale. War crimes, defined in the Charter of the International Military Tribunal as "violations of the laws or customs of war" and including acts such as the ill-treatment and murder of prisoners of war and the murder or enslavement of civilian populations, were clearly offenses under international law that had been codified in treaties such as The Hague Convention of 1907 and the Geneva Convention of 1929. To be sure, as many Germans were quick to point out, Allied countries had also been guilty of some of the same offenses, a fact demonstrating Allied hypocrisy rather than German innocence.

The Nuremberg trials were not an exercise in thinly camouflaged lynch law, in spite of the fact that the victors were trying the vanquished. Defendants were represented by German attorneys of their choice, many of them highly competent, and were allowed to express themselves freely in their own defense; Hermann Göring did so with great skill, to the embarrassment of American chief prosecutor Robert H. Jackson. Former admiral Karl Dönitz's defense attorney, Otto Kranzbuehler, with the support of U.S. judge Francis Biddle, was allowed to secure and introduce into evidence a statement by U.S. admiral Chester Nimitz attesting to the fact that the United States had employed its submarines in a way no less brutal than had Germany, sinking enemy merchant ships without warning and making no effort to assist survivors. U.S., British, and French judges overruled Soviet objections and permitted defense testimony pointing to the responsibility of the Soviet Union for the killing of thousands of captured Polish officers, whose bodies had been discovered by the Germans in the Katyn Forest in April 1943. That nineteen of the defendants were found guilty and twelve of them sentenced to hang was not because of unfair trial procedures and rulings but because of the overwhelming evidence of their guilt, primarily in the form of some four thousand incriminating official German documents, many of them bearing the signatures of the defendants. Only with the benefit of many

years of hindsight is it possible to question the justice of specific verdicts and sentences. Julius Streicher, editor of the virulently anti-Semitic newspaper *Der Stürmer*, had held no official position in the Nazi regime during World War II and seems to have been hanged primarily for his crudely racist ideas and offensive personality. However, the excessive harshness of Streicher's punishment was counterbalanced by the leniency shown to the educated, refined, and seemingly penitent Albert Speer, wartime minister for armaments and war production, who was sentenced to only twenty years in prison. One might, of course, question the fairness of Speer's punishment to the memory of the many thousands of slave laborers who perished in German armaments plants.

The 22 defendants tried by the largely American-devised International Military Tribunal were a tiny fraction of the total number of Germans who stood trial in postwar U.S. courts. An additional 185 defendants were judged in 12 exclusively American proceedings at Nuremberg between 1946 and 1949. These trials dealt with the responsibility of lower-ranking Germans for a wide range of offenses: conducting murderous medical experiments on human subjects; employment of slave labor in industry; the production of poison gas for use in the Holocaust; the perversion of law by jurists; the violation of the laws of war by military commanders; the extermination of Jews by SS killing squads in the Soviet Union; and participation in unleashing aggressive war. The vast majority of Germans tried by U.S. courts, more than 1,600, was tried by army courts in 489 proceedings between 1945 and 1948, most of which were held in the former Nazi concentration camp at Dachau. These cases dealt primarily with the operation of specific concentration camps and the murder of American prisoners of war. It is difficult and dangerous to attempt generalizations on so many trials, but the quality of justice dispensed by the subsequent Nuremberg courts was, as a rule, higher than that of the army tribunals. The subsequent Nuremberg proceedings were conducted before panels of three civilian judges, most of whom were retired justices of state supreme courts. Stanley Kramer's 1961 motion picture, *Judgment at Nuremberg*, and Spencer Tracy's role as the fictional "Judge Dan Haywood" were suggested by Case III, the "Justice Case," in which former Nazi legal officials and judges were tried for having destroyed the moral and ethical content of the German legal system and having used the forms of justice to enslave and exterminate vast numbers of victims. Again, the prosecution built its case largely on documentary evidence that the defendants and their attorneys could hardly refute. Instead, the defendants argued that if they had not been willing to cooperate with

TWENTY-ODD BROKEN MEN

On 21 November 1945 American jurist Robert H. Jackson opened the International Military Tribunal at Nuremberg with an eloquent address. Aside from delineating the charges against the accused, he carefully established the validity of the legal proceedings.

The privilege of opening the first trial in history for crimes against the peace of the world imposes a grave responsibility. The wrongs which we seek to condemn and punish have been so calculated, so malignant, and so devastating, that civilization cannot tolerate their being ignored, because it cannot survive their being repeated. That four great nations, flushed with victory and stung with injury stay the hand of vengeance and voluntarily submit their captive enemies to the judgment of the law is one of the most significant tributes that Power has ever paid to Reason.

This Tribunal, while it is novel and experimental, is not the product of abstract speculations nor is it created to vindicate legalistic theories. This inquest represents the practical effort of four of the most mighty of nations, with the support of 17 more, to utilize international law to meet the greatest menace of our times—aggressive war. The common sense of mankind demands that law shall not stop with the punishment of petty crimes by little people. It must also reach men who possess themselves of great power and make deliberate and concerted use of it to set in motion evils which leave no home in the world untouched. It is a cause of that magnitude that the United Nations will lay before Your Honors.

In the prisoners' dock sit twenty-odd broken men. . . .

What makes this inquest significant is that these prisoners represent sinister influences that will lurk in the world long after their bodies have returned to dust. We will show them to be living symbols of racial hatreds, of terrorism and violence, and of the arrogance and cruelty of power. They are symbols of fierce nationalisms and of militarism, of intrigue and war-making which have embroiled Europe generation after generation, crushing its manhood, destroying its homes, and impoverishing its life. They have so identified themselves with the philosophies they conceived and with the forces they directed that any tendencies to them is a victory and an encouragement to all the evils which are attached to their names. Civilization can afford no compromise with the social forces which would gain renewed strength if we deal ambiguously or indecisively with the men in whom those forces now precariously survive.

Source: *Michael R. Marrus, ed.,* The Nuremberg War Crimes Trial 1945–1946: A Documentary History *(Boston & New York: Bedford, 1997), pp. 79–83.*

Adolf Hitler's regime, people even less principled than they would have taken their place and that, in any case, what they had done was not in violation of existing international law. The judges found the first argument untruthful and illogical, and the second an interpretation of international law that would prevent its necessary development. Four of the defendants were sentenced to life imprisonment, six to shorter terms, and four were acquitted. Those who might have believed that the defendants in the Justice Case had been unfairly victimized by an overly broad understanding of international law were likely to have felt more comfortable with the outcome of Case VII, the "Hostage Case." Here the defendants were twelve high-ranking German army officers accused of having violated the laws of war by killing huge numbers of civilians in reprisal for guerrilla attacks on German forces. One of the defendants had ordered that one hundred Serbs be killed for every German soldier injured or killed by partisans. Even the prosecution conceded that, in some situations, reprisals were justified under the laws of war but argued that the Germans had reacted with disproportionate savagery. The judges showed some sympathy for the difficult problem the defendants had faced in dealing with guerrilla warfare and although expressing abhorrence of the deaths of innocent civilians, argued that it was their responsibility to apply international law as it was written, not as they would like it to be. Two of the defendants were acquitted, while those found guilty were given relatively mild sentences in light of the loss of civilian life that they had caused. Two were given terms of life in prison, and the remaining defendants received sentences of twenty years or less. However one might regard the verdicts and punishments meted out by the U.S. Nuremberg tribunals, it is beyond serious dispute that the accused received trials in which both law and evidence had been carefully weighed.

The trials conducted by the U.S. Army were in a different category. The numbers of defendants tried were often much larger, and verdicts and punishments were determined by regular army officers, most of whom had no formal legal training. Attorneys serving as prosecutors and defenders often had little or no experience in trying criminal cases. The most controversial of these many trials was held at Dachau in 1946. In what was popularly known as the "Malmedy massacre trial," seventy-three former members of the Waffen-SS (the combat arm of the elite Nazi organization) were tried for their role in the murder of American prisoners of war and Belgian civilians during the Battle of the Bulge (1944–1945). Following deliberation by the army judges that averaged less than two minutes per defendant, all were found guilty and more than half were sentenced to death. Yet, it was alleged by defense attorneys that many of the confessions on which the convictions had been largely based had been gotten from the Germans by beatings and psychological pressure, and there was some credible evidence to support this allegation. The Malmedy massacre trial appeared to be far from fair. However, the judges did not have the last word on the fate of the defendants. Both the subsequent Nuremberg trials and the Dachau trials were subject to reviews in which the fairness of the proceedings and the appropriateness of punishments were examined. As a result, many sentences were substantially reduced. In the case of the Malmedy massacre trial, all of the death sentences were eventually commuted to prison terms, and prison terms were, themselves, later shortened. By the end of 1956 all of the Malmedy defendants had been set free. Sentences in many trials were commuted in an effort to be fair to Germans whose guilt, in some cases, appeared to be less glaring as wartime emotions cooled. It is also clear that part of the motivation behind the reduction of sentences by United States authorities was to improve relations with West Germany, which came to be regarded as an important ally against the Soviet Union in the escalating Cold War.

At the start of the first Nuremberg trial, Jackson observed that the willingness of the United States and its allies to "stay the hand of vengeance and voluntarily submit their captive enemies to the judgment of the law is one of the most significant tributes that Power has ever paid to Reason." At Nuremberg and in the hundreds of American trials that followed, vengeance and incompetence occasionally held their own

against reason, but the system of American war-crimes justice moved cautiously and with restraint, and questionable verdicts and sentences were often substantively corrected in the post-trial review process. In light of the magnitude of the program, the complexity of the undertaking, and the overwhelming horror of Nazi Germany's offenses, the trials as a whole were fair.

–JAMES J. WEINGARTNER,
SOUTHERN ILLINOIS UNIVERSITY

Viewpoint:
No. In spite of charges of victors' justice and the questionable inclusion of Soviet judges, the Nuremberg trials were fair.

Perhaps the single greatest criticism of the International Military Tribunal (IMT) at Nuremberg involved the charge of victors' justice. Compounding that issue was the inclusion of the Soviet Union as a member of that judicial tribunal, especially in light of certain shadows that hovered above the record of Soviet activities from 1939 to 1945. Were the victors entitled to accuse and try the vanquished just because they had won, especially when at least one of those victors might have itself been guilty of equally horrendous crimes? Generally, an argument could be made that both Allied and Axis powers had committed atrocities during World War II (1939–1945) and more particularly that the U.S.S.R.'s aggression against Finland, Latvia, Estonia, Lithuania, and Poland, the latter three through secret alliance with Nazi Germany, certainly strained the credibility of that state as a prosecutor for war crimes at Nuremberg.

Many questions surfaced regarding the inclusion of the Soviet Union in a war-crimes tribunal, not the least among which were accusations of Soviet crimes of war (for example, the Katyn Forest massacre of 1940), rising postwar political tensions, fear of Soviet attempts to hijack the legal process, and apprehension that their presence would substantiate criticism of the process as simple victors' justice rather than a fair and impartial hearing on Nazi war crimes.

Yet, in fact, the rationale for inclusion of the Soviet Union, along with the United States, the United Kingdom, and France, was equally compelling. Exclusion could have been used by Moscow as an anti-Western propaganda tool, which would certainly have undermined the integrity of the IMT process. Exclusion would clearly have violated wartime agreements and policies established for the postwar period. Exclusion would have been counter to President Franklin D. Roosevelt's postwar intentions of containment by integration regarding the Soviet Union. Inclusion involved the Soviets in an international process concerning the accused, thus preventing an unlimited, unilateral system of victor's revenge by the Soviet Union that was almost certain to have followed. Above all, inclusion was justified by the Soviet Union's war record and the unparalleled losses suffered by the Soviets at the hands of the Nazis. Finally, inclusion represented a clear attempt on the part of the Allies at international justice, even though the membership of the tribunal, out of necessity, had to be limited to only four states. Inclusion of the U.S.S.R. certainly complicated the process but was necessary to the cause of justice.

The issue of inclusion of the U.S.S.R. as a member of the IMT became more of a controversy from the perspective of the late twentieth and early twenty-first centuries than it was in 1945. As the tribunal process took form and unfolded, there were certainly procedural problems with the Soviets, but the larger question of inclusion seems to have been a moot point, even with the suggestion that it might aggravate the claim of victors' justice. More-immediate concerns arose about differences in judicial philosophies and personalities. However, the former were smoothed over, and oddly, on an individual level, the Soviets proved to be "charming, courteous and friendly." Even later, when serious doubts were raised as Soviet policies were scrutinized, the tendency was to focus on the issues at hand, accusations of Nazi war crimes.

That there was to be a tribunal of any kind was not settled until 1945, and, curiously, it was the Soviets who insisted on a legal framework. As late as that year there was still a good deal of support for the idea of simply shooting Nazi leaders as they were captured. The semblance of a Carthaginian peace, in this instance, was not rejected completely by either Roosevelt or Winston Churchill. Indeed, it seems to have been Joseph Stalin's insistence that there must be trials and that "they should not be rigged," that convinced Churchill, who had traveled to Moscow in October 1944, of the necessity of a trial. According to historian Martin Gilbert, it was to be "a judicial rather than a political act." Roosevelt later responded that "it should not be too judicial." He did not want to involve the press and photographers until the guilty were dead.

The notion of a judicial framework had already appeared but with no designation regarding membership. In 1941 representatives from nine European governments in exile established an "Inter-Allied Commission on the Punishment of War Crimes" and issued from London the so-called Declaration of St. James, which insisted

on "the punishment, through the channel of organized justice, of those guilty of or responsible for these crimes." Reference to a legal tribunal was also made in the Moscow Declaration (1 November 1943) and at two wartime conventions, the Teheran Conference (November 1943) and the Yalta Conference (February 1945). In all of the latter three cases there was no question that the U.S.S.R. would be an equal participant in a legal solution to Nazis accused of war crimes. In those days how could there be a question? Stalin and the Soviet Union were integral parts of "The Big Three" along with Churchill and Great Britain and Roosevelt and the United States. Moreover, the Soviets had incurred substantial losses at the hands of the Nazis, much of this loss clearly in the form of what was suspected as war crimes, and to an extent equal to or surpassing any of the other Allies. Beyond those difficulties, exclusion would have meant breaking major agreements made at Teheran and Yalta.

The first actual meeting of the legal representatives of the victorious Allies took place in London, July 1945, the so-called London Conference. Four Allied states were present with the addition of France. Brief as it was, the conference marked the first meetings, and disagreements, between the national delegations. Compromises were made concerning charges and procedure, but no serious consideration was given to treating the Soviet Union as anything but an equal partner. The culmination of all of the general discussions concerning a legal solution was the Charter of the International Military Tribunal signed on 8 August 1945 forming the basis for the "just and prompt trial and punishment of the major war criminals of the European Axis." Article I of that document listed the United States, the United Kingdom, France, and the Soviet Union as the tribunal's four members. There was no major controversy.

No less important than these formal agreements were the intentions of President Roosevelt. Beyond the obvious practicality of retaining the U.S.S.R. as an ally against Germany and gaining its help against Japan, Roosevelt unfolded a policy of integration with Stalin and the Soviet Union for the sake of a stable postwar world. Put simply, if Stalin and the Soviets were made fundamental participants in the postwar order, they would be less inclined to cause trouble. Inclusion of the Soviets in the legal solution was a necessary part of Roosevelt's policy of containment by integration. Despite the president's death (12 April 1945), that policy held, at least as regarded the IMT.

Beyond the essential importance of integrating the Soviets into an accepted Allied legal solution, the Soviet presence on the IMT, more or less, prevented the Soviet Union from initiating a national campaign of revenge through national trials and procedures that clearly would have taken place and would have amounted to victors' justice of the worst kind, rigged show trials akin to Stalin's purges of the 1930s. The potential for Soviet excesses (indeed, extreme behavior by any of the four members) was checked by participation in the tribunal. The bare semblance of an international tribunal was also strengthened by the inclusion of the Soviets. Anglo-American law, Continental European law, and Soviet law all contributed to the legal basis of the tribunal. It was certainly not a universal representation, but it was clearly diverse enough to be called international.

Finally, embryonic Cold War suspicions also came into play. Exclusion of the Soviet Union almost certainly would have been used by the Soviets to discredit the tribunal and the western democracies. And from the beginning the American, British, and French members of the tribunal feared a Soviet attempt to hijack the proceedings legally. Curiously, it seems, the Soviets were even more afraid of an Anglo-American effort to control the trial entirely.

More than any of the other three Allies on the tribunal, the Soviets were themselves vulnerable to accusations of war crimes that both questioned their presence on the tribunal and clearly gave substance to accusations of victors' justice. The potential extent of those suspicions nearly impeached the Allied prosecution when the Soviets unwisely attempted to further the case against the Nazis by reference to the discovery of the bodies of some eleven thousand Polish military officers found in mass graves in the Katyn Forest. Only in the 1990s would the former Soviet Union acknowledge Soviet guilt in the Katyn massacre, but during the Nuremberg trials the evidence was ambiguous enough that the tribunal determined to drop the question. The guilt of the Axis prisoners was, after all, the issue at hand for the tribunal. Testimony by American admiral Chester M. Nimitz, procured by the defense in the case of German admiral Karl Dönitz, clearly suggested that acts involving the survivors of ships attacked by submarines, portrayed as crimes of war by the prosecution, were committed by the Allies as well in other theaters of the war, further suggesting victors' justice. As victors, the prosecution had the distinct advantage of determining the focus of the tribunal, which, in reflection on the previous examples, was substantial.

General debate over the question of victors' justice will, no doubt, continue, and for good reason. The judgment of the IMT at Nuremberg can be justified by the absence of an alternative legal apparatus and by the magnitude of the crimes committed by individuals acting on behalf of the Nazi State that demanded legal action. The argument that the judgment was flawed, "good justice but bad law," is generally conceded. In hindsight, one of the most prescient justifications for the tribunal was written at the time by Professor A. N. Trainin, a Russian legal authority: "There might come a time when there will be a permanent international tribunal of the United Nations organization to try all violations of international law." In the absence of such a platform he argued that the IMT "has a definite purpose in view, that is, to try criminals of the European Axis." The more particular question of whether inclusion of the Soviet Union on the IMT added substance to that accusation is a different matter. From the perspective of 1945, there was no question that the Soviets would be part of the legal proceedings: they were long-suffering members of the victorious alliance, and indeed a legal course of action was in large part at their insistence. From that perspective, the IMT represented not a collection of vengeful allies so much as a symbol of vain hopes for a united postwar world. Despite the issue of victors' justice, the IMT represented one of the few successful acts of a truly united postwar world until 1991 and the beginning of the breakup of the U.S.S.R. The inclusion of the Soviet Union as a member of the IMT was fundamental to that success.

–G. MICHAEL STATHIS,
SOUTHERN UTAH UNIVERSITY

References

Konrad Adenauer, *Memoirs,* translated by Beate Ruhm von Oppen (Chicago: Regnery, 1966).

John H. Backer, *Priming the German Economy* (Durham, N.C.: Duke University Press, 1950).

Dennis L. Bark and David R. Gress, *A History of West Germany,* volume 1, *From Shadow to Substance, 1945–1963* (Oxford & New York: Blackwell, 1989).

Michael Burleigh, *The Third Reich: A New History* (New York: Hill & Wang, 2000).

Frank M. Buscher, *The U.S. War Crimes Trial Program in Germany, 1946-1955* (Westport, Conn.: Greenwood Press, 1989).

Robert E. Conot, *Justice at Nuremberg* (New York: Harper & Row, 1983).

Eugene Davidson, *The Trial of the Germans* (New York: Macmillan, 1966).

Norman Davies, *Europe: A History* (Oxford: Oxford University Press, 1996).

Martin Gilbert, *Winston Churchill, 1941–1945: Road to Victory* (London: Heinemann, 1986).

Whitney R. Harris, *Tyranny on Trial: The Evidence at Nuremberg* (Dallas: Southern Methodist University Press, 1954).

International Military Tribunal, *Trial of the Major War Criminals Before the International Military Tribunal, Nuremberg, 14 November 1945–1 October 1946*, 42 volumes (Nuremberg: International Military Tribunal, 1947–1949).

Arieh J. Kochavi, *Prelude to Nuremberg: Allied War Crimes Policy and the Question of Punishment* (Chapel Hill: University of North Carolina Press, 1998).

Peter H. Maguire, *Law and War: An American Story* (New York: Columbia University Press, 2000).

Malmedy Massacre Investigation: Hearings Before a Subcommittee of the Committee on Armed Services, United States Senate, Eighty-First Congress, First Session, Pursuant to S. Res. 42 (Washington, D.C.: U.S. Government Printing Office, 1949).

Michael R. Marrus, ed., *The Nuremberg War Crimes Trial 1945-1946: A Documentary History* (Boston & New York: Bedford, 1997).

Richard Overy, *Interrogations: The Nazi Elite in Allied Hands, 1945* (New York: Viking, 2001).

Joseph E. Persico, *Nuremberg: Infamy on Trial* (New York: Viking/Penguin, 1994).

Simon Serfaty, *Stay the Course: European Unity and Atlantic Solidarity* (Westport, Conn.: Praeger, 1997).

Dusan Sjdjanski, *The Federal Future of Europe: From the European Community to the European Union* (Ann Arbor: University of Michigan Press, 2000).

Bradley F. Smith, *Reaching Judgment at Nuremberg* (New York: Basic Books, 1977).

Smith, ed., *The American Road to Nuremberg: The Documentary Record, 1944–1945* (Stanford, Cal.: Hoover Institution Press, 1982).

Jean Edward Smith, *Lucius D. Clay: An American Life* (New York: Holt, 1990).

Roger Spiller, "The Fuhrer in the Dock: A Speculation on the Banality of Evil," in *What If? 2: Eminent Historians Imagine What Might Have Been*, edited by Robert Cowley (New York: Putnam, 2001).

Paul Graham Taylor, *The European Union in the 1990s* (New York: Oxford University Press, 1996).

Telford Taylor, *The Anatomy of the Nuremberg Trials* (New York: Knopf, 1992).

A. N. Trainin, *Hitlerite Responsibility Under Criminal Law*, edited by A. Y. Vishinski and translated by Andrew Rothstein (London & New York: Hutchinson, 1945).

Trials of War Criminals Before the Nuremberg Military Tribunals Under Control Council Law No. 10, 15 volumes (Washington, D.C.: U.S. Government Printing Office, 1949–1953).

William Wallace, *The Transformation of Western Europe* (New York: Council on Foreign Relations Press, 1990).

James J. Weingartner, *A Peculiar Crusade: Willis M. Everett and the Malmedy Massacre* (New York: New York University Press, 2000).

WILLING EXECUTIONERS

Were Nazi soldiers who participated in the Holocaust committed anti-Semites who believed extermination was necessary for the preservation of social order?

Viewpoint: Yes. Though only a small minority of Germans killed Jews, they would not have done so had they not had good reason to believe that many other Germans shared their eliminationist anti-Semitic attitudes.

Viewpoint: No. The testimony of perpetrators, victims, and bystanders suggests that most Germans were ordinary people caught up in extraordinary circumstances and under enormous pressure to engage in or acquiesce to genocide.

In 1996 a young political scientist from Harvard, Daniel Jonah Goldhagen, published his dissertation, an event that rarely attracts much media attention. This occasion would be an exception. Goldhagen's *Hitler's Willing Executioners: Ordinary Germans and the Holocaust* claimed to overthrow virtually all contemporary scholarship on the Holocaust by arguing (a) that "eliminationist anti-Semitism" was, before the beginning of the twentieth century, a cultural norm in German society and would become "exterminationist" under the Nazis, (b) that the men and women who murdered the Jews did so because they shared this attitude toward the Jews with Adolf Hitler, and (c) that most "ordinary Germans" shared this attitude as well. Hitler had not, according to Goldhagen, forced the Holocaust onto Germany. Rather, he released German anti-Semitism from its earlier constraints of civility and permitted (rather than compelled or persuaded) quite ordinary Germans to torture, starve, and murder six million Jews. Goldhagen's book was effectively promoted by his publisher, Knopf, and though it ran to six hundred pages of often gruesome detail, it became an immediate best-seller and Goldhagen, a newcomer to the field, became one of the best known—if not the only widely recognized—scholar of the Holocaust in the United States.

Other Holocaust scholars were less impressed. Goldhagen based his arguments largely on the recorded experiences of a reserve police battalion that had carried out massacres in Poland. Christopher R. Browning had published *Ordinary Men: Reserve Police Battalion 101 and the Final Solution in Poland* (1992) based on the records of the same putatively "ordinary" Germans. Browning argued that these German killers were in no way the exterminationist anti-Semites Goldhagen would portray them to be four years later. Rather, they were, with some exceptions, pliable and frightened men who undertook a "terrible" task because they were told to. Only later, as they became hardened to the killing, did some of them seem to enjoy it. Browning, unlike Goldhagen, implied that any society could, in the right circumstances, produce genocidal killers.

The "Goldhagen thesis" was widely condemned by traditional historians of the Holocaust—most stridently at a conference attended by Goldhagen and his critics at the United States Holocaust Memorial Museum in Washington, D.C., on 8 April 1996. But more recently, other scholars have become more receptive to elements of Goldhagen's argument, thus continuing the debate.

Viewpoint:
Yes. Though only a small minority of Germans killed Jews, they would not have done so had they not had good reason to believe that many other Germans shared their eliminationist anti-Semitic attitudes.

Two books written in the 1990s gave a new focus to Holocaust studies: the question of the perpetrators and their motives. Both authors, Christopher R. Browning (*Ordinary Men: Reserve Police Battalion 101 and the Final Solution in Poland*, 1992) and Daniel Jonah Goldhagen (*Hitler's Willing Executioners: Ordinary Germans and the Holocaust*, 1996), based their research on Reserve Police Battalion 101 and their contribution to the Final Solution. Although their later conclusions clearly differ, Goldhagen and Browning come to one common important conclusion about the Order Police Reservists—a unit of approximately five hundred men that engaged in many mass shootings in the District of Lublin between June 1942 and the beginning of 1944—that they could be said to be representative of ordinary Germans. Central to the arguments is the fact that these middle-aged men "represented an age cohort that was socialized and educated in the pre-Nazi period and was fully aware of the moral norms of a pre-Nazi political culture."

The long-neglected question for the motivation of the perpetrators is answered by Browning, who explains their behavior with "universal aspects of human nature" such as conformity, obedience, and peer pressure. In this respect Goldhagen's approach of asking for the "historic specificity of the perpetrators themselves and of the society that nurtured them" is much more sophisticated. Unlike Browning, Goldhagen does not speak of ordinary men but stresses the particular social and historical setting. He accepts the relevance of the victims' and the perpetrators' identities. In this sense the historical record tells of ordinary Germans and their specific way of thinking about Jews. Goldhagen also reveals the blind spot of common explanations. Commonly, Holocaust historians' research has been based on the presupposition that the mass of the perpetrators had to be induced to kill against their will. However, Goldhagen clearly showed—and most critics failed to mention this point as being central—that the German perpetrators *understood* why they were supposed to kill Jews"; in other words, that "the annihilation of the Jews *made sense to them*." Moreover, Goldhagen is right in asking why nearly no member of the battalion took advantage of an opportunity to avoid killing Jews and in questioning why

the perpetrators so often inflicted unnecessary suffering upon their victims. These questions become more significant when contrasted with the fact that there are no reports of serious punishment incurred by any German who refused to kill. There were substantial opportunities for the Order Police Reservists to excuse themselves from these duties. Before embarking on the killing engagements, they were asked whether they were able to take part in killing helpless Jews; few of these men chose to opt out of taking part in the killing.

The question of the historic specificity and of the "political culture that produced the perpetrators and their actions," indeed, seems to be the right one to expand the historical debate. However, is Goldhagen correct in his assumption that a unique "eliminationist" anti-Semitism moved these "ordinary" Germans to kill Jews? First, it is important to sort out some misunderstandings. Of course, this cognitive model of eliminationist anti-Semitism cannot give a determinate or monocausal explanation of the Holocaust, nor does it represent some kind of biological collectivism (as misunderstood by some German historians). Instead, eliminationist anti-Semitism should be viewed as having its roots in the widespread anti-Jewish discourse in Germany in the nineteenth century and became—in the more radical and deadly form of exterminationist anti-Semitism—hegemonic by the 1930s at the latest. This German anti-Semitic discourse can explain the readiness of ordinary Germans to become "Hitler's willing executioners." At the same time, it does not deny the importance of other supplementary factors, which were necessary for the Holocaust to have been carried out.

Although initially most historians strongly rejected Goldhagen's thesis throughout the "Goldhagen Debate," a closer look at the latest research gives a rather different account. Even Browning acknowledges the necessity for a partial revision of the conclusions he reached about the killers. He states that he underestimated the group of "eager killers." Indeed, there were many who were ready to kill Jews from the start. The behavior of these perpetrators did not need to be altered by situational or organizational factors. Although Browning still speaks of this group as a "significant minority, not a majority," they nevertheless played a major role within the Holocaust. The perpetrators on the local level formed, along with the "initiators at the middle echelons and Adolf Hitler, Heinrich Himmler and Reinhard Heydrich at the top," a "crucial nucleus for the killing process." In other words, Browning concedes that a specific form of deadly anti-Semitism existed within all sectors of German society and that this eliminationist anti-

German soldiers posing
by twelve Poles, hung as
a retaliatory measure,
Rozki-Radom, 1942

(Bildarchiv Preussischer
Kulturbesitz, Berlin)

WILLING EXECUTIONERS

Semitism has to be central to an understanding of the destruction of the European Jews.

Saul Friedländer makes a similar point in his great study *Nazi Germany and the Jews* (1997). What he calls "redemptive" anti-Semitism substantially differs from other brands of European anti-Semitism. This "synthesis of a murderous rage and an 'idealistic' goal" derives from a "particularly German, mystical form" of anti-Semitism, stressing the sacredness of Aryan blood and the religious vision of German/Aryan Christianity. Though Friedländer holds the view that this most-radical kind of anti-Semitism was not shared by the majority of Germans, he makes clear that in no other European country was anti-Semitism so infused into the heart of society. Moreover, different from other countries, "a full blown antisemitic ideology was systematically elaborated" in Germany before 1933. This German specificity can be explained by a structural difference between Germany and, for example, France concerning national integration. In Germany the idea of the nation always was connected closely to the "existence of inherited characteristics belonging to a preexisting organic community." "Nation" in Germany meant a "closed ethnocultural community." Whereas Jews in France could become French, because the construction of national identity in Germany was implied in the idea itself, Jews always had to be the alien other, "regardless of formal emancipation and equality of civic rights."

Even if there can be no doubt of the existence of radical anti-Semitism in almost all European countries, one essential difference of the German development should be emphasized. According to an article by Herbert A. Strauss in *Hostages of Modernization: Studies on Modern Anti-semitism 1870-1933/39: Germany–Great Britain–France* (1993), among the German middle and elite classes before World War I (1914–1918), anti-Semitism was already a "social norm"—after the German defeat a more radical form of anti-Semitism with murderous potential came to the fore. This strain predominated among young elites at universities throughout the Weimar Republic. This anti-Semitism was opposed to other types of personal hatred and succeeded in both objectifying and radicalizing anti-Semitism. Fighting Jews was now thought of in "scientific" terms of a natural problem that necessarily has to be "solved."

Put to this context, Goldhagen's explanation that the perpetrators, ordinary Germans, were animated "by a particular *type* of anti-Semitism that led them to conclude that the Jews *ought to die*" clearly makes sense and is not really as incompatible with the tasks of other historians, as it has often been stated. As Yehuda Bauer observes, there can be no doubt that by the mid 1930s most Germans had adopted the Nazi ideology with its radical anti-Semitic content, but he also adds that the reason this fact was so pervasive "has not been sufficiently dealt with." Goldhagen's approach gives an adequate answer to this question. First, one must understand anti-Semitism as a cognitive model more complex and subtle than a mere prejudice. Certain conceptions of Jews were already being produced by German discourse, which made the last stage of radicalization a logical step for the perpetrators. A central component of this view has been "the idea of Jewish work-shirking parasitism," which had deep historical roots in Germany.

In the traditional German discourse, Jews shirked physical work and did all they could to avoid "honest" work. Opposed to this model, being German and taking work seriously were closely connected. Hard, productive work was equated with the notion of "German work." This binary opposition of hardworking Germans and work-shirking Jews preceded the Nazis, but they turned this belief into ideological capital. By at least the 1920s there were widespread anticapitalist resentments in all strata of society, which were not scornful of work and industrialism, because concrete labor appeared as a natural, creative process. Only the abstract dimension of capitalism, finance and interest capital, was criticized for being "rootless" and "parasitic," or simply put, as being "Jewish." The Nazi movement was both a part of and a means to advance this discourse. Thinking of anti-Semitism in this way, Moishe Postone called Nazism "a foreshortened anti-capitalist movement," one characterized by a hatred of the abstract and a hypostatization of the concrete. The Nazis gave themselves one mission: "to rid the world of the source of all evil." In other words, at the root of their ideology, as well as their intended actions, were components of eliminationist anti-Semitism.

As Goldhagen has conclusively shown, only this mind-set can explain the German treatment of the Jews in its economically self-injurious way. What happened in work camps such as Majdanek provides a good record of this attitude. On one hand, factories useful to war production had to be closed in order to continue the mass killing of Jews. On the other hand, Jews were the only group of victims who were compelled to perform senseless work. Singled out for especially miserable conditions, Jews suffered mortality rates in the work camps that far exceeded those of other groups of prisoners. These seemingly irrational actions gain significance when observed within the context of eliminationist anti-Semitism and German notions about Jews and work, which explains why Germans forced them to perform primarily noninstrumental labor. Jewish labor in German camps was clearly set apart from the ordinary ideas of work—it even differed from other kinds of forced labor at the camps. Jewish work was always a means to death; in Goldhagen's words, "it was death itself."

If one accepts the compelling record of a murderous anti-Semitism that derived from specific developments within German political culture, the question remains as to what extent this ideology affected Germans. First and foremost, many perpetrators of the Holocaust were ordinary Germans. Browning tells us that the reservists of the Order Police Reservists were "conscripted virtually at random from the population of those middle-aged men who enjoyed no exemption for providing skilled labor essential to the war economy." It is not possible to show each one of the perpetrators as either ready to kill Jews right from the start or as needing to be radicalized by situational factors. However, there remains one more detail that strengthens Goldhagen's thesis: the willingness of perpetrators to have their wives among them or to take photos and give written witness to their deeds. One does not have to verify that every German perpetrator did so, but the mere existence of a multitude of such evidence shows that the men had to have good reason for expecting their relatives to accept the killing of Jews as a necessary or even a beneficial act. The killers rightly expected other ordinary Germans to understand that the Jews had to be killed. This attitude surely is something that cannot be easily explained if most Germans of that time had not been eliminationist in their anti-Semitic attitudes.

−KARSTEN UHL,
UNIVERSITY OF OLDENBURG

Viewpoint:
No. The testimony of perpetrators, victims, and bystanders suggests that most Germans were ordinary people caught up in extraordinary circumstances and under enormous pressure to engage in or acquiesce to genocide.

Generalizations are easy. It takes no great leap of historical imagination to find the Germans collectively guilty of genocide. Any number of examples can be found within any particular topic to support an author's position, and so it is with this topic. Given the horrors perpetrated by the Nazis in Germany and the *Wehrmacht* (German army) in Russia and the

Ukraine, thousands of examples can be produced to attest to the callous behavior of the Germans against people they deemed inferior. With regard to "ordinary" Germans, the Holocaust historian Christopher R. Browning in *Nazi Policy, Jewish Workers, German Killers* (2000) has rightfully stated, "One of the most elusive tasks facing historians of any event is to uncover the attitudes and mindset of the 'ordinary' people who 'make history' but leave behind no files of official documents and precious few diaries and letters." This statement epitomizes the difficulty that an historian faces when confronted with a question that forces him or her, with ambiguous evidence, to explain the actions and attitudes of a large group of people.

The Nazi regime caused the German people to suppress their traditional standards of morality and to act in ways they would have otherwise found repugnant. Resistance to Nazi policies was possible and was moderately successful against the T–4 "euthanasia" program, but it had to be undertaken by a broad enough section of the population that trying to quash the opposition would threaten the Nazis' hold on power. Resistance conducted by small groups, such as the White Rose in Munich, was ruthlessly and publicly crushed. In a society such as Nazi Germany, silence does not imply acceptance or consent to the actions of the ruling regime. Knowledge of the Final Solution might have been widespread and anti-Semitism endemic, but the Nazis, not Germans as a whole, were responsible for the Holocaust. There is no reason to believe that the German people, even those who supported the Nazi regime, were uniquely "eliminationist" or "exterminationist" in their attitudes toward the Jews. Centuries of anti-Semitism may have bred indifference to the fate of the Jews and hostility to their social and political influence, but no more so among Germans than among the French, the Greeks, or even the Danes, who undertook enormous risks to rescue virtually their entire Jewish community.

The German population in Wilhelmine and Weimar Germany had its fair share of anti-Semites. In Poland in the late 1930s the government was seeking a solution to its own Jewish Question. In October 1938 the Polish ambassador to Great Britain proposed sending a specified number of Jews each year to the British colony of Rhodesia. The presence of anti-Semitism, however, does not correlate to a desire to exterminate the Jewish race. The Nazi Party, after achieving power, concentrated on an ever-increasing process of marginalization and exclusion against a population that numbered 500,000, or less than 1 percent of the German population, of which 20 percent were unassimilated Jews from eastern Europe. It is safe to say that most Germans had

little contact with Jews, given that most Jews lived in the larger German cities and not the towns and countryside where the majority of the German population resided.

Early attempts by the Nazis to marginalize the Jews met with widespread resistance. The American consul general in Berlin, George S. Messersmith, reported the 1 April 1933 boycott of Jewish businesses as not being popular because it harmed the economy and damaged the image of Germany abroad. Messersmith declared that many Germans did not take the boycott seriously and continued to shop at stores owned by Jews. A year later Messersmith related that although the German public was not much concerned with Jewish suffering, it was "tired and disgusted" with the persecution of the Jews. A report written by the Office of Strategic Services in 1943 stated that while previous animosity to the Jews must have existed in some sectors of society, the working class was not enthusiastic about anti-Semitism to start with and had benefited little from Nazi persecution of Jews.

Indeed, at a press conference held on 17 November 1938, instructions were given to reporters that under no circumstances was the impression to be given that any part of the population did not agree with anti-Jewish measures. It would seem that anti-Semitism was regarded as not well enough entrenched in society but that a concerted press campaign would bring the German population around to support the measures taken. The chief spokesman of the Ministry of Propaganda, Alfred-Ingemar Berndt, went so far as to acknowledge that the impression should not be created "that only the party and the state are antisemitic." In 1941 Joseph Goebbels, writing in the weekly magazine *Das Reich,* defended action against the Jews "because there had been some indications of solidarity with them by segments of the non-Jewish population." Even eight years of increasingly hostile anti-Jewish propaganda did not seem to affect the attitudes of Germans toward the Jews. This resistance begs the question: If the German population was behind the destruction of the Jews, then why were press campaigns necessary to convince people that the Jews were their eternal, racial enemies?

Regional studies undertaken in Germany have shown that the Jewish Question was of minimal importance to the population, especially in the war years. Reports from the German Security Service (SD) reveal a remarkable lack of commentary, positive or negative, from the Germans on this topic. Most of the remarks approving measures against the Jews came from within Nazi Party circles. Even these comments must be taken with a grain of salt; a private survey of Nazi Party members undertaken about their opinion toward the Jews reveals a remarkable apathy. In

THEY KNEW

Although Belzec death camp was in Poland, many Germans knew of its purpose, as seen in this passage. On 31 August 1942 a German officer recorded his conversations with other passengers while traveling by rail past the camp in which more than 550,000 Jews lost their lives:

I talked to a policeman on duty at the railway station. Upon my question as to where the Jews actually came from, he answered: "Those are probably the last from Lvov. That has been going on now for 5 weeks uninterruptedly. In Jaroslav they let remain only 8, no one knows why." I asked: "How far are they going?" Then he said: "To Belzec." "And then?" "Poison." I asked: "Gas?" He shrugged his shoulders. Then he said only: "At the beginning they always shot them, I believe."

Here in the German House I just talked with two soldiers from front-line prisoner-of-war camp 325. They said that these transports had lately passed through every day, mostly at night. Yesterday a 70-car one is supposed to have gone through.

In the train from Rawa Ruska to Cholm,
5:30 P.M.

When we boarded at 4:40 P.M. an empty transport had just arrived. I walked along the train twice and counted 56 cars. On the doors had been written in chalk: 60, 70, once 90, occasionally 40—obviously the number of Jews that were carried inside. In my compartment I spoke with a railway policeman's wife who is currently visiting her husband here. She says these transports are now passing through daily, sometimes also with German Jews. Yesterday 6 children's bodies were found along the track. . . .

5:40 P.M.

Short stop. Opposite us another transport. I talk to the policemen who rode on the passenger car in front. I ask: "Going back home to the Reich?" Grinning one of them says: "You know where we come from, don't you? Well, for us the work does not cease." Then the transport train continued—the cars were empty and swept clean; there were 35. In all probability that was the train I saw at 1 P.M. on the station in Rawa Ruska.

6:20 P.M.

We passed camp Belzec. Before then, we traveled for some time through a tall pine forest. When the woman called, "Now it comes," one could see a high hedge of fir trees. A strong sweetish odor could be made out distinctly. "But they are stinking already," says the woman. "Oh nonsense, that is only the gas," the railway policeman said laughing. Meanwhile—we had gone on about 200 yards—the sweetish odor was transformed into a strong smell of something burning. "That is from the crematory," says the policeman. A short distance farther the fence stopped. In front of it, one could see a guard house with an SS post. A double track led to the camp. One track branched off from the main line, the other ran over a turntable from the camp to a row of sheds about 250 yards away. A freight car happened to stand on the table. Several Jews were busy turning the disk. SS guards, rifle under the arm, stood by. One of the sheds was open; one could distinctly see that it was filled with bundles of clothes to the ceiling. As we went on, I looked back one more time. The fence was too high to see anything at all. The woman says that sometimes, while going by, one can see smoke rising from the camp, but I could notice nothing of the sort.

Source: "Behind the Fence," in Documents of Destruction: Germany and Jewry 1933–1945, *edited by Raul Hilberg (Chicago: Quadrangle Books, 1971), pp. 208–211.*

1938 one-third of those surveyed revealed indifference toward the Jewish Question; in 1942 that had risen to 69 percent. The crudely anti-Semitic "documentary" film *Der Ewige Jude* (The Eternal Jew, 1940), though promoted aggressively, was poorly attended.

The diaries of Victor Klemperer, a German Jewish professor of romantic literature in Dresden, reveals contradictions in the attitudes of the German population toward the Jews. Klemperer was interested in the Nazi Party's use of language and its impact on the Germans. He concluded that Nazi propaganda was effective because of its simplification and repetition. But not everyone got the message. On 6 February 1942, Gestapo chief Heinrich Müller reported that anonymous letters were coming from all over Germany complaining about incidents of executions of Jews. It can be inferred that the press campaigns, such as those conducted from 1938 onward, had a profound effect on the German population, one that was both positive and negative. Along with this propaganda campaign was a simultaneous effort by the Nazi regime to keep the death camps, or at least what went on inside them, secret.

If the Germans were exterminationist with regard to the Jews, as Daniel Jonah Goldhagen has argued, then why was it necessary to keep the Final Solution a secret? The Nazis went to great lengths to keep the German public and local populace ignorant of what went on inside the camps. This effort failed mainly because most of the camps were built in or near large cities, and the camp authorities could not easily explain away the glimpses of brutality or the smells emanating from the camps. An example of this policy is the concentration camp Mauthausen near Linz, Austria, and its forty outlying camps. While explanations offered did not convince the population that nothing was going on, they permitted them to ignore or rationalize what they had seen. For example, when the crematorium at the euthanasia facility in Hartheim, Austria, went into operation, the SS tried to convince the local population that the pervasive odor of burning flesh was caused by a "chemical treatment."

The German population was affected by what they saw, heard, and smelled. Following the war, a priest from Ebensee, where one of Mauthausen's satellite camps was located, reported speaking with the townspeople regarding the camp. He stated that he found women whose nerves suffered and farmers who avoided working certain fields too near the camp. Some farmers reported seeing funeral pyres where they could see bodies being incinerated. While this account does not record what tone the townspeople used in relating their stories, it can be assumed that it was not gleeful or happy since it would have been noted. This reaction does not seem to be one of a population who wanted the Jews exterminated. One could assume that the images the townspeople saw were augmented by the implicit knowledge that they themselves could be on the other side of the fence should they step out of line, though no overt threats were recorded.

With regard to perpetrators, studies undertaken of those individuals who performed the "dirty work" of the Holocaust, such as the roundup of Jews and mass executions, have shown a remarkable disparity of opinions on the Jewish Question. The most rewarding studies have been undertaken on the Order Police, especially the Reserve Police Battalions that were made up of older individuals whose formative years took place before the rise of the Nazis. Even survivors have given accounts of the Order Police who offered assistance to Jews in the form

of identity papers stating they were Polish instead of Jewish.

References from documents indicate that the *Schutzpolizei* in East Upper Silesia felt favorably toward the Jews. In November their commander warned his men that no Jewish greetings were to be acknowledged and that anyone who had contact with Jews outside of official business could be sent to a concentration camp. As late as May–June 1942 reports reached the *Schutzpolizei* commander that his men were not sufficiently harsh toward the Jews. These reports follow survivor testimony that indicates some Germans were sympathetic toward the Jews, even while they carried out their orders. The testimony of Oswald Rufeisen serves as an example, given that his recollections have been corroborated by other documentation.

Rufeisen served as a translator for the German police in the village of Mir in Silesia. He relates that the atmosphere among the men was formal and that there was little talk of politics; he did not even know who was or was not a Nazi Party member. Of the thirteen policemen stationed in Mir, Rufeisen characterized four of them as sadistic, gleeful killers; three did not actively take part in any killings; and the rest were "passive executors of orders." The three non-killers' absence from the killing operations passed without comment among the others. For Rufeisen, the sergeant in charge of the detachment, Reinhold Hein, was the most confusing individual. He told Rufeisen that he could not shoot a Jew, yet he planned every killing expedition. He was always courteous toward the *Judenrat* members and even promised them they would "die a humanitarian death" when confronted by one of them.

In the village of Marcinkance, located in the district of Bialystok, there was an example of overt resistance by a German official that resulted in charges being brought against him. Hans Lehmann was a forty-one-year-old official with the forestry office and an *Alte Kämpfer* (old fighter) who joined the Nazi Party before it came to power in 1933. During a ghetto-clearing operation in the village where some Jews tried to escape, Lehmann was accused of allowing them to run past him. Sergeant Albert Wietzke, who was in charge, accused Lehmann of leaving his post without orders and allowing Jews to escape by failing to fire his weapon at them. During the investigation Lehmann stated that he had worked well with the Jews for nine months and did not want to be responsible for their deaths. Fellow officers agreed that Lehmann had sympathetic feelings toward the Jews.

Paul Oschewski, another old Party member, implied that Lehmann did not understand the racial question but that he was fully aware of it.

WILLING EXECUTIONERS

Before the clearing operation, a customs official who was to take part committed suicide, which could suggest that he too was unwilling to participate. During this action two other men refrained from shooting at escaping Jews. Lehmann's subordinate suffered a shoulder injury while tackling an escaping Jew; this incident would imply that he too had been unwilling to shoot any Jews. It would seem that passive protest, such as not taking part in shootings, was allowed, but crossing the line into active protest over the Jewish Question was not tolerated. Not only did Lehmann refuse to fire his weapon, he also wrote a strong letter of protest concerning the action in Marcinkance, stating that the men had gunned down "peaceful Jews." The investigating officer questioned Lehmann's moral scruples and stated "that as a National Socialist he [Lehmann] must know that there is no such thing as peaceful Jews, otherwise we would have been spared the present war."

In both of these examples, between 20 and 30 percent of the men were willing, eager killers: four of thirteen in Mir and four of seventeen in Marcinkance. The same percentages of men actively avoided taking part in these actions: three or four of fourteen in Mir and as many as five of seventeen in Marcinkance. Abstention from shooting did not have any disciplinary consequences. Consequences resulted only from challenging the system, as Lehmann did. He was subjected to intense investigation and was eventually discredited and transferred.

Ordinary Germans also engaged in active resistance by ignoring laws not to fraternize with Jews. Klemperer describes a woman named Frieda who ignored orders not to talk with Jews. She occasionally brought him an apple. As the war went on, Klemperer noticed contradictions in the reactions of Germans toward the Jews. He noted that there were offerings of sympathy, food, and comforting words, especially from non-Jewish workers he met while performing forced labor in 1943–1944. In other instances he encountered hostility from passersby in the streets who became increasingly hostile as the Allied bombing campaign reached its peak. When Dresden, Klemperer's hometown, was firebombed on 13–14 February 1945, he tore off his yellow star out of fear that Jews would be murdered, since the German population increasingly blamed Jews for the bombing.

Studies that have been conducted on large segments of the population, such as those in Bavaria, have shown that the Jewish Question was of minimal importance to the German population. This work has also suggested that the anti-Semitism exhibited by the Nazi leadership was not an integrating element between the Party and the population, whatever its binding function was within the Party itself. Additionally, studies conducted by the U.S. Army in October 1945 found that 20 percent of Germans went along with Hitler regarding the Jewish Question, and another 19 percent were generally in favor but felt that he had gone too far. This finding would seem to follow the conclusions reached by historians, such as Ian Kershaw and others, who place the blame for the Holocaust squarely on the shoulders of the Nazis and a minority of other Germans.

It is impossible to say with any certainty how much the German population knew regarding the Final Solution or what their attitudes were toward it. Studies based on a broad variety of sources have shown that there was German ambiguity with regard to the Jewish Question. Even victims of Nazi persecution, such as Klemperer, have shown that ordinary Germans ignored orders against fraternization and even helped Jews, if only in small ways. The percentage of Germans sympathetic to the Jews found by the U.S. Army in October 1945 are similar to the percentage of Germans who were willing and even gleeful killers, approximately 20 percent. Given the variety of sources from perpetrators, victims, and bystanders, it would seem that Germans were not uniquely exterminationist but instead were ordinary people caught up in extraordinary circumstances under enormous stresses precipitated by the Nazi regime.

–RICHARD MCGAHA,
BREMERTON, WASHINGTON

References

Yehuda Bauer, "Overall Explanations, German Society and the Jews or: Some Thoughts about Context," in *Probing the Depths of German Antisemitism: German Society and the Persecution of the Jews, 1933–1941*, edited by David Bankier (New York: Berghahn Books, 2000), pp. 3–16.

Christopher R. Browning, *Nazi Policy, Jewish Workers, German Killers* (Cambridge & New York: Cambridge University Press, 2000).

Browning, "Ordinary Men or Ordinary Germans?" in *Unwilling Germans?: The Goldhagen Debate*, edited by Robert R. Shandley, translated by Jeremiah Reimer (Minneapolis: University of Minnesota Press, 1998), pp. 55–73.

Browning, *Ordinary Men: Reserve Police Battalion 101 and the Final Solution in Poland* (New York: HarperCollins, 1992).

Norman G. Finkelstein and Ruth Bettina Birn, *A Nation on Trial: The Goldhagen Thesis and*

Historical Truth (New York: Metropolitan, 1998).

Saul Friedländer, *Nazi Germany and the Jews*, volume 1, *The Years of Persecution, 1933–1939* (New York: HarperCollins, 1997).

Christian Gerlach, "The Wannsee Conference, The Fate of German Jews, and Hitler's Decision in Principle to Exterminate All European Jews," in *Holocaust: Origins, Implementation, Aftermath,* edited by Omer Bartov (London: Routledge, 2000).

Daniel Jonah Goldhagen, "The Failure of the Critics," in *Unwilling Germans?: The Goldhagen Debate,* edited by Shandley (Minneapolis: University of Minnesota Press, 1998), pp. 129–150.

Goldhagen, *Hitler's Willing Executioners: Ordinary Germans and the Holocaust* (New York: Knopf, 1996).

Susanne Heim, "The German-Jewish Relationship in the Diaries of Victor Klemperer," in *Probing the Depths of German Antisemitism: German Society and the Persecution of the Jews, 1933–1941,* edited by Bankier (New York: Berghahn Books, 2000).

Ulrich Herbert, "The Right Question," in *Unwilling Germans?: The Goldhagen Debate,* edited by Shandley (Minneapolis: University of Minnesota Press, 1998), pp. 109–116.

Gordon J. Horwitz, "Places Far Away, Places Very Near: Mauthausen, the Camps of the Shoah, and the Bystanders," in *The Holocaust: Origins, Implementation, Aftermath,* edited by Bartov (New York: Routledge, 2000).

Ian Kershaw, "The Führer Image and Political Integration: The Popular Conception of Hitler in Bavaria during the Third Reich," in *Der "Führerstaat," Mythos und Realität: Studien zur Struktur und Politik des Dritten Reiches* (The "Führer State," Myth and Reality: Studies on the Structure and Politics of the Third Reich), edited by Gerhard Hirschfeld and Lothar Kettenacker (Stuttgart: Klett-Cotta, 1981).

Kershaw, *Popular Opinion and Political Dissent in the Third Reich: Bavaria 1933–1945* (Oxford: Clarendon Press / New York: Oxford University Press, 1983).

Otto Dov Kulka, "The German Population and the Jews: State of Research and New Perspectives," in *Probing the Depths of German Antisemitism: German Society and the Persecution of the Jews, 1933–1941,* edited by Bankier (New York: Berghahn Books, 2000).

Franklin H. Littell, ed., *Hyping the Holocaust: Scholars Answer Goldhagen* (East Rockaway, N.Y.: Cummings & Hathaway, 1997).

Alf Lüdtke, "German Work and German Workers: The Impact of Symbols on the Exclusion of Jews in Nazis Germany," in *Probing the Depths of German Antisemitism: German Society and the Persecution of the Jews 1933–1941,* edited by Bankier (New York: Berghahn Books, 2000), pp. 296–311.

Herbert Obenaus, "The Germans: 'An Antisemitic People': The Press Campaign After 9 November 1938," in *Probing the Depths of German Antisemitism: German Society and the Persecution of the Jews, 1933–1941,* edited by Bankier (New York: Berghahn Books, 2000), pp. 155–156.

Moishe Postone, "Anti-Semitism and National Socialism," in *Germans and Jews Since the Holocaust: The Changing Situation in West Germany,* edited by Anson Rabinbach and Jack Zipes (London & New York: Holmes & Meier, 1986), pp. 302–314.

Nicholas Stargardt, "The Final Solution," in *Twentieth-Century Germany: Politics, Culture and Society, 1918–1990,* edited by Mary Fulbrook (London: Arnold / New York: Oxford University Press, 2001).

Herbert A. Strauss, "Hostages of 'World Jewry': On the Origin of the Idea of Genocide in German History," in *Hostages of Modernization: Studies on Modern Antisemitism, 1870–1933/39: Germany–Great Britain–France,* edited by Strauss (Berlin & New York: De Gruyter, 1993), pp. 165–173.

Frank Wesley, *The Holocaust and Anti-Semitism: The Goldhagen Argument and Its Effects* (San Francisco: International Scholars, 1999).

Edward B. Westermann, "'Ordinary Men' or 'Ideological Soldiers'? Police Battalion 310 in Russia," *German Studies Review,* 21 (1998): 41–68.

Robert S. Wistrich, *Hitler and the Holocaust* (London: Weidenfeld & Nicolson, 2001).

APPENDIX

The documentary record of the Holocaust (1933–1945) is unimaginably complex. As a bureaucratic venture, the Final Solution to the Jewish Question generated, in a little over a decade, whole warehouses full of letters, orders, receipts, blueprints, and assorted memoranda. It required the coordinated participation of the German military, police, judiciary, and transportation sectors. Cattle cars had to be requisitioned; rail schedules had to be coordinated; contractors had to be paid; reports had to be written; and orders had to be issued. Modern states do not do such things without leaving a paper trail. As the Allies closed in on Germany in 1945, some of this evidence was destroyed by the perpetrators, but the Holocaust had generated far too many documents for the record to have been erased.

Germany's allies generated their own documentation, as did the businesses that participated, either as service providers or beneficiaries of slave labor. The Red Cross, the Vatican, as well as the intelligence services of the United States, Soviet Union, Great Britain, Switzerland, and even Japan confronted, in one way or another, the destruction of the Jews and left documentary records thereof. Many of these archives, particularly those in the former Soviet Union, have only become available to scholars. Other documents remain classified, hidden, lost, or forgotten. Even after sixty years, the documentary record of World War II (1939–1945) and the Holocaust has much uncharted territory. Making research even more daunting is the fact that the documents are written in German, Russian, Yiddish, French, English, Polish, Hungarian, and a score of other languages. No one could hope to comprehend all of them.

In all of this wealth of documentation, there is no "smoking gun"; no single document tells the complete story. Rather, they must be collected,

analyzed, and compared to put together a reliable account of the Holocaust. Because the documentary record is so rich, the final story remains incomplete. The five documents collected here are neither representative of the whole of Holocaust archival resources, nor are they fundamentally more important than others. They do provide, however, a glimpse of the diversity and of the compelling nature of many similar sources. Alone, they tell little; within the context of other documents, the memories of survivors, liberators, bystanders, and perpetrators and the broader history of World War II, they cast light on the intellectual origins of the Holocaust ("Adolf Hitler's First Anti-Semitic Writing"), the planning of the Final Solution ("Wannsee Protocol"), its implementation ("The Warsaw Ghetto Is No More"), the liberation of the camps ("Liberators"), and the problem of rendering justice after the fact ("Rudolf Höss, Commandant of Auschwitz").

DOCUMENT 1

ADOLF HITLER'S FIRST ANTI-SEMITIC WRITING

Below is a letter written in 1919 by Hitler to the Bavarian politician Adolf Gemlich. This missive is considered by many historians as the launching point of the future Nazi leader's political career. Hitler advocates the segregation and expulsion of Jews from European society, although he does not yet call for their systematic liquidation.

September 16, 1919

Dear Herr Gemlich,

The danger posed by Jewry for our people today finds expression in the undeniable aversion of wide sections of our people. The cause of this aversion is not to be found in a clear recognition of the consciously or unconsciously systematic and pernicious effect of the Jews as a totality upon our nation. Rather, it arises mostly from personal contact and from the personal impression which the individual Jew leaves—almost always an unfavorable one. For this reason, antisemitism is too easily characterized as a mere emotional phenomenon. And yet this is incorrect. Antisemitism as a political movement may not and cannot be defined by emotional impulses, but by recognition of the facts. The facts are these: First, Jewry is absolutely a race and not a religious association. Even the Jews never designate themselves as Jewish Germans, Jewish Poles, or Jewish Americans but always as German, Polish, or American Jews. Jews have never yet adopted much more than the language of the foreign nations among whom they live. A German who is forced to make use of the French language in France, Italian in Italy, Chinese in China does not thereby become a Frenchman, Italian, or Chinaman. It's the same with the Jew who lives among us and is forced to make use of the German language. He does not thereby become a German. Neither does the Mosaic faith, so important for the survival of this race, settle the question of whether someone is a Jew or non-Jew. There is scarcely a race whose members belong exclusively to just one definite religion.

Through thousands of years of the closest kind of inbreeding, Jews in general have maintained their race and their peculiarities far more distinctly than many of the peoples among whom they have lived. And thus comes the fact that there lives amongst us a non- German, alien race which neither wishes nor is able to sacrifice its racial character or to deny its feeling, thinking, and striving. Nevertheless, it possesses all the political rights we do. If the ethos of the Jews is revealed in the purely material realm, it is even clearer in their thinking and striving. Their dance around the golden calf is becoming a merciless struggle for all those possessions we prize most highly on earth.

The value of the individual is no longer decided by his character or by the significance of his achievements for the totality but exclusively by the size of his fortune, by his money.

The loftiness of a nation is no longer to be measured by the sum of its moral and spiritual powers, but rather by the wealth of its material possessions.

This thinking and striving after money and power, and the feelings that go along with it, serve the purposes of the Jew who is unscrupulous in the choice of methods and pitiless in their employment. In autocratically ruled states he whines for the favor of "His Majesty" and misuses it like a leech fastened upon the nations. In democracies he vies for the favor of the masses, cringes before the "majesty of the people," and recognizes only the majesty of money.

He destroys the character of princes with byzantine flattery, national pride (the strength of a people), with ridicule and shameless breeding to depravity. His method of battle is that public opinion which is never expressed in the press but which is nonetheless managed and falsified by it. His power is the power of money, which multiplies in his hands effortlessly and endlessly through interest, and which forces peoples under the most dangerous of yokes. Its golden glitter, so attractive in the beginning, conceals the ultimately tragic consequences. Everything men strive after as a higher goal, be it religion, socialism, democracy, is to the Jew only means to an end, the way to satisfy his lust for gold and domination.

In his effects and consequences he is like a racial tuberculosis of the nations. The deduction from all this is the following: an antisemitism based on purely emotional grounds will find its ultimate expression in the form of the pogrom. An antisemitism based on reason, however, must lead to systematic legal combatting and elimination of the privileges of the Jews, that which distinguishes the Jews from the other aliens who live among us (an Aliens Law). The ultimate objective [of such legislation] must, however, be the irrevocable removal of the Jews in general.

For both these ends a government of national strength, not of national weakness, is necessary.

The Republic in Germany owes its birth not to the uniform national will of our people but the sly exploitation of a series of circumstances which found general expression in a deep, universal dissatisfaction. These circumstances however were independent of the form of the state and are still operative today. Indeed, more so now than before. Thus, a great portion of our people recognizes that a changed state-form cannot in itself change our situation. For that it will take a rebirth of the moral and spiritual powers of the nation.

And this rebirth cannot be initiated by a state leadership of irresponsible majorities, influenced by certain party dogmas, an irresponsible press, or internationalist phrases and slogans. [It requires] instead the ruthless installation of nationally minded leadership personalities with an inner sense of responsibility.

But these facts deny to the Republic the essential inner support of the nation's spiritual forces. And thus today's state leaders are compelled to seek support among those who draw the exclusive benefits of the new formation of German conditions, and who for this reason were the driving force behind the revolution–the Jews. Even though (as various statements of the leading personalities reveal) today's leaders fully realized the danger of Jewry, they (seeking their own advantage) accepted the readily proffered support of the Jews and also returned the favor. And this pay-off consisted not only in every possible favoring of Jewry, but above all in the hindrance of the struggle of the betrayed people against its defrauders, that is in the repression of the antisemitic movement.

Respectfully,
Adolf Hitler

Source: Eberhard Jäckel, ed., *Hitler. Sämtliche Aufzeichnungen 1905–1924* (Stuttgart: Deutsche Verlags-Anstalt, 1980), pp. 88–90. Translation by Richard S. Levy.

APPENDIX

DOCUMENT 2

WANNSEE PROTOCOL

On 20 January 1942 senior Nazi officials met in the Berlin suburb of Wannsee to formalize the Final Solution of the Jewish Question. The minutes of the conference are reproduced below.

I.

The following persons took part in the discussion about the final solution of the Jewish question which took place in Berlin, am Grossen Wannsee No. 56/58 on 20 January 1942.

Gauleiter Dr. Meyer and Reichsamtleiter Dr. Leibbrandt	Reich Ministry for the Occupied Eastern territories
Secretary of State Dr. Stuckart	Reich Ministry for the Interior
Secretary of State Neumann	Plenipotentiary for the Four Year Plan
Secretary of State Dr. Freisler	Reich Ministry of Justice
Secretary of State Dr. Bühler	Office of the Government General
Under Secretary of State Dr. Luther	Foreign Office
SS-Oberführer Klopfer	Party Chancellery
Ministerialdirektor Kritzinger	Reich Chancellery
SS-Gruppenführer Hofmann	Race and Settlement Main Office
SS-Gruppenführer Müller SS-Obersturmbannführer Eichmann	Reich Main Security Office
SS-Oberführer Dr. Schongarth Commander of the Security Police and the SD in the Government General	Security Police and SD
SS-Sturmbannführer Dr. Lange Commander of the Security Police and the SD for the General-District Latvia, as deputy of the Commander of the Security Police and the SDfor the Reich Commissariat "Eastland".	Security Police and SD

II.

At the beginning of the discussion Chief of the Security Police and of the SD, SS-Obergruppenführer Heydrich, reported that the Reich Marshal had appointed him delegate for the preparations for the final solution of the Jewish question in Europe and pointed out that this discussion had been called for the purpose of clarifying fundamental questions. The wish of the Reich Marshal to have a draft sent to him concerning organizational, factual and material interests in relation to the final solution of the Jewish question in Europe makes necessary an initial common action of all central offices immediately concerned with these questions in order to bring their general activities into line.

The Reichsfuhrer-SS and the Chief of the German Police (Chief of the Security Police and the SD) was entrusted with the official central handling of the final solution of the Jewish question without regard to geographic borders.

The Chief of the Security Police and the SD then gave a short report of the struggle which has been carried on thus far against this enemy, the essential points being the following:

a) the expulsion of the Jews from every sphere of life of the German people,
b) the expulsion of the Jews from the living space of the German people.

In carrying out these efforts, an increased and planned acceleration of the emigration of the Jews from Reich territory was started, as the only possible present solution.

By order of the Reich Marshal, a Reich Central Office for Jewish Emigration was set up in January 1939 and the Chief of the Security Police and SD was entrusted with the management. Its most important tasks were

a) to make all necessary arrangements for the preparation for an increased emigration of the Jews,
b) to direct the flow of emigration,
c) to speed the procedure of emigration in each individual case.

The aim of all this was to cleanse German living space of Jews in a legal manner.

All the offices realized the drawbacks of such enforced accelerated emigration. For the time being they had, however, tolerated it on account of the lack of other possible solutions of the problem.

The work concerned with emigration was, later on, not only a German problem, but also a problem with which the authorities of the countries to which the flow of emigrants was being directed would have to deal. Financial difficulties, such as the demand by various foreign governments for increasing sums of money to be presented at the time of the landing, the lack of shipping space, increasing restriction of entry permits, or the cancelling of such, increased extraordinarily the difficulties of emigration. In spite of these difficulties, 537,000 Jews were sent out of the country between the takeover of power and the deadline of 31 October 1941. Of these

- approximately 360,000 were in Germany proper on 30 January 1933

- approximately 147,000 were in Austria (Ostmark) on 15 March 1939
- approximately 30,000 were in the Protectorate of Bohemia and Moravia on 15 March 1939.

The Jews themselves, or their Jewish political organizations, financed the emigration. In order to avoid impoverished Jews' remaining behind, the principle was followed that wealthy Jews have to finance the emigration of poor Jews; this was arranged by imposing a suitable tax, i.e., an emigration tax, which was used for financial arrangements in connection with the emigration of poor Jews and was imposed according to income.

Apart from the necessary Reichsmark exchange, foreign currency had to be presented at the time of landing. In order to save foreign exchange held by Germany, the foreign Jewish financial organizations were—with the help of Jewish organizations in Germany—made responsible for arranging an adequate amount of foreign currency. Up to 30 October 1941, these foreign Jews donated a total of around 9,500,000 dollars.

In the meantime the Reichsführer-SS and Chief of the German Police had prohibited emigration of Jews due to the dangers of an emigration in wartime and due to the possibilities of the East.

III.

Another possible solution of the problem has now taken the place of emigration, i.e. the evacuation of the Jews to the East, provided that the Führer gives the appropriate approval in advance.

These actions are, however, only to be considered provisional, but practical experience is already being collected which is of the greatest importance in relation to the future final solution of the Jewish question.

Approximately 11 million Jews will be involved in the final solution of the European Jewish question, distributed as follows among the individual countries:

COUNTRY	NUMBER
A. Germany proper	131,800
Austria	43,700
Eastern territories	420,000
General Government	2,284,000
Bialystok	400,000
Protectorate Bohemia and Moravia	74,200
Estonia	-free of Jews-
Latvia	3,500
Lithuania	34,000
Belgium	43,000
Denmark	5,600
France / occupied territory	165,000
unoccupied territory	700,000
Greece	69,600
Netherlands	160,800
Norway	1,300

B. Bulgaria	48,000
England	330,000
Finland	2,300
Ireland	4,000
Italy including Sardinia	58,000
Albania	200
Croatia	40,000
Portugal	3,000
Rumania including Bessarabia	342,000
Sweden	8,000
Switzerland	18,000
Serbia	10,000
Slovakia	88,000
Spain	6,000
Turkey (European portion)	55,500
Hungary	742,800
USSR	5,000,000
Ukraine	2,994,684
White Russia excluding Bialystok	446,484

Total over 11,000,000

The number of Jews given here for foreign countries includes, however, only those Jews who still adhere to the Jewish faith, since some countries still do not have a definition of the term "Jew" according to racial principles.

The handling of the problem in the individual countries will meet with difficulties due to the attitude and outlook of the people there, especially in Hungary and Rumania. Thus, for example, even today the Jew can buy documents in Rumania that will officially prove his foreign citizenship.

The influence of the Jews in all walks of life in the USSR is well known. Approximately five million Jews live in the European part of the USSR, in the Asian part scarcely 1/4 million.

The breakdown of Jews residing in the European part of the USSR according to trades was approximately as follows:

Agriculture	9.1 %
Urban workers	14.8 %
In trade	20.0 %
Employed by the state	23.4 %
In private occupations such as medical profession, press, theater, etc.	32.7%

Under proper guidance, in the course of the final solution the Jews are to be allocated for appropriate labor in the East. Able-bodied Jews, separated according to sex, will be taken in large work columns to these areas for work on roads, in the course of which action doubtless a large portion will be eliminated by natural causes.

The possible final remnant will, since it will undoubtedly consist of the most resistant portion, have to be treated accordingly, because it is the product of natural selection and would, if

APPENDIX

released, act as a the seed of a new Jewish revival (see the experience of history.)

In the course of the practical execution of the final solution, Europe will be combed through from west to east. Germany proper, including the Protectorate of Bohemia and Moravia, will have to be handled first due to the housing problem and additional social and political necessities.

The evacuated Jews will first be sent, group by group, to so-called transit ghettos, from which they will be transported to the East.

SS-Obergruppenführer Heydrich went on to say that an important prerequisite for the evacuation as such is the exact definition of the persons involved.

It is not intended to evacuate Jews over 65 years old, but to send them to an old-age ghetto—Theresienstadt is being considered for this purpose.

In addition to these age groups—of the approximately 280,000 Jews in Germany proper and Austria on 31 October 1941, approximately 30% are over 65 years old—severely wounded veterans and Jews with war decorations (Iron Cross I) will be accepted in the old-age ghettos. With this expedient solution, in one fell swoop many interventions will be prevented.

The beginning of the individual larger evacuation actions will largely depend on military developments. Regarding the handling of the final solution in those European countries occupied and influenced by us, it was proposed that the appropriate expert of the Foreign Office discuss the matter with the responsible official of the Security Police and SD.

In Slovakia and Croatia the matter is no longer so difficult, since the most substantial problems in this respect have already been brought near a solution. In Rumania the government has in the meantime also appointed a commissioner for Jewish affairs. In order to settle the question in Hungary, it will soon be necessary to force an adviser for Jewish questions onto the Hungarian government.

With regard to taking up preparations for dealing with the problem in Italy, SS-Obergruppenführer Heydrich considers it opportune to contact the chief of police with a view to these problems.

In occupied and unoccupied France, the registration of Jews for evacuation will in all probability proceed without great difficulty.

Under Secretary of State Luther calls attention in this matter to the fact that in some countries, such as the Scandinavian states, difficulties will arise if this problem is dealt with thoroughly and that it will therefore be advisable to defer actions in these countries. Besides, in view of the small numbers of Jews affected, this deferral will not cause any substantial limitation.

The Foreign Office sees no great difficulties for southeast and western Europe.

SS-Gruppenführer Hofmann plans to send an expert to Hungary from the Race and Settlement Main Office for general orientation at the time when the Chief of the Security Police and SD takes up the matter there. It was decided to assign this expert from the Race and Settlement Main Office, who will not work actively, as an assistant to the police attaché.

IV.

In the course of the final solution plans, the Nuremberg Laws should provide a certain foundation, in which a prerequisite for the absolute solution of the problem is also the solution to the problem of mixed marriages and persons of mixed blood.

The Chief of the Security Police and the SD discusses the following points, at first theoretically, in regard to a letter from the chief of the Reich chancellery:

1) Treatment of Persons of Mixed Blood of the First Degree.

Persons of mixed blood of the first degree will, as regards the final solution of the Jewish question, be treated as Jews.

From this treatment the following exceptions will be made:

a) Persons of mixed blood of the first degree married to persons of German blood if their marriage has resulted in children (persons of mixed blood of the second degree). These persons of mixed blood of the second degree are to be treated essentially as Germans.

b) Persons of mixed blood of the first degree, for whom the highest offices of the Party and State have already issued exemption permits in any sphere of life. Each individual case must be examined, and it is not ruled out that the decision may be made to the detriment of the person of mixed blood.

The prerequisite for any exemption must always be the personal merit of the person of mixed blood. (Not the merit of the parent or spouse of German blood.)

Persons of mixed blood of the first degree who are exempted from evacuation will be sterilized in order to prevent any offspring and to eliminate the problem of persons of mixed blood once and for all. Such sterilization will be voluntary. But it is required to remain in the Reich. The sterilized "person of mixed blood" is thereafter free of all restrictions to which he was previously subjected.

2) Treatment of Persons of Mixed Blood of the Second Degree.

Persons of mixed blood of the second degree will be treated fundamentally as persons of German blood, with the exception of the following cases, in which the persons of mixed blood of the second degree will be considered as Jews:

a) The person of mixed blood of the second degree was born of a marriage in which both parents are persons of mixed blood.

b) The person of mixed blood of the second degree has a racially especially undesirable appearance that marks him outwardly as a Jew.

c) The person of mixed blood of the second degree has a particularly bad police and political record that shows that he feels and behaves like a Jew.

Also in these cases exemptions should not be made if the person of mixed blood of the second degree has married a person of German blood.

3) Marriages between Full Jews and Persons of German Blood.

Here it must be decided from case to case whether the Jewish partner will be evacuated or whether, with regard to the effects of such a step on the German relatives, [this mixed marriage] should be sent to an old-age ghetto.

4) Marriages between Persons of Mixed Blood of the First Degree and Persons of German Blood.

a) Without Children.

If no children have resulted from the marriage, the person of mixed blood of the first degree will be evacuated or sent to an old-age ghetto (same treatment as in the case of marriages between full Jews and persons of German blood, point 3.)

b) With Children.

If children have resulted from the marriage (persons of mixed blood of the second degree), they will, if they are to be treated as Jews, be evacuated or sent to a ghetto along with the parent of mixed blood of the first degree. If these children are to be treated as Germans (regular cases), they are exempted from evacuation as is therefore the parent of mixed blood of the first degree.

5) Marriages between Persons of Mixed Blood of the First Degree and Persons of Mixed Blood of the First Degree or Jews.

In these marriages (including the children) all members of the family will be treated as Jews and therefore be evacuated or sent to an old-age ghetto.

6) Marriages between Persons of Mixed Blood of the First Degree and Persons of Mixed Blood of the Second Degree.

In these marriages both partners will be evacuated or sent to an old-age ghetto without consideration of whether the marriage has produced children, since possible children will as a rule have stronger Jewish blood than the Jewish person of mixed blood of the second degree.

SS-Gruppenführer Hofmann advocates the opinion that sterilization will have to be widely used, since the person of mixed blood who is given the choice whether he will be evacuated or sterilized would rather undergo sterilization.

State Secretary Dr. Stückart maintains that carrying out in practice of the just mentioned possibilities for solving the problem of mixed marriages and persons of mixed blood will create endless administrative work. In the second place, as the biological facts cannot be disregarded in any case, State Secretary Dr. Stuckart proposed proceeding to forced sterilization.

Furthermore, to simplify the problem of mixed marriages possibilities must be considered with the goal of the legislator saying something like: "These marriages have been dissolved."

With regard to the issue of the effect of the evacuation of Jews on the economy, State Secretary Neumann stated that Jews who are working in industries vital to the war effort, provided that no replacements are available, cannot be evacuated.

SS-Obergruppenführer Heydrich indicated that these Jews would not be evacuated according to the rules he had approved for carrying out the evacuations then underway.

State Secretary Dr. Bühler stated that the General Government would welcome it if the final solution of this problem could be begun in the General Government, since on the one hand transportation does not play such a large role here nor would problems of labor supply hamper this action. Jews must be removed from the territory of the General Government as quickly as possible, since it is especially here that the Jew as an epidemic carrier represents an extreme danger and on the other hand he is causing permanent chaos in the economic structure of the country through continued black market dealings. Moreover, of the approximately 2 1/2 million Jews concerned, the majority is unfit for work.

State Secretary Dr. Bühler stated further that the solution to the Jewish question in the General Government is the responsibility of the Chief of the Security Police and the SD and that his efforts would be supported by the officials of the General Government. He had only one request, to solve the Jewish question in this area as quickly as possible.

In conclusion the different types of possible solutions were discussed, during which discussion both Gauleiter Dr. Meyer and State Secretary Dr. Bühler took the position that certain preparatory activities for the final solution should be carried out immediately in the territories in question, in which process alarming the populace must be avoided.

The meeting was closed with the request of the Chief of the Security Police and the SD to the participants that they afford him appropriate support during the carrying out of the tasks involved in the solution.

Source: John Mendelsohn, ed., *The Holocaust: Selected Documents in Eighteen Volumes.* Volume 11: *The Wannsee Protocol and a 1944 Report on Auschwitz by the Office of Strategic Services* (New York: Garland, 1982), pp. 18–32.

APPENDIX

DOCUMENT 3

THE WARSAW GHETTO IS NO MORE

The following is a translation of a German government document (1061–PS) detailing the destruction of the Warsaw ghetto in 1943:

For the Fuehrer and their country the following fell in the battle for the destruction of Jews and bandits in the former Ghetto of Warsaw:

[follow 15 names]

Furthermore, the Polish Police Sergeant Julian Zielinski, born 13 November 1891, 8th Commissariat * * * fell on 19 April I 1943 while fulfilling his duty. * * * They gave their utmost, their life. We shall never forget them. The following were wounded:

[follow the names of-
60 Waffen SS personnel.
11 "Watchmen" from Training Camps, probably Lithuanians, to judge by their names.
12 Security Police Officers in SS Units.
5 men of the Polish Police
2 regular Army personnel engineers]

Units used in the action	Average number of personnel used per day
SS Staff & Police Leader	6/5

Waffen SS:

SS Panzer Grenadier Training and Reserve Battalion 3, Warsaw	4/440
SS Cav. Training and Res Bat. Warsaw	5/381

Police:

SS Police Regiment 22 I. Bat.	3/94
III. Bat.	3/134
Engineering Emergency Service	1/6
Polish Police	4/363
Polish Fire Brigade	166

Security Police:

Wehrmacht

Light AA Alarm Battery III/8 Warsaw	2/22
Engineers Det. of Railway Armored Trains	
Res. flat. Rembertow	2/42
Res. Eng. 14 Gora-Kalwaria	1/34

Foreign Racial Watchmen:

1 Bat. "Trawniki" men	2/335
Total:	36/2054

[Translator's note: This obviously means; 36 officers, 2054 men]

The creation of special areas to be inhabited by Jews, and the restriction of the Jews with regard to residence and trading is nothing new in the history of the East. Such measures were first taken far back in the Middle Ages; they could be observed as recently as during the last few centuries. These restrictions were imposed with the intention of protecting the aryan population against the Jews.

Identical considerations led us as early as February, 1940 to conceive the project of creating a Jewish residential district in Warsaw. The initial intention was to establish as the Ghetto that part of the City of Warsaw which has the Vistula as its Eastern frontier. The particular situation on prevailing in Warsaw seemed at first to frustrate this plan. It was moreover opposed by several authorities particularly by the City Administration. They pointed in particular that disturbances in industry and trade would ensue if a Ghetto were founded in Warsaw, and that it would be impossible to provide the Jews with food if they were assembled in a closed area.

At a conference held in March 1940, it was decided to postpone the plan of creating a Ghetto for the time being, owing to the above objections. At the same time a plan was considered to declare the District of Dublin the collecting area for all Jews within the Government General, especially for the evacuated or fugitive Jews arriving from the Reich. But as early as April 1940, the Higher SS and Police Leader, East, Cracow, issued a declaration that there was no intention of assembling the Jews within the Lublin District. In the meantime, the Jews had increasingly taken to crossing the frontiers without permission and illegally. This noted especially at the limits of the Districts of Lowicz and Skierniewice. Conditions in the town of Lowicz became dangerous from the point of view of hygiene as well as from that of the Security Police, owing to these illegal migrations of Jews. The District President of Lowicz therefore, began to install Ghettos in his district in order to avoid these dangers.

The experiences in the district of Lowicz, after Ghettos had been installed, showed that this method is the only one suitable for dispelling the dangers which emanate repeatedly from the Jews.

The necessity of erecting a Ghetto in the City of Warsaw as well became more and more urgent in the summer of 1940, since more and more troops were being assembled in the district of Warsaw after termination of the French campaign. At that time the Department for Hygiene urged the speedy erection of a Ghetto in the interest of preserving the health of the German Forces and of the native population as well. The original plan of establishing the Ghetto in the suburb of Praga as intended in February 1940, would have taken at least 4 to 5 months, since almost 600,000 persons had to be moved. But since experience showed that greater outbreaks of epidemics might be expected in the winter months and since for this reason the District Medical Officer urged that the resettling action ought to be completed by 15 November 1940 at the latest, the plan of establishing a suburban ghetto in Praga was dropped; and instead, the area which hitherto had been used as a quarantine area for epidemics was selected for use as a Jewish residential area. In October 1940, the Governor ordered the Commissioner of the District, President for the City of Warsaw, to complete the resettlement necessary for establishing the Ghetto within the City of Warsaw by 15 November 1940.

The Ghetto thus established in Warsaw was inhabited by about 400,000 Jews. It contained 27,000 apartments with an average of 2 1/2 rooms each. It was separated from the rest of the city by partition and other walls and by walling-up of thoroughfares, windows, doors, open spaces, etc.

It was administered by the Jewish Board of Elders, who received their instructions from the Commissioner for the Ghetto, who was immediately subordinated to the Governor. The Jews were granted self-administration in which the German supervising authorities intervened only where German interests were touched. In order to enable the Jewish Board of Elders to execute its orders, a Jewish Police force was set up, identifiers by special armbands and a special beret and armed with rubber truncheons. This Jewish Police force was charged with maintaining order and security within the Ghetto and was subordinated to the German and Polish Police.

II

It soon became clear, however, that not all dangers had been removed by this confining the Jews to one place. Security considerations required removing the Jews from the city of Warsaw altogether. The first large resettlement action took place in the period from 22 July to 3 October 1942. In this action 310,322 Jews were removed. In January 1943 a second resettlement action was carried out by which altogether 6,500 Jews were affected.

When the Reichsfuehrer SS visited Warsaw in January 1943 he ordered the SS and Police Leader for the District of Warsaw to transfer to Lublin the armament factories and other enterprises of military importance which were installed within the Ghetto including their personnel and machines. The execution of this transfer order proved to be very difficult, since the managers as well as the Jews resisted in every possible way. The SS and Police Leader thereupon decided to enforce the transfer of the enterprises in a large-scale action which he intended to carry out in three days. The necessary preparations had been taken by my predecessor, who also had given the order to start the large-scale action. I myself arrived in Warsaw on 17 April 1943 and took over the command of the action on 19 April 1943, 0800 hours, the action itself having started the same day at 0600 hours.

Before the large-scale action began, the limits of the former Ghetto had been blocked by an external barricade in order to prevent the Jews from breaking out. This barricade was maintained from the start to the end of the action and was especially reinforced at night.

When we invaded the Ghetto for the first time, the Jews and the Polish bandits succeeded in repelling the participating units, including tanks and armored cars, by a well-prepared concentration of fire. When I ordered a second attack, about 0800 hours, I distributed the units, separated from each other by indicated lines, and charged them with combing out the whole of the Ghetto, each unit for a certain part. Although firing commenced again, we now succeeded in combing out the blocks according to plan. The enemy was forced to retire from the roofs and elevated bases to the basements, dugouts, and sewers. In order to prevent their escaping into the sewers, the sewerage system was dammed up below the Ghetto and filled with water, but the Jews frustrated this plan to a great extent by blowing up the turning off valves. Late the first day we encountered rather heavy resistance, but it was quickly broken by a special raiding party. In the course of further operations we succeeded in expelling the Jews from their prepared resistance bases, sniper holes, and the like, and in occupying during 20 and 21 April the greater part of the so-called remainder of the Ghetto to such a degree that the resistance continued within these blocks could no longer be called considerable.

The main Jewish battle group, mixed with Polish bandits, had already retired during the first and second day to the so-called Muranowski Square. There, it was reinforced by a considerable number of Polish bandits. Its plan was to hold the Ghetto by every means in order to prevent us from invading it. The Jewish and Polish standards were hoisted at the top of a concrete building as a challenge to us. These two standards, however, were captured on the second day of the action by a special raiding party. SS Untersturmfuehrer Dehmke fell in this skirmish with the bandits; he was holding in his hand a handgrenade which was hit by the enemy and exploded, injuring him fatally. After only a few days I realized that the original plan had no prospect of success, unless the armament factories and other enterprises of military importance distributed throughout the Ghetto were dissolved. It was therefore necessary to approach these firms and to give them appropriate time for being evacuated and immediately transferred. Thus one of these firms after the other was dealt with, and we very soon deprived the Jews and bandits of their chance to take refuge time and again in these enterprises, which were under the supervision of the Armed Forces. In order to decide how much time was necessary to evacuate these enterprises thorough inspections were necessary. The conditions discovered there are indescribable. I cannot imagine a greater chaos than in the Ghetto of Warsaw. The Jews had control of everything, from the chemical substances used in manufacturing explosives to clothing and equipment for the Armed Forces. The managers knew so little of their own shops that the Jews were in a position to produce inside these shops arms of every kind, especially hand grenades, Molotov cocktails, and the like.

Moreover, the Jews had succeeded in fortifying some of these factories as centers of resistance. Such a center of resistance in an Army accommodation office had to be attacked as early as the second day of the action by an Engineer's Unit equipped with flame throwers and by artillery. The Jews were so firmly established in this shop that it proved to be impossible to induce them to leave it voluntarily; I therefore resolved to destroy this shop the next day by fire.

The managers of these enterprises, which were generally also supervised by an officer of the Armed Forces, could in most cases make no specified statements on their stocks and the whereabouts of these stocks. The statements which they made on the number of Jews employed by them were in every case incorrect. Over and over again we discovered that these labyrinths of edifices belonging to the armament concerns as residential blocks, contained rich Jews who had succeeded in finding accommodations for themselves and their families under the name of "armament workers" and were leading marvelous lives there. Despite all our orders to the managers to make the Jews leave those enterprises, we found out in several cases that managers simply concealed the Jews by shutting them in, because they expected that the action would be finished within a few days and that they then would be able to continue working with the remaining Jews. According to the statements of arrested Jews, women also seem to have played a prominent part. The Jews are said to have endeavored to keep up good relations with officers and men of the armed forces. Carousing is said to have been frequent, during the course of which business deals are said to have been concluded between Jews and Germans.

The number of Jews forcibly taken out of the buildings and arrested was relatively small during the first few days. It transpired that the Jews had taken to hiding in the sewers and in specially erected dug-outs. Whereas we had assumed during the first days that there were only scattered dug-outs, we learned in the course of the large-scale action that the whole Ghetto was systematically equipped with cellars, dug-outs, and passages. In every case these passages and dug-outs were connected with the sewer system. Thus, the Jews were able to maintain undisturbed subterranean traffic. They also used this sewer network for escaping subterraneously into the Aryan part of the city of Warsaw. Continuously, we received reports of attempts of Jews to escape through the sewer holes. While pretending to build airraid shelters they had been erecting dug-outs within the former Ghetto ever since the autumn of 1942. These were intended to conceal every Jew during the new evacuation action, which they had expected for quite a time, and to enable them to resist the invaders in a concerted action. Through posters, handbills, and whisper propaganda, the communistic resistance movement actually brought it about that the Jews entered the dug-outs as soon as the new large-scale operation started. How far their precautions went can be seen from the fact that many of the dug-outs had been skilfully equipped with furnishings sufficient for entire families, washing and bathing facilities, toilets, arms and munition supplies, and food supplies sufficient for several months. There were differently equipped dug-outs for rich and for poor Jews. To discover the individual dug-outs was difficult for the units, as they had been efficiently camouflaged. In many cases, it was possible only through betrayal on the part of the Jews.

When only a few days had passed, it became apparent that the Jews no longer had any intention to resettle voluntarily, but were determined to resist evacuation with all their force and by using all the weapons at their disposal. So-called battle groups had been formed, led by Polish-Bolshevists; they were armed and paid any price asked for available arms.

During the large-scale action we succeeded in catching some Jews who had already been evacuated and resettled in Lublin or Treblinka, but had broken out from there and returned to the Ghetto, equipped with arms and ammunition. Time and again Polish bandits found refuge in the Ghetto and remained there undisturbed, since we had no forces at our disposal to comb out this maze. Whereas it had been possible during the first days to catch considerable numbers of Jews, who are cowards by nature, it became more and more difficult during the second half of the action to capture the bandits and Jews. Over and over again new battle groups consisting of 20 to 30 or more Jewish fellows, 18 to 25 years of age, accompanied by a corresponding number of women kindled new resistance. These battle groups were under orders to put up armed resistance to the last and if necessary to escape arrest by committing suicide. One such battle group succeeded in mounting a truck by ascending from a sewer in the so-called Prosta, and in escaping with it (about 30 to 35 bandits). One bandit who had arrived with this truck exploded 2 hand grenades, which was the agreed signal for the bandits waiting in the sewer to climb out of it. The bandits and Jews—there were Polish bandits among these gangs armed with carbines, small arms, and in one case a light machine gun, mounted the truck and drove away in an unknown direction. The last member of this gang, who was on guard in the sewer and was detailed to close the lid of the sewer hole, was captured. It was he who gave the above information. The search for the truck was unfortunately without result.

During this armed resistance the women belonging to the battle groups were equipped the same as the men; some were members of the Chaluzim movement. Not infrequently, these women fired pistols with both hands. It happened time and again that these women had pistols or hand grenades (Polish "pineapple" hand grenades) concealed in their bloomers up to the last moment to use against the men of the Waffen SS, Police, or Wehrmacht.

The resistance put up by the Jews and bandits could be broken only by relentlessly using all our force and energy by day and night. *On 23 April 1943 the Reichsfuehrer SS issued through the higher SS and Police Fuehrer East at Cracow his order to complete the combing out of the Warsaw Ghetto with the greatest severity and relentless tenacity.* I therefore decided to destroy the entire Jewish residential area by setting every block on fire, including the blocks of residential buildings near the armament works. One concern after the other was systematically evacuated and subsequently destroyed by fire. The Jews then emerged from their hiding places and dug-outs in almost every case. Not infrequently, the Jews stayed in the burning buildings until, because of the heat and the fear of being burned alive they preferred to jump down from the upper stories after having thrown mattresses and other upholstered articles into the street from the burning buildings. With their bones broken, they still tried to crawl across the street into blocks of buildings which had not yet been set on fire or were only partly in flames. Often Jews changed their hiding places during the night, by moving into the ruins of burnt-out buildings, taking refuge there until they were found by our patrols. Their stay in the sewers also ceased to be pleasant after the first week. Frequently from the street, we could hear loud voices coming through the sewer shafts. Then the men of the Waffen SS, the Police or the Wehrmacht Engineers courageously climbed down the shafts to bring out the Jews and not infrequently they then stumbled over Jews already dead, or were shot at. It was always necessary to use smoke candles to drive out the Jews. Thus one day we opened 183 sewer entrance holes and at a fixed time lowered smoke candles into them, with the result that the bandits fled from what they believed to be gas to the center of the former Ghetto, where they could then be pulled out of the sewer holes there. A great number of Jews, who could not be counted, were exterminated by blowing up sewers and dug-outs.

The longer the resistance lasted, the tougher the men of the Waffen SS, Police, and Wehrmacht became; they fulfilled their duty indefatigably in faithful comradeship and stood together as models and examples of soldiers. Their duty hours often lasted from early morning until late at night. At night, search patrols with rags wound round their feet remained at the heels of the Jews and gave them no respite. Not infrequently they caught and killed Jews who used the night hours for supplementing their stores from abandoned dug-outs and for contacting neighboring groups or exchanging news with them.

Considering that the greater part of the men of the Waffen-SS had only been trained for three to four weeks before being assigned to this action, high credit should be given for the pluck, courage, and devotion to duty which they showed. It must be stated that the Wehrmacht Engineers, too, executed the blowing up of dug-outs, sewers, and concrete buildings with indefatigability and great devotion to duty. Officers and men of the Police, a large part of whom had already been at the front, again excelled by their dashing spirit.

Only through the continuous and untiring work of all involved did we succeed in catching a total of 56,065 Jews whose extermination can be proved. To this should be added the number of Jews who lost their lives in explosions or fires but whose numbers could not be ascertained.

During the large-scale operation the Aryan population was informed by posters that it was strictly forbidden to enter the former Jewish Ghetto and that anybody caught within the former Ghetto without a valid pass would be shot. At the same time these posters informed the Aryan population again that the death penalty would be imposed on anybody who intentionally gave refuge to a Jew, especially lodged, supported, or concealed a Jew outside the Jewish residential area.

Permission was granted to the Polish police to pay to any Polish policeman who arrested a Jew within the Aryan part of Warsaw one third of the cash in the Jew's possession. This measure has already produced results.

The Polish population for the most part approved the measures taken against the Jews. Shortly before the end of the largescale operation, the Governor issued a special proclamation which he submitted to the undersigned for approval before publication, to the Polish population; in it he informed them of the reasons for destroying the former Jewish Ghetto by mentioning the assassinations carried out lately in the Warsaw area and the mass graves found in Catyn; at the same time they were asked to assist us in our fight against Communist agents and Jews (see enclosed poster).

The large-scale action was terminated on 16 May 1943 with the blowing up of the Warsaw synagogue at 2015 hours.

Now, there are no more factories in the former Ghetto. All the goods, raw materials, and machines there have been moved and stored somewhere else. All buildings etc., have been destroyed. The only exception is the so-called

Dzielna Prison of the Security Police, which was exempted from destruction.

III

Although the large-scale operation has been completed, we have to reckon with the possibility that a few Jews are still living in the ruins of the former Ghetto; therefore, this area must be firmly shut off from the Aryan residential area and be guarded. Police Battalion III/23 has been charged with this duty. This Police Battalion has instructions to watch the former Ghetto, particularly to prevent anybody from entering the former Ghetto, and to shoot immediately anybody found inside the Ghetto without authority. The Commander of the Police Battalion will continue to receive further direct orders from the SS and Police Fuehrer. In this way, it should be possible to keep the small remainder of Jews there, if any, under constant pressure and to exterminate them eventually. The remaining Jews and bandits must be deprived of any chance of survival by destroying all remaining buildings and refuges and cutting off the water supply.

It is proposed to change the Dzielna Prison into a concentration camp and to use the inmates to remove, collect and hand over for reuse the millions of bricks, the scrap-iron, and other materials.

IV

Of the total of 56,065 Jews caught, about 7,000 were exterminated within the former Ghetto in the course of the large-scale action, and 6,929 by transporting them to T.II, which means 14,000 Jews were exterminated altogether. Beyond the number of 56,065 Jews an estimated number of 5,000 to 6,000 were killed by explosions or in fires.

The number of destroyed dug-outs amounts to 631.
Booty:

Polish rifles, 1 Russian rifle, 1 German rifle 59 pistols of various calibers

Several hundred hand grenades, including Polish and home-made ones.

Several hundred incendiary bottles

Home-made explosives

Infernal machines with fuses

A large amount of explosives, ammunition for weapons of all calibers, including some machine-gun ammunition.

Regarding the booty of arms, it must be taken into consideration that the arms themselves could in most cases not be captured, as the bandits and Jews would, before being arrested, throw them into hiding places or holes which could not be ascertained or discovered. The smoking out of the dug-out by our men, also often made the search for arms impossible.

As the dug-outs had to be blown up at once, a search later on was out of the question.

The captured hand grenades, ammunition, and incendiary bottles were at once reused by us against the bandits.
Further booty:

1,240 used military tunics (part of them with medal ribbons-Iron Cross and East Medal)

600 pairs of used trousers

Other equipment and German steel helmets

108 horses, 4 of them still in the former Ghetto (hearse) Up to 23 May 1943 we had counted:

4.4 million Zloty; furthermore about 5 to 6 million Zloty not yet counted, a great amount of foreign currency, e.g. $14,300 in paper and $9,200 in gold, moreover valuables (rings, chains, watches, etc.) in great quantities.

State of the Ghetto at the termination of the large-scale operation:

Apart from 8 buildings (Police Barracks, hospital, and accommodations for housing working-parties) the former Ghetto is completely destroyed. Only the dividing walls are left standing where no explosions were carried out. But the ruins still contain a vast amount of stones and scrap material which could be used.

Warsaw, 16 May, 1943.
The SS and Police Fuehrer in the
District of Warsaw.
SS Brigadefuehrer and Majorgeneral of Police.
Copy
Warsaw, 20 April 1943.
Journal No. 516/43 secret.
(Daily reports)
SS Service Teletype message
From: The SS and Police Fuehrer in the District of Warsaw
Ref. No.: I ab/St/Gr-16 07
Re: Ghetto Operation.
To: The Higher SS and Police Fuehrer East, Cracow
Progress of Ghetto Operation on 19 April 1943:

Closing of Ghetto commenced 0300 hours. At 0600 order to Waffen-SS (strength: 16/850) to comb out the remainder of the Ghetto. Hardly had the units fallen in, strong concerted fire-concentration by the Jews and bandits. The tank used in this action and the two heavy armored cars pelted with Molotov cocktails (incendiary bottles). Tank twice set on fire. Owing to this enemy counterattack, we had at first to take the units back. Losses in first attack: 12 men (6 SS-men, 6 Trawniki-men). About 800 hours. Second attack by the units, under the command of the undersigned. Although the counterattack was reported, this time we succeeded in combing out the blocks of buildings according to plan. We caused the enemy to retire from the roofs and elevated prepared positions into the cellars or dug-outs and sewers. During this combing-out we caught only about 200 Jews. Immediately afterwards raiding parties were directed to dug-outs known to us with the order to pull out the Jews and to destroy the dug-outs. About 380 Jews captured. We found out that the Jews had taken to the sewers. Sewers were completely inundated, to make staying there impossible. About 1730 hours we encountered very strong resistance from one block of buildings including machine gun fire. A special raiding party invaded that block and defeated the enemy, but could not catch the resisters. The Jews and criminals resisted from base to base, and escaped at the last moment across lofts or through subterranean passages. About 2030 hours. the external barricade was reinforced. All units were withdrawn from the Ghetto and dismissed to their barracks. Reinforcement of the barricade by 250 Waffen-SS men. Continuation of operation on 20 April 1943.

Units at my disposal:

SS-Panzer-Gren. Res. Batl.	6/400
SS-Cav. Res. Batl.	10/450
Police	6/165
Security Service	2/48
Trawniki-men	1/150

Wehrmacht:

1 10-cm-Howitzer	1/7
Flame thrower	1
Engineers	2/16
Medical detachments	1/1
3 2.28-cm A.A. Guns	2/24
1 French tank of the Waffen-SS	
2 heavy armored cars of the Waffen-SS	

Total:	31/1262

I put Major of Police Sternagel in command of today's operations subject to my further instructions if necessary.

At 0700 hours. 9 raiding parties were formed, each 1/36 strong, consisting of mixed units, to comb out and to search the remainder of the Ghetto intensively. This search is still in progress; its first objective will be completed by 1100 hours. In the meantime it has been ascertained that part of the Ghetto which is no longer inhabited but not yet released and which contains several armament factories and the like, there are several centers of resistance, which were so strong that the tank could not go through. 2 raiding parties defeated these centers of resistance and made a passage for the tank men. In this operation we already had two wounded (Waffen-SS).

Enemy is much more cautious than yesterday, since he has of course learned of the heavy arms at our disposal.

My intention is first to comb out completely the remainder of the Ghetto and then to clean out in the same manner the socalled uninhabited Ghetto, which so far has not been released. It had been ascertained in the meantime that the latter part of the Ghetto contains at least 10 to 12 dugouts, some of which are even in armament factories. The whole operation is made more difficult because there are still factories in the Ghetto which must be protected against bombardment and fire, because they contain machines and tools.

A further report will follow tonight.
The SS and Police Fuehrer in the District of Warsaw.
/s/ stroop
SS-Brigadefuehrer and Majorgeneral of Police.
Certified copy:
SS-Sturmbannfuehrer.
Copy
Teletype message
From the SS and Police Fuehrer in the District of Warsaw
Warsaw, 20 April 1943.
Ref. No. I ab St/Gr 16 07-Journal No. 517/43 secret.
Re: Ghetto Operation.
To the Higher SS and Police Fuehrer East, SS-Obergruppenfuehrer and General of Police Krueger-or deputy.
Cracow

Supplementing my teletype message of 20 April 1943-Ref. St/Gr

16 07, re Ghetto Operation—I beg to report as follows:

The resistance centers ascertained with the uninhabited but not yet released part of the Ghetto were crushed by a battle group of the Wehrmacht-Engineers and flame throwers. The Wehrmacht had one wounded in this operation, shot through the lungs. Nine raiding parties broke through as far as the northern limit of the Ghetto. 9 dug-outs were found, their inmates crushed when they resisted, and the dug-outs blown up. What losses the enemy suffered cannot be ascertained accurately. Altogether the 9 raiding parties caught 505 Jews today; those among them who are able-bodied were kept ready for transport to Poniatowo. At about 1500 hrs. I managed to arrange that the block of buildings occupied by the Army Accommodation Office said to be occupied by 4,000 Jews is to be evacuated at once. The German manager was asked to call upon the Jewish workers to leave the block voluntarily. Only 28 Jews obeyed this order. Thereupon I resolved either to evacuate the block by force or to blow it up. The A.A. Artillery-3 2-cm. guns used for this operation had two men killed. The 10-cm howitzer, which also was used, expelled the gangs from their strong fortifications and also inflicted losses on them, as far as we were able to ascertain. This action had to be broken off owing to the fall of darkness. On 21 April 1943 we shall attack this resistance center again, as far as possible it will remain blocked off during the night.

APPENDIX

In today's action we caught, apart from the Jews reported above, considerable stores of incendiary bottles, hand grenades, ammunition, military tunics, and equipment.

Losses:

2 dead (Wehrmacht) 7 wounded (6 Waffen SS, 1 Trawniki-man)

In one case the bandits had laid pressure mines. I have succeeded in causing the firms W.C. Toebens, Schultz and Co., and Hoffman to be ready for evacuation with their entire personnel on 21 April 1943 at 0600 hrs. In this way, I hope to get the way free at last for cleaning out the Ghetto. The Trustees Toebens has pledged himself to induce the Jews, numbering about 4,000 to 5,000, to follow him voluntarily to the assembling point for being resettled. In case this has as little success as was attained in the case of the Army Accommodation Office, I am going to clean out this part of the Ghetto as well by force. I beg to acknowledge receipt of the order which the Obergruppenfuehrer communicated to me by telephone today, and of the powers granted to me.

Next report on 21 April 1943 at noon.

The SS and Police Fuehrer in the
District of Warsaw
Signed: Stroop
SS-Brigadefuehrer and Majorgeneral of Police.
Certified copy:
SS-Sturmbannfuehrer.
Copy
Teletype message
From: The SS and Police Fuehrer in the District of Warsaw
Warsaw, 21 April 1943.
Ref. Nr. I ab/St/Gr-16 07-Journal Nr. 527/43.
Re: Ghetto Operation.
To the Higher SS and Police Fuehrer East,
SS-Obergruppenfuehrer and General of Police, Krueger-or deputy.
Cracow

Progress of Ghetto Operation on 21 April 1943.

Supplementing the report which I made today about 1400 hours. by telephone, I beg to report:

Forces at my disposal as of 20 April 1943.

Start of operation: 0700 hours. The whole of the Ghetto has continued to be cordoned off since the start of the operations on 19 April 1943.

Inasmuch as the special operation concerning the block of buildings occupied by the Army Accommodation Office had to be interrupted yesterday because of darkness, one battle group reinforced by Engineers and heavy artillery was again sent into the block of buildings, which was found to contain an enormous quantity of dugouts and subterranean passages firing from time to time. I resolved therefore to blow up these passages which we had discovered and subsequently to set the entire block on fire. Not until the building was well aflame did screaming Jews make their appearance, and they were evacuated at once. We had no losses in this operation. Precautionary measures were taken in order to ensure that the conflagration remained localized.

The main body of our forces was detailed to cleanse the so called uninhabited, but not yet released, part of the Ghetto by proceeding from South to North. Before we started this action, we caught 5,200 Jews who had been employed in enterprises under the supervision of the Commissioner for Armament [Ru KoBetrieben] and transported them under armed guard to the Railway Station which had been chosen for use in the resettlement. I formed 3 search-parties to which were attached special raiding parties who had the duty to attack or blow up the dug-outs which were known to us. This operation had to be interrupted when darkness set in, after one half of the area mentioned had been combed out.

Continued on 22 April 1943, 0700 hours.

Apart from the Jews who were to be evacuated, 150 Jews or bandits were killed in battle and about 80 bandits were killed when their dug-outs were blown up. The enemy today used the same arms as on the previous day, particularly home-made explosives. Samples have been kept by the SS and Police Fuehrer. For the first time we observed the participation of members of the Jewish Women's Battle Association (Chaluzim Movement). We captured rifles, pistols, hand grenades, explosives, horses, and parts of SS uniforms.

Own losses: 2 policemen, 2 SS-men, 1 Trawniki-man. (light wounds)

The SS and Police Fuehrer
in the District of Warsaw.
Signed: Stroop
SS-Brigadefuehrer and Majorgeneral of Police.
Certified copy:
SS-Sturmbannfuehrer.
Copy
Teletype message
From the SS and Police Fuehrer in the District of Warsaw
Warsaw, 22 April 1943.
Ref. No. I ab St/Gr 16 07-Journal Nr. 530/43 secret.
Re: Ghetto Operation. (supplement to par. 1 of letter of 21 April 1943).
To: The Higher SS and Police Fuehrer of Police Krueger-or deputy
Cracow

Our setting the block on fire achieved the result in the course of the night that those Jews whom we had not been able to find despite all our search operations left their hideouts under the roofs, in the cellars, and elsewhere, and appeared at the outside of the buildings, trying to escape the flames. Masses of them—entire families—were already aflame and jumped from the windows or endeavored to let themselves down by means of sheets tied together or the like. Steps had been taken so that these Jews as well as the remaining ones were liquidated at once. During the whole night there were shots from buildings which were supposed to be evacuated. We had no losses in our cordoning forces. 5,300 Jews were caught for the evacuation and removed.

The SS and Police Fuehrer in the District of Warsaw.
Signed: Stroop
Certified copy:
SS-Sturmbannfuehrer.
Copy
Teletype message
From The SS and Police Fuehrer in the District of Warsaw
Warsaw, 22 April 1943.
Ref. Nr. I ab/St/Gr-l6 07-Journal Nr. 531/43 secret.
Re: Ghetto Operation.
To: The Higher SS and Police Fuehrer East, SS-Obergruppenfuehrer and General of Police Krueger or deputy.
Cracow

Progress of the Ghetto Operation on 22 April 1943 up to 1200 hours. One raiding party was dispatched to invade once more the block of buildings which for the greater part had burned out or was still aflame, in order to catch those Jews who were still inside.

When shooting again started from one block against the men of the Waffen-SS, this block also was set on fire, with the result that a considerable number of bandits were scared from their hideouts and shot while trying to escape. Apart for those, we caught about 180 Jews in the yards of the buildings. The main body of our units continued the cleansing action from the line where we terminated this action yesterday. This operation is still in progress. As on the preceding days local resistance was broken and the dug-outs we discovered were blown up. Unfortunately there is no way of preventing part of the Jews and bandits from taking refuge in the sewers below the Ghetto, where we can hardly catch them since they have stopped the flooding. The city administration is not in a position to frustrate this nuisance. Neither did the use of smoke candles or the introduction of creosote into the water have the desired result. Cooperation with the Wehrmacht splendid.

The SS and Police Fuehrer in the District of Warsaw.
Signed: Stroop
SS-Brigadefuehrer and Majorgeneral of Police.

Certified copy:
SS-Sturmbannfuehrer.
Copy
Teletype message
From the SS and Police Fuehrer in the District of Warsaw
Warsaw, 22 April 1943.
Ref. Nr.: ab/St/Gr-16 07-Journal Nr. 532/43 secret.
Re: Ghetto Operation.
The Higher SS and Police Fuehrer East, SS-Obergruppenfuehrer and General of Police Krueger-or deputy.
Cracow

Progress of operation of 22 April 1943. Report on action up to 1200 hours. has already been submitted by my message of today. Continuing, I beg to report:

When the special raiding party searched the remainder of the blocks as already reported, they met with resistance at some places; they had the following success: 1,100 Jews caught for evacuation, 203 bandits and Jews killed, 15 dug-outs blown up. They captured 80 incendiary bottles and other booty. Units at my disposal: as reported by teletype message on 20 April 1943. Journal No. 516/43 secret.

Our losses: SS-Untersturmfuehrer Dehmke (dead); enemy hit a hand grenade which he carried. (SS-Cav.Res. Batl.)

1 Sergeant of Police (shot through the lungs)

When the Engineers blew up the dug-outs, a considerable number of Jews and bandits were buried under the ruins. In a number of cases it was found necessary to start fires in order to smoke the gangs out.

I must add that since yesterday some of the units have been shot at time and again from outside the Ghetto, that is, from the Aryan part of Warsaw. Raiding parties at once entered the area in question and in one case succeeded in capturing 35 Polish bandits, Communists, who were liquidated at once. Today it happened repeatedly when we found it necessary to execute some bandits, that they collapsed shouting "Long live Poland," "Long live Moscow."

The operation will be continued on 23 April 1943, 0700 hours.

The SS and Police Fuehrer in the District of Warsaw.
Signed: Stroop
SS-Brigadefuehrer and Maj. Gen. of Police.
Certified copy:
SS-Sturmbannfuehrer.
Copy
Teletype message
From the SS and Police Fuehrer in the District of Warsaw
Warsaw, 23 April 1943.

Ref. No.: I ab/St/Gr-16 07-Journal No. 538/43 secret.

Re: Ghetto Operation.
To: The Higher SS and Police Fuehrer East, SS-Obergruppenfuehrer and General of Police Krueger-or deputy.
Cracow

Progress of Ghetto Operation on 23 April 1943. Start: 0700 hours.

The whole of the former Ghetto had been divided for the purposes of today's combing-out operations into 24 districts. One reinforced searching party was detailed to each district with special orders. These assignments had to be carried out by 1600 hours.

Result of this action: 600 Jews and bandits ferreted out and captured, about 200 Jews and bandits killed, 48 dug-outs, some of them of a quite elaborate character, blown up. We captured apart from valuables and money—some gas masks.

The units had been informed that we intended to terminate the operation today. In the morning the Jews had already become aware of this—instruction. This is why a renewed search by the searching parties was undertaken after an interval of 1 to 1 1/2 hours. The result was, as always, that again Jews and bandits were discovered to be in various blocks. From one block shots were even fired against the cordoning units. An attack by a special battle group was ordered and in order to smoke the bandits out, every building was now set on fire. The Jews and bandits held out, every building was now set on fire. The Jews and bandits held their fire up to the last moment and then concerted their fire against the units. They even used carbines. A number of bandits who were shooting from balconies were hit by our men and crashed down.

Furthermore, today we discovered a place said to have been the headquarters of the "P PR"; we found it unoccupied and destroyed it. It was on this 5th day of operations that obviously we found the worst of the terrorists and activists, who so far had always found ways and means to dodge every searching or evacuation action.

A racial German reported that again some Jews had escaped through the sewers into the Aryan part of the city. We learned from a traitor that there were some Jews in a certain house. A special motorized raiding party invaded the building and caught 3 Jews, 2 of them females. During this operation their motor-car was pelted with one incendiary bottle and one explosive; 2 policemen were wounded.

The whole operation is rendered more difficult by the cunning way in which the Jews and bandits act; for instance, we discover that the hearses which were used to collect the corpses lying around at the same time bring living Jews to the Jewish cemetery, and thus they are enabled to escape, from the Ghetto. Now this way of escape also is barred by continuous control of the hearses.

At the termination of today's operation about 2200 hours, we discovered that again about 30 bandits had passed into a so-called armaments factory, where they had found refuge. Since the forces are storing goods of great value in this enterprise, this factory was requested to evacuate the building by noon on 24 April; this will enable us to cleanse that labyrinth of a building tomorrow.

Today 3,500 Jews were caught who are to be evacuated from the factories. A total of 19,450 Jews have been caught for resettlement or already evacuated up to today. Of these about 2,500 Jews are still to be loaded. The next train will start on 24 April 1943.

Strength as of 22 April 1943, without 150 Trawniki men; these have already been put at the disposal of the Eastern Command as reinforcement for another assignment.

Our losses:
2 Police corporals ("SB") wounded 1 Trawniki man wounded.

The operation will be continued on 24 April 1943, 1000 hours. This hour was chosen so that Jews who may still be in the Ghetto will believe that the operation was actually terminated today.

The SS and Police Fuehrer in the District of Warsaw.
Signed: Stroop
SS-Brigadefuehrer and Major general of Police.
Certified copy:
SS-Sturmbannfuehrer.
Copy
Teletype message
From The SS and Police Fuehrer in the District of Warsaw
Warsaw, 24 April 1943.
Ref. Nr.: I ab/St/Wdt-16 07-Journal No. 545/43 secret.
Re: Ghetto operation.
The Higher SS and Police Fuehrer East, SS-Obergruppenfuehrer and general of the Police-Krueger-or deputy.
Cracow

Progress of operation on 24 April 1943, start 1000 hours.

Contrary to the preceding days, the 24 searching parties which had again been formed did not start at one end of the Ghetto, but proceeded from all sides at the same time. Apparently the Jews still in the Ghetto were deceived by the fact that the operation did not start until 1000 hours into believing that the action really had been terminated yesterday. The search action, therefore, had especially satisfactory results today. This success is furthermore due to the fact that the noncommissioned officers and men have meanwhile become accustomed to the cunning fighting, methods and tricks used by the Jews and bandits and that they have acquired great skill in tracking down the dug-outs which are found in such great number. The raiding parties having returned, we set about to clean a certain block of buildings.

Dated the northeastern part of the former Ghetto. In this labyrinth of buildings there was a so-called armaments firm which reportedly had goods worth millions for manufacture and storage. I had notified the Wehrmacht of my intentions on 23 April 1943 about 2100 hours, and had requested them to remove their goods by 1200 hours. Since the Wehrmacht did not start this evacuation until 1000 hours I felt obliged to extend the term until 1800 hours. At 1815 hours a search party entered the premises, the building having been cordoned off, and found that a great number of Jews were within the building. Since some of these Jews resisted, I ordered the building to be set on fire. Not until all the buildings along the street and the back premises on either side were well aflame did the Jews, some of them on fire, emerge from these blocks, some of them endeavored to save their life by jumping into the street from windows and balconies, after having thrown down beds, blankets, and the like. Over and over again we observed that Jews and bandits, despite the danger of being burned alive, preferred to return into the flames rather than risk being caught by us. Over and over again the Jews kept up their firing almost to the end of the action; thus the engineers had to be protected by a machine gun when toward nightfall they had to enter forcibly a concrete building which had been very strongly fortified. Termination of today's operation; on 25 April 1943 at 0145 hours. 1,660 Jews were caught for evacuation, pulled out of dug-outs, about 330 shot. Innumerable Jews were destroyed by the flames or perished when the dug-outs were blown up. 26 dug-outs were blown up and an amount of paper money, especially dollars was captured; this money has not yet been counted.

Our forces; as on the preceding day, minus 50 men of the Waffen-SS.

Our losses: 2 SS men and 1 Trawniki man wounded.

Altogether there have now been caught in this action 25,500 Jews who lived in the former Ghetto. Since there are only vague estimates available of the actual number of inhabitants I assume that now only very small numbers of Jews and bandits still remain within the Ghetto.

Operation will be continued on 25 April 1943, 1300 hours.

I beg to acknowledge receipt of teletype messages Nos. 1222 and 1223 of 24 April 1943. As far as can be predicted, the present large-scale operation will last until Easter Monday inclusive.

Today large posters were affixed to the walls surrounding the Ghetto, announcing that every-body who enters the former Ghetto without being able to prove his identity will be shot.

The SS and Police Fuehrer in the District of Warsaw.
Signed: Stroop
SS-Brigadefuehrer and Major general of Police.
Certified copy:
SS-Sturmbannfuehrer.
Copy
Teletype message
From: The SS and Police Fuehrer in the District of Warsaw
Warsaw, 25 April 1943
Ref. No. I ab/St/Wdt-16 07-Journal No. 549/43 secret.
Re: Ghetto operation.
To: The Higher SS and Police Fuehrer East, SS-Obergruppenfuehrer and General of Police Krueger-or deputy.
Cracow

Progress of operation on 25 April 1943, start 1300 hours.

For today 7 search parties were formed, strength 1/70 each, each allotted to a certain block of buildings.

Their order was: "Every building is to be combed out once more; dug-outs have to be discovered and blown up, and the Jews have to be caught. If any resistance is encountered or if dug-outs cannot be reached, the buildings are to be burnt down." Apart from the operations undertaken by these 7 search parties, a special operation was undertaken against a center of bandits, situated outside the wall surrounding the former Ghetto and inhabited exclusively by Poles.

Today's operations of the search parties ended almost everywhere in the starting of enormous conflagrations. In this manner the Jews were forced to leave their hideouts and refuges. A total of 1,960 Jews were caught alive. The Jews informed us that among them were certain parachutists who were dropped here and bandits who had been equipped with arms from some unknown source. 274 Jews were killed. As in the preceding days, uncounted Jews were buried in blown up dug-outs and, as can be observed time and again, burned with this bag of Jews today. We have, in my opinion, caught a very considerable part of the bandits and lowest elements of the Ghetto. Intervening darkness prevented immediate liquidation. I am going to try to obtain a train for T II tomorrow. Otherwise liquidation will be carried out tomorrow. Today also, some armed resistance was encountered; in a dug-out three pistols and some explosives were captured. Furthermore, considerable amounts of paper money, foreign currency, gold coins, and jewelry were seized today.

The Jews still have considerable property. While last night a glare of fire could be seen above the former Ghetto, today one can observe a giant sea of flames. Since we continue to discover great numbers of Jews whenever we search and comb out, the operation will be continued on 26 April 1943. Start: 1000 hours.

Including today, a total of 27,464 Jews of the former Warsaw Ghetto, have been captured.

Our forces; as on the previous day.

Our losses; 3 members of the Waffen-SS and one member of the Security Police wounded.

Total losses up to date:

Waffen SS	27 Wounded
Police	9 Wounded
Security Police	4 Wounded
Wehrmacht	1 Wounded
Trawniki men	9 Wounded
50 Wounded	
and 5 dead:	
Waffen-SS	2 Dead
Wehrmacht	2 Dead
Trawniki men	1 Dead
5 Dead	

The SS and Police Fuehrer in the District of Warsaw.
Signed: Stroop
SS-Brigadefuehrer and Major general of Police.
Certified copy:
SS-Sturmbannfuehrer.
Copy
Teletype message
From: The SS and Police Fuehrer in the District of Warsaw
Warsaw, 26 April 1943.
Ref. No.: I ab/St/Wdt-16 07-Journal Nr. 550/43 secret.
Re: Ghetto operation-supplementary report.
To: The Higher SS and Police Fuehrer East, SS-Obergruppenfuehrer and General of Police Krueger-or deputy.
Cracow

1. The operation on 25 April 1943, was terminated at 2200 hours. 2. General effects of the execution of this operation.

The Poles resident in Warsaw are much impressed by the toughness of our operations in the former Ghetto. As can be seen from the daily reports, the general situation has greatly calmed down since the beginning of that operation within the city area of Warsaw. From this fact one may conclude that the bandits and saboteurs resided in the former Ghetto, and that now all of them have been destroyed.

In this connection the fact may be of some interest, that an illegal ammunition store was seen to explode when we burned down a certain building in the dwelling area on which we were working at the time.

The SS and Police Fuehrer in the District of Warsaw.
Signed: Stroop

SS-Brigadefuehrer and Major general of Police.
Certified copy:
SS-Sturmbannfuehrer.
Copy
Teletype message
From: The SS and Police Fuehrer in the District of Warsaw
Warsaw, 26 April 1943.
Ref. Nr.: I ab/St/Wdt-16 07 Journal Nr. 551/43 secret.
To: The Higher SS and Police Fuehrer East, SS-Obergruppenfuehrer and General of Police Krueger-or deputy.
Cracow

Start of operation: 1000 hrs.

The whole of the former Ghetto was once more combed through today by the same search parties, each of them allotted to the same district as before. In this way I tried to bring about that the leaders of these parties work in thoroughfares, blocks of buildings, and courtyards which they know already and that thus they are able to penetrate deeper and deeper into the maze of dug-outs and subterranean passages. Almost every search party reported resistance, which however they broke either by returning fire or by blowing up the dug-outs. It becomes clearer and clearer that it is now the turn of the toughest and strongest among the Jews and bandits. Several times dug-outs have been forcibly broken open, the inmates of which had not come to the surface during the whole of this operation. In a number of cases the inmates of the dug-outs were hardly in a condition, when the dug-out had been blown up, to crawl to the surface. The captured Jews report that many of the inmates of the dug-outs became insane from the heat, the smoke, and the explosions. Several Jews were arrested who had kept close liaison with the group of Polish terrorists and collaborated with it. Outside the former Ghetto we arrested 29 Jews. During today's operation several blocks of buildings were burned down. This is the only and final method which forces this trash and subhumanity to the surface. We again captured arms, incendiary bottles, explosive charges and considerable amounts of cash and foreign currency. Today I also arranged that several so-called armament and defense enterprises will evacuate their stores from the buildings at once, so that these buildings in which the Jews now have taken refuge, under the protection of the army of the German Wehrmacht and police, can be combed out. In one case we again discovered, as previously, that in a building which had been said to contain a giant enterprise there existed in fact almost no stores or goods. One factory was closed without further ado, and the Jews were evacuated.

Result of today's operation:

30 Jews evacuated, 1,330 Jews pulled out of dug-outs and immediately destroyed, 362 Jews

killed in battle. Caught today altogether: 1,722 Jews. This brings the total of Jews caught to 29,186. Moreover, it is very probable that numerous Jews have perished in the 13 dug-outs blown up today and in the conflagrations.

At the time of writing not one of the Jews caught still remains within Warsaw. The scheduled transport to T. II had no success. [Note of translator: This probably means that no Jews were available for regular transport to the extermination camp.] Strength: as on preceding day.

Our losses: none.

End of today's operation at 2145 hours. Will be continued on 27 April 1943 at 0900 hours.

The SS and Police Fuehrer in the District of Warsaw.
Signed: Stroop
SS-Brigadefuehrer and Major general of Police.
Certified copy:
SS-Sturmbannfuehrer.
Copy
Teletype message
From: The SS and Police Fuehrer in the District of Warsaw
Warsaw, 27 April 1943.
Ref. No.: I ab/St/Gr-16 07-Journal No. 555/43 secret.
Re: Ghetto Operation
To: the Higher SS and Police Fuehrer East, SS-Obergruppenfuehrer and General of Police Krueger-or deputy.
Cracow

Progress of operation on 27 April 1943. Start: 0900 hrs.

For today's operation I formed 24 raiding parties with the same task as on several days of last week; they had to search the former Ghetto in smaller groups. These search parties pulled 780 Jews out of dug-outs and shot 115 Jews who resisted. This operation was terminated about 1500 hrs.; some of the parties had to continue to operate because they had found more dug-outs.

At 1600 hours. a special battle group, 320 officers and men strong, started cleansing a large block of buildings situated on both sides of the so-called Niska Street in the Northeastern part of the former Ghetto. After the search the entire block was set on fire, after having been completely cordoned off. In this action a considerable number of Jews were caught. As before, they remained in the dug-outs, which were either below the ground or in the lofts of the buildings until the end. They fired their arms to the last moment, and then jumped down into the street, sometimes from as far up as the fourth floor, having previously thrown down beds, mattresses, etc., but not until the flames made any other escape impossible. A total of 2,560 Jews were caught today within the former Ghetto, of whom 547 were shot. Moreover, Jews in a not ascertainable number perished

when dug-outs were blown up, or in the flames. The sum total of Jews, formerly residing in the Ghetto caught in this action, now amounts to 31,746.

We learned from an anonymous letter that there were a considerable number of Jews in a block of buildings adjoining the Northeastern part of the Ghetto, but outside of it. A special raiding party under the command of 1st. Lt. of Police Diehl was dispatched to attack these buildings. The raiding party discovered a gang of about 120 men, strongly armed with pistols, rifles, hand grenades, and light machine guns, who resisted. They succeeded in destroying 24 bandits in battle and arresting 52 bandits. The remainder could not be caught or destroyed, since darkness intervened. The buildings, however, were surrounded at once, so that an escape will hardly be possible. This cleansing action will be continued tomorrow. Moreover, we arrested 17 Poles, among whom 2 Polish Policemen, who should have been aware, among other things, of the existence of this gang. In this operation we captured 3 rifles, 12 pistols, partly of heavier caliber, 100 Polish "pineapple" hand grenades, 27 German steel helmets, quite a number of German uniforms, tunics and coats which were even furnished with ribbon of the East medal, some reserve magazines for machine guns, 300 rounds of ammunition, etc. The leader of the raiding party had a difficult task because the bandits were disguised in German uniform, but despite this fact, he did his duty with great efficiency. Among the bandits who were caught or killed, there were some Polish terrorists who were identified with certainty. Today we succeeded furthermore in discovering and liquidating one of the founders and leaders of the Jewish-Polish resistance movement. The external appearance of the Jews whom we are catching now shows that it is now the turn of those Jews who were the leaders of the entire resistance movement. They jumped from the burning windows and balconies, abusing Germany and the Fuehrer and cursing the German soldiers.

SS-men who descended into the sewers discovered that a great number of corpses of perished Jews are being washed away by the water.

Our strength:
288 German Police
200 Trawniki men

Cordon-
From 0700 to
1900 hours. 140 Polish Police
From 1900 to
0700 hours. 288 German Police forces
250 Waffen-SS
140 Polish Police

Strength in the operation:
3/115 German Police
4/400 Waffen-SS
1/6 Engineering Serv.
2/30 Security Police
2/21 Engineers.

Our losses:
3 wounded:
2 Waffen-SS
1 Trawniki-man
Termination of operation: 2300 hours. Will be continued on 28 April 1943 at 1000 hours.

The SS and Police Fuehrer in the District of Warsaw.
Signed: Stroop
SS-Brigadefuehrer and Major general of Police.
Certified copy:
SS-Sturmbannfuehrer.
Copy
Teletype message
From: The SS and Police Fuehrer in the District of Warsaw
Warsaw, 28 April 1943.
Ref. Nr. I ab/St/Gr-16 07 Journal Nr. 562/43 secret.
Re: Ghetto operation
To: The Higher SS and Police Fuehrer East, SS-Obergruppenfuehrer and General of Police Krueger-or deputy.
Cracow

Progress of operation on 28 April 1943. Start 1000 hrs.

Today, 10 raiding parties were formed for combing out the whole of the Ghetto. These raiding parties again discovered proceeding step by step, a number of dug-outs, which were found to have been prepared as far ago as the middle of last year for use in the resistance of the Jews. A total of 335 Jews were forcibly pulled out of these dug-outs. Apart from these operations, we continued to cleanse the resistance center used by the Jewish military organization, situated at the borders of the Ghetto. We succeeded in shooting 10 more bandits, and in arresting 9, beyond those caught yesterday, and in capturing more arms, ammunition, and military equipment. In the afternoon a battle group again was directed against a block of buildings which had already been combed out; the block was set on fire during this operation.

As on previous days, masses of Jews emerged, forced out by the flames and the enormous clouds of smoke. At another point an

Engineer officer, attached by the Wehrmacht to the units with great trouble opened a dug-out situated about 3 meters below ground. From this dug-out, which had been ready since October of last year and was equipped with running water, toilet, and electric light, we pulled out 274 of the richest and most influential Jews. Today again we encountered very strong resistance in many places and broke it. It becomes clearer every day that we are now encountering the real terrorists and activists, because of the duration of the operation.

Result of today: 1,655 Jews caught for evacuation, of whom 110 were killed in battle.

Many more Jews were killed by the flames; moreover, Jews in an unascertainable number were destroyed the dug-outs being blown up. By the results of today the number of Jews caught or destroyed rises to 33,401 altogether. This number does not include the Jews who were killed by fire or destroyed in the dugouts.

Our strength: as on the previous day. Our losses: 3 wounded (1 Police, 2 Waffen-SS)

Termination of operation: 2200 hours. Will be continued on 29 April 1943. 1000 hours.

The SS and Police Fuehrer in the District of Warsaw.
Signed: Stroop
SS-Brigadefuehrer and Major general of Police.
Certified copy:
SS-Sturmbannfuehrer.
Copy
Teletype message
From: The SS and Police Fuehrer in the District of Warsaw
Warsaw, 29 April 1943.
fief. Nr. I ab/St/Gr-16 07-Journal Nr. 566/43 secret.
Re: Ghetto Operation.
To: The Higher SS and Police Fuehrer East, SS-Obergruppenfuehrer and General of Police Krueger-or deputy.
Cracow

Progress of large-scale operation of 29 April 1943. Start 1000 hrs.

As on the previous day I formed search parties, who red the special task of searching those blocks of buildings which had been recently separated. A larger raiding party was detailed to clean a certain block of buildings (formerly the Hall- j mann concern) and to burn this block down. 36 more dug-outs used for habitation were discovered altogether, and from them and other hideouts and from the burning buildings, 2,359 Jews, were caught, of whom 106 were killed in battle.

Captured are 2 rifles, 10 pistols, 10 kilograms of explosives, and ammunition of various types.

When a large dug-out was blown up, the entire building collapsed and everyone of the bandits perished. In the ensuing conflagration loud detonations and darting flames showed that the building must have contained large stores of ammunition and explosives. Some sewer entrances were blown up. Two exits discovered outside the Ghetto were also made unusable by blowing them up or walling them up.

The depositions of some of the inmates of the dug-outs are to the effect that these Jews have been unable to leave the dug-outs for the last 10 days and that their food, etc., is now beginning to grow short because the large-scale operation has lasted so long. Furthermore, the Jews testify that bandits appeared at night who were Jews or sometimes Poles, wearing black masks, who walled the dug-outs up from the outside and admonished them not to give any signs of life, so that they could continue to live in the Ghetto when the action was finished. Some of the armaments factories are being evacuated very slowly. In several cases one gains the impression that this is done intentionally. Thus I discovered with regard to one firm, Schulz and Co., which I had visited on Easter Monday and then instructed to start evacuation at once and to have it completed within 3 days, that up till today, Thursday, nothing had been done. Our strength: as on the previous day. Our losses: none.

Termination of operation at 2100 hrs. Will be continued on 30 April 1943, 0900 hrs.

Total caught or destroyed: 35,760.

The SS and Police Fuehrer in the District of Warsaw.
Signed: Stroop
SS-Brigadefuehrer and Major general of Police.
Certified copy:
SS-Sturmbannfuehrer.
Copy
Teletype message
From: The SS and Police Fuehrer in the District of Warsaw
Warsaw, 30 April 1943.
Ref No.: I ab/St/Gr-16 07-Journal No. 579/43 secret.
Re: Ghetto operation.
To: The Higher SS and Police Fuehrer East, SS-Obergruppenfuehrer and General of Police Krueger-or deputy.
Cracow

Progress of large-scale operation on 30 April 1943. Start 0900 hrs.

Combing out by search parties was continued. Although some giant blocks of buildings now are completely burned out, the Jews continue to stay in the dug-outs 2 to 3 meters below ground. In many cases we are not able to discover those dug-outs unless some Jew, whom we have already caught, gives us a hint as to their whereabouts. Repeatedly, during the last few days, Jews have testified that some armed Jews emerge at night from some hideouts or dug-outs and threaten the other Jews with shooting if they give any signs of life. We were able to ascertain beyond all doubt that several dug-outs had been closed from the outside by these bandits, who tried in this manner to prove that they meant business. Altogether, 30 dug-outs were discovered, evacuated, and blown up today. Again we caught a great number of bandits and subhumans. Apart from the bombing-out operations effected by small parties, two larger battle groups were occupied with bombing out and destroying by fire several interconnected blocks of buildings.

A total of 1599 Jews were caught today, of whom 179 were killed in battle. The sum total of

Jews caught up to date thereby rises to 37,359. 3,855 Jews were loaded today. The number of Jews in possession of arms was much higher than before among the Jews caught during the last few days. Today, we again captured arms and particularly parts of German uniforms from them. The operation against Fort Traugutta did not have any positive results. So far as we were able to discover subterranean exits, we either occupied them or blew them up. In attacking one of the blocks we had to use a gun today.

Our strength:
Used in the operation:

Police	5/133
Security Police	3/36
Waffen SS	6/432
Engineer	2/40
Staff	3/7

Cordoning forces:

Waffen SS	3/318
German Police	2/89
Trawniki men	200

moreover some Polish Police

Our losses: 1 wounded (Police)

Termination of today's large scale action: 2100 hours. Will be continued on 1 May 1943, 0900 hours.

The SS and Police Fuehrer in the District of Warsaw.
Signed: Stroop
SS-Brigadefuehrer and Major general of Police.
Certified copy:
SS-Sturmbannfuehrer.
Copy
Teletype message
From: The SS and Police Fuehrer in the District of Warsaw
Warsaw, May 1, 1943.
ref: Nr.: I ab/St/Gr-16 07-Journal No. 583/43 secret.
Re: Large-scale Ghetto operation.
To: The Higher SS and Police Fuehrer East, SS Obergruppenfuehrer and General of Police Krueger-or deputy.
Cracow

Progress of large scale operation on 1 May 1943. Start 0900 hours. 10 searching parties were detailed, moreover a larger battle group was detailed to comb out a certain block of buildings, with the added instruction to burn that block down. Within this block of buildings there existed a so-called armament factory which had not yet been entirely evacuated, although it had had enough time to do so. It was not exempted from the operation. Today's operation a total of 1,026 Jews were caught, of whom 245 were killed, either in battle or while resisting. Moreover, a considerable number of bandits and ringleaders were also caught. In one case a Jew who had already been made ready for transport fired three shots against a 1st Lieutenant of Police, but missed his mark. All the Jews caught today were forcibly pulled out of dug-outs. Not a single one gave himself up voluntarily, after his dug-out had been opened. A considerable part of the Jews caught were pulled out of the sewers. We continued systematically blowing up or blocking up the sewer entrances. In one case the Engineers laid a strong concentrated charge and had to proceed to an adjoining entrance where they had something to do. In the meantime a Jew emerged from the sewer, removed the fuse from the concentrated charge, and appropriated the charge. In the further course of this operation we succeeded in catching the Jew, still in possession of the concentrated charge.

In order to ascertain the movements of the Jews during the night, today I used for the first time 5 scouting parties, each 1/9 strong, at irregular intervals during the night. In general, it has to be stated that our men need extraordinary diligence and energy to discover the Jews who are still in so-called dug-outs, caves, and in the sewerage system. It can be expected that the remainder of the Jews who formerly inhabited the Ghetto will now be caught. The sum total of Jews caught so far has risen to 38,385. Not included in this figure are those who died in the flames or in the dug-outs. One patrol discovered an unascertainable number of corpses floating in a main sewer under the Ghetto. Outside of the Ghetto, in the immediate vicinity of Warsaw, the gendarmerie has shot a total of 150 Jews who could be proved to have escaped from Warsaw.

Again we captured pistols and explosives.

Our strength, used in operation:

Police (German)	4/102
Waffen SS	7/350
Engineers (Wehrmacht)	2/38
Engineering Emergency Service	1/6
Security Police	2/1

Cordoning units:

Waffen SS	300
German Police	1/71
Trawniki	250

Our losses: 1 policeman—wounded yesterday, died from wounds.

Termination of today's large-scale action: 2200 hours. Will be continued on 2 May 1943, 1000 hours.

The SS and Police Fuehrer in the District of Warsaw.
Signed: Stroop
SS-Brigadefuehrer and Major general of Police.
Certified copy:
SS-Sturmbannfuehrer.
Copy
Teletype message
From The SS and Police Fuehrer in the District of Warsaw
Warsaw, 2 May 1943.

Ref. No.: I ab St/Gr-16 07-Journal No. 584/43 secret.
Re: Large-scale Ghetto operation.
To: The Higher SS and Police Fuehrer East, SS-Obergruppenfuehrer and General of Police Krueger-or deputy.
Cracow

Progress of large-scale operation on 2 May 1943, start 1000 hrs. 9 raiding parties combed out the whole area of the former Ghetto; moreover a larger detachment was detailed to clean out or destroy one block of buildings grouped around the two armament enterprises Transavia and Wischniewski. To find more dug-outs, the raiding parties took along with them some Jews caught on the previous day to act as guides. In these operations the raiding parties pulled out 944 Jews from dugouts; 235 more Jews were shot on this occasion. When the block of buildings mentioned above was destroyed, 120 Jews were caught and numerous Jews were destroyed when they jumped from the attics to the inner courtyards, trying to escape the flames. Many more Jews perished in the flames or were destroyed when the dug-outs and sewer entrances were blown up. The Jews were removed from two armaments concerns and the managers were requested to evacuate within a short time.

Altogether we caught today: 1,852 Jews. The sum total of Jews caught thereby rises to 40,237 Jews. 27 dug-outs were discovered, forcibly opened and destroyed, arms and ammunition captured. When the external barricade was shot at and when some Jews who broke out from a sewer entrance outside the Ghetto made an attack, we suffered 7 losses, 4 Policemen and 3 Polish Policemen. The scouting parties used during the night encountered armed resistance from some Jews who under the protection of darkness ventured to emerge from their holes and dug-outs. We did not suffer losses thereby. On the other hands a considerable number of Jews were killed or wounded in this operation.

Our strength, used in operation:

German Police	3/98
Engineering Em Service	1/6
Security Police	3/12
Engineers (Wehrmacht)	2/37
SS-Gren	11/409
SS-Cav.	3/7

Cordoning forces:

German Police	2/9
SS-Gren	1/300
Trawniki	200

Our losses:

4 Policemen wounded
3 Polish policemen wounded

Present at today's large-scale operation was the Higher SS and Police Fuehrer East, SS-

Obergruppenfuehrer and General of Police Krueger.

Termination of operation: 2030 hours. Will be continued on 3 May 1943, 0900 hours.

The SS and Police Fuehrer in the District of Warsaw.
Signed: Stroop
SS-Brigadefuehrer and Major general of Police.
Certified copy:
SS-Sturmbannfuehrer.
Copy
Teletype message
From: The SS and Police Fuehrer in the District of Warsaw
Warsaw, 3 May 1943.
Ref. Nr.: I ab-St/Gr-16 07-Journal Nr. 597/43 secret.
Re: Large-scale Ghetto operation.
To: The Higher SS and Police Fuehrer East, SS-Obergruppenfuehrer and General of Police Krueger-or deputy.
Cracow

Progress of large-scale operation on 3 May 1943, start 0900 hours. I In the combing-out operation of the former Jewish Ghetto today 19 more dug-outs were discovered and the result was as follows:

Pulled out of dug-outs—1,392 Jews

Shot—95

Evacuated from former armament factories —177

The sum total of Jews caught thereby rises to 41,806 Jews. In most cases the Jews offered armed resistance before they left the dug-outs. We had two casualties (wounded). Some of the Jews and bandits fired pistols from both hands. Since we discovered several times today, that Jew-esses had pistols concealed in their bloomers, every Jew and bandit will be ordered from today on, to strip completely for the search. We captured among other things, one German rifle, model 98, two 08 pistols and other calibers, also home-made hand grenades. The Jews cannot be induced to leave their dug-outs until several smoke candles have been burned. According to depositions made yesterday and today, the Jews were asked during the second half of 1942 to erect air-raid shelters. At that time under the camouflage of erecting air-raid shelters, they began to build the dug-outs which they are now inhabiting, in order to use them for an anti-Jewish operation. Some of the scouting parties used in the Ghetto were shot at last night. One casualty (wounded). These scouting parties reported that groups of armed bandits marched through the Ghetto.

Strength: as on the previous day.

Losses: 3 SS-men wounded.

Termination of today's operation: 2100 hours. Will be continued on 4 May 1943. 0900 hours.

3,019 Jews were loaded.

The SS and Police Fuehrer in the District of Warsaw.
Signed: Stroop
SS-Brigadefuehrer and Major general of Police.
Certified copy:
SS-Sturmbannfuehrer.
Copy
Teletype message
From: The SS and Police Fuehrer in the District of Warsaw
Warsaw, 4 May 1943.
Ref. No.: I ab-St/Gr-16 07-Journal No. 603/43 secret.
Re: Large-scale Ghetto operation.
To: The Higher SS and Police Fuehrer East, SS-Obergruppenfuehrer and General of Police Krueger-or deputy.
Cracow

Progress of large-scale operation on 4 May 1943, start 0900 hours. For mopping up the dug-outs a raiding party was used, 1/60 strong and reinforced by an Engineers' detachment provided by the Wehrmacht. This raiding party pulled 550 Jews out of dugouts and killed in battle 188 Jews. Discovering the dug-outs becomes more and more difficult. Often they can only be discovered by betrayal through other Jews. If the Jews are requested to leave their dug-out voluntarily, they hardly ever obey; they can only be forced to do so by the use of smoke-candles.

The main forces were detailed about 1100 hours to comb out, mop up, and destroy two large blocks of buildings, containing the former firms Toebbens, Schulz and Co., and others. After these blocks had been completely cordoned off, we requested the Jews who were still within the buildings to come forward voluntarily. By this measure, we caught 456 Jews for evacuation. Not until the blocks of buildings were well aflame and were about to collapse did a further considerable number of Jews emerge, forced to do so by the flames and the smoke. Time and again the Jews try to escape even through burning buildings. Innumerable Jews whom we saw on the roofs during the conflagration perished in the flames. Others emerged from the upper stories in the last possible moment and were only able to escape death in the flames by jumping down. Today we caught a total of 2,283 Jews, of whom 204 were shot and innumerable Jews were destroyed in dug-outs and in the flames. The sum total of Jews caught rises to 44,089.

As is learned from depositions made by the Jews, today we caught part of the governing body of the so-called "Party." One member of the committee which leads the gang will be used tomorrow for mopping up some more fortified dug-outs with armed Jews inside. When the armament enterprises were evacuated, we again observed that the goods carted away were by no means valuable military equipment, as had been pretended, but trifles, like used furniture and other requisitioned items. We took appropriate measures against this at once.

The scouting parties who patrolled during the night in the former Ghetto again reported movements of the Jews in the burned out and destroyed streets and courtyards. In order to be better able to take the Jews by surprise, the scouting parties at night tie rags and other stuff round their shoes. In skirmishes between the scouting parties and Jews, 30 Jews were shot.

We captured 1 carbine, 3 pistols, and some ammunition. During the conflagration a considerable amount of stored ammunition exploded.

Our strength, used in operation:

German Police	4/101
Engineering Em. Service	1/6
Security Police	2/14
Engineers	2/41
Waffen SS	11/407

Cordoning forces:	**Day**	**Night**
German Police	2/87	1/11
Waffen SS	25	1/300
Trawniki	200	
Polish Police	1/180	1/180

Our losses: None.

Termination of operation: 2330 hours. Will be continued on 5 May 1943, 1000 hours.

The SS and Police Fuehrer in the District of Warsaw.
Signed: Stroop
SS-Brigadefuehrer and Major general of Police.
Certified copy:
SS-Sturmbannfuehrer.
Copy
Teletype message
From: The SS and Police Fuehrer in the District of Warsaw
Warsaw, 5 May 1943.
Ref. Nr.: I ab/St/Gr-16 07-Journal No. 607/43 secret.
Re: Large-scale Ghetto Operation.
To: The Higher SS and Police Fuehrer East, SS-Obergruppenfuehrer and General of Police Krueger-or deputy.
Cracow

Progress of large-scale operation on 5 May 1943. Start 1000 hours. In the beginning of today's operations the raiding parties seemed to have less results than on the preceding days. When the operation terminated, however, quite a number of dug-outs had again been discovered, owing to the tracking ability of the men and to betrayal; 40 of these dug-outs were destroyed. As far as possible, the Jews in these dug-outs were caught (1,070 altogether). The combing out patrols shot about 126 Jews. Today again the Jews resisted in several places until they were captured. In several cases the entrances (hatches) of the dugouts were forcibly held or bolted from the inside, so that only by using a strong explo-

sive charge could we force them open and destroy the inmates. Today, we again captured arms and ammunition, including one pistol. From one enterprise still in existence (so-called Prosta) 2,850 Jews were caught for evacuation. This figure was included in the sum total reported earlier, so that only 1,070 have to be added; the present sum total therefore is 45,159.

Our strength: as on the preceding day.

Our losses: 1 SS man wounded, 1 Policeman wounded.

Sum total of losses to date: 8 dead, 55 wounded.

Termination of operation: 2200 hours.— Will be continued on 6 May 1943, 0900 hours.

The SS and Police Fuehrer in the District of Warsaw.
Signed: Stroop
SS-Brigadefuehrer and Major general of Police.
Certified copy:
SS-Sturmbannfuehrer.
Copy
Teletype message
From: The SS and Police Fuehrer in the District of Warsaw
Warsaw, 6 May 1943.
Ref. No.: ab/St/Gr-16 07-Journal No. 614/43 secret.
Re: Ghetto large-scale operation.
To: The Higher SS and Police Fuehrer East, SS Obergruppenfuehrer and General of Police Krueger-or deputy.
Cracow

Progress of large-scale operation on 6 May 1943, start 0930 hours.

Today we combed especially those blocks of buildings which were destroyed by fire on 4 May 1943. Although it was hardly to be expected that any living person could still exist in those blocks, we discovered quite a number of dug-outs in which a burning heat had developed. From these dug-outs and from other dugouts which we discovered in other parts of the Ghetto, we pulled out 1,553 Jews. While resisting, and in a skirmish, 356 Jews were shot. In this skirmish the Jews fired from 08 pistols and other calibers and threw Polish "pineapple" hand grenades. One SS Unterscharfuehrer was wounded and a total of 47 dug-outs were destroyed.

2 men of the external cordoning forces were wounded. The Jews who had broken out from the Ghetto seem to be returning now with the intention of assisting the Ghetto Jews by force or liberating them. One Jew who had escaped from Lublin was caught just outside of the Ghetto wall. He was armed as follows: 1 08 pistol, ample reserve ammunition, 2 Polish "pineapple" hand grenades. It could not be reliably ascertained so far whether the so-called "Party Directorate" of the Jews ("PPR") have been caught or destroyed. We are on their traces. It is to be hoped that

tomorrow we shall succeed in tracing down this so-called Party Directorate. In order to enable us to intercept more effectively the Jews and bandits who approach the Ghetto, covering detachments of the external barricade were shifted farther inside the Aryan part. The former miniature Ghetto "Prosta" was searched by raiding parties today. We caught some Jews who had stayed behind. The firm Toebbens was requested to evacuate, this miniature Ghetto by noon on 10 May 1943. The so-called library, situated outside the Ghetto, was put at their disposal for temporary storage of their raw materials, etc.

The sum total of Jews caught so far rises to 47,068. The Polish Police take pains to deliver to my office every Jew who turns up within the city, because they are eager to win such premiums as have been paid in earlier cases. The undersigned received some anonymous letters in which he was notified of the fact that some Jews are staying in the Aryan part of the city. One anonymous letter draws a parallel between Katyn and the large-scale action within the Ghetto.

Our strength:

Used in operation:

German Police	4/101
Engineering Em. Service	1/6
Security Police	2/14
Engineers	3/72
Waffen SS	10/500

Cordoning forces:	**Day**	**Night**
German Police	2/87	1/11
Waffen SS	25	1/300
Trawniki	200	
Polish Police	1/180	1/180

Our losses:

1 Policeman dead
1 Policeman seriously wounded
1 SS Unterscharfuehrer less seriously wounded

Termination of operation: 2100 hours. Will be continued on 7 May 1943, 0930 hours.

The SS and Police Fuehrer in the District of Warsaw.
Signed: Stroop
SS-Brigadefuehrer and Major general of Police.
Certified copy:
SS-Sturmbannfuehrer.
Copy
Teletype message
From: The SS and Police Fuehrer in the District of Warsaw
Warsaw, 7 May 1943.
Ref. Nr.: I ab/St/Gr-16 07-Journal Nr. 616/43 secret
Re:Large-scale Ghetto Operation.
To: The Higher SS and Police Fuehrer East, SS-Obergruppenfuehrer and General of Police Krueger-or deputy.
Cracow

Progress of large-scale operation on 7 May 1943, start 1000 hours. The combing-out parties today obtained the following results: 49 dug-outs discovered. Part of the Jews were caught. A considerable, not ascertainable, number of Jews who refused to leave the dug-outs and offered armed resistance were destroyed when the dug-outs were blown up. Altogether 1,019 Jews were caught alive today, 255 shot. The sum total of Jews caught so far rises to 48,342. Today we again encountered armed resistance in several cases, whereby we lost 1 SS man (wounded). We captured 4 pistols of various calibers and some stores of ammunition.

The location of the dug-out used by the so-called select "Party Directorate" is now known. It is to be forced open tomorrow. The Jews testify that they emerge at night to get fresh air, since it is unbearable to stay permanently within the dug-outs owing to the long duration of the operation. On the average the raiding parties shoot 30 to 50 Jews each night. From these statements it was to be inferred that a considerable number of Jews are still underground in the Ghetto. Today we blew up a concrete building which we had not been able to destroy by fire. In this operation we learned that the blowing up of a building is a very lengthy process and takes an enormous amount of explosives. The best and only method for destroying the Jews therefore remains the setting of fires.

Our strength: as on the preceding day. Our losses: 1 Waffen-SS man wounded.

Termination of operation: 2100 hours, will be continued on 8 May 1943 1000 hours.

The SS and Police Fuehrer in the District of Warsaw.
Signed: Stroop
SS-Brigadefuehrer and Major general of Police.
Certified copy:
SS-Sturmbannfuehrer.
Copy
Teletype message
From The SS and Police Fuehrer in the District of Warsaw
Warsaw, 8 May 1943.
Ref. No.: I ab/St/Gr-16 07-Journal No. 624/43 secret.
Re: Large-scale Ghetto Operation.
To: The Higher SS and Police Fuehrer East, SS Obergruppenfuehrer and General of Police Krueger-or deputy.
Cracow

Progress of operation on 8 May 1943, start 1000 hours.

The whole former Ghetto was searched today by raiding parties for the remaining dug-outs and Jews. As reported some days a number of subhumans, bandits, and terrorists still remain in the dug-outs, where heat has become intolerable by reason of the fires. These creatures know only too well that their only choice is between remaining in hiding as long as possible or coming to the surface and trying to wound or kill off the men of the Waffen-SS, Police, and Wehrmacht who keep up the pressure against them.

We continued today the operation against the dug-out of the so-called select "Party Directorate" which we had discovered yesterday, as reported in my teletype message yesterday. We succeeded in forcing open the dug-out of the Party Directorate and in catching about 60 heavily armed bandits. We succeeded in catching and liquidating Deputy Leader of the Jewish Military Organization "ZWZ" and his so-called Chief of Staff. There were about 200 Jews in this dug-out, of whom 60 were caught and 140 were destroyed, partly owing to the strong effect of smoke-candles, and partly owing to heavy explosive charges which were laid in several places. The Jews whom we caught had already reported that innumerable Jews had been killed by the effect of the smoke-candles. The fight of the first six days was hard, but now we are able to state that we are catching those Jews and Jewesses who were the ringleaders in those days. Every time a dug-out is forced open, the Jews in it offer resistance with the arms at their disposal, light machine guns, pistols, and hand grenades. Today we again caught quite a number of Jewesses who carried loaded pistols in their bloomers, with the safety catch released. Some depositions speak of 3 to 4,000 Jews who still remain in underground holes, sewers, and dug-outs. The undersigned is resolved not to terminate the large-scale operation until the last Jew has been destroyed.

A total of 1,091 Jews were caught today in dug-outs; about 280 Jews were shot in battle, innumerable Jews were destroyed in the 43 dug-outs which were blown up. The sum total of Jews caught has risen to 49,712. Those buildings which had not yet been destroyed by fire, were set on fire today and we discovered that a few Jews were still hiding somewhere within the walls or in the staircases.

Our strength:
Used in operation:

German Police	4/101
Engineering Em Service	1/6
Security Police	2/14
Engineers	3/69
Waffen SS	13/527

Cordoning forces:	**Day**	**Night**
German Police	1/87	1/36
Waffen SS	25	1/300
Trawniki	160	
Polish Police	1/160	1/160

Our losses:
2 Waffen SS dead
2 Waffen SS wounded
1 Engineer wounded

A policeman wounded on 7 May 1943 died today from wounds. We captured about 15 to 20 pistols of various calibers, considerable stores of ammunition for pistols and rifles, moreover a number of hand grenades, made in the former armament factories.

Termination of action; 2130 hours, will be continued on 9 May 1943 1000 hours.

The SS and Police Fuehrer in the District of Warsaw.
Signed: Stroop
SS-Brigadefuehrer and Major general of Police.
Certified copy:
SS-Sturmbannfuehrer.
Copy
Teletype message
From: The SS and Police Fuehrer in the District of Warsaw
Warsaw, 9 May 1943.
Ref. No.: I ab/St/Gr 1607 Journal No. 625/43.
Re: Large-scale Ghetto Operation.
To: The Higher SS and Police Fuehrer East, SS-Obergruppenfuehrer and General of Police Krueger-or deputy.
Cracow

Progress of large-scale operation on 9 May 1943, start 1000 hours.

The operation carried out today had the following result: The raiding parties at work today discovered 42 dug-outs. From these dug-outs we pulled out alive 1,037 Jews and bandits. In battle 319 bandits and Jews were shot, moreover an uncertain number were destroyed when the dug-outs were blown up. The block of buildings which formerly contained the "Transavia" concern was destroyed by fire; in this operation we again caught a number of Jews, although this block had been combed through several times.

Again we captured some pistols and hand grenades.

Our strength:
Used in operation:

German Police	4/103
Security Police	2/12
Engineers	3/67
Waffen SS	13/547

Cordoning Forces:	**Day**	**Night**
German Police	1/87	1/36
Waffen SS		1/300
Trawniki	160	
Polish Police	1/160	1/160

Our losses: None.

The total of Jews caught up to date has risen to 51,313. Outside the former Ghetto 254 Jews and bandits were shot.

Termination of operation: 2100 hours, will be continued on 10 May 1943, 1000 hours.

The SS and Police Fuehrer in the District of Warsaw.
Signed: Stroop
SS-Brigadefuehrer and Major general of Police.

Certified copy:
SS-Sturmbannfuehrer.
Copy
Teletype message
From: The SS and Police Fuehrer in the District of Warsaw,
Warsaw, 10 May, 1943.
Ref. Nr. I ab St/Gr 16 07 Journal No. 627/43 secret.
Re: Large-scale Ghetto Operation.
To: The Higher SS and Police Fuehrer East, SS-Obergruppenfuehrer and General of Police Krueger-or deputy.
Cracow

Progress of large-scale action on 10 May 1943 start 1000 hours.

Today raiding parties again combed out the area of the former Ghetto. As on preceding days we again pulled out of the dug-outs, against all expectations, a considerable number of Jews. The resistance offered by the Jews had not weakened today. In contrast to the previous days, it seems that those members of the main body of the Jewish battle group who are still in existence and have not been destroyed have retired into the ruins still within their reach, with the intention of firing from there against our men and inflicting casualties.

Today we caught a total of 1,183 Jews alive, 187 bandits and Jews were shot. Again a not ascertainable number of Jews and bandits were destroyed in the blown-up dug-outs. The total of Jews caught up to date has risen to 52,693.

Today at 0900 hours a truck drove up to a certain sewer in the so-called Prosta. Someone in the truck exploded two hand grenades, which was the signal for the bandits who were standing ready in the sewer to climb out of it. The bandits and Jews—there are always some Polish bandits among them armed with carbines, small arms, and one machine gun, climbed into the truck and drove away in an unknown direction. The last man of the gang, who stood sentry in the sewer and had the duty of closing the sewer lid, was captured. It is he who gave the above information. He testified that most of the members of the gang, which had been divided into several battle groups, had either been killed in battle or had committed suicide because they had realized the futility of continuing the fight. The search for the truck, which was ordered at once, had no results. The bandits testified further that the Prosta is now the refuge for the still existing Jews because the Ghetto has become too hot for them. For this reason, I resolved to deal with the Prosta in the same manner as with the Ghetto, and to destroy this miniature Ghetto.

Today, we again captured small arms and some ammunition.

The Security Police yesterday succeeded in capturing a workshop outside the Ghetto which manufactured 10,000 to 11,000 explosive charges and other ammunition.

Our strength: as on the preceding day. Our losses: 3 SS men wounded.

Owing to the excellent understanding between us and the Wehrmacht, the detachment of Engineers was reinforced. Moreover, a considerable amount of explosives was put at our disposal.

Termination of operation: 2200 hours. Will be continued on 11 May 1943, 0930 hours.

The SS and Police Fuehrer in the District of Warsaw.
Signed: Stroop
SS-Brigadefuehrer and Major general of Police.
Certified copy:
SS-Sturmbannfuehrer.
Copy
Teletype message
From: The SS and Police Fuehrer in the District of Warsaw
Warsaw, 11 May 1943.
Ref. No.: I ab-St/Gr-16 07 Journal No. 629/43 secret.
Re: Ghetto large-scale Operation.
To: The Higher SS and Police Fuehrer East, SS Obergruppenfuehrer and General of Police Krueger-or deputy.
Cracow

Progress of large-scale operation on 11 May 1943, start 0930 hours.

The scouting parties sent out last night again reported that there must still be some Jews within the dug-outs, since some Jews were seen in the ruined streets. The scouting parties shot 12 Jews. On the basis of these reports, today I again formed raiding parties who in combing-out operations discovered, captured, and destroyed a total of 47 dug-outs. Today again we caught some Jews who had taken refuge in ruins which were still protected by a roof. The Jews and bandits are still seeking this new refuge, because staying in the dug-outs has become unbearable. One dug-out was discovered which contained about 12 rooms equipped with plumbing, running water, and separate bathrooms for men and women. Considerable amounts of food were captured or secured, in order to make it more and more difficult for them to get necessary food.

A total of 931 Jews and bandits were caught. 53 bandits were shot. More of them perished when dug-outs were blown up and when a small block of buildings was destroyed by fire. The total of Jews caught up to date has risen to 53,667. We captured several pistols, hand grenades, and ammunition.

We have not been able to smoke out the sewers systematically once more, since we are short of smoke-candles. "OFK" is ready to provide new smoke-candles.

Our strength:

Used in operation:

German Police	6/126
Engineering Em. Service	1/6
Security Police	2/14
Engineers	4/76
Waffen SS	12/308

Cordoning forces:	Day	Night
German Police	1/112	1/86
Waffen SS	—	1/130
Trawniki	160	—
Polish Police	1/160	1/160

Our losses: 1 SS man wounded.

Total of losses up to date: 71 wounded, 12 dead.

Termination of today's operation: 2145 hours, will be continued on 12 May 1943, 0930 hours.

The SS and Police Fuehrer in the District of Warsaw.

Signed: Stroop

SS-Brigadefuehrer and Major general of Police.

Certified copy:

SS-Sturmbannfuehrer.

Copy

Teletype message

From: The SS and Police Fuehrer in the District of Warsaw

Warsaw, 12 May 1943

Ref. No.: I ab-St/Gr-16 07-Journal No. 637/43 secret.

Re: Large-scale Ghetto Operation.

To: The Higher SS and Police Fuehrer East, SS-Obergruppenfuehrer and General of Police Krueger-or deputy.

Cracow

Progress of large-scale operation on 12 May 1943, start 0930 hours.

When the raiding parties combed out the area for remaining dug-outs in which Jews were hiding, they succeeded in discovering 30 dug-outs. 663 Jews were pulled out of them and 133 Jews were shot. The sum total of Jews caught has arisen to 54,463.

Furthermore today the units cordoning off the miniature Ghetto were reinforced and destroyed by fire. Probably a considerable number of Jews perished in the flames, no accurate information in this regard could be obtained since the fire was still burning when darkness set in. One concrete building in the Prosta, from which Jews had been removed, was heavily damaged by blowing-up operations in order to make it impossible for the bandits to use it as a base later.

It is noteworthy that the Poles, without having been warned, took appropriate measures for protecting their window-panes, etc., before the blowing-up started.

The transports of Jews leaving here will be directed to T.II beginning today.

Our strength:

Used in operation:

German police	5/126
Engineering Em. Service	1/6
Security Police	2/14
Engineers	4/74
Waffen SS	12/508

Cordoning forces:	Day	Night
German Police	1/112	1/86
Waffen SS	—	1/300
Trawniki	160	—
Polish Police	1/160	1/160

Our losses:

1 Waffen SS man wounded.

Termination of today's operation: 2160 hours, will be continued on 13 May 1943, 1000 hours.

The SS and Police Fuehrer in the District of Warsaw.

Signed: Stroop

SS-Brigadefuehrer and Major general of Police.

Certified copy:

SS-Sturmbannfuehrer.

Copy

Teletype message

From: The SS and Police Fuehrer in the District of Warsaw

Warsaw, 13 May, 1943.

Ref. No.: I ate/ St/Gr 16 07 Journal No. 641/43 secret. Re: Large-scale Ghetto Operation.

To: The Higher SS and Police Fuehrer East, SS-Obergruppenfuehrer and General of Police Krueger-or deputy.

Cracow

Progress of large-scale operation on 13 May 1943, start 1000 hours. In combing out the Ghetto and the miniature Ghetto (Prosta) today we found 234 Jews. 155 Jews were shot in battle. Today it became clear that the Jews and bandits whom we are catching now belong to the so-called battle groups. All of them are young fellows and females between 18 and 25 years of age. When we captured one, a real skirmish took place, in which the Jews not only fired from 08 pistols and Polish Vis pistols, but also threw Polish "pineapple" hand grenades at the Waffen-SS men. After part of the inmates of the dug-out had been caught and were about to be searched, one of the females as quick as lightning put her hand under her shirt, as many others had done, and fetched from her bloomers a "pineapple" hand grenade, drew the safety-catch, threw the grenade among the men who were searching her, and jumped quickly to cover. It is only thanks to the presence of mind of the men that no casualties ensued.

The few Jews and criminals still staying in the Ghetto have for the last few days been using the hideouts they can still find among the ruins, retiring at night into the dug-outs whose location is known to them, to eat and get provisions for the next day. Lately we have been unable to extract information on the whereabouts of further dug-outs from the captured Jews. The remainder of the inmates of that dug-out where the skirmish took place were destroyed by using heavier explosive charges. From a Wehrmacht concern we evacuated 327 Jews today. The Jews we catch now are sent to T.II.

The total of Jews caught has risen to 55,179.

Our strength:

Used in operation:

German police	4/182
Engineering Em. Service	1/6
Security Police	2/14
Engineers	4/74
Waffen SS	12/517

Cordoning forces:	**Day**	**Night**
German Police	2/137	1/87
Waffen SS	—	1/300
Trawniki	270	
Polish Police	1/160	

Our losses:

2 Waffen SS dead
3 Waffen SS wounded
1 Policeman wounded.

The 2 Waffen SS men lost their lives in the air attack against the Ghetto.

33 dug-outs were discovered and destroyed. Booty: 6 pistols, 2 hand grenades, and some explosive charges.

Termination of today's operation: 2100 hours, will be continued on 14 May 1943, 1000 hours.

My intention is to terminate the large-scale operation on 16 May 1943 and to turn all further measures over to Police battalion III/23. Unless ordered otherwise, I am going to submit to the conference of SS and Policefuehrers a detailed report of the operation, including an appendix containing photos.

The SS and Police Fuehrer in the District of Warsaw.
Signed: Stroop
SS-Brigadefuehrer and Major general of Police.
Certified copy:
SS-Sturmbannfuehrer.
Copy
Teletype message
From: The SS and Police Fuehrer in the District of Warsaw
Warsaw, 14 May 1943.
Ref. No. I ab/St/G 16 07 Journal No. 646/43 secret.
Re: Large-scale Ghetto Operation.
To: The Higher SS and Police Fuehrer Fast, SS Obergruppenfuehrer and General of Police Krueger-or deputy.
Cracow

Progress of large-scale operation on 14 May 1943, start 1000 hours.

The raiding parties formed today went to work within the areas allotted to each of them under orders to force open further dwelling dug-outs and to catch the Jews. In this way a considerable number of bandits and Jews were caught, especially as some traces had been discovered during the night which were now followed up with good results. The night patrols clashed with armed bandits several times. These bandits fired a machine gun and small arms. In this operation we had four casualties—3 Waffen-SS men and 1 Policeman. Repeatedly, shots were fired from the Aryan part against the external barricade. In the skirmishes about 30 bandits were shot and 9 Jews and bandits, members of an armed gang, were captured. One dug-out was taken during the night, the Jews captured, and some pistols, among them one of 12-mm caliber, were captured. In one dug-out inhabited by 100 persons, we were able to capture 2 rifles, 16 pistols, some hand grenades and incendiary appliances. Of the bandits who resisted, some again wore German military uniform, German-steel helmets and "knobeloecher." Apart from the carbines, we captured 60 rounds of German rifle ammunition. One raiding party had a skirmish with a gang, 10 to 14 strong, on the roofs of a block of buildings at the border of the Ghetto (Aryan part). The bandits were destroyed; we suffered no losses.

The captured bandits repeatedly testify that still not all persons in the Ghetto have been caught. They confidently expect that the action will soon be over, and that they will then be able to continue to live in the Ghetto. Several bandits stated that they had long been in a position to kill off the leader of the action, the "General," as they call him, but that they would not do so, since they had orders to that effect to avoid the risk of a further intensification of the anti-Jewish measures.

Today again some concrete buildings in which the bandits find refuge time and again were blown up by the engineers.

In order to force the bandits in the sewers to come to the surface, 183 sewer entrances were opened at 1500 hours, and smokecandles were lowered into them at an ordered x-time, thereupon the bandits, seeking escape from what they supposed to be poison gas, crowded together in the center of the former Ghetto, and we were able to pull them out of the sewer entrances there.

I shall come to a decision after tomorrow's operations regarding termination of the action.

Today SS-Gruppenfuehrer and Lieutenant General of Waffen-SS von Horff was present during the operations.

Our strength:

Used in operation:

German Police	4/184
Engineering Em. Serv	1/6

Security Police		2/16
Engineers		4/73
Waffen-SS		12/51

Cordoning forces:	Day	Night
German Police	2/138	1/87
Waffen SS	—	1/300
Trawniki	—	270
Polish Police	1/160	1/160

Our losses:

5 wounded, 4 Waffen SS, 1 Police

A total of 398 Jews were caught today, furthermore 154 Jews and bandits were shot in battle. The total of the Jews caught has risen to 55,731.

Booty: rifles, pistols, and ammunition. Further, a number of incendiary bottles (Molotov cocktails).

Termination of action; 2155 hours, will be continued on 15 May 1943 0900 hours.

The SS and Police Fuehrer in the District of Warsaw.
Signed: Stroop
SS-Brigadefuehrer and Major general of Police.
Certified copy:
SS-Sturmbannfuehrer.
Copy
Teletype message
From: The SS and Police Fuehrer in the District of Warsaw
Warsaw, May 15th 1943.
Ref. No.: I ab/St/Gr 16 07 Journal No. 648/43 secret.
Re: Large-scale Ghetto Operation.
To: The Higher SS and Police Fuehrer East, SS-Obergruppenfuehrer and General of Police Krueger-or deputy.
Cracow

Progress of large-scale operation on 15 April 1943. Start 0900 hours.

The 5 scouting parties who patrolled the Ghetto last night reported that they encountered Jews only sporadically. In contrast to the preceding nights, they were able to shoot 6 or 7 Jews. The combing-out actions today also had little result. 29 more dug-outs were discovered, but part of them were no longer inhabited. A total of 87 Jews were caught today and 67 bandits and Jews were shot in battle. In a skirmish which developed around noon, and in which the bandits again resisted by using Molotov cocktails, pistols, and home-made hand grenades, the gang was destroyed; but subsequently a policeman was wounded by a shot through the right thigh. A special unit once more searched the last block of buildings which was still intact in the Ghetto, and subsequently destroyed it. In the evening the chapel, mortuary, and all other buildings on the Jewish cemetery were blown up or destroyed by fire.

The sum total of Jews caught has risen to 55,885.

Our strength:
Used in operation:

German Police		4/184
Engineering Em. S		1/6
Security Police		2/16
Waffen-SS		12/510

Cordoning forces:	Day	Night
German Police	2/138	1/87
Waffen-SS	—	1/300
Trawniki	270	—
Polish Police	1/160	1/160

Our losses:

1 Policeman wounded.

We captured 4 pistols of larger calibers, 1 infernal machine with fuse, 10 kilograms of explosives, and a considerable amount of ammunition. Termination of operation: 2130 hours. Will be continued on 16 May 1943, 1000 hours.

I will terminate the large-scale operation on 16 May 1943 at dusk, by blowing up the Synagogue, which we did not succeed in accomplishing today, and will subsequently charge Police Battalion III/23 with continuing and completing the measures which are still necessary.

The SS and Police Fuehrer in the District of Warsaw.
Signed: Stroop
SS-Brigadefuehrer and Major general of Police.
Certified copy:
SS-Sturmbannfuehrer.
Copy
Teletype message
From: The SS and Police Fuehrer in the District of Warsaw
Warsaw, May 16th, 1943.
Ref. No.: I ab-St/Gr 16 07 Journal Nr. 652/43 secret.
Re: Large-scale Ghetto Operation.
To: The Higher SS and Police Fuehrer East, SS-Obergruppenfuehrer and General of Police Krueger-or deputy.
Cracow

Progress of large-scale operation on 16 May 1943, start 1000 hours.

180 Jews, bandits, and subhumans were destroyed. The former Jewish quarter of Warsaw is no longer in existence. The large-scale action was terminated at 2015 hours by blowing up the Warsaw Synagogue.

The measures to be taken with regard to the established banned areas were handed over to the commander of police battalion III/23, whom I instructed carefully.

Total number of Jews dealt with 56,065, including both Jews caught and Jews whose extermination can be proved.

No losses today.

I will submit a final report to the Conference of SS Police Fuehrer on 18 May 1943.

The SS and Police Fuehrer in the District of Warsaw.
Signed: Stroop
SS-Brigadefuehrer and Major general of Police.
Certified copy:
SS-Sturmbannfuehrer.
Copy
Teletype message
From: The SS and Police Fuehrer in the District of Warsaw
Warsaw, 24 May 1943.
Ref. No.: I ab-St/Gr 16 07 Journal Nr. 663/43 secret.
Re: Large-scale Ghetto Operation.
Ref: Your teletype message Nr. 946 of 21 May 1943.
To: The Higher SS and Police Fuehrer East, SS-Obergruppenfuehrer and General of Police Krueger-or deputy.
Cracow

I beg to reply to the above teletype message:
No. 1:

Of the total of 56,065 caught, about 7,000 were destroyed in the former Ghetto during large-scale operation. 6,929 Jews were destroyed by transporting them to T.II; the sum total of Jews destroyed is therefore 13,929. Beyond the number of 56,065 an estimated number of 5 to 6,000 Jews were destroyed by being blown up or by perishing in the flames.

No. 2:
A total of 631 dug-outs were destroyed.

No. 3 (booty):
7 Polish rifles, 1 Russian rifle, 1 German rifle.
59 pistols of various calibers.
Several 100 hand grenades, including Polish and homemade ones.
A few 100 incendiary bottles.
Home-made explosive charges.
Infernal machines with fuses.
Large amounts of explosives, ammunition for all calibers, including machine-gun ammunition.

With regard to the bag of arms one must take into consideration that in most cases we were not able to capture the arms themselves, since the Jews and bandits before they were captured threw them away into hideouts and holes which we could not discover or find. The smoke which we had developed in the dug-outs also prevented our men from discovering and capturing the arms. Since we had to blow up the dug-outs at once we were not in a position to search for the arms later on.

The hand grenades, explosive charges, and incendiary bottles captured were used at once against the bandits.
Furthermore, we captured:
1,240 used uniform tunics (partly equipped with medal ribbons, Iron Cross, and East Medal).
600 pairs of used trousers.
Pieces of equipment, and German steel helmets.
103 horses, 4 of them in the former Ghetto (hearse)
We counted up to 23 May 1943:
4.4 million Zloty. We captured moreover about 5 to 6 million Zloty, not yet counted, a considerable amount of foreign currency, including—
$14,300 in paper.
$ 9,200 in gold.
Large amounts of valuables (rings, chains, watches etc.)

No. 4:
With the exception of 8 buildings (police barracks, hospital and accommodations for working parties) the former Ghetto has been completely destroyed. Where blowing-up was not carried out, only partition walls are still standing. But the ruins still contain enormous amounts of bricks and scrap material which could be used.

Source: "Nazi Conspiracy and Aggression, Volume 3: Document No. 1061-PS," Avalon Project at Yale Law School <http://www.yale.edu/lawweb/avalon/imt/ document/1061-ps.htm>.

DOCUMENT 4

LIBERATORS

In 1945 the 71st Infantry Division of the U.S. Army liberated Gunskirchen Lager, a subunit of the Mauthausen concentration camp complex in Austria. Afterward, the U.S. government printed a pamphlet of the liberators' experiences at the camp.

FOREWARD

The damning evidence against the Nazi war criminals found at Gunskirchen Lager is being recorded in this booklet in the hope that the lessons learned in Germany will not soon be forgotten by the democratic nations or the individual men who fought to wipe out a government built on hate, greed, race myths and murder. This is a true record. I saw Gunskirchen Lager myself before the 71st Division had initiated its merciful task of liberation. The horror of Gunskirchen must not be repeated. A permanent, honest record of the crimes committed there will serve to remind all of us in future years that the freedom and privileges we enjoy in a democratic nation must be jealously guarded and protected.
WILLARD G. WYMAN
Major General, USA
Commanding

"THE AMERICANS HAVE COME—AT LAST"

Capt. J. D. Pletcher, Berwyn, Ill., of the 71st Division Headquarters and Cpl. James DeSpain, Allegan, Michigan, arrived at Gunskirchen Lager the same morning the camp was found by elements of the Division. Capt. Pletcher's account of the scenes he witnessed follows:

"When the German SS troops guarding the concentration camp at Gunskirchen heard the Americans were coming, they suddenly got busy burying the bodies of their victims—or rather, having them buried by inmates—and gave the prisoners who were still alive what they considered an extremely liberal food ration: One lump of sugar per person and one loaf of bread for every seven persons. Then, two days or a day and half before we arrived, the SS left. All this I learned from talking to inmates of the camp, many of whom spoke English. Driving up to the camp in our jeep, Cpl. DeSpain and I, first knew we were approaching the camp by the hundreds of starving, half crazed inmates lining the roads, begging for food and cigarettes. Many of them had been able to get only a few hundred yards from the gate before they keeled over and died. As weak as they were, the chance to be free, the opportunity to escape was so great they couldn't resist, though it meant staggering only a few yards before death came.

"Then came the next indication of the camp's nearness—the smell. There was something about the smell of Gunskirchen I shall never forget. It was strong, yes, and permeating, too. Some six hours after we left the place, six hours spent riding in a jeep, where the wind was whistling around us, we could still detect the Gunskirchen smell. It had permeated our clothing, and stayed with us.

"Of all the horrors of the place, the smell, perhaps, was the most startling of all. It was a smell made up of all kinds of odors—human excreta, foul bodily odors, smoldering trash fires, German tobacco—which is a stink in itself—all mixed together in a heavy dank atmosphere, in a thick, muddy woods, where little breeze could go. The ground was pulpy throughout the camp, churned to a consistency of warm putty by the milling of thousands of feet, mud mixed with feces and urine. The smell of Gunskirchen nauseated many of the Americans who went there. It was a smell I'll never forget, completely different from anything I've ever encountered. It could almost be seen and hung over the camp like a fog of death.

"As we entered the camp, the living skeletons still able to walk crowded around us and, though we wanted to drive farther into the place, the milling, pressing crowd wouldn't let us. It is not an exaggeration to say that almost every inmate was insane with hunger. Just the sight of an American brought cheers, groans and shrieks. People crowded around to touch an American, to touch the jeep, to kiss our arms—perhaps just to make sure that it was true. The people who couldn't walk crawled out toward our jeep. Those who couldn't even crawl propped themselves up on an elbow, and somehow, through all their pain and suffering, revealed through their eyes the gratitude, the joy they felt at the arrival of Americans.

"An English-speaking inmate offered to show us around the camp. We accepted his offer. Another inmate organizer asked me if he could climb on the jeep to say a few words to his people. We helped him up on the hood and he yelled for order. He spoke in his native tongue—Hungarian I believe—and my guide interpreted for us. He was asking the inmates to remain in the camp and not clutter up the roads, some 3,000 had already left, and he wanted his fellow prisoners to help the Yanks by staying off the roads. He told them that the Americans were bringing food and water and medical help. After every sentence he was interrupted by loud cheers from the crowd. It was almost like a political speech. Everyone was hysterical with joy at being found by the Americans, yet in a frenzy of hunger, for they had had no food since the Germans left two days before, and not enough to keep anyone alive for months before.

"During the talk of the man on our jeep hood, a tall, blonde haired man approached me. He spoke excellent English. He was an engineer, educated in New York. He had committed the crime of letting Jewish blood infiltrate into his family stream some generations back. As hungry as he was for food, he was hungry for news. He said the camp inmates had known all about the movements of the Yanks for the past five days. Every day they had known we were coming closer, and as we approached, the anticipation in the stinking hole of Gunskirchen heightened. Through the last few, foodless days, the inmates had lived on faith alone, he said. Faith that the Americans would come soon. He was vitally interested in knowing about all phases of the European War. He asked about the other armies, how far they had advanced, how fast they were moving, about the Russians. He eagerly listened to all the news I could give him.

"The man on the jeep hood spoke for about five minutes. At the completion he asked the people to clear the road so that we might proceed. Many of the more energetic waved the cheering crowds back to clear a path just wide enough for our vehicle.

"All wanted to get close enough to see and many wanted to touch us as we moved slowly on. It was like a triumphal procession with the milling crowd cheering and waving their arms in exaltation.

"The thousands of prisoners had been crammed into a few low, one-story, frame buildings with sloppy, muddy floors. Those who were able had come out of the buildings, but there

APPENDIX

were hundreds left in them—the dead, the near-dead, and those too weak to move. Sometimes, my guide said, it was so crowded in the buildings that people slept three-deep on the floor, one on top of the other. Often, a man would awake in the morning and find the person under him dead. Too weak to move even the pathetically light bodies of their comrades, the living continued sleeping on them.

"I want to make it clear that human beings subjected to the treatment these people were given by the Germans results in a return to the primitive. Dire hunger does strange things. The inmates of Gunskirchen were a select group of prisoners—the intellectual class of Hungarian Jews, for the most part professional people, many distinguished doctors, lawyers, representatives of every skilled field. Yet, these people, who would naturally be expected to maintain their sense of values, their human qualities, longer than any others, had been reduced to animals by the treatment of the Germans—the deliberate prolonged starvation, the indiscriminate murder on little or no provocation, the unbelievable living conditions gradually brought about a change in even the strongest.

"The camp was littered with bodies. Since the Germans had left, the inmates had been unable to cope with the swiftly mounting death rate. As long as the SS men were in charge, they made the stronger inmates dig crude pits and bury the dead, not for sanitary reasons, but in an attempt to hide some of the evidence of the inhuman treatment given their prisoners.

"For the thousands of prisoners in Gunskirchen, there was one 20-hole latrine. The rule of the SS men was to shoot on sight anyone seen relieving himself in any place but the latrine. Many of the persons in the camp had diarrhea. There were always long lines at the latrine and it was often impossible for many to reach it in time because of hours spent waiting. Naturally, many were shot for they could not wait in line. Their bodies were still lying there in their own filth. The stench was unbelievable.

"Cpl. DeSpain and I both remarked later about the appearance of the inmates—that they all seemed to look alike. When men are reduced to skeletons, as these men were, they all resembled one another—the only difference being in their height and the color of their hair.

"My guide explained that many of the new prisoners at Gunskirchen had recently been forced to march from the vicinity of Hungary to Gunskirchen. There was very little food. They died like flies. If they fell out and were too weak to continue, the SS men shot then. The air-line distance from Hungarian border to Gunskirchen is 150 miles. The intervening territory is full of mountains and winding roads, so the actual distance these people walked was far greater than 150 miles. It is not hard to imagine the thousands of skeletons that mark their route.

"The hunger in evidence is hard to imagine. We found huge animal bones in camp—the bones of a horse or cow the prisoners had found and smuggled into camp. Usually these prizes were eaten raw, the flesh torn from the bones and swallowed in great gulps.

"Rarely did a prisoner have the strength to curb his hunger long enough to cook what food he got. Outside the gate of the camp was the carcass of a horse that had been killed by shellfire. There was a great, gaping wound in his belly. As we passed it, one of the inmates was down on his knees, eating off the carcass. It had been dead several days. The next day when we came back, the whole side had been sliced away. Though our troops got food to them as soon as possible, many could not wait. Of course, we quickly gave away all the rations and cigarettes we had. It was strange to see them eat the cigarettes instead of smoking them. Not one cigarette did I see smoked. They were all swallowed in a hurry.

"American troops soon organized things. Water was hauled in German tank wagons. All horses and wagons in the vicinity were put on a food hauling detail. We found a German food warehouse three miles from Gunskirchen stocked with dried noodles, potatoes, soups, meats and other food. German civilians took it to Gunskirchen under the supervision of American military government personnel, and before we could establish proper control some of the prisoners had gobbled down the food, gorged themselves and died. A starving person must learn to eat all over again.

"None of the inmates of Gunskirchen will ever be the same again. I doubt if any of us who saw it will ever forget it—the smell, the hundreds of bodies that looked like caricatures of human beings, the frenzy of the thousands when they knew the Americans had arrived at last, the spark of joy in the eyes of those who lay in the ditches and whispered a prayer of thanks with their last breaths. I felt, the day I saw Gunskirchen Lager, that I finally knew what I was fighting for, what the war was all about."

"THIS ACTUALLY HAPPENED..."

It was V-E Day. While the world celebrated, the weary men of Company "K", 5th Regiment, 71st Infantry Division, commanded by Capt. Horace S. Berry of Spartanburg, S. C., faced the task of cleaning up Gunskirchen Lager, a German concentration camp near Lambach, Austria; of sending the living to hospitals, of supervising the burying of the dead, of trying to cover the stench coming from the half-finished buildings in the woods. They had been working at the job since May 5, the day after Company "M" and Company "K", like all others who saw it, will never forget.

In order that more people may know about the record of German inhumanity and barbarity revealed at Gunskirchen, the 71st Division publishes this booklet. As strong as the words in these eyewitness accounts may be, as gruesome as the photographs and paintings may seem, they fall far short of expressing the horror that was Gunskirchen—a horror that no words or pictures could fully show.

On V-E Day Pfc. Norman Nichols, former Detroit art student, placed on a roving assignment by Major General Willard G. Wyman, commanding general of the 71st Division, set up his easel in the stinking patch of woods at Gunskirchen Lager and faithfully recorded the depths of degradation and suffering reached by "non-ayran" prisoners of the Reich. Pfc. Nichols was with rifle companies of the 71st when the big push of the war's closing weeks was on. He was under fire and shared the many discomforts of the infantryman's life, but this was his most unpleasant job of all.

But because he and the men who have seen such camps in all part of Germany believe that the people back home should know, his pictures include all the details as they actually appeared that bright May morning. The pain-racked, starving, skeleton-like figures of the prisoners are not caricatures. These people actually were that skinny. The piles of bodies and parts of bodies jumbled in death's grotesque postures are not exaggeration. The buildings, the woods, the roads near Gunskirchen Lager were choked with bodies. Artist Nichols has given a faithful picture of a German concentration camp. Cynical persons who have put-down as "propaganda" the stories of brutality in the Nazi prison camps may call Nichols' sketches "just another atrocity" story. To Pfc. Nichols and the men of the 71st Division, "atrocity" is a mild word for what they saw.

This actually happened.

German soldiers carry half-dead and dying prisoners from one of the stinking huts to a German truck for transportation to a hospital. The several day-old body in the foreground, one of many left where they fell, is ignored by both soldiers and prisoners.

"The German soldiers who were detailed to carry out the living, bury the dead and clean up the buildings denied any connection with the camp", Artist Nichols said. "They said it was another SS mess." The half-crazed, starving Jews were so glad to see the Americans they kissed the hands of embarrassed, nauseated Yanks who came away from the scenes of Nazi horror with an almost irresistible desire to shoot every German soldier on sight.

As the living were bring removed, the job of collecting and burying the dead was begun. None of the bodies was heavy for they were little more than bones. One detail of Germans collected the dead and placed them in a clearing, while another group dug graves. The kneeling boy to the right of Artist Nichols' picture sat most of the day staring at the body of his brother, sobbing quietly and begging the Germans to give him a decent burial in an individual grave.

"Every time the Germans would go anywhere in the woods, they'd find more bodies of prisoners who had gone off from their comrades to die". Nichols said. Almost any disease in the book could be recognized in the dead and dying men, though the few women in the camp who had been on "friendly" terms with the guards were apparently well-fed and buxom. One of these women walked back of the above burial scene and Nichols shows her in the right background.

"Sometimes we slept three deep in the mud of the barracks", an inmate related. "We were too weak to move out the dead, too weak to move ourselves, so we slept with the bodies." All the inmates were vermin-infested and many were covered with huge, open sores. This is a scene inside one of the buildings at Gunskirchen Lager.

THE STATES HEARD

Major Cameron Coffman, Fort Thomas, Kg., Public Relations Officer of the 71st Division, visited Gunskirchen Lager on the afternoon of May 4, 1945, shortly after its liberation by American troops. The news release he wrote about Gunskirchen, which was published in several United States papers, is printed below in full:

BY MAJOR CAMERON COPPMAN

With the 71st Division of the Third Army in Austria, May 4, 1945: Nazism at its worst was unfolded in stark reality before Doughboys of the 71st Infantry Division today when they stumbled upon a carefully concealed concentration camp six kilometers north of Lambach, Austria, which held 18,000 persons who were not true "Aryan" or whose political opinions were contrary to Hitler's "New Order".

My days of reading about Hun atrocities were over. I visited that camp today. The living and dead evidence of horror and brutality beyond one's imagination was there, lying and crawling and shuffling, in stinking, ankle-deep mud and human excrement. The sight and smell made your stomach do funny things like an egg-beater churning within. It was impossible to count the dead, but 200 emaciated corpses would be a very conservative estimate. For the most part they had died during the past two days, but there were many other rotting bodies inside the barracks beside living human beings who were too weak to move.

It is practically impossible to describe in decent or printable words the state of degradation in which the German guards had permitted the camp to fall. Located in a dense patch of pine trees, well-hidden from the main highway as well as from the air, the site was well-suited for the slimy, vermin-infested living conditions that existed there. To call the camp a pig sty would be doing injustice to a self-respecting pig. The sight was appalling, and the odor that reached you a hundred yards or so from the camp site was nauseating.

Traveling into the camp along a narrow wagon road was an experience in dodging the multitude of dazed men, women, and children fleeing from the horrors of this living hell. The natural impulse of these people after the Americans arrived was one of hysteria—a desire to escape—to leave that place forever behind them. The road was clogged with hundreds, but many did not get far. Dozens died before they had gone but a few hundred yards from their "hellhole" prison, Americans soldiers cussed violently in disgust as their trucks roared past the grotesque figures in the ditches and shuffling feebly along the road.

As we entered the first building the sight that met our startled gaze was enough to bring forth a censorable exclamation from a sergeant who had seen the bloodiest fighting this war has offered. He spat disgustedly on the filthy dirt floor and left the building which was originally built for 300 but now housed approximately 3,000. Row upon row of living skeletons, jammed so closely together that it was impossible for some to turn over, even if they could have generated enough strength to do so, met our eyes. Those too weak to move defecated where they lay. The place was crawling with lice. A pair of feet, black in death, protruded from underneath a tattered blanket just six inches from a haggard old Jew who was resting on his elbow and feebly attempting to wave to us.

A little girl, doubled with the gnawing pains of starvation, cried pitifully for help. A dead man rotted beside her. An English-speaking Jew from Ohio hummed, "The Yanks Are Coming", then broke out crying. A Jewish Rabbi tripped over a dead body as he scurried toward me with strength he must have been saving for the arrival of the American forces. He kissed the back of my gloved hand and clutched my sleeve with a talon-like grip as he lifted his face toward heaven. I could not understand what he said, but it was a prayer. I did not have to understand his spoken word.

Few of those remaining in the building could stand on their feet. The earth was dank and a chilled wind cut the smell of death and filth. Small fires of straw added to the revolting odors that filled the air. One man crawled over several prostrate bodies and patted the toe of my muddy combat boot in child-like manner.

Everywhere we turned the pathetic cry of "wasser" (water) met our ears. An English-speaking Czechoslovakian woman told us that they had received no food or water for five days. The appearances of the starving horde more than verified her statement. A lieutenant stooped to feed one creature a bit of chocolate. The man died in his arm. That lieutenant, formerly an officer in the Czech Army, fingered his pistol nervously as he eyed a group of German soldiers forcibly digging a grave outside. I also pumped a cartridge in my automatic. As I left him there were tears streaming down his face. His mother was last reported in a concentration camp "somewhere in Germany".

Before our arrival conditions had been so crowded that all could not lie down to sleep at one time. Those with strength enough to stand took turns sleeping. The dead were buried in mass graves behind the so-called barracks, but the death rate became so high that unburied piles of dead remained with the living. Many of these unfortunates were using the corpses as pillows. I counted 27 in one heap in a dark pine grove in the camp area. It was not a pretty sight.

An unforgettable drama was enacted when a sergeant of our group of five raced out of one building, his face flaming with rage. The sergeant, a Jewish boy of Polish descent, had found three of his relatives lying in the filth of that barracks. They are sleeping tonight between white sheets for the first time in three years in one of the better homes in Lambach. Their diet of a daily cup of anemic soup has suddenly changed to eggs, milk, and bread. A Yank with an M-l rifle casually drops in at regular intervals to see how they are faring.

Military government and medical personnel of the 71st Division were busy at work before we left the camp two hours later attempting to bring relief to the chaos of suffering the fleeing Germans had left behind.

Extended supply lines made the food situation a major problem until ingenious doughboys discovered a German supply train nearby. Captain William R. Swope, Lexington, Ky., assisted by an excited Austrian girl brakeman, drove the train onto a siding near the camp. Physical force was necessary for order when the first food lines were organized as it was the first these hunger-sated persons had seen in many days.

A scene on the return trip to Lambach was a fitting climax to the horror we had left. Two "fugitives from hell" were ravenously tearing the entrails from a long-dead horse and gulping huge bites. Another sergeant, whose mother and father disappeared into a Nazi concentration camp three long years, ago, turned his head and in a tear-choked voice remarked:

"And Hitler wanted to rule the world."

AND AFTERWARDS. . .

BY CPL. JERRY TAX

We pulled into Wels, Austria, that morning in two jeeps and a three quarter ton radio truck. In the lead jeep were Colonel Augustus Regnier, C. O., 66th Infantry Regiment, his driver and his machine-gunner, in the next were four MPs, and then came four of us in our 571st Signal Company truck with a battered but serviceable Signal Corps radio.

The day was bright, sunny and warm, and full of rumors that the war was over. As it turned out, it took three more days before the rumors became official news.

Our little convoy drove along hushed streets for a while here and there a shell-burst or a bomb-crater seemed the only familiar, almost friendly, sight in the city. A few buildings, pock-marked by machine-gun and rifle fire, attested to what must have been an extremely feeble attempt to defend the city.

We followed Colonel Regnier around as he took the surrender of two German garrisons, one at the airport and one in the large compound in the heart of town. He also secured all bridges and posted guards at their approaches. At the airport, we were about to drive out on the runways to inspect the few German fighter planes left there intact when we discovered that the area around each one was carefully mined.

It was just about then that the inhabitants of Wels began to realize that the event they had been anticipating, some eagerly to be sure, was taking place before their shuttered windows and sealed-up entrances to air-raid shelters. The Americans were here.

Colonel Regnier selected as the site of his temporary CP an office building on the largest open square in town. We parked there and continued sending out routine messages concerning the bridges we'd secured, the number of prisoners taken, and other administrative matters. Then came the deluge.

By the thousands, civilians crowded into the huge square, examining our vehicles and our clothing, marvelling at what little equipment we carried, and assuring us that there were no Nazis among them, only good Austrians who loved Americans and hated Hitler and Company. It's happened to all of you, in every town Americans took from Normandy to wherever we finally stopped.

About two o'clock in the afternoon, for some reason not apparent to us at the time, the crowd began to melt away . . . back into shuttered hones, down twisting alleyways to storm shelters . . . by twos and groups they left us, in quiet contrast to their noisy, enthusiastic approach. It wasn't long before we discovered why.

Drifting down into the great square, in every conceivable conveyance, on foot, on hands and knees—utilizing every inch of the wide streets—came the former inmates of Gunskirchen Lager near Lambach. With hardly a sound, they slowly engulfed the cobble-stoned avenues that led inwards, like an irresistible but languid flood, driving the civilians back to their homes before them. The news of our coming had reached the camp that morning, and practically all of the estimated 18,000 in the camp who were able to move or be moved were en route the eleven miles into town to look upon their liberators.

Neither words nor pictures—and thousands of both have been printed—have ever told the full story of these wretched people, or the incredible misery of existence at Lambach. That story, however, could be read in the faces and what passed for the bodies of the swarm of pitiful humanity that flowed into the square and surrounded our vehicles.

No more than one in a hundred walked upright, dozens were dragged into town full-length on rude carts; with their last ounce of strength, still others shuffled along leaning on sticks, crude crutches and each other. Their garments came out of a wild costumer's hallucination. They ran the gamut from tattered uniforms that had been worn twenty-four hours a day for three or four years to wrappings of rags. None, obviously, had been washed in that time. Lice and vermin of every sort crawled among the folds of these filthy rag-bag costumes and on the misshapen, emaciated bodies of the men.

The hands that clutched at what scraps of food and candy we distributed until we had no more were skin and bone and blue-black nail . . . like the claw of some predatory owl who had enjoyed a profitable night among the field-mice. Skin and bone . . . skin and bone and filthy rags and bodies crawling with vermin . . . row on row, endless . . . filling the square. And not a sound. Not one human sound came from those thousands of throats. Perhaps they hadn't the strength to speak, even in gratitude. Perhaps words of thanks were long forgotten . . . forgotten under the lash and the pistol-butt, the abyssmal degradation.

It would be fine and thrilling to say that despite their pitiful condition, despite their rags, the years of torture and abject slavery and starvation, hope and joy shone from the eyes of these men. But it wasn't so. To be sure, the eyes were far from blank, but there was no joy, no hope in them. These were not the eyes of men set free. Perhaps the gigantic, impossible fact of liberation was just too big, too miraculous to grasp. Perhaps, in their incredible weakened physical condition, liberation was too great a shock to be assimilated. Whatever the reason, these were simply broken, beaten men we looked out on, row on row.

And in their eyes, you read the story of the past four or five years. You didn't have to look at that one's back to see the scars where the whip had dug deep; the scars were in his eyes. Would they ever leave them?

You didn't have to stare in helpless fascination at that walking skeleton to learn what systematic starvation can do to a man's body; from the depth of his soul that hunger came to you from his eyes, blinding insatiable hunger. Would it ever again leave them?

And that one lying there on the cobblestones, a heap of filth and rags. Neither water nor food nor miracle drug could heal him. Perhaps he knew it. Perhaps he only asked to be carried here to look upon the miracle before he died. What of his eyes? You looked deep and all you saw were impotence and hopelessness. And his hours were too few for a madman to entertain the dream that they would ever again leave them in this world.

For hours it seemed we stared out on this sea of human misery. There was little we could say, and less we could do after all our food, candy and cigarettes were gone. Intermittently, as the work of setting up his Command Post got underway, Colonel Regnier had messages for us to send out. One I'll never forget. I sent it myself. You'll never see any like it in training manuals or practice code books. It was marked "urgent" and read something like this: "Send medical supplies and food immediately . . . 15,000 people in urgent need of delousing. . . ."

About four o'clock, we could feel that something was going on out of our sight. The crowd before us had started to move towards one side of the square . . . more accurately, it was compressing itself slowly away from the other side. Faintly we heard the rhythmic step of marching men on cobblestones suddenly a column of German soldiers came down one of the streets leading towards the center of the square and began filing into it. They were we supposed, the garrisons who had surrendered earlier in the day. As they came in, they lined up, in regular ranks, in the space just recently left vacant. And now they were all in . . . perhaps two or three hundred of them.

Here was a sight, here was a scene a master of stagecraft would have called an achievement. Maybe some Master of human props and sets had staged it. On one side of the square, in neat ranks, stood the would-be Herrenvolk. Their smart grey uniforms were pressed; chubby pink cheeks and an occasional paunch left no doubt they had fed well on their loot and what they could extract from slave labor on their farms. In their eyes was still the arrogance of the conqueror. (Would it ever leave them?)

Facing them, in disorder, in indescribable disarray, standing up in oxcarts, lying on their bellies, leaning on each other . . . were the free men of Russia, France, Poland, Yugoslavia, the Balkans . . . a heterogeneous collection of skin, bone and filth. About twenty yards separated the two groups . . . twenty yards and the whole world. And the square was as still as a tomb.

For a half hour that dragged interminably the two groups stood there, immobile. Not a voice was raised, not a fist shaken . . . not a stir. MPs were busy about the task of arranging for transportation for the Germans. That was all.

And yet I could have sworn something was taking place out there. I climbed out of the truck and walked slowly through the crowd. Was it my imagination? Was it wishful thinking? To this day, I can't answer those questions, and I wish I

could. But I saw, or thought I saw, in those eyes, the faintest glimmer of what I had looked for vainly but a half hour before. Perhaps the shock was wearing off. As they looked upon their well-fed erstwhile jailers standing in neat ranks, waiting to be led away, the huge, impossible truth began to dawn in their consciousness and in their eyes. The long years were over. The Germans were captives. They were free men at last.

Within another hour, the square was empty. Germans were on their way to internment. Every wheeled vehicle within miles was commandeered to take the sick and starving ex-prisoners to places already being set up to feed and care for them. Our CP was established and functioning smoothly.

That night, as the free men of France, Poland, Russia, Yugoslavia and the Balkans prepared for their first untroubled sleep since a madman with a comic mustache took control of an ambitious Germany, the spirit of a new Europe was being born in their hearts.

Who knows what the Germans were thinking?

Source: "The Seventy-First Came to Gunskirchen Lager" (Washington, D.C.: U.S. Army, 1945).

DOCUMENT 5

RUDOLF HÖSS, COMMANDANT OF AUSCHWITZ

Below is a portion of Rudolf Höss's signed testimony at the International Military Tribunal held at Nuremberg in 1946.

I, RUDOLF FRANZ FERDINAND HOESS, being first duly sworn, depose and say as follows:

1. I am forty-six years old, and have been a member of the NSDAPI since 1922; a member of the SS since 1934; a member of the Waffen SS since 1939. I was a member from 1 December 1934 of the SS Guard Unit, the so-called Deathshead Formation (Totenkopf Verband).

2. I have been constantly associated with the administration of concentration camps since 1934, serving at Dachau until 1938; then as Adjutant in Sachsenhausen from 1938 to 1 May, 1940, when I was appointed Commandant of Auschwitz. I commanded Auschwitz until 1 December, 1943, and estimate that at least 2,500,000 victims were executed and exterminated there by gassing and burning, and at least another half million succumbed to starvation and disease, making a total dead of about 3,000,000. This figure represents about 70% or 80% of all persons sent to Auschwitz as prisoners, the remainder having been selected and used for slave labor in the concentration camp industries. Included among the executed and burnt were approximately 20,000 Russian prisoners of war (previously screened out of Prisoner of War cages by the Gestapo) who were delivered at

Auschwitz in Wehrmacht transports operated by regular Wehrmacht officers and men. The remainder of the total number of victims included about 100,000 German Jews, and great numbers of citizens (*mostly* Jewish) from Holland, France, Belgium, Poland, Hungary, Czechoslovakia, Greece, or other countries. We executed about 400,000 Hungarian Jews alone at Auschwitz in the summer of 1944.

4. Mass executions by gassing commenced during the summer 1941 and continued until fall 1944. I personally supervised executions at Auschwitz until the first of December 1943 and know by reason of my continued duties in the Inspectorate of Concentration Camps WVHA2 that these mass executions continued as stated above. All mass executions by gassing took place under the direct order, supervision and responsibility of RSHA. I received all orders for carrying out these mass executions directly from RSHA.

6. The "final solution" of the Jewish question meant the complete extermination of all Jews in Europe. I was ordered to establish extermination facilities at Auschwitz in June 1941. At that time there were already in the general government three other extermination camps; BELZEK, TREBLINKA and WOLZEK. These camps were under the Einsatzkommando of the Security Police and SD. I visited Treblinka to find out how they carried out their exterminations. The Camp Commandant at Treblinka told me that he had liquidated 80,000 in the course of one-half year. He was principally concerned with liquidating all the Jews from the Warsaw Ghetto. He used monoxide gas and I did not think that his methods were very efficient. So when I set up the extermination building at Auschwitz, I used Cyclon B, which was a crystalized Prussic Acid which we dropped into the death chamber from a small opening. It took from 3 to 15 minutes to kill the people in the death chamber depending upon climatic conditions. We knew when the people were dead because their screaming stopped. We usually waited about one-half hour before we opened the doors and removed the bodies. After the bodies were removed our special commandos took off the rings and extracted the gold from the teeth of the corpses.

7. Another improvement we made over Treblinka was that we built our gas chambers to accommodate 2,000 people at one time, whereas at Treblinka their 10 gas chambers only accommodated 200 people each. The way we selected our victims was as follows: we had two SS doctors on duty at Auschwitz to examine the incoming transports of prisoners. The prisoners would be marched by one of the doctors who would make spot decisions as they walked by. Those who were fit for work were sent into the Camp. Others were sent immediately to the extermination plants. Children of tender years were invari-

ably exterminated since by reason of their youth they were unable to work. Still another improvement we made over Treblinka was that at Treblinka the victims almost always knew that they were to be exterminated and at Auschwitz we endeavored to fool the victims into thinking that they were to go through a delousing process. Of course, frequently they realized our true intentions and we sometimes had riots and difficulties due to that fact. Very frequently women would hide their children under the clothes but of course when we found them we would send the children in to be exterminated. We were required to carry out these exterminations in secrecy but of course the foul and nauseating stench from the continuous burning of bodies permeated the entire area and all of the people living in the surrounding communities knew that exterminations were going on at Auschwitz.

8. We received from time to time special prisoners from the local Gestapo office. The SS doctors killed such prisoners by injections of benzine. Doctors had orders to write ordinary death certificates and could put down any reason at all for the cause of death.

9. From time to time we conducted medical experiments on women inmates, including sterilization and experiments relating to cancer. Most of the people who died under these experiments had been already condemned to death by the Gestapo.

10. Rudolf Mildner was the chief of the Gestapo at Kattowicz and as such was head of the political department at Auschwitz which conducted third degree methods of interrogation from approximately March 1941 until September 1943. As such, he frequently sent prisoners to Auschwitz for incarceration or execution. He visited Auschwitz on several occasions. The Gestapo Court, the SS Standgericht, which tried persons accused of various crimes, such as escaping Prisoners of War, etc., frequently met within Auschwitz, and Mildner often attended the trial of such persons, who usually were executed in Auschwitz following their sentence. I showed Mildner throughout the extermination plant at Auschwitz and he was directly interested in it since he had to send the Jews from his territory for execution at Auschwitz.

I understand English as it is written above. The above statements are true; this declaration is made by me voluntarily and without compulsion; after reading over the statement, I have signed and executed the same at Nurnberg, Germany on the fifth day of April 1946.

Source: Rudolf Franz Ferdinand Höss, "Affidavit, 5 April 1946," in *Trial of the Major War Criminals Before the International Tribunal, Nuremberg, 14 November 1945–1 October 1946*, Doc. 3868PS, vol. 33, 27579. (Nuremberg: Secretariat of the International Military Tribunal, 1949).

REFERENCES

1. ANTI-SEMITISM

Almog, Shmuel, ed. *Antisemitism Through the Ages.* Translated by Nathan H. Reisner. New York: Pergamon Press, 1988.

Bankier, David, ed. *Probing the Depths of German Antisemitism: German Society and the Persecution of the Jews, 1933–1941.* New York: Berghahn Books, 2000.

Cohn, Norman. *Warrant for Genocide: The Myth of the Jewish World-conspiracy and the Protocols of the Elders of Zion.* London: Eyre & Spottiswoode, 1967.

Davies, Alan, ed. *Antisemitism and the Foundations of Christianity.* New York: Paulist Press, 1979.

Flannery, Edward H. *The Anguish of the Jews: Twenty-Three Centuries of Anti-Semitism.* New York: Macmillan, 1965.

Friedländer, Saul. *Nazi Germany and the Jews.* Volume 1. *The Years of Persecution, 1933–1939.* New York: HarperCollins, 1997.

Gager, John G. *The Origins of Anti-Semitism: Attitudes toward Judaism in Pagan and Christian Antiquity.* New York: Oxford University Press, 1983.

Kertzer, David I. *The Popes Against the Jews: The Vatican's Role in the Rise of Modern Anti-Semitism.* New York: Knopf, 2001.

Langmuir, Gavin I. *History, Religion, and Antisemitism.* Berkeley: University of California Press, 1990.

Levy, Richard, comp. *Antisemitism in the Modern World: An Anthology of Texts.* Lexington, Mass. & Toronto: D.C. Heath, 1991.

Littell, Franklin H. *The Crucifixion of the Jews.* New York: Harper & Row, 1975.

Parkes, James. *The Conflict of the Church and the Synagogue: A Study in the Origins of Antisemitism.* London: Soncino, 1934.

Pulzer, Peter. *The Rise of Political Anti-Semitism in Germany and Austria,* revised edition. Cambridge, Mass.: Harvard University Press, 1988.

Rose, Paul Lawrence. *Revolutionary Antisemitism in Germany from Kant to Wagner.* Princeton: Princeton University Press, 1990.

Ruether, Rosemary Radford. *Faith and Fratricide: The Theological Roots of Anti-Semitism.* New York: Seabury Press, 1974.

Strauss, Herbert A., ed. *Hostages of Modernization: Studies on Modern Antisemitism, 1870–1933/39: Germany–Great Britain–France.* Berlin & New York: Walter de Gruyter, 1993.

Taylor, Miriam S. *Anti-Judaism and Early Christian Identity: A Critique of the Scholarly Consensus.* Edited by David S. Katz. Leiden & New York: Brill, 1995.

Wesley, Frank. *The Holocaust and Anti-Semitism: The Goldhagen Argument and Its Effects.* San Francisco: International Scholars, 1999.

2. BIOGRAPHIES

Bethge, Eberhard. *Dietrich Bonhoeffer: Man of Vision, Man of Courage.* Translated by Eric Mosbacher. New York: Harper & Row, 1970.

Breitman, Richard. *The Architect of Genocide: Himmler and the Final Solution.* New York: Knopf, 1991.

Gilbert, Martin. *Winston Churchill, 1941–1945: Road to Victory.* London: Heinemann, 1986.

Harrington, Dale. *Mystery Man: William Rhodes Davis, Nazi Agent of Influence.* Washington, D.C.: Brassey's, 1999.

Hatch, Alden and Seamus Walshe. *Crown and Glory: The Life of Pope Pius XII.* New York: Hawthorn Books, 1957.

Pollak, Richard. *The Creation of Dr. B.: A Biography of Bruno Bettelheim.* New York: Simon & Schuster, 1997.

Raines, Theron. *Rising to the Light: A Portrait of Bruno Bettelheim.* New York: Knopf, 2002.

Sereny, Gitta. *Albert Speer: His Battle with Truth.* New York: Knopf, 1995.

Smith, Jean Edward. *Lucius D. Clay: An American Life.* New York: Holt, 1990.

Wyden, Peter. *Stella.* New York: Simon & Schuster, 1992.

3. CHRISTIAN CHURCH

Abbott, Walter M., ed. *The Documents of Vatican II: In a New and Definitive Translation With Commentaries and Notes by Catholic, Protestant, Orthodox Authorities.* London: Geoffrey Chapman, 1966.

Baranowski, Shelley. *The Confessing Church, Conservative Elites, and the Nazi State.* Lewiston, N.Y.: Edwin Mellen Press, 1986.

Barnett, Victoria J. *For the Soul of the People: Protestant Protest Against Hitler.* New York: Oxford University Press, 1992.

Bergen, Doris L. *Twisted Cross: The German Christian Movement in the Third Reich.* Chapel Hill: University of North Carolina Press, 1996.

Blet, Pierre. *Pius XII and the Second World War: According to the Archives of the Vatican.* Translated by

Lawrence J. Johnson. New York: Paulist Press, 1999.

Conway, John S. *The Nazi Persecution of the Churches, 1933–45.* New York: Basic Books, 1968.

Cornwell, John. *Hitler's Pope: The Secret History of Pius XII.* London & New York: Viking, 1999.

Craughwell, Thomas J. *The Wisdom of the Popes.* New York: Thomas Dunne Books/St. Martin's Press, 2000.

Falconi, Carlo. *Il silenzio di Pio XII.* Milano: Sugar, 1965. Translated by Bernard Wall as *The Silence of Pius XII.* London: Faber & Faber, 1970.

Fredriksen, Paula. *Jesus of Nazareth, King of the Jews: A Jewish Life and the Emergence of Christianity.* New York: Knopf, 1999.

Garbe, Detlef. *Zwischen Widerstand und Martyrium: Die Zeugen Jehovas im "Dritten Reich."* Munich: Oldenbourg, 1994.

Hesse, Hans, ed. *Persecution and Resistance of Jehovah's Witnesses During the Nazi Regime, 1933–1945.* Bremen: Edition Temmen, 2001.

Jehovah's Witnesses: Victims of the Nazi Era, 1933–1945. Washington, D.C.: United States Holocaust Memorial Museum, 1995.

King, Christine Elizabeth. *The Nazi State and the New Religions: Five Case Studies in Non-Conformity.* New York: Edwin Mellen Press, 1982.

Matheson, Peter, ed. *The Third Reich and the Christian Churches.* Edinburgh: T. & T. Clark / Grand Rapids, Mich.: Eerdmans, 1981.

McInerny, Ralph. *The Defamation of Pius XII.* South Bend, Ind.: St. Augustine's Press, 2001.

Pakter, Walter. "De His Qui Foris Sunt: The Teachings of the Medieval Canon and Civil Lawyers Concerning the Jews." Dissertation, Johns Hopkins University, 1974.

Phayer, Michael. *The Catholic Church and the Holocaust, 1930–1965.* Bloomington: Indiana University Press, 2000.

Rittner, Carol, Stephen D. Smith, and Irena Steinfeldt, eds. *The Holocaust and the Christian World: Reflections on the Past, Challenges for the Future.* New York: Continuum, 2000.

Rivkin, Ellis. *What Crucified Jesus?* Nashville: Abingdon Press, 1984.

Sánchez, José M. *Pius XII and the Holocaust: Understanding the Controversy.* Washington, D.C.: Catholic University of America Press, 2002.

Schaff, Philip and Henry Wace, eds. *A Select Library of the Nicene and Post-Nicene Fathers.* 14 volumes. New York: Christian Literature Company, 1890–1900.

Scholder, Klaus. *The Churches and the Third Reich.* London: SCM Press / Philadelphia: Fortress Press, 1987.

Sheils, W. J., ed. *Persecution and Toleration: Papers Read at the Twenty-Second Summer Meeting and the Twenty-Third Winter Meeting of the Ecclesiastical History Society.* Oxford: Blackwell, 1984.

4. CHRISTIANS & JEWS

Chazan, Robert, ed. *Church, State, and Jew in the Middle Ages.* New York: Behrman House, 1979.

Chrysostom, John. *Discourses Against Judaizing Christians.* Translated by Paul W. Harkins. Washington, D.C.: Catholic University of America Press, 1979.

Falk, Gerhard. *The Jew in Christian Theology: Martin Luther's Anti-Jewish Vom Schem Hamphoras, Previously Unpublished in English, and Other Milestones in Church Doctrine Concerning Judaism.* Jefferson, N.C.: McFarland, 1992.

Gerlach, Wolfgang. *And the Witnesses Were Silent: The Confessing Church and the Persecution of the Jews.* Translated by Victoria J. Barnett. Lincoln: University of Nebraska Press, 2000.

Glick, Leonard B. *Abraham's Heirs: Jews and Christians in Medieval Europe.* Syracuse, N.Y.: Syracuse University Press, 1999.

Grayzel, Solomon, ed. *The Church and the Jews in the XIIIth Century.* Revised edition. New York: Hermon Press, 1966.

Haynes, Stephen R. *Reluctant Witnesses: Jews and the Christian Imagination.* Louisville, Ky.: Westminster John Knox Press, 1995.

Limor, Ora and Guy G. Stroumsa, eds. *Contra Judaeos: Ancient and Medieval Polemics between Christians and Jews.* Tübingen: Mohr, 1996.

Manuel, Frank E. *The Broken Staff: Judaism through Christian Eyes.* Cambridge, Mass.: Harvard University Press, 1992.

Parkes, James. *Prelude to Dialogue: Jewish-Christian Relationships.* New York: Schocken Books, 1969.

Perry, Marvin and Frederick M. Schweitzer, eds. *Jewish-Christian Encounters over the Centuries: Symbiosis, Prejudice, Holocaust, Dialogue.* New York: Peter Lang, 1994.

Saperstein, Marc. *Moments of Crisis in Jewish-Christian Relations.* London: SCM Press / Philadelphia: Trinity Press International, 1989.

Simon, Marcel. *Verus Israel: A Study of the Relations between Christians and Jews in the Roman Empire, 135–425.* Translated by H. McKeating. Oxford & New York: Oxford University Press, 1986.

Simonsohn, Shlomo. *The Apostolic See and the Jews: Documents, 492–1404.* Toronto: Pontifical Institute of Mediaeval Studies, 1988.

Stroll, Mary. *The Jewish Pope: Ideology and Politics in the Papal Schism of 1130.* Leiden & New York: Brill, 1987.

Wilken, Robert L. *John Chrysostom and the Jews: Rhetoric and Reality in the Late 4th Century.* Berkeley: University of California Press, 1983.

5. COMPARATIVE STUDIES

Andrist, Ralph K. *The Long Death: The Last Days of the Plains Indian.* New York: Macmillan, 1964.

Auron, Yair. *The Banality of Indifference: Zionism and the Armenian Genocide.* New Brunswick, N.J.: Transaction Publication, 2000.

Brown, Dee. *Bury My Heart at Wounded Knee: An Indian History of the American West.* New York: Holt, Rinehart & Winston, 1970.

Chorbajian, Levon and George Shirinian, eds. *Studies in Comparative Genocide.* New York: St. Martin's Press, 1999.

Diamond, Jared. *Guns, Germs, and Steel: The Fates of Human Societies.* New York: Norton, 1997.

McCormick, Anita Louise. *Native Americans and the Reservation in American History.* Springfield, N.J.: Enslow, 1996.

Moulton, Candy. *Everyday Life Among the American Indians.* Cincinnati, Ohio: Writer's Digest Books, 2001.

Thomas, Laurence Mordekhai. *Vessels of Evil: American Slavery and the Holocaust.* Philadelphia: Temple University Press, 1993.

Trigger, Bruce G. and Wilcomb E. Washburn, eds. *The Cambridge History of the Native Peoples of the Americas.* Volume 1. *North America.* Cambridge & New York: Cambridge University Press, 1996.

Utter, Jack. *American Indians: Answers to Today's Questions*. Lake Ann, Mich.: National Woodlands Publishing, 1993.

Walliman, Isidor and Michael N. Dobkowski, eds. *Genocide and the Modern Age: Etiology and Case Studies of Mass Death*. New York: Greenwood Press, 1987.

Wilson, James. *The Earth Shall Weep: A History of Native America*. London: Picador, 1998.

6. DISPLACED PERSONS AND ISRAEL

Bauer, Yehuda. *Flight and Rescue: Brichah*. New York: Random House, 1970.

Bauer. *Out of the Ashes: The Impact of American Jews on Post-Holocaust European Jewry*. Oxford & New York: Pergamon Press, 1989.

Benson, Michael T. *Harry S. Truman and the Founding of Israel*. Westport, Conn.: Praeger, 1997.

Cohen, Michael J. *Truman and Israel*. Berkeley: University of California Press, 1990.

Dinnerstein, Leonard. *America and the Survivors of the Holocaust*. New York: Columbia University Press, 1982.

Hyman, Abraham S. *The Undefeated*. Jerusalem: Gefen, 1993.

Penkower, Monty Noam. *The Holocaust and Israel Reborn: From Catastrophe to Sovereignty*. Urbana: University of Illinois Press, 1994.

Sachar, Howard M. *A History of Israel: From the Rise of Zionism to Our Time*. New York: Knopf, 1976.

Segev, Tom. *One Palestine, Complete: Jews and Arabs under the British Mandate*. Translated by Haim Watzman. New York: Metropolitan, 2000.

Segev. *The Seventh Million: Israelis and the Holocaust*. Translated by Haim Watzman. New York: Hill & Wang, 1993.

Yehoshua, A. B. *Between Right and Right*. Translated by Arnold Schwartz. Garden City, N.Y.: Doubleday, 1981.

7. EMIGRATION OF JEWS

Abella, Irving and Harold Troper. *None Is Too Many: Canada and the Jews of Europe, 1933–1948*. Toronto: Lester & Orpen Dennys, 1982.

Avni, Haim. *Argentina & the Jews: A History of Jewish Immigration*. Translated by Gila Brand. Tuscaloosa: University of Alabama Press, 1991.

Bauer, Yehuda. *American Jewry and the Holocaust: The American Joint Distribution Committee, 1939–1945*. Jerusalem: Institute of Contemporary Jewry, Hebrew University / Detroit: Wayne State University Press, 1981.

Bauer. *Jews for Sale?: Nazi-Jewish Negotiations, 1933–1945*. New Haven: Yale University Press, 1994.

Cohen, Israel. *Travels in Jewry*. New York: Dutton, 1953.

Feingold, Henry L. *Politics of Rescue: The Roosevelt Administration and the Holocaust, 1938–1945*. New Brunswick, N.J.: Rutgers University Press, 1970.

Kranzler, David. *Japanese, Nazis, & Jews: The Jewish Refugee Community of Shanghai, 1938–1945*. New York: Yeshiva University Press, 1976.

London, Louise. *Whitehall and the Jews, 1933–1948: British Immigration Policy, Jewish Refugees, and the Holocaust*. New York: Cambridge University Press, 2000.

Quack, Sibylle. *Zuflucht Amerika: Zur Sozialgeschichte der Emigration Deutsch-Jüdischer Frauen in die USA 1933–1945*. Bonn: Dietz, 1995.

Sanders, Ronald. *Shores of Refuge: A Hundred Years of Jewish Emigration*. New York: Holt, 1988.

Wasserstein, Bernard. *Britain and the Jews of Europe, 1939–45*. London: Institute of Jewish Affairs / New York: Oxford University Press, 1979.

Wyman, David S. *Paper Walls: America and the Refugee Crisis, 1938–1941*. Amherst: University of Massachusetts Press, 1968.

8. FRANCE

Marrus, Michael R. and Robert O. Paxton. *Vichy France and the Jews*. New York: Basic Books, 1981.

Ryan, Donna F. *The Holocaust & the Jews of Marseille: The Enforcement of Anti-Semitic Policies in Vichy France*. Urbana: University of Illinois Press, 1996.

9. GENERAL HISTORIES

Arendt, Hannah. *The Origins of Totalitarianism*. New York: Harcourt, Brace, 1951.

Bartov, Omer. *Mirrors of Destruction: War, Genocide, and Modern Identity*. Oxford & New York: Oxford University Press, 2000.

Berenbaum, Michael. *The World Must Know: The History of the Holocaust as Told in the United States Holocaust Memorial Museum*. Boston: Little, Brown, 1993.

Cowley, Robert. *What If? 2: Eminent Historians Imagine What Might Have Been*. New York: Putnam, 2001.

Davies, Norman. *Europe: A History*. Oxford: Oxford University Press, 1996.

Dawidowicz, Lucy S., ed. *A Holocaust Reader*. New York: Behrman House, 1976.

Fischel, Jack R. *Historical Dictionary of the Holocaust*. Lanham, Md.: Scarecrow Press, 1999.

Gilbert, Martin. *The Macmillan Atlas of the Holocaust*. New York: Macmillan, 1982.

Glover, Jonathan. *Humanity: A Moral History of the Twentieth Century*. London: Cape, 1999.

Gutman, Israel, ed. *Encyclopedia of the Holocaust*. 4 volumes. New York: Macmillan, 1990.

Halberstam, Michael. *Totalitarianism and the Modern Conception of Politics*. New Haven: Yale University Press, 1999.

Holocaust. Jerusalem: Keter Publishing House, 1974.

Mitchell, Joseph R. and Helen Buss Mitchell, eds. *The Holocaust: Readings and Interpretations*. New York: McGraw-Hill, 2001.

Serfaty, Simon. *Stay the Course: European Unity and Atlantic Solidarity*. Westport, Conn.: Praeger, 1997.

Simpson, Christopher. *The Splendid Blond Beast: Money, Law, and Genocide in the Twentieth Century*. New York: Grove, 1993.

Sjdjanski, Dusan. *The Federal Future of Europe: From the European Community to the European Union*. Ann Arbor: University of Michigan Press, 2000.

Taylor, Paul Graham. *The European Union in the 1990s*. New York: Oxford University Press, 1996.

Totten, Samuel, William S. Parsons, and Israel W. Charny, eds. *Century of Genocide: Eyewitness Accounts and Critical Views*. New York: Garland, 1997.

Wallace, William. *The Transformation of Western Europe*. New York: Council on Foreign Relations Press, 1990.

10. GERMANY

Allen, William Sheridan. *The Nazi Seizure of Power: The Experience of a Single German Town, 1922–1945*. Chicago: Quadrangle, 1965.

Backer, John H. *Priming the German Economy*. Durham, N.C.: Duke University Press, 1950.

Banny, Leopold. *Schild im Osten: Der Südostwall zwischen Donau und Untersteiermark 1944/45.* Lackenbach: L. Banny, 1985.

Bark, Dennis L. and David R. Gress. *A History of West Germany.* Volume 1. *From Shadow to Substance, 1945–1963.* Oxford & New York: Blackwell, 1989.

Bock, Gisela. *Zwangssterilisation im Nationalsozialismus: Studien zur Rassenpolitik und Frauenpolitik.* Opladen: Westdeutscher Verlag, 1986.

Breitman, Richard. *Official Secrets: What the Nazis Planned, What the British and Americans Knew.* New York: Hill & Wang, 1998.

Burleigh, Michael. *The Third Reich: A New History.* New York: Hill & Wang, 2000.

Fischer, Klaus P. *Nazi Germany: A New History.* New York: Continuum, 1995.

Fulbrook, Mary, ed. *Twentieth-century Germany: Politics, Culture and Society, 1918–1990.* London: Arnold / New York: Oxford University Press, 2001.

Helmuth Greiner, Geführt von and Percy Ernst Schramm. *Kriegstagebuch des Oberkommandos der Wehrmacht (Wehrmachtführungsstab) 1940–1945.* Volume 1. Edited by Hans-Adolf Jacobsen. Frankfurt: Bernard & Graefe, 1965.

Hirschfeld, Gerhard and Lothar Kettenacker, eds. *Der "Führerstaat," Mythos und Realität: Studien zur Struktur und Politik des Dritten Reiches.* Stuttgart: Klett-Cotta, 1981.

Kershaw, Ian. *The Nazi Dictatorship: Problems and Perspectives of Interpretation.* London & Baltimore: Arnold, 1985.

Kershaw. *Popular Opinion and Political Dissent in the Third Reich: Bavaria 1933–1945.* Oxford: Clarendon Press / New York: Oxford University Press, 1983.

Mayer, Milton Sanford. *They Thought They Were Free: The Germans, 1933–45.* Chicago: University of Chicago Press, 1955.

Sayer, Ian and Douglas Botting. *Nazi Gold: The Story of the World's Greatest Robbery–And Its Aftermath.* London & New York: Granada, 1984.

Shirer, William L. *The Rise and Fall of the Third Reich: A History of Nazi Germany.* New York: Simon & Schuster, 1960.

Smith, Arthur L., Jr. *Hitler's Gold: The Story of the Nazi War Loot.* Oxford & New York: Berg, 1989.

Weindling, Paul. *Health, Race, and German Politics Between National Unification and Nazism, 1870–1945.* Cambridge & New York: Cambridge University Press, 1989.

Zabludoff, Sidney. *Movements of Nazi Gold: Uncovering the Trail.* New York: World Jewish Congress, 1997.

11. GERMANY AND JEWS

Aly, Götz. *"Final Solution": Nazi Population Policy and the Murder of the European Jews.* Translated by Belinda Cooper and Allison Brown. London & New York: Arnold / New York: Oxford University Press, 1999.

Aly, Peter Chroust and Christian Pross. *Cleansing the Fatherland: Nazi Medicine and Racial Hygiene.* Translated by Belinda Cooper. Baltimore: Johns Hopkins University Press, 1994.

Barkai, Avraham. *From Boycott to Annihilation: The Economic Struggle of German Jews, 1933–1945.* Hanover, N.H.: Brandeis University Press by University Press of New England, 1989.

Bartov, Omer, ed. *Holocaust: Origins, Implementation, Aftermath.* London: Routledge, 2000.

Bauer, Yehuda. *A History of the Holocaust.* New York: Watts, 1982.

Bauer. *The Holocaust in Historical Perspective.* London: Sheldon Press / Seattle: University of Washington Press, 1978.

Bauer. *Rethinking the Holocaust.* New Haven: Yale University Press, 2001.

Berghe, Gie van de. *De uitbuiting van de Holocaust.* Antwerp: Houtekiet, 1990.

Blumenthal, W. Michael. *The Invisible Wall: Germans and Jews: A Personal Exploration.* Washington, D.C.: Counterpoint, 1998.

Braham, Randolph L. *Eichmann and the Destruction of Hungarian Jewry.* New York: World Federation of Hungarian Jews, 1961.

Browning, Christopher R. *Fateful Months: Essays on the Emergence of the Final Solution.* New York: Holmes & Meier, 1985.

Browning. *The Final Solution and the German Foreign Office.* New York: Holmes & Meier, 1978.

Browning. *Nazi Policy, Jewish Workers, German Killers.* Cambridge & New York: Cambridge University Press, 2000.

Browning. *The Path to Genocide: Essays on Launching the Final Solution.* Cambridge & New York: Cambridge University Press, 1992.

Burleigh, Michael. *Ethics and Extermination: Reflections on Nazi Genocide.* New York: Cambridge University Press, 1997.

Cesarani, David, ed. *The Final Solution: Origins and Implementation.* London & New York: Routledge, 1994.

Dawidowicz, Lucy S. *The War against the Jews, 1933–1945.* New York: Holt, Rinehart & Winston, 1975.

Des Pres, Terrence. *The Survivor: An Anatomy of Life in the Death Camps.* New York: Oxford University Press, 1976.

Dwork, Debórah. *Children with a Star: Jewish Youth in Nazi Europe.* New Haven: Yale University Press, 1991.

Finkielkraut, Alain. *La mémoire vaine: Du crime contre l'humanité.* Paris: Gallimard, 1989.

Goldhagen, Daniel Jonah. *Hitler's Willing Executioners: Ordinary Germans and the Holocaust.* New York: Knopf, 1996.

Kaplan, Marion. *Between Dignity and Despair: Jewish Life in Nazi Germany.* New York: Oxford University Press, 1998.

Lang, Berel. *Act and Idea in the Nazi Genocide.* Chicago: University of Chicago Press, 1990.

Levin, Nora. *The Holocaust: The Destruction of European Jewry, 1933–1945.* New York: Schocken Books, 1975.

Limberg, Margarete and Hubert Rübsaat. *Sie Durften Nicht Mehr Deutsche Sein: Jüdischer Alltag in Selbstzeugnissen, 1933–1938.* Frankfurt & New York: Campus, 1990.

Marrus, Michael R. *The Holocaust in History.* Hanover, N.H.: University Press of New England, 1987.

Marrus, ed. *The "Final Solution": The Implementation of Mass Murder,* 2 volumes. Westport, Conn.: Meckler, 1989.

Mendes-Flohr, Paul. *German Jews: A Dual Identity.* New Haven: Yale University Press, 1999.

Paucker, Arnold, ed. *Die Juden im Nationalsozialistischen Deutschland* (The Jews in Nazi Germany, 1933–1943). Tübingen: Mohr, 1986.

Rabinbach, Anson and Jack Zipes, eds. *Germans and Jews Since the Holocaust: The Changing Situation in West Germany.* London & New York: Holmes & Meier, 1986.

Reinharz, Jehuda and Walter Schatzberg, eds. *The Jewish Response to German Culture: From the Enlightenment to the Second World War.* Hanover, N.H.: University Press of New England, 1985.

Reitlinger, Gerald. *The Final Solution: The Attempt to Exterminate the Jews of Europe.* London: Valentine, Mitchell, 1953.

Schleunes, Karl A. *The Twisted Road to Auschwitz: Nazi Policy toward German Jews, 1933–1939.* Urbana: University of Illinois Press, 1970.

Walk, Joseph, ed. *Das Sonderrecht für die Juden im NS-Staat: Eine Sammlung der Gesetzlichen Massnahmen und Richtlinien, Inhalt und Bedeutung.* Heidelberg & Karlsruhe: Müller Juristischer Verlag, 1981.

Yahil, Leni. *The Holocaust: The Fate of European Jewry, 1932–1945.* Translated by Ina Friedman and Haya Galai. New York: Oxford University Press, 1990.

12. GHETTOS

Altman, Linda Jacobs. *The Holocaust Ghettos.* Springfield, Mass.: Enslow, 1998.

Arad, Yitzhak. *Ghetto in Flames: The Struggle and Destruction of the Jews in Vilna in the Holocaust.* Jerusalem: Yad Vashem, Martyrs' and Heroes' Remembrance Authority / New York: Ktav, 1981.

Dobroszycki, Lucjan, ed. *The Chronicle of the Lodz Ghetto, 1941–1944.* Translated by Richard Lourie, Joachim Neugroschel, and others. New Haven: Yale University Press, 1984.

Gutman, Israel. *The Jews of Warsaw, 1939–1943: Ghetto, Underground, Revolt.* Translated by Ina Friedman. Bloomington: Indiana University Press, 1982.

Gutman. *Resistance: The Warsaw Ghetto Uprising.* Boston: Houghton Mifflin, 1994.

Trunk, Isaiah. *Judenrat: The Jewish Councils in Eastern Europe under Nazi Occupation.* New York: Macmillan, 1972.

Tushnet, Leonard. *The Pavement of Hell.* New York: St. Martin's Press, 1972.

Wiesel, Elie. *The Forgotten.* Translated by Stephen Becker. New York: Summit, 1992.

13. HITLER

Bracher, Karl Dietrich. *The German Dictatorship: The Origins, Structure, and Effects of National Socialism.* Translated by Jean Steinberg. New York: Praeger, 1970.

Bullock, Alan. *Hitler: A Study in Tyranny.* Revised edition. New York: Harper, 1960.

Fest, Joachim C. *Hitler.* Translated by Richard Winston and Clara Winston. New York: Harcourt Brace Jovanovich, 1974.

Fleming, Gerald. *Hitler and the Final Solution.* Berkeley: University of California Press, 1984.

Gordon, Sarah Ann. *Hitler, Germans, and the "Jewish Question."* Princeton: Princeton University Press, 1984.

Hitler, Adolf. *Mein Kampf.* Translated by Ralph Manheim. Boston: Houghton Mifflin, 1943.

Kershaw, Ian. *Hitler.* 2 volumes. New York: Norton, 1999, 2001.

Lukacs, John. *The Hitler of History.* New York: Knopf, 1997.

Rosenbaum, Ron. *Explaining Hitler: The Search for the Origins of His Evil.* New York: Random House, 1998.

Rychlak, Ronald J. *Hitler, the War, and the Pope.* Huntington, Ind.: Our Sunday Visitor Press, 2000.

Stern, J. P. *Hitler: The Führer and the People.* Berkeley: University of California Press, 1975.

Wistrich, Robert S. *Hitler and the Holocaust.* London: Weidenfeld & Nicolson, 2001.

14. HOLOCAUST STUDIES

Baldwin, Peter, ed. *Reworking the Past: Hitler, the Holocaust, and the Historians' Debate.* Boston: Beacon, 1990.

Bartov, Omer. *Murder in Our Midst: The Holocaust, Industrial Killing, and Representation.* New York: Oxford University Press, 1996.

Bauman, Zygmunt. *Modernity and the Holocaust.* Ithaca, N.Y.: Cornell University Press, 1989.

Bernstein, Michael André. *Foregone Conclusions: Against Apocalyptic History.* Berkeley: University of California Press, 1994.

Braham, Randolph L. *The Psychological Perspectives of the Holocaust and of Its Aftermath.* Boulder, Colo.: Social Science Monographs / New York: Csengeri Institute for Holocaust Studies of the Graduate School and University Center of the City University of New York, 1988.

Diner, Dan. *Beyond the Conceivable: Studies on Germany, Nazism, and the Holocaust.* Berkeley: University of California Press, 2000.

Evans, Richard J. *In Hitler's Shadow: West German Historians and the Attempt to Escape from the Nazi Past.* London: I. B. Tauris / New York: Pantheon, 1989.

Evans. *Lying About Hitler: History, Holocaust, and the David Irving Trial.* New York: BasicBooks, 2001.

Finkelstein, Norman G. and Ruth Bettina Birn. *A Nation on Trial: The Goldhagen Thesis and Historical Truth.* New York: Metropolitan, 1998.

Hayes, Peter, ed. *Lessons and Legacies: The Meaning of the Holocaust in a Changing World.* Evanston, Ill.: Northwestern University Press, 1991.

Kren, George and Leon Rappoport. *The Holocaust and the Crisis in Human Behavior.* New York: Holmes & Meier, 1980.

Langer, Lawrence L. *Holocaust Testimonies: The Ruins of Memory.* New Haven: Yale University Press, 1991.

Levy, Margot, ed. *Remembering for the Future: The Holocaust in an Age of Genocide,* 3 volumes. New York: Palgrave, 2001.

Littell, Franklin H., ed. *Hyping the Holocaust: Scholars Answer Goldhagen.* East Rockaway, N.Y.: Cummings & Hathaway, 1997.

Niewyk, Donald L., ed. *The Holocaust: Problems and Perspectives of Interpretation.* Lexington, Mass.: D.C. Heath, 1992.

Roth, John K., ed. *Ethics after the Holocaust: Perspectives, Critiques, and Responses.* St. Paul, Minn.: Paragon House, 1999.

Roth and Michael Berenbaum, eds. *Holocaust: Religious and Philosophical Implications.* New York: Paragon House, 1989.

Rubenstein, Richard L. and Roth. *Approaches to Auschwitz: The Holocaust and Its Legacy.* Atlanta: John Knox Press, 1987.

Shandley, Robert R., ed. *Unwilling Germans?: The Goldhagen Debate.* Translated by Jeremiah Reimer. Minneapolis: University of Minnesota Press, 1998.

Wiesel, Elie. *Against Silence: The Voice and Vision of Elie Wiesel.* Edited by Irving Abrahmson. New York: Holocaust Library, 1985.

Young, James E. *Writing and Rewriting the Holocaust: Narrative and the Consequences of Interpretation.* Bloomington: Indiana University Press, 1988.

15. HOMOSEXUALS

Beck, Gad and Frank Heibert. *An Underground Life: Memories of a Gay Jew in Berlin.* Translated by Allison Brown. Madison: University of Wisconsin Press, 1999.

Duberman, Martin Bauml, Martha Vinicus, and George Chauncey Jr., eds. *Hidden from History: Reclaiming the Gay and Lesbian Past.* New York: New American Library, 1989.

Grau, Günter, ed., with a contribution by Claudia Schoppmann. *The Hidden Holocaust?: Gay and Lesbian Persecution in Germany 1933–45.* Translated by Patrick Camiller. London: Cassell / Chicago: Fitzroy Dearborn, 1995.

Haggerty, George, ed. *Gay Histories and Cultures: An Encyclopedia.* New York: Garland, 2000.

Heger, Heinz. *The Men with the Pink Triangle.* Translated by David Fernbach. London: Gay Men's Press / Boston: Alyson, 1980.

Le Bitoux, Jean. *Les Oublies de la Memoire: Le Persecution des Homosexuels en Europe au temps du Nazisme.* Paris: Hachette, 2002.

Plant, Richard. *The Pink Triangle: The Nazi War Against Homosexuals.* New York: Holt, 1986.

Schoppmann. *Days of Masquerade: Life Stories of Lesbians During the Third Reich.* Translated by Brown. New York: Columbia University Press, 1996.

16. INTERNATIONAL RELATIONS

Bowen, Wayne H. *Spaniards and Nazi Germany: Collaboration in the New World Order.* Columbia: University of Missouri Press, 2000.

Herzstein, Robert Edwin. *Roosevelt & Hitler: Prelude to War.* New York: Paragon House, 1989.

Leach, Barry A. *German Strategy Against Russia, 1939–1941.* Oxford: Clarendon Press, 1973.

Leitz, Christian. *Sympathy for the Devil: Neutral Europe and Nazi Germany in World War II.* New York: New York University Press, 2001.

Packard, Jerrold M. *Neither Friend nor Foe: The European Neutrals in World War II.* New York: Scribners/Toronto & New York: Macmillan, 1992.

Vincent, Isabel. *Hitler's Silent Partners: Swiss Banks, Nazi Gold, and the Pursuit of Justice.* New York: Morrow, 1997.

17. INTERNET WEBSITES

The Avalon Project at Yale Law School: The Nuremberg War Crimes Trials <http://www.yale.edu/lawweb/avalon/imt/imt.htm>.

A Cybrary of the Holocaust, Remember.Org <http://www.remember.org/witness/dachlib.html>.

The Holocaust Centre: Beth Shalom <http://www.holocausthistory.net>.

The Holocaust History Project <http://www.holocaust-history.org>.

The Holocaust: TeacherNet <http://members.aol.com/TeacherNet/Holocaust.html>.

Museum of Tolerance and Learning, Simon Wiesenthal Center <http://motlc.wiesenthal.com/>.

United States Holocaust Memorial Museum <http://www.ushmm.org>.

Voice Vision: Holocaust Survivors Oral Histories <http://holocaust.umd.umich.edu>.

Yad Vashem <htttp://www.yadvashem.org>.

18. JEWISH HISTORY

Avni, Haim. *Spain, the Jews, and Franco.* Translated by Emanuel Shimoni. Philadelphia: Jewish Publication Society, 1982.

Eidelberg, Shlomo, ed. *The Jews and the Crusaders: The Hebrew Chronicles of the First and Second Crusades.* Translated by Shlomo Eidelberg. Madison: University of Wisconsin Press, 1977.

Hilberg, Raul. *The Destruction of the European Jews.* Chicago: Quadrangle, 1961.

Jäckel, Eberhard. *The Jews in European History: Seven Lectures.* Cincinnati: Hebrew Union College Press, 1993.

Keller, Werner. *Diaspora: The Post-Biblical History of the Jews.* Translated by Richard Winston and Clara Winston. New York: Harcourt, Brace & World, 1969.

Marcus, Jacob R. *The Jew in the Medieval World: A Source Book, 315–1791.* Cincinnati: Union of American Hebrew Congregations, 1938.

Monneray, Henry. *La Persecution des Juifs dans les pays de l'Est.* Paris: Editions du Centre, 1949.

Vital, David. *A People Apart: The Jews in Europe, 1789–1939.* Oxford & New York: Oxford University Press, 1999.

19. MEDICAL EXPERIMENTATION

Alexander, Leo. *The Treatment of Shock From Prolonged Exposure to Cold, Especially in Water, 1945.* Washington, D.C.: Office of the Publication Board, Department of Commerce, Report no. 250, n.d.

Annas, George J. and Michael A. Grodin, eds. *The Nazi Doctors and the Nuremberg Code: Human Rights in Human Experimentation.* New York: Oxford University Press, 1992.

Caplan, Arthur L., ed. *When Medicine Went Mad: Bioethics and the Holocaust.* Totowa, N.J.: Humana Press, 1992.

Crigger, Bette-Jane, ed. *Cases in Bioethics.* Third edition. New York: St. Martin's Press, 1998.

Lederer, Susan E. *Subjected to Science: Human Experimentation in America before the Second World War.* Baltimore: Johns Hopkins University Press, 1995.

Lifton, Robert Jay. *The Nazi Doctors: Medical Killing and the Psychology of Genocide.* New York: Basic Books, 1986.

Mitscherlich, Alexander and Fred Mielke. *Doctors of Infamy: The Story of the Nazi Medical Crimes.* New York: Schuman, 1949.

Proctor, Robert N. *The Nazi War on Cancer.* Princeton: Princeton University Press, 1999.

20. MEMOIRS & AUTOBIOGRAPHIES

Adenauer, Konrad. *Memoirs.* Translated by Beate Ruhm von Oppen. Chicago: Regnery, 1966.

Améry, Jean. *At the Mind's Limits: Contemplations by a Survivor on Auschwitz and Its Realities.* Translated by Sidney Rosenfeld and Stella P. Rosenfeld. Bloomington: Indiana University Press, 1980.

Berenbaum, Michael, ed. *Witness to the Holocaust.* New York: HarperCollins, 1997.

Brecher, Elinor J. *Schindler's Legacy: True Stories of the List Survivors.* New York: Dutton, 1994.

Cargas, Harry James, ed. *Voices from the Holocaust.* Lexington: University of Kentucky Press, 1993.

Delbo, Charlotte. *Auschwitz and After.* Translated by Rosette C. Lamont. New Haven: Yale University Press, 1995.

Eisenberg, Azriel, ed. *Witness to the Holocaust.* New York: Pilgrim Press, 1981.

Eisner, Ruth. *Nicht Wir Allein: Aus dem Tagebuch einer Berliner Jüdin.* Berlin: Arani Verlags-GmbH, 1971.

Foster, John, ed. *Community of Fate: Memoirs of German Jews in Melbourne.* Sydney & Boston: Allen & Unwin, 1986.

Frankl, Viktor E. *Man's Search for Meaning: An Introduction to Logotherapy.* Boston: Beacon, 1963. Revised edition of *From Death-Camp to Existentialism: A*

Psychiatrist's Path to a New Therapy. Translated by Ilse Lasch. Boston: Beacon, 1959.

Friedrich, Otto. _The Kingdom of Auschwitz._ New York: HarperPerennial, 1994.

Heller, Fanya Gottesfeld. _Strange and Unexpected Love: A Teenage Girl's Holocaust Memories._ Hoboken, N.J.: Ktav Publishing House, 1993.

Höss, Rudolf. _Commandant of Auschwitz: The Autobiography of Rudolf Hoess._ Translated by Constantine FitzGibbon. Cleveland: World, 1959.

Hyatt, Felicia Berland. _Close Calls: The Autobiography of a Survivor._ New York: Holocaust Library, 1991.

Isaacman, Clara. _Clara's Story._ As told to Joan Adess Grossman. Philadelphia: Jewish Publication Society of America, 1984.

Isaacson, Judith Magyar. _Seed of Sarah: Memoirs of a Survivor._ Urbana: University of Illinois Press, 1990.

Klüger, Ruth. _Still Alive: A Holocaust Girlhood Remembered._ New York: Feminist Press at the City University of New York, 2001.

Klüger. _Weiter leben: Eine Jugend._ Göttingen: Wallstein, 1992.

Lengyel, Olga. _I Survived Hitler's Ovens: The Story of Auschwitz._ New York: Avon, 1947.

Levi, Primo. _The Drowned and the Saved._ Translated by Raymond Rosenthal. New York: Summit, 1988.

Levi. _The Reawakening._ Translated by Stuart Woolf. New York: Collier, 1965.

Levi. _Survival in Auschwitz: The Nazi Assault on Humanity._ Translated by Woolf. New York: Collier, 1961.

Liebster, Simone Arnold. _Facing the Lion: Memoirs of a Young Girl in Nazi Europe._ New Orleans: Grammaton Press, 2000.

Lundholm, Anja. _Das Höllentor: Bericht einer Überlebenden._ Hamburg: Rowohlt, 1988.

Rothchild, Sylvia, ed. _Voices from the Holocaust._ New York: New American Library, 1981.

Seel, Pierre. _I, Pierre Seel, Deported Homosexual: A Memoir of Nazi Terror._ Translated by Joachim Neugroschel. New York: BasicBooks, 1995.

Segal, Lore. _Other People's Houses._ New York: Harcourt, Brace &World, 1964.

Spiegel, Marga. _Retter in der Nacht: Wie Eine Jüdische Familie Münsterland Urberlebte._ Münster: Lit, 1999.

Strauss, Herbert A. _In the Eye of the Storm: Growing Up Jewish in Germany, 1918–1943: A Memoir._ New York: Fordham University Press, 1999.

Unsdorfer, S. B. _The Yellow Star._ New York: Yoseloff, 1961.

Wiesel, Elie. _Night._ Translated by Stella Rodway. New York: Hill & Wang, 1960.

21. PAPERS, DOCUMENTS, & DIARIES

Baynes, Norman H., ed. _The Speeches of Adolf Hitler: April 1922–August 1939._ London: Oxford University Press, 1942.

Bonhoeffer, Dietrich. _Letters and Papers from Prison._ Edited by Eberhard Bethge. Translated by Reginald H. Fuller. London: SCM Press, 1953.

Czerniakow, Adam. _The Warsaw Diary of Adam Czerniakow: Prelude to Doom._ Edited by Raul Hilberg, Stanislaw Staron, and Josef Kermisz. Translated by Staron and the staff of Yad Vashem. New York: Stein & Day, 1979.

Documents on German Foreign Policy, 1918–1945. Washington, D.C.: U.S. Government Printing Office, 1949.

Eichmann, Adolf. _Eichmann Interrogated: Transcripts from the Archives of the Israeli Police._ Edited by

Jochen von Lang, in collaboration with Claus Sibyll. Translated by Ralph Manheim. New York: Farrar, Straus & Giroux, 1983.

Eichmann. _The Trial of Adolf Eichmann: Record of Proceedings in the District Court of Jerusalem._ 9 volumes. Jerusalem: Trust for the Publication of the Proceedings of the Eichmann Trial, in cooperation with the Israel State Archives and Yad Vashem, the Holocaust Martyrs' and Heroes' Remembrance Authority, 1992.

Goebbels, Joseph. _The Goebbels Diaries, 1939–1941._ Translated and edited by Fred Taylor. London: Hamilton, 1982.

Halder, Franz. _The Halder War Diary, 1939–1942._ Edited by Charles Burdick and Hans-Adolf Jacobsen. Novato, Cal.: Presidio, 1988.

Hitler, Adolf. _Monologe im Führerhaupquartier 1941–1944._ Edited by Werner Jochmann. Hamburg: Knaus, 1980.

Kaplan, Chaim A. _Scroll of Agony: The Warsaw Diary of Chaim A. Kaplan._ Translated and edited by Abraham I. Katsch. New York: Macmillan, 1965.

Klemperer, Victor. _I Will Bear Witness: A Diary of the Nazi Years._ 2 volumes. Translated by Martin Chalmers. New York: Random House, 1998.

Noakes, J. and G. Pridham, eds. _Nazism, 1919–1945: A History in Documents and Eyewitness Accounts._ New York: Schocken, 1990.

Ringelblum, Emmanuel. _Notes from the Warsaw Ghetto: The Journal of Emmanuel Ringelblum._ Edited and translated by Jacob Sloan. New York: McGraw-Hill, 1958.

Shirer, William L. _Berlin Diary: The Journal of a Foreign Correspondent, 1934–1941._ New York: Knopf, 1941.

United States, Department of State. _Foreign Relations of the United States: Diplomatic Papers, 1938._ 5 volumes. Washington, D.C.: U.S. Government Printing Office, 1954–1956.

Weizmann, Chaim. _The Letters and Papers of Chaim Weizmann._ 23 volumes. New Brunswick, N.J.: Transaction Books / Jerusalem: Israel Universities Press, 1968–1980.

22. RACISM

Mosse, George L. _Toward a Final Solution: A History of European Racism._ New York: Fertig, 1978.

Olender, Maurice. _The Languages of Politics: Race, Religion, and Philology in the Nineteenth Century._ Translated by Arthur Goldhammer. Cambridge, Mass.: Harvard University Press, 1992.

Poliakov, Léon. _The Aryan Myth: A History of Racist and Nationalist Ideas in Europe._ Translated by Edmund Howard. New York: Basic Books, 1974.

23. REPRESENTATIONS & MEMORY: LITERATURE & THE ARTS

Adorno, Theodor W. _Kulturkritik und Gesellschaft._ 2 volumes. Frankfurt: Suhrkamp, 1977.

Avisar, Ilan. _Screening the Holocaust: Cinema's Images of the Unimaginable._ Bloomington: Indiana University Press, 1988.

Berger, James. _After the End: Representations of Post-Apocalypse._ Minneapolis: University of Minnesota Press, 1999.

Borowski, Tadeusz. _This Way for the Gas, Ladies and Gentlemen: And Other Stories._ Translated by Barbara Vedder. London: Cape / New York: Viking, 1967.

Braham, Randolph L., ed. _Reflections of the Holocaust in Art and Literature._ Boulder, Colo.: Social Science Monographs / New York: Csengeri Institute for Holocaust Studies of the Graduate School and

REFERENCES

University Center of the City University of New York, 1990.

Cole, Tim. *Selling the Holocaust: From Auschwitz to Schindler: How History is Bought, Packaged, and Sold*. New York: Routledge, 1999.

Doneson, Judith E. *The Holocaust in American Film*. Philadelphia: Jewish Publication Society, 1987.

Ezrahi, Sidra DeKoven. *By Words Alone: The Holocaust in Literature*. Chicago: University of Chicago Press, 1980.

Federman, Raymond. *The Twofold Vibration*. Bloomington: Indiana University Press / Brighton, U.K.: Harvester Press, 1982.

Flanzbaum, Hilene, ed. *The Americanization of the Holocaust*. Baltimore: Johns Hopkins University Press, 1999.

Friedländer, Saul. *Memory, History, and the Extermination of the Jews of Europe*. Bloomington: Indiana University Press, 1993.

Friedländer. *Reflections of Nazism: An Essay on Kitsch and Death*. Translated by Thomas Weyr. New York: Harper & Row, 1984.

Friedländer. *When Memory Comes*. Translated by Helen R. Lane. New York: Farrar, Straus & Giroux, 1979.

Friedländer, ed. *Probing the Limits of Representation: Nazism and the "Final Solution."* Cambridge, Mass.: Harvard University Press, 1992.

Gottlieb, Roger S., ed. *Thinking the Unthinkable: Meanings of the Holocaust*. New York: Paulist Press, 1990.

Grossman, David. *See Under–Love*. Translated by Betsy Rosenberg. New York: Noonday Press, 1989.

Hartman, Geoffrey H., ed. *Bitburg in Moral and Political Perspective*. Bloomington: Indiana University Press, 1986.

Hartman, ed. *Holocaust Remembrance: The Shapes of Memory*. Oxford, U.K. & Cambridge, Mass.: Blackwell, 1994.

Horowitz, Sara. *Voicing the Void: Muteness and Memory in Holocaust Fiction*. Albany: State University of New York Press, 1997.

LaCapra, Dominick. *History and Memory after Auschwitz*. Ithaca, N.Y.: Cornell University Press, 1998.

Lang, Berel, ed. *Writing and the Holocaust*. New York: Holmes & Meier, 1988.

Langer, Lawrence L. *The Holocaust and the Literary Imagination*. New Haven: Yale University Press, 1975.

Langer. *Versions of Survival: The Holocaust and the Human Spirit*. Albany: State University of New York Press, 1982.

Loshitzky, Yosefa, ed. *Spielberg's Holocaust: Critical Perspectives on Schindler's List*. Bloomington: Indiana University Press, 1997.

Lyotard, Jean-François. *The Différend: Phrases in Dispute*. Translated by Georges Van Den Abbeele. Minneapolis: University of Minnesota Press, 1988.

Mächler, Stefan. *The Wilkomirski Affair: A Study in Biographical Truth*. Translated by John E. Woods. New York: Schocken, 2001.

Meyer, Michael J., ed. *Literature and Ethnic Discrimination*. Amsterdam & Atlanta: Rodopi, 1997.

Mintz, Alan. *Popular Culture in the Shaping of Holocaust Memory in America*. Seattle: University of Washington Press, 2001.

Reiter, Andrea. *Auf daß sie entsteigen der Dunkelheit: Die literarische Bewältigung von KZ-Erfahrung*. Vienna: Löcker, 1995. Translated by Patrick Camiller as *Narrating the Holocaust*. London & New York: Continuum, 2000.

Rosenfeld, Alvin H. *A Double Dying: Reflections on Holocaust Literature*. Bloomington: Indiana University Press, 1980.

Rothberg, Michael. *Traumatic Realism: The Demands of Holocaust Representation*. Minneapolis: University of Minnesota Press, 2000.

Spiegelman, Art. *Maus: A Survivor's Tale*. New York: Pantheon, 1986.

Spiegelman. *Maus II: A Survivor's Tale: And Here My Troubles Began*. New York: Pantheon, 1992.

Steiner, George. *Language and Silence: Essays on Language, Literature, and the Inhuman*. New York: Atheneum, 1967.

Wiesel, Elie. *Dimensions of the Holocaust: Lectures at Northwestern University*. Evanston, Ill.: Northwestern University Press, 1977.

24. RESISTENCE, SURVIVAL, & COMPLICITY

Barnett, Victoria J. *Bystanders: Conscience and Complicity during the Holocaust*. Westport, Conn.: Greenwood Press, 1999.

Bethge, Eberhard. *Friendship and Resistance: Essays on Dietrich Bonhoeffer* (Geneva: WCC Publications / Grand Rapids, Mich.: Eerdmans, 1995).

Bettelheim, Bruno. *Surviving and Other Essays*. New York: Knopf, 1979.

Bower, Tom. *Blood Money: The Swiss, the Nazis and the Looted Billions*. London: Macmillan, 1997.

Bridgman, Jon. *The End of the Holocaust: The Liberation of the Camps*. Portland, Ore.: Areopagitica, 1990.

Gellately, Robert. *Backing Hitler: Consent and Coercion in Nazi Germany*. Oxford & New York: Oxford University Press, 2001.

Hass, Aaron. *The Aftermath: Living with the Holocaust*. Cambridge & New York: Cambridge University Press, 1995.

Hilberg, Raul. *Perpetrators, Victims, Bystanders: The Jewish Catastrophe, 1933–1945*. New York: Asher, 1992.

Jaspers, Karl. *The Question of German Guilt*. Translated by E. B. Ashton. New York: Capricorn, 1961.

Klemperer, Klemens von. *German Resistance Against Hitler: The Search for Allies Abroad, 1938–1945*. Oxford: Clarendon Press / New York: Oxford University Press, 1993.

Laqueur, Walter and Richard Breitman. *Breaking the Silence*. New York: Simon & Schuster, 1986.

LeBor, Adam. *Hitler's Secret Bankers: The Myth of Swiss Neutrality during the Holocaust*. Secaucus, N.J.: Carol, 1997.

Levin, Itamar. *The Last Deposit: Swiss Banks And Holocaust Victims' Accounts*. Translated by Natasha Dornberg. Westport, Conn.: Praeger, 1999.

Paldiel, Mordecai. *The Path of the Righteous: Gentile Rescuers of Jews During the Holocaust*. Hoboken, N.J.: Ktav, 1993.

Paldiel. *Sheltering the Jews: Stories of Holocaust Rescuers*. Minneapolis: Fortress Press, 1996.

Pross, Christian. *Paying for the Past: The Struggle over Reparations for Surviving Victims of the Nazi Terror*. Translated by Belinda Cooper. Baltimore: Johns Hopkins University Press, 1998.

Rohrlich, Ruby, ed. *Resisting the Holocaust*. Oxford & New York: Berg, 1998.

Shaw, Stanford J. *Turkey and the Holocaust: Turkey's Role in Rescuing Turkish and European Jewry from Nazi Persecution, 1933–1945*. New York: New York University Press, 1993.

Todorov, Tzvetan. *Facing the Extreme: Moral Life in the Concentration Camps.* Translated by Arthur Denner and Abigail Pollak. New York: Metropolitan, 1996.

Ziegler, Jean. *The Swiss, the Gold, and the Dead: How Swiss Bankers Helped Finance the Nazi War Machine.* Translated by John Brownjohn. New York: Harcourt Brace, 1998.

25. STATE TERROR

Browning, Christopher R. *Ordinary Men: Reserve Battalion 101 and the Final Solution in Poland.* New York: HarperCollins, 1992.

Burleigh, Michael. *Death and Deliverance: "Euthanasia" in Germany, c. 1900-1945.* Cambridge & New York: Cambridge University Press, 1994.

Burleigh. *Ethics and Extermination: Reflections on Nazi Genocide.* Cambridge & New York: Cambridge University Press, 1997.

Friedlander, Henry. *The Origins of Nazi Genocide: From Euthanasia to the Final Solution.* Chapel Hill: University of North Carolina Press, 1995.

Johnson, Eric A. *Nazi Terror: The Gestapo, Jews, and Ordinary Germans.* New York: BasicBooks, 1999.

Krausnick, Helmut. *Anatomy of the SS State.* Translated by Richard Barry, Marian Jackson, and Dorothy Long. New York: Walker, 1968.

Lifton, Robert Jay. *The Nazi Doctors: Medical Killings and the Psychology of Genocide.* New York: Basic Books, 1986.

Zillmer, Eric A. and others. *The Quest for the Nazi Personality: A Psychological Investigation of Nazi War Criminals.* Hillsdale, N.J.: Erlbaum, 1995.

26. UNITED STATES AND THE ALLIES

Abzug, Robert H. *America Views the Holocaust, 1933-1945: A Brief Documentary History.* Boston: Bedford/St. Martin's Press, 1999.

Breitman, Richard. *Official Secrets: What the Nazis Planned, What the British and Americans Knew.* New York: Hill & Wang, 1998.

Favez, Jean-Claude. *The Red Cross and the Holocaust.* Edited and translated by Beryl and John Fletcher. New York: Cambridge University Press, 1999.

Feingold, Henry L. *The Politics of Rescue: The Roosevelt Administration and the Holocaust, 1938-1945.* New Brunswick, N.J.: Rutgers University Press, 1970.

Gilbert, Martin. *Auschwitz and the Allies.* New York: Holt, Rinehart & Winston, 1981.

Hersh, Burton. *The Old Boys: The American Elite and the Origins of the CIA.* New York: Scribners/Toronto: Maxwell Macmillan Canada/New York: Maxwell Macmillan International, 1992.

Higham, Charles. *Trading with the Enemy: An Exposé of the Nazi-American Money Plot, 1933-1949.* New York: Delacorte, 1983.

Lipstadt, Deborah E. *Beyond Belief: The American Press and the Coming of the Holocaust, 1933-1945.* New York: Free Press, 1986.

Morse, Arthur D. *While Six Million Died: A Chronicle of American Apathy.* New York: Ace, 1967.

Novick, Peter. *The Holocaust in American Life.* Boston: Houghton Mifflin, 1999.

Shandler, Jeffrey. *While America Watches: Televising the Holocaust.* New York: Oxford University Press, 1999.

Stembler, Charles Herbert and others. *Jews in the Mind of America.* Edited by George Salomon. New York: Basic Books, 1966.

Wyman, David S. *The Abandonment of the Jews: America and the Holocaust, 1941-1945.* New York: New Press, 1998.

27. WAR CRIMES TRIALS

Arendt, Hannah. *Eichmann in Jerusalem: A Report on the Banality of Evil.* Revised edition. New York: Penguin, 1964.

Brager, Bruce L. *The Trial of Adolf Eichmann: The Holocaust on Trial.* San Diego: Lucent Books, 1999.

Braham, Randolph L. *The Eichmann Case: A Source Book.* New York: World Federation of Hungarian Jews, 1969.

Buscher, Frank M. *The U.S. War Crimes Trial Program in Germany, 1946-1955.* Westport, Conn.: Greenwood Press, 1989.

Conot, Robert E. *Justice at Nuremberg.* New York: Harper & Row, 1983.

Davidson, Eugene. *The Trial of the Germans.* New York: Macmillan, 1966.

Glock, Charles Y., Gertrude J. Selznick, and Joel L. Spaeth. *The Apathetic Majority: A Study Based on Public Responses to the Eichmann Trial.* New York: Harper & Row, 1966.

Harris, Whitney R. *Tyranny on Trial: The Evidence at Nuremberg.* Dallas: Southern Methodist University Press, 1954.

Hausner, Gideon. *Justice in Jerusalem.* New York: Harper & Row, 1966.

International Military Tribunal. *Trial of the Major War Criminals Before the International Military Tribunal, Nuremberg, 14 November 1945-1 October 1946.* 42 volumes. Nuremberg: International Military Tribunal, 1947-1949.

Kochavi, Arieh J. *Prelude to Nuremberg: Allied War Crimes Policy and the Question of Punishment.* Chapel Hill: University of North Carolina Press, 1998.

Maguire, Peter H. *Law and War: An American Story.* New York: Columbia University Press, 2000.

Malkin, Peter Z. and Harry Stein. *Eichmann in My Hands.* New York: Warner, 1990.

Malmedy Massacre Investigation: Hearings Before a Subcommittee of the Committee on Armed Services, United States Senate, Eighty-First Congress, First Session, Pursuant to S. Res. 42. Washington, D.C.: U.S. Government Printing Office, 1949.

Marrus, Michael R., ed. *The Nuremberg War Crimes Trial, 1945-1946: A Documentary History.* Boston & New York: Bedford, 1997.

Overy, Richard. *Interrogations: The Nazi Elite in Allied Hands, 1945.* New York: Viking, 2001.

Papadatos, Peter. *The Eichmann Trial.* London: Stevens / New York: Praeger, 1964.

Persico, Joseph E. *Nuremberg: Infamy on Trial.* New York: Viking/Penguin, 1994.

Robinson, Jacob. *And the Crooked Shall Be Made Straight: The Eichmann Trial, the Jewish Catastrophe and Hannah Arendt's Narrative.* New York: Macmillan, 1965.

Rogat, Yosal. *The Eichmann Trial and the Rule of Law.* Santa Barbara, Cal.: Center for the Study of Democratic Institutions, 1961.

Sharpe, Barry. *Modesty and Arrogance in Judgment: Hannah Arendt's Eichmann in Jerusalem.* Westport, Conn.: Praeger, 1999.

Smith, Bradley F. *Reaching Judgment at Nuremberg.* New York: Basic Books, 1977.

Smith, ed. *The American Road to Nuremberg: The Documentary Record, 1944-1945.* Stanford, Cal.: Hoover Institution Press, 1982.

Taylor, Telford. *The Anatomy of the Nuremberg Trials.* New York: Knopf, 1992.

Taylor. *Nuremberg Trials: War Crimes and International Law.* New York: Carnegie Endowment for International Peace, 1949.

Trainin, A. N. *Hitlerite Responsibility Under Criminal Law.* Edited by A. Y. Vishinski. Translated by Andrew Rothstein. London & New York: Hutchinson, 1945.

Trial of the Major War Criminals Before the International Military Tribunal, Nuremberg, 14 November 1945 – 1 October 1946. 42 volumes. Nuremberg, 1947–1949.

Trials of War Criminals Before the Nuremberg Military Tribunals Under Control Council Law No. 10. 15 volumes. Washington, D.C.: U.S. Government Printing Office, 1949–1953.

Weingartner, James J. *A Peculiar Crusade: Willis M. Everett and the Malmedy Massacre.* New York: New York University Press, 2000.

Wighton, Charles. *Eichmann: His Career and Crimes.* London: Odhams, 1961.

Woetzel, Robert K. *The Nuremberg Trials in International Law with a Postlude on the Eichmann Case.* London: Stevens / New York: Praeger, 1962.

28. WOMEN & GENDER

Bridenthal, Renate, Atina Grossmann, and Marion Kaplan, eds. *When Biology Became Destiny: Women in Weimar and Nazi Germany.* New York: Monthly Review Press, 1984.

Gilligan, Carol. *In a Different Voice: Psychological Theory and Women's Development.* Cambridge, Mass.: Harvard University Press, 1982.

Kaplan. *The Making of the Jewish Middle Class: Women, Family, and Identity in Imperial Germany.* New York: Oxford University Press, 1991.

Katz, Esther and Joan Miriam Ringelheim, eds. *Proceedings of the Conference on Women Surviving the Holocaust.* New York: Institute for Research in History, 1983.

Koonz, Claudia. *Mothers in the Fatherland: Women, the Family, and Nazi Politics.* New York: St. Martin's Press, 1987.

Kremer, S. Lillian. *Women's Holocaust Writing: Memory and Imagination.* Lincoln: University of Nebraska Press, 1999.

Ofer, Dalia and Lenore J. Weitzman, eds. *Women in the Holocaust.* New Haven: Yale University Press, 1998.

Quack, Sibylle, ed. *Between Sorrow and Strength: Women Refugees of the Nazi Period.* Washington, D.C.: German Historical Institute; Cambridge & New York: Cambridge University Press, 1995.

Rittner, Carol and John K. Roth, eds. *Different Voices: Women and the Holocaust.* New York: Paragon House, 1993.

Rupp, Leila J. *Mobilizing Women for War: German and American Propaganda, 1939-1945.* Princeton: Princeton University Press, 1978.

Stephenson, Jill. *Women in Nazi Society.* London: Croom Helm / New York: Barnes & Noble, 1975.

CONTRIBUTORS' NOTES

BOWEN, Wayne: Assistant Professor of History at Ouachita Baptist University, where he teaches courses on modern Germany, military history, and twentieth-century Europe; earned his B.A. from the University of Southern California and his M.A. and Ph.D. from Northwestern University; author of *Spaniards and Nazi Germany: Collaboration in the New Order* (2000); author of articles on the Holocaust, modern Turkey, World War II, and the Franco regime.

BUSSE, Kristina: Received her doctorate in English from Tulane University for her work on postmodern representations of the Holocaust; currently teaches at the Alabama School of Mathematics and Science.

BUTLER, J. Michael: Assistant Professor of History, South Georgia College; received his M.A. and Ph.D. in History from the University of Mississippi; author of articles in *Journal of Southern History*, *Popular Music and Society*, and *Journal of Mississippi History*.

CASEY, Michael S.: Associate Professor of Humanities at Graceland University in Iowa; earned his Ph.D. from Salve Regina University and is a specialist in the U.S. military "experience"; was a career naval officer and taught at the Naval War College; author of *America's Technological Sailor: A Retrospective on a Century of "Progress" in the United States Navy* (1998).

CHU, Jolene: Social historian with an M.A., who specializes in Jehovah's Witnesses during the Nazi period; researcher at the Watch Tower Society (New York); serves on the board of directors of Jehovah's Witness Holocaust-Era Survivors Fund, Inc.; author of many articles and book chapters on historical and religious aspects of the Nazi persecution of Jehovah's Witnesses.

DAVIS, John: Independent scholar, Athens, Alabama.

EHLY, Victor: Norwich University, Northfield, Vermont.

ERSPAMER, Peter R.: Fort Hays State University, Hays, Kansas; studied at Grinnell College, the University of Freiburg, the University of Bonn, the University of Wisconsin, Madison, and other universities; author of *The Elusiveness of Tolerance: The "Jewish Question" from Lessing to the Napoleonic Wars* (1997) and *The Holocaust and the Survival of Human Dignity* (forthcoming).

FEUER, Menachem: M.A. in Philosophy and Ph.D. in Comparative Literature from State University of New York at Binghamton; research focuses on postmodern Holocaust fiction.

FRANÇOIS, Pieter: Researcher at the Department of Modern History at the University of Ghent (Belgium); studied history at the University of Ghent and the University of Leiden (The Netherlands); research interests in theoretical and historiographical aspects of the Holocaust.

HOLLAND, Carolsue: Professor of International Relations at Troy State University; earned her Ph.D. in History and Diplomacy at the University of Pennsylvania in 1967; co-author, with Tom Rothbart, of an article on SS booty in *After the Battle* (August 1996); consultant to the British Holocaust Educational Trust (1996–1998); participant in Scholars and Churchmen Conferences on the Holocaust; research interests in the Holocaust and Holocaust denial.

HUTTENBACH, Henry R.: History Professor at the City College of New York; earned his Ph.D. in Russian history at the University of Washington, Seattle; founder/editor of the *International Journal of Genocide Research* (1999–   ) and *The Genocide Forum* (1994–   ).

JACOBS, Steven Leonard: Aaron Aronov Chair of Judaic Studies at the University of Alabama, Tuscaloosa and Associate Professor in the Department of Religious Studies; earned his undergraduate degree from Pennsylvania State University and graduate degrees from the Hebrew Union College-Jewish Institute of Religion; author, editor, or translator of more than fifty articles and reviews and several books dealing primarily with the Holocaust and genocide.

KAPLAN, Marion: Professor of History in the Department of Hebrew and Judaic Studies and the Department of History at New York University; author of *The Jewish Feminist Movement in Germany: The Campaigns of the Jüdischer Frauenbund, 1904–1938* (1979); *The Making of the Jewish Middle Class: Women, Family, and Identity in Imperial Germany* (1990); and *Between Dignity and Despair: Jewish Life in Nazi Germany* (1996).

KAY, Judith W.: Teaches courses on capital punishment and anti-Semitism at the University of Puget Sound; earned her Ph.D. in Social Ethics from the Graduate Theological Union in Berkeley, Cal.;

author of "In the Shadow of the Execution Chamber: Affirming Wholeness in a Broken Place" (an essay on spiritual advisers to death-row inmates) in *Practice What You Preach: Virtues, Ethics, and Power in the Lives of Pastoral Ministers and Their Congregations,* edited by James Keenan and Joseph Kotva Jr. (1999); currently writing a book on revenge and retribution.

KLIMA, Cynthia: State University of New York, Geneseo.

KUYKENDALL, John: Currently completing his Ph.D. in History at the University of South Carolina; earned his B.A. from Erskine College and an M.A. in History from the University of South Carolina.

LAFFER, Dennis R., M.D.: A physician in private practice in Tampa, Florida; specializes in gastrointestinal and liver disease; has a strong interest in history, especially focusing on the Holocaust era; currently serving on the board of directors of the Florida Holocaust Museum, St. Petersburg, Florida.

MAGRATH, Leslie: Independent scholar, Hopkins, South Carolina.

MAHONY, Mary Ann: Columbia College, Columbia, South Carolina.

MAIER, Wendy A.: Lecturer in European, American, and women's history at several Illinois colleges; earned her M.A. from Roosevelt University, Chicago; research interests include investigations into female Nazi perpetrators; contributor to *History: Review of New Books, Oxford Dictionary of National Biography,* and *Encyclopedia of World War II.*

MCCONNELL, Tandy: Associate Professor of History and department chairman at Columbia College, Columbia, South Carolina; earned his Ph.D. from the University of South Carolina; editor of *American Decades: 1990–1999* (2001).

MCCORMICK, Robert: Newman University, Wichita, Kansas.

MCCULLOCH, Anne: Columbia College, Columbia, South Carolina.

MCGAHA, Richard: Independent scholar, Bremerton, Washington.

MICHAEL, Robert: Professor Emeritus of European History at the University of Massachusetts, Dartmouth, where he taught the Holocaust for thirty years; a Phi Beta Kappa graduate of Boston University in Philosophy; he has published poetry and more than fifty articles and six books on the Holocaust and the history of anti-Semitism; a founder of the scholarly e-mail list H-ANTISEMITISM; offered the world's first distance-education course on the Holocaust in 1994.

PAULY, Robert J., Jr.: Adjunct Professor of History and Political Science at Midlands Technical College; earned his Ph.D. in International Studies from Old Dominion University; author of *U.S. Foreign Policy and the Persian Gulf: Safeguarding American Interests Through Selective Multilateralism* (forthcoming).

PING, Larry L.: Professor of History at Southern Utah University; earned his B.A. and Ph.D. at the University of Oregon and his M.A. at Purdue; has taught German History for twelve years at Southern Utah University; contributed articles and book reviews on German History to several state and national journals.

PORTER, Clifford F.: Historian for the Defense Language Institute, Presidio of Monterey, California, and an adjunct instructor at the Marine Corps University.

PROLL, Lauren S.: Assistant Professor of English at Wittenberg University, Springfield, Ohio; she earned her Ph.D. in English at Indiana University in Bloomington.

RUBINSTEIN, William D.: University of Wales-Aberystwyth.

SAGE, Steven F.: Independent scholar, Rockville, Maryland; holds a Ph.D. in History; a former U.S. diplomat who has investigated Holocaust and human-rights-related matters in eastern Europe; researches compensation cases for the conference on Jewish Material Claims Against Germany.

SCHAUMANN, Caroline: Emory University, Atlanta.

SHARPE, Barry: Assistant Professor of Political Science at Tusculum College; has a Ph.D. in Political Science from the University of South Carolina and a J.D. from the University of Texas School of Law; author of *Modesty and Arrogance in Judgment: Hannah Arendt's* Eichmann in Jerusalem (1999).

SHAW, Susan M.: Director of Women Studies at Oregon State University; she earned her B.A. at Berry College, MAIS at Oregon State University, and M.A. and Ph.D. at Southern Seminary; author of *Storytelling in Religious Education* (1999); co-author, with Janet Lee, of *Women's Voices, Feminist Visions: Classic and Contemporary Readings* (2001); currently co-authoring *Girls Rock!: 50 Years of Women Making Music* (forthcoming).

STACKELBERG, Rod: Robert K. and Ann J. Powers Professor of Humanities at Gonzaga University; author of *Hitler's Germany: Origins, Interpretations, Legacies* (1999); co-editor, with Sally A. Winkle, of *The Nazi Germany Sourcebook: An Anthology of Texts* (2002).

STATHIS, G. Michael: Associate Professor of Political Science and International Relations and Director for the International Relations Certificate at Southern Utah University; earned his B.S. in Political Science (1971), M.A. in Middle Eastern Studies (Persian, 1976) at the Middle East Center, and Ph.D. in International Relations (1995) at the University of Utah; has published many scholarly papers and newspaper articles; is a regular radio guest on the British Forces Broadcasting System commenting on world affairs.

STEELE, Meili: Professor of English and Comparative Literature at the University of South Carolina, Columbia.

STERLING, Eric: Holds a Ph.D. from Indiana University; currently Distinguished Research Professor of English at Auburn University, Montgomery, Alabama.

STERNBERG, Frances Glazer: Program Associate at the Midwest Center for Holocaust Education in Overland Park, Kansas; Adjunct Graduate Instructor in the Department of History at the University of Missouri, Kansas City.

TAYLOR, Melissa Jane: Ph.D. candidate at the University of South Carolina; she received her M.A. in Modern European History from USC in 2001.

UHL, Karsten: Independent historian and museologist currently working as a freelance teacher and researcher at the University of Oldenburg, Germany; earned M.A. in History at the University of Hamburg (Germany, 1998) and Ph.D. in Modern History at the University of Munich (Germany, 2000); wrote her Ph.D. thesis on crime, gender, and punishment in criminological and literary discourses during the nineteenth and twentieth centuries; author of "The Auschwitz Sketchbook," in *The Last Expression: Art and Auschwitz,* edited by The Block Museum of Art (forthcoming).

UNGER, Nancy C.: Assistant Professor of History, Women and Gender Studies, and Environmental Studies at Santa Clara University, where she teaches Gay and Lesbian History; author of *Fighting Bob La Follette: The Righteous Reformer* (2000); working on a book on the significance of gender in women's responses to the environment and environmental issues in American history.

UNTERSEHER, Lisa A.: Assistant Professor of Religion at Columbia College (South Carolina) and the assistant director of the Honors program; graduated Phi Beta Kappa from the University of Texas at Austin with a B.A. in History; completed an M.Div. and a Ph.D. in Religious Studies with a concentration on the History of the Christian Tradition, from Southern Methodist University in Dallas, Texas; author of "The Mark of Cain and the Jews: Augustine's Theology of Jews," in *Augustinian Studies* (2002); her research focuses on Jewish-Christian relations in late antiquity; currently working on a book that examines Augustine of Hippo's theology of Jews and Judaism.

WEINGARTNER, James J.: Professor of History at Southern Illinois University, Edwardsville; earned his Ph.D. from the University of Wisconsin at Madison; author of books and articles on World War II and Nazi Germany.

WELLS, John W.: Associate Professor of Political Science, Carson-Newman College, Jefferson City, Tennessee.

WRAIGHT, Jamie L.: Curator and historian of the Voice/Vision Holocaust Survivor Oral History Archive at the University of Michigan, Dearborn; he received his M.A. in Modern European History from the University of Toledo, where he is currently a doctoral candidate in the same field.

INDEX

Association of Professional NGOs for Social Assistance
in Baia Mare (ASSOC) VII 252
Association of South-East Asian Nations (ASEAN) VI
271
Assyria XI 125, 169
Astoria, Oregon VII 53
Aswan Dam II 146, 148
Aswan High Dam (Egypt) VII 3
Ataturk, Kemal VIII 118, 211–214
Atchafalaya River VII 161
Atkins, J. D. C. VII 56
Atlanta Exposition (1895) III 268, 271
Atlantic Charter (1941) I 301; II 99; V 45, 146–149;
VI 9, 78–79; IX 250; XI 110
Atlantic Ocean IX 77, 79, 140, 142, 181, 245; XI 174
atmospheric nuclear testing VI 16
atomic bomb II 228; III 10, 16; V 48–55; VI 20, 57,
136, 154, 254–255; VIII 195
American I 260, 262–263
Anglo-American cooperation on VI 10
data passed to Soviet Union II 231
development V 44
Hiroshima and Nagasaki III 10
impact on World War II II 268; III 11
introduction I 4
Soviet Union development of II 229
"Stockholm Appeal" II 47
Atomic Energy Act (1946) I 220–221
Atomic Energy Act (1954) VII 175
Atomic Energy Commission (AEC) I 27, 29–31, 214,
220; II 82; VII 174–175, 178
Atoms for Peace I 216–217, 221; II 51
Attaturk Dam (Turkey) VII 82
Attila the Hun XI 71
Attlee, Clement VI 11, 250
Attorney General's List I 76
Auchinleck, Sir Claude John Eyre V 76, 172
Audubon Society VII 31, 258
Auden, Wystan VIII 191
Aufmarschplan I (Deployment Plan I) VIII 247
Aufmarschplan II (Deployment Plan II) VIII 247–248
Ausgleich agreement (1867) IX 137
August Revolution (1945) V 146
Augustine of Hippo X 20, 80–81, 84–85, 103–104, 229,
277; XI 19–20, 23, 169
Aurul SA cyanide spill (Romania) VII 248–250, 252–
255
Auschwitz (concentration camp) I 138; III 253–254,
256; V 54, 56–57, 60, 158, 160–163, 219;
VIII 94; XI 2, 4, 9, 11, 16, 45, 50, 69–70, 79,
102–104, 111, 114, 131, 148, 180, 186, 188,
206, 213–214, 217–221, 224, 227–228, 230–
231, 235–237, 239–240, 250
theories of formation V 156
Australia VI 136; VIII 33, 133, 137, 160–161, 208; IX
76, 173; XI 62, 93, 96
Aborigines XI 57
grain reserves VIII 290
immigrants XI 57, 59, 62
Japanese immigration to IX 162
motivation of soldiers VIII
represented at Evian Conference XI 55
World War I VIII 54, 117–123, 220
Australia (Australian ship) VIII 137
Australian and New Zealand Army Corps (ANZAC)
VIII 121–122
Australia Light Horse IX 72
Australia Mounted Division IX 67
Austria I 253, 293; VI 136; VIII 18, 82, 106, 251–252,
266, 281; IX 49, 82, 93, 120, 158, 225–226;
XI 14, 36, 56, 59, 88, 110, 123, 167, 175, 179,
211
alliance with Germany (1879) VIII 35
Central European Model I 108
contribution of Jews in VIII 167
customs union with Germany forbidden VIII 283
dam agreement with Hungary VII 101
dams in VII 101

East German emigration through VI 118, 121
Jehovah's Witnesses in XI 129
Jews in XI 55, 60, 93
occupation of I 108
pre-World War I alliances VIII 225–231
Socialists in VIII 260
supports Slovak anti-nuclear activists VII 103
union with Nazi Germany VIII 284
Austria-Hungary VIII 76, 95, 98, 104, 172, 178, 226,
228, 230, 266–267, 280, 299; IX 30, 64–65,
99, 102, 140, 154, 192–193, 204, 206, 225,
227, 248, 266–272
army VIII 69; IX 134, 158
collapse of VIII 216–217; IX 81
invades Poland VIII 72
invades Serbia VIII 72
relations with Germany concerning Slavic lands
VIII 94
Socialists in VIII 257, 261
U. S. trade with IX 22
World War I VIII 11, 43–49; IX 133–138
aircraft IX 13
casualties VIII 125, 268
defense budget VIII 44
Jews in VIII 164
mobilization in VIII 125
motivation of soldiers VIII 266
war against the United States VII 11
Austrian Refugee Foundation XI 62
Auténtico Party I 91
automobile
impact on interstate highway development II 106
impact on United States II 109
recreation II 108
Axis I 3; V 62–67
defeat in Tunisia IV 144
North African campaign V 66
parallel war theory V 63–65
Ayyubids X 48–49, 139, 183, 185, 187–188, 274
Azerbaijan VI 255; VIII 96, 216; X 183, 187

B

B-1 bomber I 191; II 57
B-1B "Lancer" supersonic nuclear bomber VI 109, 234
B-17 bomber V 4, 5, 6, 98
B-17C bomber V 5
B-17E bomber V 5
B-24 bomber V 7, 98
B-26 bomber V 5
B-29 bomber V 3, 7, 49, 52,
B-36 bomber I 3– 8
B-52 I 189, 193
B-58 I 193
Babbitt (1922) II 109; III 177
Baby Boomers VI 24–25
Baby M II 80
Babylon XI 125
Babylonian Captivity X 210
Bach, Johann Sebastian XI 2
Back to Africa movement III 121
Backfire bomber VI 259
Bacon, Francis VI 195
Bacon, Roger X 53, 65, 67, 69, 79, 181, 235
Badeni crisis (1897) IX 138
Badoglio, Marshall Pietro V 178
Italian campaign IV 144
Baghdad X 48, 52, 77, 172, 193
Baghdad Pact (1955) I 161, 277; II 146
Iraq I 277
Turkey I 277
Baghdad Railway VIII 212
Baia Mare Environmental Protection Agency VII 248,
253
Baia Mare Task Force VII 248, 252, 254
Baia Mare, Romania VII 247, 249, 253, 255
Baker v. *Carr* (1962) II 139, 281–282, 286

March on Washington (1963) II 25, 91–92
media coverage of II 20–22
President's Committee on Civil Rights (1946) II 42
relationship with labor movement II 192
resistance to II 25, 140
Scottsboro case III 188
"separate but equal" doctrine II 137
use of civil disobedience II 140
voter registration II 27
Civil War (1861–1865) VI 26, 28, 57; VIII 14, 18, 23, 25, 68, 136, 149, 199, 226, 296, 299; IX 19, 22, 116, 158, 209; XI 123
Civil Works Administration (CWA, 1933) III 154
Civilian Conservation Corps (CCC, 1933) III 154
Clark, Mark W. IV 146; V 125–126, 187
Italian campaign IV 144
Clark, William P. VI 231
Clark Amendment (1975) VI 1–4
Clay, Lucius I 35–36; XI 179, 255
Clausewitz, Carl von VIII 16, 71, 112–113, 199
Clean Air Act Amendments (1970) II 183
Clean Water Act (1972) VII 256, 258, 262–264, 267–269, 274, 303–305
reauthorization VII 274
Clemenceau, Georges VIII 11, 19, 78, 147, 149–150, 256, 278, 283–283; IX 203, 207, 250
assassination attempt upon VIII 278
Clement III X 216, 219, 221, 227, 229
Clement IV X 145
Cleveland VII 116, 122–123, 262, 265
Clifford, Clark M. I 160; II 6, 205
Clifford-Elsey report II 205, 208
Clift, Montgomery XI 158
Clinton, Bill I 97–98; II 80; VI 8, 58, 61, 231, 235; VII 224; VIII 11
abortion legislation II 223
and dam protests VII 221
Dayton accords II 154
impact of 1960s on presidency II 163
Israel I 159
Lewinsky scandal VI 231
pro-choice stand II 223
re-election of II 200
Clinton administration
arms-control agreements VI 20
defense spending VI 220
foreign policy of VI 58
nuclear nonproliferation I 224
on flood control VII 214
Clovis X 104
Cluniac Reform X 17–18, 36, 94
Cluny X 85, 141, 220, 279
CNN Cold War television series VI 66
Coastal Zone Management Act (1972) II 183
Cobra helicopter VI 173
Coffin, Howard IX 21
Colautti v. *Franklin* (1979) II 222
Colby, William E. VI 257
Cold War I 27–32, 82–90, 101–106, 115–122, 148–155, 165–203, 216–224, 271–276, 300–303; II 4, 9, 30–63, 68, 104, 163; III 10, 48; V 46, 119, 145, 149, 191, 199; VI 1–6, 8–11, 30–33, 108–115, 130–133, 160–162, 168–172, 175–178; VII 31, 53, 97, 174, 188; X 55, 63; XI 181, 253, 257, 260, 262
casualties in VI 50
causes of VI 252
conclusion of VI 47–51, 213–216
dam building in VII 29
effect of nuclear weapons I 250–257
end of VI 150, 214
impact on development of space programs II 241
impact on federal highway development II 107
impact on U.S. space program development II 257
late 1970s intensification II 172
military buildup II 43

mutual assured destruction (MAD) I 251–252
origins of I 258–264; II 30
Reagan's role in ending VI 221–241
Stalin's role in starting VI 250–252
vindicationist interpretation VI 155
Cole v. *Young* I 80
Collier, John, Commissioner of Indian affairs III 141–142
Collins, J. Lawton I 6; V 122
colonialism X 55–56, 63
Colorado VII 10, 13, 112, 181, 182
farmers' use of water in VII 13
production of crops on irrigated land in VII 11
Colorado River VII 27, 31, 151–153, 155, 168, 211, 214
dams on VII 108–115, 152
Colorado River Compact (CRC) VII 152–153
Colorado River Irrigation District VII 157
Colorado River Land Company VII 152
Colorado River Storage Project (CRSP) VII 27, 112
Columbia Basin VII 29
dams in VII 196
Columbia Basin Project VII 202
Columbia River VII 25, 27–28, 31, 51–61, 197, 199, 202, 219–220, 222, 225, 227
as salmon producer VII 53
first major navigation project on VII 52
hydroelectric dams on VII 198
Columbia River Fisherman's Protective Union VII 53
Columbia River Highway VII 57
Columbia River Inter-Tribal Fish Commission VII 61
Columbia River Packers Association VII 53
Columbus, Christopher X 7–8, 304
combat effectiveness
Germany V 282, 284
Japan V 281–282
Leyte campaign V 281
Normandy invasion V 282
psychological limits IV 47–52
United States V 278–286
Combined Bomber Offensive IX 223
Combined Chiefs of Staff (CCS) V 20, 23, 25, 38, 42–45
Commission on Polish Affairs VIII 281
Committee on Political Refugees XI 60
Commission on Presidential Debates II 196, 199
Committee on Public Information (CPI) VIII 296; IX 78
Committee on the Present Danger VI 256, 262
Committee to Re-Elect the President (CREEP) II 177; VI 24
Commonwealth of Independent States (CIS) VI 54
Commonwealth of Nations VI 13
communism I 148–155; II 31–32, 56–57, 160; VI 49; IX 83
atheism of VI 176
attraction for women VI 49
China II 267
collapse of II 153
global II 130
ideology I 258–262; VI 49
infiltration of federal government II 133
world domination VI 175–182
Communist Control Act (1954) I 74, 77
Communist Information Bureau (Cominform) I 36–113; VI 179, 246
Communist International (Comintern) I 113; III 224, 226; IV 80; VI 178, 254, 277
Communist Manifesto (1848) VI 178
Communist Party I 74; III 182, 221
in Chile I 124
in Guatemala I 123
of the Soviet Union III 224; VI 179, 276
of Yugoslavia (CPY) VI 273–278, 280–281
Communist Party of the United States of America (CPUSA) II 46–48; III 237; VI 123, 154, 157
1932 presidential candidate III 182

INDEX

INDEX

INDEX

Index

INDEX

INDEX

INDEX

water shortage in VII 280
World War I 37–42
Midwest Holocaust Education Center, Overland Park, Kansas XI 238
Migratory Bird Conservation Act (1929) VII 277
Mihajlovic, Draza VI 275, 277–278
Mikva, Abner Joseph VII 121
military gap between U.S. and Soviet Union I 188–194
Military Intelligence Service (MIS) III 14–15
Military Service Act (1916) IX 58
Milites X 14, 16, 34
Millerand, Alexandre VIII 152, 255
Milliken v. *Bradley* (1974) II 293, 298
Milne, George VIII 214, 216; IX 206
Milosovic, Slobodan XI 71, 75
Milyukov, Pavel VIII 173–174
Minow, Newton II 121, 23
Miranda, Ernesto II 284
Miranda v. *Arizona* (1966) II 281, 284, 286
Missao do Fomento e Powoamento dio Zambeze (MFPZ) VII 240
missile gap I 182–194; II 260; VI 21, 141
Mississippi River VII 27, 29, 31, 182, 211
Mitchell Act (1938) VII 202
Mitchell, William A. (Billy) IV 2; V 3, 14, 126; IX 11, 223
Mitterand, François-Maurice VI 102, 104
Mobutu Sese Seko VI 81
Mohammad Reza Pahlavi (shah of Iran) I 11, 141–146; II 97
Molotov, Vyacheslav I 36, 113, 175, 177, 238, 303; II 35; VI 101, 255, 280
Molotov Plan I 178; II 40
Soviet nuclear spying I 245
Molotov-Ribbentrop Pact I 110
Moltke, Helmuth von (the Elder) VIII 73, 75, 184, 248–249, 252; IX 98
Moltke, Helmuth von (the Younger) VIII 72, 114, 179–180, 182, 184, 226, 248; IX 41, 46, 52, 98–99, 101, 103, 124, 227, 263
Mongke (Mangu Khan) X 183, 186–187
Mongols X 30, 48, 52–53, 60, 66, 144, 180, 182–189
Monroe, James IX 96, 246
Monroe Doctrine (1823) I 124–125, 132; II 98, 156, 257; III 45–46, 243, 247; VI 75; IX 96, 173, 246
as applied to Cuba VI 71
Roosevelt Corollary (1904) III 46
Montenegro IX 267, 270
Montgomery bus boycott II 22–24, 90, 140
Montgomery, Field Marshal Bernard Law II 50; IV 64, 66, 144, 177–184; V 16, 19–25, 28, 34, 42, 44, 122–125, 129
Moors X 2, 8, 10, 41, 128, 133, 260, 265, 269, 290
Moravia 60, 205–206, 208
Morelos Dam (Mexico) VII 152, 155, 157–159
Morgan, J. P. IX 19, 57, 248
Morgenthau, Hans J. I 266; II 8
Morgenthau, Henry III 257; XI 11, 257
Morgenthau Plan (1944) II 210
Moriscos (converted Muslims) X 4, 6
Morrill Act (1862) III 2
Morocco VIII 32, 152, 227; IX 91, 114, 226; X 270, 278, 289
soldiers in France IX 118
Moroccan Crisis (1905) VIII 35
Mosaddeq, Mohammad I 66, 69, 211; II 146; VI 131
Moscow Conference (1944) V 311
Moscow Declaration (1943) XI 261
Moscow Olympics (1980) VI 166, 237
U.S. boycott VI 43
Mountbatten, Lord Louis V 42, 196
Movies, represenatations of the Holocaust XI 45–50
Movimiento de Izquierda Revolucionaria (MIR) I 127,130
Movimiento Nacionalista Revolucionario (MRN) I 125–126
Moynihan, Daniel Patrick II 166, 271, 276

Mozambique VI 1–7, 188, 221, 256, 261; VII 236–237, 239–240
aid from Soviet Union VI 2
independence VI 2
Porgtuguese immigration to VII 237
Mozambique Liberation Front (*Frente da Libertação de Moçambique* or FRELIMO) VI 2, 6; VII 239
Mozambique National Resistance Movement (*Resistência Nacional Moçambicana* or RENAMO) VI, 2, 4, 6
Mozarabs X 2, 202, 242, 244
Mubarak, Hosni I 163, 317
Mudejars X 2, 180
Mudros Armistice (1918) VIII 217
Muhammad X 10, 29, 43, 45, 59, 64–66, 132–133, 198–199, 201, 273, 288
mujahidin (mujahideen) I 10–16; VI 2, 133, 165, 238
U.S. support VI 229
Müller, Ludwig XI 27, 29
Mundt, Karl E. I 74, 306; II 131, 211
Mundt-Nixon Bill I 74
Munich Agreement (1938) I 293, 300
Munich Conference (1938) IV 127
Municipality of Metropolitan Seattle (Metro) 188–195
Munitions of War Act (1915) IX 56
Murphy, Charles Francis III 262
Murphy, Justice Frank V 188
Murray, Wallace XI 57, 62
music
"folk revival" II 214
as political force II 214
music industry
impact of television II 218
record companies at Monterey Music Festival II 219
sheet music production II 217
technological advances II 216
youth market II 219
Muskie, Edmund Sixtus VII 176, 261, 263–264, 268
Muslims X 8, 10, 17, 19, 27, 29, 33–34, 37, 43–44, 47–48, 52, 54, 59–60, 65, 69, 78, 81, 88–90, 95, 101, 105, 108–109, 117, 128, 133, 140, 149–150, 153, 159, 169, 174, 176, 179–181, 195, 209, 212, 219–220, 223–224, 238, 248, 255, 265–266, 280–281, 284, 287, 289, 292, 297: XI 17
Christian treatment of X 177
cultural interaction with Christians X 197–203
in Spain X 1–6, 40–45, 241–246
Latinization of X 43
treatment of in Crusader States X 190–196
treatment of Jews X 272–278
Mussolini, Benito I 134; IV 14, 80; V 36, 108–109, 117, 135, 169, 175–177, 226, 233; VIII 95; IX 96, 175; X 305; XI 74, 167
alliance with Hitler V 179
downfall V 2
invasion of Ethiopia V 118, 120
proposal of the Four Power Pact V 120
removal from power V 178, 179
support of Franco IV 224, 226
Muste, A. J. II 7; III 184
Mutual Assured Destruction (MAD) I 154, 169–171, 191, 198, 202, 226–227, 230–232, 251–252; II 67; VI 31, 168, 174
Mutual Defense Assistance Act (1949) I 59
Mutual Security Act I 175
Mutual Security Program (MSP) I 175
MX missile VI 17–18

N

Nader, Ralph VII 178, 265, 269
Nagasaki I 30, 230, 239, 242–245, 249, 268; III 12, 15; V 3, 8, 49, 52, 111, 154, 192; VI 31; VII 174; XI 159
Nagy, Imre VI 130–131, 134, 270
Nagymaros Dam (Hungary) VII 100–101, 104
Namibia VI 1 6; VII 7, 38, 236–237, 240–242

INDEX

INDEX

INDEX

INDEX

INDEX

INDEX

World War II V 303–304
    economic gain III 64
    entry XI 14
United States Employment Service VIII 301
United States Fish Commission (USFC) VII 201
United States Holocaust Memorial Museum XI 16, 45, 264
United States Military Academy, West Point VIII 16, 22
United States Railroad Administration IX 24
United States v. Winans (1905) VII 57
United Steelworkers Union VII 267
United Towns Organization VII 143
Universalism I 284–289
Universal Negro Improvement Association (UNIA) IX 4
University of California Japanese American Evacuation and Resettlement Study (1942–1946) V 186
University of Chicago VII 262
University of Halle XI 28
University of Heidelberg XI 28
University of Idaho VII 225
University of Maryland VII 48
University of Oregon VII 60
University of Vienna XI 149
University of Washington VII 60, 202
Untermenschen (subhumans) IV 86, 99, 131
Unterseeboote (U-boats) V 2, 79–83, 135; VIII 106, 134–135, 138, 196, 223, 287–294, 296; IX 21, 53, 58, 74–79, 104, 120, 142, 144, 181, 183–188, 247–248
    bases in World War I VIII 219
    blockade IX 194
    technology V 83
    Type IX V 80
    Type VII V 79, V 80
    Type VIIC V 83
    unrestricted warfare IX 77, 120, 142, 187, 246, 248, 256
Upper Colorado River Storage Project VII 30
Upper Stillwater Dam (United States) VII 31
Uprising (2001) XI 155, 158, 161
Urban II X 13–20, 24, 26, 32, 35, 59, 71–72, 77, 88, 98–105, 116–119, 121–122, 124–127, 130–131, 135–136, 148–150, 171, 175, 191, 205, 209, 211–221, 223–224, 227, 231–233, 238, 245, 256, 265, 267–269, 279–294, 297–298
Urban III X 254, 259
Urban political bosses III 259–265
Uruguay
    communist guerrilla movements I 125
    in War of the Triple Alliance I 125
    military coups I 26
    reduction of U.S. military aid I 141
Utah VII 31, 112

V

Vaal River VII 7–8, 240–241
Valencia X 2, 6, 159
Vance, Cyrus R. I 143, 145; VI 42, 263
Vandenberg, Arthur I 306, 203, 205, 207–208
Vandenberg, Hoyt Sanford I 6, 236
Van der Kloof Dam (South Africa) VII 243
Van Devanter, Justice Willis III 25, 27, 31
Vanishing Air (1970) VII 269
Vanzetti, Bartolomeo III 229–238
Vardar Valley IX 204–205
Vargha, Janos VII 101
Vatican VIII 208–209; XI 131, 192–193
Vatican Radio XI 192
V-E Day IV 62; V 60
Velsicol Chemical Company VII 162–165
Velvet Divorce (1992) VII 100
Velvet Revolution (1989) VII 101
Venereal Disease VIII 128
Venice IX 107; X 30, 75, 108–109, 112–114, 128, 148–157, 198

Venona Project I 242–243; 247; VI 123, 126, 154, 156
Ventura, Jesse II 199, 201
Vernichtungskrieg (war of annihilation) IV 88, 141
Venizelos, Eleutherios IX 208
Versailles Treaty (1919) I 255, 285, 293, 300; II 99, 145; III 99, 180; IV 17–18, 86, 164, 266–273; V 148, 202, 292; VI 176; VIII 20, 58, 95–96, 156, 166, 173, 207, 264, 277–285, 295, 298–299 ; IX 21, 27, 93, 95–96, 172–174, 268; XI 15, 82, 98, 168
    Article 231, War Guilt Clause IV 267; VIII 280, 282, 284
    impact on German economy IV 269
    impact on World War II IV 267
Vichy France IV 275–280; IX 84; XI 177
    anti-Semitism IV 277, 280
    cooperation with Nazis IV 276, 278
    National Renewal IV 276
    Statut des juifs (Statute on the Jews) IV 277
    support of the Wehrmacht (German Army) IV 277
Victoria, Queen of England VIII 30, 32, 35
Vidovian Constitution (1921) IX 268
Vienna Declaration I 253
Viet Minh V 146–148; VI 106; IX 260
Vietcong I 40–42, 296–297; VI 93, 96
    attacks on U.S. bases (1965) I 291
    begins war with South Vietnam I 290
Vietnam I 41, 46, 50, 54, 82, 87, 89, 273, 290–294, 298–299; II 3–5, 7–10, 40, 173, 269; VI 32, 50, 59, 64, 80–81, 98, 101, 107, 201, 203, 229, 261, 270–272; VIII 35, 193; IX 260
    as a colony of France I 290
    Buddhist dissidents VI 92
    French withdrawal from I 213; II 266; VI 102, 106
    imperialism I 151
    peace agreement with France I 290, 297
    seventeenth parallel division II 267; VI 98
    U.S. bombing of I 183
    U.S. military buildup I 183; VI 96
Vietnam War (ended 1975) I 40, 44–45, 89, 101, 140, 142, 144, 290–299; II 3–10, 97, 177, 180, 224, 257, 260, 263–265, 273; VI 8, 23–29, 33, 38, 56–57, 61, 85, 88, 98–99, 103, 138–145, 173, 185, 202, 222, 266, 283–285; VIII 60, 188, 266; IX 262
    comparison to Soviet invasion of Afghanistan I 14
    domino theory I 266, I 297–298
    doves II 263
    folly of U.S. militarism I 183
    Gulf of Tonkin Resolution I 291
    hawks II 263
    impact on Republican and Democratic concensus II 208
    impact on U.S. domestic programs II 270; VI 185, 202
    labor movement support of II 193
    number of casualties I 291
    Operation Duck Hook II 6
    Operation Flaming Dart I 291
    Operation Rolling Thunder I 291
    reasons for U.S. involvement I 292, 295, 297–298
    result of containment policy II 265
    result of French colonial system II 267
    television coverage II 124–125; VI 145
    Tet Offensive II 9, 180, 275
    U.S. troop buildup I 291
    U.S. troops leave I 291
    Vietminh I 290
    Vietnamization VI 99
Vikings X 122, 213, 280, 287
Villa, Francisco "Pancho" III 125–130; VIII 16, 18, 22; IX 6
Villard, Henry VII 57
Vilna Ghetto XI 144
A Vindication of the Rights of Women (Mary Wollstonecraft) II 74